Introduction to Information Systems

Supporting and Transforming Business

Third Canadian Edition

R. Kelly Rainer, Jr.
Casey G. Cegielski
Ingrid Splettstoesser
Cristóbal Sánchez-Rodríguez

WILEY

Library and Archives Canada Cataloguing in Publication

Rainer, R. Kelly, Jr., 1949-, author

Introduction to information systems: supporting and transforming business / R. Kelly Rainer, Jr., Casey G. Cegielski, Ingrid Splettstoesser-Hogeterp, Cristóbal Sánchez-Rodríguez. - Third Canadian edition.

Includes index.

ISBN 978-1-118-47699-4 (pbk.)

1. Information technology—Management—Textbooks. 2. Management information systems—Textbooks. I. Cegielski, Casey G, author II. Splettstoesser-Hogeterp, Ingrid, 1954-, author III. Sánchez-Rodríguez, Cristóbal, 1973-, author

T58.6.I64 2013 658.4'038011 C2013-903785-3

Production Credits

Acquisitions Editor: Darren Lalonde
Vice President & Publisher: Veronica Visentin
Marketing Manager: Aida Krneta
Editorial Manager: Karen Staudinger
Developmental Editor: Daleara Jamasji Hirjikaka
Media Editor: Channade Fenandoe
Editorial Assistant: Luisa Begani
Production Manager: Tegan Wallace
Associate Production Manager: Joel Balbin
Cover and Interior Design: Joanna Vieira
Cover Credits: ©iStockphoto.com/blackred, ©iStockphoto.com/chris_lemmens, ©iStockphoto.com/art12321
Typesetting: Aptara
Printing & Binding: Quad Graphics

Printed and bound in the United States of America
1 2 3 4 5 QG 18 17 16 15 14

John Wiley & Sons Canada, Ltd.
5353 Dundas Street West, Suite 400
Toronto, ON M9B 6H8
Visit our website at www.wiley.ca

About the Authors

R. Kelly Rainer, Jr.

R. Kelly Rainer, Jr, is George Phillips Privett Professor of Management Information Systems at Auburn University, Auburn, Alabama. He received his bachelor of science degree in Mathematics from Auburn and his Doctor of Dental Medicine (DMD) from the University of Alabama in Birmingham. After practising dentistry for 10 years, Dr. Rainer returned to school and received his doctorate at the University of Georgia. He has published numerous articles in leading journals. His research interests include enterprise resource planning (particularly using SAP), business process reengineering, and object-oriented technology.

Casey G. Cegielski

Casey G. Cegielski is an assistant professor of management information systems. His current research interests are in the areas of innovation diffusion, computer-facilitated speech recognition, and the strategic use of information technology. His research has appeared in numerous international information technology journals. Currently, he teaches courses in object-oriented application development and systems analysis and design. Dr. Cegielski earned a doctorate in business administration with a concentration in management information systems from the University of Mississippi. Additionally, he holds a master's degree in accountancy as well as a bachelor's degree, both from the University of Alabama.

Ingrid Splettstoesser

Ingrid Splettstoesser teaches management information systems, auditing, and information systems auditing using a multidisciplinary approach at York University in Toronto. Her research and publications are based on real-world cases involving the documentation and analysis of e-commerce systems. Dr. Splettstoesser believes in continuing education, as shown by her educational background, which includes mathematics, management sciences, psychology, and forensics. She is also a qualified Chartered Accountant (FCA), Certified Information Systems Auditor (CISA), and Certified Fraud Examiner (CFE).

Cristóbal Sánchez-Rodríguez

Cristóbal Sánchez-Rodríguez is a professor of audit and management information systems at the School of Administrative Studies at York University in Toronto, where he teaches courses in management information systems and enterprise resource planning systems. Dr. Sánchez-Rodríguez has published research papers on a number of operations management and information systems topics. His research has been published in the *International Journal of Operations and Production Management, International Journal of Production Economics, and International Journal of Enterprise Information Management*, among others. Dr. Sánchez-Rodríguez research interests include e-procurement and enterprise resource planning (particularly using SAP).

Preface

What Do Information Systems Have to Do with Business?

Rainer, Cegielski, Splettstoesser, and Sánchez-Rodríguez's *Introduction to Information Systems* will answer this question for you. In every chapter, you will see h3ow real global businesses use technology and information systems to manage their daily operations, improve their customer service, and, in turn, gain market share and increase their profitability. In other words, information systems provide the foundation for business.

Our goal is to teach all business majors, especially undergraduates, how to use IT (information technology) to master their current or future jobs and to help ensure the success of their organization. Our focus is not merely on *learning* the concepts of information technology but rather on *applying* those concepts to facilitate business processes. We concentrate on placing information systems in the context of business so that students will more readily grasp the concepts presented in the text.

The theme of this book is *What's in IT for Me?*, which is a question asked by most students who take this course. Our book will show you that IT is the backbone of any business, whether you're majoring in accounting, finance, marketing, production/operations management, human resource management, or management information systems (MIS).

New to This Edition

The third edition contains many exciting additions and changes. These elements make our book more interesting and readable for students of all majors while still providing the most current information possible in the rapidly changing field of information systems. The chapters have been reorganized and renumbered as a result of these changes.

Overall

- A new chapter on Web 2.0 and social networks (Chapter 7) that addresses the recent developments in social media such as crowdfunding and provides current examples of how businesses are embracing social media.
- The splitting of the second edition's ethics and security chapter into two separate chapters (Chapter 12 on ethics and privacy, and Chapter 13 on information security and controls) to provide greater focus on these two critical areas.

- A new Technology Guide (Technology Guide 3) on emerging types of enterprise computing, including a thorough discussion of cloud computing.
- All-new chapter-opening and chapter-closing cases featuring Canadian and international businesses.
- All-new or updated IT's About Business features in every chapter.
- All-new or updated examples in every chapter.
- New spreadsheet activities at the end of each chapter, providing valuable hands-on experience about how information systems manipulate data to obtain information and assist in decision making.
- A new Case Assignment at the end of each chapter to give students the chance to apply the concepts explained in the chapter to the particular case of a company.
- New and updated PowerPoint slides incorporating extensive images and video.
- A new and updated Test Bank with questions labelled according to difficulty—easy, medium, and hard—and new Apply the Concepts questions that require critical thinking or analysis.

Specifically

- Chapter 1 (Introduction to Information Systems) has been extensively reorganized. It focuses on the importance of information systems to you the student, to organizations, and to society in general.
- Chapter 2 (Organizational Strategy, Competitive Advantage, and Information Systems) has also been extensively reorganized. It opens with an expanded discussion of business processes, business process management, and business process reengineering. The remainder of Chapter 2 focuses on organizational strategy and how information systems help organizations gain a competitive advantage in the marketplace.
- Chapter 3 (Data and Knowledge Management) includes an expanded discussion about entity relationship (ER) diagrams and the specific notation that is used in drawing an ER diagram.
- Chapter 4 (Networks) has been reorganized for enhanced readability. The chapter begins by describing the main technical aspects of computer networks. Next, it briefly addresses the basics of the Internet and the World Wide Web. The chapter concludes by exploring what networks enable us to do: namely, to discover, communicate, and collaborate.
- Chapter 5 (E-Business and E-Commerce) starts with a discussion of social commerce, a recent phenomenon where businesses are taking advantage of social media in their relations with business partners, whether they are customers, suppliers, or other organizations.
- Chapter 6 (Wireless, Mobile Computing, and Mobile Commerce) talks about the rapidly evolving wireless payment revolution that has resulted in a battle for our mobile wallets, and the burgeoning new forms of mobile business.
- Chapter 9 includes both customer relationship management (CRM) and supply chain management (SCM). This chapter helps students understand how an organization's information systems reach outside the company to enable business with customers and suppliers. Several examples in this chapter also introduce the role of social media in CRM and SCM.
- Chapter 10 has been refocused on business intelligence (BI) and extensively rewritten. The chapter begins with an overview of managers and decision making, and continues with a definition of business intelligence. It then covers BI data analysis applications, followed by BI presentation applications. The chapter concludes by focusing on corporate performance management.

Key Features

We have been guided by the following goals that we believe will enhance the teaching and learning experience.

What's in IT for Me? Theme

We show why IT is important by calling attention in each chapter to how that chapter's IT topic relates to students in each major.

- A new feature of this edition is chapter-opening teasers that list specific tasks for each major that the chapter will help prepare students to do.
- Throughout each chapter, icons guide the reader to relevant issues for their specific functional area—accounting (ACC), finance (FIN), marketing (MKT), production/operations management (POM), human resources management (HRM), and management information systems (MIS).
- Every chapter concludes with a summary of how the concepts relate to each functional area (What's in IT for Me?).

Active Learning

We recognize the need to actively involve students in problem solving, creative thinking, and capitalizing on opportunities. Therefore, we have included in every chapter a variety of hands-on exercises, activities, and mini-cases, including exercises that require students to use software application tools. Through these activities and an interactive website, we enable students to apply the concepts they learn. Examples of these applications are improving a business through IT, configuring products, and using spreadsheets to facilitate problem solving.

Diversified and Unique Examples from Different Industries

Extensive use of vivid examples from large corporations, small businesses, and government and not-for-profit organizations helps to enliven concepts by demonstrating the capabilities of IT, its cost and justification, and innovative ways in which real corporations are using IT in their operations. Each chapter constantly highlights the integral connection between IT and business. This is especially evident in the IT's About Business boxes and a new IT's About Small Business box in each chapter.

Successes and Failures

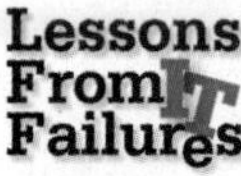

Like other textbooks, this one presents many examples of IT success. But we also provide numerous examples of IT failures, in the context of lessons that can be learned from such failures. Misuse of IT can be very expensive, as we illustrate.

Innovation and Creativity

In today's rapidly changing environment, creativity and innovation are essential for a business to operate effectively and profitably. Throughout the text, we demonstrate how IT facilitates these concepts.

Global Focus

Because an understanding of global competition, partnerships, and trading is essential to success in business, we provide a broad selection of international cases and examples. We discuss how IT facilitates export and import, the management of multinational companies, and electronic trading around the globe. These global examples are highlighted with the global icon.

Focus on Ethics

With corporate scandals appearing almost daily in the news, ethics and ethical questions have come to the forefront of business people's minds. In addition to a chapter that concentrates on ethics and privacy (Chapter 12), we have included examples and cases that focus on business ethics throughout the book. These examples are highlighted with the ethics icon.

Pedagogical Structure

Other pedagogical features provide a structured learning system that reinforces the concepts through chapter-opening organizers, study aids throughout the chapter, and end-of-chapter study aids.

Chapter-opening organizers include the following pedagogical features:

- The Learning Objectives provide an overview of the key concepts students should come away with after reading the chapter.
- The Chapter Outline lists the major chapter headings.
- Web Resources highlight ancillary materials available on the book companion site and within *WileyPLUS* for both instructors and students.
- An opening case identifies a business problem faced by an actual company, describes the IT solution applied to the business problem, presents the results of the IT solution, and summarizes what students can learn from the case.
- New What's in IT for Me? Teasers give students a quick hint about skills in their majors for which each chapter will help prepare them.

Study aids are provided throughout each chapter. These include the following:

- IT's About Business boxes provide real-world applications, with questions that relate to concepts covered in the text. Icons relate these sections to the specific functional areas.
- New IT's About Small Business boxes show examples of small businesses that students may relate to more closely than to large corporations.
- Highlighted Examples interspersed throughout the text illustrate the use (and misuse) of IT by real-world organizations, thus making the conceptual discussion more concrete.
- Tables list key points or summarize different concepts.
- End-of-section reviews (Before You Go On . . .) prompt students to pause and test their understanding of basic concepts before moving on to the next section.

End-of-chapter study aids provide extensive opportunity for the student to review and actually "do something" with the concepts they have just studied:

- What's in IT for Me? is a unique chapter summary section that demonstrates the relevance of topics for different functional areas (accounting, finance, marketing, production/operations management, human resources management, and management information systems).
- The chapter Summary, keyed to learning objectives listed at the beginning of the chapter, enables students to review the major concepts covered in the chapter.
- The Chapter Glossary facilitates studying by listing and defining all of the key terms introduced in the chapter.
- Discussion Questions, Problem-Solving Activities, Spreadsheet Activities, Case Assignments, and Team Assignments provide practice through active learning. These exercises are hands-on opportunities to use the concepts discussed in the chapter.
- The closing case presents a case study organized around a business problem and explains how IT helped to solve it. Questions at the end of the case relate it to concepts discussed in the chapter.
- Interactive Case: Ruby's Club gives the student an assignment as an intern for Ruby's Club, a downtown music venue that needs help redesigning its website and overhauling its technological infrastructure, among other things. Students are referred to *WileyPLUS* or the Student Companion Site for support, information, and assignments.

On-line Supplements

www.wiley.com/go/rainercanada

This textbook also facilitates the teaching of an introductory information systems course by providing extensive support materials for instructors and students. Go to www.wiley.com/go/rainercanada to access the student and instructor websites.

Instructor's Manual

The Instructor's Manual, prepared by Gokul Bhandari of the University of Windsor, includes a chapter overview, teaching tips and strategies, answers to all end-of-chapter questions, supplemental mini-cases with essay questions and answers, and experiential exercises that relate to particular topics.

Test Bank

The Test Bank, written by Raul Valverde of Concordia University, is a comprehensive resource for test questions. It contains multiple-choice, true/false, short answer, and essay questions for each chapter. The multiple-choice and true/false questions are labelled according to difficulty: easy, medium, or hard. New to this edition are Apply the Concept questions that require the students to use critical thinking to solve a problem.

The Test Bank is available for use in Respondus's easy-to-use software. Respondus is a powerful tool for creating and managing exams that can be printed to paper or published directly to Blackboard, WebCT, Desire2Learn, eCollege, ANGEL, and other e-learning systems. For more information on Respondus and the Respondus Test Bank Network, visit www.respondus.com.

PowerPoint Presentations

The media-enriched PowerPoint presentations created by Kelly Rainer and Debbie Gorval of Kwantlen Polytechnic University consist of series of slides that are designed around the text content for each chapter, incorporating key points from the text and all text illustrations as appropriate. In addition, the slides include links to relevant websites, videos, and articles to enhance classroom discussion. The presentations make extensive use of images and video clips.

Weekly Updates

Weekly updates, harvested from around the web, provide the latest IT news and issues. These are posted every Monday morning throughout the year at www.wileyISupdates.ca and include video and article links as well as discussion questions to assign or use in class.

Image Library

All textbook figures are available for download from the website. These figures can easily be added to PowerPoint presentations.

Online Chapter

A new chapter discussing the emerging area of Enterprise Resource Planning Systems is available for download.

WileyPLUS

This on-line teaching and learning environment integrates the entire digital textbook with the most effective instructor and student resources to fit every learning style.

With *WileyPLUS*:

- Students can achieve concept mastery in a rich, structured environment that's available 24/7.
- Instructors can personalize and manage their course more effectively with assessment, assignments, grade tracking, and more.

WileyPLUS can complement the textbook or replace the printed textbook altogether for about half the price of a new textbook.

For Students:

Each of your students is unique, having different learning styles, different levels of proficiency, and different levels of preparation. *WileyPLUS* empowers them to take advantage of their individual strengths.

– Integrated, multimedia resources provide multiple study paths to fit each student's learning preferences and encourage more active learning. Resources include:

  - Author podcasts, several for each chapter, to use for review
  - Manager videos
  - Ruby's Club Interactive Case
  - Student lecture slides (PowerPoint) for note-taking
  - Microsoft Office lab manual and how-to animations

– *WileyPLUS* includes many opportunities for self-assessment linked to the relevant portions of the text. Students can take control of their own learning and practise until they master the material. Resources include:

  - Automatically graded practice questions from the Test Bank
  - Pre- and post-lecture quizzes
  - Vocabulary flash cards and quizzes

For Instructors:

WileyPLUS empowers you with the tools and resources you need to make your teaching even more effective.

– You can customize your classroom presentation with a wealth of resources and functionality. You can even add your own materials to your *WileyPLUS* course. Resources include:

  - Media-enriched PowerPoint presentations, created by Kelly Rainer
  - A completely revised Test Bank with a wide range of levels and new Apply the Concepts questions

– With *WileyPLUS*, you can identify those students who are falling behind and intervene accordingly, without having to wait for them to come to see you during office hours.

– *WileyPLUS* simplifies and automates such tasks as student performance assessment, making assignments, scoring student work, keeping grades, and more.

For more information on *WileyPLUS* or for a demo, contact your Wiley sales representative or visit www.wileyplus.com.

Wiley Custom Select

One size doesn't fit all. Wiley Custom Select gives you the freedom to create your course materials exactly the way you want them. You can browse from our extensive collection of Wiley content, add your own material, arrange the sequence of content, choose the output method, and a lot more in just three easy steps. Find out more at www.customselect.wiley.com.

Acknowledgements

Creating, developing, and producing a text for an introductory course to information technology is a formidable undertaking. First of all, we would like to thank our students, to whom this book is dedicated. We would like to reiterate our commitment to them and thank them for their feedback in improving this textbook. Also, we would like to extend our thanks to all those instructors who use this textbook in the classroom. You are the reason for the third edition. Thank you as well to supplement contributors Gokul Bhandari, Debbie Gorval, Dennis Kira, and Raul Valverde. Many thanks to our acquisitions editor, Darren Lalonde, and the team at John Wiley & Sons Canada for all their work and effort. Along the way, we were fortunate to receive continuous evaluation, criticism, and direction from many colleagues who regularly teach this course. Reviewers for this text were:

Anteneh Ayanso, Brock University
Gokul Bhandari, University of Windsor
Dale Foster, Memorial University of Newfoundland
Debbie Gorval, Kwantlen Polytechnic University
Rebecca Grant, University of Victoria
Marcelo Machado, Kwantlen Polytechnic University
Al Pilcher, Algonquin College
Raul Valverde, Concordia University
John Walker, Brock University

Ingrid Splettstoesser
Cristóbal Sánchez-Rodríguez
Toronto, Ontario

August 2013

Brief Contents

Contents

Chapter 1

Introduction to Information Systems

[LEARNING OBJECTIVES]	[CHAPTER OUTLINE]	[WEB RESOURCES]

[LEARNING OBJECTIVES]

1. Begin the process of becoming an informed user of your organization's information systems.
2. Define the terms "data," "information," and "knowledge," and give examples of each.
3. Define the terms "information technology," "information system," "computer-based information system," and "application" and give examples of each.
4. Identify three ways in which you depend on information technology in your daily life.
5. Provide three ways in which information technology can impact managers and three ways in which it can impact non-managerial workers.
6. List three positive and three negative societal effects of the increased use of information technology.

[CHAPTER OUTLINE]

1.1 Why Should I Study Information Systems?
1.2 Overview of Computer-Based Information Systems
1.3 How Does IT Impact Organizations?
1.4 Importance of Information Systems to Society

[WEB RESOURCES]

Student Companion Site
wiley.com/college/rainer

- Student PowerPoints for note taking
- Interactive Case: Ruby's Club Assignments
- Complete glossary

WileyPLUS

All of the above and

- E-book
- Mini-lecture by author for each chapter section
- Practice quizzes
- Flash Cards for vocabulary review
- Additional "What's in IT for Me?" cases
- Video interviews with managers
- Lab Manual for Microsoft Office 2010
- How-to Animations for Microsoft Office 2010

What's In IT For Me?
THIS CHAPTER WILL HELP PREPARE YOU TO ...
ACCT
Forecast revenues
FIN
Determine best sources for funds
MKT
Develop new goods and services
POM
Process customer orders
HR
Hire new employees
MIS
Directly support all functional areas

[Case 1.1 Will BlackBerry Survive?]

The Problem

In 2012, BlackBerry (formerly Research In Motion, or RIM) was losing money. The Canadian company laid off thousands of employees in an attempt to reduce costs by as much as $1 billion. How is it possible that a company that was an innovator in smart phones, with an international telecommunications infrastructure, came to such losses? How could a company with 79 million subscribers (as of January 2013) and sales of over 14 million smart phones in the six months ended December 1, 2012, be in such a financial mess?

After several other wireless products, RIM (founded in 1985) had a highly successful BlackBerry e-mail service in 1999. At the time, the BlackBerry was the first wireless product that provided for synchronization of wireless e-mail on a hand-held device with corporate e-mail systems. Highly successful, it was primarily alone until 2007, when Apple launched the iPhone, which quickly gained popularity over the BlackBerry because of its ease of use.

The problem is that the environment for smart phones changed dramatically. BlackBerry is no longer an only player. Instead, we have seen several competitors constantly introduce new smart phones (hardware) and the operating systems and applications that run on them (software). Like the BlackBerry proprietary operating system, the iPhone also has its own proprietary operating system, the iOS. In addition, the Android operating system, now owned by Google, was developed as an open source system that can operate on phones made by several manufacturers, which has enabled many smart phones to share common software applications (or apps). This means that developers write more apps for Android and Apple phones, since they expect to have higher sales of their apps. BlackBerry users are poor cousins, with only about 70,000 apps, while Android and Apple phone users have more than 10 times as many apps to choose from (as of early 2013). It is not only hardware and software innovation, but what you can do with the smart phone that makes it useful.

BlackBerry's original niche was to provide text and e-mail services over a secure network. Now smart phones are portable computing devices that search the web, play games, and search for the user's location. They have become true multipurpose devices, used for everything from making payments to listening to music.

The result of this increased competition without a solid response from BlackBerry meant that in February 2013, BlackBerry was ranked third behind Apple and Google Android for smart phone sales, capturing just 5 percent of sales by volume.

The Solution

RIM must compete with Apple and Android phones, providing the functionality of the iPhone, while leading in its corporate stronghold. In early 2013, RIM renamed its company BlackBerry and launched new smart phones that focused on its traditional strengths. They were well-built phones with a versatile message centre. New features included remote screen sharing (which is great for technical support) and the ability to be used by Visa card holders for credit card transactions. The screen resolution on the new BlackBerry devices was higher than that of the iPhone 5 and of most Android phones, such as the popular Samsung Galaxy S3. The new BlackBerry phones were accompanied by an aggressive marketing campaign, which included marketing to software developers to encourage them to develop more apps for the phone.

The Results

Media coverage of the 2013 BlackBerry phones was high, with articles about features and reviews comparing the BlackBerry with other phones (such as the Apple iPhone 5) resulting in favourable comments for the BlackBerry.

When this text went to press, BlackBerry (as a company) was still alive, selling its phones and talking about more new products to come. It was too early to tell whether the new products would increase the company's market share or its bottom line, regaining some of its earlier glory.

What We Learned from This Case

The chapter-opening case illustrates how rapid changes in information technology can make products obsolete and drive non-responsive businesses to the brink of destruction. It is you, the consumer, who drives this demand.

Before we proceed, we need to define information technology and information systems. **Information technology (IT)** relates to any computer-based tool that people use to work with information and to support the information and information-processing needs of an organization. An **information system (IS)** collects, processes, stores, analyzes, and disseminates information for a specific purpose.

Case 1.1 is a dramatic example of the far-reaching effects of IT on individuals, organizations, and our planet. Although this text is largely devoted to the many ways in which IT has transformed modern organizations, you will also learn about the significant impacts of IT on individuals and societies, the global economy, and our physical environment. In addition, IT is making our world smaller, enabling more and more people to communicate, collaborate, and compete, thereby levelling the digital playing field.

When you graduate, you either will start your own business or will go to work for an organization, whether it is public sector, private sector, for-profit, or not-for-profit. Your organization will have to survive and compete in an environment that has been radically changed by information technology. This environment is global, massively interconnected, intensely competitive, 24/7/365, real-time, rapidly changing, and information-intensive. To compete successfully, your organization must effectively use IT. Moreover, your organization does not have to be large to benefit from IT, as you will see in the case of eMeals in IT's About Small Business 1.1.

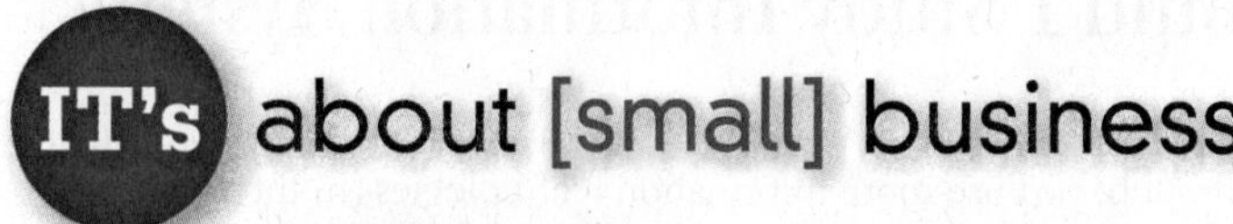

1.1 E-Meals

Jane DeLaney grew up in a home where family meals around the table were the norm. She wanted the same for her family, but she found it very difficult due to their busy schedules. She would go from one week of a somewhat organized meal plan to another week of sheer chaos.

In 2003, Jane decided it was time to do something about the problem. She created a meal-planning service, E-Mealz (now called eMeals, *www.emeals.com*), that she could both use herself and offer to other families. How does eMeals work? Essentially, Jane and a few employees create a weekly meal plan for different-sized families. They then draw up a grocery list with prices from various grocery stores. Customers pay for the service—in January 2013, the cost was $1.25 to $1.75 a week—and they receive their grocery list at the beginning of the week.

Jane needed information technology to put her great idea to work. The eMeals website promotes her products and convinces customers to sign up for her service. If you visit her site, you will find that she also uses Twitter and Facebook to promote her product and to create a community of customers. Visitors can submit their own recipes to be included in the system. Members can sign up for newsletters, and they can manage their accounts to determine which particular plan they will join. The website offers plans for couples and families, and it provides information about a host of nutritional needs, all of which is updated weekly. Although the tools that Jane uses are not complicated, she could not have transformed her dream into a reality without them.

When Jane DeLaney started eMeals, her objective was not to create a huge meal-planning service. Rather, her goal was simply to provide a way for families to spend time together, save money, and enjoy delicious meals. Since its inception, eMeals has been acclaimed for improving family meals while helping families control their budgets. Members testify that they are able to shop more quickly and spend less money while feeling confident that they have purchased all the ingredients they will need for the week. Jane has successfully used IT to accomplish her goal of helping families spend time together, much as they did when she was growing up.

Questions

1. Provide two examples of how Jane uses information technology to provide her service.
2. Provide two additional examples of how Jane might use information technology to improve her service. Be specific.

Sources: Compiled from A. Caldwell, "E-Mealz.com—Meal Planning Resource Review," *Blissfully Domestic*, February 17, 2011; *www.emeals.com*; *http://blog.emeals.com/*; *www.daveramsey.com/recommends/dave-recommends*, accessed January 30, 2013.

Sources: Compiled from "5 Reasons to Buy a BlackBerry Z10," *http://buyblackberryz10.com*; Canadian Press, "RIM Stock Up 5% After Visa OK's Mobile Payment Tech," February 11, 2013, *www.cbc.ca*; J. Martin, "BlackBerry Z10 vs Apple iPhone 5 Comparison Review," *www.pcadvisor.co.uk*, February 8, 2013; H. Solomon, "RIM's Big Day: Meet the BlackBerry Z10. Is It Enough?" *ITbusiness.ca*, January 31, 2013; B. Womack and A. Satariano, "Apple App Advantage Eroded as Google Narrows iPhone Lead," *www.mercurynews.com*, February 5, 2013.

As the case of eMeals illustrates, small business owners do not need to be experts in technology to be successful. The core competency of Jane DeLaney's business is not technology. Rather, it is the service of saving time and money. However, she has effectively employed social media and available Internet-related tools to create a successful business.

As you read this chapter and this text, keep in mind that the information technologies you will learn about are important to businesses of all sizes. No matter what area of business you major in, what industry you work for, or the size of your company, you will benefit from learning about IT. Who knows? Maybe you will use the tools you learn about in this class to make your great idea a reality much the way Jane DeLaney has!

The modern environment is intensely competitive not only for your organization, but for you as well. You must compete with human talent from around the world. Therefore, you will also have to make effective use of IT.

Accordingly, this chapter begins with a discussion of why you should become knowledgeable about IT. It also distinguishes among data, information, and knowledge, and it differentiates computer-based information systems from application programs. Finally, it considers the impacts of information systems on organizations and on society in general.

1.1 Why Should I Study Information Systems?

You are part of the most connected generation in history: You have grown up on-line; you are, quite literally, never out of touch; you use more information technologies (in the form of digital devices), for more tasks, and are bombarded with more information, than any generation in history. The *MIT Technology Review* refers to you as *Homo conexus*. Information technologies are so deeply embedded in your lives that your daily routines would be almost unrecognizable to a college student just 20 years ago.

Essentially, you practise continuous computing, surrounded by a movable information network. This network is created by constant co-operation between the digital devices you carry (for example, laptops, media players, and smart phones); the wired and wireless networks that you access as you move about; and web-based tools for finding information and communicating and collaborating with other people. Your network enables you to pull information about virtually anything from anywhere, at any time, and to push your own ideas back to the web, from wherever you are, via a mobile device. Think of everything you do on-line, often with your smart phone: register for classes; take classes (and not just at your university); access class syllabi, information, PowerPoints, and lectures; research class papers and presentations; conduct banking; pay your bills; research, shop, and buy products from companies or other people; sell your "stuff"; search for, and apply for, jobs; make your travel reservations (hotel, airline, rental car); create your own blog and post your own podcasts and videocasts to it; design your own page on Facebook; make and upload videos to YouTube; take, edit, and print your own digital photographs; "burn" your own custom-music CDs and DVDs; use RSS feeds to create your personal electronic newspaper; text and tweet your friends and family throughout your day; and many other activities. (Note: If any of these terms are unfamiliar to you, don't worry. You will learn about everything mentioned here in detail later in this text.)

The Informed User—You!

So, the question is: Why should you learn about information systems and information technologies? After all, you can comfortably use a computer (or other electronic devices) to perform many activities, you have been surfing the web for years, and you feel confident that you can manage any IT application that your organization's IT department installs.

The answer lies in your becoming an **informed user**; that is, a person knowledgeable about information systems and information technology. There are several reasons why you should be an informed user.

In general, informed users tend to get more value from whatever technologies they use. You will enjoy many benefits from being an informed user of IT. First, you will benefit more from your organization's IT applications because you will understand what is "behind" those applications (see Figure 1.1). That is, what you see on your computer screen is brought to you by your IT department operating "behind" your screen. Second, you will be in a position to enhance the quality of your organization's IT applications with your input. Third, even as a new graduate, you will quickly be in a position to recommend—and perhaps help select—the IT applications that your organization will use. Fourth, being an informed user will keep you abreast of both new information technologies and rapid developments in existing technologies. Remaining "on top of things" will help you to anticipate the impacts that "new and improved" technologies will have on your organization and to make recommendations on the adoption and use of these technologies. Finally, you will understand how using IT can improve your organization's performance and teamwork as well as your own productivity.

Managing the IS function within an organization is no longer the exclusive responsibility of the IS department. Rather, users now play key roles in every step of this process. The overall objective in this text is to be able to immediately contribute to managing the IS function in your organization from the user's perspective. In short, the goal is to help you become a very informed user!

In addition, if you have ideas of becoming an entrepreneur, then being an informed user will help you use IT when you start your own business. IT's About Business 1.2 illustrates how one couple uses IT to run their own multinational businesses from their home.

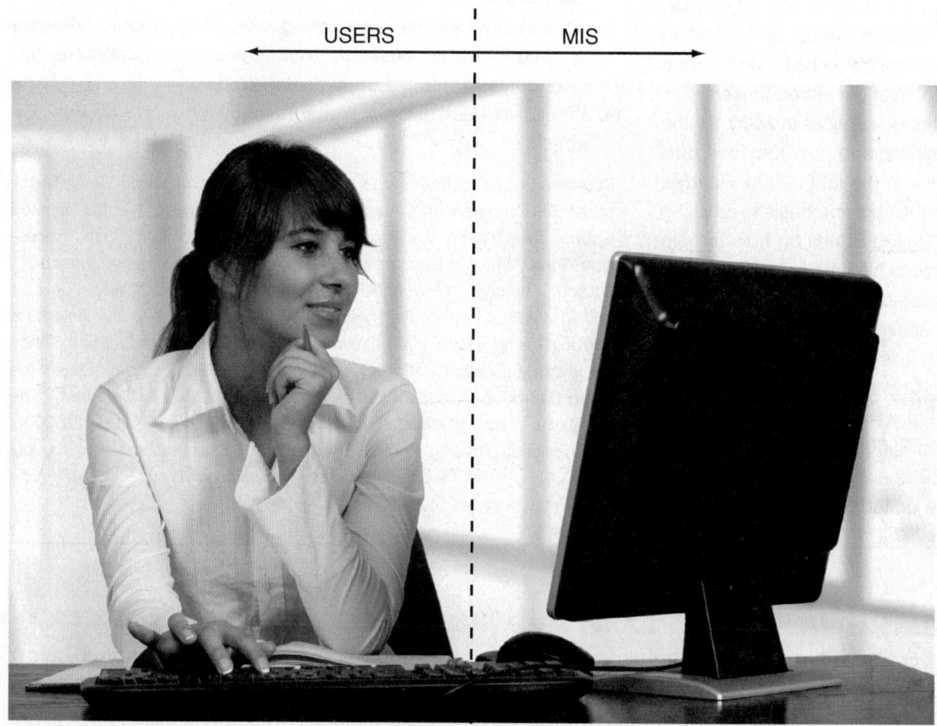

FIGURE 1.1 IT skills open many doors because IT is so widely used. What do you think is this woman's job? (*Source:* © Slawomir Fajer/iStockphoto)

IT's [about business]

1.2 Build Your Own Multinational Company

If you want to run a multinational company, you no longer need to rent office space and hire an army of employees. More small businesses are operated inside someone's home, with functions such as software development, accounting, support services, and design work being outsourced to professionals around the globe thanks to the technology that allows remote working. This is not only a boost to the growing on-line services industry, but to the businesses that use them. Companies in this industry include Elance (*www.elance.com*), Guru (*www.guru.com*), Brickwork India (*www.brickworkindia.com*), DoMyStuff (*www.domystuff.com*), and Freelancer.com (*www.freelancer.com*). To help allay customers' concerns about working with people they can't directly supervise or don't know personally, Guru has launched a system to avoid disputes over payments by holding buyers' funds until the work is received. Elance, meanwhile, has helped further reduce customers' administrative tasks by developing software so they can track work in progress and to handle billing, payments, and tax records.

An example of customers who successfully use global outsourcing is Randy and Nicola Wilburn. The Wilburns operate a multinational company with real estate, consulting, design, and baby food enterprises out of their home.

Just a mouse click away, professionals from around the world do everything from design to marketing to administration. For example, Nicola paid an Indian artist $300 to design the letterhead and logo for her line of "Baby Fresh Organic Baby Foods." A writer in London provided promotional materials. Randy uses "virtual assistants" in Jerusalem to transcribe voice mail, update his website, and design graphics. He farms out real estate paperwork to retired brokers.

The Wilburns began using outsourcing services in 2000. As the economy changed, so has their business and how they use outsourcing. After the U.S. housing crisis in the late 2000s, Randy's real estate business slowed, so he shifted his emphasis to advising non-profit organizations across the United States on how to help homeowners avoid foreclosure. To focus his time on adding value to his clients, Randy hires virtual assistants to handle routine correspondence and put together business materials while he travels. The bill for this outsourcing comes to less than $10,000 per year.

After having their second child, Nicola decided to work from home, cooking and selling organic baby food. When setting up a website for that business, she offered $500 for the design work to bidders around the world. Of the 20 freelancers who responded via Elance, 18 were from outside the United States.

The couple has been using two primary offshore vendors. One is GlobeTask (*www.globetask.com*), a Jerusalem-based outsourcing firm that employs graphic artists, web designers, writers, and virtual assistants in Israel, India, and the United States. The company generally charged around $8 per hour. The other vendor is Webgrity (*www.webgrity.com*), headquartered in Kolkata, India. Randy was able to get a logo for his real estate business for $125, which he maintains would have cost as much as $1,000 in the United States.

Global outsourcing brings together people who are part of a growing lifestyle trend: the digital nomads. Both the customers, such as the Wilburns, and the freelancers are digital nomads. A *digital nomad* is someone who uses information technologies such as smart phones, wireless Internet access, and web-based applications to work remotely—from home, a coffee shop, an airport, and similar locations. Digital nomads have location independence, and they frequently work as knowledge workers such as writers, photographers, affiliate marketers, web designers, developers, graphic designers, and computer programmers.

Questions

1. Identify and evaluate the advantages and disadvantages of outsourcing work overseas.
2. Can anyone do what Randy and Nicola Wilburn are doing? Or does their strategy require special qualifications or knowledge? Support your answer.
3. Explain how global outsourcing can affect people who are starting their own business. (Hint: Consider capital outlay, labour costs, IT infrastructure costs, etc.)
4. Would you like to be a digital nomad? Why or why not? Be specific.

Sources: Compiled from M. Elgan, "Is Digital Nomad Living Going Mainstream?" *Computerworld*, August 1, 2009; M. Rosenwald, "Digital Nomads Choose Their Tribes," *The Washington Post*, July 26, 2009; M. Elgan, "Recession Woes? Why Not Become a Digital Nomad?" *Computerworld*, March 23, 2009; P. Engardio, "Mom-and-Pop Multinationals," *BusinessWeek*, July 14 and 21, 2008; T. Ferriss, *The 4-Hour Workweek: Escape 9–5, Live Anywhere and Join the New Rich*, 2007, Crown Publishing Group; B. McDermott, "Ahoy the Micro-Multinational," *Forbes*, September 14, 2007; S. Harris, "Rise of the Micro Giants," *San Jose Mercury News*, July 14, 2007; A. Campbell, "The Trend of the Micro-Multinationals," *Small Business Trends*, February 20, 2007; M. Copeland, "The Mighty Micro-Multinational," *Business 2.0 Magazine*, July 28, 2006; H. Varian, "Technology Levels the Business Playing Field," *The New York Times*, August 25, 2005.

IT Offers Career Opportunities

Because information technology is vital to the operation of modern businesses, it offers many employment opportunities. The demand for traditional IT staff—programmers, business analysts, systems analysts, and designers—is substantial. In addition, many well-paid jobs exist in areas such as the Internet and electronic commerce (e-commerce), mobile commerce, network security, telecommunications, and multimedia design.

The information systems field includes the people in organizations who design and build information systems, the people who use those systems, and the people responsible for managing those systems. At the top of the list is the chief information officer (CIO).

The CIO is the executive who is in charge of the IS function. In most modern organizations, the CIO works with the chief executive officer (CEO), the chief financial officer (CFO), and other senior executives. Therefore, he or she actively participates in the organization's strategic planning process. In today's digital environment, the IS function has become increasingly important and strategic within organizations. As a result, although most CIOs still rise from the IS department, a growing number are coming up through the ranks in the business units (such as marketing and finance). So, regardless of your major, you could become the CIO of your organization one day. This is another reason to be an informed user of information systems!

Table 1.1 provides a list of IT jobs along with a description of each one. For further details about careers in IT, see *www.computerworld.com/careertopics/careers* and *www.monster.ca*. Career opportunities in IS are strong and are projected to remain strong over the next decade.

Table 1.1

Information Technology Jobs

Position	Job Description
Chief Information Officer	Highest-ranking IS manager; is responsible for all strategic planning in the organization
IS Director	Manages all systems throughout the organization and the day-to-day operations of the entire IS organization
Information Centre Manager	Manages IS services such as help desks, hot lines, training, and consulting
Applications Development Manager	Coordinates and manages new systems development projects
Project Manager	Manages a particular new systems development project
Systems Manager	Manages a particular existing system
Operations Manager	Supervises the day-to-day operations of the data and/or computer centre
Programming Manager	Coordinates all applications programming efforts
Systems Analyst	Interfaces between users and programmers; determines information requirements and technical specifications for new applications
Business Analyst	Focuses on designing solutions for business problems; interfaces closely with users to demonstrate how IT can be used innovatively
Systems Programmer	Creates the computer code for developing new systems software or maintaining existing systems software
Applications Programmer	Creates the computer code for developing new applications or maintaining existing applications
Emerging Technologies Manager	Forecasts technology trends; evaluates and experiments with new technologies
Network Manager	Coordinates and manages the organization's voice and data networks
Database Administrator	Manages the organization's databases and oversees the use of database-management software
Auditing or Computer Security Manager	Manages the ethical and legal use of information systems and evaluates the quality or effectiveness of such systems
Webmaster	Manages the organization's World Wide Website
Web Designer	Creates World Wide Websites and pages

IT Manages Information Resources

Managing information systems in modern organizations is a difficult, complex task. Several factors contribute to this complexity. First, information systems have enormous strategic value to organizations. Firms rely on them so heavily that, in some cases, when these systems are not working (even for a short time), the firm cannot function. (This situation is called "being hostage to information systems.") Second, information systems are very expensive to acquire, operate, and maintain.

Table 1.2

The Changing Role of the Management Information Systems (MIS) Department

Traditional Functions of the MIS Department

- Managing systems development and systems project management
  - As a user, you will have critical input into the systems development process. You will learn about systems development in Chapter 11.
- Managing computer operations, including the computer centre
- Staffing, training, and developing IS skills
- Providing technical services
- Infrastructure planning, development, and control
  - As a user, you will provide critical input about the IS infrastructure needs of your department.

New (Consultative) Functions of the MIS Department

- Initiating and designing specific strategic information systems
  - As a user, your information needs will often mandate the development of new strategic information systems. You will decide which strategic systems you need (because you know your business needs better than the MIS department does), and you will provide input into developing these systems.
- Incorporating the Internet and electronic commerce into the business
  - As a user, you will be primarily responsible for effectively using the Internet and electronic commerce in your business. You will work with the MIS department to accomplish this task.
- Managing system integration including the Internet, intranets, and extranets
  - As a user, your business needs will determine how you want to use the Internet, your corporate intranets, and extranets to accomplish your goals. You will be primarily responsible for advising the MIS department on the most effective use of the Internet, your corporate intranets, and extranets.
- Educating the non-MIS managers about IT
  - Your department will be primarily responsible for advising the MIS department on how best to educate and train your employees about IT.
- Educating the MIS staff about the business
  - Communication between the MIS department and the business units is a two-way street. You will be responsible for educating the MIS staff on your business, its needs, and its goals.
- Partnering with business-unit executives
  - Essentially, you will be in a partnership with the MIS department. You will be responsible for seeing that this partnership is one "between equals" and ensuring its success.
- Managing outsourcing
  - Outsourcing is driven by business needs. Therefore, the outsourcing decision resides largely with the business units (i.e., with you). The MIS department, working closely with you, will advise you on technical issues such as communications bandwidth and security.
- Proactively using business and technical knowledge to seed innovative ideas about IT
  - Your business needs often will drive innovative ideas about how to effectively use information systems to accomplish your goals. The best way to bring these innovative uses of IS to life is to partner closely with your MIS department. Such close partnerships have amazing synergies!
- Creating business alliances with business partners
  - The needs of your business unit will drive these alliances, typically along your supply chain. Again, your MIS department will act as your advisor on various issues, including hardware and software compatibility, implementation of extranets, communications, and security.

A third factor contributing to the difficulty in managing information systems is the evolution of the management information systems (MIS) function within the organization. When businesses first began to use computers in the early 1950s, the MIS department "owned" the only computing resource in the organization, the mainframe. At that time, end users did not interact directly with the mainframe.

In contrast, in the modern organization, computers are located in all departments, and almost all employees use computers in their work. This situation is known as *end user computing*. End-user computing has two components: end-user data entry, reporting, and inquiry (commonly referred to as simply *users*); and end-user development, where users develop usable systems, such as spreadsheets or programs using programming languages or other development tools.

As a result of these developments, the responsibility for managing information resources is now divided between the MIS department and the users. This arrangement raises several important questions: Which resources are managed by whom? What is the role of the MIS department, its structure, and its place within the organization? What is the appropriate relationship between the MIS department and the users? Regardless of who is doing what, it is essential that the MIS department and the users work in close co-operation.

There is no standard way to divide responsibility for developing and maintaining information resources between the MIS department and the users. Instead, that division depends on several factors: the size and nature of the organization, the amount and type of IT resources, the organization's attitudes toward computing, the attitudes of top management toward computing, the maturity level of the technology, the amount and nature of outsourced IT work, and even the countries in which the company operates. At large organizations, the MIS department is responsible for corporate-level and shared resources, and the users are responsible for departmental resources. Table 1.2 identifies both the traditional functions and various new, consultative functions of the MIS department.

So, where do the users come in? Take a close look at Table 1.2. Under the traditional MIS functions, you will see two functions for which you provide vital input. Under the consultative MIS functions, you will see how you exercise the primary responsibility for each function, and how the MIS department acts as your advisor.

before you go on...

1. Rate yourself as an informed user. (Be honest; this isn't a test!)
2. Explain the benefits of being an informed user of information systems.
3. Discuss the various career opportunities offered in the IT field.

1.2 Overview of Computer-Based Information Systems

Organizations refer to their management information system's functional area by several names, including the MIS Department, the Information Systems Department, the Information Technology Department, and the Information Services Department. Regardless of the name, however, this functional area deals with the planning for—and the development, management, and use of—information technology tools to help people perform all the tasks related to information processing and management. Information technology relates to any computer-based tool that people use to work with information and to support the information and information-processing needs of an organization.

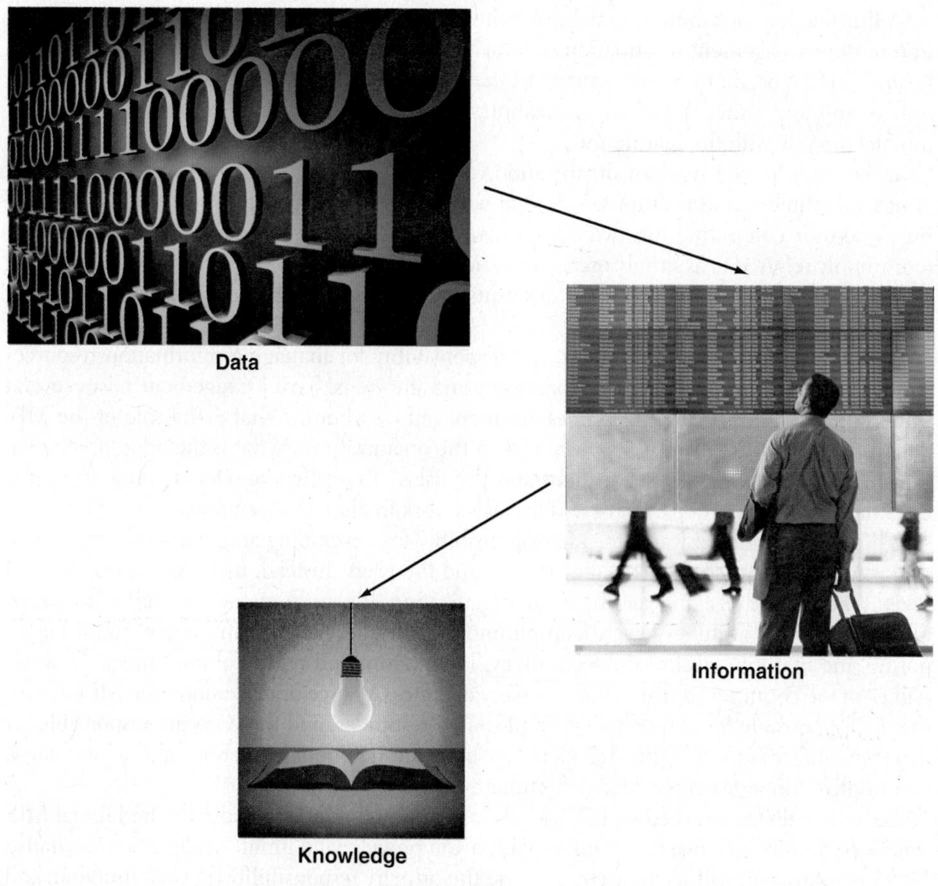

FIGURE 1.2 Binary code, the foundation of information and knowledge, is the key to making complex decisions. (*Sources:* © janaka Dharmasena-Fotolia.com; Exactostock/SuperStock; uttam gurjar/Shutterstock)

An information system collects, processes, stores, analyzes, and disseminates information for a specific purpose. It has been said that the purpose of information systems is to get the right information to the right people, at the right time, in the right amount, and in the right format. Because information systems are intended to supply useful information, we need to differentiate between information and two closely related terms: data and knowledge (see Figure 1.2).

Data items are an elementary description of things, events, activities, and transactions that are recorded, classified, and stored but are not organized to convey any specific meaning. Data items can be numbers, letters, figures, sounds, and images. Examples of data items are collections of numbers (e.g., 3.11, 2.96, 3.95, 1.99, 2.08) and characters (e.g., B, A, C, A, B, D, F, C).

Information is data that have been organized so that they have meaning and value to the recipient. For example, a grade point average (GPA) by itself is data, but a student's name coupled with his or her GPA is information. The recipient interprets the meaning and draws conclusions and implications from the information. Consider the examples of data provided in the preceding paragraph. Within the context of a university, the numbers could be GPAs, and the letters could be grades in an Introduction to MIS class.

Knowledge consists of data and/or information that have been organized and processed to convey understanding, experience, accumulated learning, and expertise as they apply to a current problem. For example, suppose that a company recruiting at your school has found over time that students with GPAs over 3.0 have experienced the greatest success in its management program. Based on this accumulated knowledge, that company may decide to interview only those students with GPAs over 3.0. Organizational knowledge, which reflects the experience and expertise of many people, has great value to all employees.

Consider this example:

Data	Information	Knowledge
[No context]	**[University context]**	
3.16	3.16 + John Sladowski = GPA	* Job prospects
2.92	2.92 + Marie Gagnon = GPA	* Graduate school prospects
1.39	1.39 + Kyle Owens = GPA	* Scholarship prospects
3.95	3.95 + Tom Elias = GPA	
[No context]	**[Professional baseball pitcher context]**	
3.16	3.16 + Ken Rice = ERA	
2.92	2.92 + Eduardo Diaz = ERA	* Keep pitcher, trade pitcher, or send pitcher to minor leagues
1.39	1.39 + Hugh Carr = ERA	* Salary/contract negotiations
3.95	3.95 + Nick Ford = ERA	

GPA = grade point average (higher is better)
ERA = earned run average (lower is better); ERA is the number of runs per nine innings accountable to a pitcher

You see that the same data items, with no context, can mean entirely different things in different contexts.

Now that you have a clearer understanding of data, information, and knowledge, the focus shifts to computer-based information systems. As you have seen, these systems process data into information and knowledge that you can use.

A **computer-based information system** (**CBIS**) is an information system that uses computer technology to perform some or all of its intended tasks. Although not all information systems are computerized, today most are. For this reason the term "information system" is typically used synonymously with "computer-based information system." The basic components of computer-based information systems are listed below. The first four are called **information technology components**. Figure 1.3 shows how these four components interact to form a CBIS.

1. **Hardware** consists of devices such as the processor, monitor, keyboard, and printer. Together, these devices accept, process, and display data and information.
2. **Software** is a program or collection of programs that enable the hardware to process data.

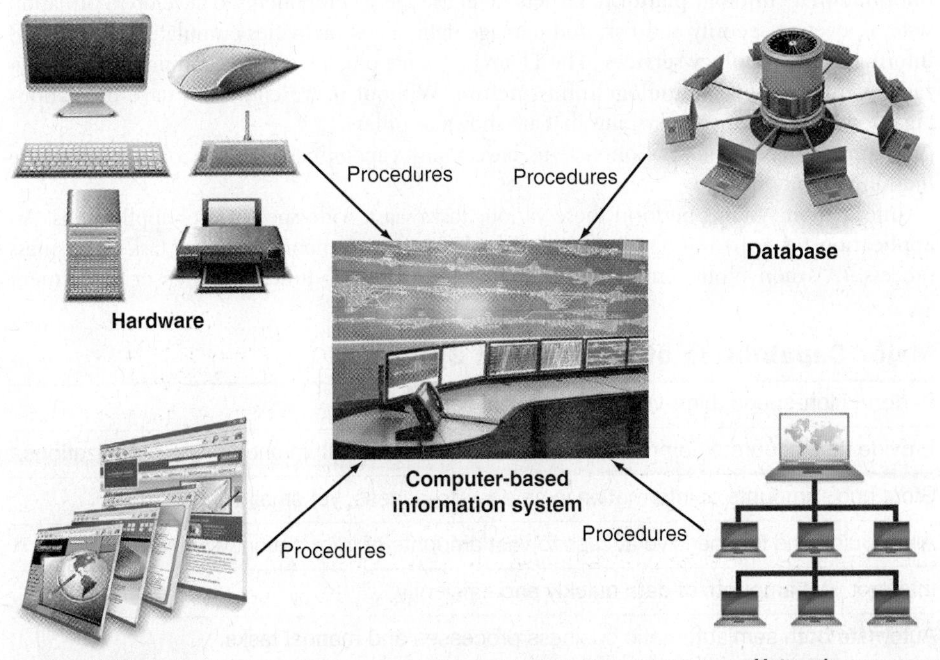

FIGURE 1.3 It takes technology (hardware, software, databases, and networks) with appropriate procedures to make a CBIS useful for people. (*Sources:* Nasonov/Shutterstock; Angela Waye/Shutterstock; alexmillos/Shutterstock; broukoid/Shutterstock; zhu difeng/Shutterstock)

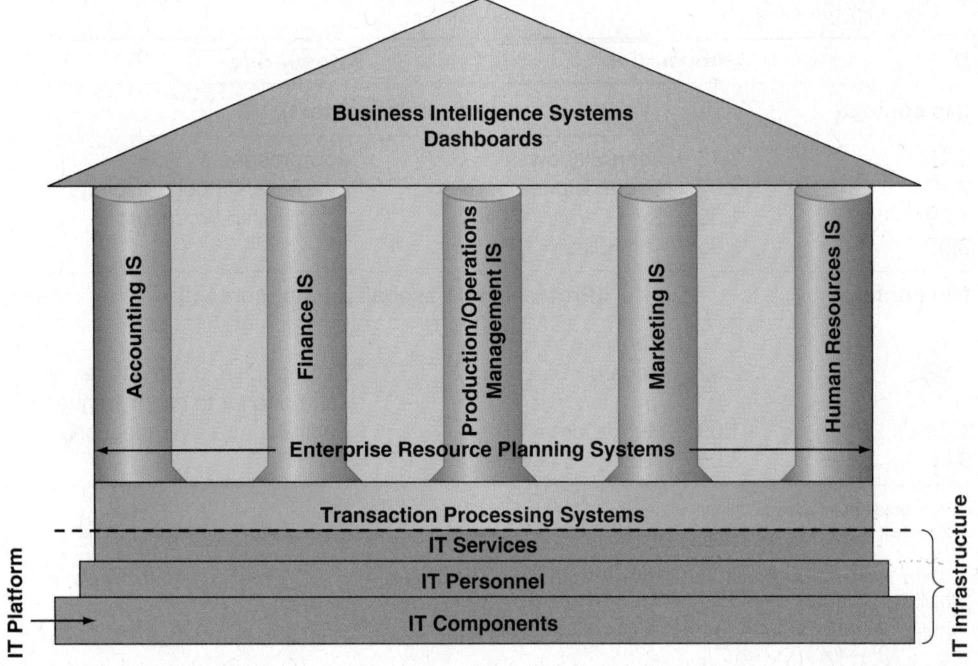

FIGURE 1.4 Information technology inside your organization.

3. A **database** is a collection of related files or tables containing data.
4. A **network** is a connecting system (wireline or wireless) that permits different computers to share resources.
5. **Procedures** are the instructions for combining the above components in order to process information and generate the desired output.
6. People are those individuals who use the hardware and software, interface with it, or use its output.

Figure 1.4 shows how these components are integrated to form the wide variety of information systems in an organization. Starting at the bottom of the figure are the IT components of hardware, software, networks (wireline and wireless), and databases that form the **information technology platform.** IT personnel use these components to develop information systems, oversee security and risk, and manage data. These activities cumulatively are called **information technology services**. The IT components plus IT services comprise the organization's **information technology infrastructure**. Without it, we could not have the various organizational information systems that are shown as pillars.

Computer-based information systems have many capabilities. Table 1.3 summarizes the most important ones.

Information systems perform these various tasks via a wide spectrum of applications. An **application** (or **app**) is a computer program designed to support a specific task or business process. (A synonymous term is *application program*.) Each functional area or department

Table 1.3

Major Capabilities of Information Systems
Perform high-speed, high-volume numerical computations.
Provide fast, accurate communication and collaboration within and among organizations.
Store huge amounts of information in an easy-to-access, yet small space.
Allow quick and inexpensive access to vast amounts of information, worldwide.
Interpret vast amounts of data quickly and efficiently.
Automate both semiautomatic business processes and manual tasks.

within a business organization uses many application programs grouped into application systems. For instance, the human resources department sometimes uses one application system for screening job applicants and another for monitoring employee turnover. The collection of application systems in a single department is usually referred to as a *departmental information system* (also known as a *functional area information system*). For example, the collection of application systems in the human resources area is called the *human resources information system (HRIS)*. There are collections of application systems—that is, departmental information systems—in the other functional areas as well, such as accounting, finance, marketing, and production/operations. IT's About Business 1.3 illustrates how electronic discovery software applications improve the efficiency and effectiveness of the legal discovery process.

IT's [about business]

1.3 Electronic E-Discovery Software Replaces Lawyers

One of the most routine yet important aspects of legal work is the discovery process, when lawyers can obtain evidence from the opposing party in a lawsuit or criminal trial. It's time-consuming and can be very expensive. For example, when the U.S. Justice Department sued CBS for antitrust violations in 1978, lawyers and paralegals for five television studios examined 6 million documents at a cost of $2.2 million. Today, much of that process can be automated thanks to electronic discovery (e-discovery) software applications, which can analyze documents in a fraction of the time at a fraction of the cost. For example, in January 2006, Deloitte and Touche used e-discovery software to find evidence of unauthorized plans for sales of data at Motion Picture Distribution LP.

E-discovery software can quickly find documents using relevant search terms. But some go beyond that, extracting relevant concepts without having specific terms, and deducing patterns of behaviour that may have gone unnoticed by lawyers examining millions of documents.

E-discovery software generally operates using either a "linguistic" or a "sociological" approach. Linguistic software can find and sort information using specific search words or using a large number of interrelated word and phrase definitions.

In contrast, sociological applications take a broader approach. They can add inferential analysis, closely resembling human reasoning. For example, software from Cataphora (*www.cataphora.com*) examines information relating to the activities and interactions of people—who did what and when, and who talked to whom. The software then manipulates this information to theorize what might have happened. This can be particularly helpful in white-collar crime investigations. The software identifies instances when an employee, for example, writes in an e-mail for the recipient to "call me." The software envisions that the sender and recipient could have carried on their conversation via instant messaging, telephone, or in person, to try to hide their tracks.

The Cataphora software also can interpret the sentiment in an e-mail message, such as whether the sender is being positive or negative, or whether the e-mail contains unusual emphasis that hints that at illegal activity, such as an abrupt change in the sender's tone and writing style.

Another e-discovery service, Clearwell (*www.clearwellsystems.com*), part of Symantec, has developed software that sifts through documents to find concepts rather than specific keywords, speeding up the process of finding relevant legal evidence. Clearwell's software, and software like it, often uses language analysis to search through information and then presents the general concepts in a visual way. In 2006, for example, such software was used when Air Canada was required to analyze 75,000 documents after allegations of corporate spying against WestJet. Results of this analysis were not disclosed, however, since the case was settled out of court.

E-discovery software is not only speeding up the discovery process, but it's making it increasingly automated, scientific, and objective. One lawyer went back to files his company's lawyers worked on in the 1980s and 1990s. Using e-discovery software to reanalyze the work, he discovered that his colleagues had been only 60 percent accurate.

What impact do these software applications have on people's jobs? Even though software can do the work rapidly, it can still uncover massive numbers of documents, which still need to be examined manually. Wortzman Nickle, a Canadian law firm, said that in one example, it used a team of six lawyers to look at 2,000 documents after using e-discovery software in order to narrow the number of documents that needed to be examined.

Questions

1. What are the advantages of e-discovery software? Provide specific examples.
2. What are the disadvantages of e-discovery software? Provide specific examples.
3. Based on this scenario, how do you think e-discovery software will affect the legal profession?

Sources: Compiled from B. Kerschberg, "E-Discovery and the Rise of Predictive Coding," *Forbes*, March 23, 2011; J. Markoff, "Armies of Expensive Lawyers, Replaced by Cheaper Software," *The New York Times*, March 4, 2011; J. McNish, "Electronic Paper Trail Tells the Tale," *www.theglobeandmail.com*, May 23, 2007; K. Fogarty, "E-Discovery: How a Law Firm Slashes Time and Costs," *CIO*, February 15, 2011; M. Pratt, "E-Discovery Moves In-House," *Computerworld*, December 30, 2010; *www.autonomy.com*, *www.clearwellsystems.com*, *www.cataphora.com*, *www.blackstonediscovery.com*, *www.wortzmannickle.com*, accessed January 30, 2013.

Types of Computer-Based Information Systems

Modern organizations employ many different types of information systems. Figure 1.4 illustrates the different types of information systems that function *within* a single organization, and Figure 1.5 shows the different types of information systems that function *among* multiple organizations. You will study transaction processing systems, management information systems, and enterprise resource planning systems in Chapter 8. You will learn about systems used by multiple organizations such as customer relationship management (CRM) systems and supply chain management (SCM) systems in Chapter 9.

In the next section you will learn about the numerous and diverse types of information systems employed by modern organizations. You will also read about the types of support these systems provide.

Breadth of Support of Information Systems

Certain information systems support parts of organizations, others support entire organizations, and still others support groups of organizations. This section addresses all of these systems.

Recall that each department or functional area within an organization has its own collection of application programs, or information systems. These **functional area information systems (FAISs**, groups of application systems) are supporting pillars for the information systems located at the top of Figure 1.4, namely, business intelligence systems and dashboards. As the name suggests, each FAIS supports a particular functional area within the organization. Examples are accounting IS, finance IS, production/operations management (POM) IS, marketing IS, and human resources IS.

In sales and marketing, managers use information technology to perform the following functions:

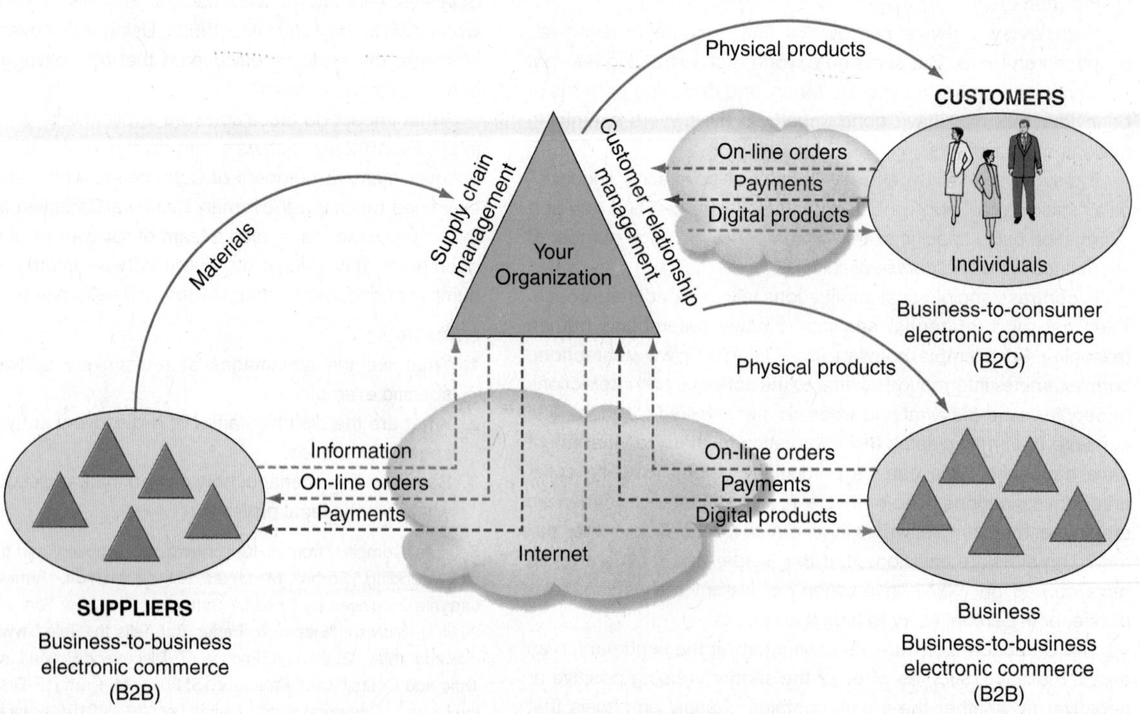

FIGURE 1.5 Information systems that function among multiple organizations as part of the supply chain.

- *Product analysis:* developing new goods and services
- *Site analysis:* determining the best location for production and distribution facilities
- *Promotion analysis:* identifying the best advertising channels
- *Price analysis:* setting product prices to obtain the highest total revenues

Marketing managers also use IT to manage their relationships with their customers. In *manufacturing*, managers use IT to process customer orders, develop production schedules, control inventory levels, and monitor product quality. They also use IT to design and manufacture products called *computer-assisted design* (CAD) and *computer-assisted manufacturing* (CAM).

Managers in *human resources* use IT to manage the recruiting process, analyze and screen job applicants, and hire new employees. They also employ IT to help employees manage their careers, to administer performance tests to employees, and to monitor employee productivity. Finally, they rely on IT to manage compensation and benefits packages.

Two information systems support the entire organization: enterprise resource planning systems and transaction processing systems. **Enterprise resource planning (ERP) systems** are designed to correct a lack of communication among the functional area ISs. For this reason, Figure 1.4 shows ERP systems spanning the FAISs. ERP systems were an important innovation because the various functional area ISs were often developed as stand-alone systems and did not communicate effectively (if at all) with one another. ERP systems resolve this problem by tightly integrating the functional area ISs via a common database. In doing so, they enhance communications among the functional areas of an organization. Experts credit ERP systems with greatly increasing organizational productivity.

A **transaction processing system (TPS)** supports the monitoring, collection, storage, and processing of data for a particular functional area. Each of the organization's basic business transactions generates data. When you are checking out at Walmart, for example, a transaction occurs each time the cashier swipes an item across the bar code reader. There also are different definitions of a transaction in an organization. In accounting, for example, a transaction is anything that changes a firm's chart of accounts. The information system definition of a transaction is broader: A transaction is anything that changes the firm's database. The chart of accounts is only part of the firm's database. Consider a scenario in which a student transfers from one section of an Introduction to MIS course to another section. This move would be a transaction to the university's information system, but not to the university's accounting department.

The TPS collects data continuously, typically in *real time*—that is, as soon as the data are generated—and provides the input data for the corporate databases. TPSs are considered critical to the success of any enterprise because they support core operations. Significantly, nearly all ERP systems are also TPSs, but not all TPSs are ERP systems. In fact, modern ERP systems incorporate many functions that previously were handled by the organization's functional area information systems. You study both TPSs and ERP systems in detail in Chapter 8.

ERP systems and TPSs function primarily within a single organization. Information systems that connect two or more organizations are referred to as **interorganizational information systems (IOSs)**. IOSs support many interorganizational operations, of which supply chain management is the best known. An organization's **supply chain** is the flow of materials, information, money, and services from suppliers of raw materials through factories and warehouses to the end customers.

Note that the supply chain in Figure 1.5 shows physical flows, information flows, and financial flows. Digitizable products are those that can be represented in electronic form, such as music and software. Information flows, financial flows, and digitizable products go through the Internet, whereas physical products are shipped separately. For example, when you order a computer from *www.dell.ca*, your information goes to Dell via the Internet. When your transaction is completed (that is, your credit card is approved and your order is processed), Dell ships your computer to you.

Electronic commerce (e-commerce) systems are another type of interorganizational information system. These systems enable organizations to conduct transactions, called business-to-business (B2B) electronic commerce, and customers to conduct transactions with businesses, called business-to-consumer (B2C) electronic commerce. E-commerce systems typically are Internet-based. Figure 1.5 illustrates B2B and B2C electronic commerce. Electronic commerce systems are so important that we discuss them in detail in Chapter 5, with additional examples interspersed throughout the text.

Support for Organizational Employees

So far, you have concentrated on information systems that support specific functional areas and operations. Now you will learn about information systems that typically support particular employees within the organization.

Clerical workers, who support managers at all levels of the organization, include bookkeepers, secretaries, electronic file clerks, and insurance claim processors. *Lower-level managers* handle the day-to-day operations of the organization, making routine decisions such as assigning tasks to employees and placing purchase orders. *Middle managers* make tactical decisions for activities such as short-term planning, organizing, and control.

Knowledge workers are professional employees such as financial and marketing analysts, engineers, lawyers, and accountants. All knowledge workers are experts in a particular subject area. They create information and knowledge, which they integrate into the business. In turn, they act as advisors to middle managers and executives. Finally, *executives* make decisions that deal with situations that can significantly change the manner in which business is done. Examples of executive decisions are introducing a new product line, acquiring other businesses, and relocating operations to a foreign country.

Office automation systems (OASs) typically support the clerical staff, lower and middle managers, and knowledge workers. These employees use OASs to develop documents (word processing and desktop publishing software), schedule resources (electronic calendars), and communicate (via e-mail, voice mail, videoconferencing, and groupware).

Functional area information systems summarize transaction data entered by clerical staff (or others) and prepare reports, primarily for middle managers, but sometimes for lower-level managers as well. Because these reports typically concern a specific functional area, report generators (RPGs) used to generate one-time reports are an important type of functional area IS.

Business intelligence (BI) systems provide computer-based support for complex, nonroutine decisions, primarily for middle managers and knowledge workers. (They also support lower-level managers, but to a lesser extent.) These systems are typically used with a data warehouse, and they enable users to perform their own data analysis. You learn about BI systems in Chapter 10.

Expert systems (ESs) attempt to duplicate the work of human experts by applying reasoning capabilities, knowledge, and expertise within a specific domain. They have become valuable in many application areas, primarily but not exclusively areas involving decision making. For example, navigation systems use rules to select routes, but we do not typically think of these systems as expert systems. Significantly, expert systems can operate as stand-alone systems or be embedded in other applications. We examine ESs in greater detail in Technology Guide 4.

Dashboards (also called "digital dashboards") are a special form of IS that support all managers of the organization. They provide rapid access to timely information and direct access to structured information in the form of reports. Dashboards that are tailored to the information needs of executives are called *executive dashboards*. Chapter 10 provides a thorough discussion of dashboards.

Table 1.4 provides an overview of the types of information systems used by organizations.

Table 1.4

Types of Organizational Information Systems

Type of System	Function	Example
Functional area IS	Supports the activities within specific functional areas.	System for processing payroll
Transaction processing system	Processes transaction data from business events.	Walmart checkout point-of-sale terminal
Enterprise resource planning	Integrates all functional areas of the organization.	Oracle, SAP system
Office automation system	Supports daily work activities of individuals and groups.	Microsoft Office
Management information system	Produces reports summarized from transaction data, usually in one functional area.	Report on total sales for each customer
Decision support system	Provides access to data and analysis tools.	Microsoft Excel for "What-if" analysis of changes in budget
Expert system	Mimics human expert in a particular area and makes decisions.	Credit card approval analysis
Executive dashboard	Presents structured, summarized information about aspects of business important to executives.	Status of sales by product
Supply chain management system	Manages flows of products, services, and information among organizations.	Walmart Retail Link system connecting suppliers to Walmart
Electronic commerce system	Enables transactions among organizations and between organizations and customers.	Payment processes on *www. dell.ca*

before you go on...

1. What is a computer-based information system?
2. Describe the components of computer-based information systems.
3. What is an application program?
4. Explain how information systems provide support for knowledge workers.
5. As we move up the organization's hierarchy from clerical workers to executives, how does the type of support provided by information systems change?

1.3 How Does IT Impact Organizations?

Throughout this text you will encounter numerous examples of how IT affects various types of organizations. This section provides an overview of the impact of IT on modern organizations. As you read this section you will learn how IT will affect you as well.

IT Reduces the Number of Middle Managers

IT makes managers more productive and increases the number of employees who can report to a single manager. Thus, IT ultimately decreases the number of managers and experts. It is reasonable to assume, therefore, that in coming years organizations will have fewer managerial levels and fewer staff and line managers. If this trend materializes, promotional opportunities will decrease, making promotions much more competitive. Bottom line: Pay attention in school!

IT Changes the Manager's Job

One of the most important tasks of managers is making decisions. A major consequence of IT has been to change the manner in which managers make their decisions. In this way, IT ultimately has changed managers' jobs.

IT often provides managers with near real-time information, meaning that they have less time to make decisions, making their jobs even more stressful. Fortunately, IT also provides many tools—for example, business intelligence applications such as dashboards, search engines, and intranets—to help managers handle the volumes of information they must deal with on an ongoing basis.

So far in this section, we have been focusing on managers in general. Now, let's focus on you. Due to advances in IT, you will increasingly supervise employees and teams who are geographically dispersed. Employees can work from anywhere at any time, and teams can consist of employees who are dispersed throughout the world. Information technologies such as telepresence systems (discussed in Chapter 4) can help you manage these employees even though you do not often see them face-to-face. For these employees, electronic or "remote" supervision will become the norm. Remote supervision places greater emphasis on completed work and less emphasis on personal contacts and office politics. You will have to reassure your employees that they are valued members of the organization, thereby diminishing any feelings they might have of being isolated and "out of the loop."

Will IT Eliminate Jobs?

One major concern of every employee, part-time or full-time, is job security. Relentless cost-cutting measures in modern organizations often lead to large-scale layoffs. Put simply, organizations are responding to today's highly competitive environment by doing more with less. Regardless of your position, then, you consistently will have to add value to your organization and to make certain that your superiors are aware of this value.

Many companies have responded to difficult economic times, increased global competition, demands for customization, and increased consumer sophistication by increasing their investments in IT. In fact, as computers continue to advance in terms of intelligence and capabilities, the competitive advantage of replacing people with machines is increasing rapidly. This process frequently leads to layoffs. At the same time, however, IT creates entirely new categories of jobs, such as electronic medical record keeping and nanotechnology.

IT Impacts Employees at Work

Many people have experienced a loss of identity because of computerization. They feel like "just another number" because computers reduce or eliminate the human element present in noncomputerized systems.

The Internet threatens to exert an even more isolating influence than computers and television have done. Encouraging people to work and shop from their living rooms could produce some unfortunate psychological effects, such as depression and loneliness.

IT Impacts Employees' Health and Safety. Although computers and information systems are generally regarded as agents of "progress," they can adversely affect individuals' health and safety. To illustrate this point, we consider two issues associated with IT: job stress and long-term use of the keyboard.

An increase in an employee's workload and/or responsibilities can trigger *job stress*. Although computerization has benefited organizations by increasing productivity, it also has created an ever-expanding workload for some employees. Some workers feel overwhelmed and have become increasingly anxious about their job performance. These feelings of stress and anxiety can actually diminish rather than improve workers' productivity while jeopardizing their physical and mental health. Management can help alleviate these problems by providing training, redistributing the workload among workers, and hiring more workers.

On a more specific level, the long-term use of keyboards can lead to *repetitive strain injuries* such as backaches and muscle tension in the wrists and fingers. *Carpal tunnel syndrome* is a particularly painful form of repetitive strain injury that affects the wrists and hands.

Designers are aware of the potential problems associated with the prolonged use of computers. To address these problems, they continually attempt to design a better computing environment. The science of designing machines and work settings that minimize injury and illness is called **ergonomics**. The goal of ergonomics is to create an environment that is safe, well lit, and comfortable. Examples of ergonomically designed products are antiglare screens that alleviate problems of fatigued or damaged eyesight and chairs that contour the human body to decrease backaches. Figure 1.6 displays some sample ergonomic products.

(a)

(b)

(c)

(d)

FIGURE 1.6 Ergonomic products protect computer users.
(a) Wrist support. (*Source*: Media Bakery)
(b) Back support. (*Source*: Media Bakery)
(c) Eye-protection filter (optically coated glass). (*Source*: Media Bakery)
(d) Adjustable foot rest. (*Source*: Media Bakery)

IT Provides Opportunities for People with Disabilities. Computers can improve employment opportunities for people with disabilities by integrating speech- and vision-recognition capabilities. For example, individuals who cannot type can use a voice-operated keyboard, and individuals who cannot travel can work at home.

Going further, adaptive equipment for computers enables people with disabilities to perform tasks they normally would not be able to do. The web and graphical user interfaces (e.g., the Windows operating system) can be difficult to use for people with impaired vision. Audible screen tips and voice interfaces added to deal with this problem essentially restore the functionality of computers to the way it was before graphical interfaces become standard.

Other devices help improve the quality of life in more mundane but useful ways for people with disabilities. Examples are a two-way writing telephone, a robotic page turner, a hair brusher, and a hospital-bedside video trip to the zoo or the museum. Several organizations specialize in IT designed for people with disabilities.

before you go on...

1. Why should employees in all functional areas become knowledgeable about IT?
2. Describe how IT might change the manager's job.
3. Discuss several ways in which IT impacts employees at work.

1.4 Importance of Information Systems to Society

As you saw in the chapter-opening case, millions of smart phones are sold quarterly, changing the way we interact with information. This section will explain in greater detail why IT is important to society as a whole. Other examples of the impact of IT on society appear throughout the text.

IT Affects Our Quality of Life

IT has significant implications for our quality of life. The workplace can be expanded from the traditional 9-to-5 job at a central location to 24 hours a day at any location. IT can provide employees with flexibility that can significantly improve the quality of leisure time, even if it doesn't increase the total amount of leisure time.

From the opposite perspective, however, IT also can place employees on "constant call," which means they are never truly away from the office, even when they are on vacation. In fact, a recent poll revealed that 80 percent of respondents took their laptop computers on their most recent vacations and 100 percent took their cell phones. Going further, 80 percent did some work while vacationing, and almost all of them checked their e-mail.

Robot Revolution on the Way. Once restricted largely to science fiction movies, robots that can perform practical tasks are becoming more common. In fact, "cyberpooches," "nursebots," and other mechanical beings may be our companions before we know it. Around the world, quasi-autonomous devices have become increasingly common on factory floors, in hospital corridors, and in farm fields. For home use, iRobot (*www.irobot.com*) produces the Roomba to vacuum our floors, the Scooba to wash our floors, the Mint to sweep our garages, the Mirra to clean our pools, and the Looj to clean our gutters.

Telepresence robots are a recent development in the field of robotics. The following example illustrates how organizations use these robots.

Example 1.1

Telepresence robots have been humorously described as a cross between a Segway and a Wall-E. These robots are designed to help companies save money on travel and on expensive teleconferencing technology. The robots enable people in remote offices or locations to have a rich communications experience without using a complicated video conference system.

A telepresence robot has both a video camera and a video screen embedded in its "head." It also has wheels and can be moved around remotely by computer. It is designed to steer its way clear of obstacles and people.

The robots enable a person to maintain a consistent connection with co-workers, customers, or clients. The user places the robot at a remote location and directs it to move around, for example, in a conference room during a meeting, broadcasting what is going on to the human controlling it from afar. Interestingly, the robots actually break down barriers of awkwardness that people sometimes feel in person-to-person meetings.

Although this technology is rather expensive, some companies are buying multiple units to place in their remote locations. That way, someone running a meeting could, for example, easily hear what is being said—or see what is being written on a whiteboard—in each location, without having to spend thousands of dollars on travel costs.

Business managers are using telepresence robots to walk factory floors. Storage companies are using them for security. In the retail environment, a robot could wander the floor with a customer who asks it purchasing or support questions. The person controlling the robot could answer the questions, essentially making the robot a mechanical sales clerk.

Health care organizations are employing them for home care and for servicing remote areas. The town of Nairn, on Labrador's north coast, is remote. If someone needs to see a doctor, it takes three days of travel (round trip) to go to Happy Valley (in Goose Bay). Since November 2009, Nairn has had a telepresence robot called Rosie that is coordinated by a nurse stationed in the community. Initially, the robot was there for two trial six-month periods before becoming a "permanent resident." It is used via laptop for multiple doctors to see and hear patients in Nairn. The doctors can recommend treatment and print prescriptions using wireless communications, no matter their location. The robot is about the size of a human being, with large rubber wheels for mobility, and an LCD screen where the face would be. That screen shows the face of the doctor that is working with Rosie. The cost of a robot like Rosie (as of September 2012) was about $140,000.

In an example of precision agriculture, Carnegie Mellon University in Pittsburgh has developed self-directing tractors that harvest hundreds of acres of crops around the clock in California. These "robot tractors" use global positioning systems (GPSs) combined with video image processing that identifies rows of uncut crops.

It probably will be a long time before we see robots making decisions by themselves, handling unfamiliar situations, and interacting with people on their own. Nevertheless, robots are extremely helpful in various environments, particularly those that are repetitive, harsh, or dangerous to humans.

Improvements in Health Care. IT has brought about major improvements in health care delivery. Medical personnel use IT to make better and faster diagnoses and to monitor critically ill patients more accurately. IT also has streamlined the process of researching and developing new drugs. Expert systems now help doctors diagnose diseases, and machine vision is enhancing the work of radiologists. Surgeons use virtual reality to plan complex surgeries. They also use surgical robots to perform long-distance surgery. Finally, doctors discuss complex medical cases via videoconferencing. New computer simulations recreate the sense of

Sources: Compiled from D. Bennett, "I'll Have My Robots Talk to Your Robots," *Bloomberg BusinessWeek*, February 21–27, 2011; A. Diana, "12 Advances in Medical Robotics," *InformationWeek*, January 29, 2011; D. Terdiman, "The Telepresence Robots Are Coming," CNET.com, May 18, 2010; A. Randell, "A Robot Called Rosie," *www.thelabradorian.ca*, July 15, 2010; E. Sparling, "Dr. Robot," *www.cumberlandnewsnow.com*, September 5, 2012, *www.vgocom.com*, *www.anybots.com*, accessed April 8, 2013.

touch, allowing doctors-in-training to perform virtual procedures without risking harm to an actual patient.

Of the thousands of other applications related to health care, administrative systems are critically important. These systems perform functions ranging from detecting insurance fraud, to creating nursing schedules, to financial and marketing management.

The Internet contains vast amounts of useful medical information (see *www.webmd.com*, for example). In an interesting study, researchers at the Princess Alexandra Hospital in Brisbane, Australia, identified 26 difficult diagnostic cases published in the *New England Journal of Medicine*. They selected three to five search terms from each case and then conducted a Google search. The researchers selected and recorded the three diagnoses that Google ranked most prominently and that appeared to fit the symptoms and signs. They then compared these results with the correct diagnoses as published in the journal. They discovered that their Google searches had found the correct diagnosis in 15 of the 26 cases, a success rate of 57 percent. The researchers caution, however, against the dangers of self-diagnosis. They maintain that people should use diagnostic information gained from Google and medical websites such as WebMD (*www.webmd.com*) only to ask questions of their physicians.

before you go on...

1. What are some of the quality-of-life improvements made possible by IT? Has IT had any negative effects on our quality of life?
2. Describe the robotic revolution, and consider its possible implications for humans.
3. Explain how IT has improved health care practices.

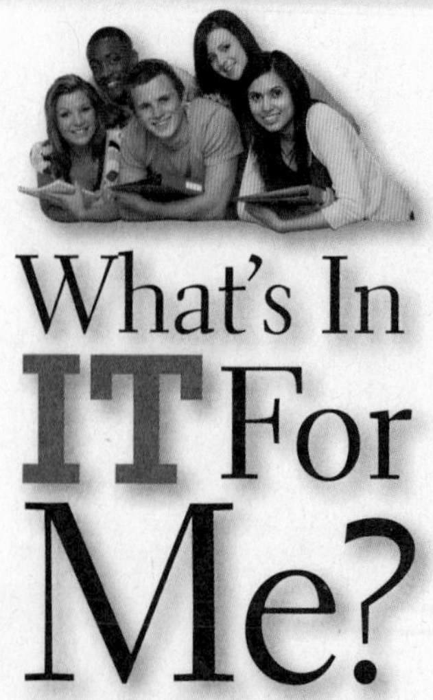

What's In IT For Me?

In section 1.2, we discussed how IT supports each of the functional areas of the organization. Here we examine the MIS function.

For the MIS Major

The MIS function directly supports all other functional areas in an organization. That is, the MIS function is responsible for providing the information that each functional area needs in order to make decisions. The overall objective of MIS personnel is to help users improve performance and solve business problems using IT. To accomplish this objective, MIS personnel must understand both the information requirements and the technology associated with each functional area. Given their position, however, they must think "business needs" first and "technology" second.

[Summary]

1. Begin the process of becoming an informed user of your organization's information systems.

The benefits of being an informed user of IT include:

- You will benefit more from your organization's IT applications because you will understand what is "behind" those applications.
- You will be able to provide input into your organization's IT applications, thus improving the quality of those applications.
- You will quickly be in a position to recommend or participate in the selection of IT applications that your organization will use.
- You will be able to keep up with rapid developments in existing information technologies, as well as the introduction of new technologies.
- You will understand the potential impacts that "new and improved" technologies will have on your organization and therefore will be qualified to make recommendations concerning their adoption and use.
- You will play a key role in managing the information systems in your organization.
- You will be in a position to use IT if you decide to start your own business.

2. Define the terms "data," "information," and "knowledge," and give examples of each.

Data items are an elementary description of things, events, activities, and transactions that are recorded, classified, and stored, but are not organized to convey any specific meaning. Examples of data items are collections of numbers (e.g., 3.11, 2.96, 3.95, 1.99, 2.08) and characters (e.g., B, A, C, A, B, D, F, C).

Information is data that have been organized so that they have meaning and value to the recipient. For example, a grade point average (GPA) by itself is data, but a student's name coupled with his or her GPA is information. In the above examples, the numbers could be GPAs, and the letters could be grades in an Introduction to MIS class.

Knowledge consists of data and/or information that have been organized and processed to convey understanding, experience, accumulated learning, and expertise as they apply to a current business problem. For example, a company recruiting at your school has found over time that students with GPAs over 3.0 have enjoyed the greatest success in its management program. Based on this accumulated knowledge, that company may decide to interview only those students with GPAs over 3.0.

3. Define the terms "information technology," "information system," "computer-based information system," and "application" and give examples of each.

Information technology (IT) is any computer-based tool that people use to work with information and to support the information and information-processing needs of an organization. An example is word processing or spreadsheet software. An *information system* (IS) collects, processes, stores, analyzes, and disseminates information for a specific purpose. An example is an online point of sale system. A *computer-based information system* (CBIS) is an information system that uses computer technology to perform some or all of its intended tasks. An example is an automated teller machine. An *application* (or *app*) is a computer program designed to support a specific task or business process, such as a payroll cheque payment system.

4. Identify three ways in which you depend on information technology in your daily life.

You are practising continuous computing, where you are surrounded with a movable information network. Think of all you do on-line, often with your phone: register for classes;

take classes, and not just classes from your university; access class syllabi, information, PowerPoints, and lectures; conduct banking; pay your bills; research, shop, and buy products from companies or other people; sell your "stuff"; search for, and apply for, jobs; have your own page on Facebook; text and tweet your friends and family throughout your day; and many other activities.

5. **Provide three ways in which information technology can impact managers and three ways in which it can impact non-managerial workers.**

   Potential IT impacts on managers include:

   - IT may reduce the number of middle managers.
   - IT will provide managers with real-time or near real-time information, meaning that managers will have less time to make decisions.
   - IT will increase the likelihood that managers will have to supervise geographically dispersed employees and teams.

   Potential IT impacts on non-managerial workers include:

   - IT may eliminate jobs.
   - IT may cause employees to experience a loss of identity.
   - IT can cause job stress and physical problems, such as repetitive stress injury.

6. **List three positive and three negative societal effects of the increased use of information technology.**

   Positive societal effects include:

   - IT can provide opportunities for people with disabilities.
   - IT can provide people with flexibility in their work (e.g., work from anywhere, anytime).
   - Robots will take over mundane chores.
   - IT will enable improvements in health care.

   Negative societal effects include:

   - IT can cause health problems for individuals.
   - IT can place employees on constant call.
   - IT can potentially misinform patients about their health problems.

[Chapter Glossary]

application (or **app**) A computer program designed to support a specific task or business process.

business intelligence (BI) system An information system that provides computer-based support for complex, nonrouine decisions, primarily for middle managers and knowledge workers.

computer-based information system (CBIS) An information system that uses computer technology to perform some or all of its intended tasks.

dashboards A special form of IS that support all managers of the organization by providing rapid access to timely information and direct access to structured information in the form of reports.

data items An elementary description of things, events, activities, and transactions that are recorded, classified, and stored but are not organized to convey any specific meaning.

database A collection of related files or tables containing data.

electronic commerce (e-commerce) systems A type of interorganizational information system that enables organizations to conduct transactions (business-to-business or B2B electronic commerce), and customers to conduct transactions with businesses (business-to-consumer or B2C electronic commerce).

enterprise resource planning (ERP) systems Information systems that correct a lack of communication among the functional area information systems by tightly integrating the functional area ISs via a common database.

ergonomics The science of adapting machines and work environments to people; focuses on creating an environment that is safe, well lit, and comfortable.

expert systems (ESs) Systems that attempt to duplicate the work of human experts by applying reasoning capabilities, knowledge, and expertise within a specific domain.

functional area information systems (FAISs) Information systems that support a particular functional area within the organization.

hardware A device such as a processor, monitor, keyboard, or printer. Together, these devices accept, process, and display data and information.

information Data that have been organized so that they have meaning and value to the recipient.

information system (IS) A system that collects, processes, stores, analyzes, and disseminates information for a specific purpose.

information technology (IT) Any computer-based tool that people use to work with information and support the information and information-processing needs of an organization.

information technology components Hardware, software, databases, and networks.

information technology infrastructure IT components plus IT services.

information technology platform An underlying system formed by the IT components of hardware, software, networks (wireline and wireless), and databases.

information technology services Services performed by IT personnel—using IT components—such as developing information systems, overseeing security and risk, and managing data.

informed user A person knowledgeable about information systems and information technology.

interorganizational information systems (IOSs) Information systems that connect two or more organizations.

knowledge Data and/or information that have been organized and processed to convey understanding, experience, accumulated learning, and expertise as they apply to a current problem or activity.

knowledge workers Professional employees such as financial and marketing analysts, engineers, lawyers, and accountants, who are experts in a particular subject area and create information and knowledge, which they integrate into the business.

network A connecting system (wireline or wireless) that permits different computers to share resources.

office automation systems (OASs) Information systems that typically support the clerical staff, lower and middle managers, and knowledge workers.

procedures The set of instructions for combining hardware, software, database, and network components in order to process information and generate the desired output.

software A program or collection of programs that enable the hardware to process data.

supply chain The flow of materials, information, money, and services from suppliers of raw materials through factories and warehouses to the end customers.

transaction processing system (TPS) A system that supports the monitoring, collection, storage, and processing of data from the organization's basic business transactions, each of which generates data.

[Discussion Questions]

1. Describe a business that you would like to start. Discuss how you would use global outsourcing to accomplish your goals.
2. Your university wants to recruit high-quality high school students from your home province. Provide examples of (1) the data that your recruiters would gather in this process, (2) the information that your recruiters would process from these data, and (3) the types of knowledge that your recruiters would infer from this information.
3. Can the terms "data," "information," and "knowledge" have different meanings for different people? Support your answer with examples.
4. Information technology makes it possible to never be out of touch. Discuss the pros and cons of always being available to your employers and clients (regardless of where you are or what you are doing).
5. Robots have the positive impact of being able to relieve humans from working in dangerous conditions. What are some negative impacts of robots in the workplace?
6. Is it possible to endanger yourself by accessing too much medical information on the web? Why or why not? Support your answer.
7. Is the vast amount of medical information on the web a good thing? Answer from the standpoint of a patient and from the standpoint of a physician.

8. Describe other potential impacts of IT on societies as a whole.
9. What are the major reasons why it is important for employees in all functional areas to become familiar with IT?
10. Refer to the study at Princess Alexandra Hospital in Australia (in the "Improvements in Health Care" section). How do you feel about Google searches finding the correct diagnosis in 57 percent of the cases? Are you impressed with these results? Why or why not? What are the implications of this study for self-diagnosis?

[Problem-Solving Activities]

1. Visit some websites that offer employment opportunities in IT. Prominent examples are: *www.dice.com, www.monster.ca, www.collegerecruiter.com, www.careerbuilder.ca, www.jobcentral.com, www.career.com,* and *www.simplyhired.ca*. Compare the IT salaries with salaries offered to accountants, marketing personnel, financial personnel, operations personnel, and human resources personnel. For other information on IT salaries, check *Computerworld*'s annual salary survey (*www.computerworld.com/s/article/9224243/IT_Salary_Survey_2012*).
2. Enter the website of UPS (*www.ups.com/canada/engindex.html*).
   a. Find out what information is available to customers before they send a package.
   b. Find out about the "package tracking" system.
   c. Calculate the cost of delivering a 10″ × 20″ × 15″ (25 cm × 50 cm × 25 cm) box, weighing 40 pounds (18 kg), from your hometown to Montreal, Québec (or to Vancouver, British Columbia, if you live in or near Montreal). Compare the fastest delivery against the least cost.
3. Surf the Internet for information about the federal Department of Public Safety and Emergency Preparedness. Examine the available information, and comment on the role of information technologies in the department.
4. Access *www.irobot.com* and investigate the company's education and research robots. Surf the web for other companies that manufacture robots, and compare their products with those of iRobot.

[Spreadsheet Activity]

Objective: A spreadsheet is a software tool that allows large amounts of data to be stored, organized, analyzed, and presented in graphical form. A spreadsheet is extremely useful because of its ability to make simple work of a mundane task (such as calculating the average inventory turnover time for 1,000 products). Although it is not difficult to calculate averages, the sheer volume of the work makes it very time-consuming. A spreadsheet allows you to create your own "formula" and then apply that formula to all 1,000 products at the same time, reducing the amount of necessary work dramatically. Given these possibilities, you need to take some time to consider the possible applications of a spreadsheet. It is the endless application of the spreadsheet that makes it so powerful. This activity will show you that this tool can be used for a variety of situations and purposes.

Chapter Connection: Data, information, and knowledge are the main focus of this chapter. Spreadsheets are just one of many tools (albeit the most widespread and easily accessible) that can be used to manage data, information, and knowledge.

Activity: As the text introduces the concepts of data, information, and knowledge, this activity will introduce you to the vast possibilities of using spreadsheets to help manage and control data. Unmanaged data will never provide information or knowledge, and so it is imperative to understand not only how to use a spreadsheet but the possibilities of when to use it. Consider the following three examples, and then develop your own ideas about how spreadsheets can be used.

- *Individual:* Money is something everyone has to deal with. A spreadsheet is a great tool to help track and manage personal finances. Someone with a spreadsheet budget can quickly see where his or her money is being spent and make plans for where it will go in the future. With a little creativity and experience, one can quickly create a personal spreadsheet that will help track finances without purchasing a separate money management software program.
- *Organizations:* It is still the simple things that make a big difference. Companies continue to seek better ways to manage inventory, and often these systems incorporate a spreadsheet. Many supply chain management tools will export data into spreadsheets for

analysis. Once in a spreadsheet, charts and graphs can be used to easily display how inventory is being handled.

- *Society:* Most governments periodically perform a census. Much of the resulting information is available to the public. A good deal of interesting information can be gained by placing these data in a spreadsheet. Charts and graphs can be used to analyze population changes, employment rates, demographic information, and trends over time. Spreadsheets can be used to tell a story with this information.

Having read these descriptions, describe to your professor how you might use a spreadsheet to help manage the required maintenance on your vehicle (or a vehicle that you would like to purchase in the future). Think about things like gas mileage, oil changes, and maintenance costs. What math formulas would you use that a spreadsheet could help with? If it will help, search the web for "vehicle maintenance spreadsheets" to see what other people do with it!

Deliverable: You will provide a written description that demonstrates the ways a spreadsheet can be used to help keep up with routine maintenance on a vehicle.

Discussion Questions

1. For data to be turned into information, they often need to be cleaned, organized, calculated, and ultimately presented in some graphical format. Spreadsheets are excellent at all of these. Discuss three tools that help spreadsheets accomplish all of these goals.
2. You have generated your own ideas for using spreadsheets. Be prepared to discuss your ideas with the class at large.

[Case Assignment]

Happy Pets Company (HPC) is an international company that makes pet food. HPC has many manufacturing locations around the world. It sells its products to a wide variety of outlets: pet stores, grocery stores, and department stores. Retailers can order products via the Internet using HPC's secure extranet, or via many other more traditional methods (e-mail, telephone, or paper orders).

HPC produces both dry and wet pet food products for various animals, including special products for older dogs and for hypo-allergenic diets. It also produces pet food treats in many flavours and shapes. The only products that have seasonal demand are the pet food treats, which seem to sell more around holiday times.

HPC conducts research into its brands and about pet food dietary needs, and regularly updates its products, providing at least one new type of pet food every two years.

Required

Describe data items, information, and knowledge, providing a clear example of how HPC would use each of these during the conduct of its business. Use a two-column table to record your answer. Show the description of data item, information, and knowledge in one column, and examples applied to HPC in the second column.

[Team Assignments]

1. Create an on-line group for studying IT or an aspect of IT that you are interested in. Use either Yahoo! groups or Google groups. Read about these groups and describe the differences between Yahoo! and Google groups.
2. Review the *Wall Street Journal*, *Toronto Star*, *Globe and Mail*, and local newspapers for the last three months to find stories about the use of computer-based information systems in organizations. Each group will prepare a report describing five applications. The reports should emphasize the role of each application and its benefit to the organization. Present and discuss your work.

[Case 1.2 L'Oréal Retools Its Information Systems]

The Problem

Headquartered in France, the L'Oréal Group (*www.loreal.com*) is the world's largest cosmetics and beauty company. With 23 global brands, the company focuses on products in the areas of hair colour, skin care, sun protection, makeup, perfumes, and hair care. The company's philosophy is that everyone aspires to beauty, and its core mission is to help people around the world realize that aspiration.

L'Oréal has more than 67,000 employees in 130 countries. The firm's products are manufactured in more than 40 factories located around the world. The company has a tremendous challenge to produce high-quality, consistent products globally. It must ensure that all of its products are created with uniform production processes and quality control.

By 2010, L'Oréal had come to realize that its current enterprise resource planning (ERP) system, based on software manufactured by SAP, could not support its goal of global product uniformity without consolidating its many different information systems located around the world. For example, L'Oréal had multiple versions of SAP running in different regions and countries. As a result, the company used to take between two and five years to upgrade to the latest version of SAP. L'Oréal also wanted to improve productivity, safety, and quality by standardizing the production processes throughout the firm.

The Solution

To accomplish its mission, L'Oréal reengineered its entire manufacturing process to work more efficiently while still supporting the quality of its brands. The company integrated its SAP ERP system with Apriso's (*www.apriso.com*) FlexNet for operations management. FlexNet is a unified set of manufacturing software applications that coordinate a company's manufacturing operations within a plant, between plants, and across an entire supply chain. The integration of SAP and FlexNet resulted in a global, central IT system called the Integrated Solution for Industrial Systems (ISIS). ISIS consists of all the transactional applications, financial controls, and purchasing transactions integrated into the manufacturing operations on the plant floor. FlexNet and ISIS support all factory processes—including production, quality assurance, and purchasing—while promoting L'Oréal's best practices.

ISIS runs in L'Oréal's central data centre in Montpellier, France, where the master data for the business are stored. FlexNet runs on servers located in individual factories so that each factory can continue operations in case a problem arises in the central data centre.

The Results

In its reengineering process, L'Oréal implemented a single, global instance of SAP and FlexNet, so the last upgrade took only one weekend. By upgrading so quickly, the firm was able to update its systems without disrupting its factories.

The new software implementation also allows L'Oréal to bring factories on-line much more quickly. In the past, when L'Oréal acquired a factory, it took years to bring it online. In contrast, the new software enabled L'Oréal to integrate an Yves St. Laurent factory that it had acquired, along with its quality assurance, safety, and efficiency practices, in two months.

Every L'Oréal factory can have thousands of products going through its production lines. Workers must follow the recipes for its cosmetic products exactly, including testing every ingredient for quality. With such exacting standards, human error is inevitable, which can affect quality, slow production, and lead to waste. With SAP and FlexNet, production workers are guided through each step of every recipe, including weighing each ingredient to ensure the amounts are accurate. As another quality control measure, workers must scan in the labels of ingredients that have been tested for quality before they are added to the product. Forklift drivers use the labels on the materials so they will know which ones are to be carried to which packaging stations. The labels also provide information on shelf life. Shop workers find that the new system has reduced the process's complexity.

By deploying a single, global instance of SAP and FlexNet, L'Oréal has increased its overall production capacity, decreased the gap in its actual-versus-planned production, and reduced its wasted materials. As a result, the company is able to maintain lower, better-managed inventories at significant cost savings.

Questions

1. Describe several reasons why L'Oréal needed to re-engineer its information systems.
2. Describe the benefits of L'Oréal's new information systems. Explain how the benefits you describe are related to L'Oréal's strategic goals, using specific examples to support your arguments.

Sources: Compiled from J. Playe, "L'Oreal's Manufacturing Makeover," *Baseline Magazine*, January 28, 2011; "Business Process Management in Manufacturing," *Aberdeen Research Report*, January 20, 2011; M. Littlefield, "Business Process Management in Manufacturing: Paving the Way for Effective Collaboration," *Aberdeen Research Report*, November 30, 2010; M. Johnson, "What's Happening with ERP Today," *CIO*, January 27, 2010; E. Lai, "Microsoft Brings BI to the Cloud," *Computerworld*, April 30, 2009; "Case Study: Siemens," *www.acresso.com*, 2008; *www.loreal.com*, *www.apriso.com*, accessed April 8, 2013.

[Interactive Case]

Planning a New Website for Ruby's Club

Go to the Ruby's Club link at the Student Companion website or *WileyPLUS* where you will find a description of your internship at Ruby's Club, a downtown music venue, and information for your assignment. Your assignment will include providing input on Ruby's new website design in a memo to the club's managers.

Chapter 2

Organizational Strategy, Competitive Advantage, and Information Systems

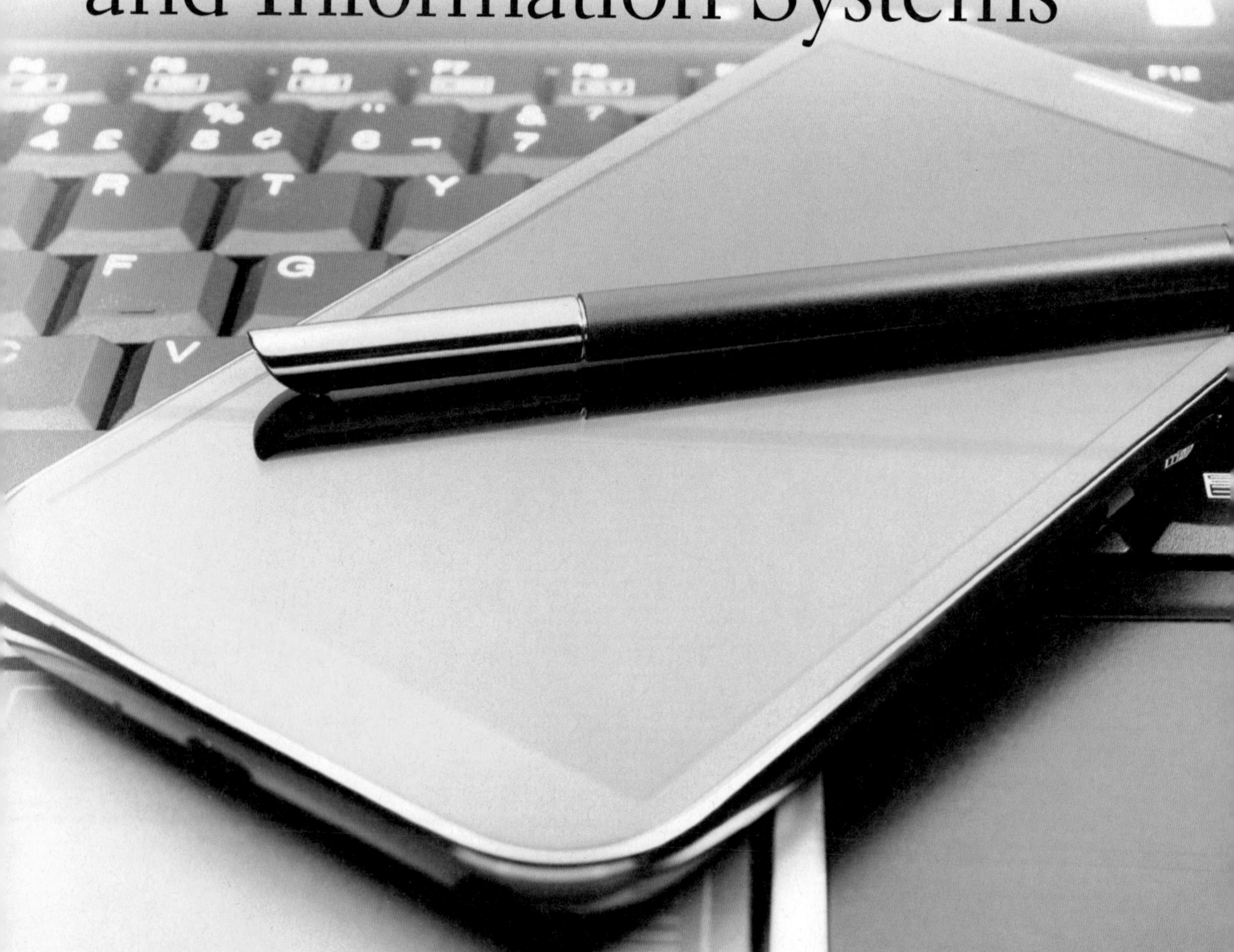

[LEARNING OBJECTIVES]

1. Understand the concept of business processes, and provide examples of business processes in the functional areas of an organization.
2. Differentiate between the terms "business process reengineering" and "business process management."
3. List and provide examples of the three types of business pressures, and describe one IT response to each.
4. Identify the five competitive forces described by Porter, and explain how the web has an impact on each one.
5. Describe the strategies that organizations typically adopt to counter the five competitive forces and achieve competitive advantage.
6. Define the term "business–information technology alignment," and describe the characteristics of effective alignment.
7. Define the term "IT governance" and explain why information systems need to be effectively managed and planned.

[CHAPTER OUTLINE]

2.1 Business Processes

2.2 Business Process Reengineering and Business Process Management

2.3 Business Pressures, Organizational Responses, and Information Technology Support

2.4 Competitive Advantage and Strategic Information Systems

2.5 Business–Information Technology Alignment

[WEB RESOURCES]

Student Companion Site
wiley.com/college/rainer

- Student PowerPoints for note taking
- Interactive Case: Ruby's Club Assignments
- Complete glossary

WileyPlus

All of the above and

- E-book
- Practice quizzes
- Flash Cards for vocabulary review
- Additional "What's in IT for Me?" cases
- Video interviews with managers
- Lab Manual for Microsoft Office 2010
- How-to Animations for Microsoft Office 2010

What's In IT For Me?
THIS CHAPTER WILL HELP PREPARE YOU TO ...
ACCT
Perform audits
FIN
Determine best uses for funds
MKT
Conduct price analyses
POM
Monitor product quality
HR
Help employees manage their careers
MIS
Develop systems to support firm's strategy

[Case 2.1 Double Trouble For BP]

BP's First Problem

In 2008, CEO Tony Hayward of BP (*www.bp.com*) gathered his top 500 managers and told them the stark news: the giant oil company had become a serial underperformer. Among those who listened to their leader was Dana Deasy, BP's chief information officer (CIO). Deasy knew that his IT group would have to do a much better job of supporting Hayward's goals: to reignite revenue growth across the enormous company (with annual revenues of $300 billion), to refocus the company's behaviour around high performance and accountability, and to reduce BP's complexity. With 4,200 employees and a $3-billion annual budget, BP's IT group was big, sluggish, unaccountable, and unfocused.

Media Bakery

Deasy wanted to slash IT expenses by $800 million and change the IT function from a cost centre into a strategic tool. To do this, Deasy came up with a three-year plan to overhaul the IT group, including halving the number of IT vendors, evaluating and reducing the number of IT employees, and reducing the 8,500 software applications in use at BP globally.

The Solution to BP's First Problem

Deasy set his sights first on BP's IT workers—only half of whom were actually BP employees. About 1,900 of them were contractors, and Deasy eliminated 1,000 full-time contractor positions. But he didn't stop there: Deasy also replaced 80 percent of BP's top IT managers.

Next, Deasy hired IBM to assess the strengths and identify talent gaps of the top 1,000 IT employees (excluding the remaining contractors). The biggest gaps identified were in the areas of the organizational location of the IT function, project and portfolio management, and vendor management.

With his new team in place, Deasy shuffled the IT organizational structure, moving from a hierarchy to more of a matrix. Each of BP's business units has a CIO. Deasy mandated that these CIOs report to the business unit leader as well as to Deasy. In addition, those CIOs were made accountable for the bottom line. That is, Deasy ensured that their primary responsibility was to help the business units use IT effectively to increase revenue and reduce costs.

Deasy's cost-cutting moves then affected BP's vendors, of whom there were more than 2,000—although the 20 largest vendors accounted for only 30 percent of IT spending. This arrangement was not only costly, but was unwieldy. BP put nearly two thirds of its annual global IT spending—about $1.5 billion—up for rebid in one year. As a result, BP eliminated 1,200 IT vendors and saved $900 million over the next five years.

In the area of application development and maintenance, the high number of IT vendors—about 50—was causing additional problems. Most of them refused to talk with one another for fear of losing their share of BP's business. By issuing a new request for proposals for multi-year application development and maintenance contracts, totalling about $2 billion, BP ended up with just five vendors. By following a standard operating model, these vendors ensure their work is done according to standards and is integrated, saving an estimated $500 million.

Crucial to BP's business is its enterprise software, including that from SAP. BP created a team focused on standardizing how it implemented and managed SAP applications around the world. BP's goal was to deliver SAP upgrades and new features 50 percent faster and 40 percent cheaper than under the existing system.

The Results

Deasy and his team finished their overhaul a year ahead of schedule. BP saved $800 million in IT spending, reduced the number of vendors by 60 percent, significantly reduced the number of software applications, and overhauled the IT reporting structure in the business units.

Beyond the number-crunching, though, BP's IT transformation yielded two major benefits that are difficult to quantify:

- The almost complete turnover in IT personnel, which resulted in replacing generalists with specialists in a certain technology or business.
- The turnaround in the IT organization's culture, which went from being indifferent about cost and results to being committed to relentless improvement, innovation, and a focus on business growth.

BP's Second Problem

BP had little time to bask in the success of its IT transformation. Soon after, in April 2010, the company's Deepwater Horizon offshore oil-drilling rig, located in the Gulf of Mexico, exploded, killing 11 crewmembers and creating a fireball visible 60 kilometres away. The company spent the next three months capping the well. As oil continued to pour into the Gulf, it caused the world's largest-ever marine oil spill.

The explosion was investigated by the National Commission on the BP Deepwater Horizon Oil Spill and Offshore Drilling, a U.S. federal authority. The commission laid most of the blame on BP's monitoring IT systems, finding that they had failed to provide automatic alerts that there was something wrong with the Deepwater Horizon oil platform. Instead of relying on automated systems, BP's engineers had to manually monitor and analyze complex data from the well over long work days.

The commission further added to BP's IT woes, finding that the company had ignored the data from a cement modelling software implemented by Halliburton, the cement contractor. The software, OptiCem, had indicated that more stabilizers were needed to support the underwater cement work. The commission's report found a breakdown in communication, criticizing Halliburton for failing to share data from tests on its cement mix with BP.

While not mentioned in the commission's report, BP also failed to take advantage of social media to open a clear line of communication with people living nearby and around the world. BP could have used sites such as Facebook, YouTube, and Twitter to report on what steps the company was taking to cap the spill and contain the damage.

The Solution (?) to BP's Second Problem

In addition to technological efforts to cap the spill, BP spent huge amounts on public relations. For example, it paid large sums of money to buy Google ads, which directed people to BP's own website. Media reports claimed that BP was buying Google ads to catapult its own website to the top of the list of advertisements that appeared when Internet users searched on terms such as "oil spill," "volunteer," and "claims." The BP website contained press releases and photographs of people involved in the oil cleanup, but did not show the spill or its effects on the landscape or animals.

The Results

While BP capped the spill after three months, scientists said that the damage from the oil would continue for many years.

Several months after the spill, the U.S. government launched a $21.1-billion lawsuit against BP and its drilling partners, alleging that they had "failed … to use the best available and safest drilling technology" to monitor pressure in the well. Legal experts predict that all the lawsuits involved could take up to 20 years to complete.

On October 1, 2010, BP CEO Tony Hayward resigned his position.

What We Learned from This Case

The BP case illustrates the importance of information systems in helping a company respond to business pressures and in supporting the company's global strategy. The case demonstrates that any information system can be *strategic*, meaning that it can provide a competitive advantage if used properly.

The case also demonstrates the incredible complexity of the information systems employed by a large, international company. BP did an excellent job of revamping the information systems that support its business operations. However, the company seemed to neglect those information systems that support its drilling operations, which are clearly just as strategic as the firm's business information systems.

Information systems can be just as strategic to a small or medium-sized company as they are to a large firm. IT's About Small Business 2.1 illustrates how information systems are strategically important to Shopcaster.

Strategy and competitive advantage come in many forms. (**Competitive advantage** is an advantage over competitors in some measure such as cost, quality, or speed; it leads to control of a market and to larger-than-average profits.)

Amazon, the world's largest on-line retailer, is always looking for unique business ideas. What could you do with an Amazon store?

As you study this chapter, think of the small businesses in your area that are doing interesting things with popular technologies. Do any of them use Twitter in an interesting way? Facebook? Amazon? PayPal? If not, can you think of any businesses that would benefit from using these technologies?

This chapter is important for you for several reasons. First, the business pressures addressed here will affect your organization, but they also will affect you. As a result, you must understand how information systems can help you, and eventually your organization, respond to these pressures.

IT's about [small] business

2.1 Boosting Store Power

Retail store owners set up shop because they believe that they have something powerful to sell: something that is useful, priced right, and perhaps the best in its field. A website is often the last thing that retailers think of, and they often do not think of the website as a place that will help them drive people into their store. The founders of Canadian start-up Shopcaster (*http://shopcaster.com*) were looking for a way to help retailers sell their products, and had originally thought to create a classification scheme that would cross-list and supplement selling sites such as Craigslist and Kijiji. However, they did their homework and talked to local retailers instead. It turned out that the biggest problem was for stores to show their latest and greatest products on-line without having to spend large dollars on website development or on specialist staff.

So, the company built a platform for showcasing products instead. Member retailers can use any digital camera (or even their cell phone) to take photographs of their new inventory, then upload these to a shopping interface at Shopcaster.com. As of February 2012, there were over 300 Toronto stores using Shopcaster, with more than 10 times as many products.

Retailers say that the use of Shopcaster increases traffic in their stores, since people come into the store to buy the product that they have seen on-line. This software is local—it is for people living in the area. Customers can browse with their smart phones, then drop in to the store and touch and feel the product before buying. In this way, wireless computing and the Internet facilitate local businesses, in addition to e-commerce.

The idea is so successful that the company raised $1 million of private investor capital in mid-2012 to enable expansion to other cities across Canada and the United States.

Questions

1. Would you buy a membership in Shopcaster if you were a store owner? Why or why not? What type of product do you think would benefit most from the software?
2. Would you invest in Shopcaster? Why or why not?

Sources: Compiled from E. Bury, "We Heard, Then Built It," *business.financialpost.com*, February 21, 2012; Canada Newswire, "Local E-commerce Platform Shopcaster Announces $2 Million Round of Financing, Plans to Expand to New Cities," *www.newswire.ca*, July 9, 2012; *http://shopcaster.com*, accessed April 9, 2013.

Sources: Compiled from L. King, "BP Oil Spill IT Systems Lacked Key Alarms," *Computerworld*, January 6, 2011; S. Mufson, "BP, Transocean, Halliburton Blamed by Presidential Gulf Oil Spill Commission," *The Washington Post*, January 5, 2011; D. Bates, "BP Accepts Blame for Gulf of Mexico Spill After Leaked Memo Reveals Engineer Misread Pressure Reading," *The Daily Mail*, August 30, 2010; S. Gaudin, "BP, in Crisis Mode, Misses Social Networking Target," *Computerworld*, June 15, 2010; P. Gralla, "BP's Disaster Containment Plan—Throw Plenty of Money at Google," *Computerworld*, June 11, 2010; S. Power, R. Gold, and N. King, "Staffing Levels on Deepwater Horizon Are Questioned," *The Wall Street Journal*, June 8, 2010; B. Evans, "BP's IT Transformation," *InformationWeek*, March 8, 2010; J. Stempel, "Special Report: BP Oil Spill a Gusher for Lawyers," Reuters, June 30, 2010; *www.bp.com*, accessed February 26, 2013.

In addition, acquiring competitive advantage is essential for your organization's survival. Many organizations achieve competitive advantage through the efforts of their employees. Therefore, becoming knowledgeable about strategy and how information systems have an impact on strategy and competitive position will help you throughout your career.

This chapter encourages you to become familiar with your organization's strategy, mission, and goals and to understand its business problems and how it makes (or loses) money. It will help you understand how information technology contributes to organizational strategy. Further, you likely will become a member of business/IT committees that decide (among many other things) whether to adopt new technologies and how to use existing technologies more effectively. After studying this chapter, you will be able to make immediate contributions to these committees when you join your organization.

In many cases, organizations gain competitive advantage by managing their business processes better than their competitors do. Therefore, we begin this chapter with a brief introduction to business processes and business process management. You will then see how information systems enable organizations to respond to business pressures. Next, you will learn how information systems help organizations gain competitive advantages in the marketplace. The chapter concludes by discussing business–IT alignment; in other words, how an organization's IT function supports the organization's strategy.

2.1 Business Processes

A **business process** is an ongoing collection of related activities that create a product or a service of value to the organization, its business partners, and/or its customers. A process has inputs and outputs, and its activities can be measured. Many processes cross functional areas in an organization. For example, product development involves research, design, engineering, manufacturing, marketing, and distribution. Other processes involve only a single functional area.

Functional Processes

Table 2.1 identifies the fundamental business processes performed in an organization's functional areas.

Cross-Functional Processes

All of the business processes discussed above fall within a single functional area of the company. However, many other business processes, such as materials procurement and order fulfillment, cut across multiple functional areas; that is, they are **cross-functional business processes**, meaning that no single functional area is responsible for their execution. Rather, multiple functional areas collaborate to perform the process. For a cross-functional process to be successfully completed, each functional area must execute its specific process steps in a coordinated, collaborative way. To clarify this point, let's examine the procurement and fulfillment cross-functional processes in more detail.

The materials procurement process includes all of the tasks involved in acquiring needed materials externally from a vendor. Procurement comprises five steps that are completed in three different functional areas of the firm: warehouse, purchasing, and accounting.

The process begins when the warehouse recognizes the need to procure materials, perhaps due to low inventory levels. The warehouse documents this need with a purchase requisition, which it sends to the purchasing department (Step 1). In turn, the purchasing department identifies a suitable vendor, creates a purchase order based on the purchase requisition, and sends the order to the vendor (Step 2). When the vendor receives the purchase order, it ships the materials, which are received in the warehouse (Step 3). The vendor then sends an invoice, which is received by the accounting department (Step 4). Accounting sends payment to the vendor, thereby completing the procurement process (Step 5).

The fulfillment process is concerned with efficiently processing customer orders. Fulfillment is triggered by a customer purchase order that is received by the sales department. Sales

Table 2.1

Examples of Business Processes

Accounting Business Processes
- Managing accounts payable
- Managing accounts receivable
- Reconciling bank accounts
- Managing cash receipts
- Managing invoice billings
- Managing petty cash
- Producing month-end close
- Producing virtual close

Finance Business Processes
- Managing account collection
- Managing bank loan applications
- Producing business forecasts
- Applying customer credit approval and credit terms
- Producing property tax assessments
- Managing stock transactions
- Generating financial cash flow reports

Marketing Business Processes
- Managing post-sale customer follow-up
- Collecting sales taxes
- Applying copyrights and trademarks
- Using customer satisfaction surveys
- Managing customer service
- Handling customer complaints
- Handling returned goods from customers
- Producing sales leads
- Entering sales orders
- Training sales personnel

Production/Operations Management Business Processes
- Processing bills of materials
- Processing manufacturing change orders
- Managing master parts list and files
- Managing packing, storage, and distribution
- Processing physical inventory
- Managing purchasing
- Managing quality control for finished goods
- Auditing for quality assurance
- Receiving, inspecting, and stocking parts and materials
- Handling shipping and freight claims
- Handling vendor selection, files, and inspections

Human Resources Business Processes
- Applying disability policies
- Managing employee hiring
- Handling employee orientation
- Managing files and records
- Applying health care benefits
- Managing pay and payroll
- Producing performance appraisals and salary adjustments
- Managing resignations and terminations
- Applying training/tuition reimbursement
- Managing travel and entertainment
- Managing workplace rules and guidelines
- Overseeing workplace safety

Management Information Systems Business Processes
- Implementing antivirus controls
- Reporting computer security incidents
- Training computer users
- Applying disaster recovery procedures
- Applying electronic mail policy
- Generating Internet use policy
- Managing service agreements and emergency services
- Applying user workstation standards
- Managing the use of personal software

then validates the purchase order and creates a sales order. The sales order communicates data related to the order to other functional areas within the organization, and it tracks the progress of the order. The warehouse prepares and sends the shipment to the customer. Once accounting is notified of the shipment, it creates an invoice and sends it to the customer. The customer then makes a payment, which accounting records.

An organization's business processes can create a competitive advantage if they enable the company to innovate or to execute better than its competitors. They can also be liabilities if they make the company less responsive and efficient. Consider the airline industry. It has become a competitive necessity for all airlines to offer electronic ticket purchases via their websites. At the same time, however, these sites must be highly responsive and provide the most current information on flights and prices. An up-to-date, user-friendly site will attract customers and increase revenues. In contrast, a site that provides outdated or inaccurate information will hurt rather than improve business. Figure 2.1 illustrates the e-ticket purchasing business process.

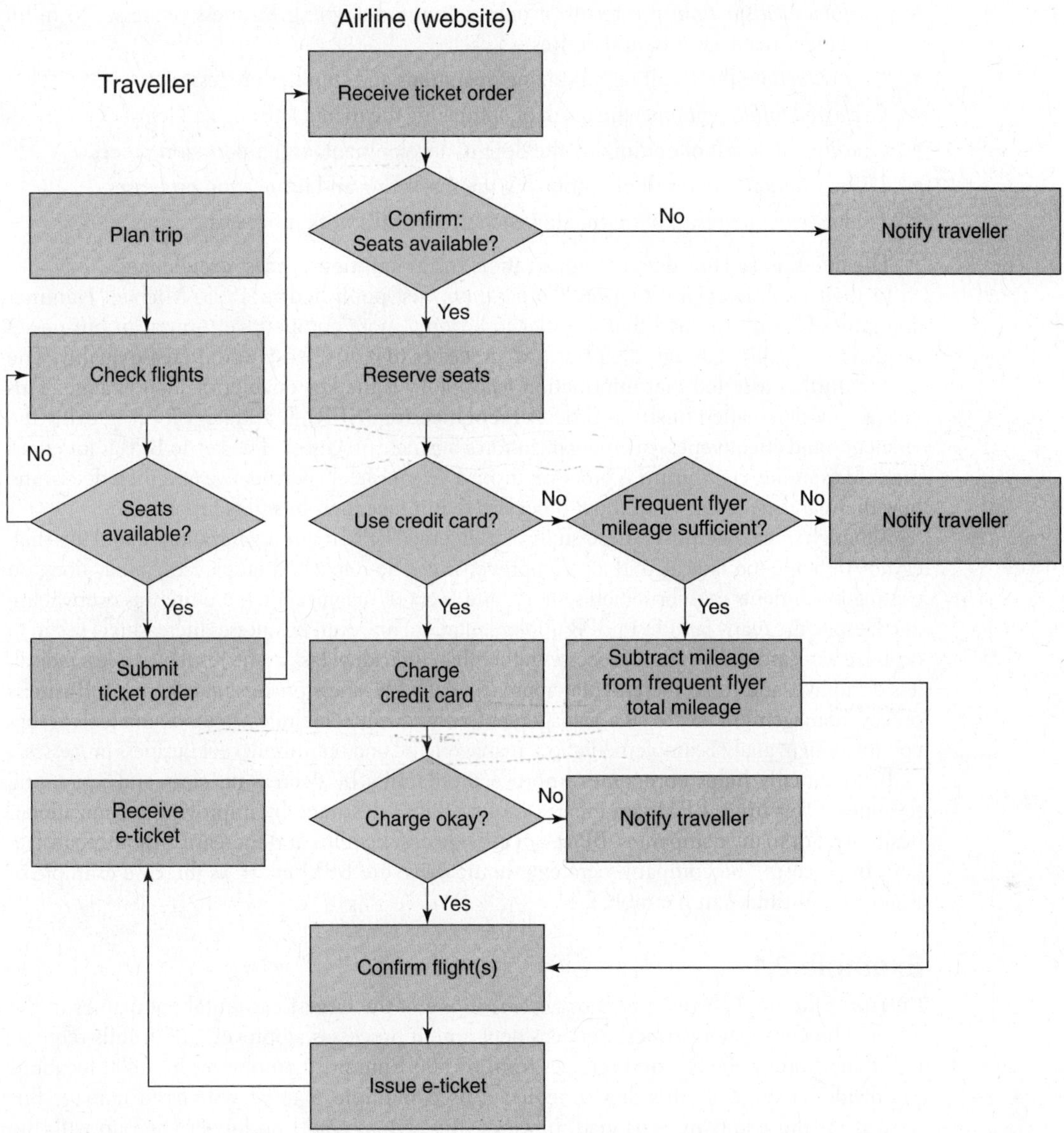

FIGURE 2.1 Business process for ordering an e-ticket from an airline website.

before you go on...

1. What is a business process?
2. Describe several business processes carried out at your university.
3. Define a cross-functional business process, and provide several examples of such processes.

2.2 Business Process Reengineering and Business Process Management

It is widely recognized that all of an organization's significant measures of competitive performance have excellence in executing business processes as their underlying basis. Consider the following outcomes that can be measured, for example:

- *Customer satisfaction*: the result of optimizing and aligning business processes to fulfill customers' needs, wants, and desires
- *Cost reduction*: the result of optimizing operations and supplier processes
- *Cycle and fulfillment time*: the result of optimizing the manufacturing and logistics processes
- *Quality*: the result of optimizing the design, development, and production processes
- *Differentiation*: the result of optimizing the marketing and innovation processes
- *Productivity*: the result of optimizing each individual's work processes

The question is: How does an organization ensure business process excellence?

In their book *Reengineering the Corporation*, first published in 1993, Michael Hammer and James Champy argued that in order to become more competitive, American businesses needed to radically redesign their business processes to reduce costs and increase quality. The authors further asserted that information technology is the key enabler of such change. This radical redesign, called **business process reengineering (BPR)**, is a strategy for improving the efficiency and effectiveness of an organization's business processes. The key to BPR is for enterprises to examine their business processes from a "clean sheet" perspective and then determine how they can best reconstruct those processes to improve their business functions.

Although some enterprises successfully implemented BPR, many organizations found this strategy too difficult, too radical, and too comprehensive. The impact on employees, on facilities, on existing investments in information systems, and even on organizational culture was overwhelming. Despite the many failures in BPR implementation, however, businesses increasingly began to organize work around business processes rather than individual tasks. The result was a less radical, less disruptive, and more incremental approach, called business process management. **Business process management (BPM)** is a management technique that includes methods and tools to support the design, analysis, implementation, management, and optimization of business processes.

BPM initially helps companies improve profitability by decreasing costs and increasing revenues. Over time, BPM can create a competitive advantage by improving organizational flexibility. For many companies, BPM can provide cost benefits and increase customer satisfaction. In all cases, the company's strategy should drive the BPM effort, as the case example of Enterprise illustrates in Example 2.1.

Example 2.1

Enterprise Rent-A-Car (*www.enterprise.com*) is one of the largest car rental companies in the world. The company's Request Services department processes, approves, and fulfills requests for IT hardware, software, and services from 65,000 Enterprise employees in 7,000 locations worldwide. Historically this department had used multiple manual systems to manage this process. As the company expanded, however, this system could no longer keep up with the growing number of IT requests. Determined to improve this process, Enterprise initiated a BPM project and selected a product from Appian (*www.appian.com*).

Before Enterprise actually started the project, the company made certain that its strategy was in place. Enterprise recognized that implementing a new process would transform the company's traditional work behaviours. Therefore, the Request Services department engaged key stakeholders—primarily the people who approve IT product and service requests and the people who fulfill these requests—early in the project. The company also educated employees about BPM in general as well as in how to use the new Appian system.

Enterprise has used its new platform to expand its van-pool services offered by one of its affiliates (see *www.enterpriserideshare.com*), which signs up users for van sharing. Sales staff can do all of their work remotely using an iPad while still having access to the power of the in-house Appian system.

Sources: Compiled from B. Violino, "BPM Success at Enterprise," *Baseline Magazine*, March 13, 2009; B. Violino, "BPM: Strategy Before Software," *CIO Insight*, March 13, 2009; D. Byron, "Appian BPM at Enterprise: Can Renting BPM Be Like Renting a Car?," *www.ebizq.net/blogs/bpminaction/2008/03/appian_bpm_at_enterprise_can_r.php*, February 16, 2013; "Enterprise Rent-A-Car Goes Live with Appian Enterprise," Appian press release (*www.appian.com/bpm-company/news/press/enterprise-rent-a-car-goes-live-with-appian-enterprise.jsp*), February 16, 2013; *www.enterprise.com*, accessed February 16, 2013; *www.appian.com*, "Enterprise Holdings, Inc. Runs Enterprise Rideshare on Appian Worksocial," accessed February 16, 2013.

After the BPM system was implemented, Enterprise eliminated its manual processes entirely. Its employees now use the Appian system to request IT products and services. Significantly, Request Services now fulfill requests more promptly while making fewer errors than they did with the manual system. In addition, the new process contains business rules that provide appropriate restrictions on fulfillment (e.g., what IT hardware, software, or service an employee is entitled to).

Important components of BPM are process modelling, web-enabled technologies, and business activity monitoring. BPM begins with *process modelling,* which is a graphical depiction of all the steps in a process. Process modelling helps employees understand the interactions and dependencies among the people, the information systems they rely on, and the information they require to optimally perform their tasks.

Web-enabled technologies display and retrieve data via a web browser. They enable an organization to integrate the necessary people and applications into each process.

Business activity monitoring (BAM) is a real-time approach for measuring and managing business processes. Companies use BAM to monitor their business processes, identify failures or exceptions, and address these failures in real time. Further, because BAM tracks process operations and indicates whether they succeed or fail, it creates valuable records of process behaviours that organizations can use to improve their processes.

before you go on...

1. What is business process reengineering? What are its advantages and disadvantages?
2. What is business process management? What are its advantages?

2.3 Business Pressures, Organizational Responses, and Information Technology Support

Modern organizations compete in a challenging environment. To remain competitive they must react rapidly to problems and opportunities that arise from extremely dynamic conditions. In this section we examine some of the major pressures confronting modern organizations and the strategies that organizations employ to respond to these pressures.

Business Pressures

The **business environment** is the combination of social, legal, economic, physical, and political factors in which businesses conduct their operations. Significant changes in any of these factors are likely to create business pressures on organizations. Organizations typically respond to these pressures with activities supported by IT. Figure 2.2 illustrates the relationships among business pressures, organizational performance and responses, and IT support. You will learn about three major types of business pressures: market, technology, and societal pressures.

Market Pressures.

Market pressures are generated by the global economy, intense competition, the changing nature of the workforce, and powerful customers. Let's look more closely at each of these factors.

Globalization. **Globalization** is the integration and interdependence of economic, social, cultural, and ecological facets of life, made possible by rapid advances in information technology. In his book *The World Is Flat,* Pulitzer Prize-winning author Thomas Friedman argues that technology is levelling the global competitive playing field, thereby making it "flat."

Friedman identifies three eras of globalization. The first era, Globalization 1.0, lasted from 1492 to 1800. During this era, the force behind globalization was how much muscle, horsepower, wind power, or steam power a country could deploy.

The second era, Globalization 2.0, lasted from 1800 to 2000. In this era, the force behind globalization was the emergence of multinational companies; that is, companies had their headquarters in one country but operated in several countries. In the first half of this era, globalization

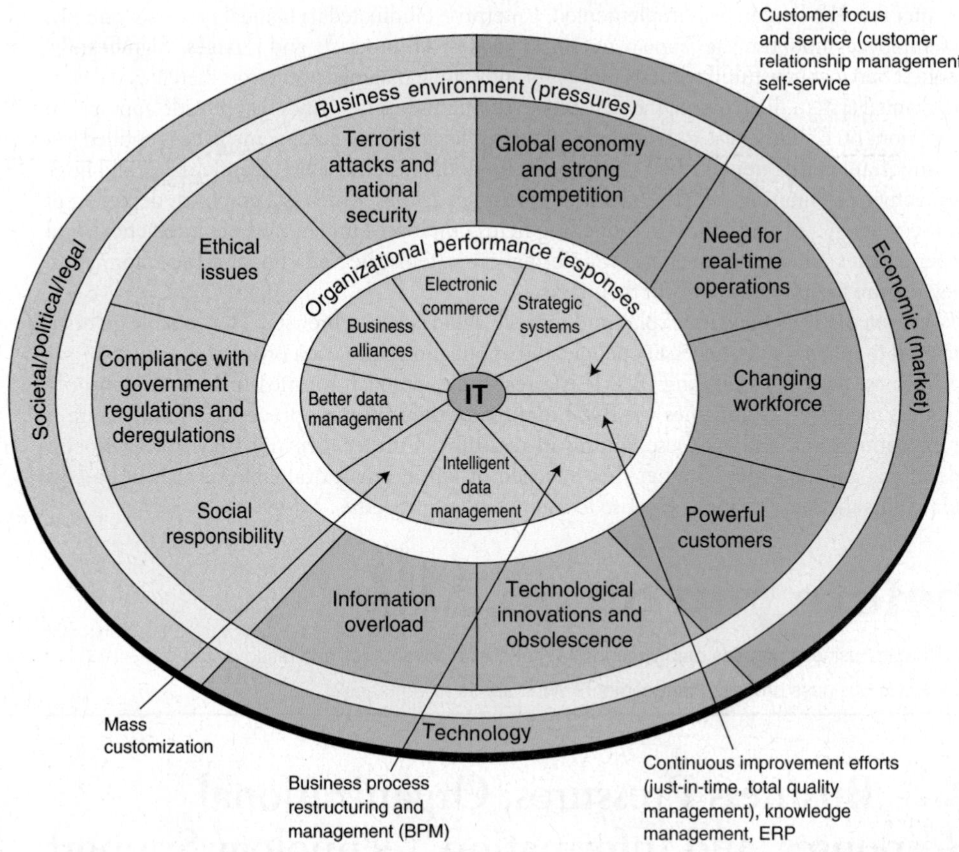

FIGURE 2.2 Business pressures, organizational performance and responses, and IT support.

was driven by falling transportation costs, generated by the development of the steam engine and the railroads. In the second half, the driving force was falling telecommunications costs resulting from the telegraph, telephones, computers, satellites, fibre-optic cable, and the Internet and World Wide Web. The modern global economy began to evolve during this era.

Around the year 2000, the world entered Globalization 3.0. In this era, globalization has been driven by the convergence of 10 forces that Friedman calls "flatteners." Table 2.2 identifies these forces.

According to Friedman, each era has been characterized by a distinctive focus. The focus of Globalization 1.0 was on countries, the focus of Globalization 2.0 was on companies, and the focus of Globalization 3.0 is on groups and individuals.

As you look at Table 2.2, note that nine of Friedman's 10 flatteners directly relate to IT (all except the fall of the Berlin Wall). These flatteners enable individuals to connect, compute, communicate, collaborate, and compete everywhere and anywhere, anytime and all the time; to access limitless amounts of information, services, and entertainment; to exchange knowledge; and to produce and sell goods and services. People and organizations can now operate without regard to geography, time, distance, or even language barriers. The bottom line? Globalization is markedly increasing competition.

These observations highlight the importance of market pressures for you. Simply put, you and the organizations you join will be competing with people and organizations from all over a flat world.

Let's consider some examples of globalization. Regional agreements such as the North American Free Trade Agreement (NAFTA), which includes Canada, the United States, and Mexico, have contributed to increased world trade and increased competition. Further, the rise of India and China as economic powerhouses has increased global competition.

One important pressure that businesses in a global market must contend with is the cost of labour, which varies widely among countries. In general, labour costs are higher in developed countries like Canada and Japan than in developing countries such as China and El Salvador. Also, developed

Table 2.2

Friedman's 10 Flatteners

- **Fall of the Berlin Wall on November 9, 1989**
  - Shifted the world toward free-market economies and away from centrally planned economies.
  - Led to the emergence of the European Union and early thinking about the world as a single, global market.
- **Netscape goes public on August 9, 1995**
  - Popularized the Internet and the World Wide Web.
- **Development of workflow software**
  - Enabled computer applications to work with one another without human intervention.
  - Enabled faster, closer collaboration and coordination among employees, regardless of their location.
- **Uploading**
  - Empowered all Internet users to create content and put it on the web.
  - Led the transition from a passive approach to content to an active, participatory, collaborative approach.
- **Outsourcing**
  - Involved contracting with an outside company to perform a specific function that your company was doing itself and then integrating their work back into your operation; for example, moving customer call centres to India.
- **Offshoring**
  - Involved relocating an entire operation, or certain tasks, to another country; for example, moving an entire manufacturing operation to China.
- **Supply chaining**
  - Supported by the technological revolution, resulted in the creation of networks composed of companies, their suppliers, and their customers, all of which could collaborate and share information for increased efficiency.
- **Insourcing**
  - Involved delegating operations or jobs within a business to another company that specializes in those operations; for example, Dell hires FedEx to "take over" Dell's logistics process.
- **Informing**
  - Led to the ability to search for information, best illustrated by search engines.
- **The steroids** (computing, instant messaging and file sharing, wireless technologies, Voice over Internet Protocol, videoconferencing, and computer graphics)
  - Technologies that amplify the other flatteners.
  - Enable all forms of computing and collaboration to be digital, mobile, and personal.

countries usually offer greater benefits, such as enhanced health care, to employees, driving the cost of doing business even higher. Therefore, many labour-intensive industries have moved their operations to countries with low labour costs. IT has made such moves much easier to implement.

However, IT's About Business 2.2 illustrates the problems that can arise when companies outsource their manufacturing processes overseas.

The Changing Nature of the Workforce. The workforce, particularly in developed countries, is becoming more diversified. Increasing numbers of women, single parents, minorities, and persons with disabilities are now employed in all types of positions. IT is easing the integration of these employees into the traditional workforce. IT is also enabling people to work from home, which can be a major benefit for parents with young children and for people confronted with mobility and/or transportation issues.

Powerful Customers. Consumer sophistication and expectations increase as customers become more knowledgeable about the products and services they acquire. Customers can use the Internet to find detailed information about products and services, to compare prices, and to purchase items at electronic auctions.

Organizations recognize the importance of customers and have increased their efforts to acquire and retain them. Modern firms strive to learn as much as possible about their customers to better anticipate and address their needs. This process, called *customer intimacy*, is an important component of *customer relationship management* (CRM), an organization-wide effort toward maximizing the customer experience. You will learn about CRM in Chapter 9.

Technology Pressures. The second category of business pressures consists of those pressures related to technology. Two major technology-related pressures are technological innovation and information overload.

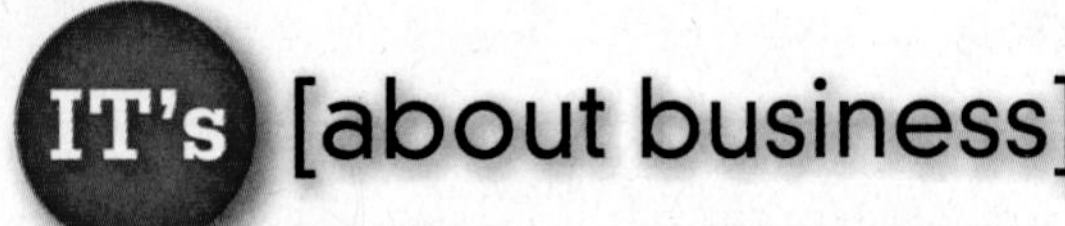

2.2 Sleek Audio

The CEO of Sleek Audio (*www.sleek-audio.com*) was frustrated with a contract factory in Dongguan, China, that assembled the majority of his company's products. Not only did he have to travel to China every few months to troubleshoot quality flaws, but manufacturing problems in the factory threatened to bankrupt his company. In one case, Sleek Audio had to discard an entire shipment of 10,000 earphones because they were improperly welded—a mistake that cost the company millions of dollars. Further, delivery delays caused by the factory's lax approach to deadlines forced Sleek Audio to spend huge amounts of money air-freighting products to the United States. As a result, the company had far too much money tied up in inventory that took months to arrive after the prototypes were developed.

Lessons From IT Failures

Sleek Audio decided to search for a manufacturing partner that possessed the necessary tools and expertise to produce their earphones. They found one, Dynamic Innovations, located close to their headquarters in Palmetto, Florida. One year later, Sleek Audio had a full-scale manufacturing operation that could be reached with a 15-minute car ride rather than a 24-hour flight. Each earphone costs roughly 50 percent more to produce in Florida than in China. Sleek Audio is happy to pay the premium, however, for the assurance that botched orders and shipping delays will not ruin the company. Based on enthusiastic customer response, Sleek Audio had projected 2011 to be its most profitable year ever.

When Sleek Audio was considering how the company could return manufacturing to the United States with its higher labour costs, company executives realized that the only way to make the move feasible was to minimize the role of humans on the assembly line. This process meant redesigning products to take advantage of automated tools and robots.

Sleek Audio's earphones featured plastic side panels that the Chinese factory had to weld into place by hand. In the U.S. factory the company automated this process by replacing human labour with robots. Managers redesigned the entire product around a solid aluminum centre into which robots insert the speaker. This new assembly process requires neither welding nor human hands. Moreover, as shown in Chapter 1, robots are becoming more skilled and less expensive.

Questions

1. Which of Friedman's flatteners apply to Sleek Audio's decision to bring its manufacturing back to the United States? Support your answer.
2. Identify some potential negative implications of Sleek Audio's increasing reliance on robots in its manufacturing processes.

Sources: Compiled from "Bring Manufacturing Jobs Home!" *Deloitte Debates* (*www.deloitte.com*), 2011; R. Read, "In Reverse of Offshore Trend, Oregon Manufacturing Thrives When High-Tech, High-Quality Products Are Needed," *The Oregonian*, September 18, 2010; T. George, "U.S. Sourcing Firms Bid to Reverse Offshoring Trend," *Nearshore Americas*, April 8, 2010; B. Koerner, "Made in the USA," *Wired*, March, 2011; "Is Reverse Offshoring a Trend?," *Supply Chainer*, October 25, 2008; J. Aitoro, "Offshore Manufacturing: A Risky Proposition?," *CRN.com*, June 25, 2007; *www.sleek-audio.com*, accessed February 16, 2013.

Technological Innovation and Obsolescence. New and improved technologies rapidly create or support substitutes for products, alternative service options, and superb quality. As a result, today's state-of-the-art products may be obsolete tomorrow. For example, how fast are new versions of your smart phone being released? How quickly are electronic versions of books, magazines, and newspapers replacing traditional hard copy versions? These changes force businesses to keep up with consumer demands.

Consider the Apple iPad (*www.apple.com/ipad*). Apple released the first iPad in April 2010 and sold 3 million of the devices in 80 days. Rather than taking time to enjoy its success, Apple made its iPad2 available for sale on March 11, 2011, only 11 months later, while in early 2013 it was up to the iPad5.

Information Overload. The amount of information available on the Internet doubles approximately every year, and much of it is free. The Internet and other telecommunications networks are bringing a flood of information to managers. To make decisions effectively and efficiently, managers must be able to access, navigate, and use these vast stores of data, information, and knowledge. Information technologies, such as search engines (discussed in Chapter 4) and data mining (Chapter 10), provide valuable support in these efforts.

Societal/Political/Legal Pressures. The third category of business pressures includes social responsibility, government regulation/deregulation, spending for social programs, spending to protect against terrorism, and ethics. This section will explain how all of these elements affect modern businesses.

Social Responsibility. Social issues that affect businesses and individuals range from the state of the physical environment, to company and individual philanthropy, to education. Some corporations and individuals are willing to spend time and/or money to address various social problems. These efforts are known as **organizational social responsibility** or **individual social responsibility**.

One critical social problem is the state of the physical environment. A growing IT initiative, called *green IT*, is addressing some of the most pressing environmental concerns. Example 2.2 illustrates how IT is instrumental in organizational efforts to "go green."

Example 2.2

Companies are "going green," and IT professionals are facing increasing pressures to help their companies accomplish their environmental goals. Organizations consider IT to be a natural choice to lead their sustainability efforts, because IT touches every area of an organization. In a series of interviews, several IT executives listed four areas where IT is particularly valuable for going green.

1. Facilities Design and Management

Organizations are creating more sustainable work environments. Many organizations are pursuing Leadership in Energy and Environmental Design (LEED) certification from the Canada Green Building Council (*www.cagbc.org*), a non-profit group that promotes the construction of environmentally friendly buildings. For example, the Burlington Performing Arts Centre in Burlington, Ontario, received LEED gold certification for its construction. One impact of this development is that IT professionals are expected to help create green facilities. Consequently, IT personnel have to consider how their computing decisions have an impact on sustainable design and, in turn, how the building's design affects the IT infrastructure. Green design influences the type of IT devices used and the locations where IT clusters personal computers, people, and servers. IT must become familiar with the metering and monitoring systems used in green buildings and the requirements of buildings' computerized infrastructure.

2. Carbon Management

As companies try to reduce their carbon footprints, they are turning to IT executives to develop the systems needed to calculate and track carbon throughout the organization and its supply chain, which can be global in scope. Therefore, IT employees need to become knowledgeable about embedded carbon and how to measure it in the company's products and processes.

Consider, for example, application development. IT managers will have to ask whether an application will require new hardware to test and run, or how much additional server space (and thus energy) it will require—and how these issues translate into carbon output.

3. International and Canadian Environmental Laws

IT executives must deal with provincial, federal, and international laws and regulations that affect everything from the IT products they buy, to how they dispose of them, to their company's carbon footprint. IT managers must understand environmental compliance issues so they can ask their vendors the right questions regarding specific provincial, federal, and international environmental standards before buying, deploying, and disposing of equipment. In short, IT managers must have an equipment strategy from cradle to grave.

4. Energy Management

IT executives must understand their entire organization's energy needs. They also need to establish a good relationship with their company's electrical utilities, for several reasons. First, energy management systems are becoming increasingly sophisticated. To employ these systems effectively and make intelligent consumption decisions, IT personnel must familiarize themselves with the system's complex monitors and sensors. Second, more utilities are developing an expertise in creating energy-efficient IT departments. IT managers should tap that expertise to improve their own departments' energy performance. Third, utilities are offering incentives to commercial customers who take certain energy conservation steps, such as enabling computer

Sources: Compiled from J. Matthews, "For IT Managers, Going Green Can Save You Some Long Green," *Forbes*, March 31, 2011; A. Diana, "15 Green Tech Innovations," *InformationWeek*, January 5, 2011; A. Nguyen, "Hire Green IT Managers Now, Forrester Urges," *CIO*, November 23, 2010; M. Pratt, "How to Get Your Green IT Cred," *Computerworld*, September 2, 2010; C. Penttila, "Why—and How—Your Company Should Go Green," *InformationWeek*, January 30, 2009; *www.usgbc.org*, accessed February 16, 2013.

power management across their networks and designing energy-efficient data centres. Finally, utilities are offering variable rate incentives depending on when companies use electricity and how much they use. These issues require IT systems that can regulate electricity use.

Continuing our discussion of social responsibility, social problems all over the world may be addressed through corporate and individual philanthropy. In some cases, questions arise as to what percentage of contributions actually goes to the intended causes and recipients and what percentage goes to the charity's overhead. Another problem that concerns contributors is that they often exert little influence over the selection of projects their contributions will support. As you will see in IT's About Business 2.3, the Internet can act as a facilitator of generosity.

Still another social problem that affects modern business is the digital divide. The **digital divide** refers to the wide gap between those who have access to information and communications technology and those who do not. This gap exists both within and among countries.

Many government and international organizations are trying to close the digital divide. As technologies develop and become less expensive, the speed at which the gap can be closed will accelerate.

One project trying to close the digital divide is the One Laptop per Child (OLPC) project (*http://one.laptop.org*). OLPC is a non-profit association dedicated to research and develop a very inexpensive laptop—a technology that aims to revolutionize how the world can educate its children.

The first generation of inexpensive laptops appeared in 2007 with a price of $188, which was too high. The second generation of the laptop was scrapped because the price remained

IT's [about business]

2.3 The Internet Facilitates Generosity

The Internet can facilitate acts of generosity and true connection. Consider, for example, a website such as PatientsLikeMe (*www.patientslikeme.com*), or any of the thousands of message boards dedicated to infertility, cancer, and various other health issues. People use these sites and message boards to obtain information about life-and-death decisions based on volunteered information, while also receiving much-needed emotional support from strangers.

Sociologists contend that contributing to such communities helps people gain self-esteem by donating their time and experiences to people in need. People will most readily share information, followed by time, and then physical goods.

Many websites help concerned individuals provide goods and services to others. These hubs translate the peer-to-peer principles of sharing from the virtual world to the real world. For example, CouchSurfing (*www.couchsurfing.org*) has helped over 8 million travellers find willing and free hosts throughout the world. What is the main reason that people allow strangers to sleep on their couch for free? The answer is that they give away something that has little marginal cost in exchange for the opportunity to meet people from all over the world.

Let's look at some additional examples of websites that enable generosity.

- *GiftFlow* (*www.giftflow.org*): GiftFlow is a virtual community where you can obtain things you need for free and find people who need the "stuff" you have to give away. GiftFlow connects community organizations, businesses, governments, and neighbours in a network of reciprocity, where they can share resources, meet one another's needs, and coordinate their efforts to build a better world.
- *Place2Give* (*www.place2give.com*): This site enables searches of registered Canadian charities (and related government websites) so that donors can find out about the charity. Users can search the site to find out which charities help out in their community, while the site also provides help to charities with fundraising.
- *Kiva* (*www.kiva.org*): Kiva is a non-profit enterprise that provides a link between lenders in developed countries and entrepreneurs in developing countries. Users pledge interest-free loans starting at $25 rather than giving tax-deductible donations. Kiva directs 100 percent of the loans to borrowers.
- *Canadian Red Cross* (*www.redcross.ca/donate.asp*): At this site, potential donors can decide where their money can be directed, stating whether it goes to a particular disaster relief fund. Other large charities similarly provide selection to their donors in deciding where their money will be used.

Questions

1. Discuss why people will give away their time and knowledge for free.
2. Describe the various ways in which the Internet can facilitate generosity.

Sources: Compiled from A. Kamenetz, "The Case for Generosity," *Fast-Company*, March, 2011; N. Ferraro, "Lending and Philanthropy in the Internet Age," *InformationWeek*, February 2, 2008; *www.giftflow.org, www.thredup.com, http://blog.p2pfoundation.net, www.collaborativeconsumption.com, www.kiva.org, www.place2give.com, www.redcross.ca/donate.asp*, accessed February 16, 2013.

too high. The next generation of devices is inexpensive tablets, called the UbiSlate and Aakash, which are being sold by a U.K. company, Datawind (*http://datawind.com*), for $20 to India. This is 50 percent subsidized from the retail cost of $40.

Compliance with Government Regulations. Another major source of business pressures is government regulations regarding health, safety, environmental protection, and equal opportunity. Businesses tend to view government regulations as expensive constraints on their activities. In general, government deregulation intensifies competition.

Protection against Fraud or Terrorist Attacks. Computer systems can be used to create fraudulent or fictitious transactions that are used to steal funds from banks or other organizations, or to engage in identity theft—the use of another person's identity for financial gain. Individuals and organizations need to protect their information to help prevent these actions. This is discussed further in Technology Guide 5. You can learn more about fraud from organizations such as the Association of Certified Fraud Examiners, at *www.acfe.com*.

Since September 11, 2001, organizations have been under increased pressure to protect themselves against terrorist attacks. Canada responded to these attacks in 2001 by passing an Anti-Terrorism Act, which made changes to the Criminal Code, the Official Secrets Act, the Canada Evidence Act, and the National Defence Act. Organizations responsible for Canada's security include the Royal Canadian Mounted Police, Canadian Security Intelligence Service, and the Communications Security Establishment.

Information technology can help protect businesses by providing security systems and possibly identifying patterns of behaviour associated with terrorist activities, including cyber attacks (discussed in Chapter 13).

Ethical issues. Ethics relates to general standards of right and wrong. Information ethics relates specifically to standards of right and wrong in information-processing practices. Ethical issues are very important because, if handled poorly, they can damage an organization's image and destroy its employees' morale. The use of IT raises many ethical issues, ranging from monitoring e-mail to invading the privacy of millions of customers whose data are stored in private and public databases. Chapter 12 covers ethical issues in detail.

Clearly, then, the pressures on organizations are increasing, and organizations must be prepared to take responsive actions if they are to succeed. You will learn about these organizational responses in the next section.

Organizational Responses

Organizations are responding to the various pressures just discussed by implementing IT such as strategic systems, customer focus, make-to-order and mass customization, and e-business. This section explores each of these responses.

Strategic Systems. Strategic systems provide organizations with advantages that enable them to increase their market share or profits, to better negotiate with suppliers, and to prevent competitors from entering their markets. As an example, the IT department at Procter & Gamble (P&G) (*www.pg.com*) developed a virtualized environment that the company uses for product design work, product placement research, and consumer feedback studies. P&G uses these virtual reality models to test design ideas for the next breakthroughs in products such as diapers and cosmetics. Within these "cyberworlds," P&G can rapidly test product performance as well as consumer responses to various kinds of ingredient and packaging choices.

Customer Focus. Organizational attempts to provide superb customer service can make the difference between attracting and keeping customers and losing them to competitors. Numerous IT tools and business processes have been designed to keep customers happy. Consider Amazon, for example. When you visit Amazon's website anytime after your first visit, the site welcomes you back by name and presents you with information about items that you might like, based on your previous purchases. In another example, Dell guides you through the process of buying a computer by providing information and choices that help you make an informed buying decision.

Make-to-Order and Mass Customization. **Make-to-order** is a strategy of producing customized (made to individual specifications) products and services. The business problem is how to manufacture customized goods efficiently and at a reasonably low cost. Part of the solution is to change manufacturing processes from mass production to mass customization. In mass production, a company produces a large quantity of identical items. In **mass customization**, it also produces a large quantity of items, but it customizes them to fit the needs and preferences of individual customers. Mass customization is simply an attempt to perform make-to-order on a large scale. Bodymetrics (*www.bodymetrics.com*) is an excellent example of mass customization involving men's and women's jeans, as shown in Example 2.3.

Example 2.3

Well-fitting jeans are notoriously difficult to find. To address this problem, Bodymetrics developed a "body scanner" that scans the customer's body, captures more than 150 measurements, and produces a digital replica of his or her size and shape. This scan is then used to provide three services: made-to-measure jeans, body-shape jeans, and on-line virtual try-on.

With made-to-measure jeans, the scan is used to create a pattern for the jeans, which are hand-tailored to the exact lines and contours of the customer's body. The jeans are ready in three to six weeks, at which time the customer has a final fitting with a Bodymetrics tailor.

Based on its experience with made-to-measure jeans, Bodymetrics has identified three body shapes: straight, semicurvy, and curvy. Body-shape jeans are specifically designed to fit these different body shapes. After customers are scanned, a Bodymetrics jeans expert helps them determine their body shapes. Customers can then instantly purchase jeans matching their body shapes off the rack in the store.

The on-line virtual try-on allows customers who have been scanned to try on jeans virtually on their own bodies without physically trying on jeans in a dressing room. The service creates an *avatar* (a three-dimensional graphical representation of the customer), which has an amazing resemblance to her or him. Then, the customer can choose various styles of jeans and "virtually see" what the jeans look like on her or his avatar.

E-Business and E-Commerce. Conducting business electronically is an essential strategy for companies that are competing in today's business environment. *Electronic commerce* (EC or e-commerce) describes the process of buying, selling, transferring, or exchanging products, services, or information via computer networks, including the Internet. *E-business* is a somewhat broader concept. In addition to the buying and selling of goods and services, e-business also refers to servicing customers, collaborating with business partners, and performing electronic transactions within an organization. Chapter 5 focuses extensively on this topic. In addition, e-commerce applications appear throughout the text.

You now have a general overview of the pressures that affect companies in today's business environment and the responses that organizations choose to manage these pressures. To plan for the most effective responses, companies formulate strategies. In the new digital economy, these strategies rely heavily on information technology, especially strategic information systems. We examine these topics in the next section.

before you go on...

1. What are the characteristics of the modern business environment?
2. Discuss some of the pressures that characterize the modern global business environment.
3. Identify some of the organizational responses to these pressures. Are any of these responses specific to a particular pressure? If so, which ones?

Sources: Compiled from "The First Time I Had a Bodymetrics Scan," *http://howfayeseesit.wordpress.com*, March 23, 2011; L. Talbot, "Bodymetrics: What's Your Jean Shape?," *http://lisatalbot.blogspot.com*, February 2, 2011; Asmita, "Custom-Fit Jeans with Bodymetrics," *www.styleguru.com*, January 18, 2007; R. Young, "Turning Tailoring Over to a Computer," *International Herald Tribune*, January 15, 2007; *www.bodymetrics.com*, accessed February 16, 2013.

2.4 Competitive Advantage and Strategic Information Systems

A *competitive strategy* is a statement that identifies a business's approach to compete, its goals, and the plans and policies that will be required to carry out those goals (Porter, 1985). A strategy, in general, can apply to a desired outcome, such as gaining market share. A competitive strategy focuses on achieving a desired outcome when competitors want to prevent you from reaching your goal. Therefore, when you create a competitive strategy, you must plan your own moves, but you must also anticipate and counter your competitors' moves.

Through its competitive strategy, an organization seeks a competitive advantage in an industry. That is, it seeks to outperform its competitors in a critical measure such as cost, quality, and time-to-market. Competitive advantage helps a company function profitably within a market and generate larger-than-average profits.

Competitive advantage is increasingly important in today's business environment, as you will note throughout the text. In general, the *core business* of companies has remained the same. That is, information technologies simply offer tools that can enhance an organization's success through its traditional sources of competitive advantage, such as low cost, excellent customer service, and superior supply chain management. **Strategic information systems (SISs)** provide a competitive advantage by helping an organization implement its strategic goals and improve its performance and productivity. Any information system that helps an organization gain a competitive advantage, or reduce a competitive disadvantage, qualifies as a strategic information system.

Porter's Competitive Forces Model

The best-known framework for analyzing competitiveness is Michael Porter's **competitive forces model** (Porter, 1985). Companies use Porter's model to develop strategies to increase their competitive edge. Porter's model also demonstrates how IT can make a company more competitive.

Porter's model identifies five major forces that can endanger or enhance a company's position in a given industry. Figure 2.3 highlights these forces. Although the web has changed the nature of competition, it has not changed Porter's five fundamental forces. In fact, what makes

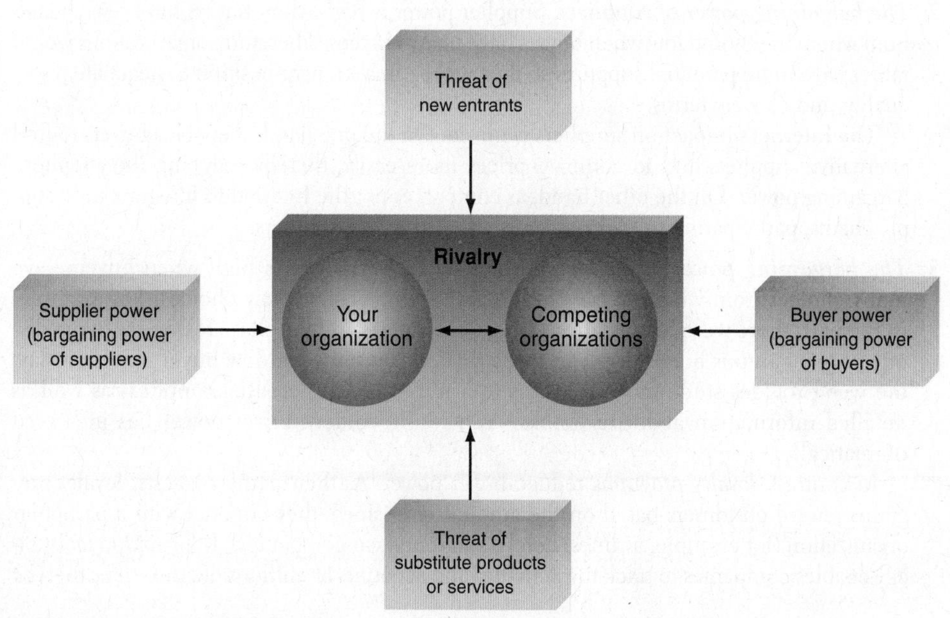

FIGURE 2.3 Porter's competitive forces model.

these forces so valuable as analytical tools is that they have not changed for centuries. Every competitive organization, no matter how large or small, or what business it is in, is driven by these forces. This observation applies even to organizations that you might not consider competitive, such as local governments. Although local governments are not for-profit enterprises, they compete for businesses to locate in their areas, for funding from higher levels of government, for employees, and for many other things.

Significantly, Porter (2001) concludes that the *overall* impact of the web is to increase competition, which generally diminishes a firm's profitability. Let's examine Porter's five forces and the ways that the web influences them.

1. ***The threat of entry of new competitors (entrants).*** The threat that new competitors will enter your market is high when entry is easy and low when there are significant barriers to entry. An **entry barrier** is a product or service feature that customers have learned to expect from organizations in a certain industry. A competing organization must offer this feature in order to survive in the marketplace. There are many types of entry barriers. Consider, for example, legal requirements such as admission to the bar to practise law or a licence to serve liquor, where only a certain number of licences are available.

   Suppose you want to open a gasoline station. In order to compete in that industry, you would have to offer pay-at-the-pump service to your customers. Pay-at-the-pump is an IT-based barrier to entering this market because you must offer it for free. The first gas station that offered this service gained first-move advantage and established barriers to entry. This advantage did not last, however, because competitors quickly offered the same service and thus overcame the entry barrier.

   For most firms, the web *increases* the threat that new competitors will enter the market because it sharply reduces traditional barriers to entry, such as the need for a sales force or a physical storefront. Today, competitors frequently need only to set up a website. This threat of increased competition is particularly acute in industries that perform an *intermediation role*, which is a link between buyers and sellers (for example, stock brokers and travel agents), as well as in industries where the primary product or service is digital (for example, the music industry). In addition, the geographical reach of the web enables distant competitors to compete more directly with an existing firm.

   In some cases the web increases barriers to entry. This scenario occurs primarily when customers have come to expect a nontrivial capability from their suppliers. For example, the first company to offer web-based package tracking gained a competitive advantage from that service. Competitors were forced to follow.

2. ***The bargaining power of suppliers.*** Supplier power is high when buyers have few choices from whom to buy and low when buyers have many choices. Therefore, organizations would rather have more potential suppliers so they will be in a stronger position to negotiate price, quality, and delivery terms.

   The Internet's impact on suppliers is mixed. On the one hand, it enables buyers to find alternative suppliers and to compare prices more easily, thereby reducing the supplier's bargaining power. On the other hand, as companies use the Internet to integrate their supply chains, participating suppliers prosper by locking in customers.

3. ***The bargaining power of customers (buyers).*** Buyer power is high when buyers have many choices from whom to buy and low when buyers have few choices. For example, in the past, there were few locations where students could purchase textbooks (typically, one or two campus bookstores). In this situation, students had low buyer power. Today, the web provides students with access to a multitude of potential suppliers as well as detailed information about textbooks. As a result, student buyer power has increased dramatically.

   In contrast, *loyalty programs* reduce buyer power. As their name suggests, loyalty programs reward customers based on the amount of business they conduct with a particular organization (for example, airlines, hotels, and rental car companies). Information technology enables companies to track the activities and accounts of millions of customers, thereby reducing buyer power. That is, customers who receive "perks" from loyalty programs are less likely to do business with competitors. (Loyalty programs are associated with customer relationship management, which you will study in Chapter 7.)

4. ***The threat of substitute products or services.*** If there are many alternatives to an organization's products or services, then the threat of substitutes is high. If there are few alternatives, then the threat is low. Today, new technologies create substitute products very rapidly. For example, customers today can purchase wireless telephones instead of land-line telephones, Internet music services instead of traditional CDs, and ethanol instead of gasoline in cars.

   Information-based industries experience the greatest threat from substitutes. Any industry in which digitized information can replace material goods (for example, music, books, and software) must view the Internet as a threat because the Internet can convey this information efficiently and at low cost and high quality.

   Even when there are many substitutes for their products, however, companies can create a competitive advantage by increasing switching costs. *Switching costs* are the costs, in money and time, of a decision to buy elsewhere. For example, contracts with smart phone providers typically include a substantial penalty for switching to another provider until the term of the contract expires (quite often, two years). This switching cost is monetary.

   As another example, when you buy products from Amazon, the company develops a profile of your shopping habits and recommends products targeted to your preferences. If you switch to another on-line vendor, that company will need time to develop a profile of your wants and needs. In this case, the switching cost involves time rather than money.

5. ***The rivalry among existing firms in the industry.*** The threat from rivalry is high when there is intense competition among many firms in an industry. The threat is low when the competition is among fewer firms and is not as intense.

   In the past, proprietary information systems—systems that belong exclusively to a single organization—have provided strategic advantage to firms in highly competitive industries. Today, however, the visibility of Internet applications on the web makes proprietary systems more difficult to keep secret. In simple terms, when a company sees its competitor's new system on-line, it will rapidly match those features in order to remain competitive. The result is fewer differences among competitors, which leads to more intense competition in an industry.

   To understand this concept, consider the highly competitive grocery industry, where Walmart, Price Chopper, Food Basics, Loblaws, and other stores compete essentially on price. Some of these companies have IT-enabled loyalty programs in which customers receive discounts and the store gains valuable business intelligence on customers' buying preferences. Stores use this business intelligence in their marketing and promotional campaigns. (You will learn about business intelligence in Chapter 10.)

   Grocery stores are also experimenting with wireless technologies such as *radio-frequency identification* (RFID, discussed in Chapter 6) to speed the checkout process, track customers through the store, and notify customers of discounts as they pass by certain products. Grocery companies also use IT to tightly integrate their supply chains for maximum efficiency and thus reduce prices for shoppers.

   Competition also is being affected by the extremely low variable cost of digital products. That is, once a digital product has been developed, the cost of producing additional "units" approaches zero. Consider the music industry as an example. When artists record music, their songs are captured in digital format. Physical products, such as CDs or DVDs of the songs for sale in music stores, involve costs. The costs of a physical distribution channel are much higher than those involved in delivering the songs digitally over the Internet.

   In fact, in the future companies might give away some products for free. For example, some analysts predict that commissions for on-line stock trading will approach zero because investors can search the Internet for information to make their own decisions regarding buying and selling stocks. At that point, consumers will no longer need brokers to give them information that they can obtain themselves, virtually for free.

Porter's Value Chain Model

Organizations use the Porter competitive forces model to design general strategies. To identify specific activities where they can use competitive strategies for greatest impact, they use his **value chain model** (1985). The value chain model also identifies points where an organization can use information technology to achieve competitive advantage (see Figure 2.4).

According to Porter's value chain model, the activities conducted in any organization can be divided into two categories: primary activities and support activities. **Primary activities** relate to the production and distribution of the firm's products and services. These activities create value for which customers are willing to pay. The primary activities are buttressed by **support activities**. Unlike primary activities, support activities do not add value directly to the firm's products or services. Rather, as their name suggests, they contribute to the firm's competitive advantage by supporting the primary activities.

Next, you will see examples of primary and support activities in the value chain of a manufacturing company. Keep in mind that other types of firms, such as transportation, health care, education, retail, and others, have different value chains. The key point is that every organization has a value chain: a sequence of activities through which the organization's inputs, whatever they are, are transformed into more valuable outputs, whatever they are.

In a manufacturing company, primary activities involve purchasing materials, processing the materials into products, and delivering the products to customers. Companies typically perform five primary activities in the following sequence:

1. Inbound logistics (inputs)
2. Operations (manufacturing and testing)

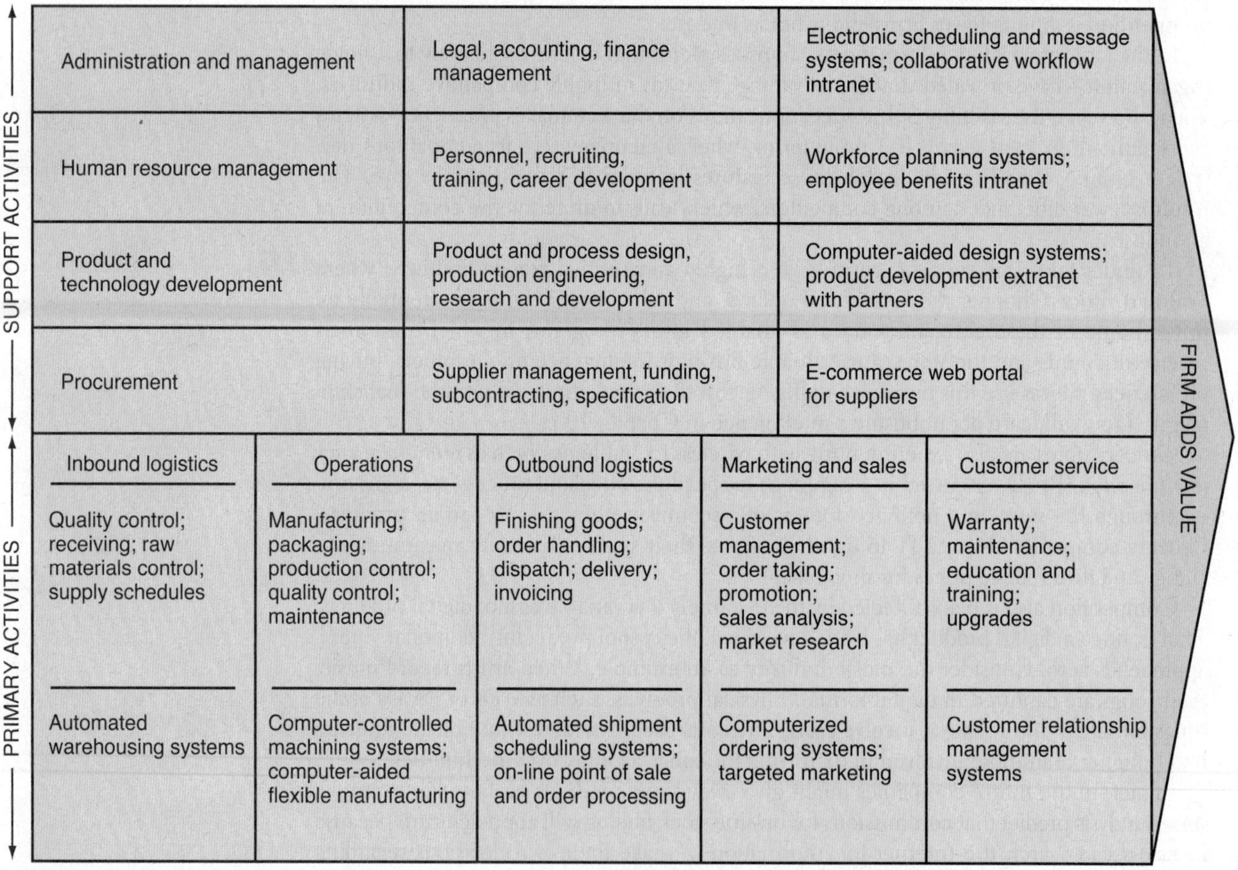

SUPPORT ACTIVITIES

Administration and management	Legal, accounting, finance management	Electronic scheduling and message systems; collaborative workflow intranet
Human resource management	Personnel, recruiting, training, career development	Workforce planning systems; employee benefits intranet
Product and technology development	Product and process design, production engineering, research and development	Computer-aided design systems; product development extranet with partners
Procurement	Supplier management, funding, subcontracting, specification	E-commerce web portal for suppliers

PRIMARY ACTIVITIES

Inbound logistics	Operations	Outbound logistics	Marketing and sales	Customer service
Quality control; receiving; raw materials control; supply schedules	Manufacturing; packaging; production control; quality control; maintenance	Finishing goods; order handling; dispatch; delivery; invoicing	Customer management; order taking; promotion; sales analysis; market research	Warranty; maintenance; education and training; upgrades
Automated warehousing systems	Computer-controlled machining systems; computer-aided flexible manufacturing	Automated shipment scheduling systems; on-line point of sale and order processing	Computerized ordering systems; targeted marketing	Customer relationship management systems

FIRM ADDS VALUE

FIGURE 2.4 Porter's value chain model.

3. Outbound logistics (storage and distribution)
4. Marketing and sales
5. Services

As work progresses in this sequence, value is added to the product in each activity. Specifically, the following steps occur:

1. The incoming materials are processed (in receiving, storage, and so on) in activities called *inbound logistics*.
2. The materials are used in operations, where value is added by turning raw materials into products.
3. These products are prepared for delivery (packaging, storing, and shipping) in the outbound logistics activities.
4. Marketing and sales sell the products to customers, increasing product value by creating demand for the company's products.
5. Finally, the company performs after-sales service for the customer, such as warranty service or upgrade notification, adding further value.

As noted above, the primary activities are buttressed by support activities. Support activities consist of:

1. The firm's infrastructure (accounting, finance, management)
2. Human resources management
3. Product and technology development (R & D)
4. Procurement

Each support activity can be applied to any or all of the primary activities. In addition, the support activities can also support one another.

A firm's value chain is part of a larger stream of activities, which Porter calls a **value system**. A value system, or an *industry value chain*, includes the suppliers that provide the inputs necessary to the firm along with their value chains. After the firm creates products, these products pass through the value chains of distributors (which also have their own value chains), all the way to the customers. All parts of these chains are included in the value system. To achieve and sustain a competitive advantage, and to support that advantage with information technologies, a firm must understand every component of this value system.

Strategies for Competitive Advantage

Organizations continually try to develop strategies to counter the five competitive forces identified by Porter. You will learn about five of those strategies here. Before we go into specifics, however, it is important to note that an organization's choice of strategy involves trade-offs. For example, a firm that concentrates only on cost leadership might not have the resources available for research and development, leaving the firm unable to innovate. As another example, a company that invests in customer happiness (customer-orientation strategy) will experience increased costs.

Companies must select a strategy and then stay with it, because a confused strategy cannot succeed. This selection, in turn, decides how a company will use its information systems. A new information system that can improve customer service but will increase costs slightly will be welcomed at a higher-end retailer such as Hudson's Bay (*www.thebay.com*), but not at a discount store like Walmart. The following list presents the most commonly used strategies below. Figure 2.5 provides an overview of these strategies.

1. ***Cost leadership strategy.*** Produce products and/or services at the lowest cost in the industry. An example is Walmart's automatic inventory replenishment system, which enables Walmart to reduce inventory storage requirements. As a result, Walmart stores use floor space only to sell products, and not to store them, thereby reducing inventory costs.

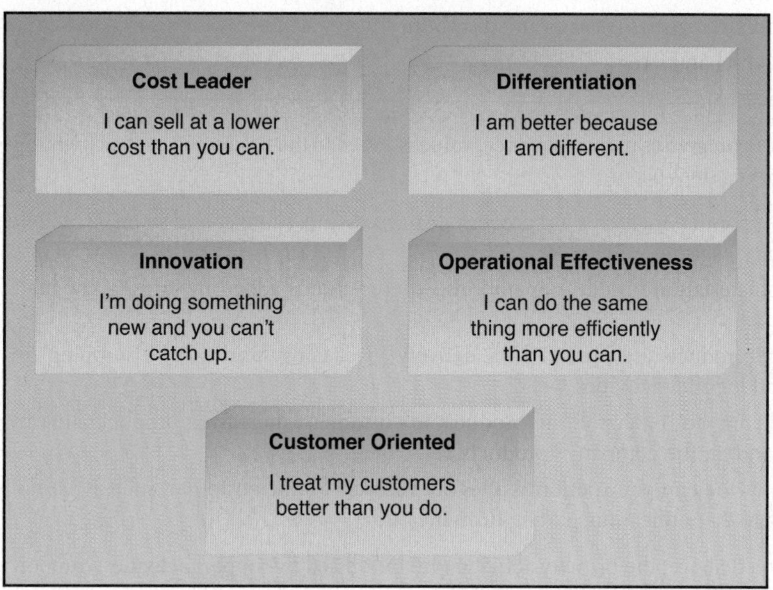

FIGURE 2.5 Strategies for competitive advantage.

2. ***Differentiation strategy.*** Offer different products, services, or product features than your competitors. WestJet Airlines, for example, has differentiated itself as a low-cost, Canadian airline that offers regional service. This has proved to be a winning strategy for competing in the highly competitive airline industry. Also, Dell has differentiated itself in the personal computer market through its mass-customization strategy.
3. ***Innovation strategy.*** Introduce new products and services, add new features to existing products and services, or develop new ways to produce them. A classic example is the introduction of automated teller machines (ATMs) by Citibank of New York (*https://online.citibank.com*). The convenience and cost-cutting features of this innovation gave Citibank a huge advantage over its competitors. Like many innovative products, the ATM changed the nature of competition in the banking industry. Today, an ATM is a competitive *necessity* for any bank.
4. ***Operational effectiveness strategy.*** Improve the manner in which internal business processes are executed so that a firm performs these activities better than its rivals. Such improvements increase quality, productivity, and employee and customer satisfaction while decreasing time to market.
5. ***Customer-orientation strategy.*** Concentrate on making customers happy. Web-based systems are particularly effective in this area because they can provide a personalized, one-to-one relationship with each customer.

before you go on...

1. What are strategic information systems?
2. According to Porter, what are the five forces that could endanger a firm's position in its industry or marketplaces?
3. Describe Porter's value chain model. Differentiate between Porter's competitive forces model and his value chain model.
4. What strategies can companies use to gain competitive advantage?

2.5 Business–Information Technology Alignment

The "holy grail" of organizations is business–information technology alignment, or strategic alignment (which we will call simply *alignment*). **Business–information technology alignment** is the tight integration of the IT function with the strategy, mission, and goals of the organization. That is, the IT function directly supports the business objectives of the organization. There are six characteristics of excellent alignment:

- Organizations view IT as an engine of innovation that continually transforms the business, often creating new revenue streams.
- Organizations view their internal and external customers and their customer service function as supremely important.
- Organizations rotate business and IT professionals across departments and job functions.
- Organizations provide overarching goals that are completely clear to each IT and business employee.
- Organizations ensure that IT employees understand how the company makes (or loses) money.
- Organizations create a vibrant and inclusive company culture.

Unfortunately, many organizations fail to achieve this type of close alignment. In fact, according to a McKinsey & Company survey on IT strategy and spending, only 16 percent of the IT and business executives who participated agreed that their organization had adequate alignment between IT and the business. Given the importance of business–IT alignment, why do so many organizations fail to implement this policy? The major reasons are:

- Business managers and IT managers have different objectives.
- The business and IT departments are ignorant of the other group's expertise.
- There is a lack of communication.

Put simply, some business executives know little about information technology, and IT executives understand the technology but may not understand the real needs of the business.

The good news is that some organizations "get it right." IT's About Business 2.4 illustrates business–IT alignment at two Canadian companies: Unhaggle and Shopify. In fact, both companies maintain that business and IT are virtually indistinguishable in their strategy and operations. It is IT governance that helps organizations effectively manage their IT operations so that it aligns with their business strategies.

Organizational strategies take account of risks or potential problems that could occur and the opportunities that organizations have to serve their customers better or create more value for their stakeholders. Large organizations expect the board of directors and executives to effectively manage the organization, which is called *corporate governance*.

IT governance, as defined by the Information Systems Audit and Control Association (*www.isaca.org*), is "a structure of relationships and processes to direct and control the enterprise in order to achieve the enterprise's goals by adding value while balancing risk versus return over IT and its processes." We can see that this definition has three parts. First, it talks about relationships and processes; these would be designed by those who lead the organization. These actions are taken to meet the organization's goals. For example, if an organization wants to efficiently process its sales transactions, then systems are needed to capture, store, and organize those sales transactions. The second part of the definition is that these actions should add value; that is, they should make money or bring some kind of intangible benefit to the organization. So any new systems should have a reasonable cost. Finally, there should be a balance between risks and profits; for example, systems should be secure so that they cannot be hacked into and private data exposed.

Chapter 13 explains how an *IT steering committee* is an important part of managing information technology in organizations. However, IT governance is about managing IT throughout the organization. This includes planning, acquisition, implementation, and ongoing support, as well as monitoring and evaluation so that decisions can be made about potential changes.

Without effective IT governance, there are many things that could go wrong. Information systems might not meet organizational business objectives, or systems could be error prone, over budget, or hard to use. If there was poor security, data and programs could be damaged or copied by unauthorized individuals.

Smaller businesses implement IT governance by having an aware and knowledgeable owner-manager who actively selects business practices and software.

before you go on...

1. What is business–IT alignment?
2. Give examples of business–IT alignment at your university, regarding student systems. (Hint: What are the "business" goals of your university with regard to student registration, fee payment, grade posting, and communications?)
3. What is IT governance and why is it important?

[about business]

2.4 Unhaggle and Shopify: Strategically Meeting Customer Needs

Unhaggle's strategy is to remove a long-time dislike from our lives: haggling for a new car. Started after one of the owners had an unpleasant car purchase process, Unhaggle (*www.unhaggle.com*) charges a fixed fee for membership and provides multiple quotes from car dealers in your area (unless you live in a remote region of Canada where there are very few car dealers). The owners went beyond their own experiences, though, and did market research: they consulted with other car purchasers. The company earns its revenue from customer fees and also from small dealer fees when an actual sale is made based upon information provided in the site. The weak link in Unhaggle's strategy is that dealers must sign up to the service. It turns out that the opportunity to sell a slow-moving vehicle at a discounted price (perhaps because of an unpopular colour) has resulted in many dealers signing up to the service.

The site also provides added value to consumers, by providing announcements, such as about automobile shows, and by providing information about manufacturer incentives that are available by vehicle. Apparently, these incentives change frequently as manufacturers attempt to encourage their dealers to sell vehicles, and are not always communicated to buyers. So Unhaggle has several full-time employees to track down and provide these details.

Ottawa-based Shopify (*www.shopify.ca*) also fulfills a need, but is focused on retail stores rather than on individuals. Tobias Luetke was starting a snowboard shop and was unhappy with the standard storefront software available to sell his products. He could not afford to have a customized system written for him, so he wrote his own (since he had trained as a programmer before starting his snowboard shop). The result was easy-to-use software that is being sold to thousands of clients around the world (with over 1,000 in Canada).

Organizations as large as Shopify (with over 100 employees and widely dispersed customers) need to use IT governance to manage their systems development and maintenance processes effectively. They also need to stay responsive to their customers to provide high-quality products that improve, since success breeds competition in the marketplace.

Questions

1. Consider the cases of Unhaggle and Shopify. What does it mean that the business strategy and information technology go hand-in-hand (i.e., neither comes before the other)?
2. Provide specific examples of problems that could occur at Unhaggle and Shopify if the companies did not manage their IT systems properly (i.e., if they had ineffective IT governance).

Sources: Compiled from M. Anderson, "Canada's Smartest Company: Shopify," *www.profitguide.com*, November 28, 2012; T. Kiladze, "A New, Hassle-Free Way to Get a Deal on a New Car," *The Globe and Mail*, January 9, 2013; E. Roseman, "Websites Offer Haggle-Free Way to Purchase a New Car," *Toronto Star*, p. B1, B2, September 26, 2012; *www.unhaggle.com*, *www.shopify.ca*, accessed April 16, 2013.

For all Majors

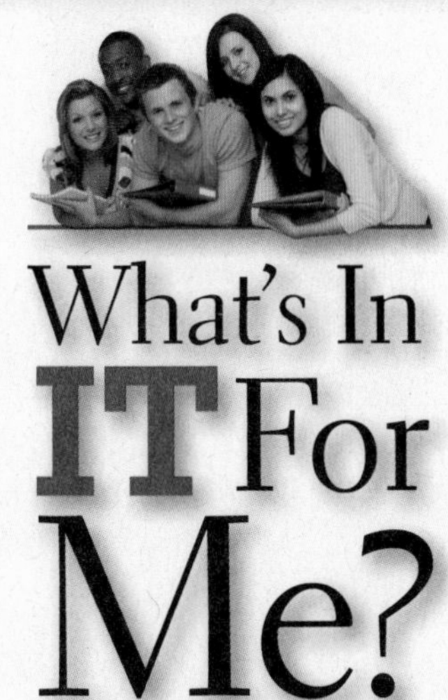

All of the functional areas of any organization are composed of a variety of business processes. Regardless of your major, you will be involved in a variety of business processes from your first day on the job. Some of these processes you will do by yourself, some will involve only your group or department, and others will involve several (or all) of the organization's functional areas.

It is important for you to be able to visualize processes, understand the inputs and outputs of each process, and identify the "customer" of each process. These capabilities will enable you to make the organization's business processes more efficient and effective. This task generally involves incorporating information technology in the process. It is also important for you to appreciate how each process fits in to your organization's strategy.

All functional areas in any organization must work together in an integrated fashion in order for the firm to respond adequately to business pressures. These responses typically require each functional area to use a variety of information systems. In today's competitive global marketplace, the timeliness and accuracy of these responses is even more critical.

Closely following this discussion, all functional areas must work together for the organization to gain competitive advantage in its marketplace. Again, the functional areas use a variety of strategic information systems to achieve this goal.

You have seen why companies must be concerned with strategic advantage. But why is this chapter so important for you? There are several reasons. First, the business pressures you have learned about have an impact on your organization, but they also affect you as an individual. So, it is critical that you understand how information systems can help you, and eventually your organization, respond to these pressures.

In addition, achieving competitive advantage is essential for your organization's survival. In many cases, you, your team, and all your colleagues will be responsible for creating a competitive advantage. Therefore, having general knowledge about strategy, information technology governance, and how information systems affect the organization's strategy and competitive position will help you in your career.

You also need a basic knowledge of your organization's strategy, mission, and goals, as well as its business problems and how it makes (or loses) money. You now know how to analyze your organization's strategy and value chain, as well as the strategies and value chains of your competitors. You also have acquired a general knowledge of how information technology contributes to organizational strategy. This knowledge will help you to do your job better, to be promoted more quickly, and to contribute significantly to the success of your organization.

[Summary]

1. **Understand the concept of business processes, and provide examples of business processes in the functional areas of an organization.**

A business process is an ongoing collection of related activities that produce a product or a service of value to the organization, its business partners, and/or its customers. Examples of business processes in the functional areas are managing accounts payable, managing accounts receivable, managing post-sale customer follow-up, managing bills of materials, managing manufacturing change orders, applying disability policies, hiring employees, training staff and computer users, and applying Internet use policy.

2. Differentiate between the terms "business process reengineering" and "business process management."

Business process reengineering (BPR) is a radical redesign of an organization's business processes that is intended to improve the efficiency and effectiveness of these processes. The key to BPR is for enterprises to examine their business processes from a "clean sheet" perspective (that is, from scratch) and then determine how they could best reconstruct those processes to improve their business functions. Because BPR proved difficult to implement, organizations have turned to business process management (BPM). BPM is a management technique that includes methods and tools to support the design, analysis, implementation, management, and optimization of business processes.

3. List and provide examples of the three types of business pressures, and describe one IT response to each.

- *Market pressures:* An example of a market pressure is powerful customers. Customer relationship management is an effective IT response that helps companies achieve customer intimacy.
- *Technology pressures:* An example of a technology pressure is information overload. Search engines and business intelligence applications enable managers to access, navigate, and use vast amounts of information.
- *Societal/political/legal pressures:* An example of a societal/political/legal pressure is social responsibility, such as the state of the physical environment. Green IT is one response that is intended to improve the environment.

4. Identify the five competitive forces described by Porter, and explain how the web has an impact on each one.

Porter's five competitive forces:

- *The threat of entry of new competitors (entrants):* For most firms, the web increases the threat that new competitors will enter the market by reducing traditional barriers to entry. Frequently, competitors need only to set up a website to enter a market. The web can also increase barriers to entry, as when customers come to expect a nontrivial capability from their suppliers.
- *The bargaining power of suppliers:* The web enables buyers to find alternative suppliers and to compare prices more easily, thereby reducing suppliers' bargaining power. From a different perspective, as companies use the web to integrate their supply chains, participating suppliers can lock in customers, thereby increasing suppliers' bargaining power.
- *The bargaining power of customers (buyers):* The web provides customers with incredible amounts of choices for products, as well as information about those choices. As a result, the web increases buyer power. However, companies can implement loyalty programs where they use the web to monitor the activities of millions of customers. Such programs reduce buyer power.
- *The threat of substitute products or services:* New technologies create substitute products very rapidly, and the web makes information about these products available almost instantly. As a result, many industries (particularly information-based industries) are in great danger from substitutes (e.g., music, books, newspapers, magazines, software). However, the web also can enable a company to build in switching costs, so that it will cost customers time and/or money to switch from that company to a competitor.
- *The rivalry among existing firms in the industry:* In the past, proprietary information systems provided strategic advantage for firms in highly competitive industries. The visibility of Internet applications on the web makes proprietary systems more difficult to keep secret. Therefore, the web makes strategic advantage more short-lived.

5. Describe the strategies that organizations typically adopt to counter the five competitive forces and achieve competitive advantage.

The five strategies are as follows:

- *Cost leadership strategy*—Produce products and/or services at the lowest cost in the industry.
- *Differentiation strategy*—Offer different products, services, or product features.

- *Innovation strategy*—Introduce new products and services, put new features in existing products and services, or develop new ways to produce them.
- *Operational effectiveness strategy*—Improve the manner in which internal business processes are executed so that a firm performs similar activities better than its rivals.
- *Customer-orientation strategy*—Concentrate on making customers happy.

6. **Define the term "business–information technology alignment," and describe the characteristics of effective alignment.**

Business–IT alignment is the tight integration of the IT function with the strategy, mission, and goals of the organization. There are six characteristics of effective alignment:

- Organizations view IT as an engine of innovation that continually transforms the business.
- Organizations view customers and customer service as supremely important.
- Organizations rotate business and IT professionals across departments and job functions.
- Organizations provide clear, overarching goals for all employees.
- Organizations ensure that IT employees understand how the company makes (or loses) money.
- Organizations create a vibrant and inclusive company culture.

7. **Define the term "IT governance" and explain why information systems need to be effectively managed and planned.**

IT governance is the structure of relationships and processes used to direct and control organizations in order to achieve the enterprise's goals by adding value while balancing risk versus return over IT and its processes. Without IT governance, errors in information systems or excess costs would be more likely. Also, without IT governance, organizations could implement information systems that do not meet their needs or that do not help them meet their business objectives.

[Chapter Glossary]

business environment The combination of social, legal, economic, physical, and political factors in which businesses conduct their operations.

business–information technology alignment The tight integration of the IT function with the strategy, mission, and goals of the organization.

business process A collection of related activities that produce a product or a service of value to the organization, its business partners, and/or its customers.

business process management (BPM) A management technique that includes methods and tools to support the design, analysis, implementation, management, and optimization of business processes.

business process reengineering (BPR) A radical redesign of a business process that improves its efficiency and effectiveness, often by beginning with a "clean sheet" (from scratch).

competitive advantage An advantage over competitors in some measure such as cost, quality, or speed; leads to control of a market and to larger-than-average profits.

competitive forces model A business framework devised by Michael Porter that analyzes competitiveness by recognizing five major forces that could endanger a company's position.

cross-functional business process A process in which no single functional area is responsible for its completion; multiple functional areas collaborate to perform the function.

digital divide The gap between those who have access to information and communications technology and those who do not.

entry barrier Product or service feature that customers expect from organizations in a certain industry; an organization trying to enter this market must provide this product or service at a minimum to be able to compete.

globalization The integration and interdependence of economic, social, cultural, and ecological facets of life, enabled by rapid advances in information technology.

individual social responsibility (see **organizational social responsibility**)

IT governance A structure of relationships and processes to direct and control the enterprise in order to achieve the enterprise's goals by adding value while balancing risk versus return over IT and its processes.

make-to-order The strategy of producing customized products and services.

mass customization A production process in which items are produced in large quantities but are customized to fit the desires of each customer.

organizational social responsibility (also called **individual social responsibility**) Efforts by organizations or individuals to solve various social problems.

primary activities Those business activities related to the production and distribution of the firm's products and services, thus creating value.

strategic information systems (SISs) Systems that help an organization gain a competitive advantage by supporting its strategic goals and/or increasing performance and productivity.

support activities Business activities that do not add value directly to a firm's product or service under consideration but support the primary activities that do add value.

value chain model Model that shows the primary activities that sequentially add value to the profit margin; also shows the support activities.

value system A system that includes the producers, suppliers, distributors, and buyers, all with their value chains.

[Discussion Questions]

1. Consider the student registration business process at your university:
   - Describe the steps necessary for you to register for your classes each semester.
   - Describe how information technology is used in each step of the process (or is not used).
2. Why is it so difficult for an organization to actually implement business process reengineering?
3. Explain why IT is both a business pressure and an enabler of response activities that counter business pressures.
4. What does a flat world mean to you in your choice of a major? In your choice of a career? Will you have to be a "lifelong learner"? Why or why not?
5. What might the impact of a flat world be on your standard of living?
6. Is IT a strategic weapon or a survival tool? Discuss.
7. Why might it be difficult to justify a strategic information system?
8. Describe the five forces in Porter's competitive forces model, and explain how the Internet has affected each one.
9. Describe Porter's value chain model. What is the relationship between the competitive forces model and the value chain model?
10. Discuss the idea that an information system by itself can rarely provide a sustainable competitive advantage.
11. Explain why large organizations need IT governance.
12. Should all organizations have IT governance? Why or why not?

[Problem-Solving Activities]

1. Surf the Internet for information about Public Safety Canada. Examine the available information and comment on the role of information technologies in the federal department.
2. Experience customization by designing your own shoes at *www.nike.com*, your car at *www.jaguar.com*, your CD at *www.easternrecording.com*, your business card at *www.iprint.com*, and your diamond ring at *www.bluenile.com*. Summarize your experiences.
3. Access *www.go4customer.com*. What does this company do and where is it located? Who are its customers? Which of Friedman's flatteners does this company fit? Provide examples of how a Canadian company would use its services.
4. Visit the website of Walmart China (*www.wal-martchina.com/english/index.htm*). How does Walmart China differ from your local Walmart? (Consider products, prices, services, etc.) Describe these differences.
5. Apply Porter's value chain model to Costco (*www.costco.ca*). What is Costco's competitive strategy? Who are Costco's major competitors? Describe Costco's business model. Describe the tasks that Costco must accomplish for each primary value chain activity. How would Costco's information systems contribute to Costco's competitive strategy, given the nature of its business?
6. Apply Porter's value chain model to Dell (*www.dell.ca*). What is Dell's competitive strategy? Who are Dell's major competitors? Describe Dell's business model. Describe the tasks that Dell must accomplish for each primary value chain activity. How would Dell's information systems contribute to Costco's competitive strategy, given the nature of its business?
7. The market for optical copiers is shrinking rapidly. It is expected that in the coming years, 90 percent or more of all duplicated documents will be done on computer printers. Can a company such as Xerox Corporation survive?
   a. Read about the problems and solutions of Xerox from 2000 to 2010 by searching *http://money.cnn.com/magazines/fortune/*, *www.search.com/*, and *www.google.com*.
   b. Identify all the business pressures on Xerox.
   c. Find some of Xerox's response strategies (see *www.xerox.com*, *www.yahoo.com*, and *www.google.com*).
   d. Identify the role of IT as a contributor to the business technology pressures (for example, obsolescence).
   e. Identify the role of IT as a facilitator of Xerox's critical response activities.

[Spreadsheet Activity]

Objective: Strategic information systems are designed to help create some type of competitive advantage. This activity teaches you that something as simple as sorting and filtering within a spreadsheet can be a form of a strategic information system since it will help make strategic decisions.

Chapter Connection: Porter's five forces are demonstrated in this activity. The two most focused on are the bargaining power of customers and industry rivalry. These will be evaluated in the activity by working with multiple pages within one workbook. Each page will provide a different comparison that will provide new or different information.

Activity: There are many factors that play a role in determining the final cost of a product. There are even more decisions that play into which options are chosen for a given product. Often, strategic information systems are used to help create competitive advantage. The recreational vehicle (RV) industry is no exception. Companies try to fit as many options into a camper as they can without dramatically increasing the weight, sacrificing the durability of the unit, or driving manufacturing costs so high that the price is uncompetitive. Industry innovations quickly become standard, customer desires change as gas prices go up and down, and businesses are left to sort everything out.

Visit *www.wiley.com/go/rainer/spreadsheet* and find the links provided for Chapter 2. The first link will be a video about sorting and filtering within spreadsheets. It will explain the process and how something this simple can be used to help make strategic decisions. Then click on the second link to download the file for this activity "MIS–Chapter 2.xlsx." It includes a customer survey regarding RV options and customer preferences as well as a list of competitive offerings and prices.

Then sort and filter the information based on criteria given to you by your professor. By sorting and filtering, you are creating information from your data (the raw facts). You will then use this information to make strategic business decisions to help your RV company create a competitive advantage within the marketplace.

Deliverable: The final product will be a spreadsheet filtered to show rankings of the organization among different criteria relative to its competition. Once you have filtered and ranked the data, you will make suggestions as to the best course of action that will provide the strongest possible competitive advantage for the company. This recommendation will come in the form of a business letter.

Discussion Questions

1. Too often, information systems are viewed as complicated computer programs that are difficult to understand. However, spreadsheets can provide much of the needed functionality. At what point is it cost-effective to purchase a more legitimate program than to use simple tools found within a spreadsheet?
2. Given the fact that information systems are there to support decisions, why do you think many opt for more expensive systems than the relatively easy-to-use spreadsheet?

[Case Assignment]

Car dealerships are heavily linked to their suppliers and their customers by means of automation. When a customer orders a car, the dealership can link to the vehicle production schedule or to other dealerships to obtain the appropriate model and colour. Then, customer transactions are tracked in internal information systems, while service department software helps the dealership remind users about when they should bring their vehicle in for service such as an oil change.

Lesser known systems help dealerships collect money when customers do not pay for their lease or their car loans that are financed via the dealership. Vehicle on-board computing systems can have remote access systems installed that enable the dealer to prevent the car from being started or have its horn honk incessantly. Then, the customer must pay amounts owed before the vehicle will start or to have the horn honking turned off.

Required

Using Porter's competitive forces model, explain how the Internet has affected competition at organizations like car dealerships.

[Team Assignments]

1. As a class, describe the business pressures on your university. Each group will then create an on-line group for studying one of these business pressures, and how your university uses IT to respond to this pressure. Each member of the group must have a Yahoo! e-mail account (free). Form your groups in Google Groups (*http://groups.google.com*).
2. Divide the class into teams. Each team will select a country government and visit its official website (for example, try Australia, Canada, Denmark, France, Germany, the

Netherlands, New Zealand, Norway, Singapore, the United Kingdom, or the United States). The official web portal for Canada is *www.canada.gc.ca* and for the U.S. government is *www.usa.gov*. Review and compare the services offered by each country. How does Canada compare? Are you surprised at the number of services offered by countries through websites? Which country offers the most services? The least?

[Case 2.2 Can Lululemon Sustain Competitive Advantage?]

The Problem

Lululemon athletica inc. (*www.lululemon.com*), founded in Vancouver in 1998, has a reputation for top-quality clothes that consumers pay top prices for. From a single store, the company has grown to sales over $1 billion, with over 10 percent of those sales from its Internet store. The company continues to innovate with new fabrics and new designs in women's and men's athletic clothing. This success has encouraged copycats and competition from the likes of Nike and the Gap.

These competing companies have launched yoga lines of clothing (albeit at lower prices), and have created yoga environments, including free yoga classes, in their stores. Free yoga classes were started by Lululemon, which strives to attract customers who want to take care of their bodies, and wear high-quality, attractive clothing while doing so. Lululemon's edge was the design of new fabrics that would not slip or slide or crumple while doing the yoga exercises. However, as synthetic fabrics have increased in availability, other companies have been able to design good yoga wear.

Lululemon has continued to grow, with most recent results of sales growth in the 8 or 9 percent range in the last part of 2012, versus 18 percent the year before. These growth figures are significantly less than the previous growth rates of the company, which have exceeded 30 percent or even 50 percent—amazing results when many retailers are struggling to do well.

Do these figures mean that Lululemon will continue to lose ground to more and more competition?

The Solution

Lululemon uses people and technology to keep its customers happy and keep costs down. The company implemented Vocollect's Voice technology to improve communication and speed up processing at its distribution centres. This means that the voice technology will be implemented for picking (taking products from the shelves and readying shipments), for organizing shipments to stores, and for moving products within the distribution centres. By implementing technology that saves time, the company improves employee productivity and lowers costs.

Lululemon also implemented FlexPLM (PLM stands for "product life cycle management"), which is used to manage the creation, production, and distribution of products. This type of software allows the company to manage the different stages of the product life cycle, setting targets for work, tracking what has been done, and following up tasks that are not on target. This means that customer marketing can be more effectively planned and tie in with the actual availability of products.

Since Lululemon has relatively short product life cycles, this helps the company implement new products quickly. Lululemon has basic products (such as black yoga apparel) that it stocks all the time, but it has special products that come in with smaller cycles, lasting from two to 12 weeks. The products in the cycle are not repeated, so the company creates a perception of unusual products and scarcity, with the intention of having customers buy something that they like when they see it, because it will not be in the store again if they come back many weeks later. Business analysts who analyze corporate performance believe that this is one of Lululemon's weaknesses, yet the company continues to use short product cycles and does not have "sales" of merchandise, instead selling products at full price.

The company limits the money that it spends on information technology; for example, it does not have customer relationship systems nor does it spend time on intensive data analytics. Instead, Chief Executive Officer Christine Day, walks around stores, listening to customers for some of her time, and the company has implemented practices that encourage employees to treat customers well, while listening to customer complaints. Clothing that customers have difficulty putting on (such as tops that are too tight in the arms) are not re-ordered.

Thus, Lululemon is creating a brand environment, a culture of high quality, uniqueness, and customer service, enhanced with information technology that supports efficient distribution.

The Results

Lululemon continues to outperform other rivals in the clothing industry. For the fourth quarter of 2012, net revenue was 31 percent higher than in the previous fourth quarter (at $485.5 million, making it the second year in a row that the company was a billion-dollar company, with sales of \$1.4 billion in 2012 and \$1.0 billion in 2011. Clearly the company is doing something right.

Questions

1. What type of competitive strategies is Lululemon employing?
2. Describe the business pressures that Lululemon is facing and how it is dealing with them.

Sources: Compiled from "Creativity Is Maximized when You Are Living in the Moment: Strategy and Technology, Lululemon Strategic Management Study," *http://hawksquawkblog.edublogs.org*, October 9, 2012; S. Freeman, "Lululemon Does Downward Dog," *Toronto Star*, January 5, 2013, p. B2; A. Lutz, "Rivals Rush to Copy Lululemon's Yoga Pose," *www.businessweek.com*, September 8, 2011; "Lululemon Athletic Partners with Vitech to Implement Vocollect Voice," January 29, 2010, *http://your-story.org/lululemon-athletic-partners-with-vitech-ti-implement-vocollect-voice-92769/*; *www.lululemon.com*, accessed April 16, 2013.

[Interactive Case]

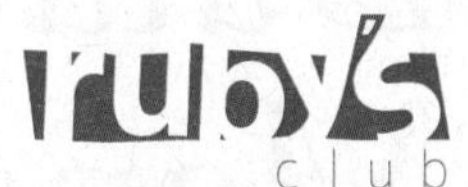

Supporting a Customer-Oriented Strategy at Ruby's Club

Go to the Ruby's Club link at the Student Companion website or *WileyPLUS* for information about your current internship assignment. Your assignment will entail outlining how Ruby's members' site can best support its customer-oriented strategy and creating a presentation for the club's managers.

Chapter 3

Data and Knowledge Management

[LEARNING OBJECTIVES]

1. Identify three common challenges in managing data, and describe one way organizations can address each challenge using data governance.
2. Name six problems that can be minimized by using the database approach.
3. Demonstrate how to draw and interpret relationships depicted in an entity-relationship diagram.
4. Discuss at least one main advantage and one main disadvantage of relational databases.
5. Identify the six basic characteristics of data warehouses and data marts.
6. Demonstrate the use of a multidimensional model to store and analyze data.
7. List two main advantages of using knowledge management, and describe the steps in the knowledge management system cycle.

[CHAPTER OUTLINE]

[WEB RESOURCES]

Student Companion Site

wiley.com/college/rainer

- Student PowerPoints for note taking
- Interactive Case: Ruby's Club Assignments
- Complete glossary

WileyPlus

All of the above and

- E-book
- Mini-lecture by author for each chapter section
- Practice quizzes
- Flash Cards for vocabulary review
- Additional "What's in IT for Me?" cases
- Video interviews with managers
- Lab Manual for Microsoft Office 2010
- How-to Animations for Microsoft Office 2010

ACCT	FIN	MKT	POM	HR	MIS
Cost justify firm's databases	Use data for internal investment decisions	Use customer data to plan marketing campaigns	Analyze data for quality control	Use employee data for performance evaluations	Provide infrastructure to store firm's data

[Case 3.1 Big Data]

The Problem

In today's information-centred environment, organizations and individuals must contend with an unimaginably vast amount of data that is growing ever more rapidly. In fact, the amount of digital data increases tenfold every five years. Consider these examples:

- Walmart processes more than 1 million customer transactions every hour, sending this information to its databases and data warehouses, which are estimated to contain more than 2.5 petabytes of data (1 petabyte equals 1,000 trillion bytes, or terabytes).
- Facebook contains more than 40 billion photographs, totalling hundreds of terabytes of data. More than 1 billion people use Facebook every month, sharing more than 2.4 billion content items every day. Facebook's data are stored in four data centres located in the United States and Sweden in buildings the size of small factories.
- To probe the inner workings of matter and better understand the make-up of the universe, the Large Hadron Collider at CERN, Europe's particle physics laboratory near Geneva, Switzerland, smashes tiny particles of matter and snaps pictures of the collisions. The collider has 5 collision detectors. Each one is about 5 storeys tall and contains 150 million sensors, each taking 40 million pictures per second. The collider generates 40 terabytes of data every second, much more data than can be stored or analyzed, so much of the information is simply thrown away.

Anna Tyukhmeneva/Shutterstock

Scientists say that we are undergoing a new revolution, the "Industrial Revolution of Data," and they have coined the term "Big Data" to describe the superabundance of data available today. Big Data allows us to do many things not previously possible; for example, to spot business trends more rapidly and accurately, to prevent disease, and to track crime.

At the same time, however, Big Data is creating numerous problems. First, beginning in 2007, there are more data available than the space to store them, and the gap continues to widen. Second, the quantity of data is growing faster than the ability of networks—particularly the Internet—to carry it. Third, the speed with which the amount of data grows and is shared around the world makes it more difficult to protect data security and personal privacy. Fourth, the sheer volumes of data are making them increasingly inaccessible. Fifth, individuals are swamped with data, making decision making sometimes overwhelming. Finally, only 5 percent of the data are structured; that is, saved in a standard format that computers can read.

IT Solutions

For many organizations, the first step in managing Big Data was to deal with the problem of *information silos*. Silos are information that is stored and isolated in separate functional areas. Organizations began to integrate this information into a database environment and then to develop data warehouses to serve as decision-making tools. Next, they turned their attention to the business of data and information management; that is, making sense of their proliferating data. Seeing a market need for data management, software vendors Oracle, IBM, Microsoft, and SAP together have spent more than $15 billion in recent years to purchase software firms specializing in data management and business intelligence (discussed in Chapter 10). IBM alone has recently invested $12 billion, opening six business intelligence centres with 4,000 employees worldwide.

The growing mounds of data have given rise to a new type of professional, the data scientist. Data scientists combine the skills of software programmers, statisticians, and storytellers to find valuable hidden "nuggets of information."

The Results

The way information is managed touches all areas of life. At the turn of the twentieth century, mass manufacturing was supported by new flows of information through channels such as the telegraph and telephone. Today, the availability of abundant yet small-scale data enables companies to cater to niche markets, and even individual customers, anywhere in the world. For example, Best Buy (*www.bestbuy.ca*), a retailer of consumer electronics, discovered that 7 percent of its customers accounted for 43 percent of its sales, so it reorganized its stores to concentrate on those customers' needs.

Some industries have led the way in gathering and exploiting data. Consider these examples:

- Credit card companies monitor every purchase and can accurately identify fraudulent ones, using rules derived by analyzing billions of transactions.
- Insurance companies analyze data to spot suspicious claims.
- Mobile-phone companies analyze subscribers' calling patterns to determine whether most of the people they call are using a rival network. If that rival network is offering a promotion that might lure its subscribers away, then the company can offer subscribers an incentive to stay.
- Retailers analyze customer transactions to tailor promotions to individual needs.
- The oil industry examines seismic data before drilling new wells.

There are many success stories of organizations using effective data management. Consider the global food products company Nestlé, for example. Nestlé sells more than 100,000 products in 200 countries, using 550,000 suppliers. But its supply chain was not effective, in part because its databases had severe problems. Roughly half of the company's 9 million records of vendors, customers, and materials were obsolete or duplicated, and about one-third of the remainder were inaccurate or incomplete. To improve the quality of its data, Nestlé overhauled its databases. The company could finally tap into its huge buying power and profit from its scale. For example, for just one ingredient, vanilla, the company's U.S. operation was able to use fewer suppliers, saving $30 million per year.

In contrast to these success stories, there are still cases where organizations have plenty of data but poor ways to manage and share it. For example, law enforcement and intelligence agencies' databases are not particularly well integrated despite years of effort. Similarly, in the health care field, large-scale efforts to computerize health records have encountered bureaucratic, technological, and ethical problems.

What We Learned From This Case

"Big Data" represents a very real problem that every business faces, as the data keep getting "bigger." The opening case describes the numerous problems caused by Big Data, the solutions that organizations are employing to manage these data, several good results, and a few poor results. The important idea here is that Big Data will continue to grow, and organizations will have to find ever more creative solutions to manage it.

Just as an example, the amount of digital information created, captured, and replicated in a recent four-year period equals about 18 million times as much information as that contained in all the books ever written. Images captured by billions of devices around the world, from digital cameras and smart phones to medical scanners and security cameras, make up the largest component of this digital information.

We are accumulating data and information at a frenzied pace from such diverse sources as company documents, e-mails, web pages, credit card swipes, phone messages, stock trades, memos, address books, and radiology scans. New sources of data and information include blogs, social media sites, podcasts, videocasts (think of YouTube), digital video surveillance, and radio frequency identification (RFID) tags and other wireless sensors (discussed in Chapter 6). We are awash in data, which we have to manage and make sense of. To deal with the growth and the diverse nature of digital data, organizations must use sophisticated techniques for data management.

Information technologies and systems support organizations in managing—that is, acquiring, organizing, storing, accessing, analyzing, and interpreting—data. As noted in Chapter 1, when these data are managed properly, they become *information* and then *knowledge*. Information and knowledge are valuable organizational resources that can provide a competitive advantage. This chapter will examine the processes whereby data are transformed first into information and then into knowledge.

Big Data is certainly a problem for large organizations. However, even small organizations can have problems with their data. Take the example of a small restaurant.

Restaurants must be highly coordinated businesses due to the shelf life of much of their inventory. For example, poor inventory management will result in overstocked or understocked shelves, and poor table management will result in long wait times and unhappy customers. To coordinate these activities, a manager needs timely information. A restaurant does not have to install an expensive ERP system (discussed in Chapter 8) to provide such information. In many cases, existing databases can be connected and a simple software package (such as Microsoft Access or FileMaker Pro) can be used to access that information. The problem for many small businesses is not gathering data, it is having that data in an accessible format so that they will be useful.

Few business professionals are comfortable making or justifying business decisions that are not based on solid information. This is especially true today, when modern information systems make access to that information quick and easy. For example, we have technology that formats data in a way that managers and analysts can easily understand. Consequently, these professionals can access these data themselves and analyze them according to their needs, using a variety of tools. The result is useful information. Executives can then apply their experience to use this information to address a business problem, thereby producing knowledge. Knowledge management, enabled by information technology, captures and stores knowledge in forms that all organizational employees can access and apply, thereby creating the flexible, powerful "learning organization."

Clearly, data and knowledge management are vital to modern organizations. But, why should you learn about them? The reason is that you will have an important role in the development of database applications. The structure and content of your organization's database depends on how users (you) look at your business activities. For example, when database developers in the firm's MIS group build a database, they use a tool called *entity-relationship (ER) modelling*, which we will discuss in Section 3.2. This tool creates a model of how users view a business activity. When you understand how to create and interpret an ER model, then you can evaluate whether the developers have captured your business activity correctly.

Keep in mind that decisions about data last longer, and have a broader impact, than decisions about hardware or software. If decisions concerning hardware are wrong, then the equipment can be replaced relatively easily. If software decisions turn out to be incorrect, they can be modified, though not always painlessly or inexpensively. Database decisions, in contrast, are much harder to undo. Database design constrains what the organization can do with its data for a long time. Remember that those who will be stuck with a bad database design are the business users, and not the database programmers, who will quickly move on to their next projects. This is why it is so important to get database designs right the first time—and you will be playing a key role in these designs.

Regarding relational databases, to be discussed in Section 3.3, when you know how data are stored in tables, then you know what types of data you have available for analysis and decision

Sources: Compiled from D. McCafferty, "The Big Data Conundrum," *CIO Insight*, November 9, 2010; D. Henschen, "What's At Stake in the Big Data Revolution?" *InformationWeek*, August 18, 2010; S. Nunziata, "Business Analytics: Turning IP into Opportunity," *CIO Insight*, August 17, 2010; D. Henschen, "The Big Data Era: How Data Strategy Will Change," *InformationWeek*, August 7, 2010; "Data, Data Everywhere," *The Economist*, February 25, 2010; D. Bollier, "The Promise and Peril of Big Data," *The Aspen Institute*, January 1, 2010; T. Davenport, J. Harris, and R. Morison, "Analytics at Work: Smarter Decisions, Better Results," *Harvard Business Press*, 2010; "Big Data—It's Not Just for Google Anymore," *AMD White Paper*, 2010; L. Gomes, "Parsing Data at the Large Hadron Collider," *Forbes*, August 30, 2010; J. Parikh, "A New Data Center for Iowa," Facebook newsroom, April 22, 2013; *www.nestle.com*, *www.ibm.com*, *www.rsc.org.uk*, accessed February 19, 2011.

making. Of course, your familiarity with data warehouses will serve the same purpose. Also, understanding relational databases will help you work with database developers in defining a new database or suggesting improvements to an existing one. It is one thing to say to a database developer, "I wish I could get this information from the database," but quite another to say, "If you could add this column of data to Table A and this other column of data to Table B, then I could get this information from the database." Database developers enjoy responding to specific, knowledgeable requests from users!

In addition, you might want to create a small, personal database using a software product such as Microsoft Access. In that case, you will want to know at least the basics of the product.

After the data are stored in your organization's databases, they must be accessible to users in a form that helps them make decisions. Organizations accomplish this objective by developing data warehouses. You should become familiar with data warehouses because they are invaluable decision-making tools and for this reason we will cover them in Section 3.4.

You will also make extensive use of your organization's knowledge base to perform your job. For example, when you are assigned a new project, you will likely research your firm's knowledge base to identify factors that contributed to the success of previous, similar projects. Thus, the chapter finishes by taking a look at knowledge management.

3.1 Managing Data

IT applications require data. These data should be of high quality, meaning they should be accurate, complete, timely, consistent, accessible, relevant, and concise. Unfortunately, the process of acquiring, keeping, and managing data is becoming increasingly difficult, as you see below.

The Difficulties of Managing Data

Because data are processed in several stages and often in several places, there are frequently problems and difficulties. Managing data in organizations is difficult for many reasons.

First, the amount of data increases exponentially with time. Much historical data—data that include time as a variable—must be kept for a long time, and new data are added rapidly. For example, to support millions of customers, large companies such as the Hudson's Bay Company or The Coca-Cola Company have to manage petabytes of data.

In addition, data are also scattered throughout organizations and are collected by many individuals using different methods and devices. These data are frequently stored in numerous servers and locations and in different computing systems, databases, formats, and human and computer languages.

Another problem is that data are obtained from multiple sources: internal sources (for example, corporate databases and company documents), personal sources (for example, personal thoughts, opinions, and experiences), and external sources (for example, commercial databases, government reports, and corporate websites). Data also are downloaded from the web, in the form of clickstream data. **Clickstream data** are produced by visitors and customers when they visit a website and click on hyperlinks. These data provide a trail of the users' activities in the website, including user behaviour and browsing patterns.

Further, data degrade over time. For example, customers move to new addresses or change their names, companies go out of business or are bought, new products are developed, employees are hired or fired, companies expand into new countries, and so on.

Data are also subject to *data rot*, a term that refers primarily to problems with the media on which the data are stored. Over time, temperature, humidity, and exposure to light can cause physical problems with storage media and thus make it difficult to access the data. Compounding this problem is the fact that finding the machines needed to access the data can be difficult. For example, it is almost impossible to find eight-track players anymore. This means that a library of eight-track tapes has become relatively worthless, unless you convert the tapes to a modern medium such as a DVD.

Data security, quality, and integrity are critical, yet they are easily jeopardized. In addition, legal requirements relating to data differ among countries as well as industries, and they change frequently.

Another problem arises from the fact that, over time, organizations have developed information systems for specific business processes, such as transaction processing, supply chain management, customer relationship management, and others. Information systems that specifically support these processes impose unique requirements on data, thereby creating repetition and conflicts across an organization. For example, the marketing function might maintain information on customers, sales territories, and markets that duplicates data within the billing or customer service functions. This situation produces inconsistent data in the enterprise. Inconsistent data prevent a company from developing a unified view of core business information—data concerning customers, products, finances, and so on—across the organization and its various information systems.

Two other factors complicate data management. First, federal government regulations—most significantly, Bill 198, the Canadian equivalent to the U.S. Sarbanes-Oxley Act—require companies to account for how information is being managed within their organizations. The law in Canada mandates that (1) public companies evaluate and disclose the effectiveness of their internal financial controls and (2) independent auditors for these companies confirm this disclosure. The law also holds CEOs and CFOs personally responsible for these disclosures. If their companies lack satisfactory data management policies and fraud or a security breach occurs, then these executives could be held personally responsible and face prosecution.

To address these myriad problems, modern organizations are turning to data governance. Let's take a closer look at this practice.

Data Governance

Data governance is an approach to managing information across an entire organization. It involves a formal set of business processes and policies designed to ensure that data are handled in a certain, well-defined fashion. That is, the organization follows unambiguous rules for creating, collecting, handling, and protecting its information. The objective is to make information available, transparent, and useful for the people authorized to access it, from the moment it enters an organization until it is outdated and deleted.

One strategy for implementing data governance is master data management. **Master data management** is a process that spans all of an organization's business processes and applications. It provides companies with the ability to store, maintain, exchange, and synchronize a consistent, accurate, and timely "single version of the truth" for the company's master data.

Master data are a set of core data, such as customer, product, employee, vendor, and geographic location, that span all of the enterprise's information systems. It is important to distinguish between master data and transaction data. *Transaction data*, which are generated and captured by operational systems, describe the activities, or transactions, of the business. In contrast, master data involve multiple transactions and are used to categorize, aggregate, and evaluate the transaction data.

To clarify this difference, let's look at an example of a transaction. You (Mary Jones) purchase one Samsung 42-inch plasma television, part number 1234, from Yves Gagnon at Best Buy, for $2,000, on August 20, 2013. In this example, the master data are "product sold," "vendor," "salesperson," "store," "part number," "purchase price," and "date." When specific values are applied to the master data, a transaction is represented. Therefore, the transaction data would be, respectively, "42-inch plasma television," "Samsung," "Yves Gagnon," "Best Buy," "1234," "$2,000," and "August 20, 2013."

IT's About Business 3.1 portraits the example of hardware retailer Ace Hardware and its efforts in managing master data.

Along with data governance, organizations use the database approach to efficiently and effectively manage their data. We turn our attention to the database approach in the next section.

IT's [about business]

3.1 Ace Hardware Standardizes Master Data

With 4,600 stores in more than 60 countries, Ace Hardware Corporation is one of the largest retailer-owned co-operatives worldwide. With 130 stores in Canada, its main competition still remains Home Hardware as well as other home hardware retailers such as Canadian Tire, Home Depot, or Rona. In their stores you can find items for your home improvement or repair projects, such as paint, plumbing supplies, and hammers and screwdrivers, along with gardening products such as shovels and rakes. Ace Hardware says that what sets it apart is friendly, expert advice from staff who can help customers select from thousands of home improvement and hardware products.

To better arm its staff with information on its 90,000 products, Ace Hardware developed ACENET, a system where. Ace retailers and associates can look up products at the click of a button, and they do so about 129,000 times each day.

ACENET was working well, but the company thought it could do better. For example, it wanted the ability for staff to use ACENET to compare products, which would be especially useful in finding a comparable product for a customer if the one they were looking for is out of stock. Providing Ace retailers and store associates with up-to-date, accurate product information is therefore of paramount importance.

Ace Hardware quickly realized the need to improve its master data in ACENET, starting with product names and description, manufacturer names, brands, and item attributes. This was necessary in order to improve search effectiveness, increase accuracy, and streamline new product entry into the database management system.

Therefore, Ace Hardware turned to Oracle software in an effort to improve its master data management, a project that was implemented in three phases. First, the company evaluated attributes that every item should have. It first identified brand and product type as two classifications that would provide an immediate return on investment. Second, the team worked on standardizing the navigation and product description for thousands of products in more than 900 categories of hardware merchandise. Finally, in the third phase, Ace created user-friendly expanded descriptions, introducing subcategory product-specific attributes, such as units of measure, material types, and finishes and colours.

Questions

1. Which of the difficulties about managing data can be applied to ACE Hardware? Support your answer.
2. Why was it important to standardize data for Ace Hardware? How does this concept tie in with data governance?
3. Why is it important to have a structured process in deciding which data to store in a database?

Sources: Compiled from "Ace Hardware Corporation: New Retail Focus and Customer Insight Make Ace Hardware a Fast-Growing Place," Teradata case study, *www.teradata.com*, accessed March 20, 2013; "Ace Hardware Corporation Standardized Product Attribute Information to Improve Online Product Search," Oracle case study, *www.oracle.com*, accessed May 17, 2013; *www.ace-canada.com/en/about-ace/history*, accessed March 20, 2013.

before you go on...

1. Identify and explain six major difficulties involved in managing data.
2. Define data governance.
3. Compare and contrast master data and transactional data, and provide an example of each one.

3.2 The Database Approach

From the time of the first computer applications in business (mid-1950s) until the early 1970s, organizations managed their data in a *file management environment*. This environment evolved because organizations typically began automating one application at a time. Thus, these systems grew independently from one another (again, in information silos), without overall planning. Each application required its own data, which were organized in a data file.

Therefore, in a file management environment, each application has a specific data file related to it that contains all the data records needed by the application. Over time, organizations developed numerous applications, each with an associated, application-specific data file.

As an illustration, imagine a situation where most of your information is stored in your university's central database, but a club to which you belong has its own files, the athletics department has separate files for student-athletes, and your instructors maintain grade data on their personal computers. Clearly, this type of arrangement lends itself to inconsistencies and inaccuracies. For example, your name could be misspelled in one of these files, but not in the others. If you move, your address might be updated correctly in one file, but not in the others. Using databases eliminates many problems that arose from previous methods of storing and accessing data, such as file management systems. **Databases** are arranged so that one set of software programs—the database management system—provides all users with access to all the data. (You will study database management systems later in this chapter.) This system minimizes the following problems:

- *Data redundancy*: The same data are stored in many places.
- *Data isolation*: Applications cannot access data associated with other applications.
- *Data inconsistency*: Various versions of the data do not agree.

In addition, database systems maximize the following strengths:

- *Data security*: Because data are "put in one place" in databases, there is a potential for losing a lot of data at once. Therefore, databases have extremely high security measures in place to deter mistakes and attacks. (You will learn about information security in Chapter 13.)
- *Data integrity*: Data meet certain constraints, such as no alphabetic characters in a Social Insurance Number field.
- *Data independence*: Applications and data are not linked to each other, so that all applications are able to access the same data.

Figure 3.1 illustrates a university database. Note that university applications from the Registrar's office, the Accounting department, and the Athletics department access data through the database management system.

A database can contain vast amounts of data. To make these data more understandable and useful, they are arranged in a hierarchy. In the next subsection, you will become familiar with the data hierarchy. You will then see how databases are designed.

The Data Hierarchy

Data are organized in a hierarchy that begins with bits and proceeds all the way to databases (see Figure 3.2). A **bit** (*b*inary dig*it*) represents the smallest unit of data a computer can process. The term "binary" means that a bit can consist only of a 0 or a 1. A group of eight bits, called a **byte**,

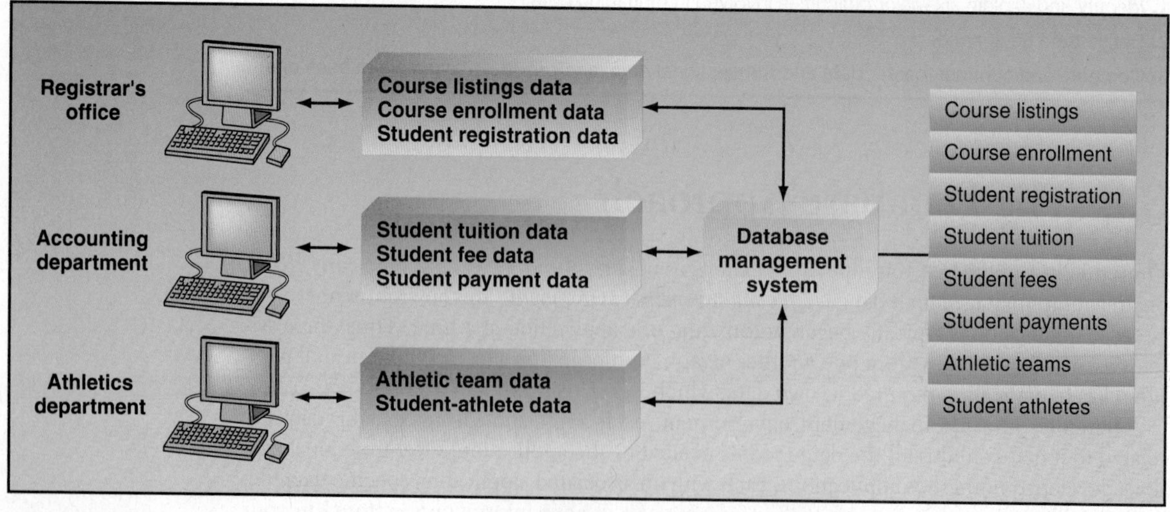

FIGURE 3.1 Database management system.

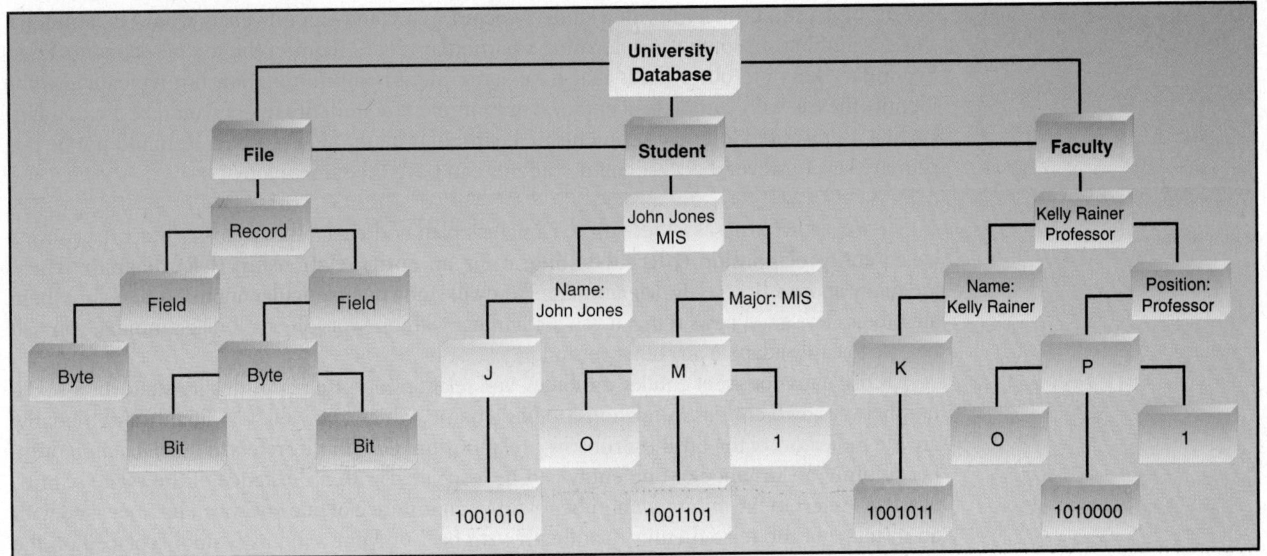

FIGURE 3.2 Hierarchy of data in database.

represents a single character. A byte can be a letter, a number, or a symbol. A logical grouping of characters into a word, a small group of words, or an identification number is called a **field**. For example, a student's name in a university's computer files would appear in the "name" field, and her or his Social Insurance Number would appear in the "Social Insurance Number" field. In addition to text and numbers, fields can also contain images and any other type of multimedia. Examples include a motor vehicle department's licensing database containing a person's photograph; a field containing a voice sample to authorize access to a secure facility; and the Apple iTunes Store, in which a song is a field in a record, with other fields giving the song's title, its price, and the album it is part of.

A logical grouping of related fields—such as the student's name, the courses taken, the date, and the grade—comprise a **record**. A logical grouping of related records is called a **file** or a **table**. For example, the records from a particular course, consisting of course number, professor, and students' grades, would constitute a data file for that course. A logical grouping of related files constitutes a database. Using the same example, the student course files could be grouped with files on students' personal histories and financial backgrounds to create a student database.

Now that you understand how data are arranged in a database, you will examine how modern organizations design their databases. The focus will be specifically on entity-relationship (ER) modelling and normalization procedures.

Designing the Database

Database Concepts. To be valuable, a database must be organized so that users can retrieve, analyze, and utilize the data they need. A key to designing an effective database is the data model. A **data model** is a diagram that represents the entities in the database and the relationships among them. An **entity** is a person, place, thing, or event—such as a customer, an employee, or a product—about which an organization maintains information. Entities can typically be identified in the user's work environment. A record generally describes an entity. An **instance** of an entity is a specific, unique representation of the entity. For example, an instance of the entity STUDENT would be a specific student, "Dominic Fisher."

Each characteristic or quality of a particular entity is called an **attribute**. For example, if our entity was a student, then entity attributes would be student name, student identification number, student address, student major, and so on.

Every record in a file must contain at least one field that uniquely identifies that record so that it can be retrieved, updated, and sorted. This identifier field is called the **primary key**.

For example, the primary key in a student record in a Canadian university would be a unique student number. In some cases, locating a particular record requires the use of secondary keys. **Secondary keys** are other fields that have some identifying information but typically do not identify the file with complete accuracy. For example, the student's major would be a secondary key if a user wanted to find all students in a particular major field of study. It should not be the primary key, however, because many students can have the same major.

Entity-Relationship Modelling. Designers plan and create the database through a process called **entity-relationship (ER) modelling**, using an **entity-relationship (ER) diagram**. There are many approaches to ER diagramming. You will study one particular approach here, but there are others. The good news is that if you are familiar with one version of ER diagramming, you will be able to easily adapt to any other version.

ER diagrams consist of entities, attributes, and relationships. Relationships illustrate an association between two entities. A relationship has a name, which is a verb. Cardinality and modality are the indicators of the business rules in a relationship. *Cardinality* refers to the *maximum* number of times an instance of one entity can be associated with an instance of the related entity. *Modality* refers to the *minimum* number of times an instance of one entity can be associated with an instance of the related entity. Cardinality can be 1 or Many, and its symbol is placed on the outside of the relationship line, closest to the entity. Modality can be 1 or 0, and its symbol is placed on the inside of the relationship line, next to the cardinality symbol. Figure 3.3 illustrates the cardinality and modality symbols. Figures 3.4a and 3.4b display an entity-relationship diagram. Entities are pictured in boxes, and relationships are displayed in diamonds. The attributes for each entity are listed in tables, and the primary key within a table is underlined.

As defined earlier, an entity is something that can be identified in the users' work environment. Consider student registration at a university. Students register for courses, and those who drive to campus also register their cars for parking permits. In this example, STUDENT, PARKING PERMIT, CLASS, and PROFESSOR are entities, as indicated in Figure 3.4.

Entities of a given type are grouped in **entity classes**. In our example, STUDENT, PARKING PERMIT, CLASS, and PROFESSOR are entity classes. An instance of an entity class is the representation of a particular entity. Therefore, a particular STUDENT (Peng Xu, 145-89-7123) is an instance of the STUDENT entity class; a particular parking permit (91778) is an instance of the PARKING PERMIT entity class; a particular class (76890) is an instance of the CLASS entity class; and a particular professor (Teresa De Carvalho, 115-65-7632) is an instance of the PROFESSOR entity class.

Entity instances have **identifiers** (primary keys), which are attributes that are unique to that instance. For example, STUDENT instances can be identified with *StudentIdentificationNumber*; PARKING PERMIT instances can be identified with *PermitNumber*; CLASS instances can be identified with *ClassNumber*; and PROFESSOR instances can be identified with *ProfessorIdentificationNumber*. These identifiers are underlined on ER diagrams, as in Figure 3.4b.

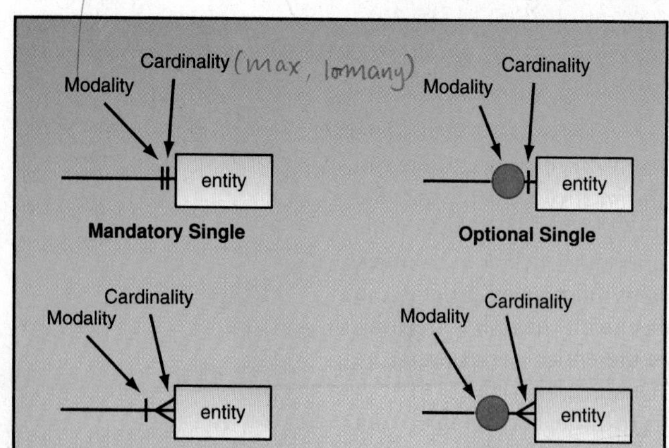

FIGURE 3.3 Cardinality and modality symbols.

In our example, examples of attributes for STUDENT are *StudentName* and *StudentAddress*. Examples of attributes for PARKING PERMIT are *StudentIdentificationNumber* and *CarType*. Examples of attributes for CLASS are *ClassName*, *ClassTime*, and *ClassPlace*. Examples of attributes for PROFESSOR are *ProfessorName* and *ProfessorDepartment*. (We assume that each course at this university has one professor—no team teaching.)

Why is StudentIdentificationNumber an attribute of both the STUDENT and PARKING PERMIT entity classes? That is, why do we need the PARKING PERMIT entity class? The reason is that the PARKING PERMIT entity class is needed for other applications, such as fee payments, parking tickets, and external links to the province's Ministry of Transportation.

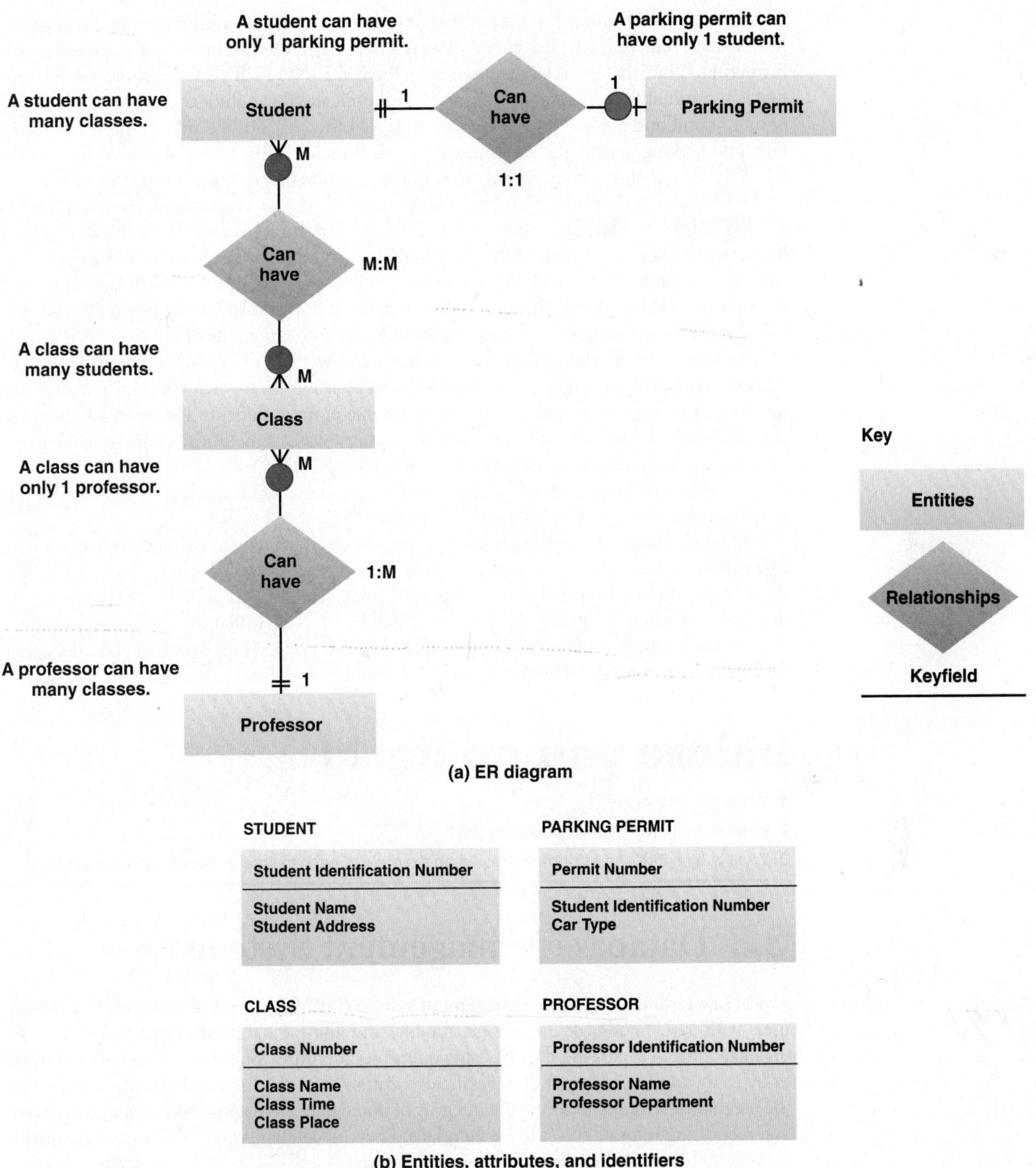

FIGURE 3.4 Entity-relationship diagram model.

Entities are associated with one another in relationships, which can include many entities. (Remember that relationships are noted by diamonds on ER diagrams.) The number of entities in a relationship constitutes the degree of the relationship. Relationships between two items are called *binary relationships*. There are three types of binary relationships: one-to-one, one-to-many, and many-to-many.

In a *one-to-one (1:1)* relationship, a single-entity instance of one type is related to a single-entity instance of another type. Figure 3.4a presents STUDENT-PARKING PERMIT as a 1:1

relationship. The relationship means that a student can have a parking permit, but does not need to have one. (Clearly, if a student does not have a car, then he or she will not need a parking permit.) Note that the relationship line on the PARKING PERMIT side shows zero or one; that is, a cardinality of 1 and a modality of 0. This indicates that a student can have a maximum of one permit and a minimum of zero permits. On the STUDENT side of the relationship, only one parking permit can be assigned to one student. Thus, the relationship line on the STUDENT side shows one and only one; that is, a cardinality of 1 and a modality of 1.

The second type of relationship, *one-to-many (1:M)*, is represented by the CLASS–PROFESSOR relationship in Figure 3.4a. This relationship means that a professor can have one or more courses (or none if the professor is not teaching that semester), but each course can have only one professor. Thus, the relationship line on the PROFESSOR side shows one and only one; that is, a cardinality of 1 and a modality of 1. The relationship line on the CLASS side shows one or many; that is, a cardinality of Many and a modality of 0.

The third type of relationship, *many-to-many (M:M)*, is represented by the STUDENT–CLASS relationship in Figure 3.4a. This M:M relationship means that typically a student can have one or more courses, and a course can have one or more students. However, a student can also take a semester off and not be enrolled in any courses; and sometimes a course might have no students enrolled. Note that the relationship line on the STUDENT side shows one or more; that is, a cardinality of Many and a modality of 0. Further, the relationship line of the CLASS side shows one or more; that is, a cardinality of Many and a modality of 0.

Entity-relationship modelling is valuable because it allows database designers to communicate with users throughout the organization to ensure that all possible entities and the relationships among them are represented. This process underscores the importance of taking all users into account when designing organizational databases. Notice that all entities and relationships in our example are labelled in terms that users can understand. Now that you understand how a database is designed, you can turn your attention to database management systems.

before you go on...

1. What is a data model?
2. What is a primary key? A secondary key?
3. What is an entity? An attribute? Provide an example of each in a sales department database.

3.3 Database Management Systems

As you saw earlier, a **database management system (DBMS)** is a set of programs that provide users with tools to add, delete, access, modify, and analyze data stored in one location. An organization can access the data by using query and reporting tools that are part of the DBMS or by using application programs specifically written to access the data. DBMSs also provide the mechanisms for maintaining the integrity of stored data, managing security and user access, and recovering information if the system fails. Because databases and DBMSs are essential to all areas of business, they must be carefully managed.

There are a number of different database architectures, but we focus on the relational database model because it is popular and easy to use. Other database models—for example, the hierarchical and network models—are the responsibility of the MIS function and are not used by organizational employees. Popular examples of relational databases products are Microsoft Access or FileMaker Pro for small business and for large businesses Oracle 11g, IBM DB2, SAP HANA, and Microsoft SQL Server.

The Relational Database Model

Most business data—especially accounting and financial data—traditionally were organized into simple tables consisting of columns and rows. Tables allow people to compare information quickly by row or column. In addition, items are easy to retrieve by finding the point of intersection of a particular row and column.

The **relational database model** is based on the concept of two-dimensional tables. A relational database generally is not one big table—usually called a *flat file*—that contains all of the records and attributes. Such a design would entail far too much data redundancy. Instead, a relational database is usually designed with a number of related tables. Each of these tables contains records, which are listed in rows, and attributes, which are listed in columns.

These related tables can be joined when they contain common columns. The uniqueness of the primary key tells the DBMS which records are joined with others in related tables. This feature allows users great flexibility in the variety of queries they can make. Despite these features, however, this model has some disadvantages. Because large-scale databases may be composed of many interrelated tables, the overall design can be complex and therefore have slow search and access times.

Consider the relational database example about students diagrammed in Figure 3.5. The table contains data about the entity called *students.* Attributes of the entity are *student name*, *undergraduate major*, *grade point average*, and *graduation date.* The rows are the records on Sally Adams, John Jones, Jane Lee, Kevin Durham, Juan Rodriguez, Stella Zubnicki, and Ben Wilson. Of course, your university's database maintains much more data on you than our example indicates. In fact, it probably keeps hundreds of attributes on each student.

Query Languages. Requesting information is the most commonly performed database operation. **Structured query language (SQL)** is the most popular query language used for this purpose. SQL allows people to perform complicated searches by using relatively simple statements or key words. Typical key words are *SELECT* (to specify a desired attribute), *FROM* (to specify the table to be used), and *WHERE* (to specify conditions to apply in the query).

To understand how SQL works, imagine that a university wants to know the names of students who will graduate with Magna Cum Laude—in May 2014. The university IS staff would

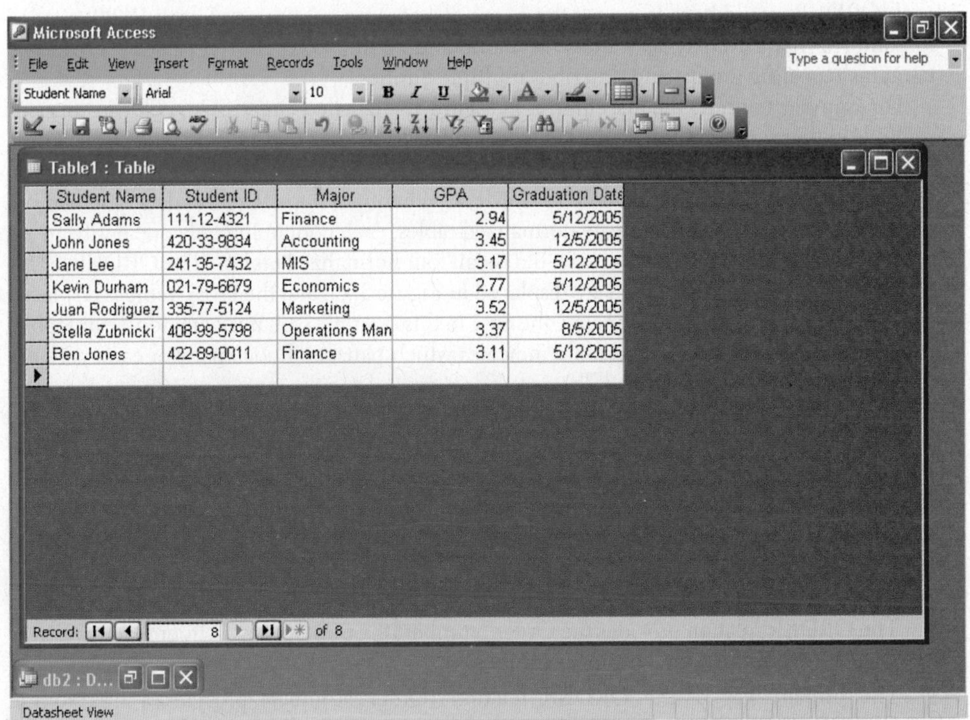

Student Name	Student ID	Major	GPA	Graduation Date
Sally Adams	111-12-4321	Finance	2.94	5/12/2005
John Jones	420-33-9834	Accounting	3.45	12/5/2005
Jane Lee	241-35-7432	MIS	3.17	5/12/2005
Kevin Durham	021-79-6679	Economics	2.77	5/12/2005
Juan Rodriguez	335-77-5124	Marketing	3.52	12/5/2005
Stella Zubnicki	408-99-5798	Operations Man	3.37	8/5/2005
Ben Jones	422-89-0011	Finance	3.11	5/12/2005

FIGURE 3.5 Student database example.

query the student relational database with an SQL statement such as: SELECT Student Name, FROM Student Database, WHERE Grade Point Average > 7.50 and Grade Point Average < 8.00. The SQL query would return John Jones and Juan Rodriguez.

Another way to find information in a database is to use **query by example (QBE)**. In QBE, the user fills out a grid or template, also known as a *form*, to construct a sample or description of the data he or she wants. Users can construct a query quickly and easily by using drag-and-drop features in a DBMS such as Microsoft Access. Conducting queries in this manner is simpler than keying in SQL commands.

Data Dictionary. When a relational model is created, the **data dictionary** defines the appropriate format for entering the data into the database. The data dictionary provides information on each attribute, such as its name, whether it is a key or part of a key, the type of data expected (e.g., alphanumeric, numeric, dates), and valid values. Data dictionaries can also specify how often the attribute should be updated, why it is needed in the database, and which business functions, applications, forms, and reports use the attribute.

Data dictionaries provide many advantages to the organization. Because they provide names and standard definitions for all attributes, they reduce the chances that the same attribute will be used in different applications under a different name. In addition, data dictionaries provide organizations with an inventory of their data resources, enabling them to manage those resources more effectively.

Normalization. For a relational database management system to be effective, the data must be carefully scrutinized to eliminate redundant data elements. **Normalization** is a method for reducing a relational database to its most streamlined form for minimum redundancy, maximum data integrity, and optimal processing performance. When data are *normalized*, attributes in the table depend only on the primary key.

As an example of normalization, consider an automotive repair garage. This business takes orders from customers whose cars need to be repaired. In this example, *ORDER*, *PART*, *SUPPLIER*, and *CUSTOMER* are entities. There can be many PARTS in an ORDER, but each PART can come from only one SUPPLIER. In a nonnormalized table (see Figure 3.6), each ORDER would have to repeat the name, description, and price of each PART needed to complete the ORDER, as well as the name and address of each SUPPLIER. This table contains repeating groups and describes multiple entities.

For example, consider the first column in Figure 3.6 (labelled *Order*). This column contains multiple entries for each Order—four rows for Order 11, six rows for Order 12, and so on. These multiple rows for an Order are called *repeating groups*. Figure 3.6 also has multiple entities: *ORDER*, *PART*, *SUPPLIER*, and *CUSTOMER*. When you normalize the data, you want to eliminate repeating groups to create normalized tables, each containing only one entity.

You might think that four entities would mean four normalized tables. (The ORDER, SUPPLIER, and CUSTOMER tables are displayed in Figure 3.7a, and the PART table is displayed in Figure 3.7b.) But, to fully normalize the data in this example, you must create an extra table, called *ORDERED-PARTS*. This table indicates which parts, and how many of each part, are in a particular order (see Figure 3.7b).

The normalization process, illustrated in Figure 3.8, breaks down the relation ORDER into smaller relations: *ORDER*, *SUPPLIER*, and *CUSTOMER* (Figure 3.7a) and *ORDERED-PARTS* and *PART* (Figure 3.7b). Each of these relations describes a single entity. This process is conceptually simpler, and it eliminates repeating groups. For example, consider an order at the automobile repair shop. The normalized relations can produce the order in the following manner (see Figure 3.8).

- The ORDER relation provides the Order Number (the primary key), Order Date, Delivery Date, Order Total, and Customer Number.
- The primary key of the ORDER relation (Order Number) provides a link to the ORDERED-PARTS relation (the link numbered *1* in Figure 3.8).

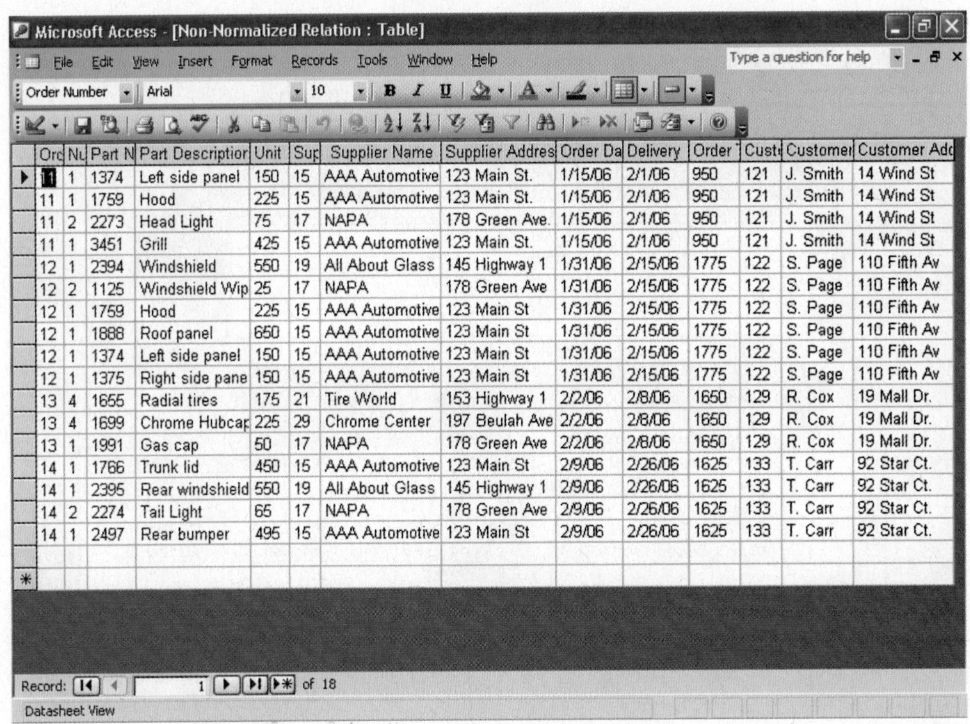
Microsoft Access - [Non-Normalized Relation : Table]

Ord	Nu	Part N	Part Descriptior	Unit	Sup	Supplier Name	Supplier Addres	Order Da	Delivery	Order	Custo	Custome	Customer Add
11	1	1374	Left side panel	150	15	AAA Automotive	123 Main St.	1/15/06	2/1/06	950	121	J. Smith	14 Wind St
11	1	1759	Hood	225	15	AAA Automotive	123 Main St.	1/15/06	2/1/06	950	121	J. Smith	14 Wind St
11	2	2273	Head Light	75	17	NAPA	178 Green Ave.	1/15/06	2/1/06	950	121	J. Smith	14 Wind St
11	1	3451	Grill	425	15	AAA Automotive	123 Main St.	1/15/06	2/1/06	950	121	J. Smith	14 Wind St
12	1	2394	Windshield	550	19	All About Glass	145 Highway 1	1/31/06	2/15/06	1775	122	S. Page	110 Fifth Av
12	2	1125	Windshield Wip	25	17	NAPA	178 Green Ave	1/31/06	2/15/06	1775	122	S. Page	110 Fifth Av
12	1	1759	Hood	225	15	AAA Automotive	123 Main St	1/31/06	2/15/06	1775	122	S. Page	110 Fifth Av
12	1	1888	Roof panel	650	15	AAA Automotive	123 Main St	1/31/06	2/15/06	1775	122	S. Page	110 Fifth Av
12	1	1374	Left side panel	150	15	AAA Automotive	123 Main St	1/31/06	2/15/06	1775	122	S. Page	110 Fifth Av
12	1	1375	Right side pane	150	15	AAA Automotive	123 Main St	1/31/06	2/15/06	1775	122	S. Page	110 Fifth Av
13	4	1655	Radial tires	175	21	Tire World	153 Highway 1	2/2/06	2/8/06	1650	129	R. Cox	19 Mall Dr.
13	4	1699	Chrome Hubcap	225	29	Chrome Center	197 Beulah Ave	2/2/06	2/8/06	1650	129	R. Cox	19 Mall Dr.
13	1	1991	Gas cap	50	17	NAPA	178 Green Ave	2/2/06	2/8/06	1650	129	R. Cox	19 Mall Dr.
14	1	1766	Trunk lid	450	15	AAA Automotive	123 Main St	2/9/06	2/26/06	1625	133	T. Carr	92 Star Ct.
14	1	2395	Rear windshield	550	19	All About Glass	145 Highway 1	2/9/06	2/26/06	1625	133	T. Carr	92 Star Ct.
14	2	2274	Tail Light	65	17	NAPA	178 Green Ave	2/9/06	2/26/06	1625	133	T. Carr	92 Star Ct.
14	1	2497	Rear bumper	495	15	AAA Automotive	123 Main St	2/9/06	2/26/06	1625	133	T. Carr	92 Star Ct.

Record: 1 of 18

Datasheet View

FIGURE 3.6 Nonnormalized table.

- The ORDERED-PARTS relation supplies the Number of Parts information to ORDER.
- The primary key of the ORDERED-PARTS relation is a composite key that consists of Order Number and Part Number. Therefore, the Part Number component of the primary key provides a link to the PART relation (the link numbered 2 in Figure 3.8).
- The PART relation supplies the Part Description, Unit Price, and Supplier Number to ORDER.
- The Supplier Number in the PART relation provides a link to the SUPPLIER relation (the link numbered 3 in Figure 3.8).
- The SUPPLIER relation provides the Supplier Name and Supplier Address to ORDER.
- The Customer Number in ORDER provides a link to the CUSTOMER relation (the link numbered 4 in Figure 3.8).
- The CUSTOMER relation supplies the Customer Name and Customer Address to ORDER.

Databases in Action

It is safe to say that almost all organizations have one or more databases. Further, there are numerous interesting database applications. IT's About Business 3.2 illustrates how China Sports Lottery Technology Development Co. used a relational database to improve its operations.

Organizations implement databases to manage their data efficiently and effectively. However, because databases typically process data in real time (or near real time), it is not practical to allow users access to the databases. To overcome this problem, organizations have developed data warehouses and data marts, which enable users to access data for decision making. You will learn about data warehouses in the next section.

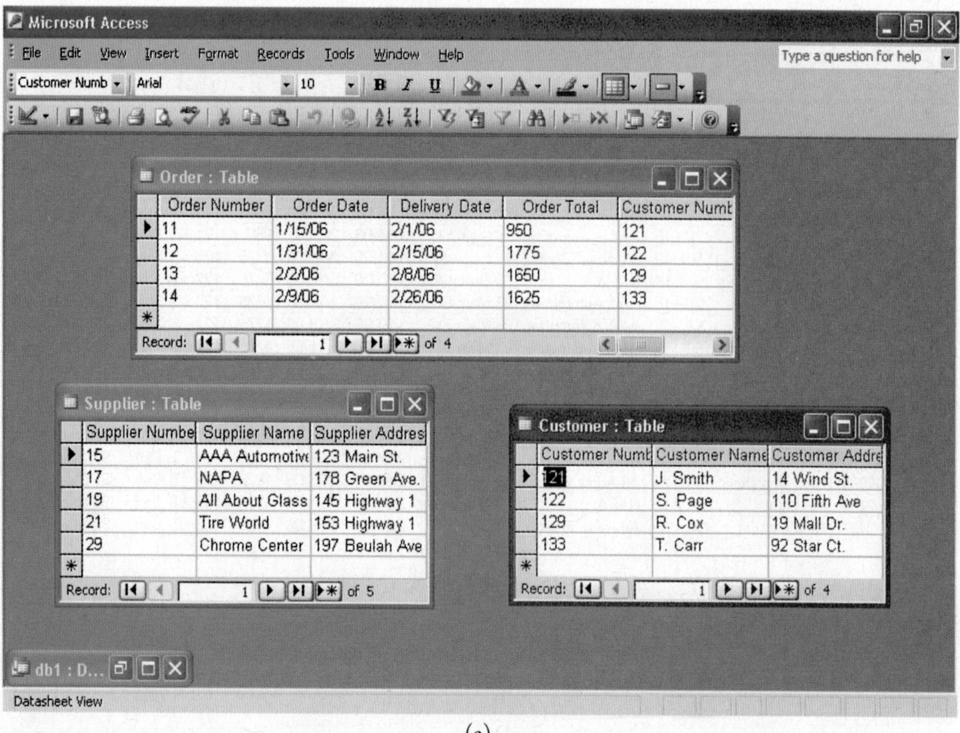

Order : Table

Order Number	Order Date	Delivery Date	Order Total	Customer Numb
11	1/15/06	2/1/06	950	121
12	1/31/06	2/15/06	1775	122
13	2/2/06	2/8/06	1650	129
14	2/9/06	2/26/06	1625	133

Supplier : Table

Supplier Numbe	Supplier Name	Supplier Addres
15	AAA Automotive	123 Main St.
17	NAPA	178 Green Ave.
19	All About Glass	145 Highway 1
21	Tire World	153 Highway 1
29	Chrome Center	197 Beulah Ave

Customer : Table

Customer Numb	Customer Name	Customer Addre
121	J. Smith	14 Wind St.
122	S. Page	110 Fifth Ave
129	R. Cox	19 Mall Dr.
133	T. Carr	92 Star Ct.

(a)

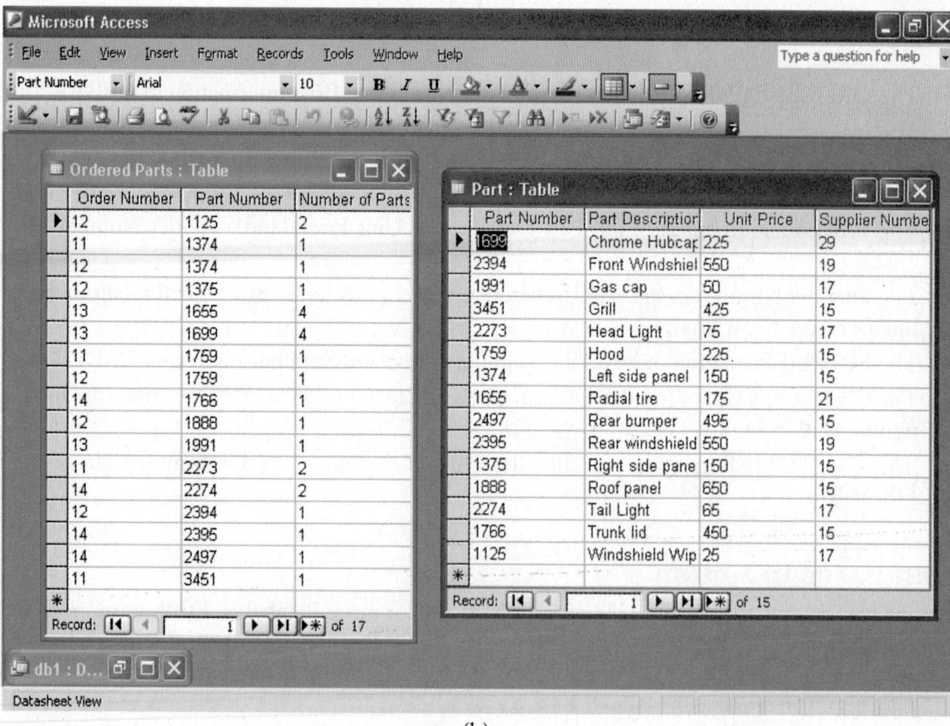

Ordered Parts : Table

Order Number	Part Number	Number of Parts
12	1125	2
11	1374	1
12	1374	1
12	1375	1
13	1655	4
13	1699	4
11	1759	1
12	1759	1
14	1766	1
12	1888	1
13	1991	1
11	2273	2
14	2274	2
12	2394	1
14	2395	1
14	2497	1
11	3451	1

Part : Table

Part Number	Part Description	Unit Price	Supplier Numbe
1699	Chrome Hubcap	225	29
2394	Front Windshiel	550	19
1991	Gas cap	50	17
3451	Grill	425	15
2273	Head Light	75	17
1759	Hood	225	15
1374	Left side panel	150	15
1655	Radial tire	175	21
2497	Rear bumper	495	15
2395	Rear windshield	550	19
1375	Right side pane	150	15
1888	Roof panel	650	15
2274	Tail Light	65	17
1766	Trunk lid	450	15
1125	Windshield Wip	25	17

(b)

FIGURE 3.7 Smaller relationships broken down from the nonnormal relations. (a) Order, Supplier, Customer. (b) Ordered Parts, Part.

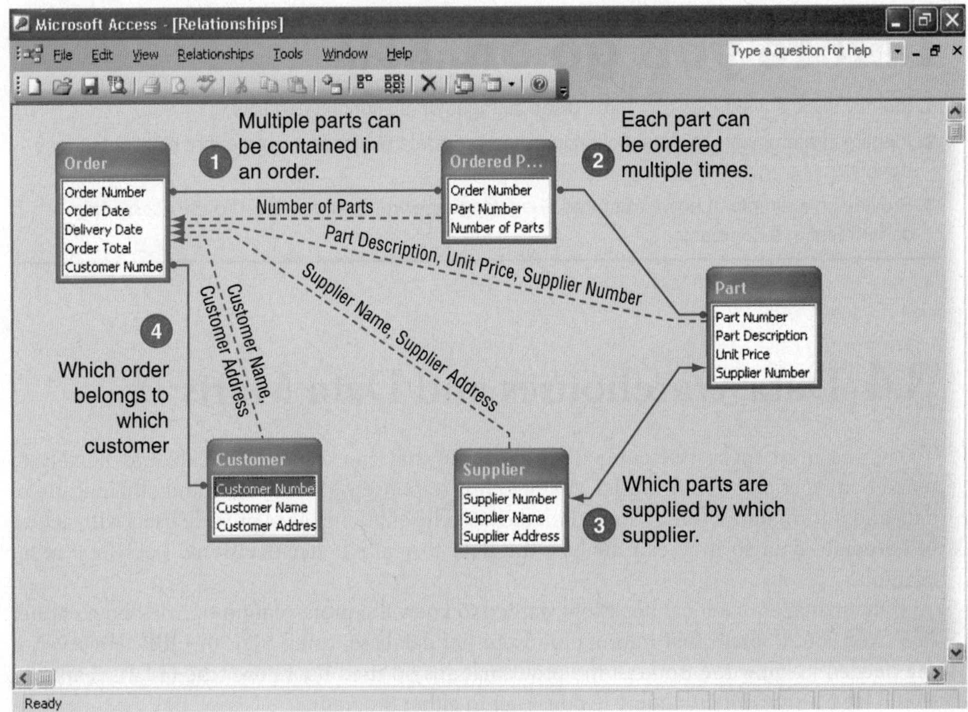

FIGURE 3.8 How normalized relations produce the order.

[about business]

3.2 DBMS at China Sports Lottery Technology Development

Lottery is big business in China, where 110,000 lottery sales terminals across the country generate about 10 million transactions every day. The development, operation, and maintenance of these terminals is done by the Beijing-based Sports Lottery Technology Development Co., Ltd. (CSLT), a state-owned high-tech company with four regional centres across China.

China's lottery system began with traditional paper tickets and scratch-type instant games, and then expanded to include computer lotteries. While this growth has boosted sales, it has also increased the volume of data that the system must handle and the difficulty of managing it.

The data management system was getting to be unwieldy, as each game had it own system, and some of the data were entered semi-manually. As a result, it was very difficult to aggregate the data, respond quickly to changes or new information, and to get a handle on how the lottery business was doing.

Faced with these challenges, CSLT selected a relational database management system from Microsoft called SQL Server 2008 R2. This improved CSLT's database administration, allowing the generation of business reports and integration with other software applications such as Microsoft Office. Users can now take advantage of features in software like Excel, such as pivot tables and pivot charts, which are data summarization and analysis tools, and formulas to perform data analysis in Microsoft Office without the help from IT personnel. The CSLT's database capacity is growing by 2 terabytes a year, and the company expects to provide data services to more than 100,000 relevant employees.

Questions

1. Discuss why the characteristics of the database approach fit the case of CSLT. Hint: Address in your discussion the benefits of database management systems.
2. What are three technical issues that need to be considered when selecting a new database management system? Use facts from this story to support your answer.
3. Why is it important for a relational database to be normalized? Discuss your answer in relation to CSLT.
4. Explain the usefulness of a data dictionary in the case of CSLT. Use an example to support your answer.

Sources: Compiled from "Microsoft Business Intelligence Boosts Development of China Sports Lottery," *www.microsoft.com/casestudies/*, January 13, 2012; "China Sports Lottery Technology Development Co., Ltd Sports Lottery Technology Operator Takes Strategic Leaps Forward in Supporting Booming Sports Lottery Industry," *www.microsoft.com/casestudies/*, May 10, 2011.

before you go on...

1. Identify three advantages and three disadvantages of relational databases.
2. Identify three benefits of data dictionaries and provide a business example that highlights those benefits.
3. Provide an example of how structured query language works and relate it to the accounting department in a company.

3.4 Data Warehouses and Data Marts

Today, the most successful companies are those that can respond quickly and flexibly to market changes and opportunities. A key to this response is the effective and efficient use of data and information by analysts and managers. The challenge is to provide users with access to corporate data so they can analyze the data to make better decisions. Let's look at an example.

If the manager of a local bookstore wanted to know the profit margin on used books at her store, she could obtain that information from her database, using SQL or QBE. However, if she needed to know the trend in the profit margins on used books over the last 10 years, she would have a very difficult query to construct in either program.

This example illustrates several reasons why organizations are building data warehouses and/or data marts. First, the bookstore's databases have the necessary information to answer the manager's query, but this information is not organized in a way that makes it easy for her to find what she needs. Second, the organization's databases are designed to process millions of transactions per day. Therefore, complicated queries might take a long time to answer and also might degrade the performance of the databases. Third, transactional databases are designed to be updated. This updating requires extra processing. Data warehouses and data marts are read-only, and the extra processing is eliminated because data already in the data warehouse are not updated. Fourth, transactional databases are designed to access a single record at a time. Data warehouses are designed to access large groups of related records.

Companies are using a variety of tools with data warehouses and data marts to make it easier and faster for users to access, analyze, and query data. You will learn about these tools in Chapter 10 (Business Intelligence).

Describing Data Warehouses and Data Marts

In general, data warehouses and data marts support business intelligence (BI) applications. As you will see in Chapter 10, business intelligence is a broad category of applications, technologies, and processes for gathering, storing, accessing, and analyzing data to help business users make better decisions. A **data warehouse** is a repository of historical data that are organized by subject to support decision makers in the organization.

Because data warehouses are so expensive, they are used primarily by large companies. A **data mart** is a low-cost, scaled-down version of a data warehouse that is designed for the end-user needs in a small organization or a strategic business unit or a department in a large organization. Data marts can be implemented more quickly than data warehouses, often in less than 90 days. Further, they support local rather than central control by conferring power on the using group. Typically, groups that need a single or a few BI applications require only a data mart rather than a data warehouse.

The basic characteristics of data warehouses and data marts include:

Organized by Business Dimension or Subject. Data are organized by subject (for example, by customer, vendor, product, price level, and region). This arrangement is different from transactional systems, where data are organized by business process, such as order entry, inventory control, and accounts receivable.

Use On-line Analytical Processing. Typically, organizational databases are oriented toward handling transactions. That is, databases use *on-line transaction processing (OLTP)*, where business transactions are processed on-line as soon as they occur. The objectives are speed and efficiency, which are critical to a successful Internet-based business operation. In contrast, data warehouses and data marts, which are designed to support decision makers rather than OLTP, use on-line analytical processing. *On-line analytical processing (OLAP)* involves the analysis of accumulated data by end users.

Integrated. Data are collected from multiple systems and are integrated around subjects. For example, customer data can be extracted from internal (and external) systems and integrated around a customer identifier to create a comprehensive view of the customer.

Time Variant. Data warehouses and data marts maintain historical data. Unlike transactional systems, which maintain only recent data (such as for the last day, week, or month), a data warehouse or data mart can store years of data. Companies need historical data to detect trends, deviations from trends, and long-term relationships.

Nonvolatile. Data warehouses and data marts are nonvolatile, meaning that only IT professionals can change or update the data. Consequently, the data warehouse or data mart reflects history, which is critical for trend analysis. Data warehouses and data marts are updated, but through IT-controlled load processes rather than by users.

Multidimensional. Recall that relational databases store data in two-dimensional tables. In contrast, data warehouses and data marts store data in a **multidimensional structure**, which consists of more than two dimensions. A common representation for this structure is the *data cube*.

The data in data warehouses and data marts are organized by *business dimensions*, which are subjects such as product, geographic area, and time period. These subjects represent the edges of the data cube. If you look ahead briefly to Figure 3.11 for an example of a data cube, you will see that the product dimension is composed of nuts, screws, bolts, and washers; the geographic area dimension is composed of East, West, and Central; and the time period dimension is composed of 2011, 2012, and 2013. Users can view and analyze data from the perspective of these business dimensions. This analysis is intuitive because the dimensions are defined in business terms that users can easily understand.

A Generic Data Warehouse Environment

The environment for data warehouses and data marts includes the following:

- Source systems that provide data to the data warehouse or data mart
- Data integration technology and processes that are needed to prepare the data for use
- Different architectures for storing data in an organization's data warehouse or data marts
- Different BI tools and applications for the variety of users (you will learn about these BI tools and applications in Chapter 10)
- The need for metadata, data quality, and governance processes to be in place to ensure that the data warehouse or data mart meets its purposes

Figure 3.9 illustrates a generic data warehouse/data mart environment. Let's drill down into the component parts.

Source Systems. There is typically some business need or business problem that motivates the development of BI capabilities in a firm. Working backwards, this business need leads to information requirements, BI applications, and source system data requirements. The data

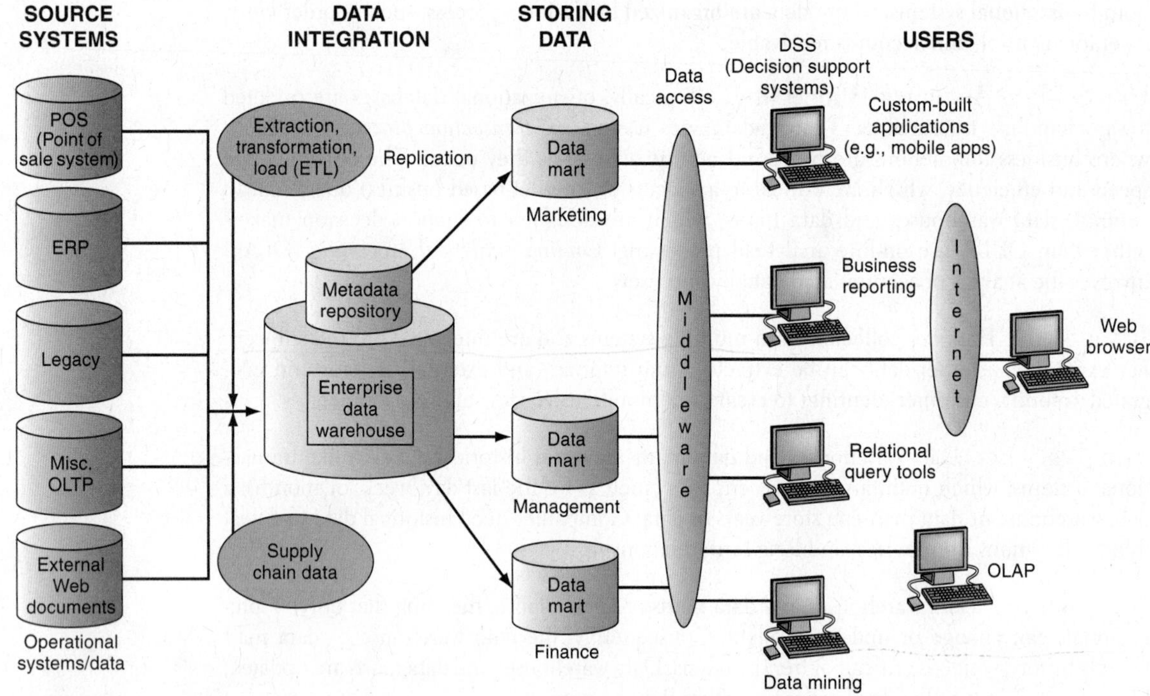

FIGURE 3.9 Data warehouse framework.

requirements may involve only a single source system, as in the case of a data mart, or hundreds of source systems, as in the case of an enterprise-wide data warehouse.

Organizations have access to a variety of source systems: operational/transactional systems, enterprise resource planning (ERP) systems, website data, third-party data (e.g., customer demographic data), and more. The current trend is to include more types of data (e.g., sensing data from RFID tags). These source systems often use different software packages (e.g., IBM, Oracle) and store data in different formats (e.g., relational, hierarchical).

A common source for the data in data warehouses is the company's operational databases, which can be relational databases. To differentiate between relational databases and multidimensional data warehouses and data marts, suppose your company has four products—nuts, screws, bolts, and washers—that have been sold in three territories—East, West, and Central—for the previous three years—2011, 2012, and 2013. In a relational database, these sales data would appear like Figures 3.10a, b, and c. In a multidimensional database, these data would be represented by a three-dimensional matrix (or data cube), as displayed in Figure 3.11. This matrix represents sales *dimensioned by* products and regions and year. Notice that in Figure 3.10a you can see sales only for 2011. Sales for 2012 and 2013 are presented in Figures 3.10b and 3.10c, respectively. Figures 3.12a, b, and c display the equivalence between these relational and multidimensional databases.

Many source systems that have been in use for years contain "bad data"—for example, missing or incorrect data—and are poorly documented. As a result, data-profiling software should be used at the beginning of a data warehousing project to evaluate the data. Data-profiling software has many capabilities, such as providing statistics on missing data, identifying possible primary keys, and revealing how derived values (e.g., column 3 = column 1 + column 2) are calculated. Subject area database specialists (e.g., marketing, human resources) can also help in understanding and accessing the data in source systems.

Other issues related to source systems must be addressed. Organizations often have multiple systems that contain the same data. In these cases the organization should select the best system as the source. Organizations must also decide how granular (i.e., the level of detail) the

(a) 2011

Product	Region	Sales
Nuts	East	50
Nuts	West	60
Nuts	Central	100
Screws	East	40
Screws	West	70
Screws	Central	80
Bolts	East	90
Bolts	West	120
Bolts	Central	140
Washers	East	20
Washers	West	10
Washers	Central	30

(b) 2012

Product	Region	Sales
Nuts	East	60
Nuts	West	70
Nuts	Central	110
Screws	East	50
Screws	West	80
Screws	Central	90
Bolts	East	100
Bolts	West	130
Bolts	Central	150
Washers	East	30
Washers	West	20
Washers	Central	40

(c) 2013

Product	Region	Sales
Nuts	East	70
Nuts	West	80
Nuts	Central	120
Screws	East	60
Screws	West	90
Screws	Central	100
Bolts	East	110
Bolts	West	140
Bolts	Central	160
Washers	East	40
Washers	West	30
Washers	Central	50

FIGURE 3.10 Relational databases.

data need to be. For example, are daily sales figures adequate, or are data at the individual transaction level needed? The conventional wisdom is that data are best stored at a highly granular level because they are likely to be requested at some point.

Data Integration. It is necessary to *e*xtract data from source systems, *t*ransform them, and *l*oad them into a data mart or warehouse. Consequently, this process is often called ETL, but the term *data integration* is increasingly being used because of the growing number of ways that source system data can be handled. For example, in some cases, the data are extracted, loaded into a mart or warehouse, and then transformed (i.e., ELT rather than ETL).

Data extraction can be performed by hand-written code (e.g., SQL queries) or by commercial data-integration software. Most companies ultimately use commercial software. This software makes it relatively easy to specify the appropriate tables and attributes in the source

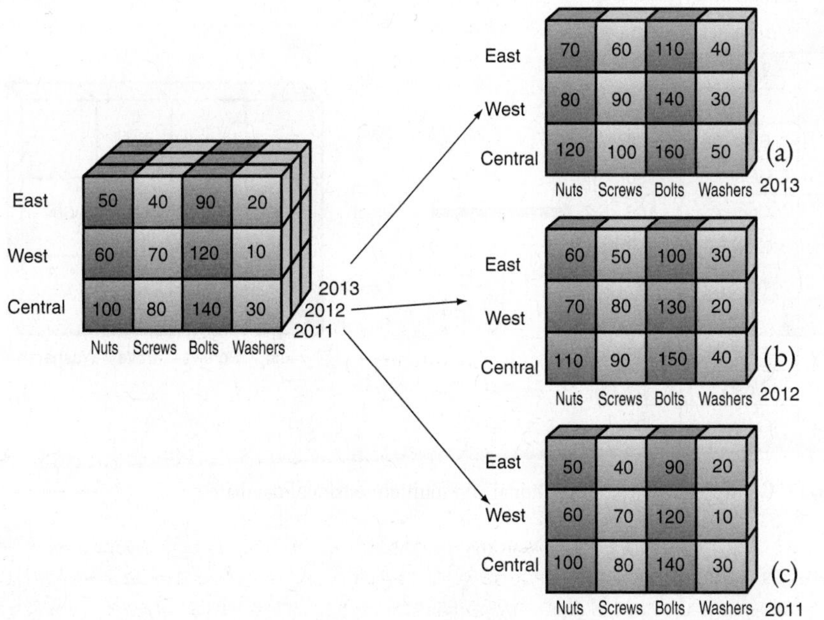

FIGURE 3.11 Data cube.

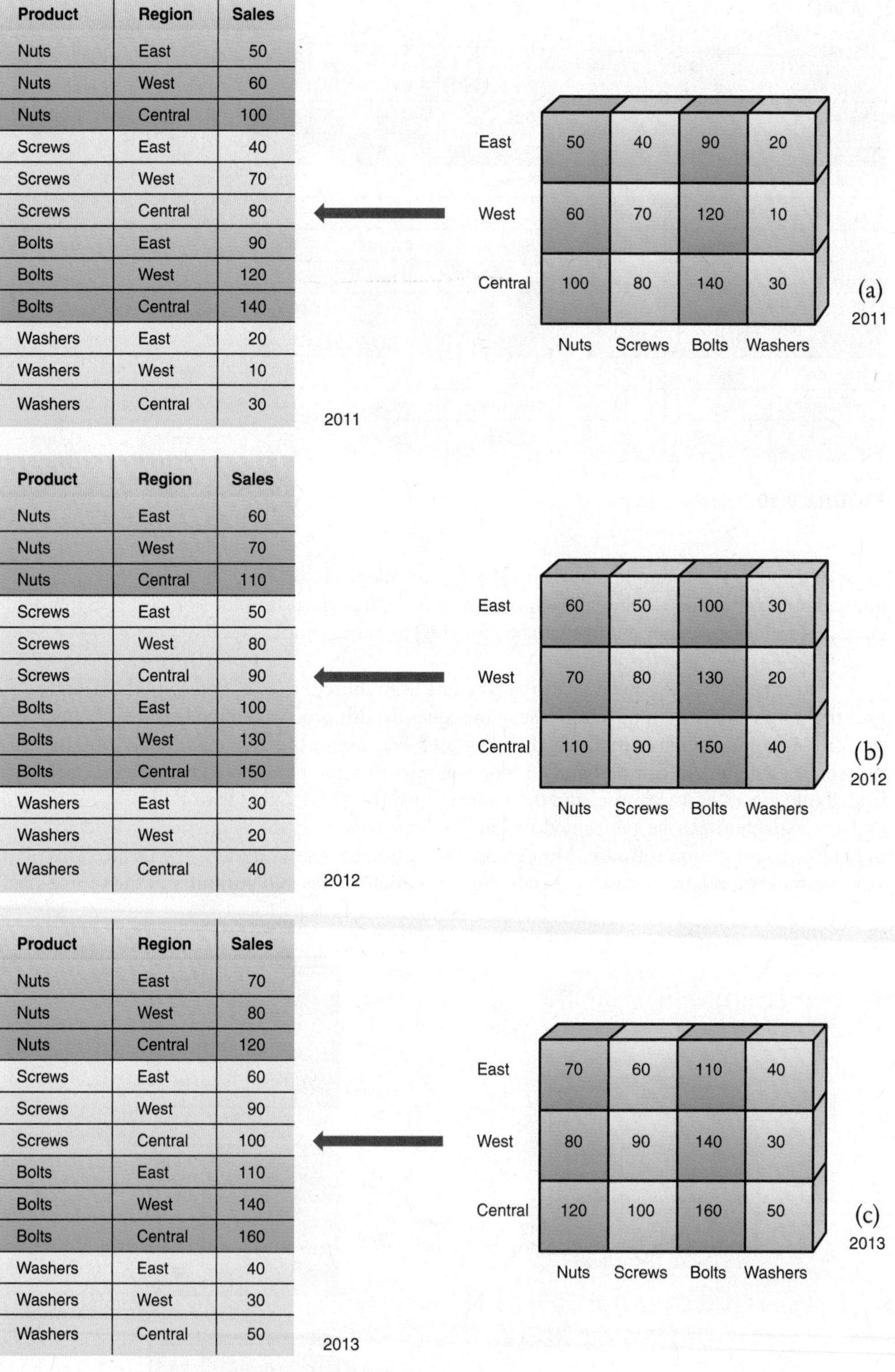

2011

Product	Region	Sales
Nuts	East	50
Nuts	West	60
Nuts	Central	100
Screws	East	40
Screws	West	70
Screws	Central	80
Bolts	East	90
Bolts	West	120
Bolts	Central	140
Washers	East	20
Washers	West	10
Washers	Central	30

(a) 2011

	Nuts	Screws	Bolts	Washers
East	50	40	90	20
West	60	70	120	10
Central	100	80	140	30

2012

Product	Region	Sales
Nuts	East	60
Nuts	West	70
Nuts	Central	110
Screws	East	50
Screws	West	80
Screws	Central	90
Bolts	East	100
Bolts	West	130
Bolts	Central	150
Washers	East	30
Washers	West	20
Washers	Central	40

(b) 2012

	Nuts	Screws	Bolts	Washers
East	60	50	100	30
West	70	80	130	20
Central	110	90	150	40

2013

Product	Region	Sales
Nuts	East	70
Nuts	West	80
Nuts	Central	120
Screws	East	60
Screws	West	90
Screws	Central	100
Bolts	East	110
Bolts	West	140
Bolts	Central	160
Washers	East	40
Washers	West	30
Washers	Central	50

(c) 2013

	Nuts	Screws	Bolts	Washers
East	70	60	110	40
West	80	90	140	30
Central	120	100	160	50

FIGURE 3.12 Equivalence between relational and multidimensional databases.

systems, to map and schedule the movement of the data to the target (e.g., a data mart or data warehouse), to make the required transformations, and ultimately to load the data.

As the data are integrated, they are also transformed to make them more useful. For example, data from different systems may be integrated around a common key, such as a customer identification number. This is the approach taken with customer data to create a 360-degree view of all interactions with customers (discussed in Chapter 9 in Section 9.2 Customer Relationship Management). Let's use a bank as an example. Customers may go to a branch, bank on-line, use an ATM, take out a car loan, and use other services. The systems for these touchpoints—the numerous ways that organizations interact with customers, such as e-mail, the web, direct contact, and the telephone—are typically separate. In order to analyze and fully understand how customers are using the bank, it is necessary to integrate the data from the various source systems in a data mart or warehouse.

Data integration can involve other kinds of transformations. For example, it might require format changes to the data, such as using *Male* and *Female* to denote gender, as opposed to 0 and 1 or M and F. Aggregations may be performed, say, on sales figures, so that queries can use the summaries rather than recalculate them each time. Data-cleansing software may be used to "clean up" the data, such as eliminating duplicate records (e.g., for the same customer).

The period of time during which new data are loaded into the warehouse or mart is known as the "load window." This window is getting smaller as companies demand ever fresher data in their warehouses. Many companies have moved to real-time data warehousing where data are moved, using data-integration processes, from source systems to the data warehouse or data mart almost immediately. For example, within 15 minutes of a purchase at Walmart, the details of the sale have been stored in a data warehouse and are available for analysis.

Storing the Data. There are a variety of possible architectures to store decision-support data. The most common architecture is *one central enterprise data warehouse*, without data marts. Most organizations use this approach, in which the data in the warehouse are accessed by all users and are the *single version of the truth*.

Another architecture is *independent data marts*, which store data for a single or a few applications, such as in marketing or finance. Limited thought is given as to how the data might be used for other applications and throughout the organization. This is a very application-centric approach to storing data.

Independent data marts are not very effective in large organizations. Although they typically meet the needs of a small organization or a department in a large organization, they do not take an enterprise-wide approach to data management. Instead, various units create independent data marts throughout the organization. Unfortunately, these marts often contain inconsistent data. For example, they may have inconsistent data definitions (such as whether a particular individual is a potential customer or a current customer) or use different source systems (which may contain different data for the same item, such as a customer address). Although independent data marts are an organizational reality, larger companies have increasingly moved to data warehouses.

Still another data warehouse architecture is the *hub and spoke*. This architecture stores data in a central data warehouse while simultaneously maintaining dependent data marts that obtain their data from the central repository. Because the marts acquire their data from the central repository, the data in the marts are still the single version of the truth for decision-support purposes.

The dependent data marts store the data in a format appropriate for how the data will be used. They provide faster response times to queries and applications.

Metadata. In addition to storing vast amounts of data in warehouses and data marts, modern organizations need to maintain data about that data. Data about data are referred to as **metadata**. Both the IT personnel who operate and manage the data warehouse and the users who access the data stored there need metadata. IT personnel need information about data sources; database, table, and column names; refresh schedules; and data usage measures. Users' needs include data definitions, the available report/query tools, report distribution information, and help desk contact information.

Data Quality. The quality of the data in the warehouse must be adequate to satisfy users' needs. If it is not, then the data will not be trusted and ultimately will not be used. Most organizations find that the quality of the data in source systems is poor and must be improved before the data can be stored in the data warehouse. Some of the data can be improved through the use of data-cleansing software, but the better, long-term solution is to improve the quality at the source system level. To accomplish this goal, the owners of the data must take responsibility for implementing any necessary changes to both the data and the data-collection system.

Lessons From IT Failures

To illustrate this point, consider the case of a large hotel chain that wanted to conduct targeted marketing promotions using postal code data collected when guests check in. When the data were analyzed, many of the postal codes were found to be the same, although the city and province was different. How did this happen? Obviously, the clerks were not asking customers for their postal codes, but they needed to enter some value in order to complete the registration process. The standard strategy was simply to enter any combination of letters and numbers that would let the clerk to advance to the next registration screen. A short-term solution to this problem was to conduct the marketing campaign using city and province data, which the clerks always entered. The long-term solution was to get the clerks to enter the actual postal codes. To implement this strategy, the hotel managers had to take the responsibility for changing the clerks' behaviours to meet the company's needs.

Governance. For an organization to ensure that BI is meeting its needs, it must practise governance to plan and control BI activities. Governance requires that people, committees, and processes be in place. Companies with effective BI governance often create a senior-level committee made up of vice-presidents and directors who prioritize projects, allocate resources, and ensure that the business and BI strategies are in alignment. These companies also put together a middle-level committee that oversees the various projects in the BI portfolio to ensure that they are being completed effectively and efficiently. Finally, lower-level operational committees perform tasks such as creating data definitions and identifying and solving data problems. All of these committees require the collaboration and contributions of business and IT personnel.

Users. Once the data are stored in a data mart or data warehouse, they can be accessed. At this point the process of receiving business value from BI begins; everything else we discussed constitutes creating BI infrastructure.

There are a large number of potential BI users, including IT developers; front-line workers; analysts; information workers; managers and executives; and suppliers, customers, and regulators. Some of these users are *information producers*, meaning that they primarily create information for others. IT developers and analysts typically fall into this category. Other users, including managers and executives, are *information consumers* who utilize information created by others.

Companies have reported hundreds of successful data-warehousing applications. You can read client success stories and case studies at the websites of vendors such as NCR Corp. (*www.ncr.com*) and Oracle (*www.oracle.com*). For a more detailed discussion, visit the Data Warehouse Institute (*www.tdwi.org*). The benefits of data warehousing include:

- End users can access needed data quickly and easily via web browsers because these data are located in one place.
- End users can conduct extensive analysis with data in ways that may not have been possible before.
- End users can obtain a consolidated view of organizational data.

These benefits can improve business knowledge, provide competitive advantage, enhance customer service and satisfaction, facilitate decision making, and streamline business processes.

[about business]

3.3 The Data Warehouse at The Isle of Capri Casinos

The Isle of Capri Casinos (*www.isleofcapricasinos.com*) is one of the largest publicly traded gaming companies in North America. The company operates 15 casinos in six U.S. states as well as a property in the Caribbean. It also provides accommodations, with a total of 3,000 hotel rooms. The properties have a total of roughly 15,000 slot machines, 400 gaming tables, and 35 restaurants, serving roughly 2 million guests annually.

The company aims to not only anticipate guests' needs, but to exceed their expectations. To do this, the company culture is focused on making every guest experience enjoyable. It uses a data platform so that employees can better understand their customers.

In the entertainment and accommodation business, marketing is key. The Isle of Capri faces a marketing challenge because its customers are diverse and geographically dispersed. The company needed to segment customers while at the same time maintaining and building an overall brand image. Historically, the firm managed its customer relationship management efforts with a piecemeal direct mail program run out of each property. However, this meant that company employees did not have a complete view of the customer. For example, the company occasionally experienced difficulties recognizing regular customers at one property who were well known at another property.

The Isle of Capri decided to implement a data warehouse that would provide a "single view of the business" as well as a "single view of the customer." The data warehouse would underpin both direct mail and e-mail marketing campaigns.

The company began to implement a data warehouse in 2004, but that had to take a back seat when Hurricane Katrina hit the U.S. Gulf Coast the next year. At that time, The Isle's headquarters were located in Biloxi, Mississippi. The company shifted its focus to recovery efforts, and it relocated its headquarters to St. Louis, Missouri. In 2006, The Isle returned to implementing the warehouse, which became operational in 2007.

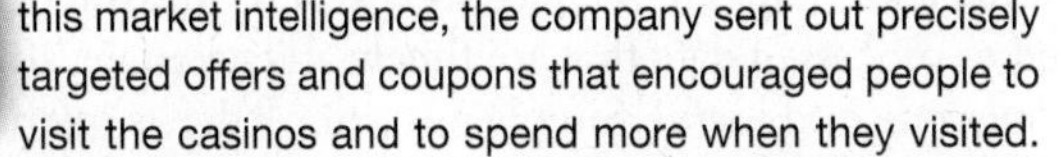

With its data warehouse in place, The Isle could quickly and easily identify and segment a key market. Armed with this market intelligence, the company sent out precisely targeted offers and coupons that encouraged people to visit the casinos and to spend more when they visited. For example, marketers segmented customers based on the frequency of their visits. The less often a customer visited, the more incentives the company offered for them to return. A company spokesperson noted that a player who visits four times a month requires a much less aggressive incentive package than one who comes only once a month.

The data warehouse enabled marketing campaign preparation times to be cut in half. Further, both the company and the individual properties can track the results of campaigns more effectively, including receiving immediate alerts when a customer redeems a coupon.

The information in the data warehouse was made available beyond the marketing team. Now, multiple business users can access, analyze, and generate reports on the company's wealth of data.

The data warehouse became even more valuable when it was expanded to include data concerning The Isle's hotels. The company tracks guests by the number of days they stay at a hotel. It then can ask a series of queries to gain further insights; for example: "Who stayed at least two or three times?" "Who gamed and who didn't?" "How much did staying in a hotel affect a customer's gaming activity?"

The results of these experiments were surprising. Customers who live close to a casino and do not need to stay overnight spend more money when they do stay over. Further, they play more frequently than hotel guests who live farther away. The Isle used this information to target marketing to local customers, enticing them to stay overnight, including offers of a free night in one of its hotels.

The Isle then added slot machine data to the warehouse. Beyond targeted marketing, these data helped the company to determine where high-value players prefer the machines to be located. The information also allowed the company to let customers know about new games they might be interested in based on their past behaviour. The company plans to closely track slot activity to increase knowledge of its customers' activities, target its promotions more precisely, and change the layout in each casino to optimize revenue and profit.

Questions

1. Why was it necessary for The Isle of Capri Casinos to develop a data warehouse?
2. Describe the variety of benefits that The Isle realized from its data warehouse.
3. Can you think of any additional ways in which The Isle can take advantage of its data warehouse? Provide specific examples.

Sources: Compiled from L. Brockaw, "In Experiments We Trust: From Intuit to Harrah's Casinos," *Sloan Management Review*, March 3, 2011; "Data Warehouse Assessment Services Leads Ameristar Casinos to Select Teradata," *PR Newswire*, February 21, 2011; "Isle of Capri Casinos Makes a Sure Bet," *Teradata Magazine*, v. 11, no. 1, 2011; "Harrah's Entertainment, Inc.," IBM Case Studies, November 2, 2010; *www.isleofcapricasinos.com*, *www.teradata.com*, accessed February 18, 2011.

IT's about Business 3.3 demonstrates the benefits of data warehousing at The Isle of Capri Casinos.

Despite their many benefits, data warehouses do have problems. First, they can be very expensive to build and to maintain. Second, incorporating data from obsolete mainframe systems can be difficult and expensive. Finally, people in one department might be reluctant to share data with other departments.

before you go on...

1. Provide three characteristics of a data warehouse.
2. Identify three differences between data warehouse and data marts.
3. Identify four components of a data warehouse environment.
4. What are three possible architectures for data warehouse and data marts in an organization?

3.5 Knowledge Management

As you have seen throughout the book so far, data and information are critically important organizational assets. Knowledge is a vital asset as well. Successful managers have always used intellectual assets and recognized their value. These efforts, however, were not systematic, and they did not ensure that knowledge was shared and dispersed in a way that benefited the overall organization. Moreover, industry analysts estimate that most of a company's knowledge assets are not housed in relational databases. Instead, they are dispersed in e-mail, electronic text documents, spreadsheets, and presentations on individual computers. This arrangement makes it extremely difficult for companies to access and integrate this knowledge. The result frequently is less-effective decision making.

Concepts and Definitions

Knowledge management (KM) is a process that helps organizations manipulate important knowledge that is part of the organization's memory, usually in an unstructured format. For an organization to be successful, knowledge, as a form of capital, must exist in a format that can be exchanged among persons. In addition, it must be able to grow.

Knowledge. In the information technology context, knowledge is distinct from data and information. As you learned in Chapter 1, data are a collection of facts, measurements, and statistics; information is organized or processed data that are timely and accurate. Knowledge is information that is *contextual*, *relevant*, and *useful*. Simply put, knowledge is *information in action*. **Intellectual capital** (or **intellectual assets**) is another term for knowledge.

To illustrate with an example, a bulletin listing all the courses offered by your university during one semester would be considered data. When you register, you process the data from the bulletin to create your schedule for the semester. Your schedule would be considered information. Awareness of your work schedule, your major, your desired social schedule, and characteristics of different faculty members could be construed as knowledge, because it can affect the way you build your schedule. This awareness is contextual and relevant (to developing an optimal schedule of classes), as well as useful (it can lead to changes in your schedule). The implication is that knowledge has strong experiential and reflective elements that distinguish it from information in a given context. Unlike information, knowledge can be exercised to solve a problem.

There are numerous theories and models that classify different types of knowledge. Here you will focus on the distinction between explicit knowledge and tacit knowledge.

Explicit and Tacit Knowledge. **Explicit knowledge** deals with more objective, rational, and technical knowledge. In an organization, explicit knowledge consists of policies, procedural guides, reports, products, strategies, goals, core competencies of the enterprise, and the IT infrastructure. In other words, explicit knowledge is the knowledge that has been codified (documented) in a form that can be distributed to others or transformed into a process or a strategy. A set of instructions on how to process a job application that is documented in a firm's human resources policy manual is an example of explicit knowledge.

In contrast, **tacit knowledge** is the cumulative store of subjective or experiential learning. In an organization, tacit knowledge consists of an organization's experiences, insights, expertise, know-how, trade secrets, skill sets, understanding, and learning. It also includes the organizational culture, which reflects the past and present experiences of the organization's people and processes, as well as the organization's prevailing values. Tacit knowledge is generally imprecise and costly to transfer. It is also highly personal. Finally, because it is unstructured, it is difficult to formalize or codify, in contrast to explicit knowledge. A salesperson who has worked with particular customers over time and has come to know their needs very well would possess extensive tacit knowledge. This knowledge is typically not recorded. In fact, it might be difficult for the salesperson to put into writing.

Knowledge Management Systems

The goal of knowledge management is to help an organization make the most effective use of the knowledge it possesses. Historically, management information systems have focused on capturing, storing, managing, and reporting explicit knowledge. Organizations now realize they need to integrate explicit and tacit knowledge in formal information systems. **Knowledge management systems (KMSs)** are those that use modern information technologies—the Internet, intranets, extranets, databases—to systematize, enhance, and expedite knowledge management within a single firm and among multiple firms. KMSs are intended to help an organization cope with turnover, rapid change, and downsizing by making the expertise of the organization's human capital widely accessible. IT's About Business 3.4 describes how Mazda implemented a new knowledge management system.

Organizations can realize many benefits with KMSs. Most importantly, they make **best practices**—the most effective and efficient ways of doing things—readily available to a wide range of employees. Enhanced access to best-practice knowledge improves the organization's overall performance. For example, account managers can make available their tacit knowledge about how best to handle large accounts. The organization can then use this knowledge to train new account managers. Other benefits include improved customer service, more efficient product development, and improved employee morale and retention.

At the same time, however, there are challenges to implementing effective KMSs. First, employees must be willing to share their personal tacit knowledge. To encourage this behaviour, organizations must create a knowledge management culture that rewards employees who add their expertise to the knowledge base. Second, the knowledge base must be continually maintained and updated. New knowledge must be added, and old, outdated knowledge must be deleted. Finally, companies must be willing to invest in the resources needed to carry out these operations.

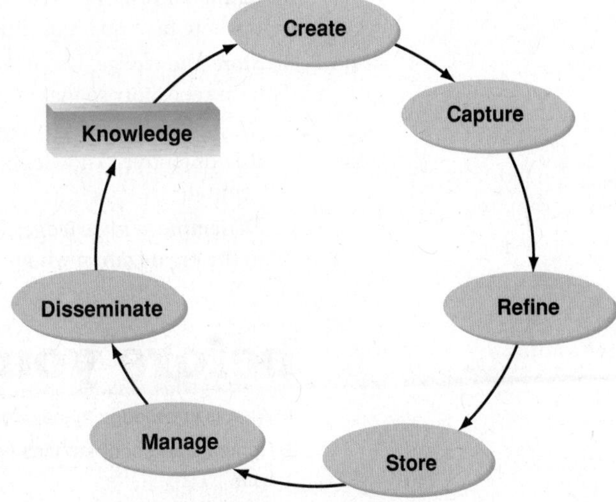

FIGURE 3.13 The knowledge management system cycle.

The Knowledge Management System Cycle

A functioning KMS follows a cycle that consists of six steps (see Figure 3.13). The reason the system is cyclical is that knowledge is dynamically refined over time. The knowledge in an

IT's [about business]

3.4 Knowledge Management at Mazda North America

Mazda North American Operations is the regional research and development, sales and marketing, distribution, parts, and customer service operation for Japan-based Mazda Motor Corporation. Spanning Canada, the United States, and Mexico, it represents approximately 27 percent of Mazda's global revenue.

The company had been using a legacy system for internal knowledge management and automotive service technician support, but it was not available in multiple languages and had no flexibility in terms of customization and maintenance. The system provided support to 170 dealerships in Canada, 650 dealers in the United States, 14 in Puerto Rico, and 32 in Mexico, as well as third-party automotive service centres. In total this knowledge management system provided support to more than 6,000 users.

In order to find the answer to their technical problems such as an engine not starting, or how to replace a thermostat sensor, mechanics at dealerships and automotive service centres had to search millions of technical documents, which made it increasing difficult to do their job in a timely manner. Because customer satisfaction is key, Mazda had to find a replacement for its outdated knowledge management system, and it found it in software from Oracle.

The software provides content in multiple languages. It is also scalable, meaning that it can accommodate growing amounts of data and users. The software allows automotive technicians to intuitively search millions of technical documents in seconds. And they can do that using categories and terms familiar to them, since the software allows Mazda to use its own metadata for a search. Mazda credits the new knowledge management system with helping to improve customer service: in 2012, Mazda North America achieved higher customer service ratings than in previous years.

Questions

1. What are the issues that made Mazda North America adopt a new knowledge management system? Use the facts from the case to support your answer.
2. What managerial factors need to be considered when implementing a knowledge management system? (Hint: Think in terms of organizational characteristics, size, industry, management style, and organizational culture.)
3. Provide examples of tacit knowledge in the case of Mazda.
4. Explain the role that knowledge management systems could play in regard to managing tacit knowledge. Use the case of Mazda to explain your answer.

Sources: Compiled from "Mazda North American Operations Delivers Technical Information to Automotive Service Professionals in Seconds Using an Advanced Knowledge Solution," Oracle case study, *www.oracle.com*, accessed March 21, 2013; *www.mazda.ca*, accessed March 21, 2013.

---

effective KMS is never finalized because the environment changes and knowledge must be updated to reflect these changes. The cycle works as follows:

1. *Create knowledge.* Knowledge is created as people determine new ways of doing things or develop know-how. Sometimes external knowledge is brought in.
2. *Capture knowledge.* New knowledge must be identified and recorded.
3. *Refine knowledge.* New knowledge must be placed in context so that it is actionable. This is where tacit qualities (human insights) must be captured along with explicit facts.
4. *Store knowledge.* Useful knowledge must then be stored in a reasonable format in a knowledge repository so that other members of the organization can access it.
5. *Manage knowledge.* Like a library, the knowledge must be kept current. To accomplish this objective, knowledge must be reviewed regularly to verify that it is relevant and accurate.
6. *Disseminate knowledge.* Knowledge must be made available in a useful format to anyone in the organization who needs it, anywhere and anytime.

before you go on...

1. What is knowledge management?
2. Compare and contrast tacit knowledge and explicit knowledge, and provide one example of each type.
3. Identify and describe the six steps in the knowledge management system cycle.

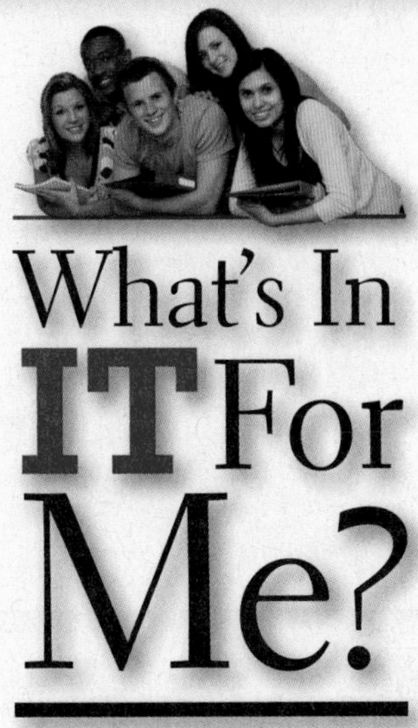

For the **Accounting Major**

The accounting function is intimately concerned with keeping track of an organization's transactions and internal controls. Modern databases enable accountants to perform these functions more effectively. Databases help accountants manage the flood of data in today's organizations so that they can keep their firms in compliance with the standards imposed by financial reporting legislation.

Accountants also play a role in cost-justifying the creation of a knowledge base and then auditing its cost-effectiveness. In addition, if you work for a large accounting firm that provides management services or sells knowledge, you will most likely use some of your company's best practices that are stored in a knowledge management system.

For the **Finance Major**

Financial managers make extensive use of computerized databases that are external to the organization, such as those of Statistics Canada or the Toronto Stock Exchange (TSX), to obtain financial data on organizations in their industry. They can use these data to determine if their organization meets industry benchmarks in return on investment, cash management, and other financial ratios.

Financial managers, who produce the organization's financial status reports, are also closely involved with financial reporting legislation.

For the **Marketing Major**

Databases help marketing managers access data from the organization's marketing transactions (for example, customer purchases) to plan targeted marketing campaigns and to evaluate the success of previous campaigns. Knowledge about customers can make the difference between success and failure. In many databases and knowledge management systems, the vast majority of information and knowledge concerns customers, products, sales, and marketing. Marketing managers regularly use an organization's knowledge base, and often they participate in its creation.

For the **Production/Operations Management Major**

Production/operations personnel access organizational data to determine optimum inventory levels for parts in a production process. Past production data enable POM personnel to determine the optimum configuration for assembly lines. Firms also maintain data concerning the quality of finished products as well as quality issues regarding incoming raw materials, production irregularities, shipping and logistics, and after-sale use and maintenance of the product.

Knowledge management is extremely important for running complex operations. The accumulated knowledge regarding scheduling, logistics, maintenance, and other functions is very valuable. Innovative ideas are necessary for improving operations and can be supported by knowledge management.

For the **Human Resources Management Major**

Organizations keep extensive data on employees, including gender, age, race, current and past job descriptions, and performance evaluations. Human resources personnel access these data to provide reports to government agencies regarding compliance with human rights legislation. HR managers also use these data to evaluate hiring practices, review salary structures, and manage any discrimination claims or lawsuits brought against the firm.

Databases help HR managers provide assistance to all employees as companies turn over more and more decisions about health care and retirement planning to the employees themselves. The employees can use the databases for help in selecting the optimal mix among these critical choices.

Human resources managers also need to use a knowledge management system frequently to find out how past cases were handled. Consistency in how employees are treated is not only important, but it protects the company against legal actions. Also, training for building, maintaining, and using the knowledge system sometimes is the responsibility of the HR department. Finally, the HR department might be responsible for compensating employees who contribute their knowledge to the knowledge base.

For the MIS Major

The MIS function manages the organization's data as well as the databases. MIS database administrators standardize data names by using the data dictionary. This process ensures that all users understand which data are stored in the database. Database personnel also help users access needed data and help them generate reports with query tools.

[Summary]

1. **Identify three common challenges in managing data, and describe one way organizations can address each challenge using data governance.**

Three common challenges in managing data are:

- Data are scattered throughout organizations and are collected by many individuals using various methods and devices. These data are frequently stored in numerous servers and locations and in different computing systems, databases, formats, and human and computer languages.
- Data come from multiple sources.
- Information systems that support particular business processes impose unique requirements on data, which results in repetition and conflicts across an organization.

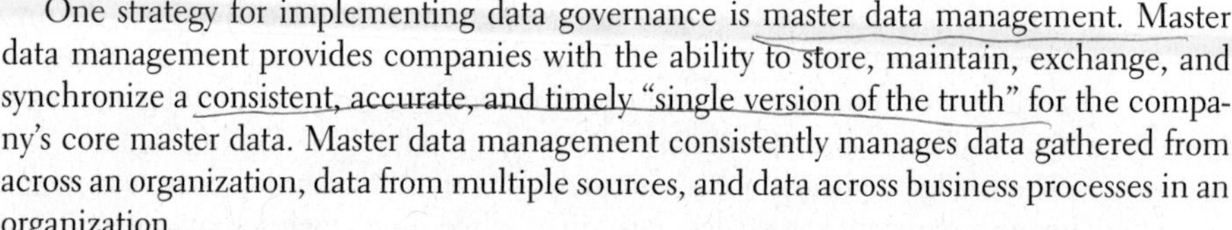

One strategy for implementing data governance is master data management. Master data management provides companies with the ability to store, maintain, exchange, and synchronize a consistent, accurate, and timely "single version of the truth" for the company's core master data. Master data management consistently manages data gathered from across an organization, data from multiple sources, and data across business processes in an organization.

2. **Name six problems that can be minimized by using the database approach.**

The database approach minimizes the following problems: data redundancy, data isolation, data inconsistency, data security, data integrity, and data independence.

3. **Demonstrate how to draw and interpret relationships depicted in an entity-relationship diagram.**

See Figures 3.3 and 3.4 for a demonstration of interpreting relationships in an ER diagram.

4. **Discuss at least one main advantage and one main disadvantage of relational databases.**

Relational databases enable people to compare information quickly by row or column. In addition, users can retrieve items by finding the point of intersection of a particular row and column. However, large-scale relational databases can be composed of many interrelated tables, making the overall design complex, with slow search and access times.

5. **Identify the six basic characteristics of data warehouses and data marts.**

The basic characteristics of data warehouses and data marts include:

- Data are collected from multiple systems and are integrated around subjects. For example, customer data may be extracted from internal (and external) systems and integrated around a customer identifier to create a comprehensive view of the customer.
- Data warehouses and data marts maintain historical data (i.e., they include time as a variable). A data warehouse or mart may store years of data. Historical data are needed to detect trends, deviations, and long-term relationships.
- Data warehouses and data marts are nonvolatile—no one can change or update the data. Nonvolatility means that the warehouse or mart reflects history, which is critical for trend analysis.
- Typically the data warehouse or data mart uses a multidimensional data structure.
- Data are organized by subject (for example, by customer, vendor, product, price level, and region). As a result, the analyses performed by users are intuitive because the dimensions are labelled in business terms.
- Data warehouses and data marts use on-line analytical processing (OLAP), which involves the analysis of accumulated data by end users. OLAP allows users to "drive" their own data analyses and to examine data in unique ways to improve job performance.

6. **Demonstrate the use of a multidimensional model to store and analyze data.**

See Figures 3.10a, b, and c; 3.11a, b, and c; and 3.12a, b, and c.

7. **List two main advantages of using knowledge management, and describe the steps in the knowledge management system cycle.**

Organizations can use knowledge management to develop best practices, the most effective and efficient ways of doing things, and to make these practices readily available to a wide range of employees. Other benefits of knowledge management include improved customer service, more efficient product development, and improved employee morale and retention.

A functioning KMS follows a cycle that consists of six steps: create knowledge, capture knowledge, refine knowledge, store knowledge, manage knowledge, and disseminate knowledge.

[Chapter Glossary]

attribute Each characteristic or quality describing a particular entity.

best practices The most effective and efficient ways to do things.

bit A binary digit; that is, a 0 or a 1.

byte A group of eight bits that represents a single character.

clickstream data Data collected about user behaviour and browsing patterns by monitoring users' activities when they visit a website.

database A group of logically related files that stores data and the associations among them.

database management system (DBMS) The software program (or group of programs) that provides access to a database.

data dictionary A collection of definitions of data elements, data characteristics that use the data elements, and the individuals, business functions, applications, and reports that use the data elements.

data governance An approach to managing information across an entire organization.

data mart A low-cost, scaled-down version of a data warehouse designed for the end-user needs in a small organization, or in a strategic business unit or department in a large organization.

data model The manner in which data in a database management system are conceptually structured.

data warehouse A repository of historical data that are organized by subject to support decision makers in the organization.

entity A person, place, thing, or event about which information is maintained in a record.

entity classes A grouping of entities of a given type.

entity-relationship (ER) diagram Document that shows data entities and attributes and relationships among them.

entity-relationship (ER) modelling The process of designing a database by organizing data entities to be used and identifying the relationships among them.

explicit knowledge The more objective, rational, and technical types of knowledge.

field A grouping of logically related characters into a word, a small group of words, or a complete number.

file A grouping of logically related records.

identifier An attribute that identifies an entity instance.

instance A particular entity within an entity class.

intellectual capital (intellectual assets) Collective knowledge that belongs to an organization

knowledge management (KM) A process that helps organizations identify, select, organize, disseminate, transfer, and apply information and expertise that are part of the organization's memory and that typically reside within the organization in an unstructured manner.

knowledge management systems (KMSs) Information technologies used to systematize, enhance, and expedite intra- and interfirm knowledge management.

master data A set of core data, such as customer, product, employee, vendor, geographic location, and so on that span the enterprise information systems.

master data management A process that provides companies with the ability to store, maintain, exchange, and synchronize a consistent, accurate, and timely "single version of the truth" for a company's core master data.

metadata Data about data.

multidimensional structure The manner in which data are structured in a data warehouse so that they can be analyzed by different views or perspectives, which are called *dimensions.*

normalization A method for analyzing and reducing a relational database to its most streamlined form for minimum redundancy, maximum data integrity, and best processing performance.

primary key The identifier field or attribute that uniquely identities a record.

query by example (QBE) Database language that enables the user to fill out a grid (form) to construct a sample or description of the data wanted.

record A grouping of logically related fields.

relational database model Data model based on the simple concept of tables in order to capitalize on characteristics of rows and columns of data.

secondary key An identifier field or attribute that has some identifying information, but typically does not identify the file with complete accuracy.

structured query language (SQL) Popular relational database language that enables users to perform complicated searches with relatively simple instructions.

table A grouping of logically related records.

tacit knowledge The cumulative store of subjective or experiential learning; it is highly personal and hard to formalize.

[Discussion Questions]

1. Explain the difficulties involved in managing data.
2. What are the problems associated with poor-quality data?
3. What is master data management? What does it have to do with high-quality data?
4. Explain why master data management is so important in companies that have multiple data sources.
5. Describe the advantages of relational databases.
6. Discuss the benefits of data warehousing to end users.
7. What is the relationship between a company's databases and its data warehouse?
8. Distinguish between data warehouses and data marts.
9. Explain why it is important to capture and manage knowledge.
10. Compare and contrast tacit knowledge and explicit knowledge.

[Problem-Solving Activities]

1. Access various employment websites (for example, *www.workopolis.com*, *www.monster.ca*), and find several job descriptions for a database administrator. Are the descriptions similar? What are the required skills in these positions?
2. Access the websites of several real estate companies. Find the sites that (1) take you through a step-by-step process for buying a home, (2) provide virtual reality tours of homes in your price range and location, (3) provide mortgage and interest rate calculators, and (4) offer financing for your home. Think about the design of the database used to build this website. Identify six different entities in the database.
3. It is possible to find many websites that provide demographic information. Access several of these sites to see what they offer. Do the sites differ in the types of demographic information they offer? If so, how? Provide an example of the data they need to collect to provide the demographic information. Would demographic information be useful to you if you wanted to start a new business? If so, how and why?
4. The Internet contains many websites that provide information on financial aid resources for students. Access

several of these sites. If you were to provide financial advise to one of your fellow students, what type of data would you need to ask for? Provide a detailed example.

5. Draw an entity-relationship diagram for a small retail store. You wish to keep track of the product name, description, unit price, and the number of items of that product sold to each customer. You also wish to record customer name, mailing address, and billing address. You must track each transaction (sale) in terms of the date, product purchased, unit price, number of units, tax, and total amount of the sale.
6. Draw the entity-relationship diagram for this patient appointment system. The business rules of this system are the following:

   A dentist can be scheduled for many appointments, but may not have any appointments scheduled at all. Each appointment is scheduled with exactly one dentist. A patient can schedule one or more appointments. One appointment is scheduled with exactly one patient. An appointment must generate exactly one bill, and a bill is generated by only one appointment. One payment is applied to exactly one bill, and one bill can be paid off over time by several payments. A bill can be outstanding, meaning that it has not been paid at all. One patient can make many payments, but a single payment is made by only one patient. Some patients are insured by an insurance company. If they are insured, they can carry insurance with only one insurance company. An insurance company can have many patients carry their policies. For patients who carry insurance, the insurance company will make payments, with each single insurance payment made by exactly one insurance company.
7. Access the websites of IBM (*www.ibm.com*), Teradata (*www.teradata.com*), Sybase (*www.sybase.com*), and Oracle (*www.oracle.com*), and trace the capabilities of their latest data management products, including data warehousing.
8. Enter the website of Gartner, Inc. (*www.gartner.com*). Examine its research studies pertaining to data management. Prepare a report on the state of the art.
9. Calculate your personal digital footprint at *www.emc.com/digital_universe*.
10. Access *http://academicprograms.teradata.com/tun/* and sign in under the student registration option. Choose one of the topics related to databases and data warehouses that are available on the website and prepare a short presentation for your class.

[Spreadsheet Activity]

Objective: Normalization is taught in this chapter. Often, normalization begins when organizations are ready to transition from a large spreadsheet to a multidimensional database. This exercise will have you work your way through this transition.

Chapter Connection: *Primary key*, *secondary key*, and *attributes*: These terms are a bit abstract until you have to make these determinations yourself. The process of normalization is best when it is practised. Spreadsheets provide the perfect opportunity.

Activity: When schools first began keeping digital records of students, they used a spreadsheet to manage the data. It did not take long before it was obvious that the spreadsheet alone was not sufficient to manage this information. The problem was that the spreadsheet recorded each student as a single event. Every time someone accessed the page to update a grade, contact information, receipt of payment, or class enrollment, that person had to access the main page to make changes. This meant that everyone had access to everything. The registrar could see financial information and the bursar could see academic information.

A database, no doubt, is more suited for this type of application and the normalization process will prepare the spreadsheet for conversion. Visit *www.wiley.com/go/rainer/spreadsheet* and download the spreadsheet for this exercise (MIS—Chapter 3.xlsx). Carefully choose a primary key according to the definitions provided in this chapter. Look for data that will uniquely identify each student. Perhaps this will be a student number or a combination of the student's last and first name. Whatever you decide, normalize the data and allow the primary key to tie the information together from one sheet to another. Your normalized spreadsheet will have multiple sheets rather than one single sheet. Perhaps you will have student information, financial information, academic enrollment, major, grades, etc. Take the single sheet and move the data into multiple sheets. Be sure to copy your primary keys onto each page so that the data can be reconciled.

Deliverable: The final product will be a normalized spreadsheet that is much easier to understand and update and that is ready to be converted to a database.

Discussion Questions

1. Even though this exercise is about normalization for a database, is it also helpful to have data normalized in a spreadsheet? Why or why not?
2. What are the differences between spreadsheets and databases when it comes to data manipulation?

[Case Assignment]

Your firm, ABM Inc., is an international software developer and hardware manufacturer. The company has locations around the world and employs thousands of people. It markets software in all sectors, by industry (for example, banking and retail) and by software type (for example, operating systems, database management systems, and functional software).

ABM's software can be used with a variety of infrastructures (small and large) and for different types of data communications. This means that organizations can purchase ABM's software for use internally or for external use, and for small internal systems through to larger systems that involve international data communications.

Required

a. Describe three reasons why it may be difficult for ABM Inc. to manage its data.

b. Following is an example of what the sales transaction information at ABM looks like:

Customer number	Invoice number	Invoice date	Invoice amount
Ang852	00095235	August 12, 2013	$1,596.35
Ojk685	00085632	August 31, 2013	$680.66
Zee153	00195732	October 14, 2013	$6,011.00

Describe the following terms and provide an example from the table for each term. Clearly explain why your example is appropriate.

1. Attribute
2. Record
3. Instance
4. Secondary key

c. For each of the following aspects of a relational database management system, explain the term, and provide an example of how ABM Inc. could use it.

1. Query language (e.g., SQL)
2. Data dictionary
3. Normalization

[Team Assignments]

1. Each team will select an on-line database such as Grocery-Gateway (*www.grocerygateway.com*), Amazon.ca (*www.amazon.ca*), or any other on-line retailer. Explore these websites to see what information they provide. List the entities and the attributes that the websites must track in their databases. Diagram the relationship between the entities you have identified.
2. In groups, create a data model for a pet store to include:
   - Customer data
   - Product data
   - Employee data
   - Financial data
   - Vendor data
   - Sales data
   - Inventory data
   - Building data
   - Other data (specify)

   Create attributes (four or more) for each entity. Create relationships between the entities, name the relationships, and create an entity-relationship diagram for the store.

[Case 3.2 Coca-Cola Thrives with Enterprise Data Warehousing Solution]

The Problem

The Coca-Cola Company is one of the most widely known companies in the world, operating in more than 200 countries, with 3,500 different products and over 16 brands valued at more than $1 billion. A big part of the reason for Coca-Cola's success lies in advertising and big data analytics. One example was the 2012 Super Bowl. Watched by more than 111 million people, the football classic is one of the sports world's most sought-after advertising events, and Coca-Cola was part of it. Advertisers can spend millions creating and airing just one Super Bowl commercial, and they want to make sure they're getting their money's worth. In order to assess the reaction to the ad, Coca-Cola collected and analyzed data from multiple sources. For example, it collected data from several survey organizations and new unstructured data from social media to gauge viewers' responses to the commercial. In addition, data from different business partners, including retail customers' transaction scan data, sales and shipment data, merchandising data, and loyalty card data, were also collected and needed to be analyzed to assess the impact of such an important adverting campaign.

The Solution

In order to respond to its ever-growing data management needs, Coca-Cola decided to implement an enterprise-wide data warehouse solution from Teradata. It did this partly for the ability to manage the ever-growing unstructured data sets that come from popular social networking websites and that must be organized so that the information can be quickly stored, recovered, and analyzed.

The Results

The new data management solution can quickly generate a single view of all retail information and convert mountains of data into usable information. This allows The Coca-Cola Company to respond to market changes, such as in consumer preferences or competitor prices, as they happen.

With these added business analytics capabilities of the new data warehouse, retailers of Coca-Cola products have become more efficient and effective in their stores. It's also helped drive sales and improve the experience for shoppers and consumers. In the end, as one company manager stated, the goal is to ensure that Coca-Cola provides "the right products in the right stores at the right time to meet shoppers' daily and seasonal consumption needs."

Questions

1. Discuss the importance of data governance in the supply chain between Coca-Cola and its business partners such as retail stores.
2. Provide three examples of components of a data warehouse environment and relate them to the case of The Coca-Cola Company.
3. How does the term "Big Data" relate to knowledge management?

Sources: Compiled from "How The Coca-Cola Company Is Using Advanced Enterprise Data Warehousing Technology and Analytics to Streamline Complex and High-Volume Data," Teradata customer success story, *www.teradata.com*, accessed March 2013; "Coca-Cola: Continuous Refreshment," Big Data Insight Group case study, October 19, 2012; *www.coca-colacompany.com*, accessed April 2013.

[Interactive Case]

Analyzing Customer Data for Ruby's Club

Go to the Ruby's Club link at the Student Companion website or *WileyPLUS* for information about your current internship assignment. Your assignment will include working with customer data in a spreadsheet and preparing them for use within a database.

Chapter 4

Networks

[LEARNING OBJECTIVES]	[CHAPTER OUTLINE]	[WEB RESOURCES]

[LEARNING OBJECTIVES]

1. Define the term "computer network," and compare and contrast the two major types of networks.
2. Describe the differences among the three types of wireline communications media, and discuss the main advantages and disadvantages of each type.
3. Differentiate between the Internet and the World Wide Web, and identify the most common methods for accessing the Internet.
4. Identify six major categories of network applications, provide an example of each, and explain how that application supports business functions.

[CHAPTER OUTLINE]

[WEB RESOURCES]

Student Companion Site

wiley.com/college/rainer

- Student PowerPoints for note taking
- Interactive Case: Ruby's Club Assignments
- Complete glossary

WileyPlus

All of the above and

- E-book
- Mini-lecture by author for each chapter section
- Practice quizzes
- Flash Cards for vocabulary review
- Additional "What's in IT for Me?" cases
- Video interviews with managers
- Lab Manual for Microsoft Office 2010
- How-to Animations for Microsoft Office 2010

What's In IT For Me?
THIS CHAPTER WILL HELP PREPARE YOU TO ...
ACCT
Collaborate with external auditors
FIN
Integrate internal and industry financial data
MKT
Coordinate activities of sales force
POM
Collaborate with project team
HR
Deliver online training to employees
MIS
Implement and manage firm's networks

[Case 4.1 The Network Neutrality Wars]

The Problem

Analysts are expecting strong results from Netflix (*www.netflix.com*) as the company moves from a DVD-delivery service to an on-demand, on-line entertainment provider. During peak periods, people streaming Netflix movies and television shows accounts for about one third of all Internet traffic, according to Sandvine (*www.sandvine.com*), which makes network-monitoring equipment.

IQoncept/Shutterstock

The CEO of Netflix was asked whether the Internet's infrastructure can withstand the strain of his expanding business, which had more than 36 million subscribers worldwide as of mid-2013. He replied: "If there's anything you'd want to bet on, it's that technology will make bandwidth faster and cheaper."

That bet may not be as safe as it seems and the explosion of streaming video and mobile technologies in recent years is beginning to cause problems. The Internet was built to transmit content such as e-mails and web pages. In contrast, media items such as high-definition movies are magnitudes greater in size. To compound this problem, there are now more than 60 million smart phone users in the United States and Canada, many of whom stream video content to their phones.

In a widely cited estimate, Cisco Systems (*www.cisco.com*) predicted that Internet traffic would triple by 2014, to 64 exabytes (1 exabyte is 1 million terabytes) a month. Moreover, by 2014, more than 90 percent of Internet traffic would consist of video. Market researcher Infonetics (*www.infonetics.com*) contends that Cisco's numbers may be conservative. Infonetics's worst-case scenario is that Internet backbone carriers will cease upgrading their technologies, leaving consumers with slow connections and hindering Internet innovation.

While technology is changing by leaps and bounds, Internet service providers (ISPs) are still constrained by the bottom line. Currently, Internet users can upload 10-minute videos to YouTube or watch a 30-gigabyte high-definition movie for the same monthly broadband fee. Unlike with power and water bills, there is no meter to make high-bandwidth users pay more.

But the free ride that some Internet consumers have been getting likely won't last forever. A study from Juniper Networks (*www.juniper.net*) predicts that Internet revenues for U.S. telecommunications companies will grow by 5 percent per year through 2020. In the same period, though, Internet traffic was expected to jump by 27 percent annually. While ISPs won't have to match investments at quite the same pace to keep up with demand, they will have to increase infrastructure spending by about 20 percent per year. By 2014, it was expected that ISPs' revenues would not match the total investment required.

Industry analysts doubted that ISPs would stop investing in new capacity, but they agreed that the current business model is likely not sustainable. ISPs will probably earn less and less per megabit of capacity as demand skyrockets. The carriers can find ways to increase their bandwidth and speed, but it will be difficult for them to reap any benefits in terms of revenue.

Consider the problem that developed between Level 3 Communications (*www.level3.com*) and Comcast (the United States' second-largest Internet service provider). Level 3, which operates Internet backbone networks, worked with Netflix to help speed delivery of its streaming videos. While the deal benefited Netflix, it took a toll on Level 3, because some of its traffic is rerouted through Comcast's cables, and the Netflix traffic caused Level 3's traffic to surge. Level 3 claimed that Comcast charged its cable customers exorbitant rates to carry the additional traffic. Comcast said it did not have the obligation to absorb the extra traffic without cost. The exchange between the two companies gets to the heart of the problem: Even if the technology is up to the task of shipping huge amounts of data, no one is sure how to pay for it.

A Net Neutrality Solution

One possible solution is net neutrality. *Network neutrality* is the concept that ISPs must allow customers equal access to content and applications, regardless of the source or nature of the content.

Telecommunications and cable companies are not in favour of net neutrality, however. Instead, they want to be able to charge differentiated prices based on the amount of bandwidth consumed by the content being delivered over the Internet. They believe that differentiated pricing is the most equitable method to finance necessary investments in their network infrastructures.

To bolster their argument in favour of differentiated pricing, ISPs point to the huge amount of bandwidth that transmitting pirated content of copyrighted materials over the Internet requires. In fact, Comcast reported that illegal file sharing of copyrighted material was consuming half of its network capacity. Thus, the company slowed down transmission of BitTorrent (*www.bittorrent.com*) files, which frequently are used for piracy and illegal sharing of copyrighted materials. In response, the Federal Communications Commission (FCC) ruled that Comcast had to stop slowing down peer-to-peer traffic. Comcast then filed a lawsuit challenging the FCC's authority to enforce network neutrality.

Further, ISPs contend that mandating net neutrality will hinder U.S. competitiveness by decreasing innovation and discouraging capital expenditures for new network technologies. In this scenario, ISPs will be unable to handle the exploding demand for Internet and wireless data transmission.

In April 2010, a federal appeals court ruled in favour of Comcast, declaring that the FCC did not have the authority to regulate how an ISP manages its network. This ruling favoured differentiated pricing of transmissions over the Internet and was a blow to net neutrality.

Meanwhile, proponents of network neutrality petitioned the U.S. Congress to regulate the industry to prevent network providers from adopting strategies like those of Comcast. They argued that the risk of censorship increases when network providers can selectively block or slow access to certain content, such as access to competing low-cost services like Skype and Vonage. They also asserted that a neutral network encourages everyone to innovate without permission from the phone and cable companies or other authorities, and that the neutral Internet has helped create many new businesses.

The Results

Most analysts expect that the heaviest data consumers eventually will have to pay more, most likely in the form of tiered pricing plans. Americans, however, have never experienced limits on the amount of data they upload and download. Nevertheless, wireless networks have already moved in the direction of these plans. For example, AT&T (a U.S. provider of wireless networks) discontinued its all-you-can-use $30-a-month data plan, forcing mobile consumers to choose between two plans that cap usage at 0.2 gigabytes and 2 gigabytes per month, respectively.

Despite the court ruling of April 2010, on December 21, 2010, the FCC approved network neutrality rules, prohibiting broadband providers from blocking customer access to legal web content. The new rules would bar wireline-based broadband providers—but not mobile broadband providers—from "unreasonable discrimination" against web traffic. In January 2011, telecommunications company Verizon filed a legal appeal challenging the FCC's authority to enforce these new rules.

What We Learned from This Case

The opening case illustrates the critical importance of networks, particularly the Internet, to organizations and individuals. The network neutrality battle is important not only for organizations, but for you as well. For example, which kind of Internet user are you? (See Problem-Solving Activity #1 at the end of this chapter.) If you download and upload many large files—for example, high-definition movies—then getting rid of network neutrality will most likely impact your wallet!

Sources: "Sandvine Global Report: Internet Data Usage Up 120 Percent in North America," Sandvine news release, November 7, 2012; L. Segall, "Verizon Challenges FCC Net Neutrality Rules," *CNN Money*, January 21, 2011; K. Corbin, "Net Neutrality 2011: What Storms May Come," *Internet News*, December 30, 2010; G. Gross, "FCC Approves Compromise Net Neutrality Rules," *Network World*, December 21, 2010; P. Burrows, "Will Video Kill the Internet, Too?" *Bloomberg BusinessWeek*, December 6–12, 2010; J. Nocera, "The Struggle for What We Already Have," *The New York Times*, September 4, 2010; C. Miller, "Web Plan Is Dividing Companies," *The New York Times*, August 11, 2010; A. Schatz and S. Ante, "FCC Web Rules Create Pushback," *The Wall Street Journal*, May 6, 2010; *www.comcast.com*, accessed May 3, 2011; *https://signup.netflix.com/MediaCenter/facts*, accessed May 25, 2013.

There are three fundamental points about network computing you need to know. First, computers do not work in isolation in modern organizations. Rather, they constantly exchange data with one another. Second, this exchange of data—facilitated by telecommunications technologies—provides companies with a number of very significant advantages. Third, this exchange can take place over any distance and over networks of any size.

Without networks, the computer on your desk would be merely another productivity-enhancement tool, just as the typewriter once was. The power of networks, however, turns your computer into an amazingly effective tool for accessing information from thousands of sources, thereby making both you and your organization more productive. Regardless of the type of organization (profit/not-for-profit, large/small, global/local) or industry (manufacturing, financial services, health care), networks in general, and the Internet in particular, have transformed—and will continue to transform—the way we do business.

Networks support new ways of doing business, from marketing, to supply chain management, to customer service, to human resources management. In particular, the Internet and private intranets—networks located within a single organization—have an enormous impact on our lives, both professionally and personally. In fact, for all organizations, having an Internet strategy is no longer just a source of competitive advantage. Rather, it is necessary for survival.

Computer networks are essential to modern organizations, for many reasons. First, networked computer systems enable organizations to be more flexible so they can adapt to rapidly changing business conditions. Second, networks enable companies to share hardware, computer applications, and data across the organization and among different organizations. Third, networks make it possible for geographically dispersed employees and work groups to share documents, ideas, and creative insights. This sharing encourages teamwork, innovation, and more efficient and effective interactions. Finally, networks are a critical link between businesses, their business partners, and their customers.

Clearly, networks are essential tools for modern businesses. But, why do *you* need to be familiar with networks? The simple fact is that if you operate your own business or work in a business, you cannot function without networks. You will need to communicate rapidly with your customers, business partners, suppliers, employees, and colleagues. Until about 1990, you would have used the postal system or telephone system with voice or fax capabilities for business communication. Today, however, the pace of business is much faster—almost real time. To keep up with this incredibly fast pace, you will need to use computers, e-mail, the Internet, cell phones, and mobile devices. Further, all of these technologies will be connected via networks to enable you to communicate, collaborate, and compete on a global scale.

Networking and the Internet are the foundation for commerce in the 21st century. Recall that one important objective of this book is to help you become an informed user of information systems. A knowledge of networking is an essential component of modern business literacy.

You begin this chapter by learning what a computer network is and identifying the various types of networks. You then study network fundamentals and follow by turning your attention to the basics of the Internet and the World Wide Web. The chapter concludes by showing you the many Internet network applications available to individuals and organizations—that is, what networks help you do.

4.1 What Is a Computer Network?

A **computer network** is a system that connects computers and other devices (e.g., printers) via communications media so that data and information can be transmitted among them. Voice and data communication networks are continually becoming faster—that is, their bandwidth is increasing—and cheaper. **Bandwidth** is the transmission capacity of a network; it is stated in bits per second. **Broadband** refers to network transmission capacities ranging from approximately 1 million bits per second (megabits/s) to as much as 175 megabits/s with fibre-to-the-home (discussed later in this chapter). You no doubt are familiar with certain types of broadband connections, such as digital subscriber line (DSL) and cable to your homes and dorms. DSL and cable fall within the range of transmission capacities mentioned above and thus are defined as broadband connections.

There are various types of computer networks, ranging from small to worldwide. They include (from smallest to largest) personal area networks (PANs), local area networks (LANs), metropolitan area networks (MANs), wide area networks (WANs), and the Internet. PANs are short-range networks—typically a few metres—used for communication among devices close to one person. PANs can be wired or wireless. You will learn about wireless PANs in Chapter 6. MANs are relatively large computer networks that cover a metropolitan area. MANs fall between LANs and WANs in size. WANs typically cover large geographic areas and can span the entire planet.

Local Area Networks

Regardless of their size, networks represent a compromise among three objectives: speed, distance, and cost. Organizations generally can have any two of these three. To cover long distances, organizations can have fast communication, if they are willing to pay for it, or cheap communication, if they are willing to accept slower speeds. A third possible combination of the three trade-offs is fast, cheap communication with distance limitations. This is the idea behind local area networks.

A **local area network (LAN)** connects two or more devices in a limited geographical region, usually within the same building, so that every device on the network can communicate with every other device. Most LANs today use Ethernet (discussed later in this chapter). Figure 4.1 illustrates an Ethernet LAN that consists of four computers, a server, and a printer, all of which connect via a shared cable. Every device in the LAN has a *network interface card* (NIC) that allows the device to physically connect to the LAN's communications medium. This medium is typically unshielded twisted-pair wire (UTP).

Although it is not required, many LANs have a **file server** or **network server**. The server typically contains various software and data for the network. It also houses the LAN's network operating system, which manages the server and routes and manages communications on the network.

Wide Area Networks

When businesses have to transmit and receive data beyond the confines of the LAN, they use wide area networks. Interestingly, the term *wide area network* did not even exist until local area networks appeared. Before that time, what we call a wide area network today was called simply a "network."

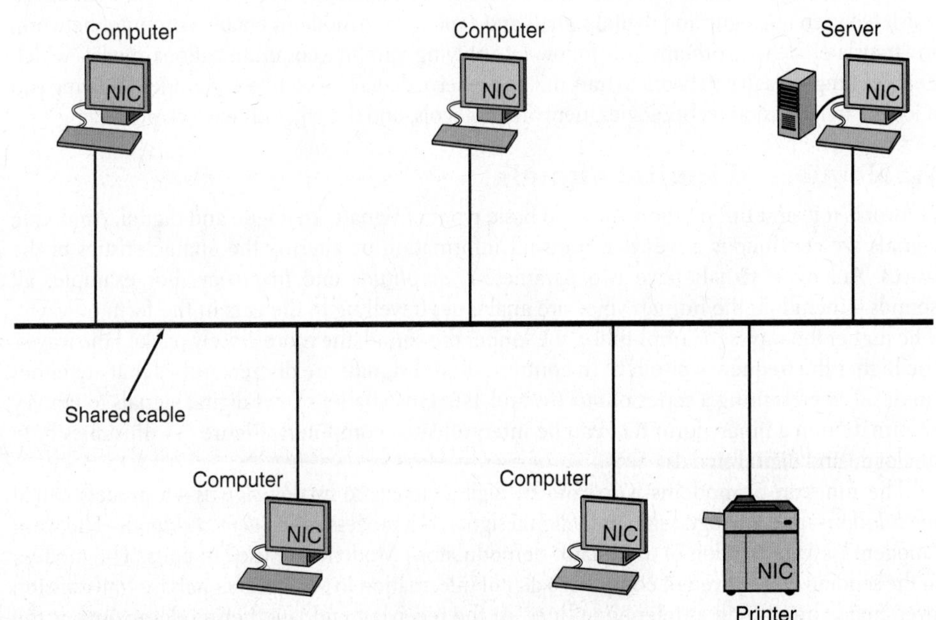

FIGURE 4.1 Ethernet local area network.

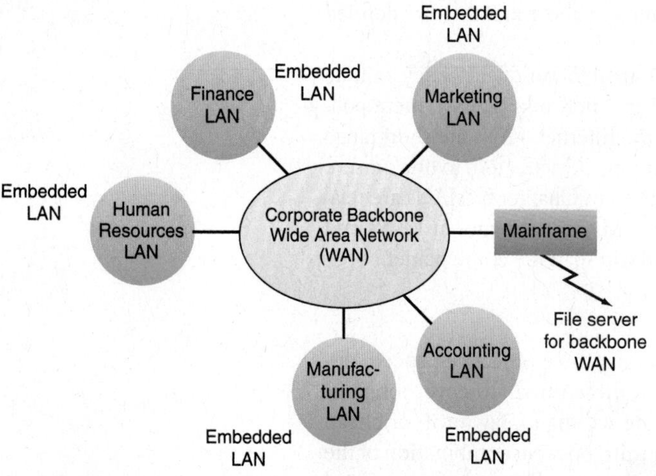

FIGURE 4.2 Enterprise network.

Wide area networks (WANs) are networks that cover large geographic areas. WANs typically connect multiple LANs. WANs generally are provided by common carriers such as telephone companies and the international networks of global communications services providers. WANs have large capacity, and they typically combine multiple channels (for example, fibre-optic cables, microwave, and satellite). The Internet is an example of a WAN.

WANs also contain routers. A **router** is a communications processor that routes messages from a LAN to the Internet, across several connected LANs, or across a wide area network such as the Internet.

Enterprise Networks

Organizations today have multiple LANs and may have multiple WANs, which are interconnected to form an **enterprise network**. Figure 4.2 displays a model of enterprise computing. Note that the enterprise network in the figure has a **backbone network**. Corporate backbone networks are high-speed central networks to which multiple smaller networks (such as LANs and smaller WANs) connect. The LANs are called embedded LANs because they connect to the backbone WAN.

before you go on...

1. Identify three primary business reasons for using networks.
2. What is the difference between LANs and WANs?
3. Describe an enterprise network.

4.2 Network Fundamentals

In this section, you will learn the basics of how networks actually operate. You will then distinguish between analogue and digital signals and explain how modems enable computer networks to "translate" between them. You follow by studying wireline communications media, which enable computers in a network to transmit and receive data. The section concludes by giving you a look at transmission technologies, network protocols, and the types of network processing.

Analogue and Digital Signals

Networks transmit information with two basic types of signals, analogue and digital. **Analogue signals** are continuous waves that transmit information by altering the characteristics of the waves. Analogue signals have two parameters, *amplitude* and *frequency*. For example, all sounds—including the human voice are analogue, travelling to the ears in the form of waves. The higher the waves (or amplitude), the louder the sound; the more closely packed the waves, the higher the frequency or pitch. In contrast, **digital signals** are discrete pulses that are either on or off, representing a series of *bits* (0s and 1s). This quality allows digital signals to convey information in a binary form that can be interpreted by computers. Figure 4.3 illustrates both analogue and digital signals.

The function of **modems** is to convert digital signals to analog signals—a process called *modulation*—and analogue signals to digital signals—a process called *demodulation*. (The word "modem" is a contraction of **modulator-demodulator**.) Modems are used in pairs. The modem at the sending end converts a computer's digital information to analogue signals for transmission over analog lines, such as telephone lines. At the receiving end, another modem converts the

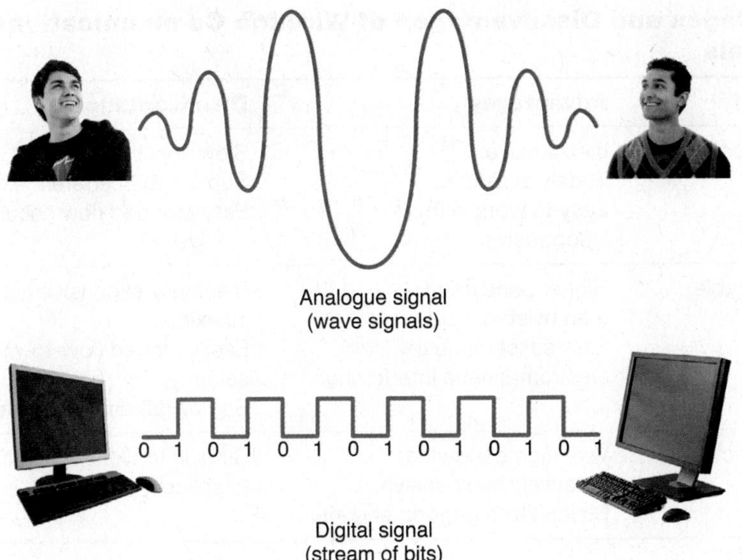

FIGURE 4.3 Analogue and digital signals. (*Sources:* Fancy/Image Source; Media Bakery; © Zoonar/Dmitry Rukhle/Age Fotostock America, Inc.)

analogue signal back to digital signals for the receiving computer. There are three types of modems: dial-up modems, cable modems, and DSL modems.

Most public telephone systems were originally designed as an analogue network to carry voice signals or sounds in an analogue wave format. In order for this type of circuit to carry digital information, that information must be converted into an analog wave pattern by a *dial-up modem*. Dial-up modems have transmission speeds of up to 56 Kbps (thousand bits per second).

Cable modems are modems that operate over coaxial cable; for example, those used for cable TV. They offer broadband access to the Internet or corporate intranets. Cable modem speeds vary widely. Most providers offer bandwidth between 1 and 6 Mbps (million bits per second) for downloads (from the Internet to your computer) and between 128 and 768 Kbps for uploads. Cable modem services share bandwidth among subscribers in a locality. That is, the same cable line connects to many households. Therefore, when large numbers of your neighbours access the Internet at the same time, cable speeds can decrease significantly during those times.

DSL (digital subscriber line, discussed later in this chapter) *modems* operate on the same lines as voice telephones and dial-up modems. DSL modems always maintain a connection, so an Internet connection is immediately available.

Communications Media and Channels

Communicating data from one location to another requires some form of pathway or medium. These pathways, called **communications channels**, are composed of two types of media: cable (twisted-pair wire, cable, and fibre-optic cable) and broadcast (microwave, satellite, radio, and infrared).

Cable or **wireline media** use physical wires or cables to transmit data and information. Twisted-pair wire and coaxial cables are made of copper, and fibre-optic cable is made of glass fibre. The alternative is communication over **broadcast** or **wireless media**. The key to mobile communications in today's rapidly moving society is data transmissions over electromagnetic media—the "airwaves." In this section you will study the three wireline channels. Table 4.1 summarizes the advantages and disadvantages of each of these channels. You will become familiar with wireless media in Chapter 6.

Twisted-Pair Wire.

Twisted-pair wire is the prevalent form of communications wiring; it is used for almost all business telephone wiring. Twisted-pair wire consists of strands of copper wire twisted in pairs (see Figure 4.4). It is relatively inexpensive to purchase, widely available, and easy to work with. However, it also has some significant disadvantages. Specifically, it is relatively slow for transmitting data, it is subject to interference from other electrical sources,

Table 4.1 Advantages and Disadvantages of Wireline Communications Channels

Channel	Advantages	Disadvantages
Twisted-pair wire	Inexpensive. Widely available. Easy to work with. Unobtrusive.	Slow (low bandwidth). Subject to interference. Easily tapped (low security).
Coaxial cable	Higher bandwidth than twisted-pair. Less susceptible to electromagnetic interference.	Relatively expensive and inflexible. Easily tapped (low-to-medium security). Somewhat difficult to work with.
Fiber-optic cable	Very high bandwidth. Relatively inexpensive. Difficult to tap (good security).	Difficult to work with (difficult to splice).

FIGURE 4.4 Twisted-pair wire. (*Source:* deepspacedave/Shutterstock)

and it can be easily tapped by unintended receivers for gaining unauthorized access to data.

Coaxial Cable. **Coaxial cable** (Figure 4.5) consists of insulated copper wire. It is much less susceptible to electrical interference than is twisted-pair wire, and it can carry much more data. For these reasons, it is commonly used to carry high-speed data traffic as well as television signals (thus the term "cable TV"). However, coaxial cable is more expensive and more difficult to work with than twisted-pair wire. It is also somewhat inflexible.

Fibre-Optic Cables. **Fibre-optic cables** (Figure 4.6) consist of thousands of very thin filaments of glass fibres that transmit information via light pulses generated by lasers. The fibre-optic cable is surrounded by cladding, a coating that prevents the light from leaking out of the fibre.

Fibre-optic cables are significantly smaller and lighter than traditional cable media. They also can transmit far more data, and they provide greater security from interference and tapping. Optical fibre has been shown to reach data transmission rates of more than 50 trillion bits (terabits) per second in laboratory experiments. Fibre-optic cable is typically used as the backbone for a network, whereas twisted-pair wire and coaxial cable connect the backbone to

FIGURE 4.5 Two views of coaxial cable. (*Sources:* GIPhoto Stock/Photo Researchers; © airborne77-Fotolia.com)

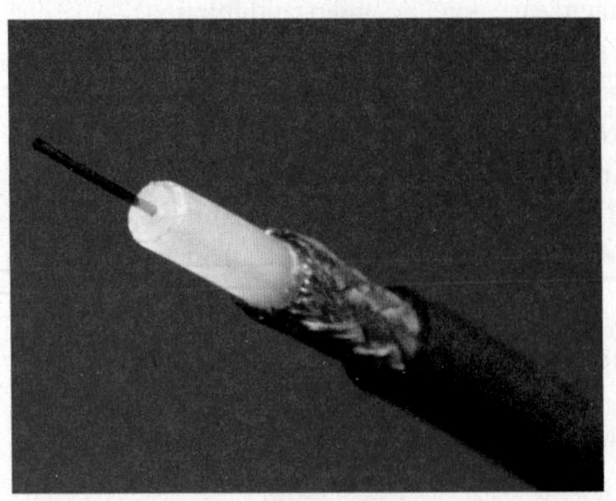

Cross-section view

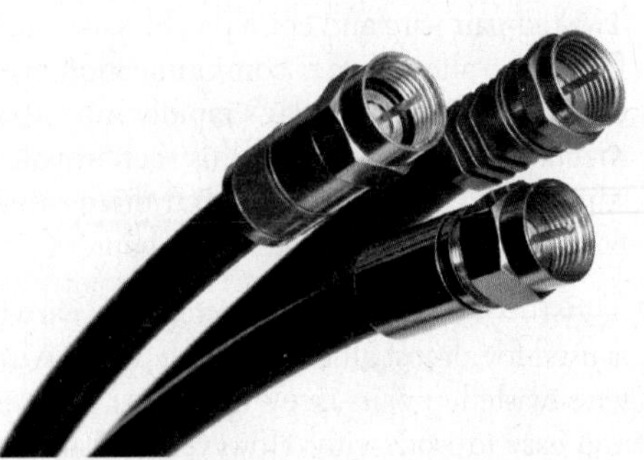

How coaxial cable looks to us

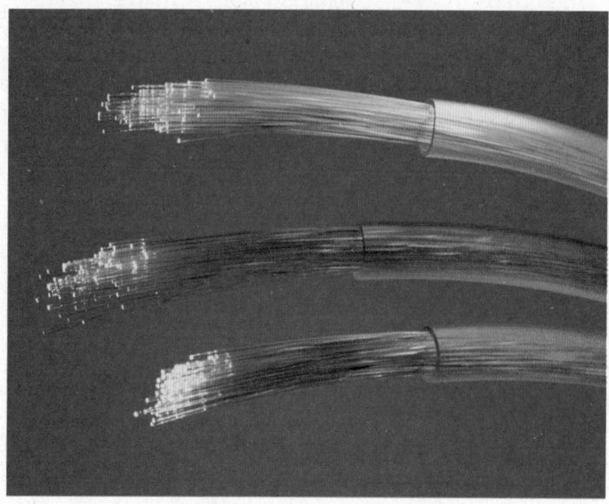
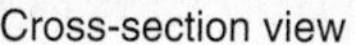
Cross-section view

How fibre-optic cable looks to us

FIGURE 4.6 Two views of fibre-optic cable. (*Sources:* Phillip Hayson/Photo Researchers; Chris Knapton/Photo Researchers)

individual devices on the network. IT's About Small Business 4.1 recounts a case in which a fibre-optics network helped a small business grow rapidly.

Transmission Technologies

A number of telecommunications technologies enable users to transmit high-volume data quickly and accurately over any type of network. You explore these technologies in this section.

about [small] business

4.1 A WAN for Mobile Payments

A Canadian company hopes it has solved the problem of drivers having to dig in their pockets and purses for change to feed parking meters. Vancouver-based PayByPhone is a small company that provides systems for parking and urban mobility payments in North America. PayByPhone allows drivers to pay for and extend their parking time using a mobile app, going on-line, or calling a local phone number. Operating in over 180 major international cities, it has more than 3 million subscribers. Three cities in Canada already use PayByPhone: Vancouver, Ottawa, and Winnipeg, plus a number of private parking operators in Calgary, Edmonton, Saskatoon, Regina, London (Ont.), Quebec City, and several smaller locales. The company had over 17 million transactions around the world in 2012.

While its smart phone app continues to gain popularity, the majority of its parking payment business still comes from mobile calling. This means PayByPhone's technology must be robust enough to handle the full capabilities of its mobile services. In addition, considering the large amount of traffic and that a large proportion of the calls are long distance, PayByPhone needs to keep operating costs low in order to ensure success.

To meet its growing needs, PayByPhone partnered with Allstream, a Canadian giant in IP communications with over 30,000 kilometres of fibre-optic cable across the country. PayByPhone was looking not only for a bulk long-distance rate, but for a solution that would reduce costs, expand capabilities, and ensure its services could be ramped up for future growth. PayByPhone serves over 100,000 North American calls per week—a mix of toll-free U.S. and local Canadian calls—over the Allstream network.

Questions

1. Describe the characteristics of the PayByPhone telecommunications network (such as geographical reach and media channel used).
2. What are the reasons that led PayByPhone to switch to an IP-based network?
3. Provide two examples of additional business applications that PayByPhone could run on its network.
4. Discuss the pros and cons of PayByPhone setting up its own WAN compared with using a telecommunications service provider such as Allstream.

Sources: "Vancouver Given Authority to Directly Collect Fees from Pay-by-Phone," *Vancouver Sun*, February 14, 2013; "PayByPhone Consolidates Service, Reduces Costs and Plans for Growth with SIP Trunking," 2012 case study, Allstream website, *www.allstream.com*, accessed May 11, 2013; "PayByPhone Adds NFC to Mobile Payments for Ottawa's Parking Spaces," PayByPhone website *www.paybyphone.com/ottawa-nfc/*, accessed May 11, 2013.

Digital Subscriber Line. **Digital subscriber lines (DSL)** provide high-speed transmission of digital data from homes and businesses over existing telephone lines. Because the existing lines are analog and the transmission is digital, DSL systems must include modems. DSLs offer bandwidth from 128 Kbps to 3 Mbps. DSL service is typically available only within 5.5 kilometres of the provider's central office.

Asynchronous Transfer Mode. **Asynchronous transfer mode (ATM)** networks allow users to access almost unlimited bandwidth on demand. In addition, ATM provides support for data, video, and voice transmissions on a single communications line. Current ATM systems can transmit up to 2.5 gigabits (billions of bits) per second. On the downside, ATM requires fibre-optic cable and is therefore about 20 percent more expensive than DSL.

Synchronous Optical Network. **Synchronous optical network (SONET)** is an interface standard designed to carry large volumes of traffic over relatively long distances using fibre-optic lines. SONET defines optical line rates, known as optical carrier (OC) signals. The base rate is 51.84 Mbps (OC-1), and higher rates are direct multiples of the base rate. For example, OC-3 runs at 155.52 Mbps, or three times the rate of OC-1.

T-Carrier System. The **T-carrier system** is a digital transmission system that defines circuits that operate at different rates, all of which are multiples of the basic 64 Kbps used to transport a single voice call. These circuits include T1 (1.544 Mbps, equivalent to 24 channels); T2 (6.312 Mbps, equivalent to 96 channels); T3 (44.736 Mbps, equivalent to 672 channels); and T4 (274.176 Mbps, equivalent to 4,032 channels).

Network Protocols

Computing devices that are connected to the network must access and share the network to transmit and receive data. These devices are often referred to as "nodes" of the network. They work together by adhering to a common set of rules that enable them to communicate with one another. This set of rules and procedures that govern transmission across a network is a **protocol**. In this section you will learn about two major protocols: Ethernet and TCP/IP.

Ethernet. A common LAN protocol is **Ethernet**. Most large corporations use 10-gigabit Ethernet, where the network provides data transmission speeds of 10 gigabits (10 billion bits) per second. However, 100-gigabit Ethernet is becoming the standard.

Transmission Control Protocol/Internet Protocol. The **transmission control protocol/Internet protocol (TCP/IP)** is the protocol of the Internet. TCP/IP uses a suite of protocols, the main ones being the transmission control protocol (TCP) and the Internet protocol (IP). The TCP performs three basic functions: (1) It manages the movement of packets (discussed below) between computers by establishing a connection between the computers; (2) it sequences the transfer of packets; and (3) it acknowledges the packets that have been transmitted. The **Internet protocol (IP)** is responsible for disassembling, delivering, and reassembling the data during transmission, a process you will see next.

Before data are transmitted over the Internet, they are broken down into small, fixed bundles of data called *packets*. The transmission technology that breaks up blocks of data into packets is called **packet switching**. Each packet carries the information that will help it reach its destination—the sender's IP address, the intended receiver's IP address, the number of packets in this message, and the number of this particular packet within the message. Each packet travels independently across the network and can be routed through different paths in the network. When the packets reach their destination, they are reassembled into the original message.

It is important to note that packet-switching networks are reliable and fault tolerant. For example, if a path in the network is very busy or is broken, packets can be dynamically ("on the fly") rerouted around that path. Also, if one or more packets do not reach the receiving computer, only those packets need to be resent.

Why do organizations use packet switching? The main reason is to achieve reliable end-to-end message transmission over sometimes unreliable networks that may have transient (short-acting) or persistent (long-acting) faults.

Website: Sending a message via HTTP (Hypertext transfer protocol)	Application	Website: Message received
Break message into packets and determine order	Transport	Packets reordered and replaced (if lost)
Assign sending and receiving IP addresses and apply to each packet	Internet	Packets routed through internal network to desired IP address
Determine path across network/ Internet to intended destination	Network Interface	Receipt of packets

FIGURE 4.7 The four layers of the TCP/IP reference model. (*Source:* Dabroost/Shutterstock.)

The packets use the TCP/IP protocol to carry their data. TCP/IP functions in four layers (see Figure 4.7). The *application layer* enables client application programs to access the other layers, and it defines the protocols that applications use to exchange data. One of these application protocols is the **hypertext transfer protocol (HTTP)**, which defines how messages are formulated and how they are interpreted by their receivers. The *transport layer* provides the application layer with communication and packet services. This layer includes TCP and other protocols. The *Internet layer* is responsible for addressing, routing, and packaging data packets. The Internet protocol (IP) is one of the protocols in this layer. Finally, the *network interface layer* places packets on, and receives them from the network medium, which can be any networking technology.

Two computers using TCP/IP can communicate even if they use different hardware and software. Data sent from one computer to another proceed downward through all four layers, beginning with the sending computer's application layer and going through its network interface layer. After the data reach the receiving computer, they travel up the layers.

TCP/IP enables users to send data across sometimes unreliable networks with the assurance that the data will arrive in uncorrupted form. TCP/IP is very popular with business organizations due to its reliability and the ease with which it can support intranets and related functions.

Let's look at an example of packet-switching across the Internet. Figure 4.8 illustrates a message being sent from Toronto to Calgary over a packet-switching network. Note that the different coloured packets travel by different routes to reach their destination in Calgary, where they are reassembled into the complete message.

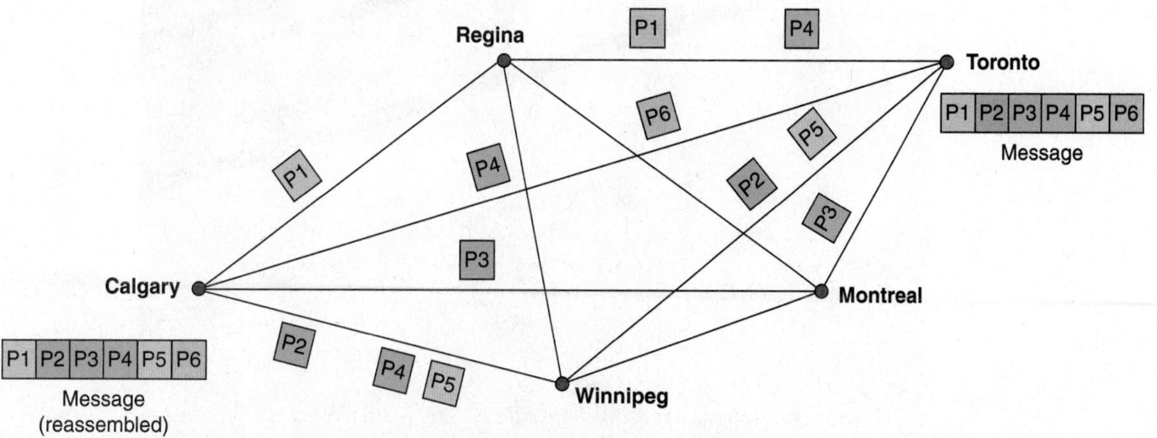

FIGURE 4.8 Packet switching.

Types of Network Processing

Organizations typically use multiple computer systems across the firm. **Distributed processing** divides processing work among two or more computers. This process enables computers in different locations to communicate with one another via telecommunications links. A common type of distributed processing is client/server processing. A special type of client/server processing is peer-to-peer processing.

Client/Server Computing.

Client/server computing links two or more computers in an arrangement in which some machines, called **servers**, provide computing services for user PCs, called **clients**. Usually, an organization performs the bulk of its processing or application/data storage on suitably powerful servers that can be accessed by less powerful client machines. The client requests applications, data, or processing from the server, which acts on these requests by "serving" the desired commodity.

Client/server computing leads to the ideas of "fat" clients and "thin" clients. As discussed in Technology Guide 1, *fat clients* have large storage and processing power and therefore can run local programs, such as a Microsoft Office application, if the network is down. In contrast, *thin clients* may have no local storage and limited processing power. Thus, they must depend on the network to run applications. For this reason they are of little value when the network is not functioning.

Peer-to-Peer Processing.

Peer-to-peer (P2P) processing is a type of client/server distributed processing where each computer acts as *both* a client and a server. Each computer can access (as assigned for security or integrity purposes) all files on all other computers.

There are three basic types of peer-to-peer processing (see Figure 4.9). The first accesses unused CPU power among networked computers. A well-known application of this type is SETI@home (*http://setiathome.ssl.berkeley.edu*). These applications are from open-source projects and can be downloaded at no cost.

The second form of peer-to-peer is real-time, person-to-person collaboration, such as Microsoft SharePoint (*http://office.microsoft.com/en-us/sharepoint/*). This product provides P2P collaborative applications that use buddy lists to establish a connection and allow real-time collaboration within the application.

The third peer-to-peer category is advanced search and file sharing. This category is characterized by natural-language searches of millions of peer systems. It enables users to discover other users, not just data and web pages. One example of this category is BitTorrent.

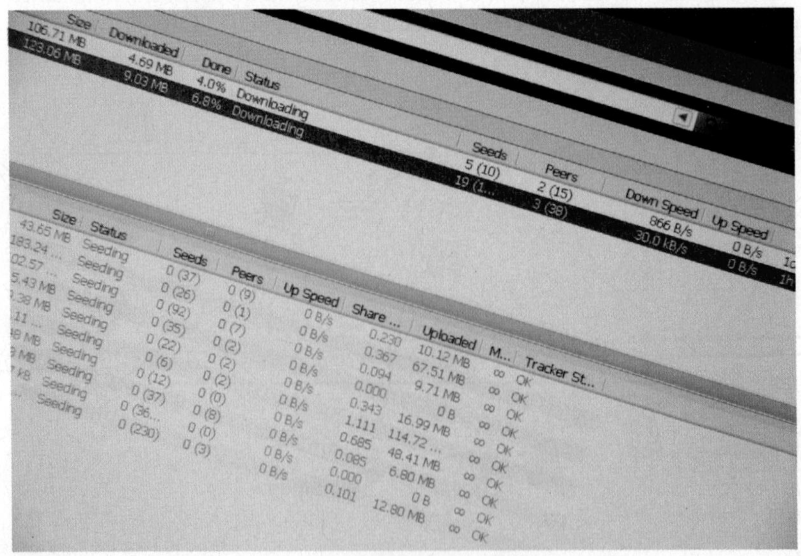

FIGURE 4.9 File-sharing website. (*Source:* © digitallife/Alamy Limited.)

BitTorrent (*www.bittorrent.com*) is an open-source, free, peer-to-peer file-sharing application that is able to simplify the problem of sharing large files by dividing them into tiny pieces, or "torrents." BitTorrent addresses two of the biggest problems of file sharing: (1) downloading bogs down when many people access a file at once, and (2) some people leech, meaning they download content but refuse to share. BitTorrent eliminates the bottleneck by enabling all users to share little pieces of a file at the same time—a process called *swarming*. The program prevents leeching because users must upload a file while they download it. This means that the more popular the content, the more efficiently it zips over a network.

before you go on...

1. Compare and contrast the three wireline communications channels.
2. Describe the various technologies that enable users to send high-volume data over any network.
3. Describe the Ethernet and TCP/IP protocols.
4. Differentiate between client/server computing and peer-to-peer processing.

4.3 The Internet and the World Wide Web

The Internet ("the Net") is a global WAN that connects approximately 1 million organizational computer networks in more than 200 countries on all continents, including Antarctica, and plays a role in the daily routine of almost 2 billion people. Participating computer systems include smart phones, PCs, LANs, databases, and mainframes.

The computers and organizational nodes on the Internet can be of different types and makes. They are connected to one another by data communications lines of different speeds. The primary network connections and telecommunications lines that link the nodes are referred to as the backbone. For the Internet, the backbone is a fibre-optic network that is operated primarily by large telecommunications companies.

As a network of networks, the Internet enables people to access data in other organizations and to communicate, collaborate, and exchange information seamlessly around the world, quickly and inexpensively. Thus, the Internet has become a necessity for modern businesses.

The Internet grew out of an experimental project of the Advanced Research Project Agency (ARPA) of the U.S. Department of Defense. The project began in 1969 as the *ARPAnet*. Its purpose was to test the feasibility of a WAN over which researchers, educators, military personnel, and government agencies could share data, exchange messages, and transfer files.

Today, Internet technologies are being used both within and among organizations. An **intranet** is a network within an organization that uses Internet protocols so that users can take advantage of familiar applications and work habits. Intranets support discovery (easy and inexpensive browsing and search), communication, and collaboration inside an organization.

In contrast, an **extranet** provides access to parts of an organization's intranets to different outside organizations. In addition, it enables business partners to communicate securely over the Internet using virtual private networks (VPNs, explained in Chapter 13). Extranets offer limited accessibility to the intranets of participating companies, as well as necessary interorganizational communications. They are widely used in the areas of business-to-business (B2B) electronic commerce (see Chapter 5) and supply chain management (SCM; see Chapter 9).

No central agency manages the Internet. Instead, the cost of its operation is shared among hundreds of thousands of nodes. Thus, the cost for any one organization is small. Organizations must pay a small fee if they wish to register their names, and they need to have their own hardware and software to operate their internal networks. The organizations are obliged to move any data or information that enters their organizational network, regardless of the source, to its destination, at no charge to the senders. The senders, of course, pay the telephone bills for using either the backbone or regular telephone lines.

Accessing the Internet

There are several ways to access the Internet. From your place of work or your university, you can access the Internet via your organization's LAN. A campus or company backbone connects all of the various LANs and servers in the organization to the Internet. You can also log on to the Internet from your home or on the road, using either wireline or wireless connections.

Connecting via an On-line Service.

You can also access the Internet by opening an account with an Internet service provider. An **Internet service provider (ISP)** is a company that offers Internet connections for a fee. Large ISPs include Bell Canada (*www.bell.ca*), RogersYahoo! (*www.rogers.com*), TekSavvy (*www.teksavvy.com*), and TELUS (*www.telus.com*). In addition, many telephone providers and cable companies sell Internet access, as do computer companies such as Microsoft. To use this service you need a modem and standard communications software. To find additional local ISPs, access *www.canadianisp.ca/index.php*. There, you can search for an ISP that services your province.

ISPs connect to one another through **network access points (NAPs)**. NAPs are exchange points for Internet traffic. They determine how traffic is routed. NAPs are key components of the Internet backbone. Figure 4.10 shows a schematic of the Internet in Canada. The blue and

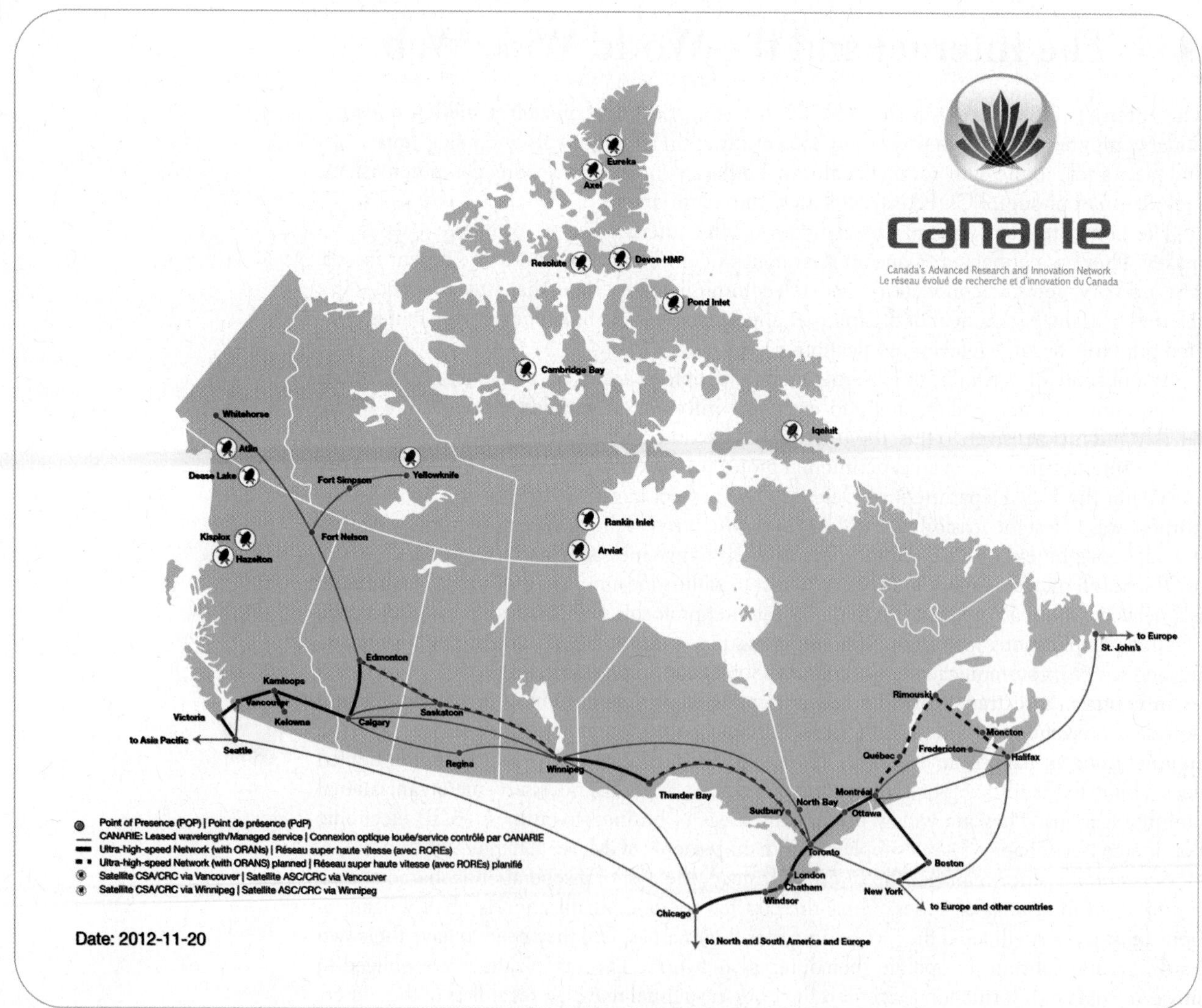

FIGURE 4.10 Internet backbone in Canada. (*Source:* http://www.canarie.ca/templates/news/docs/CANARIEMap.png)

red lines and the dotted blue lines that link the main Canadian cities in the map represent fibre-optic links and constitute the Canadian Internet backbone; the same figure also shows little satellite dishes. These small satellites provide connectivity to the Internet backbone for remote cities Canada where a fibre-optics link is still not available.

Connecting via Other Means. There have been several attempts to make access to the Internet cheaper, faster, and easier. For example, terminals known as Internet kiosks have been located in public places like libraries and airports (and even in convenience stores in some countries) for use by people who do not have their own computers. Accessing the Internet from smart phones and iPads is common, and fibre-to-the-home (FTTH) is growing rapidly. FTTH involves connecting fibre-optic cable directly to individual homes. This system initially was restricted to new residential developments, but it is rapidly spreading. Table 4.2 summarizes the various means that you can use to connect to the Internet.

Addresses on the Internet. Each computer on the Internet has an assigned address, called the **Internet protocol (IP) address**, that distinguishes it from all other computers. The IP address consists of numbers, in four parts, separated by dots. For example, the IP address of one computer might be 135.62.128.91. You can access a website by typing this number, if known, in the address bar of your browser. Because the numbers may be tedious to deal with, an IP address may also be assigned to a host name such as yorku.ca or canarie.ca, which is sometimes easier to remember. Hostnames may be looked up to find IP addresses, and vice-versa.

Currently, there are two IP addressing schemes. The first scheme, IPv4, is the most widely used. IP addresses using IPv4 consist of 32 bits, meaning that there are 232 possibilities for IP addresses, or 4,294,967,295 distinct addresses. Note that the IP address in the preceding paragraph (135.62.128.91) is an IPv4 address. At the time that IPv4 was developed, there were not as many computers that needed addresses as there are today. Therefore, a new IP addressing scheme, IPv6, has been developed.

IP addresses using IPv6 consist of 128 bits, meaning that there are 2,128 possibilities for distinct IP addresses, which is an unimaginably large number. IPv6, which is replacing IPv4, will accommodate the rapidly increasing number of devices that need IP addresses, such as smart phones.

IP addresses must be unique so that computers on the Internet know where to find one another. The Internet Corporation for Assigned Names and Numbers (ICANN) (*www.icann.org*) coordinates these unique addresses throughout the world. Without that coordination we would not have one global Internet.

Because the numeric IP addresses are difficult to remember, most computers have names as well. ICANN accredits certain companies called *registrars* to register these names, which are derived from a system called the **domain name system (DNS)**. **Domain names** consist of multiple

Table 4.2

Internet Connection Methods

Service	Description
Dial-up	Still used in the Canada where broadband is not available.
DSL	Broadband access via telephone companies.
Cable modem	Access over your cable TV coaxial cable. Can have degraded performance if many neighbours are accessing the Internet at once.
Satellite	Access where cable and DSL are not available.
Wireless	Access via Wi-Fi access point or telephone network. Very convenient.
Fibre to the home	Expensive and usually only placed in new housing developments.

parts that are read from right to left, separated by dots. For example, consider the domain name *software.ibm.com*. The rightmost part of an Internet name is its *top-level domain (TLD)*. The letters "com" in *software.ibm.com* indicate that this is a commercial site. Popular TLDs are:

com	commercial sites
edu	educational sites
mil	military government sites
gov	civilian government sites
org	organizations

To finish our domain name example, "ibm" is the name of the company (IBM), and "software" is the name of the particular machine (computer) within the company to which the message is being sent.

In other countries, the country name or designator is the TLD. For example, "ca" stands for Canada, "de" stands for Germany, "it" for Italy, and "ru" for Russia. In essence, every country decides for itself whether to use TLDs. Moreover, countries that use TLDs do not necessarily follow the U.S. system. For example, the United Kingdom uses ".co" where the U.S. uses ".com," and ".ac" (for academic) where the U.S. uses ".edu." In contrast, many other non-U.S. websites use U.S. TLDs, especially ".com."

The Future of the Internet

Consumer demand for content delivered over the Internet is increasing at 60 percent per year. According to technology giant Cisco, by the end of 2016, global IP traffic will reach 1.3 zettabytes per year or 110.3 exabytes per month (1 exabyte is equivalent to 50,000 years of DVD-quality data). Many experts are now concerned that Internet users will experience brownouts (temporary unavailability or slower speeds) due to three factors: (1) the increasing number of people who work on-line, (2) the soaring popularity of websites such as YouTube that require large amounts of bandwidth, and (3) the tremendous demand for high-definition television delivered over the Internet. These brownouts will lead to computers going off-line for several minutes at a time. Researchers assert that if Internet bandwidth is not improved rapidly, then within a few years the Internet will be able to function only at a much reduced speed (see Case 4.1).

Even today, the Internet sometimes is too slow for data-intensive applications such as full-motion video files (movies) or large medical files (X-rays). In addition, the Internet is unreliable and is not secure. As a result, research networks in different countries are working toward developing new technologies to support the growing needs of the Internet. In Canada, **CANARIE Inc.** (*www.canarie.ca*) is a not-for-profit organization supported by the government and the private sector with the goal of doing research and implementing advanced communication networks. CAnet 4 is CANARIE's most advanced network and interconnects provincial research networks, universities, research centres, government research laboratories, and schools. CANARIE develops and deploys advanced network applications essential for national and international collaboration, such as remote medical diagnosis, digital libraries, distance education, on-line simulation, and virtual laboratories. **Internet2** is the equivalent of CANARIE in the United States. Internet2 develops and deploys advanced network applications such as remote medical diagnosis, digital libraries, distance education, on-line simulation, and virtual laboratories. Internet2 is designed to be fast, always on, everywhere, natural, intelligent, easy, and trusted. Internet2 is not a separate physical network from the Internet. For more details, see *www.internet2.edu*.

The World Wide Web

Many people equate the Internet with the World Wide Web. However, they are not the same thing. The Internet functions as a transport mechanism, whereas the World Wide Web is an application that uses those transport functions. Other applications, such as e-mail, also run on the Internet.

The **World Wide Web (the web, WWW,** or **W3)** is a system of universally accepted standards for storing, retrieving, formatting, and displaying information via a client/server architecture. The web handles all types of digital information, including text, hypermedia, graphics, and sound. It uses graphical user interfaces (GUIs), so it is very easy to navigate.

Organizations that wish to offer information through the web must establish a *home page*, which is a text and graphical screen display that usually welcomes the user and provides basic information on the organization that has established the page. In most cases, the home page will lead users to other pages. All of the pages of a particular company or individual are collectively known as a **website**. Most web pages provide a way to contact the organization or the individual. The person in charge of an organization's website is its *webmaster*.

To access a website, the user must specify a **uniform resource locator (URL)**, which points to the address of a specific resource on the web. For instance, the URL for Microsoft is "http://www.microsoft.com". Recall that HTTP stands for hypertext transport protocol. The remaining letters in this URL—www.microsoft.com—indicate the domain name that identifies the web server that stores the website.

IT's [about business]

4.2 Browser Competition Heats Up

You probably surf the web every day, but haven't given much thought to the browser you use to get around. Neither had some software companies, but they're trying to catch up now. Companies are investing increasing amounts of resources in their browsers, which is good for consumers. A couple of developments are behind this trend. The first is Google, whose big plans for its Chrome (*www.google.com/chrome*) browser forced Microsoft to pay more attention to its own browser, Internet Explorer (IE). Microsoft had all but stopped efforts to enhance IE after winning the last browser war, defeating Netscape.

The second factor was a decision by the European Union (EU). Starting in March 2010, the EU required computer manufacturers to offer European customers more freedom to choose their software. Under this plan, part of an antitrust settlement with Microsoft, purchasers were to be presented with a screen at start-up that lists a dozen browsers in random order, all of which are free. Users can download any of these browsers and start roaming the web.

Regardless of which browser users select, however, they should take into consideration issues of security and privacy. Every company brags about its security features, but the term "secure browser" is questionable at best. Further, privacy is not much more dependable. All browsers offer "private" or "incognito" modes, but for the most part such settings only prevent people who might look at your computer from seeing the websites you have browsed. They do not stop those sites from keeping records of your visits.

You should also keep in mind why companies distribute their browsers for free. Chrome, for instance, is a key part of Google's strategy to make computer users comfortable with cloud computing (discussed in Technology Guide 3). The objective is to convince users to move away from using licensed software on their hard drives (e.g., from Microsoft) in favour of free services, such as Google Docs, which reside on servers and storage systems on the Internet. What's the catch? Google makes money from selling advertisements on its free services. In this way, Chrome—available in versions for Windows, Mac, and Linux—makes users dependent on Google's own ad-driven services. But for Google's strategy to work, Chrome must be a good browser. Many feel that it is, because Chrome is fast and takes up little space on users' hard drives.

Mac users should have no problem choosing a browser. Apple's own browser, Safari (*www.apple.com/safari*), is excellent, and it comes installed on every Mac (and is also available in a Windows version). Microsoft adopted the same policy with IE, but the company was charged with antitrust violations. Presumably, Apple gets away with loading its computers with its own browser because its market share is so much smaller than that of Microsoft.

Another excellent browser is Mozilla Firefox (*www.mozilla.com/*), a descendant of Netscape. Maintained by an open-source community, Firefox is the most commonly used browser behind the market-leading Microsoft IE. It is available for Windows, Mac, and Linux systems. Firefox benefits from a well-developed application base that includes thousands of add-ons for everything from speeding up YouTube downloads to Stumble-Upon, which helps users discover and share websites that match their interests.

Opera (*www.opera.com*), created by the Norwegian company Opera Software, is also a good choice for a browser. Like Firefox, it is available in Windows, Mac, and Linux versions.

Finally, there is the market leader, Microsoft Internet Explorer. In early 2013, Microsoft released the full version of IE 10 (*http://windows.microsoft.com/en-us/internet-explorer/download-ie*), which contains many enhancements, including the promise to run 20 percent faster than the previous version.

Questions

1. Given that all browsers are free, what features do the major browser companies focus on to gain competitive advantage?
2. Which browser do you use? Why?
3. Should a company determine which browser employees should use? Why or why not?

Sources: Compiled from "Internet Browser Software Review," *TopTenReviews*, May 2011; R. Jaroslovsky, "Browser Wars: The Sequel," *Bloomberg BusinessWeek*, March 8, 2010; F. Lardinois, "Microsoft Launches IE10 for Windows 7, Starts Auto-Upgrading IE9 Users and Launches New Ad Campaign," *Techcrunch.com*, February 26, 2013.

Users access the web primarily through software applications called **browsers**. Browsers provide a graphical front end that enables users to point and click their way across the web, a process called *surfing*. Web browsers became a means of universal access because they deliver the same interface on any operating system under which they run. As IT's About Business 4.2 shows, companies are pouring resources into their browsers.

before you go on...

1. Describe the various ways that you can connect to the Internet.
2. Identify the parts of an Internet address.
3. What are the functions of browsers?
4. Describe the difference between the Internet and the World Wide Web.

4.4 Internet Network Applications

Now that you have a working knowledge of what networks are and how you can access them, the key question is: How do businesses use networks to improve their operations? This section addresses that question. Stated in general terms, networks support businesses and other organizations in all types of functions.

This section will explore numerous Internet network applications, including discovery, communication, collaboration, e-learning and distance learning, virtual universities, and telecommuting. These applications, however, are merely a sampling of the many network applications currently available to users. Even if these applications formed an exhaustive list today, they would not necessarily do so tomorrow, when something new may be developed. Further, placing network applications in categories is difficult, because there will always be borderline cases. For example, the difference between chat rooms (in the communications category) and teleconference (in the collaboration category) is only one of degree.

Discovery

The Internet enables users to access information located in databases all over the world. By browsing and searching data sources on the web, users can apply the Internet's discovery capability to areas ranging from education, to government services, to entertainment, to commerce. Although having access to all this information is a great benefit, it is critically important to realize that there is no quality assurance for information on the web. The web is truly democratic in that *anyone* can post information to it.

In addition, the web's major strength—the vast stores of information it contains—also presents a major challenge. The amount of information on the web can be overwhelming, and it doubles approximately each year. As a result, navigating through the web and gaining access to necessary information are becoming more and more difficult. To accomplish these tasks, people increasingly are using search engines, directories, and portals.

Search Engines and Metasearch Engines. A **search engine** is a computer program that searches for specific information by key words and then reports the results. A search engine maintains an index of billions of web pages. It uses that index to find pages that match a set of user-specified keywords. Such indexes are created and updated by *webcrawlers*, which are computer programs that browse the web and create a copy of all visited pages. Search engines then index these pages to provide fast searches.

At the publication of this textbook, three search engines accounted for almost all searches in North America: Google (*www.google.ca*), Yahoo! (*http://ca.yahoo.com*), and Bing (*www.bing.com*). Search engine preference can vary by region. In China, for example, the leading search engine is called Baidu.

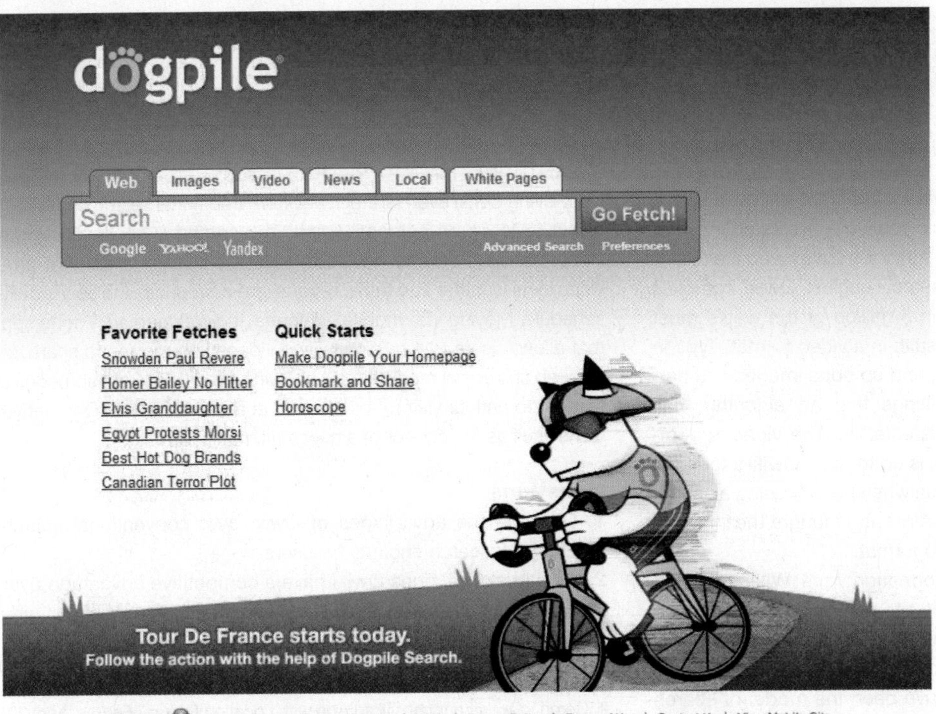

FIGURE 4.11 The Dogpile home page (*www.dogpile.com*).

For an even more thorough search, you can use a metasearch engine. **Metasearch engines** search several engines at once and then integrate the findings to answer users' queries. Examples are SurfWax (*www.surfwax.com*), Metacrawler (*www.metacrawler.com*), Mamma (*www.mamma.com*), KartOO (*www.kartoo.com*), and Dogpile (*www.dogpile.com*). Figure 4.11 illustrates the Dogpile home page.

One interesting search engine, Qwiki, provides videos as your search results. IT's About Business 4.3 explains how Qwiki works.

Publication of Material in Other Languages. Not only is there a huge amount of information on the Internet, but it is written in many different languages. How, then, do you access this information? The answer is that you use an *automatic translation* of web pages. Such translation is available to and from all major languages, and its quality is improving with time. Some major web translation tools are Bing (*www.bing.com/translator/*) and Google (*http://translate.google.com/*) (see Figure 4.12).

Should companies invest their time and resources to make their websites accessible in multiple languages, beyond Canadian English and French? The answer is an emphatic yes. In fact, multilingual websites are now a competitive necessity because of the global nature of the business environment. Companies increasingly are looking outside their home markets to grow revenues and attract new customers. At a time when companies are disseminating information around the world, getting that information correct is essential. It is not enough for companies to translate web content. They also must localize that content and be sensitive to the needs of the people in local markets.

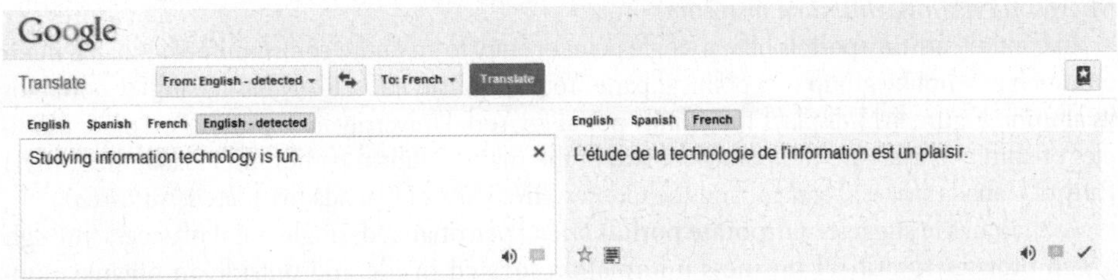

Google
Translate
From: English - detected
To: French
Translate
English Spanish French English - detected
Studying information technology is fun.
English Spanish French
L'étude de la technologie de l'information est un plaisir.

FIGURE 4.12 Google Translate. (*Source*: Google and the Google logo are registered trademarks of Google Inc., used with permission.)

IT's [about business]

4.3 Informative Videos on the Fly

What if you could have your own virtual assistant deliver a verbal and visual report on almost any topic you were interested in? That sci-fi scenario is possible now, thanks to the Qwiki website (*www.qwiki.com*). Like a supercharged search engine, Qwiki compiles the latest information on more than 3 million of the web's most popular topics and presents the results in a video format. Type in the name of a city you want to visit, and up pops images and narration with the most important things that an algorithm has decided you are probably most interested in. The video is compiled in real time, so the information is up to date. Qwiki's founder, Doug Imbruce, came up with the idea when he was using a search engine to research a trip to Buenos Aires and thought the information would be more useful in a video format.

Qwiki's algorithms compile information from Wikipedia and other sources with each search. The site can also suggest videos on related topics, such as neighbouring cities you're interested in visiting on your trip. Qwiki wants to get away from the traditional list of links to static articles that have been the model of search engines since the early days of the web, including AltaVista, which was founded by Louis Monier, who is now Qwiki's chief technology officer.

Moving Qwiki even farther away from traditional search engines, it wants to focus on personalization. The company continued in the virtual assistant vein by developing a custom alarm clock that provides local weather and traffic reports and announces the user's daily schedule. Moving into mobile platforms, it developed an iPhone app that allows users to turn picture and videos into movies to share on the web and social media sites—showing everything from someone's first tattoo parlour visit to a day spent at a music festival. Qwiki envisions itself as the creator of a new multimedia format.

Questions

1. Describe the advantages of Qwiki over conventional search and metasearch engines for users.
2. As a business, does Qwiki have a competitive advantage over conventional search and metasearch engines? Why or why not? Provide examples to support your answer.

Sources: Compiled from "Vision Quest," *Forbes Departures*, May 23, 2011; T. Geron, "Qwiki Launches iPad App with Location Focus," *Forbes*, April 20, 2011; A. Diana, "Qwiki Launches Multimedia Search Engine," *InformationWeek*, January 25, 2011; J. Coe, "Qwiki's Visual Search Engine," *Departures* magazine, May/June 2011; *www.qwiki.com*, accessed May 25, 2013.

To reach 80 percent of the world's Internet users, a website needs to support a minimum of 10 languages: English, Chinese, Spanish, Japanese, German, Korean, French, Italian, Russian, and Portuguese. At 20 cents and more per word, translation services are expensive. Companies supporting 10 languages can spend $200,000 annually to localize information and another $50,000 to maintain the websites. Translation budgets for major multinational companies can run in the millions of dollars. Many large companies use translation software for high-quality machine translation services (for example, Systran, *www.systransoft.com*).

Portals. Most organizations and their managers encounter information overload. Information is scattered across numerous documents, e-mail messages, and databases at different locations and systems. Finding relevant and accurate information is often time consuming and may require users to access multiple systems.

One solution to this problem is to use portals. A **portal** is a web-based, personalized gateway to information and knowledge that provides relevant information from different IT systems and the Internet using advanced search and indexing techniques. After reading the next section, you will be able to distinguish among four types of portals: commercial, affinity, corporate, and industrywide.

Commercial (public) portals are the most popular portals on the Internet. They are intended for broad and diverse audiences, and they offer fairly routine content, some of it in real time (for example, a stock ticker). Examples are Yahoo Canada (*http://ca.yahoo.com*) and Microsoft Network (*http://ca.msn.com*).

In contrast, **affinity portals** offer a single point of entry to an entire community of affiliated interests, such as a hobby group or a political party. Your university most likely has an affinity portal for its alumni. Figure 4.13 displays the affinity portal for York University in Toronto. Two other examples of affinity portals are the portals for two of the major political parties in Canada, the Liberal Party of Canada (*www.liberal.ca*) and the Conservative Party of Canada (*www.conservative.ca*).

As their name suggests, **corporate portals** offer a personalized, single point of access through a web browser to critical business information located inside and outside an organization. These portals are also known as *enterprise portals*, *information portals*, and *enterprise information*

FIGURE 4.13 York University Alumni affinity portal. (Courtesy of York University.)

portals. In addition to making it easier to find needed information, corporate portals offer customers and employees self-service opportunities.

Whereas corporate portals are associated with a single company, **industrywide portals** serve entire industries. An example is TruckNet (*www.truck.net*), a portal for the trucking industry and the trucking community, including professional drivers, owner/operators, and trucking companies (see Figure 4.14). TruckNet provides drivers with personalized web-based e-mail, access to applications to leading trucking companies in the United States and Canada, and access to the Drivers Round Table, a forum where drivers can discuss issues of interest. The portal also provides a large database of trucking jobs and general information related to the trucking industry.

These four types of portals are differentiated by the audiences they serve. Another type, the mobile portal, is distinguished by its technology. **Mobile portals** are portals that are accessible from mobile devices. Significantly, any of the four portals just discussed can be accessed by mobile devices. Mobile devices are typically wireless, so they will be presented in detail in Chapter 6.

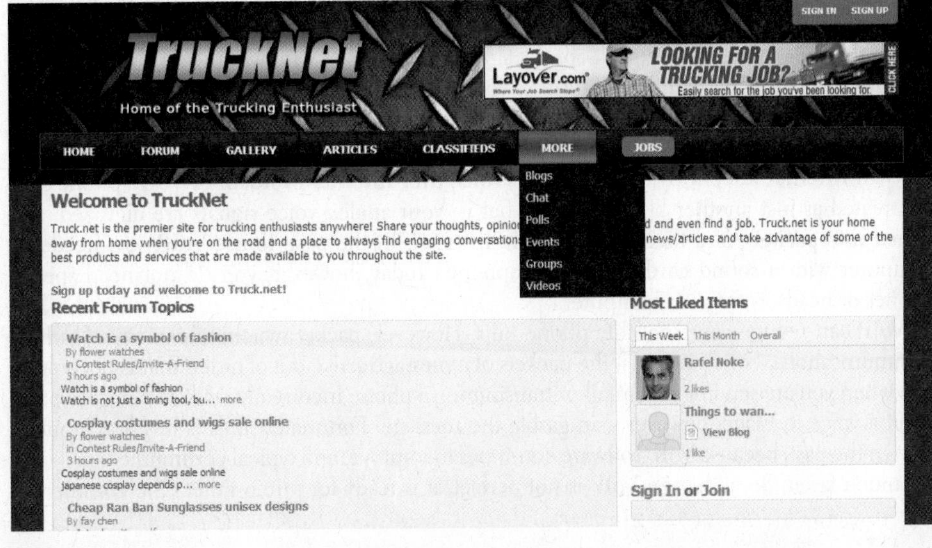

FIGURE 4.14 TruckNet portal.

Communication

The second major category of network applications is communication. There are many types of communication technologies, including e-mail, call centres, chat rooms, and voice. You learn about each one in this section. You will see another type of communication, blogging, in Chapter 7.

Electronic Mail. Electronic mail (e-mail) is the largest-volume application running over the Internet. Studies have found that almost all companies conduct business transactions via e-mail, and the vast majority confirm that e-mail is tied to their means of generating revenue. In fact, for many users, e-mail has all but replaced the telephone.

Web-Based Call Centres. Effective personalized customer contact is becoming an important aspect of web-based customer support. Such service is provided through *web-based call centres*, also known as *customer care centres*. For example, if you need to contact a software vendor for technical support, you usually will communicate with the vendor's web-based call centre, using e-mail, a telephone conversation, or a simultaneous voice/web session. Web-based call centres are sometimes located in foreign countries such as India. Such *offshoring* is an important issue for Canadian companies. For several reasons, some Canadian companies are moving their call centre operations back to Canada. First, they feel that they have less control over their call centre operations when they are overseas. They must depend on the vendor company, ensuring that it can uphold their standards, such as quality of service. Second, language difficulties can occur. Third, companies that manage sensitive information can run the risk of breaching customer confidentiality. Finally, the vendor company's call centre representatives typically work with many companies. As a result, they may not deliver the same level of customer services that you require.

Electronic Chat Rooms. *Electronic chat* is an arrangement whereby participants exchange conversational messages in real time. A **chat room** is a virtual meeting place where many people (in fact, anyone) come to "gab." Chat programs allow you to send messages to people who are connected to the same channel of communication at the same time. Anyone can join in the conversation. Messages are displayed on your screen as they arrive, even if you are in the middle of typing a message.

There are two major types of chat programs. The first type is a web-based chat program, which allows you to send messages to Internet users by visiting a web chat site (for example, *http://messenger.yahoo.com*). The second type is an e-mail-based (text-only) program called *Internet Relay Chat (IRC)*. A business can use IRC to interact with customers, provide on-line experts' answers to questions, and so on.

Voice Communication. When people need to communicate with one another from a distance, they use the telephone more frequently than any other communication device. With the plain old telephone service (POTS), every call opened up a dedicated circuit for the duration of the call. A dedicated circuit connects you to the person with whom you are talking and is devoted only to your call. In contrast, as you saw earlier in the chapter, the Internet divides data into packets, which traverse the Internet in random order and are reassembled at their destination.

With **Internet telephony**, also known as **voice over Internet protocol** or **VoIP**, phone calls are treated as just another kind of data. That is, your analog voice signals are digitized, sectioned into packets, and then sent over the Internet. In the past, to use VoIP, you needed a computer with a sound card and a microphone. Today, however, you do not need special phones or headsets for your computer.

VoIP can reduce your monthly phone bills. However, packet switching can cause garbled communications. For example, if the packets of a message arrive out of order, that is not a problem when you are sending an e-mail or transmitting a photo. Incorrectly reassembling the packets of a voice message, however, can garble the message. Fortunately, this is less of a problem than in the past, because VoIP software continues to improve, and typical communications links are much faster. So, although VoIP is not perfect, it is ready for prime time. One commercial

FIGURE 4.15 Skype 5.5 interface.

example of VoIP is Skype (*www.skype.com*), which provides several VoIP services for free: voice and video calls to users who also have Skype, instant messaging, short message service, voice mail, one-to-one and group chats, and conference calls with up to nine people (see Figure 4.15).

Unified Communications. In the past, organizational networks for wired and wireless data, voice communications, and video conferencing operated independently, and the IT department managed each network separately. This arrangement increased costs and reduced productivity.

Unified communications (UC) simplifies and integrates all forms of communications—voice, voice mail, fax, chat, e-mail, instant messaging, short message service, presence (location) services, and video conferencing—on a common hardware and software platform. Presence services enable users to know where their intended recipients are and if they are available, in real time.

UC unifies all forms of human and computer communications into a common user experience. For example, UC allows an individual to receive a voice mail message and then read it in his or her e-mail inbox. In another example, UC enables users to seamlessly collaborate with another person on a project, regardless of where the users are located. One user could quickly locate the other user by accessing an interactive directory, determine if that user were available, engage in a text messaging session, and then escalate the session to a voice call, or even a video call, all in real time.

Collaboration

The third major category of network applications is collaboration. An important feature of modern organizations is that people collaborate to perform work. **Collaboration** is efforts by two or more entities—that is, individuals, teams, groups, or organizations—who work together to accomplish certain tasks. The term **work group** refers specifically to two or more individuals who act together to perform some task.

Workflow is the movement of information as it flows through the sequence of steps that make up an organization's work procedures. Workflow management makes it possible to pass documents, information, and tasks from one participant to another in a way that is governed by the organization's rules or procedures. Workflow systems are tools for automating business processes.

If group members are in different locations, they constitute a **virtual group (team)**. Virtual groups conduct *virtual meetings*; that is, they "meet" electronically. **Virtual collaboration** (or *e-collaboration*) is the use of digital technologies that enable organizations or individuals to collaboratively plan, design, develop, manage, and research products, services, and innovative applications. Organizational employees frequently collaborate virtually with one another. In addition, organizations collaborate virtually with customers, suppliers, and other business partners to improve productivity and competitiveness.

One type of collaboration is *crowdsourcing*, which is the outsourcing of a task to an undefined, generally large group of people in the form of an open call. Let's look at some examples of crowdsourcing.

- *Crowdsourcing help desks:* IT help desks are a necessary service on university campuses because students depend on their computers and Internet access to complete their school work and attend class on-line. At one university, new IT help desks use crowdsourcing to alleviate the cost and pressure of having to answer so many calls. Students and professors post their IT problems on an on-line forum, where other students and amateur IT experts answer them.
- *IdeaBOOST:* IdeaBOOST (*www.ideaboost.ca*) is an innovative creative and business development lab sponsored by the Canadian Film Centre that uses crowdsourcing to help Canadian entertainment entrepreneurs grow ideas into products and concepts into businesses. The website serves as a platform where ideas are submitted, and based on the audience's response, the highest rated ideas are shortlisted. The chosen contestants spend four months working with industry-leading mentors to define their business model and to develop a market-ready prototype.
- *The Great Sunflower Project:* This is a project by a university professor who needed help with her studies of honeybees, but she had limited grant money. So, she contacted gardening groups around the country. Through this crowdsourcing strategy, this professor ultimately created a network of more than 25,000 gardeners and schools to assist with her research. She then sent these participants seeds for plants that attract bees. In return, the participants recorded the honeybees' visits and activity on her website.

Collaboration can be *synchronous*, meaning that all team members meet at the same time. Teams may also collaborate *asynchronously* when team members cannot meet at the same time. Virtual teams, whose members are located throughout the world, typically must collaborate asynchronously.

Various software products are available to support all types of collaboration. Among the most prominent are Microsoft SharePoint, Google Docs, IBM Lotus Quickr, and Jive. In general, these products provide on-line collaboration capabilities, workgroup e-mail, distributed databases, bulletin whiteboards, electronic text editing, document management, workflow capabilities, instant virtual meetings, application sharing, instant messaging, consensus building, voting, ranking, and various application development tools.

These products also provide varying degrees of content control. Wikis, Google Docs, Microsoft SharePoint, and Jive provide for shared content with *version management*, whereas Microsoft SharePoint and IBM Lotus Quickr offer *version control*. Products with version management track changes to documents and provide features to accommodate multiple people working on the same document at the same time. In contrast, version-control systems provide each team member with an account that includes a set of permissions. Shared documents are located in shared directories. Document directories are often set up so that users must check out documents before they can edit them. When one team member checks out a document, no other member can access it. Once the document has been checked in, it becomes available to other members.

In the following sections, you will review the major collaboration software products. You then shift your attention to two tools that support collaboration—electronic teleconferencing and video conferencing.

Microsoft SharePoint. Microsoft's SharePoint product (*www.microsoft.com/Sharepoint/default.mspx*) provides shared content with version control. SharePoint supports document directories and has features that enable users to create and manage surveys, discussion forums, wikis, member blogs, member websites, and workflow. It also has a rigorous permissions structure, which allows organizations to control users' access based on their organizational role, team membership, interest, security level, or other criteria.

One company that used SharePoint effectively is Continental Airlines, which merged with United Airlines in 2013. When new U.S. federal regulations regarding long runway delays went into effect, Continental responded by implementing a SharePoint system that puts various aspects of flight operations—aircraft status, pilots, crews, and customer care—on the same page. Using the system, the 135 general managers at the airline's domestic airports filled out a 16-page form on-line. The form included the names and numbers of airport workers—from the airport authority, to the person who drives the stairs, to planes waiting on the runway. The general managers had to specify how they would manage delays of an hour, two hours, and two-and-one-half hours. The SharePoint system included a dashboard for Continental's centralized system operations centre. People in the centre could use the dashboard to find information about delays quickly and to communicate with pilots, crews, and dispatchers to decide what to do to mitigate any delays.

Google Docs. Google Docs (*http://docs.google.com*) is a free, web-based word processor, spreadsheet, and presentation application. It enables users to create and edit documents on-line while collaborating with other users. Google Docs allows multiple users to open, share, and edit documents at the same time.

IBM Lotus Quickr. IBM's Lotus Quickr (*www.ibm.com/lotus/quickr*) product provides shared content with version control in the form of document directories with check-in and check-out features based on user privileges. Quickr provides on-line team spaces where members can share and collaborate by using team calendars, discussion forums, blogs, wikis, and other collaboration tools for managing projects and other content.

Compagnie d'Enterprises CFE, one of Belgium's largest construction companies, has put the collaboration tools of Quickr to good use. Construction projects require many parties to collaborate effectively. When these projects are conducted on a global scale and the parties are scattered throughout the world, the projects become incredibly complex. CFE needed to tap its best resources for its projects, regardless of where those resources were located. The company was using e-mail to share documents with suppliers and clients, but this process resulted in version-control errors and security vulnerabilities. To eliminate these problems, CFE deployed Quickr with its centralized document libraries and version control. The software reduced both the volume of large attachments sent through e-mail and the impact of those e-mails on the system. As a result, project teams were able to work more efficiently.

Jive. Jive's (*www.jivesoftware.com*) newest product, Clearspace, uses web collaboration and communication tools such as forums, wikis, and blogs to allow people to share content with version management, via discussion rooms, calendars, and to-do lists. For example, Nike originally used Clearspace Community to run a technical support forum on Nike Plus (*http://nikeplus.nike.com*), a website where runners track their distance ran and calories burned using a sensor in their shoes. The company soon noticed that runners were also using the forum to meet other athletes. In response, Nike expanded its forum to include a section where runners could meet and challenge one another to races. Since that time, 40 percent of visitors to the site who did not own the Nike Plus sensor ended up buying the product.

Electronic Teleconferencing. **Teleconferencing** is the use of electronic communication technology that enables two or more people at different locations to hold a simultaneous conference. There are several types of teleconferencing. The oldest and simplest is a telephone conference call, where several people talk to one another from multiple locations. The biggest

IT's [about business]

4.4 Canadian Firm Develops Video Conferencing Software

Librestream (*www.librestream.com*) is a Canadian company based in Winnipeg that makes a collaboration software named Onsight. This collaboration software runs on remote computers and hand-held devices with video capabilities and uses fourth-generation telecommunication networks to enable workers to communicate with multiple parties using video, voice, and sound.

What makes Onsight different from other video conferencing products such as Skype? The main difference is that it can be used on hand-held mobile devices, allowing for communication in such remote places as offshore oil rigs, natural gas fields, wind farms, or places that might be located in a different continent. Field workers and remote experts can connect and share live video and images, and talk and draw onscreen. This is a more cost-efficient way of collaborating than flying in an expert to solve the questions that field employees might encounter while working on a project, such as repairing a wind turbine or a gas pump in a natural gas field in the middle of Alberta, or flying an expert to an offshore oil platform off the coast of Newfoundland.

Questions

1. Make a table comparing the characteristics of remote collaboration with video conferencing and on-site collaboration.
2. What type of decisions or problems is collaboration software more suited to?
3. Provide additional examples (within a company or different industries) where Onsight collaboration software might be used.

Sources: Compiled from K. Deirdre, "Video-Collaboration Firm Can't Find Joy in Canada," *The Globe and Mail*, May 10, 2012; Librestream, *www.librestream.com*, accessed April 2013.

disadvantage of conference calls is that they do not allow the participants to communicate face to face. In addition, participants in one location cannot see graphs, charts, and pictures at other locations.

To overcome these shortcomings, organizations are increasingly turning to video teleconferencing, or video conferencing. In a **video conference**, participants in one location can see participants, documents, and presentations at other locations.

IT's About Business 4.4 discusses the example of a Canadian company providing video conferencing software.

The latest version of video conferencing, called *telepresence*, enables participants to seamlessly share data, voice, pictures, graphics, and animation by electronic means. Conferees can also transmit data along with voice and video, which allows them to work on documents together and to exchange computer files.

Several companies are offering high-end telepresence systems. For example, Hewlett-Packard's Halo system (*www.hp.com*), Cisco's TelePresence 3000 (*www.cisco.com*), and Polycom's HDX (*www.polycom.com*) use massive high-definition screens up to 2.5 metres wide to show people sitting around conference tables (see Figure 4.16). Telepresence systems also have advanced audio capabilities that let everyone talk at once without cancelling out any voices. Telepresence systems can cost up to $400,000 for a room, with network management fees ranging up to $18,000 per month. Financial and consulting firms are quickly adopting telepresence systems. For example, the Blackstone Group (*www.blackstone.com*), a private equity firm, has 40 telepresence rooms around the world, and Deloitte & Touche (*www.deloitte.com*) has 12 telepresence rooms.

Let's look at two other organizations that use telepresence systems.

- International law firm DLA Piper's (*www.dlapiper.com*) telepresence system saves the company approximately $1 million per year in travel costs and lost productivity. The firm realizes these savings by rescheduling half of its in-person board meetings as telepresence conferences and relying on at least two lawyers per week to use telepresence rather than travel. Making it possible for globally based lawyers to work closely together via telepresence helps drive home the reality that the firm has offices all over the world and therefore should have an international focus. This benefit of telepresence cannot be quantified in terms of dollars and cents.

FIGURE 4.16 Telepresence system. (*Source:* PRNews Foto/ Polycom, Inc./NewsCom.)

- The insurance giant MetLife (*www.metlife.com*) is using telepresence in three dedicated conference rooms in Chicago, New York, and New Jersey, and it is expanding the system to other offices nationally and internationally. MetLife has experienced a direct cost savings as well as better employee time efficiency. Further, telepresence is helping the company meet its "green initiative" goal of reducing its carbon emissions by 20 percent. Interestingly, one MetLife executive noted that when the company uses telepresence for meetings, employees who normally would not be asked to travel to headquarters now have the opportunity to make presentations and get valuable exposure to company executives.

4.5 E-Learning and Distance Learning

E-learning and distance learning are not the same thing, but they do overlap. **E-learning** is learning supported by the web. It can take place inside classrooms as a support to conventional teaching, such as when students work via the web during class. It also can take place in virtual classrooms, in which all coursework is done on-line and classes do not meet face-to-face. In these cases, e-learning is a part of distance learning. **Distance learning (DL)** is any learning situation in which teachers and students do not meet face-to-face.

Today, the web provides a multimedia interactive environment for self-study. Web-enabled systems make knowledge accessible to those who need it, when they need it, anytime, anywhere. For this reason, e-learning and DL can be useful for both formal education and corporate training.

There are many benefits to e-learning. For example, on-line materials can deliver up-to-date content that is of high quality (created by content experts) and consistent (presented the same way every time). It also gives students the flexibility to learn at any place, at any time, and at their own pace. In corporate training centres that use e-learning, learning time generally is shorter, which means that more people can be trained within a given timeframe. This system reduces training costs as well as the expense of renting facility space.

Despite these benefits, e-learning has some drawbacks. To begin with, students must be computer literate. Also, they may miss the face-to-face interaction with instructors. Finally, assessing students' work can be problematic because instructors really do not know who completed the assignments.

E-learning usually does not replace the classroom setting. Rather, it enhances it by taking advantage of new content and delivery technologies. Advanced e-learning support environments, such as Blackboard (*www.blackboard.com*), add value to traditional learning in higher education.

Virtual Universities

Virtual universities are on-line universities in which students take classes from home or at an off-site location, via the Internet. A large number of existing universities offer on-line education of some form. Some universities, such as Athabasca University (*www.athabascau.ca*), the University of Manitoba (*http://umanitoba.ca*), Thompson Rivers University (*www.tru.ca*), and TÉLUQ (*www.teluq.uquebec.ca*), offer hundreds of courses and dozens of degrees to students, all on-line. Other universities offer limited on-line courses and degrees but use innovative teaching methods and multimedia support in the traditional classroom.

Telecommuting

Knowledge workers are being called the *distributed workforce*, or *digital nomads*. This group of highly prized workers is now able to work anywhere and anytime, a process called **telecommuting**.

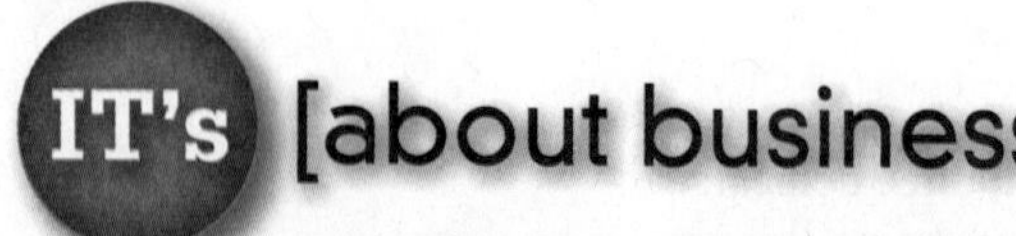

4.5 Is Telecommuting for Everyone?

It's estimated that half of all jobs in Canada are suitable for telecommuting. But is telecommuting suitable for everyone?

Canadian IT services company T4G Ltd. (*www.t4g.com*) embraces telework for its employees, allowing staff to work from home or the road almost every day. Many of them choose to do so. Its Toronto office, for example, has workspaces for at least 140 people, but usually fewer than 30 of them are occupied. Company executives say that as long as employees deliver quality work on time, it doesn't matter where they are.

The T4G employees are among the more than 1.5 million Canadians now working from home at least part-time. As the number of knowledge workers continues to grow, so will the number of teleworkers, experts predict.

There are the benefits of telecommuting. For businesses, the main pros of telecommuting are the money saved on accommodations: renting or buying office space, and maintaining it with utilities, repairs, cleaning, and so on. For employees, the main benefits are a better work-life balance and savings in transportation costs and time. Some find they're more productive at home, which can be quieter than the office.

However, telecommuting has also disadvantages. In early 2013, for example, Yahoo abolished its policy allowing working from home, saying that face-to-face collaboration among its staff is better for productivity and innovation. In some organizations, some employees still prefer to go in to the office. For example, T4G employees in some areas, particularly in human resources and accounting, find they can get more work done on-site. Another disadvantage of telecommuting is that it's harder to remotely pass along the corporate culture—the shared norms, values, and expectations.

Some companies are trying to overcome these disadvantages by adopting information technology solutions. In the case of T4G, employees are issued computers equipped with Microsoft Lync (*http://office.microsoft.com/en-ca/*), a business equivalent of Skype, and earphones. Using this technology, teams can hold daily or weekly face-to-face meetings remotely. However, the company still gathers employees together physically to share a camaraderie and corporate identity for key events, such as monthly meetings and an annual Christmas party.

The result of its successful telecommuting policy is easily measurable: T4G enjoys a low employee turnover ratio in an industry where high employee turnover is the norm.

Questions

1. Is telecommuting a consequence of information technology? Justify your answer.
2. What IT network-related issues would a company need to consider with telecommuting?
3. What IT security issues would a company need to consider with telecommuting?
4. What other challenges would telecommuting pose to the IT department in an organization?

Sources: Compiled from W. Immen, "How to Be Out of the Office but Still at Work," *The Globe and Mail*, January 15, 2013; W. Immen, "The Benefits of Telecommuting," *The Globe and Mail*, January 15, 2013; J. Christie, "For Every Benefit of Telecommuting, a Challenge," *The Globe and Mail*, January 23, 2013; W. Immen, "Still on Worker Productivity? Think of Profitability Instead," *The Globe and Mail*, January 23, 2013; C. Cain Miller and C. Rampell, "Yahoo Orders Home Workers Back to the Office," *The New York Times*, February 25, 2103.

Distributed workers are those who have no permanent office at their companies, preferring to work in home offices, airport lounges, client conference rooms, or hockey arenas. The growth of the distributed workforce is driven by globalization, extremely long commutes to work, rising gasoline prices, ubiquitous broadband communications links (wireline and wireless), and powerful laptop computers and computing devices.

Telecommuting has a number of potential advantages for employees, employers, and society. For employees, the benefits include reduced stress and improved family life. In addition, telecommuting offers employment opportunities for housebound people such as single parents and persons with disabilities. Employer benefits include increased productivity, the ability to retain skilled employees, and the ability to attract employees who don't live within commuting distance.

However, telecommuting also has some potential disadvantages, as we can see in IT's About Business 4.5. For employees, the major disadvantages are increased feelings of isolation, possible loss of fringe benefits, lower pay (in some cases), the potential for slower promotions, and lack of socialization. In addition, telecommuting employees often have difficulties "training" their families to understand that they are at work even though they are physically at home. The major disadvantages to employers are difficulties in supervising work and potential data security problems.

before you go on...

1. Discuss the network applications that you studied in this section and the tools and technologies that support each. Provide one example for each network application in a business setting.
2. Identify the business conditions that have made video conferencing more important.
3. Differentiate between e-learning and distance learning.
4. Describe virtual universities. Identify three benefits and three disadvantages of e-learning.
5. What is telecommuting? Identify three benefits and three disadvantages of telecommuting.

What's In IT For Me?

For the **Accounting Major**

Accounting personnel use corporate intranets and portals to consolidate transaction data from legacy systems to provide an overall view of internal projects. This view contains the current costs charged to each project, the number of hours spent on each project by individual employees, and an analysis of how actual costs compare with projected costs. Finally, accounting personnel use Internet access to government and professional websites to stay informed on legal and other changes affecting their profession.

For the **Finance Major**

Corporate intranets and portals can provide a model to evaluate the risks of a project or an investment. Financial analysts use two types of data in the model: historical transaction data from corporate databases via the intranet, and industry data obtained via the Internet. In addition, financial services firms can use the web for marketing and to provide services.

For the **Marketing Major**

Marketing managers use corporate intranets and portals to coordinate the activities of the sales force. Sales personnel access corporate portals via the intranet to discover updates on pricing, promotion, rebates, customer information, and information about competitors. Sales staff also can download and customize presentations for their customers. The Internet, particularly the web, opens a completely new marketing channel for many industries. Just how advertising, purchasing, and information dispensation should occur appears to vary from industry to industry, product to product, and service to service.

For the **Production/Operations Management Major**

Companies are using intranets and portals to speed product development by providing the development team with three-dimensional models and animation. All team members can access the models for faster exploration of ideas and enhanced feedback. Corporate portals, accessed via intranets, enable managers to carefully supervise their inventories as well as real-time production on assembly lines. Extranets are also proving valuable as a communication format for joint research and design efforts among companies. The Internet also is a great source of cutting-edge information for POM managers.

For the **Human Resources Management Major**

Human resources personnel use portals and intranets to publish corporate policy manuals, job postings, company telephone directories, and training classes. Many companies deliver on-line training obtained from the Internet to employees through their intranets. Human resources departments use intranets to offer employees extended health care benefits, savings, and benefit plans, as well as the opportunity to take competency tests on-line. The Internet supports worldwide recruiting efforts, and it also can be the communications platform for supporting geographically dispersed work teams.

For the **MIS Major**

As important as the networking technology infrastructure is, it is invisible to users (unless something goes wrong). The MIS function is responsible for keeping all organizational networks up and running all the time. MIS personnel, therefore, provide users with the ability to compute, communicate, and collaborate from almost anytime and anywhere. For example, organizations have access to experts at remote locations without having to duplicate that expertise in multiple areas of the firm. Virtual teaming allows experts physically located in different cities to work on projects as though they were in the same office.

[Summary]

1. **Define the term "computer network," and compare and contrast the two major types of networks.**

   A computer network is a system that connects computers via communications media so that data and information can be transmitted among them. The two major types of networks are local area networks (LANs) and wide area networks (WANs). LANs encompass a limited geographic area and usually are composed of one communications medium.

In contrast, WANs encompass a broad geographical area and usually are composed of multiple communications media.

2. **Describe the differences among the three types of wireline communications media, and discuss the main advantages and disadvantages of each type.**

Twisted-pair wire, the most prevalent form of communications wiring, consists of strands of copper wire twisted in pairs. It is relatively inexpensive to purchase, widely available, and easy to work with. However, it is relatively slow for transmitting data, it is subject to interference from other electrical sources, and it can easily be tapped by unintended receivers.

Coaxial cable consists of insulated copper wire. It is much less susceptible to electrical interference than is twisted-pair wire, and it can carry more data. However, coaxial cable is more expensive and more difficult to work with than twisted-pair wire.

Fibre-optic cables consist of thousands of very thin filaments of glass fibres that transmit information via light pulses generated by lasers. Fibre-optic cables are significantly smaller and lighter than traditional cable media. They also can transmit far more data, and they provide greater security from interference and tapping. Fibre-optic cable often is used as the backbone for a network, whereas twisted-pair wire and coaxial cable connect the backbone to individual devices on the network.

3. **Differentiate between the Internet and the World Wide Web, and identify the most common methods for accessing the Internet.**

The Internet is a global network of computer networks, using a common communications protocol, TCP/IP. The *World Wide Web* is a system that stores, retrieves, formats, and displays information accessible through a browser.

Methods for connecting to the Internet include dial-up, DSL, cable modem, satellite, wireless, and fibre to the home.

4. **Identify six major categories of network applications, provide an example of each, and explain how that application supports business functions.**

- *Discovery* involves browsing and information retrieval, and provides users the ability to view information in databases, download it, and/or process it. Discovery tools include search engines, directories, and portals. Discovery tools enable business users to efficiently find needed information.
- *Networks* provide fast, inexpensive *communications*, via e-mail, call centres, chat rooms, voice communications, and blogs. Communications tools provide business users with a seamless interface among team members, colleagues, business partners, and customers.
- *Collaboration* is mutual efforts by two or more entities (individuals, groups, or companies) who work together to accomplish tasks. Collaboration is enabled by workflow systems. Collaboration tools enable business users to collaborate with colleagues, business partners, and customers.
- *E-learning* is learning supported by the web. Distance learning is any learning situation in which teachers and students do not meet face-to-face. E-learning provides tools for business users to enable their lifelong learning.
- *Virtual universities* are on-line universities in which students take classes from home or at an off-site location, via the Internet. Virtual universities make it possible for students to obtain degrees while working full time, thus increasing their value to their firms.
- *Telecommuting* is the process where knowledge workers are able to work anywhere and anytime. Telecommuting provides flexibility for employees, with many benefits and some drawbacks.

[Chapter Glossary]

affinity portal A website that offers a single point of entry to an entire community of affiliated interests.

analogue signals Continuous waves that transmit information by altering the amplitude and frequency of the waves.

asynchronous transfer mode (ATM) Data transmission technology that uses packet switching and allows for almost unlimited bandwidth on demand.

backbone networks High-speed central networks to which multiple smaller networks (such as LANs and smaller WANs) connect.

bandwidth The transmission capacity of a network, stated in bits per second.

broadband A transmission speed ranging from approximately 1 megabit per second up to several terabits per second.

broadcast media (also called **wireless media**) Communications channels that use electromagnetic media (the "airwaves") to transmit data.

browsers Software applications through which users primarily access the web.

cable media (also called **wireline media**) Communications channels that use physical wires or cables to transmit data and information.

CANARIE A Canadian not-for-profit organization supported by the Canadian government and the private sector with the goal of doing research and implementing advanced communication networks.

chat room A virtual meeting place where groups of regulars come to "gab" electronically.

clients Computers, such as users' personal computers, that use any of the services provided by servers.

client/server computing Form of distributed processing in which some machines (servers) perform computing functions for end-user PCs (clients).

coaxial cable Insulated copper wire; used to carry high-speed data traffic and television signals.

collaboration Mutual efforts by two or more individuals who perform activities in order to accomplish certain tasks.

commercial (public) portal A website that offers fairly routine content for diverse audiences; offers customization only at the user interface.

communications channels Pathway for communicating data from one location to another.

computer network A system that connects computers and other devices via communications media so that data and information can be transmitted among them.

corporate portal A website that provides a single point of access to critical business information located inside and outside of an organization.

digital signals A discrete pulse, either on or off, that conveys information in a binary form.

digital subscriber lines (DSL) A high-speed, digital data-transmission technology using existing analog telephone lines.

distance learning (DL) Learning situations in which teachers and students do not meet face-to-face.

distributed processing Network architecture that divides processing work between two or more computers, linked together in a network.

domain names The name assigned to an Internet site, consisting of multiple parts, separated by dots, which are translated from right to left.

domain name system (DNS) The system administered by the Internet Corporation for Assigned Names and Numbers (ICANN) that assigns names to each site on the Internet.

e-learning Learning supported by the web; can be done inside traditional classrooms or in virtual classrooms.

enterprise network A network, encompassing an organization, composed of interconnected multiple LANs and WANs.

Ethernet A common local area network protocol.

extranet A network that provides access to parts of an organization's intranets to different outside business partners.

fibre-optic cables A communications medium consisting of thousands of very thin filaments of glass fibres, surrounded by cladding, that transmit information via light pulses generated by lasers.

file server (also called **network server**) A computer that contains various software and data files for a local area network, and contains the network operating system.

hypertext transport protocol (HTTP) The communications standard used to transfer pages across the WWW portion of the Internet; defines how messages are formulated and transmitted.

industrywide portal A web-based gateway to information and knowledge for an entire industry.

Internet ("the Net") The massive network that connects computer networks of businesses, organizations, government agencies, and schools around the world, quickly, seamlessly, and inexpensively.

Internet2 A new, faster U.S. telecommunications network that deploys advanced network applications such as remote medical diagnosis, digital libraries, distance education, on-line simulation, and virtual laboratories.

Internet protocol (IP) A set of rules responsible for disassembling, delivering, and reassembling packets over the Internet.

Internet protocol (IP) address An assigned address that uniquely identifies a computer on the Internet.

Internet service provider (ISP) A company that provides Internet connections for a fee.

Internet telephony (also called **voice over Internet protocol** or **VoIP**) The use of the Internet as the transmission medium for telephone calls.

intranet A private network that uses Internet software and TCP/IP protocols.

local area network (LAN) A network that connects communications devices in a limited geographical region (for example, a building), so that every user device on the network can communicate with every other device.

metasearch engine A computer program that searches several engines at once and integrates the findings of the various search engines to answer queries posted by users.

mobile portal A website that is accessible from mobile devices.

modem Device that converts signals from analog to digital and vice versa.

network access points (NAPs) Computers that act as exchange points for Internet traffic and determine how traffic is routed.

network server (see **file server**)

packet switching The transmission technology that breaks up blocks of text into packets.

peer-to-peer (P2P) processing A type of client/server distributed processing that allows two or more computers to pool their resources, making each computer both a client and a server.

portal A web-based personalized gateway to information and knowledge that provides information from disparate information systems and the Internet, using advanced search and indexing techniques.

protocol The set of rules and procedures governing transmission across a network.

router A communications processor that routes messages from a LAN to the Internet, across several connected LANs, or across a wide area network such as the Internet.

search engine A computer program that searches for specific information by key words and reports the results.

servers A computer that provides access to various network services, such as printing, data, and communications.

synchronous optical network (SONET) An interface standard for transporting digital signals over fibre-optic lines; allows the integration of transmissions from multiple vendors.

T-carrier system A digital transmission system that defines circuits that operate at different rates, all of which are multiples of the basic 64 Kbps used to transport a single voice call.

telecommuting A work arrangement whereby employees work at home, at the customer's premises, in special workplaces, or while travelling, usually using a computer linked to their place of employment.

teleconferencing The use of electronic communication that allows two or more people at different locations to have a simultaneous conference.

transmission control protocol/Internet protocol (TCP/IP) A file transfer protocol that can send large files of information across sometimes unreliable networks with assurance that the data will arrive uncorrupted.

twisted-pair wire A communications medium consisting of strands of copper wire twisted together in pairs.

unified communications (UC) Hardware and software platform that simplifies and integrates all forms of communications—voice, e-mail, instant messaging, location, and video conferencing—across an organization.

uniform resource locator (URL) The set of letters that identifies the address of a specific resource on the web.

video conference A virtual meeting in which participants in one location can see and hear participants at other locations and can share data and graphics by electronic means.

virtual collaboration The use of digital technologies that enable organizations or individuals to collaboratively plan, design, develop, manage, and research products, services, and innovative information systems and electronic commerce applications.

virtual group (team) A work group whose members are in different locations and who meet electronically.

virtual universities On-line universities from which students take classes from home or an off-site location via the Internet.

voice over Internet protocol (VoIP; see **Internet telephony**)

website Collectively, all of the web pages of a particular company or individual.

wide area network (WAN) A network, generally provided by common carriers, that covers a wide geographic area.

wireless media (see **broadcast media**)

wireline media (see **cable media**)

work group Two or more individuals who act together to perform some task, on either a permanent or temporary basis.

workflow The movement of information as it flows through the sequence of steps that make up an organization's work procedures.

World Wide Web (also called **the web, WWW,** or **W3**) A system of universally accepted standards for storing, retrieving, formatting, and displaying information via a client/server architecture; it uses the transport functions of the Internet.

[Discussion Questions]

1. What are the implications of having fibre-optic cable to everyone's home?
2. Draw a chart of your university's campuses and faculties and indicate where it would use LANs and WANs.
3. Discuss the pros and cons of P2P networks.
4. Should the Internet be regulated? If so, by whom?
5. Discuss the pros and cons of delivering this book over the Internet.

6. Explain how the Internet works. Assume you are talking with someone who has no knowledge of information technology. (In other words, keep it very simple.)
7. How are the network applications of communication and collaboration related? Do communication tools also support collaboration? Give examples.
8. Search Google for recent news about telecommuting in Canada. Identify obstacles to telecommuting and report on why firms don't use telecommuting more often. Are these factors the same for every province in Canada? Are they the same for every country?

[Problem-Solving Activities]

1. Calculate how much bandwidth you consume when using the Internet every day. How many e-mails do you send daily, and what is the size of each? (Your e-mail program may have e-mail file size information.) How many music and video clips do you download (or upload) daily, and what is the size of each? If you view YouTube often, surf the web to find out the size of a typical YouTube file. Add up the number of e-mail, audio, and video files you transmit or receive on a typical day. When you have calculated your daily Internet usage, determine whether you are a "normal" Internet user or a "power" Internet user. What impact does network neutrality have on you as a "normal" user? As a "power" user?
2. Access several P2P applications, such as SETI@home. Describe the purpose of each one, and identify which ones you would like to join.
3. Access *http://ipv6.com* and learn about the impact of IPv6 for businesses.
4. Access *www.icann.org* and learn more about this important organization.
5. You want to set up your own website using your name for the domain name (for example, KellyRainer).
   - Explain the process for registering a domain name.
   - Which top-level domain will you use and why?
6. Access *www.icann.org* and obtain the name of an agency or company that can register a domain for the TLD that you selected. What is the name of that agency or company?
7. Access the website for that agency or company to learn the process that you must use. How much will it initially cost to register your domain name? How much will it cost to maintain that name in the future?
8. You plan to take a two-week vacation in Australia this year. Using the Internet, find information that will help you plan the trip. Such information includes, *but is not limited to*, the following:
   a. Geographical location and weather conditions at the time of your trip.
   b. Major tourist attractions and recreational facilities.
   c. Travel arrangements (airlines, approximate fares).
   d. Car rental; local tours.
   e. Alternatives for accommodation (within a moderate budget) and food.
   f. Estimated cost of the vacation (travel, lodging, food, recreation, shopping, etc.).
   g. Country regulations regarding the entrance of your dog, which you would like to take with you.
   h. Shopping.
   i. Passport information (either to obtain one or to renew one).
   j. Information on the country's language and culture.

   What else do you think you should research before going to Australia?
9. From your own experience or from the vendor's information, list the major capabilities of Lotus Notes/Domino. Do the same for Microsoft Exchange. Compare and contrast the products. Explain how the products can be used to support knowledge workers and managers.
10. Visit the websites of companies that manufacture telepresence products for the Internet. Prepare a report. Differentiate between telepresence products and video conferencing products.
11. Access Google videos (or YouTube) and search for "Cisco Magic." This video shows Cisco's next-generation telepresence system. Compare and contrast it with current telepresence systems.
12. Access the website of your university. Does the website provide high-quality information (right amount, clear, accurate, etc.)? Do you think that a high school student who is thinking of attending your university would feel the same way?
13. Imagine that you wanted to set up a website for your own start-up business. Compare and contrast Google Sites (*www.google.com/sites*) and Intuit Websites (*www.intuitwebsites.ca*). Which site would you use to create your own website? Explain your choice.
14. Access the website of Music Canada, formerly the Canadian Recording Industry Association (*www.musiccanada.com*). Discuss what you find there regarding copyright infringement (that is, downloading music files through P2P networks, for example). How do you feel about Music Canada's efforts to stop music downloads? Debate this issue from your point of view and from Music Canada's point of view.
15. Research the companies involved in Internet telephony (VoIP). Compare their offerings as to price, necessary technologies, ease of installation, and so on. Which company is the most attractive to you? Which might be the most attractive for a large company?

16. Access two alternative search engines other than Google on the web and search for the same terms on all of them. Compare the results on breadth (number of results found) and precision (results are what you were looking for).
17. Second Life (*www.secondlife.com*) is a three-dimensional, on-line world built and owned by its *residents*. Residents of Second Life are avatars created by real-world people. Access Second Life, learn about it, and create your own avatar to explore this world. Learn about the thousands of people who are making "real world" money from operations in Second Life.
18. Access the Boeing Supplier Portal information page at *www.boeingsuppliers.com/*. Describe some of the many services offered there for Boeing's suppliers. What type of portal would you classify it into? What are the benefits for both Boeing and its suppliers of having this portal?

[Spreadsheet Activity: Building Charts and Tables]

Objective: Creating charts and graphs is a really useful skill to develop. Visual data can be shared more quickly, comprehended more easily, and displayed much more cleanly than numbers in a spreadsheet. This activity will require you to build both charts and tables to present data surrounding network speeds.

Chapter Connection: As you learn about network connections and speeds, this exercise will show you how to do an analysis on your own. It is possible that your Internet connection is not providing the speeds you are paying for! This tool is also useful when your Internet does not seem to be running as quickly as it should. Knowing how to test the speed will help you determine where the possible problem could be.

Prerequisites: There are no prerequisites for this activity.

Activity: Calculating return on investment (ROI) is extremely difficult when it comes to information systems. For example, when network administrators sense a strain on their network (from network diagnostics or user complaints), they may look into upgrading their network.

To get a feel for the type of information someone might see, create your own spreadsheet of data while watching your Internet connection at home. If you are not at home regularly, choose a computer in a convenient location and test the speed there. Go to *www.wiley.com/go/rainer/spreadsheet* and look for the link provided for Chapter 4. This link will take you to "speedtest.net" and the network test will be on the home page asking you to "Begin Test." The test will take only a few minutes. In a new spreadsheet, create columns for the following:

- Date
- Time
- Ping speed
- Upload speed
- Download speed
- Test location (not your location, but the host of the test)

Collect this data for a week, preferably three times a day (i.e., morning, afternoon, and evening). Once you have your 15 data points, create a chart that shows the change in bandwidth available over time. This is exactly what a network administrator might see when trying to determine if it is necessary to upgrade the system. Additionally, calculate the average, minimum, and maximum for each day and for the entire week. Place these data in a chart for quick reference.

Back at *www.wiley.com/go/rainer/spreadsheet*, you will also find a short video on creating charts and graphs to help you create your final product.

Deliverable: The deliverable will be a line chart that shows data speeds over time. *Note:* There is no correct answer, but there are wrong answers if you do not collect enough data or do not create the chart appropriately.

Discussion Questions

1. What is it about a chart that makes it easier to comprehend than raw numbers?
2. Is it possible for charts and graphs to depict real data in a way that misleads the viewer?

[Case Assignment]

Alcoa is a manufacturer of aluminum products. It has several mines around the world, smelters, storage facilities, and manufacturing plants to produce different types of aluminum products sold to distributors and other manufacturing companies. It employs about 2,500 people in 14 countries, has 12 mainframe computing systems, several server farms, and thousands of desktop computer systems in addition to its manufacturing systems. It reduced inventories by a quarter of a billion dollars in one year, while increasing sales by just under $1 billion. Alcoa did all of this because it implemented new e-business systems for the transmission of documents and funds, using new standards that were common to all locations.

Required

a. Several internal audit team members at Alcoa's Canadian subsidiary Kawneer Canada will be working at two different locations: some of you will be working in Georgetown, Ontario, while others will be in Lethbridge, Alberta. Provide four examples of how your team could use information technology to collaborate during the completion of your work.

b. Provide examples of network technology components that would be necessary to support remote collaboration among the audit teams in Toronto and Sydney.

[Team Assignments]

1. Assign each group member to a collaboration product (e.g., Jive, Google Docs, SharePoint, or Quickr). Have each member visit the website of the product and obtain information about it. As a group, prepare a comparative table of the major similarities and differences among the products.

2. Each team will choose one of the following: YourStreet, Topix, or Google Earth. Compare and contrast these products as to features and ease of use. Present each product to the class. Each group will collaborate on writing a report on its product using Google Docs.

[Case 4.2 E-Learning for Nurses]

The Problem

Any magazine with nearly 2.6 million subscribers, 390,000 monthly visits to its website, and 110,000 Facebook fans must be doing something right. But *Scrubs*, a magazine for U.S. nurses, was overdue to move parts of its operations from print to digital.

Scrubs had been providing nurses an opportunity to take continuing education credits by mail. Traditionally, nurses would buy the magazine and fill out the print copy and mail it in. This approach had several challenges for readers. On the one hand, the continuing education material would use several pages of the magazine that could be used to display some other featured material. On the other hand, the mailed-in form with the answers could get lost in the mail and it would take several weeks for the nurse to find out. In addition to that, the magazine needed the ability to process the mailed-in forms and payments.

The Solution

As part of its modernization efforts, The Scrubs Media Group, which publishes *Scrubs* magazine, launched an on-line service called The Scrubs Learning Network. It uses CoursePark.com, the cloud-based on-line e-learning platform from Bluedrop. Bluedrop is a Canadian firm that specializes in designing, developing, and delivering training content on-line.

The Scrubs Learning Network, hosted on CoursePark.com, provides nurses with the accredited nursing continuing education courses they require to meet their annual licensing requirements from the professional bodies in each U.S. state. The network contains more than 200 hours of continuing education courses on topics such as leadership, regulatory issues, and critical patient care. The courses are recognized in all U.S. states. This on-line learning offers nurses a cost-effective way to increasing their professional competence. Nurses can purchase an annual, unlimited continuing education subscription.

The Scrubs Learning Network also provides users with a lifelong learning portfolio tool for certificate management, the ability to rate and comment on courses, and discussion boards for peer-to-peer collaboration. Members of The Scrubs Learning Network also have access to scrubsmag.com, where they can comment on articles and enter giveaways.

The Results

The Scrubs Learning Network ensures that nurses have access to the latest medical industry news as well as a wide number of accredited continuing education courses. It is one more example of how bringing technology and information together can facilitate professional development by helping professionals keep current in their field and connected with colleagues.

Questions

1. What are some of the basic network infrastructure technology required to be able to provide e-learning to employees?
2. Discuss how e-learning could make use of the three main network applications (discovery, communications, and collaboration). Give specific examples of how these network applications could be used in e-learning.
3. Can all types of courses and subjects in business education be fit for delivery on-line? What types of courses are more suitable to e-learning? Justify your answer.

Sources: "Scrubs Magazine Launches New Nursing Continuing Education Program on CoursePark.com®," Bluedrop Performance Learning, press release February 18, 2013, *www.bluedrop.com*; Scrubs magazine, *www.scrubsmag.com/*, accessed April 2013.

[Interactive Case]

ruby's club

Analyzing Network Opportunities for Ruby's Club

Go to the Ruby's Club link at the Student Companion website or *WileyPLUS* for information about your current internship assignment. Your assignment will entail working with data about how Ruby's network can create a better experience for its customers.

Chapter 5

E-Business and E-Commerce

[LEARNING OBJECTIVES]	[CHAPTER OUTLINE]	[WEB RESOURCES]

1. Describe the six common types of electronic commerce; provide specific personal examples of how you have used or could use B2C, C2C, G2C, and mobile commerce; and offer a specific example of B2B and G2B.
2. Discuss the five on-line services of business-to-consumer electronic commerce, provide a specific example of each service, and state how you have used or would use each service.
3. Describe the three business models for business-to-business electronic commerce, and provide a specific example of each model.
4. Describe the four types of electronic payments and provide a specific example of each one.
5. Illustrate the ethical and legal issues relating to electronic commerce with two specific examples of each issue.

Student Companion Site

wiley.com/college/rainer

- Student PowerPoints for note taking
- Interactive Case: Ruby's Club Assignments
- Complete glossary

WileyPlus

All of the above and

- E-book
- Mini-lecture by author for each chapter section
- Practice quizzes
- Flash Cards for vocabulary review
- Additional "What's in IT for Me?" cases
- Video interviews with managers
- Lab Manual for Microsoft Office 2010
- How-to Animations for Microsoft Office 2010

What's In IT For Me?
THIS CHAPTER WILL HELP PREPARE YOU TO ...
ACCT
Audit e-commerce transactions
FIN
Trade securities on-line
MKT
Manage firm's virtual marketplace
POM
Transition from push to pull model
HR
Manage e-commerce legal issues
MIS
Provide IT infrastructure for e-commerce

[Case 5.1 From Social Networks to Social Commerce]

The Problem

We're all familiar with national advertising campaigns for big brands that spend millions on 30-second television commercials, as an example. But did you know that local advertising is also big business? In the United States, for example, advertisers spend about $100 billion every year to try to reach local customers. Much of that money is wasted, because local commerce is highly segmented and inefficient. A small company cannot acquire customers or advertise with the efficiency of a large chain that has multiple locations in the same town. The problem, therefore, is how to make local advertising more efficient and effective for small businesses.

VLADGRIN/Shutterstock

The Solution

The solution may lie in the emerging area of social commerce, as illustrated by Groupon (*www.groupon.com*). Every day, Groupon e-mails its subscribers—more than 200 million globally in 2013 and growing at a rate of 3 million per month—discounts on goods and services, but only if a minimum of people sign up for the deals. The discount could be up to 90 percent off on a hotel room, a restaurant meal, a cooking class, dental work, or just about any product or service available in dozens of cities in 48 countries where Groupon operates. Groupon's social commerce model pays off in three ways: (1) The subscriber gets a better price; (2) the merchant gets additional business and potential new customers; and (3) Groupon receives a share of the revenues generated by the deals.

When Groupon started it merely connected local merchants with local customers, advertising one deal per day because it did not have any merchant relationships. As you can imagine, such e-mail blasts were not targeted. As Groupon became more popular, however, merchants were approaching the company to form relationships and offer deals. Demand became so great that merchants were waiting months for their deal to be featured. To solve this problem, Groupon created Groupon Stores and the Deal Feed.

Instead of waiting for Groupon to organize and publicize a deal, Groupon Stores lets businesses create and launch their own deals whenever they want, without waiting to be featured as the deal of the day. Merchants create Groupon stores without any upfront fee. Groupon then promotes their deals via e-mail, Twitter, and Facebook, while the merchants collect 70 percent of the revenue from each promoted Groupon deal. As part of the promotion, Groupon members can sign up for the Deal Feed, which acts similar to a Twitter feed. Merchants can use the Deal Feed to inform their followers about new deals or special offers. Using software it developed, Groupon selects the best deals from Groupon Stores each day and matches them with customers.

Groupon then refined its business model even further, moving into a phase it calls *hyperlocal*. This involves knowing where subscribers live and what their interests are, becoming familiar with their shopping and leisure experiences, and sharing these experiences with their friends. Groupon then tailors its e-mail blasts to subscribers' cell phones based on what they might like. It also can integrate and popularize deals through social networking sites such as Twitter and Facebook.

The next phase of its business model is *Groupon Now*, offering subscribers two choices: "I'm hungry" and "I'm bored." When you click the "I'm hungry" button, Groupon displays a list of deals from nearby restaurants. Similarly, when you click "I'm bored," Groupon displays a list of nearby events and deals.

Groupon Now works by reducing inefficiencies in the market: by selling off food, labour hours, or anything else that is "perishable," merchants can make money on things that would otherwise go to waste. Groupon claims that Groupon Now will enable businesses to become more like airlines selling off empty seats, matching supply against demand to maximize revenues. For example, a spa could send out a deal on a massage because a customer cancelled, or a gym could run several days of coupons to fill the class of a new yoga instructor.

The Results

Groupon's business model has been wildly successful. The company has about 10,000 employees and sends out more than 900 deals each day in over 550 markets. The company, which launched in 2008, gained 1 million subscribers within a year and went from zero to $500 million in sales within 18 months. In 2012, gross billings rose by 35 percent to $5.4 billion.

While it was a pioneer in the field, today Groupon faces competition from more than 500 companies around the world offering similar services. And that burgeoning market has attracted the interest of Internet giants that want a foothold in social commerce. For example, when Google tried to purchase Groupon in December 2010 for $6 billion, and Groupon turned the offer down, Google promptly became a competitor and developed plans for its own social commerce site, called *Google Offers*. Groupon's biggest rival, LivingSocial (*www.livingsocial.com*), received an infusion of $175 million in 2010 from Amazon, which wanted a piece of the social commerce action. This investment enabled LivingSocial to develop a technology platform from which to expand its base of 10 million subscribers.

In addition to competition, Groupon has other problems. Running a discounted deal can attract so many customers that the deal can actually cost small businesses money. In a survey of 150 small to mid-size businesses that had used Groupon, two thirds said that their Groupon deal was profitable, while the other third found it unprofitable. And in a blow to a service that should rely on repeat business, 40 percent of the respondents stated that they would not use Groupon again, mostly because they did not know what to expect from each Groupon deal; they could be overwhelmed with customers, or not have any customers at all.

What We Learned from This Case

A profound change in the modern world of business is the emergence of electronic commerce, also known as *e-commerce*. E-commerce is transforming all business functional areas and their fundamental tasks, from advertising to paying bills. Its impact is so widespread that it is affecting almost every organization. This means that, regardless of where you work, your organization likely is practising electronic commerce.

Electronic commerce affects organizations in many significant ways. First, it increases an organization's reach, defined as the number of potential customers to whom the company can market its products. In fact, e-commerce provides unparalleled opportunities for companies to expand worldwide at a small cost, to increase market share, and to reduce costs. By using electronic commerce, many small businesses now can operate and compete in market spaces once dominated by larger companies.

Another major impact of electronic commerce has been to remove many of the barriers that previously kept entrepreneurs from starting their own businesses. E-commerce offers amazing opportunities for you to open your own business by developing an e-commerce website.

Electronic commerce also is drastically changing the nature of competition, due to the development of new on-line companies, new business models, and the diversity of electronic commerce-related products and services. Recall your study of competitive strategies in Chapter 2, particularly the impact of the Internet on Porter's five forces. You learned that the Internet can both endanger and enhance a company's position in a given industry. IT's About Small Business 5.1 shows how a small company can use e-commerce to gain a competitive edge in the marketplace.

Case 5.1 on Groupon demonstrated how the company uses social networking to build its social commerce business model. That is, Groupon realized that social networking technologies can provide a direct link between businesses and their customers.

You need to have a working knowledge of electronic commerce because your organization almost certainly will employ e-commerce applications that affect the firm's strategy and business model. This knowledge will make you more valuable to your organization and will enable you to quickly contribute to e-commerce applications in your functional area. When you read the What's in IT for Me? feature at the end of the chapter, envision yourself performing the activities discussed in your functional area.

Going further, you may decide to become an entrepreneur and start your own business. In that case, an understanding of electronic commerce is even more essential for you because e-commerce, with its broad reach, will probably be critical for your business to survive and thrive.

Social commerce is a type of electronic commerce that uses social media to assist in the on-line buying and selling of products and services. Social commerce taps into a community of enthusiasts, builds relationships, anticipates needs, and promotes products with special deals for the community's members. Social commerce efforts include shareable coupons, refer-a-friend programs, loyalty incentives, group promotions, and time-sensitive offers.

The biggest advantage that social commerce enjoys over traditional e-commerce, and even Google Search, is the ability to predict buying habits based on real-time information as opposed to historical data. Google Search cannot anticipate any one person's needs very well; in contrast, that person's friends would know, for example, that she is going to be a grandmother and probably will be shopping for baby products. Social commerce focuses squarely on one-to-one relationships. Still another advantage of social commerce is that it analyzes relationships and interactions within a social community, enabling companies to bring exciting new products to the market more effectively.

In this chapter you will discover the major applications of e-business, and you will be able to identify the services necessary for its support. You then will study the major types of electronic commerce: business-to-consumer (B2C), business-to-business (B2B), consumer-to-consumer (C2C), business-to-employee (B2E), and government-to-citizen (G2C). You conclude by examining several legal and ethical issues that have arisen as a result of the rapid growth of e-commerce.

5.1 Overview of E-Business and E-Commerce

Any entrepreneur or company that decides to practise electronic commerce must develop a strategy to do so effectively. The first step is to determine exactly *why* you want to do business over the Internet using a website. There are several reasons for employing websites:

- To sell goods and services
- To induce people to visit a physical location
- To reduce operational and transaction costs
- To enhance your reputation

A website can accomplish any and all of these goals. Unless a company (or you) has substantial resources, however, it is difficult to accomplish all of them at the same time. The appropriate website for achieving each goal will be somewhat different. When setting up your website, you must consider how the site will generate and retain traffic, as well as a host of other issues. The point here is that, when you are considering electronic commerce, keeping the strategy of the organization or entrepreneur in mind will give you a good idea as to the type of website to use.

This section examines the basics of e-business and e-commerce. First, these two concepts are defined, and then you become familiar with pure and partial electronic commerce. You then take a look at the various types of electronic commerce. Next, you focus on e-commerce mechanisms, which are the ways in which businesses and people buy and sell over the Internet. The section concludes by considering the benefits and limitations of e-commerce.

Sources: Compiled from B. Stone and D. MacMillan, "Are Four Words Worth $25 Billion for Groupon?" *Bloomberg BusinessWeek*, March 17, 2011; B. Saporito, "The Groupon Clipper," *Time*, February 21, 2011; L. Indvik, "Groupon Goes from Local to Hyperlocal with New Ad Campaign," *Forbes*, January 25, 2011; J. O'Dell, "The History of Groupon," *Forbes*, January 7, 2011; E. Anderson, "Groupon Getting It Right," *Forbes*, January 7, 2011; S. Purewal, "Groupon Nightmares (and How to Avoid Them)," *Entrepreneur*, December 10, 2010; S. Gaudin, "Google Expected to Buy or Eclipse Groupon," *Computerworld*, December 6, 2010; K. Burnham, "Groupon 2.0: More Deals and a Personalized Feed," *CIO*, December 1, 2010; J. Galante, "Groupon Coupons: The Small-Biz Challenge," *Bloomberg BusinessWeek*, June 10, 2010; *www.groupon.com*, *www.livingsocial.com*, accessed February 21, 2011; Groupon 2012 annual report.

Definitions and Concepts

Electronic commerce (EC or **e-commerce**) describes the process of buying, selling, transferring, or exchanging products, services, or information via computer networks, including the Internet. **E-business** is a somewhat broader concept. In addition to the buying and selling of goods and services, e-business also refers to servicing customers, collaborating with business partners, and performing electronic transactions within an organization.

Electronic commerce can take several forms depending on the degree of digitization involved. The *degree of digitization* is the extent to which the commerce has been transformed from physical to digital. This concept can relate to both the product or service being sold and the delivery agent or intermediary. In other words, the product can be either physical or digital, and the delivery agent can be either physical or digital.

In traditional commerce, both dimensions are physical. Purely physical organizations are referred to as **brick-and-mortar organizations**. (You may also see the term "bricks-and-mortar.") In contrast, in *pure EC* all dimensions are digital. Companies engaged only in EC are considered **virtual** (or *pure-play*) **organizations**. All other combinations that include a mix of digital and physical dimensions are considered *partial* EC (but not pure EC). **Clicks-and-mortar organizations** are those that conduct some e-commerce activities, yet carry out their primary business in the physical world. (A common alternative to the term "clicks-and-mortar" is "clicks-and-bricks." You will encounter both terms.) Therefore, clicks-and-mortar organizations are examples of partial EC. E-commerce now is so well established that people generally expect all companies to offer this service in some form.

Purchasing a shirt at Walmart.ca or a book from Amazon.ca is partial EC because the merchandise, although bought and paid for digitally, is physically delivered by courier. In contrast, buying an e-book from Amazon.ca or a software product from Buy.com is pure EC because the product itself as well as its delivery, payment, and transfer are digital. To avoid confusion, we use the term "electronic commerce" to denote both pure and partial EC.

Types of E-Commerce

E-commerce can be conducted between and among various parties. In this section, you will identify the six common types of e-commerce, and you will learn about three of them—C2C, B2E, and e-government—in detail. You then consider B2C and B2B in separate sections because they are very complex.

- **Business-to-consumer (B2C)**: In B2C, the sellers are organizations, and the buyers are individuals. You learn about B2C electronic commerce in Section 5.2.
- **Business-to-business (B2B)**: In B2B transactions, both the sellers and the buyers are business organizations. The vast majority of EC volume is of this type. You see B2B electronic commerce in Section 5.3.
- **Consumer-to-consumer (C2C)**: In C2C (also called "customer-to-customer"), an individual sells products or services to other individuals. The major strategies for conducting C2C on the Internet are auctions and classified ads.

In dozens of countries, C2C e-commerce on auction sites is exploding. Most auctions are conducted by intermediaries like eBay (*www.ebay.ca*). Consumers can select general sites such as *www.auctionanything.com*, a company that sells software and services that help individuals and organizations conduct their own auctions. In addition, many individuals are conducting their own auctions. You will learn about reverse auctions, in which buyers solicit bids from sellers, later in this section.

The major categories of on-line classified ads are similar to those found in print ads: vehicles, real estate, employment, pets, tickets, and travel. Classified ads are available through most Internet service providers (such Rogers, Bell, and SaskTel), at some portals (such as Yahoo!), and from Internet directories and on-line newspapers. Many of these sites contain search engines that help shoppers narrow their searches. Craigslist (*www.craigslist.org*) is the largest on-line classified ad provider.

Internet-based classified ads have one big advantage over traditional types of classified ads: They provide access to an international, rather than a local, audience. This wider audience greatly increases both the supply of goods and services and the number of potential buyers. It is important to note that the value of expanded geographic reach depends greatly on what is being bought or sold. For example, you might buy software from a company located 1,000 kilometres away from you, but you would not buy firewood from someone at such a distance.

- **Business-to-employee (B2E):** In B2E, an organization uses EC internally to provide information and services to its employees. For example, companies allow employees to manage their benefits and to take training classes electronically. In addition, employees can buy discounted insurance, travel packages, and tickets to events on the corporate intranet. They also can order supplies and materials electronically. Finally, many companies have electronic corporate stores that sell the company's products to its employees, usually at a discount.
- **E-government:** E-government is the use of Internet technology in general and e-commerce in particular to deliver information and public services to citizens (called *government-to-citizen* or *G2C EC*) and to business partners and suppliers (called *government-to-business* or *G2B EC*). G2B EC is much like B2B EC, usually with an overlay of government procurement regulations. That is, G2B EC and B2B EC are similar conceptually. However, the functions of G2C EC are different from anything that exists in the private sector (e.g., B2C EC).

  E-government is also an efficient way of conducting business transactions with citizens and businesses and within the governments themselves. E-government makes government more efficient and effective, especially in the delivery of public services. An example of G2C electronic commerce is electronic benefits transfer, in which governments transfer benefits, such as employment insurance and Canada Pension Plan payments, directly to recipients' bank accounts.
- **Mobile commerce (m-commerce):** The term *m-commerce* refers to e-commerce that is conducted entirely in a wireless environment. An example is using cell phones to shop over the Internet. You will learn about m-commerce in Chapter 6.

Each of the above types of EC is executed in one or more business models. A **business model** is the method by which a company generates revenue to sustain itself. Table 5.1 summarizes the major EC business models. Other classifications of EC business models include Michael Rappa's Business Models on the Web (*http://digitalenterprise.org/models*).

E-Commerce and Search

The development of e-commerce has proceeded in phases. Initial e-commerce efforts consisted of flashy brochure sites with rudimentary shopping carts and checkout systems. They were then replaced with systems that tried to anticipate customer needs and accelerate checkout.

However, one of the biggest changes in recent times has been the growing importance of search in the overall e-commerce experience. For example, Google justifies the importance of online searches because a higher number of purchases follow successful web searches compared to nonproductive searches where online shoppers tend to abandon their shopping carts. In other words, if you are able to quickly find that product you are looking for and the information you need to make a decision, then you are more likely to buy it in that online session. If, on the other hand, you are not able to find the product and/or the information you need to make an informed decision about your purchase, you are more likely to abandon your shopping cart even though you might have initially decided to buy it.

Google is confident that in the future, retailers will post tremendous amounts of additional details. Merchants will pour continuous structured feeds of data—including product listings, daily inventory, and hours of operation—into public search engines such as Google. Google currently is using Google Base, the company's on-line database, to work on this process. This process would allow customers to access much more specific and relevant search results.

Major E-Commerce Mechanisms

There are many mechanisms through which businesses and customers can buy and sell on the Internet. The most widely used are electronic catalogues, electronic auctions, e-storefronts, e-malls, and e-marketplaces.

TABLE 5.1

E-Commerce Business Models

EC Model	Description
On-line direct marketing	Manufacturers or retailers sell directly to customers. Very efficient for digital marketing of products and services. Can allow for product or service customization (*www.dell.ca*).
Electronic tendering system	Businesses request quotes from suppliers. Uses B2B with a reverse auction mechanism.
Name-your-own-price	Customers decide how much they are willing to pay. An intermediary (for example, *www.priceline.com*) tries to match a provider.
Find-the-best-price	Customers specify a need; an intermediary (for example, *www.hotwire.com*) compares providers and shows the lowest price. Customers must accept the offer in a short time or they may lose the deal.
Affiliate marketing	Vendors ask partners to place logos (or banners) on partners' sites. If customers click on the logo, go to the vendor's site, and buy, then the vendor pays commissions to partners.
Viral marketing	Receivers send information about your product to their friends.
Group purchasing (co-ops)	Small buyers aggregate demand to get a large volume. The group then conducts tendering or negotiates a low price.
On-line auctions	Companies run auctions of various types on the Internet. Very popular in C2C, but gaining ground in other types of EC (*www.ebay.ca*).
Product customization	Customers use the Internet to self-configure products or services. Sellers then price them and fulfill them quickly (*build-to-order*) (*www.jaguar.com*).
Electronic marketplaces and exchanges	Transactions are conducted efficiently (more information to buyers and sellers, lower transaction costs) in electronic marketplaces (private or public).
Bartering on-line	Intermediary administers on-line exchange of surplus products and/or company receives "points" for its contribution, which can be used to purchase other needed items (*www.bbu.com*).
Deep discounters	Companies (for example, *www.half.ebay.com*) offer deep price discounts. Appeals to customers who consider only price in their purchasing decisions.
Membership	Only members can use the services provided, including access to certain information and conducting trades (*www.egreetings.com*).

Catalogues have been printed on paper for generations. Today, however, they are available on CD-ROM and the Internet. Electronic catalogues consist of a product database, directory and search capabilities, and a presentation function. They are the backbone of most e-commerce sites.

An **auction** is a competitive process in which either a seller solicits consecutive bids from buyers or a buyer solicits bids from sellers. The primary characteristic of auctions is that prices are determined dynamically by competitive bidding. Electronic auctions (e-auctions) generally increase revenues for sellers by broadening the customer base and shortening the cycle time of the auction. Buyers generally benefit from e-auctions because they can bargain for lower prices. In addition, they don't have to travel to an auction at a physical location.

The Internet provides an efficient infrastructure for conducting auctions at lower administrative costs and with many more involved sellers and buyers. Individual consumers and corporations alike can participate in auctions. There are two major types of auctions: forward and reverse.

Forward auctions are auctions that sellers use as a channel to many potential buyers. Usually, sellers place items at sites for auction, and buyers bid continuously for them. The highest bidder wins the items. Both sellers and buyers can be individuals or businesses. The popular auction site eBay.com is a forward auction.

In **reverse auctions**, one buyer, usually an organization, wants to buy a product or a service. The buyer posts a request for quotation (RFQ) on its website or on a third-party site. The RFQ provides detailed information on the desired purchase. The suppliers study the RFQ and then submit bids electronically. Everything else being equal, the lowest-price bidder wins the auction. The reverse auction is the most common auction model for large purchases (in terms of either quantities or price). Governments and large corporations frequently use this approach, which may provide considerable savings for the buyer.

Auctions can be conducted from the seller's site, the buyer's site, or a third party's site. For example, eBay, the best-known third-party site, offers hundreds of thousands of different items in several types of auctions. Overall, more than 300 major companies, including Amazon.com and Dellauction.com, offer on-line auctions.

An *electronic storefront* is a website that represents a single store. An *electronic mall*, also known as a *cybermall* or *e-mall*, is a collection of individual shops under one Internet address. Electronic storefronts and electronic malls are closely associated with B2C electronic commerce. You will study each one in more detail in Section 5.2.

An **electronic marketplace (e-marketplace)** is a central, virtual market space on the web where many buyers and many sellers can conduct e-commerce and e-business activities. Electronic marketplaces are associated with B2B electronic commerce. You will learn about electronic marketplaces in Section 5.3.

Benefits and Limitations of E-Commerce

Few innovations in human history have provided as many benefits to organizations, individuals, and society as e-commerce has. E-commerce benefits organizations by making national and international markets more accessible and by lowering the costs of processing, distributing, and retrieving information. Customers benefit by being able to access a vast number of products and services, around the clock. The major benefit to society is the ability to easily and conveniently deliver information, services, and products to people in cities, rural areas, and developing countries.

Despite all these benefits, EC has some limitations, both technological and non-technological, that have restricted its growth and acceptance. One major technological limitation is the lack of universally accepted security standards. Also, in less-developed countries, telecommunications bandwidth often is insufficient, and accessing the web is expensive. Non-technological limitations include the perceptions that EC is insecure, has unresolved legal issues, and lacks a critical mass of sellers and buyers. As time passes, the limitations, especially the technological ones, will diminish or be overcome.

before you go on...

1. Define e-commerce, and distinguish it from e-business.
2. Differentiate among B2C, B2B, C2C, and B2E electronic commerce.
3. Define e-government.
4. Describe the key characteristics of forward and reverse auctions.
5. Identify some benefits and limitations of e-commerce.

IT's about [small] business

5.1 Vending Goes On-line

Treat America Food Services (*www.treatamerica.com*) is, among other things, a vending machine company. Doctors' offices, colleges and universities, hospitals, and other organizations contract with Treat America to provide vending services to their customers and employees. The problem is that Treat America's vending machines are unstaffed most of the time. The company has no idea how much money or product is in each machine, or even if someone has broken into it. With gas prices rapidly increasing, it is becoming prohibitively expensive for Treat America to monitor vending machines by driving to each machine's location. Many of the firm's competitors have simply raised prices. Treat America, however, found a better solution: e-business.

E-business refers to performing any "normal" business activity with the assistance of computer-based information systems and networks. Treat America determined that it essentially needed only a few simple pieces of information on each machine. Consequently, the company installed a small device on top of each machine that communicates with headquarters via a cellular connection. The device reports the amount of money in the machine at any given minute, the amount of product inventory remaining, whether the machine has been moved, and whether the door has been opened after business hours.

The company's efforts paid off. In one location, for example, when thieves broke into a vending machine, the attached device automatically alerted the customer and the police that the door was open after hours. Police caught the culprits in action and arrested them. In another store, several employees quit when they could no longer steal from the vending machine. As an added benefit, Treat America's customers now use less gas because they can check inventory on-line without having to drive to each machine to check quantities and to restock. This on-line feature costs Treat America's customers approximately $150 per machine per year—a minimal amount considering how much money the system saves customers in theft and fuel.

Questions

1. Provide two examples of how the technology added to the vending machines gives Treat America a competitive advantage.
2. Is this competitive advantage sustainable for any length of time? Why or why not? Support your answer using Porter's five forces competitive model.

Sources: Compiled from J. Smith, "Vending Machines Go High-Tech with Wireless, Web-Based Systems," *The Kansas City Star*, April 10, 2011; *http://treatamerica.com*, accessed April 21, 2011.

5.2 Business-to-Consumer (B2C) Electronic Commerce

B2B EC is much larger than B2C EC by volume, but B2C EC is more complex. The reason is that B2C involves a large number of buyers making millions of diverse transactions per day with a relatively small number of sellers. As an illustration, consider Amazon, an on-line retailer that offers thousands of products to its customers. Each customer's purchase is relatively small, but Amazon must manage that transaction as if that customer were its most important one. Each order must be processed quickly and efficiently, and the products must be shipped to the customer in a timely manner. In addition, returns must be managed. Multiply this simple example by millions, and you get an idea of the complexity of B2C EC. Overall, B2B complexities tend to be more business related, whereas B2C complexities tend to be more technical and volume related.

This section addresses the primary issues in B2C EC. You begin by studying the two basic mechanisms that customers use to access companies on the web: electronic storefronts and electronic malls. In addition to purchasing products over the web, customers also access on-line services. Therefore, the next section covers several on-line services, such as banking, securities trading, job searching, and travel. The complexity of B2C EC creates two major challenges for sellers: channel conflict and order fulfillment. You will examine these two topics in detail. Finally, companies engaged in B2C EC must "get the word out" to prospective customers. Therefore, this section concludes with a look at on-line advertising.

Electronic Storefronts and Malls

For several generations, home shopping from catalogues, and later from television shopping channels, has attracted millions of customers. Today, shopping on-line offers an alternative to catalogue and television shopping. **Electronic retailing (e-tailing)** is the direct sale of products and services through electronic storefronts or electronic malls, usually designed around an electronic catalogue format and/or auctions.

Like any mail-order shopping experience, e-commerce enables you to buy from home 24 hours a day, 7 days a week. However, EC also offers a wider variety of products and services, including unique items, often at lower prices. Further, within seconds, shoppers can access very detailed

[about business]

5.2 Luxury Goods Turn to E-Commerce

It seems the very opposite of luxury. Instead of buying an iconic Louis Vuitton bag in an exclusive store with plush fixtures and well-manicured and attentive staff, more consumers are buying luxury items while staring at a computer screen.

In recent years, more major luxury goods companies have realized that selling their items on-line does not take away from their posh image. Labels such as Richemont (*www.richemont.com*), Burberry (*www.burberry.com*), and LVMH Moët Hennessy Louis Vuitton (*www.lvmh.com*) have launched e-commerce. High-end retail websites such as Net-a-Porter (*www.net-a-porter.com*) and Yoox (*www.yoox.com*), as well as discount luxury flash sales websites such as Gilt Groupe (*www.gilt.com*) and Rue La La (*www.ruelala.com*), have forced executives in the well-known luxury brands to rethink the benefits of on-line sales. In fact, Bain & Company (*www.bain.com*) estimates that the on-line luxury market grew by 10 percent in 2012 and was on track to reach 250 billion euros in sales by 2015.

However, selling $1,000 dresses on-line is different from selling a $10 book. Luxury consumers don't want a point-and-click transaction; they want an on-line shopping experience, including a guide to the latest styles. To provide this guiding hand, Swiss luxury goods maker Richemont purchased Net-a-Porter. Richemont is the owner of brands such as Cartier (*www.cartier.com*), Montblanc (*www.montblanc.com*), Van Cleef & Arpels (*www.vancleef-arpels.com*), and Chloé (*www.chloe.com*). Net-a-Porter ups the e-tailing ante by offering an interactive shopping fashion magazine that publishes 52 weeks of editorial content each year in addition to its designer clothes sales operations.

But even luxury consumers love a bargain. In 2009, Net-a-Porter launched a sister website, theOutnet.com (*www.outnet.com*), which offers discounted designer clothes. This move enables Net-a-Porter to compete with other companies that operate flash sales of high-end merchandise at sometimes rock-bottom discounts. Competitors include Gilt, Rue La La, Amazon's MyHabit, and eBay (*www.ebay.com*).

How do the flash sales websites operate? The Gilt Groupe, for example, operates an invitation-only website, offering subscribers exclusive and short-lived sales reminiscent of the designer sample sales previously only available to shoppers in cities such as New York. Shortly before noon, Gilt sends an e-mail to its millions of members, alerting them of the day's sales. Shoppers then have only 36 hours to snap up the limited number of deeply discounted designer clothes, which stirs the impulse buying that bricks-and-mortar stores excel at.

The Gilt Group (and companies like it) has had an enormous impact on how well-known luxury brands view electronic commerce. First, Gilt has forced luxury brands to embrace the Internet. For example, while e-commerce had been entrenched for over a decade, it wasn't until 2010 that Marc Jacobs (*www.marcjacobs.com*), Jimmy Choo (*www.jimmychoo.com*), and Donna Karan (*www.donnakaran.com*) added retail sales to their websites. Burberry now offers select pieces from its runway shows for a limited time on its website just hours after its Fashion Week show. Second, discount designer websites have changed how the fashion industry works, allowing smaller brands that, unlike the better-known brands, do not have large retail outlets to sell older merchandise at a discount. Third, these companies have democratized fashion, giving consumers everywhere access to the most exclusive brands at insider prices that shoppers could formerly get only in fashion capitals such as New York City and London. Finally, these designer sites have changed the way we shop. Instead of hanging out at the mall, fashionistas now sit by their smart phones, waiting for the daily deals to pop in their inbox to scoop up the latest designer bargains.

The end result for the luxury goods market? These firms are embracing the 21st-century model for luxury fashion retailing, namely, electronic commerce.

Questions

1. Provide two specific examples of luxury shoppers' requirements that a website could not provide.
2. What features are provided by on-line luxury retailers that overcome the problems you mentioned in Question 1?

Sources: Compiled from R. Laneri, "Gilt Groupe Founders: The Most Powerful People in Fashion?" *Forbes,* November 9, 2010; P. Sonne, "Richemont to Buy Net-a-Porter," *The Wall Street Journal,* April 2, 2010; A. Lee, "Luxury Goes Digital: Fashion House Richemont Embraces E-Commerce," *Fast Company,* April 1, 2010; A. Rice, "What's a Dress Worth," *The New York Magazine,* February 14, 2010; "Worldwide Luxury Goods Continues Double-Digit Annual Growth," Bain & Company news release, May 16, 2013.

supplementary product information. In addition, they can easily locate and compare competitors' products and prices. Finally, buyers can find hundreds of thousands of sellers. Two popular on-line shopping mechanisms are electronic storefronts and electronic malls.

Electronic Storefronts. As noted earlier, an **electronic storefront** is a website that represents a single store. Hundreds of thousands of electronic storefronts can be found on the Internet. Each has its own uniform resource locator (URL), or Internet address, at which buyers can place orders. Some electronic storefronts are extensions of physical stores, such as Future Shop, Chapters, and Sears. Others are new businesses started by entrepreneurs who discovered a niche on the web (e.g., TigerDirect.ca and Abebooks.com). Manufacturers (e.g., *www.dell.ca*) and retailers (e.g., *www.staples.ca*) also use storefronts.

Despite the proliferation of e-businesses, questions have lingered about whether selling luxury goods on-line would be successful. IT's About Business 5.2 answers this question.

Electronic Malls. Whereas an electronic storefront represents a single store, an **electronic mall**, also known as a *cybermall* or an *e-mall*, is a collection of individual shops grouped under a single Internet address. The basic idea of an electronic mall is the same as that of a regular shopping mall—to provide a one-stop shopping place that offers a wide range of products and services.

There are two types of cybermalls. In the first type, known as *referral malls* (e.g., *http://yahoo.shoptoit.ca*), you cannot buy anything. Instead, you are transferred from the mall to a participating storefront. In the second type of mall (e.g., *www.shop.ca*), you can actually make a purchase (see Figure 5.1). At this type of mall, you might shop at several stores, but make only one purchase transaction at the end. You use an *electronic shopping cart* to gather items from various vendors and then pay for them all together in a single transaction. The mall organizer, such as Yahoo! or Shop.ca, takes a commission from the sellers for this service.

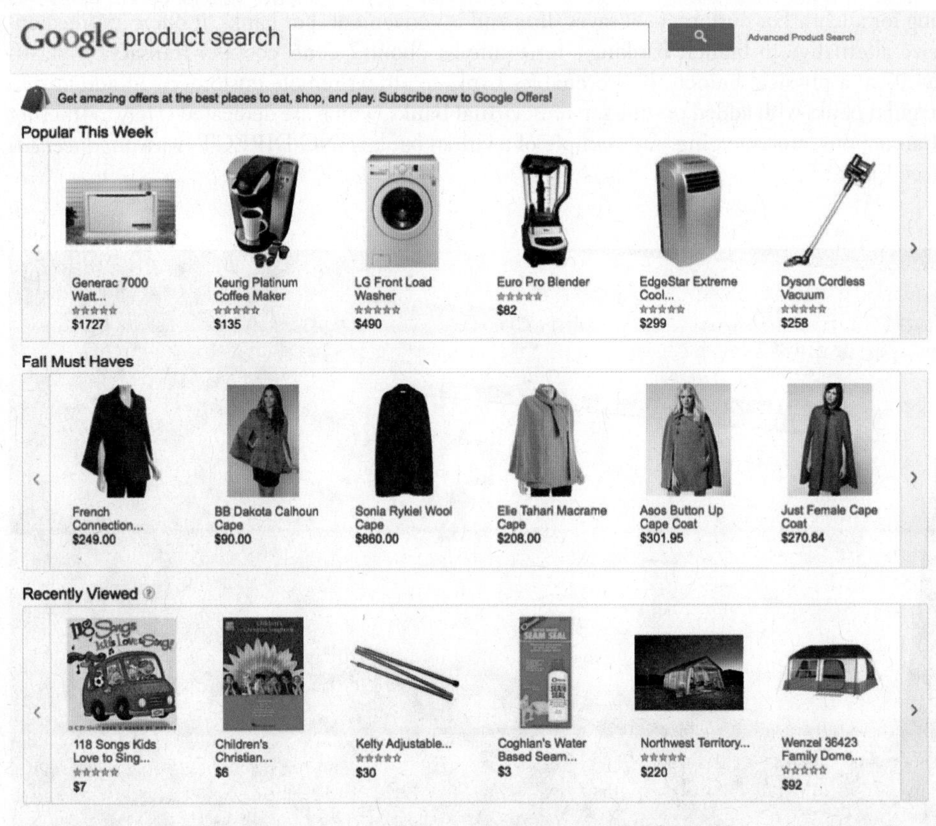

FIGURE 5.1 Electronic malls include products from many vendors. (*Source*: Google and the Google logo are registered trademarks of Google Inc., used with permission.)

On-line Service Industries

In addition to purchasing products, customers can also access needed services via the web. Selling books, toys, computers, and most other products on the Internet can reduce vendors' selling costs by 20 to 40 percent. Further reduction is difficult to achieve because the products must be delivered physically. Only a few products, such as software or music, can be digitized and then delivered on-line for additional savings. In contrast, services, such as buying an airline ticket and purchasing stocks or insurance, can be delivered entirely through e-commerce, often with considerable cost reduction. Not surprisingly, then, on-line delivery of services is growing very rapidly, with millions of new customers being added each year.

One of the most pressing EC issues relating to on-line services (as well as in marketing tangible products) is disintermediation. Intermediaries, also known as *middlemen*, have two functions: (1) they provide information, and (2) they perform value-added services such as consulting. The first function can be fully automated and most likely will be assumed by e-marketplaces and portals that provide information for free. When this occurs, the intermediaries who perform only (or primarily) this function are likely to be eliminated. This process is called **disintermediation**.

In contrast, performing value-added services requires expertise. Unlike the information function, therefore, this function can be only partially automated. Thus, intermediaries who provide value-added services not only are likely to survive, but may actually prosper. The web helps these employees in two situations: (1) when the number of participants is enormous, as with job searches, and (2) when the information that must be exchanged is complex.

In this section, you will examine some leading on-line service industries: banking, trading of securities (stocks, bonds), job matching, travel services, and on-line advertising.

Cyberbanking.

Electronic banking, also known as **cyberbanking**, involves conducting various banking activities from home, at a place of business, or on the road instead of at a physical bank location. Electronic banking has capabilities ranging from paying bills to applying for a loan. For customers, it saves time and is convenient. For banks, it offers an inexpensive alternative to branch banking—for example, about 2 cents cost per transaction versus $1.07 at a physical branch. It also enables banks to attract remote customers. In addition to regular banks with added on-line services, **virtual banks**, which are dedicated solely to Internet transactions, are emerging. An example of a virtual bank is ING DIRECT (*www.ingdirect.ca*) (see Figure 5.2).

FIGURE 5.2 ING DIRECT Canada. (*Source:* © Newscast/Alamy)

International banking and the ability to handle trading in multiple currencies are critical for international trade. Transfers of electronic funds and electronic letters of credit are important services in international banking. For example, banks and companies such as OANDA (*www.oanda.com*) provide conversions of more than 160 currencies.

On-line Securities Trading. Many Canadians use computers to trade stocks, bonds, and other financial instruments. Around the world, several well-known securities companies, including E*Trade and Charles Schwab, offer only on-line trading. In South Korea, more than half of stock traders are already using the Internet for that purpose. Why? Because it is cheaper than a full-service or discount broker. Further, on the web, investors can find a considerable amount of information regarding specific companies or mutual funds in which to invest (via, for example, *www.bnn.ca* and *www.bloomberg.com*).

For example, let's say you have an account with TDwaterhouse.ca. You access the *www.tdwaterhouse.ca* website from your personal computer or your Internet-enabled mobile device, enter your account number and password to access your personalized web page, and then click on "stock trading." Using a menu, you enter the details of your order—buy or sell, margin or cash, price limit, market order, and so on. The computer informs you of the current "ask" and "bid" prices, much as a broker would do over the telephone. You then can approve or reject the transaction.

The On-line Job Market. The Internet offers a promising new environment for job seekers and for companies searching for hard-to-find employees. Thousands of companies and government agencies advertise available positions, accept resumés, and take applications via the Internet.

Job seekers use the on-line job market to reply to employment ads, to place resumés on various job sites and social networking sites, and to use recruiting firms (e.g., *www.monster.ca*, *www.workopolis.com*, and *www.linkedin.com*). Companies that have jobs to offer advertise these openings on their websites, and they search the bulletin boards of recruiting firms. In many countries, governments must advertise job openings on the Internet.

Travel Services. The Internet is an ideal place to plan, explore, and arrange almost any trip economically. On-line travel services allow you to purchase airline tickets, reserve hotel rooms, and rent cars. Most sites also offer a fare-tracker feature that sends you e-mail messages about low-cost flights. Examples of comprehensive on-line travel services are Expedia.ca, Travelocity.ca, and itravel2000.com. On-line services are also provided by all major airline vacation services, large conventional travel agencies, car rental agencies, hotels (e.g., *www.hotels.ca*), and tour companies. In a variation of this process, Priceline.com allows you to set a price you are willing to pay for an airline ticket or hotel accommodations. It then attempts to find a vendor that will match your price.

One costly problem that e-commerce can cause is "mistake fares" in the airline industry. For example, over the weekend of May 4–6, 2007, United Airlines offered a $1,221 fare for a round trip from the United States to New Zealand in business class. This price was incorrect; the actual price was much higher. By the time United noticed the mistake and pulled the fare, however, hundreds of tickets had been sold, thanks in part to on-line travel discussion groups.

On-line Advertising. *Advertising* is the practice of disseminating information in an attempt to influence a buyer–seller transaction. Traditional advertising on TV or in newspapers is impersonal, one-way mass communication. In contrast, direct-response marketing, or telemarketing, contacts individuals by direct mail or telephone and requires them to respond in order to make a purchase. The direct-response approach personalizes advertising and marketing. At the same time, however, it can be expensive, slow, and ineffective. It also can be extremely annoying to the consumer.

Internet advertising redefines the advertising process, making it media-rich, dynamic, and interactive. It improves on traditional forms of advertising in a number of ways. First, Internet ads can be updated any time at minimal cost and therefore can be kept current. In addition, these ads can reach very large numbers of potential buyers all over the world. Further, they are generally cheaper than radio, television, and print ads. Finally, Internet ads can be interactive and targeted to specific interest groups and/or individuals.

Advertising Methods. The most common on-line advertising methods are banners, pop-ups, and e-mail. **Banners** are simply electronic billboards. Typically, a banner contains a short text or

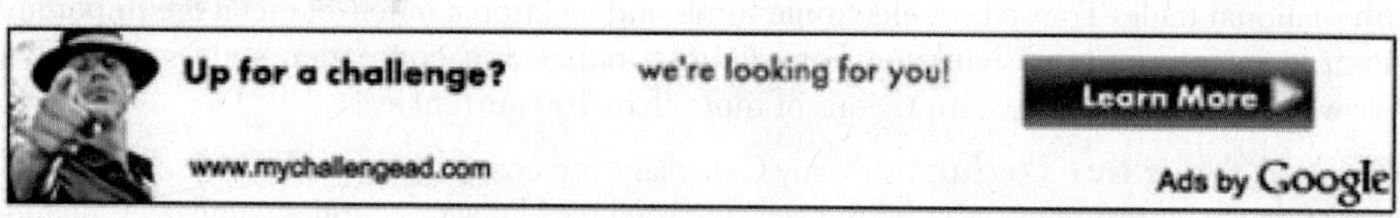

FIGURE 5.3 When customers click on a banner ad, they are transferred to the vendor's homepage. (*Source:* Google and the Google logo are registered trademarks of Google Inc., used with permission.)

graphical message that promotes a product or a vendor. It may even contain video clips and sound. When customers click on a banner, they are transferred to the advertiser's home page. Banner advertising is the most commonly used form of advertising on the Internet (see Figure 5.3).

A major advantage of banners is that they can be customized to the target audience. If the computer system knows who you are or what your profile is, it might send you a banner targeted to match your interests. A major disadvantage of banners is that they can convey only limited information due to their small size. Another drawback is that many viewers simply ignore them.

Pop-up and pop-under ads are contained in a new browser window that is automatically launched when you enter or exit a website. A **pop-up ad** appears in front of the current browser window. A **pop-under ad** appears underneath the active window, and when the active window is closed, the ad appears. Many users strongly object to these ads, which they consider intrusive. Modern browsers let users block pop-up ads, but this feature must be used with caution because some websites depend on pop-up capabilities to present content other than advertising. For example, when customers log on to their Verizon e-mail page, they also see brief (one-line) summaries of recent news stories. If you hover your mouse over one of them, a pop-up window appears with an extended summary (a few paragraphs) of that story. Another example is the WebCT Vista software for on-line instruction, where discussion group posts appear in pop-up windows. Blocking pop-ups would make the first of these two examples less useful and would eliminate important functionality from the second example.

E-mail is emerging as an Internet advertising and marketing channel. It is generally cost effective to implement, and it provides a better and quicker response rate than other advertising channels. Marketers develop or purchase a list of e-mail addresses, place them in a customer database, and then send advertisements via e-mail. A list of e-mail addresses can be a very powerful tool because the marketer can target a group of people or even individuals.

As you have probably concluded by now, there is a potential for misuse of e-mail advertising. In fact, some consumers receive a flood of unsolicited e-mail, or *spam*. **Spamming** is the indiscriminate distribution of electronic ads without the permission of the receiver. Unfortunately, spamming is becoming worse over time.

Two important responses to spamming are permission marketing and viral marketing. **Permission marketing** asks consumers to give their permission to voluntarily accept on-line advertising and e-mail. Typically, consumers are asked to complete an electronic form that asks what they are interested in and requests permission to send related marketing information. Sometimes, consumers are offered incentives to receive advertising.

Permission marketing is the basis of many Internet marketing strategies. For example, thousands of users periodically receive e-mails from airlines such as Air Canada and WestJet. Users of this marketing service can ask to be notified of low fares from their hometown or to their favourite destinations. Significantly, they can easily unsubscribe at any time. Permission marketing is also extremely important for market research (for example, see the Media Metrix suite at *www.comscore.com*).

In one particularly interesting form of permission marketing, companies such as CashSurfers.com have built customer lists of millions of people who are happy to receive advertising messages whenever they are on the web. These customers are paid $0.25 to $0.50 an hour to view messages while they do their normal surfing.

Viral marketing is on-line "word-of-mouth" marketing. The strategy behind viral marketing is to have people forward messages to friends, family members, and other acquaintances suggesting they "check this out." For example, a marketer can distribute a small game program embedded with a sponsor's e-mail that is easy to forward. The marketer releases only a few thousand copies, with the expectation that the recipients, in turn, will forward the program to many more thousands of potential customers. In this way, viral marketing enables companies to build brand awareness at a minimal cost without having to spam millions of uninterested users.

On-line Advertising on Social Networks. On-line advertising on social networks has become more successful over time. This type of advertising takes several forms, including self-service advertising, brand advertising, performance-based advertising, and impression-based advertising.

Self-service advertising is advertising purchased without the assistance of a sales representative. By eliminating the expense of a sales representative, a social networking company can offer smaller minimum ad buys than would otherwise be practical or profitable. Also, using text ads rather than banner ads makes self-service advertising easier for small businesses that do not have compelling graphical ads. Self-service advertising enables companies to carefully target very small groups. For example, Facebook allows advertisers to target "Americans who are married or engaged and are avid flyfishers."

Brand advertising relies on large advertising campaigns that emphasize the company's brand and use special features like fan pages that are unique to Facebook and other social networking sites. Typically, a company that runs a brand advertising campaign on a social networking site will create a fan page for free. The advertising company pays the social networking site for premium ad placement that drives users to the fan page, where they can interact with the brand.

With *performance-based advertising*, the advertising company pays only for measurable results; that is, when someone clicks on a company's ad and goes on to purchase something. For example, today many universities place precisely targeted ads on Facebook because the right sorts of people view the ads, click on them, and sign up for on-line courses. Facebook is paid only when customers actually enroll for classes.

Impression-based advertising occurs when a company purchases a set amount of impressions. An *impression* is a single instance of an ad appearing on a website. Impression-based advertising is typically cheaper than *click-through advertising*, where a company pays only when someone clicks on its ad.

Issues in E-Tailing

Despite e-tailing's increasing popularity, many e-tailers continue to face serious issues that can restrict their growth. Perhaps the two major issues are channel conflict and order fulfillment.

Clicks-and-mortar companies may face a conflict with their regular distributors when they sell directly to customers on-line. This situation, known as **channel conflict**, can alienate the distributors. Channel conflict has forced some companies to avoid direct on-line sales. For example, Walmart, Lowe's, and Home Depot would rather have customers come to their stores. Therefore, although all three companies maintain e-commerce websites, their sites place more emphasis on providing information—products, prices, specials, and store locations—than on on-line sales.

Channel conflict can arise in areas such as pricing and resource allocation; for example, how much money to spend on advertising. Another potential source of conflict involves the logistics services provided by the off-line activities to the on-line activities. For example, how should a company handle returns of items purchased on-line? Some companies have completely separated the "clicks" (the on-line portion of the organization) from the "mortar" or "bricks" (the traditional physical part of the organization). However, this approach can increase expenses and reduce the synergy between the two organizational channels. As a result, many companies are integrating their on-line and off-line channels, a process known as **multichannelling**. IT's About Business 5.3 illustrates how the on-line channel is causing problems for the Hong Kong Jockey Club.

The second major issue confronting e-commerce is order fulfillment, which can create problems for e-tailers as well. Any time a company sells directly to customers, it is involved in various order-fulfillment activities: quickly finding the products to be shipped; packing them; arranging for the packages to be delivered speedily to the customer's door; collecting the money from every customer, either in advance or by individual bill; and handling the return of unwanted or defective products.

IT's [about business]

5.3 Hong Kong's Jockey Club in a Race

In many jurisdictions, gamblers have dozens of opportunities for betting on horses, playing the lottery, and other ways to part with their money. In Hong Kong, however, the only legal form of horse racing and lottery is run by the Hong Kong Jockey Club (*www.hkjc.com*). The Jockey Club, established in 1884 under British rule, is one of the many clubs that form the high society in one of the world's richest cities. Unlike other clubs, the Jockey Club makes money. Although a non-profit organization, it enjoys a government-granted monopoly on horse racing and lotteries. In return, the club remits a portion of its revenues to the government, making it Hong Kong's single-largest taxpayer. Betting is big business, as the club accounts for approximately 8 percent of the government's total revenues.

Jockey Club customers bet an average of $15 billion each year. For every dollar earned, the club returned 82 cents to winning bettors as dividends and payouts. The club claimed the remaining 18 cents on the dollar as revenue. Of this, it paid 64 percent to the government. That is an unusually high tax rate for such operations around the world. The Jockey Club says it gives about $193 million a year to charity. The club has almost 27,000 full- and part-time employees, making it one of the largest private employers in Hong Kong.

Over the decades, the Jockey Club has seen its share of adversity, from equine flu and the Japanese occupation to bribery scandals and the end of British colonial rule. But what is seriously threatening its existence now is something that can't even be seen or touched: the Internet. You could call the club a "tracks and mortar" organization, as it operates two horse-racing tracks where its members still gather to bet on the races. But more and more of the money wagered is bypassing the club in favour of unauthorized betting websites.

The club estimates that its unauthorized competitors take bets on Hong Kong horse races equal to somewhere between 33 percent and 100 percent of the club's revenues. Further, because betting websites have virtually no overhead—they pay neither Hong Kong taxes nor track expenses—they can offer more attractive odds. To add insult to injury, many of these sites aren't even in Hong Kong, but are based in faraway locations such as the South Pacific island of Vanuatu and Curacao in the Caribbean, so authorities are powerless to go after them.

The Jockey Club does have a web presence. About one third of the club's bets on horse racing now come through its website or mobile devices. One potential saving grace for the club is its solid reputation as Hong Kong's only track operator, which may mean that many gamblers may not trust unregulated websites and would prefer to bet through its site.

Another option for the club to fight on-line bookmakers is to link up with racing courses elsewhere to pool bets, which would let track operators offer better odds because more money is at stake. In Hong Kong, however, the Jockey Club's overseas revenue would be taxed both at home and in the country where the bet was made, eliminating any profit. To make that business model work, the Jockey Club would need the political will to help it survive in the Internet age. To that end, the Hong Kong government would have to consider a change in its tax policy.

Questions

1. What competitive advantages does the Hong Kong Jockey Club already have in its competition with on-line betting websites?
2. Use specific examples to describe other measures that the Hong Kong Jockey Club might take to compete with betting websites.

Sources: Compiled from "For Hong Kong's Jockey Club, the Race is Online," *Bloomberg BusinessWeek*, February 21–27, 2011; S. Oster, "Scandal Hits Hong Kong's Exclusive Jockey Club," *The Wall Street Journal*, December 2, 2010; *www.hkjc.com*, accessed March 19, 2011.

It is very difficult to accomplish these activities both effectively and efficiently in B2C, because a company has to ship small packages to many customers and do it quickly. For this reason, companies involved in B2C activities often experience difficulties in their supply chains.

In addition to providing customers with the products they ordered and doing it on time, order fulfillment also provides all related customer services. For example, the customer must receive assembly and operation instructions for a new appliance. In addition, if the customer is not happy with a product, an exchange or return must be arranged. (Visit *www.fedex.com* to see how returns are handled via FedEx.)

In the late 1990s, e-tailers faced continuous problems in order fulfillment, especially during the holiday season. These problems included late deliveries, delivering wrong items, high delivery costs, and compensation to unhappy customers. For e-tailers, taking orders over the Internet is the easy part of B2C e-commerce. Delivering orders to customers' doors is the hard part. In contrast, order fulfillment is less complicated in B2B. These transactions are much larger, but they are fewer in number. In addition, these companies have had order fulfillment mechanisms in place for many years.

before you go on...

1. Describe electronic storefronts and malls.
2. Discuss various types of on-line services, such as cyberbanking, securities trading, job searches, and travel services.
3. Discuss on-line advertising, its methods, and its benefits.
4. Identify the major issues relating to e-tailing.
5. What are spamming, permission marketing, and viral marketing?

5.3 Business-to-Business (B2B) Electronic Commerce

In *business to business (B2B)* e-commerce, the buyers and sellers are business organizations. B2B comprises about 85 percent of EC volume. It covers a broad spectrum of applications that enable an enterprise to form electronic relationships with its distributors, resellers, suppliers, customers, and other partners. Organizations can use B2B to restructure their supply chains and their partner relationships.

There are several business models for B2B applications. The major ones are sell-side marketplaces, buy-side marketplaces, and electronic exchanges.

Sell-Side Marketplaces

In the **sell-side marketplace** model, organizations attempt to sell their products or services to other organizations electronically from their own private e-marketplace website and/or from a third-party website. This model is similar to the B2C model in which the buyer is expected to come to the seller's site, view catalogues, and place an order. In the B2B sell-side marketplace, however, the buyer is an organization.

The key mechanisms in the sell-side model are electronic catalogues that can be customized for each large buyer and forward auctions. Sellers such as Dell Computer (*www.dellauction.com*) use auctions extensively. In addition to conducting auctions from their own websites, organizations can use third-party auction sites, such as eBay, to liquidate items. Companies such as Ariba (*www.ariba.com*) are helping organizations auction old assets and inventories.

The sell-side model is used by hundreds of thousands of companies. It is especially powerful for companies with superb reputations. The seller can be either a manufacturer (e.g., Dell, IBM), a distributor (e.g., *www.avnet.com*), or a retailer (e.g., *www.grandandtoy.com*). The seller uses EC to increase sales, reduce selling and advertising expenditures, increase delivery speed, and lower administrative costs. The sell-side model is especially suitable to customization. Many companies allow their customers to configure their orders on-line. For example, at Dell (*www.dell.ca*), you can determine the exact type of computer that you want. You can choose the type of chip (e.g., Itanium 2), the size of the hard drive (for example, 1 terabyte), the type of monitor (e.g., 22-inch flat screen), and so on. Similarly, the Jaguar website (*www.jaguar.com*) allows you to customize the Jaguar you want. Self-customization greatly reduces any misunderstandings concerning what customers want, and it encourages businesses to fill orders more quickly.

Buy-Side Marketplaces

The **buy-side marketplace** is a model in which organizations attempt to buy needed products or services from other organizations electronically. A major method of buying goods and services in the buy-side model is the reverse auction.

The buy-side model uses EC technology to streamline the purchasing process. The goal is to reduce both the costs of items purchased and the administrative expenses involved in purchasing them. In addition, EC technology can shorten the purchasing cycle time. Procurement includes purchasing goods and materials as well as sourcing (finding goods), negotiating with suppliers, paying for goods, and making delivery arrangements. Organizations now use the Internet to accomplish all of these functions.

Purchasing by using electronic support is referred to as **e-procurement**. E-procurement uses reverse auctions, particularly group purchasing. In **group purchasing**, multiple buyers combine their orders so that they constitute a large volume and therefore attract more seller attention. In addition, when buyers place their combined orders on a reverse auction, they can negotiate a volume discount. Typically, the orders of small buyers are aggregated by a third-party vendor, such as the United Sourcing Alliance (*www.usa-llc.com*).

Electronic Exchanges

E-marketplaces, called **public exchanges** or just **exchanges**, are independently owned by a third party and connect many sellers and many buyers. Public exchanges are open to all business organizations. They frequently are owned and operated by a third party. Public exchange managers provide all the necessary information systems to the participants. Thus, buyers and sellers merely have to "plug in" in order to trade. B2B public exchanges often are the initial point for contacts between business partners. Once the partners make contact, they may move to a private exchange or to the private trading rooms provided by many public exchanges to conduct their subsequent trading activities. IT's About Business 5.4 offers the example of Biddingo.com, an Canadian electronic exchange for municipalities and other government agencies.

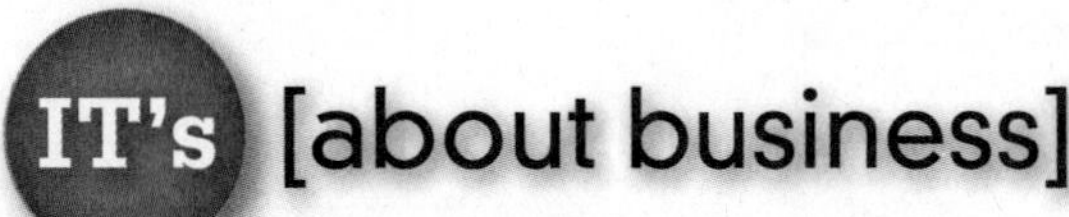

5.4 A New Electronic Exchange for the City of Kingston

Canadian municipalities have long embraced the web as a means of informing residents of important policies and offering on-line transactions, such as telling them when garbage pick-up day is or letting them reserve a book at their local library branch. But some municipalities are taking the web to the next level, leveraging its ability to procure products and services at the best cost for taxpayers.

The City of Kingston in Ontario is one such municipality. The city of 125,000 people recently underwent an updating of its website. The project objectives were to provide easier navigation and improved functionality on computers and mobile devices.

The new site includes the traditional tools for residents such as Kingston Transit's trip planner, on-line pay services, and the waste sorting look-up. But probably most importantly, the new website also incorporates a section for businesses to do business with the City of Kingston. This new system, called Biddingo (*www.biddingo.com*), is aimed at streamlining the city's purchasing process. Anything from buying a truck or cleaning products, to catering for events can be done through the Biddingo e-commerce platform.

This system is already used by multiple government agencies and other cities around Canada. It is becoming the industry standard for businesses interested in providing various goods and services to public sector buyers.

Whenever a customer, such as the City of Kingston, needs to buy a vehicle or computers, for example, it uses the Biddingo platform to issue a request for information, if they only want to find out about possible products and services and their cost, or they issue a request for proposal, which is the formal tender document seeking specific products and services. Suppliers can only win the contracts that they know about, and Biddingo ensures that they are made aware of the proposals. Suppliers get a daily e-mail alert of all the bids that match their profile, submit bid responses, and often win them! They have access to detailed reports that provide crucial business decision-making information, such as invitation lists, document taker's lists, mandatory site meetings, amendment notices, bid results, and awarded contracts. Biddingo.com helps both sides: It assists buyers with fulfilling their purchasing requirements and it assists suppliers with bidding on work that can help their businesses grow.

Questions

1. What type of B2B e-commerce exchange website is Biddingo?
2. Visit the Biddingo website (*www.biddingo.com*) and view some of the goods and services being tendered by the City of Kingston or any other city in Canada. What types of goods and services are tendered through Biddingo.com?
3. Are there any goods or services that might not be suitable to be tendered on Biddingo? Why or why not?
4. What reasons would lead the City of Kingston to set up its own buy-side marketplace instead of using Biddingo?

Sources: Compiled from D. Mathison, "City of Kingston Website Launches New Design," *Kingston Herald*, February 21, 2013; *www.biddingo.com*, accessed May 2013.

Some electronic exchanges deal in direct materials, and others in indirect materials. *Direct materials* are inputs to the manufacturing process, such as safety glass used in automobile windshields and windows. *Indirect materials* are items, such as office supplies, that are needed for maintenance, repairs, and operations (MRO). There are three basic types of public exchanges: vertical, horizontal, and functional. All three types offer diversified support services, ranging from payments to logistics.

Vertical exchanges connect buyers and sellers in a given industry. Vertical exchanges are frequently owned and managed by a *consortium*, a term for a group of major players in an industry. For example, Marriott and Hyatt own a procurement consortium for the hotel industry, and ChevronTexaco owns an energy e-marketplace. The vertical e-marketplaces offer services that are particularly suited to the community they serve.

Horizontal exchanges connect buyers and sellers across many industries and are used primarily for MRO materials. Examples of horizontal exchanges are Worldbid.com (*www.worldbid.com*), Global Sources (*www.globalsources.com*), and Alibaba (*www.alibaba.com*).

In *functional exchanges*, needed services such as temporary help or extra office space are traded on an "as-needed" basis. For example, Employease (*www.employease.com*) can find temporary labour by searching employers in its Employease Network.

before you go on...

1. Briefly differentiate between the sell-side marketplace and the buy-side marketplace.
2. Briefly differentiate among vertical exchanges, horizontal exchanges, and functional exchanges.

5.4 Electronic Payments

Implementing EC typically requires electronic payments. **Electronic payment systems** enable you to pay for goods and services electronically rather than by writing a cheque or using cash. Payments are an integral part of doing business, whether in the traditional manner or on-line. Traditional payment systems typically have involved cash and/or cheques.

In most cases, traditional payment systems are not effective for EC, especially for B2B. Cash cannot be used because there is no face-to-face contact between buyer and seller. Further, not everyone accepts credit cards or cheques, and some buyers do not have credit cards or chequing accounts. Finally, contrary to what many people believe, it may be *less* secure for the buyer to use the telephone or mail to arrange or send payments, especially from another country, than to complete a secured transaction on a computer. For all of these reasons, a better way is needed to pay for goods and services in cyberspace. This better method is electronic payment systems. We now take a closer look at four types of electronic payment: electronic cheques, electronic credit cards, purchasing cards, and electronic cash.

Electronic Cheques

Electronic cheques (e-cheques) are similar to regular paper cheques. They are used primarily in B2B. A customer who wishes to use e-cheques first must establish a chequing account with a bank. Then, when the customer buys a product or a service, he or she e-mails an encrypted electronic cheque to the seller. The seller deposits the cheque in a bank account, and funds are transferred from the buyer's account into the seller's account.

Like regular cheques, e-cheques carry a signature (in digital form) that can be verified (see *www.authorize.net*). Properly signed and endorsed e-cheques are exchanged between financial institutions through electronic clearinghouses. (Visit the Canadian Payments Association *www.cdnpay.ca* to learn more about electronic clearinghouses.)

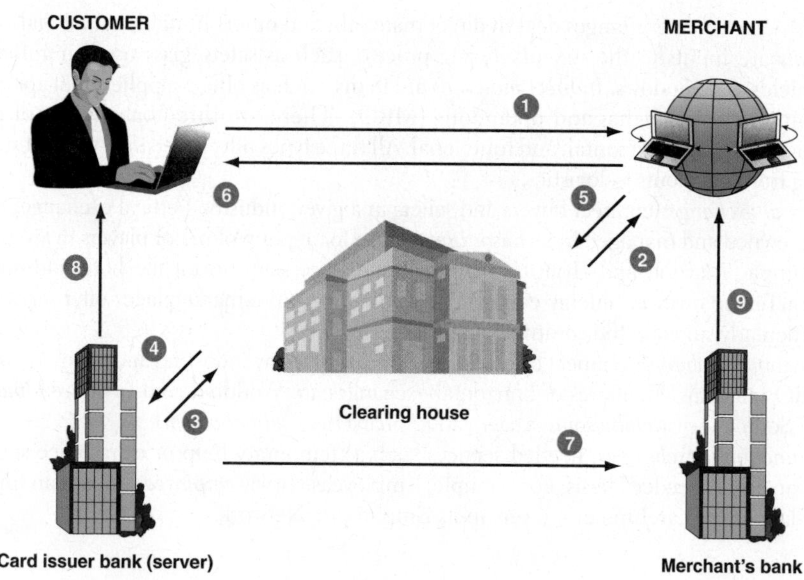

FIGURE 5.4 How e-credit cards work. The numbers 1–9 indicate the sequence of activities. (*Source:* Drawn by E. Turban)

Electronic Credit Cards

Electronic credit (e-credit) cards allow customers to charge on-line payments to their credit card account. These cards are used primarily in B2C and in shopping by small-to-medium enterprises (SMEs). Here is how e-credit cards work (see Figure 5.4).

- Step 1: When you buy a book from Amazon, for example, your credit card information and purchase amount are encrypted in your browser. This way, the information is safe while it is "travelling" on the Internet to Amazon.
- Step 2: When your information arrives at Amazon, it is not opened. Rather, it is transferred automatically (in encrypted form) to a *clearinghouse*, where it is decrypted for verification and authorization.
- Step 3: The clearinghouse asks the bank that issued you your credit card (the card issuer bank) to verify your credit card information.
- Step 4: Your card issuer bank verifies your credit card information and reports this to the clearinghouse.
- Step 5: The clearinghouse reports the result of the verification of your credit card to Amazon.
- Step 6: Amazon reports a successful purchase and amount to you.
- Step 7: Your card issuer bank sends funds in the amount of the purchase to Amazon's bank.
- Step 8: Your card issuer bank notifies you (either electronically or in your monthly statement) of the debit on your credit card.
- Step 9: Amazon's bank notifies Amazon of the funds credited to its account.

Several major credit card issuers are offering customers the option of shopping on-line with *virtual, single-use credit card numbers* (see Figure 5.5). The goal is to thwart criminals by using a different random card number every time you shop on-line. This virtual number is good only on the website where you make your purchase. An on-line purchase made with a virtual card number shows up on your bill just like any other purchase.

Purchasing Cards

The B2B equivalent of electronic credit cards is *purchasing cards* (see Figure 5.6). In some countries, purchasing cards are the primary form of payment between companies. Unlike credit cards, where credit is provided for 30 to 60 days (for free) before payment is made to the merchant, payments made with purchasing cards are settled within a week.

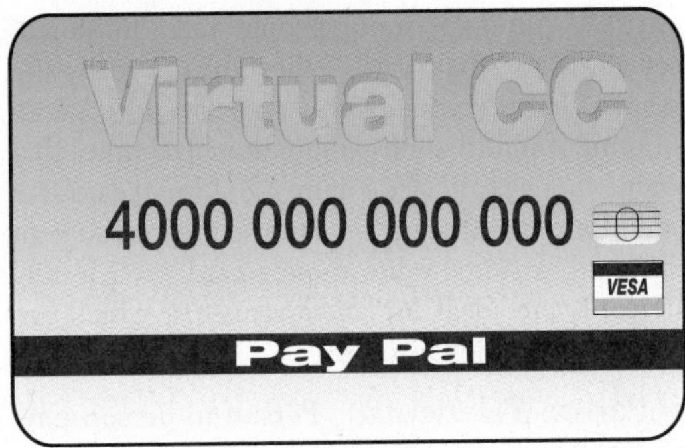

FIGURE 5.5 Example of virtual credit card.

FIGURE 5.6 Purchasing card. (*Source:* Mike Clarke/AFP/GettyImages/NewsCom)

Purchasing cards typically are used for unplanned B2B purchases, and corporations generally limit the amount per purchase, usually $1,000 to $2,000. Purchasing cards can be used on the Internet, much like regular credit cards.

Electronic Cash

Despite the growth of credit cards, cash remains the most common mode of payment in off-line transactions. Many EC sellers, and some buyers, however, prefer electronic cash. *Electronic cash (e-cash)* appears in three major forms: stored-value money cards, smart cards, and person-to-person payments.

Stored-Value Money Cards. Although **stored-value money cards** resemble credit cards, they actually are a form of e-cash. The cards that you use to pay for photocopies in your library, for transportation, and for telephone calls are stored-value money cards. They are called "stored-value" because they allow you to store a fixed amount of prepaid money and then spend it as necessary. Each time you use the card, the amount is reduced by the amount you spent. Figure 5.7 shows a stored-value money card for use at York University in Toronto.

FIGURE 5.7 York University stored-value money card. (*Source:* © York University)

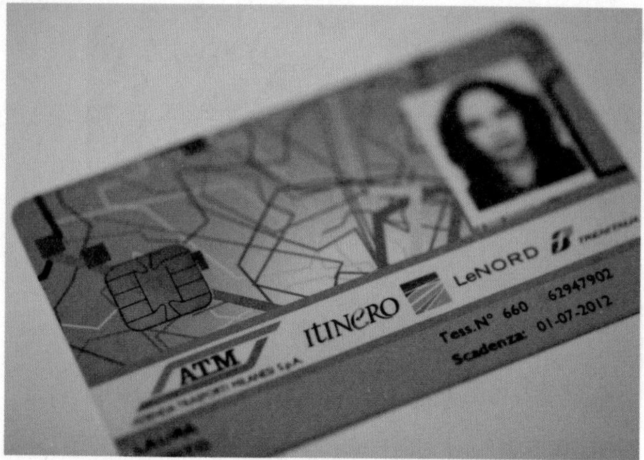

FIGURE 5.8 Smart cards are frequently multipurpose.
(*Source:* © MARKA/Alamy Limited)

Smart Cards. Although some people refer to stored-value money cards as "smart cards," they are not really the same. True **smart cards** contain a chip that can store a considerable amount of information—more than 100 times that of a stored-value money card (see Figure 5.8). Smart cards are frequently multipurpose; that is, you can use them as a credit card, a debit card, a stored-value money card, or a loyalty card. Smart cards are ideal for *micropayments*, which are small payments of a few dollars or less.

Person-to-Person Payments. **Person-to-person payments** are a form of e-cash that enables two individuals, or an individual and a business, to transfer funds without using a credit card. Person-to-person payments can be used for a variety of purposes, such as sending money to students at university, paying for an item purchased at an on-line auction, or sending a gift to a family member.

One of the first companies to offer this service was PayPal. Most recently, a new company called Stripe (*http://stripe.com/ca*) started offering similar on-line payment services as PayPal, but for small and medium businesses, as IT's About Business 5.5 describes.

All of these person-to-person payment services work in a similar way. First, you select a service and open up an account. Basically, this process entails creating a user name, selecting a password, and providing the service with a credit card or bank account number. Next, you transfer funds from your credit card or bank account to your new account. Now you're ready to send money to someone over the Internet. You access the service—for example, PayPal—with your user name and password, and you specify the e-mail address of the person to receive the money, along with the dollar amount that you want to send. The service then sends an e-mail

[about business]

5.5 Stripe, an On-line Payment System for Small Businesses

Stripe is a new on-line payment system for small businesses developed by two brothers from Ireland, Patrick and John Collison. They turned their hobby of developing software applications into a growing business by raising over $38 million in cash from investors in order to expand to other countries, including Canada.

The new payment system is geared toward small and medium businesses that want to sell their products on-line. It provides them with a quick way to accept credit card payments without a lot of technical complexity or overhead costs. An e-tailer can set up an account within minutes and it charges its customers a flat fee of 2.9 percent plus 30 cents for every transaction. Stripe has already spent several months of beta testing with companies such as Ottawa-based Shopify, one of Canada's leading e-commerce players.

But what is the difference between Stripe and on-line payment methods such as PayPal? The first difference when you visit Stripe's website is that it is easy to navigate and with a well-designed GUI. But the main difference is that Stripe doesn't require e-tailers to set up an account with them first before using their platform. This offers new e-tailers a cost advantage when setting up their payment systems on their websites.

Today, Stripe handles millions of dollars of payments per day from thousands of businesses, many of them small but some of them enormous, such as Walmart and NBC. As for the highly encrypted security system used by the company, it is certified as a Level 1 provider, which is the highest level available by the payment card industry.

Questions

1. Would Stripe be able to maintain its current competitive advantage based on ease of payment and costs? Why or why not?
2. Would Stripe be a good payment system to pay for small purchases? Why or why not? As a hint, discuss the payment of an on-line newspaper article that would cost 20 cents.
3. What are the main differences between person-to-person payment systems such as Stripe and PayPal and the use of credit cards?

Sources: Compiled from M. Evans, "Stripe 'Disrupts' Payment-Processing Market with Its Simplicity," *The Globe and Mail*, September 24, 2012; D. Kucera, "Payments Startup Stripe Expands to Canada in Challenge to PayPal," go.bloomberg.com, September 19, 2012; C. Wong, "Online Payment Startup Stripe Hits Canada," ITbusiness.ca, September 19, 2012; D. Weir, "Stripe Is the Payment System Under the Hood at Lots of Your Favorite Sites and Apps," 7x7SF, *www.7x7.com*, April 4, 2013.

to the payee's e-mail address. The e-mail contains a link back to the service's website. When the recipient clicks on the link, he or she is taken to the service. There, the recipient is asked to set up an account to which the money that you sent will be credited. The recipient can then credit the money from this account to either a credit card or a bank account. The service charges the payer a small amount, roughly $1 per transaction.

An attractive security feature of PayPal is that you have to put only enough money in the account to cover any upcoming transactions. Therefore, if anyone should gain access to your account, they he or she not have access to all of your money.

Digital Wallets. **Digital wallets** (or **e-wallets**) are not proper on-line payment systems but are software mechanisms that provide security measures, combined with convenience, to EC purchasing. The wallet stores the financial information of the buyer, such as credit card number, shipping information, and so on. Thus, the buyer does not need to re-enter sensitive information for each purchase. In addition, if the wallet is stored at the vendor's website, then it does not have to travel on the Internet for each purchase, making the information more secure. Examples of popular digital wallets are Skrill (*www.skrill.com*), Yahoo! Wallet (*http://ca.wallet.yahoo.com/*), and Google Checkout (*http://checkout.google.com/*). Convenience is the main advantage of digital wallets; however, they are not totally secured systems.

before you go on...

1. List the various electronic payment mechanisms. Which of these mechanisms are most often used for B2B payments?
2. What are micropayments?

5.5 Ethical and Legal Issues in E-Business

Technological innovation often forces a society to re-examine and modify its ethical standards. In many cases the new standards are incorporated into law. In this section, you will learn about two important ethical considerations—privacy and job loss—as well as various legal issues arising from the practice of e-business.

Ethical Issues

Many of the ethical and global issues related to IT also apply to e-business. Here you will learn about two basic issues, privacy and job loss.

By making it easier to store and transfer personal information, e-business presents some threats to privacy. To begin with, most electronic payment systems know who the buyers are. It may be necessary, then, to protect the buyers' identities. Businesses frequently use encryption to provide this protection.

Another major privacy issue is tracking. For example, individuals' activities on the Internet can be tracked by cookies, discussed in Chapter 13. Cookies store your tracking history on your personal computer's hard drive, and any time you revisit a certain website, the server recognizes the cookie. In response, antivirus software packages routinely search for potentially harmful cookies.

In addition to compromising individual privacy, the use of EC may eliminate the need for some of a company's employees, as well as brokers and agents. The manner in which these unneeded workers, especially employees, are treated can raise ethical issues: How should the company handle the layoffs? Should companies be required to retrain employees for new positions? If not, how should the company compensate or otherwise assist the displaced workers?

Legal and Ethical Issues Specific to E-Commerce

There are many legal issues that are related specifically to e-commerce. When buyers and sellers do not know one another and cannot even see one another, there is a chance that dishonest people will commit fraud and other crimes. During the first few years of EC, the public witnessed many such crimes. These illegal actions ranged from creating a virtual bank that disappeared along with the investors' deposits to manipulating stock prices on the Internet. In the following section, you explore some of the major legal issues that are specific to e-commerce.

Fraud on the Internet. Internet fraud has grown even faster than Internet use itself. In one case, stock promoters falsely spread positive rumours about the prospects of the companies they touted in order to boost the stock price. In other cases, the information provided might have been true, but the promoters did not disclose that they were paid to talk up the companies. Stock promoters specifically target small investors who are lured by the promise of fast profits.

Stocks are only one of many areas where swindlers are active. Auctions also are especially conducive to fraud, by both sellers and buyers. Other types of fraud include selling bogus investments and setting up phantom business opportunities. Due to the growing use of e-mail, financial criminals now have access to many more people. The Royal Canadian Mounted Police (RCMP) (*www.rcmp-grc.gc.ca/scams-fraudes*) regularly publishes examples of scams that are most likely to be spread via e-mail or to be found on the web. Later in this section you will see some ways in which consumers and sellers can protect themselves from on-line fraud.

Domain Names. Another legal issue is competition over domain names. Domain names are assigned by central non-profit organizations that check for conflicts and possible infringement of trademarks. Obviously, companies that sell goods and services over the Internet want customers to be able to find them easily. In general, the more closely the domain name matches the company's name, the easier the company is to locate.

A domain name is considered to be legal when the person or business who owns the name has operated a legitimate business under that name for some period of time. Companies such as Christian Dior, Nike, Deutsche Bank, and even Microsoft have had to fight or pay to get the domain name that corresponds to their company's name. Consider the case of Delta Air Lines. Delta originally could not obtain the Internet domain name delta.com because Delta Faucet had purchased it first. Delta Faucet had been in business under that name since 1954 and therefore had a legitimate business interest in the domain name. Delta Air Lines had to settle for delta-airlines.com until it bought the domain name from Delta Faucet. Delta Faucet is now at deltafaucet.com. Several cases of disputed domain names have been before the courts.

Cybersquatting. **Cybersquatting** is the practice of registering or using domain names for the purpose of profiting from the goodwill or the trademark that belongs to someone else.

Some practices that could be considered cybersquatting, however, are not illegal, although they may well be unethical. One of these practices, known as *domain tasting*, lets registrars profit from the complex money trail of pay-per-click advertising. The practice can be traced back to the policies of the organization responsible for regulating web names, the Internet Corporation for Assigned Names and Numbers (ICANN) (*www.icann.org*). In 2000, ICANN established the "create grace period," a five-day period when a company or person can claim a domain name and then return it for a full refund of the $6 registry fee. ICANN implemented this policy to allow anyone who mistypes a domain name to return it without cost.

Domain tasters exploit this policy by claiming Internet domains for five days at no cost. These domain names frequently resemble those of prominent companies and organizations. The tasters then jam these domains full of advertisements that come from Google and Yahoo!. Because this process involves zero risk and 100 percent profit margins, domain tasters register millions of domain names every day—some of them over and over again. Experts estimate that registrants ultimately purchase less than 2 percent of the sites they sample. In the vast majority of cases, they use the domain names for only a few days to generate quick profits. IT's About

IT's [about business]

5.6 Domain Name Slamming

Ever since there has been an Internet, there have been Internet scams. A new one involves owners of dot-ca top-level domains. The Canadian Internet Registration Authority (CIRA) recently warned these owners of an on-line scam involving fake renewal notices sent via e-mail from Renewdomain.ca, which was not a CIRA-certified registrar, that tried to collect payment from dot-ca site owners.

The fraudulent site sent an e-mail to legitimate dot-ca domain owners and told them that they need to renew their domain. The e-mail sender fraudulently posed as the dot-ca registrar, telling them to make a payment though PayPal in order to keep the ownership of their domain name.

Although it might seem a rather simple way of misleading businesses that operate on the Internet, this type of fraud seems to be effective, especially with small businesses since owners may not remember who their original registrar is in the first place.

In response to the scam, the Renewdomain.ca website was shut down and CIRA revoked the licence of the company that owned it. In addition, CIRA also worked with PayPal to close the fraudulent web page to process the payments.

Questions

1. What are the differences between cybersquatting and domain name slamming?
2. Why would it be so difficult to detect domain slamming cases?
3. How could a company protect itself against this kind of scam?

Sources: Compiled from B. Jackson, "CIRA Investigating dot-ca Phishing Scammers," *ITbusiness.ca,*, August 13, 2012; B. Jackson, "Canadian Web Site Owners Targeted by New Scam," *ITbusiness.ca*, August 10, 2012; "On-line Scam Warning for Internet Users," CIRA news release, 2012, *www.cira.ca*, accessed May 29, 2013.

Business 5.6 relates another recent fraudulent way of using domain names called *domain name slamming*.

Taxes and Other Fees. In off-line sales, most provinces and localities collect taxes on business transactions conducted within their jurisdiction. For online sales in Canada we must pay a federal tax on most items we purchase. In most provinces of Canada, we must also pay a provincial tax such as the QST in Québec. Some provinces however federal and provincial taxes are combined into a single, harmonized tax (HST), this is the case of provices such as Ontario or Nova Scotia.

In addition to the sales tax, in many jurisdictions around the world, there is a question about where—and in some cases, whether—electronic sellers should pay business licence taxes, franchise fees, gross-receipts taxes, excise taxes, privilege taxes, and utility taxes. Furthermore, how should tax collection be controlled?

Copyright. As you will learn in Chapter 12, intellectual property is protected by copyright laws and cannot be used freely. This point is significant because many people mistakenly believe that once they purchase a piece of software, they have the right to share it with others. In fact, what they have bought is the right to *use* the software, not to *distribute* it. That right remains with the copyright holder. Similarly, copying material from websites without permission is a violation of copyright laws. Protecting intellectual property rights in e-commerce is extremely difficult, however, because it involves hundreds of millions of people who have access to billions of web pages in about 200 countries with differing copyright laws.

before you go on...

1. List and explain some ethical issues in EC.
2. Discuss the major legal issues of EC.

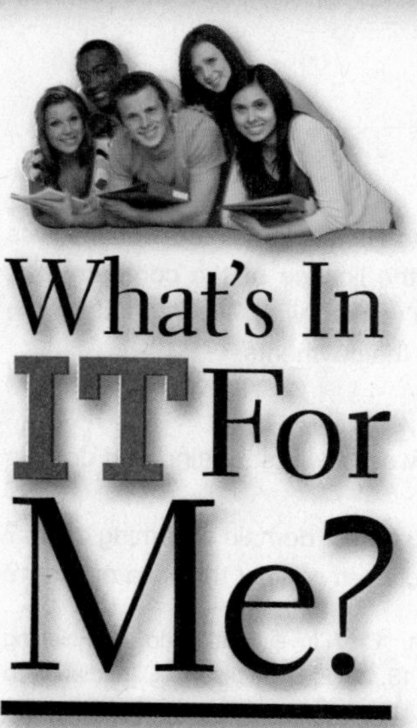

For the Accounting Major

Accounting personnel are involved in several EC activities. Designing the ordering system and its relationship with inventory management requires accounting attention. Billing and payments also are accounting activities, as are determining cost and profit allocation. Replacing paper documents with electronic means will affect many of the accountant's tasks, especially the auditing of EC activities and systems. Finally, building a cost-benefit and cost-justification system to determine which products and services to take on-line and creating a chargeback system are critical to the success of EC.

For the Finance Major

The worlds of banking, securities and commodities markets, and other financial services are being re-engineered due to EC. On-line securities trading and its supporting infrastructure are growing more rapidly than any other EC activity. Many innovations already in place are changing the rules of economic and financial incentives for financial analysts and managers. On-line banking, for example, does not recognize political boundaries, and it may create a new framework for financing global trades. Public financial information now is accessible in seconds. These innovations will dramatically change the manner in which finance personnel operate.

For the Marketing Major

A major revolution in marketing and sales is taking place due to EC. Perhaps its most obvious feature is the transition from a physical to a virtual marketplace. Equally important, though, is the radical transformation to one-on-one advertising and sales and to customized and interactive marketing. Marketing channels are being combined, eliminated, or recreated. The EC revolution is creating new products and markets and significantly altering existing ones. Digitization of products and services also has implications for marketing and sales. The direct producer-to-consumer channel is expanding rapidly and is fundamentally changing the nature of customer service. As the battle for customers intensifies, marketing and sales personnel are becoming the most critical success factor in many organizations. On-line marketing can be a blessing to one company and a curse to another.

For the Production/Operations Management Major

EC is changing the manufacturing system from product-push mass production to order-pull mass customization. This change requires a robust supply chain, information support, and re-engineering of processes that involve suppliers and other business partners. Suppliers can use extranets to monitor and replenish inventories without the need for constant reorders. In addition, the Internet and intranets help reduce cycle times. Many production/operations problems that have persisted for years, such as complex scheduling and excess inventories, are being solved rapidly with the use of web technologies. Companies now can use external and internal networks to find and manage manufacturing operations in other countries much more easily. Also, the web is re-engineering procurement by helping companies conduct electronic bids for parts and subassemblies, thus reducing cost. All in all, the job of the progressive production/operations manager is closely tied in with e-commerce.

For the Human Resources Management Major

HR majors need to understand the new labour markets and the impacts of EC on old labour markets. Also, the HRM department may use EC tools for such functions as procuring office supplies. Also, becoming knowledgeable about new government on-line initiatives and on-line training is critical. Finally, HR personnel must be familiar with the major legal issues related to EC and employment.

For the MIS Major

The MIS function is responsible for providing the information technology infrastructure necessary for electronic commerce to function. In particular, this infrastructure includes the company's networks, intranets, and extranets. The MIS function also is responsible for ensuring that electronic commerce transactions are secure.

[Summary]

1. Describe the six common types of electronic commerce; provide specific personal examples of how you have used or could use B2C, C2C, G2C, and mobile commerce; and offer a specific example of B2B and G2B.

In *business-to-consumer* (B2C) electronic commerce, the sellers are organizations, and the buyers are individuals. In *business-to-business* (B2B) electronic commerce, the sellers and the buyers are businesses. In *consumer-to-consumer* (C2C) electronic commerce, an individual sells products or services to other individuals. In *business-to-employee* (B2E) electronic commerce, an organization uses EC internally to provide information and services to its employees. *E-government* is the use of Internet technology in general and e-commerce in particular to deliver information and public services to citizens (called *government-to-citizen* or *G2C EC*), and business partners and suppliers (called *government-to-business* or *G2B EC*). *Mobile commerce* is e-commerce that is conducted entirely in a wireless environment.

We leave the examples of each type to you.

2. Discuss the five on-line services of business-to-consumer electronic commerce, provide a specific example of each service, and state how you have used or would use each service.

Electronic banking, also known as *cyberbanking*, involves conducting various banking activities from home, at a place of business, or on the road instead of at a physical bank location.

On-line securities trading involves buying and selling securities over the web.

On-line job matching over the web offers a promising environment for job seekers and for companies searching for hard-to-find employees. Thousands of companies and government agencies advertise available positions, accept resumés, and take applications via the Internet.

The Internet is an ideal place to plan, explore, and arrange almost any trip economically. *On-line travel services* allow you to purchase airline tickets, reserve hotel rooms, and rent cars. Most sites also offer a fare-tracker feature that sends you e-mail messages about low-cost flights.

On-line advertising over the web makes the advertising process media-rich, dynamic, and interactive.

We leave the examples to you.

3. Describe the three business models for business-to-business electronic commerce, and provide a specific example of each model.

In the *sell-side marketplace* model, organizations attempt to sell their products or services to other organizations electronically from their own private e-marketplace website and/or from a third-party website. Sellers such as Dell Computer (*www.dellauction.com*) use sell-side auctions extensively. In addition to auctions from their own websites, organizations can use third-party auction sites, such as eBay, to liquidate items.

The *buy-side marketplace* is a model in which organizations attempt to buy needed products or services from other organizations electronically.

E-marketplaces, in which there are many sellers and many buyers, are called *public exchanges*, or just exchanges. Public exchanges are open to all business organizations. They frequently are owned and operated by a third party. There are three basic types of public exchanges: vertical, horizontal, and functional. *Vertical exchanges* connect buyers and sellers in a given industry. *Horizontal exchanges* connect buyers and sellers across many industries. In *functional exchanges*, needed services such as temporary help or extra office space are traded on an "as-needed" basis.

4. **Describe the four types of electronic payments and provide a specific example of each one.**

Electronic cheques (*e-cheques*) are similar to regular paper cheques. They are used mostly in B2B.

Electronic credit (*e-credit*) cards allow customers to charge on-line payments to their credit card account. Electronic credit cards are used primarily in B2C and in shopping by small-to-medium enterprises.

The B2B equivalent of electronic credit cards is *purchasing cards*. Unlike credit cards, where credit is provided for 30 to 60 days (for free) before payment is made to the merchant, payments made with purchasing cards are settled within a week. Purchasing cards typically are used for unplanned B2B purchases, and the amount per purchase generally is limited (usually $1,000 to $2,000).

Electronic cash (*e-cash*) appears in three major forms: stored-value money cards, smart cards, and person-to-person payments. Although they resemble credit cards, *stored-value money cards* allow you to store a fixed amount of prepaid money and then spend it as necessary. Each time you use the card, the amount is reduced by the amount you spent. *Smart cards* contain a chip that can store a considerable amount of information. You can use them as a credit card, a debit card, or a stored-value money card. *Person-to-person payments* enable two individuals or an individual and a business to transfer funds without using a credit card.

We leave the examples to you.

5. **Illustrate the ethical and legal issues relating to electronic commerce with two specific examples of each issue.**

E-business presents some threats to privacy. To begin with, most electronic payment systems know who the buyers are. It may be necessary, therefore, to protect the buyers' identities with encryption. Another major privacy issue is tracking, where individuals' activities on the Internet can be tracked by cookies.

The use of EC may eliminate the need for some of a company's employees, as well as brokers and agents. The manner in which these unneeded workers, especially employees, are treated can raise ethical issues: How should the company handle the layoffs? Should companies be required to retrain employees for new positions? If not, how should the company compensate or otherwise assist the displaced workers?

[Chapter Glossary]

auction A competitive process in which either a seller solicits consecutive bids from buyers or a buyer solicits bids from sellers, and prices are determined dynamically by competitive bidding.

banners Electronic billboards, which typically contain a short text or graphical message to promote a product or a vendor.

brick-and-mortar organizations Organizations in which the product, the process, and the delivery agent are all physical.

business-to-business electronic commerce (B2B) Electronic commerce in which both the sellers and the buyers are business organizations.

business-to-consumer electronic commerce (B2C) Electronic commerce in which the sellers are organizations and the buyers are individuals; also known as *e-tailing*.

business-to-employee electronic commerce (B2E) An organization that uses electronic commerce internally to provide information and services to its employees.

business model The method by which a company generates revenue to sustain itself.

buy-side marketplace B2B model in which organizations buy needed products or services from other organizations electronically, often through a reverse auction.

channel conflict The alienation of existing distributors when a company decides to sell to customers directly on-line.

clicks-and-mortar organizations Organizations that do business in both the physical and digital dimensions.

consumer-to-consumer electronic commerce (C2C) Electronic commerce in which both the buyer and the seller are individuals (not businesses).

cyberbanking Various banking activities conducted electronically from home, a business, or on the road instead of at a physical bank location.

cybersquatting Registering domain names in the hope of selling them later at a higher price.

digital wallets (e-wallets) software mechanisms that stores the financial information of the buyer, such as credit card number, shipping information so the buyer does not need to re-enter this information for each purchase.

disintermediation Elimination of intermediaries in electronic commerce.

e-government The use of electronic commerce to deliver information and public services to citizens, business partners, and suppliers of government entities, and those working in the public sector.

e-procurement Purchasing by using electronic support.

electronic business (e-business) Electronic commerce, more broadly defined to include buying and selling of goods and services as well as servicing customers, collaborating with business partners, conducting e-learning, and conducting electronic transactions within an organization.

electronic commerce (EC or e-commerce) The process of buying, selling, transferring, or exchanging products, services, or information via computer networks, including the Internet.

electronic mall A collection of individual shops under one Internet address.

electronic marketplace (e-marketplace) A virtual market space on the web where many buyers and many sellers conduct electronic business activities.

electronic payment systems Computer-based systems that allow customers to pay for goods and services electronically, rather than writing a cheque or using cash.

electronic retailing (e-tailing) The direct sale of products and services through storefronts or electronic malls, usually designed around an electronic catalogue format and/or auctions.

electronic storefront The website of a single company, with its own Internet address, at which orders can be placed.

exchange (see **public exchange**)

forward auctions An auction that sellers use as a selling channel to many potential buyers; the highest bidder wins the items.

group purchasing The aggregation of purchasing orders from many buyers so that a volume discount can be obtained.

mobile commerce (m-commerce) Electronic commerce conducted in a wireless environment.

multichannelling A process in which a company integrates its on-line and off-line channels.

permission marketing Method of marketing that asks consumers to give their permission to voluntarily accept on-line advertising and e-mail.

person-to-person payments A form of electronic cash that enables the transfer of funds between two individuals, or between an individual and a business, without the use of a credit card.

pop-under ad An advertisement that is automatically launched by some trigger and appears underneath the active window.

pop-up ad An advertisement that is automatically launched by some trigger and appears in front of the active window.

public exchange (exchange) Electronic marketplace in which there are many sellers and many buyers, and entry is open to all; it is frequently owned and operated by a third party.

reverse auction An auction in which one buyer, usually an organization, seeks to buy a product or a service, and suppliers submit bids; the lowest bidder wins.

sell-side marketplace B2B model in which organizations sell to other organizations from their own private e-marketplace and/or from a third-party site.

smart card A card that contains a microprocessor (chip) that enables the card to store a considerable amount of information (including stored funds) and to conduct processing.

social commerce type of electronic commerce that uses social media to assist in the on-line buying and selling of products and services.

spamming Indiscriminate distribution of e-mail without the receiver's permission.

stored-value money card A form of electronic cash on which a fixed amount of prepaid money is stored; the amount is reduced each time the card is used.

viral marketing On-line word-of-mouth marketing.

virtual bank A banking institution dedicated solely to Internet transactions.

virtual organizations Organizations in which the product, the process, and the delivery agent are all digital; also called *pure-play organizations*.

[Discussion Questions]

1. Discuss the major limitations of e-commerce. Which of these limitations are likely to disappear? Why?
2. Discuss the reasons for having multiple EC business models.
3. Distinguish between business-to-business forward auctions and buyers' bids for requests for quotations (RFQs).
4. Discuss the benefits to sellers and buyers of a B2B exchange.

5. What are the major benefits of G2C electronic commerce?
6. Discuss the various ways to pay on-line in B2C. Which one(s) would you prefer and why?
7. Why is order fulfillment in B2C considered difficult?
8. Discuss the reasons for EC failures.
9. Should BMW or Honda sell cars on-line? (Hint: Take a look at the discussion of channel conflict in this chapter.)
10. In some cases, individuals engage in cybersquatting so that they can sell the domain names to companies expensively. In other cases, companies engage in cybersquatting by registering domain names that are very similar to their competitors' domain names in order to generate traffic from people who misspell web addresses. Discuss each practice in terms of its ethical nature and legality. Is there a difference between the two practices? Support your answer.

[Problem-Solving Activities]

1. Suppose that you are interested in buying a brand new car. You can find information about cars at numerous websites from car manufacturers. Access three of these sites and write a report analyzing the different types of on-line advertising methods they use on their main website.
2. Compare the various electronic payment methods. Specifically, collect information from the vendors cited in the chapter, and find additional vendors using Google.ca. Pay attention to security level, speed, cost, and convenience. What type of payment method has the lowest cost for the seller? Which one is the most convenient for the buyer?
3. Conduct a study on selling diamonds and gems on-line. Access such sites as *www.peoplesjewellers.com*, *www.tiffany.ca*, and *www.charmdiamondcentres.com/*
   a. What features do these sites use to educate buyers about gemstones?
   b. How do these sites attract buyers?
   c. How do these sites increase customers' trust in on-line purchasing?
   d. What customer service features do these sites provide?
4. Access Canadian payment association *www.cdnpay.ca*. What is its role? What is their vision for the year 2020?
5. Access *www.tsn.com*. Identify at least five different ways the site generates revenue.
6. Access *www.queendom.com*. Examine its offerings and try some of them. What type of electronic commerce is this? How does this website generate revenue?
7. Access *www.ediets.com*. Prepare a list of all the services the company provides. Identify its revenue model.
8. Access *www.theknot.com*. Identify the site's revenue sources.
9. Access *www.mint.com*. Identify the site's revenue model. What are the risks of giving this website your credit and debit card numbers, as well as your bank account number?
10. Research the case of *www.nissan.com*. Is Uzi Nissan cybersquatting? Why or why not? Support your answer. How is Nissan (the car company) reacting to the *www.nissan.com* website?

[Web Activities]

1. Access the Stock Market Game Worldwide (*www.smgww.org*). You will be bankrolled with $100,000 in a trading account every month. Play the game, and relate your experiences with regard to information technology. Identify the site's revenue sources.
2. Enter *www.alibaba.com*. Identify the site's capabilities. Look at the site's private trading room. Write a report. How can such a site help a person who is making a purchase?
3. Enter *www.dineoncampus.ca/* Explore the site. Why is the site so successful? Could you start a competing site? Why or why not?
4. Enter *www.dell.ca* and configure a desktop system. Register to "my account" (no obligation). What calculators are used there? What are the advantages of this process as compared with buying a computer in a physical store? What are the disadvantages?
5. Enter *www.fiserv.com/* and *www.digitalriver.com/*, and compare and contrast their product and service offerings. Prepare a report comparing the two sites' offerings.
6. Access various travel sites such as *www.travelocity.ca*, *www.orbitz.com*, *www.expedia.ca*, and *www.kayak.com*. Compare these websites for ease of use and usefulness. Note differences among the sites. If you ask each site for the itinerary, which one gives you the best information and the best deals?
7. Access *www.outofservice.com*, and answer the musical taste and personality survey. When you have finished, click on Results and see what your musical tastes say about your personality. How accurate are the findings about you?

[Spreadsheet Activity: Building Charts and Graphs]

Objective: Graphs and charts are helpful tools within most spreadsheet applications. This activity will place you in a business scenario where graphs and charts are extremely helpful in determining customer patterns and preferences.

Chapter Connection: E-business and e-commerce are much more than simply buying and selling via the Internet. Amazon.com is a perfect example of a company that has leveraged the power of the web to make product suggestions to customers and help them find the right product. This activity builds on this concept and applies spreadsheet tools to help provide this type of business data and make them useful even in a traditional bricks-and-mortar scenario.

Activity: Go to Amazon.com (or go to *www.wiley.com/go/rainer/spreadsheet* and click on the link to Amazon there) and search for a Coleman Sundome 10 x 10 tent. At the time of this writing, customers are shown items that are frequently purchased with the tent, items that customers often buy with it (but not as frequently as the other group), and finally a list of related products. This type of information is very helpful to consumers, especially when combined with customer ratings.

Another type of feedback provided by Amazon.com is the list of items that are most frequently purchased after shopping for a particular item. This type of information is invaluable to consumers and can only be provided in an on-line environment. Walmart cannot tell customers what most people buy when they are standing in the aisle, so consumers are blind and have to make a choice based on either information they found before they arrived or what is said on the box.

Imagine that you work for a small bookstore. You would like to post a chart next to a book showing that it is one of the more popular books purchased or possibly to direct someone to a more popular book (that you also sell). Search Amazon.com for three books (pick your own genre) and find Amazon's "Customers who bought this item also bought" section. You may have to search for more than three books to find this section because it is not listed on every page. Collect the 5-star rating and total number of ratings (for example, 4.5/5 stars by 1,135 reviewers) for the main book and for the five competing books and place it in a spreadsheet. You will use different columns for each of these, as shown in the table below. Be sure to also include the data from your original book.

	5-Star Rating	Total Ratings
Main book 1	4.5	568
Customers also bought 1	3.5	789
Customers also bought 2	4.0	156
Customers also bought 3	2.7	45
Customers also bought 4	4.5	9
Customers also bought 5	5.0	12

Once your data collection is complete, you will have data for each of the three books in a spreadsheet. The table above illustrates what the data may look like for one of these books. Use the tools provided in Microsoft Excel to create at least three different types of charts based on your data. Take each chart and copy and paste it in a Word document that you could place on the shelf in your bookstore to help drive customers to the right product. If you need some help with charts, watch the tutorials that are linked at *www.wiley.com/go/rainer/spreadsheet*.

Deliverable: The final product will be five separate Word documents that the owner of the small bookstore could place on the shelf in front of a product. The chart will show the percentage of Amazon.com customers who buy that product as well as what other books they purchase. The final documents demonstrate how traditional businesses can leverage the power of e-business and e-commerce in their stores with public information.

Discussion Questions

1. Given the complexity of e-business and e-commerce, is it something that everyone should engage in? Is the future of business to have a website and sell everything on-line? Will there always be a place for traditional brick-and-mortar stores?
2. On-line shopping provides many advantages to consumers. Other than the example provided in this exercise, what other ways can you think of that will help traditional businesses leverage the power of on-line tools for their in-store customers?

[Case Assignment]

Bellwood College has switched to using electronic readers rather than paper-based textbooks. Students are issued a reader that gives them access to the textbooks that are listed as required for their courses at no additional charge. The publishing fee for the texts, paid to one Canadian publisher, means that the college is now using textbooks from only that publisher. It also means that the college will be spending less on new library acquisitions, since the licence fee for the books is coming from the college library budget.

Students at the college also have access to the college's e-mail systems, websites, and a computer lab with a variety of software, as well as a wireless network.

The College Store sells a variety of products in addition to books: these include uniforms, stationery, and art supplies. There is also a full-service restaurant on campus, which is open to the public, run by students. Recently, the college has started a campaign for students to bring non-students to the restaurant, by offering free desserts to students who bring a new person to the restaurant.

The college student council has set up a website where students can sell their art work or other products that they have developed or created. Five percent of the sale price goes to the student council and the rest goes to the student.

Required

a. Provide examples of how Bellwood College could engage in or provide the following types of e-commerce:

(Note: Your examples must indicate a clear understanding of the type of e-commerce listed.)

- Business-to-consumer (B2C)
- Business-to-business (B2B)
- Consumer-to-consumer (C2C)

b. For the following four e-commerce business models, describe the business model and explain how the college or the student council could use the business model.

- On-line direct marketing
- Electronic tendering system
- Viral marketing
- Electronic marketplace or exchange

c. Describe three different types of electronic payments that Bellwood College could accept.

[Team Assignments]

1. Assign each team to one industry vertical. An industry vertical is a group of industries in the "same" business, such as financial services, insurance, manufacturing, retail, telecommunications, pharmaceuticals and chemicals, and so on. Each team will find five real-world applications of the major business-to-business models listed in the chapter. (Try success stories of vendors and EC-related magazines.) Examine the problems they solve or the opportunities they exploit.

2. 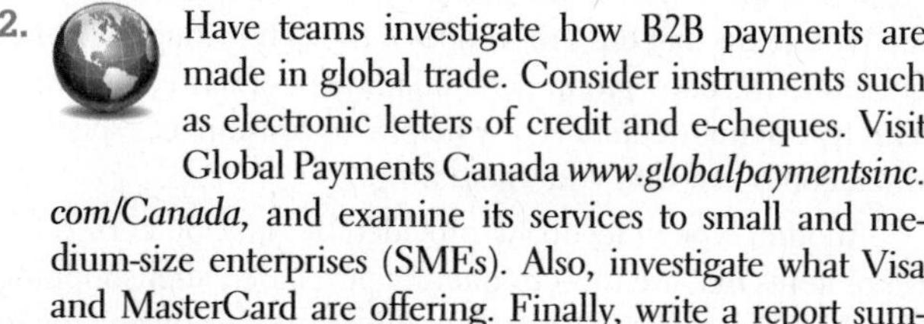
Have teams investigate how B2B payments are made in global trade. Consider instruments such as electronic letters of credit and e-cheques. Visit Global Payments Canada *www.globalpaymentsinc.com/Canada*, and examine its services to small and medium-size enterprises (SMEs). Also, investigate what Visa and MasterCard are offering. Finally, write a report summarizing your findings.

[Case 5.2 eBay Finds A Way into China]

The Problem

China is one of the world's emerging economies, and it's already an Internet powerhouse. In 2013, some 457 million Chinese had Internet access and they were doing more than $76 billion in e-commerce. In 2005, e-commerce in China amounted to just $2 billion. That exponential growth is simply too vast for any company to ignore.

Many foreign companies are seeking to do e-commerce China. For example, Groupon (*www.groupon.com*) announced the launch of a Chinese version of its group buying service, teaming up with Tencent Holdings (*www.tencent.com*), an instant messaging operator that is China's largest Internet company. Russia's Digital Sky Technologies invested $500 million in 360buy (*www.360buy.com*), a Chinese on-line retailer. And one of the pioneers of e-commerce, eBay, is also trying to capitalize on China's new capitalism.

In 2003, eBay paid $150 million to purchase EachNet, which was China's top e-commerce site at the site. eBay poured an additional $100 million in EachNet, but it didn't see a return on its investment. EachNet suffered from a combination of management mistakes—for example, not giving enough power to local executives—and intense competition from local competitor Taobao (*www.taobao.com*). Taobao, which, unlike eBay, does not charge commissions, overtook EachNet and has maintained its lead.

The Solution

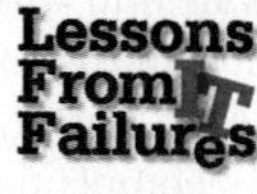

Although eBay is no longer trying to challenge Taobao, the company is still committed China. Rather than target Chinese consumers, eBay wants to link Chinese entrepreneurs and exporters to eBay consumers outside of China. One such entrepreneur is Tang Fengyan. In 2007, Tang started her own dress business, selling her $50 cocktail dresses on eBay. In 2010 alone, her sales totalled $700,000. Tang does not mind that eBay is not entrenched within China, because she is looking to attract customers beyond her borders. To reach them, eBay makes the most sense for her.

eBay looked for a niche, knowing that the Chinese electronic commerce market was dominated by Taobao's boss, Jack Ma, and his Alibaba Group (*www.alibaba.com*). While Taobao has a stranglehold in China, it has little market share outside the country. Meanwhile, Alibaba, a site connecting small and mid-size importers and exporters worldwide, does not cater much to consumers. Seeing an opportunity, eBay focused on Chinese suppliers wanting to sell to consumers outside of China. The company now has 150 service agents catering to Chinese sellers. eBay also teamed with China Post and the U.S. Postal Service to provide a way for foreign buyers to track their China purchases and also to allow sellers on the mainland to offer free shipping.

The Results

eBay's strategy worked. Thanks to its new business model and exporters like Tang Fengyan, eBay has built a formidable business in China. Transactions from China and Hong Kong on eBay and its PayPal unit amounted to $4 billion in 2010, making China eBay's fifth-largest market behind the United States, Germany, Britain, and South Korea.

Despite this success, eBay continues to face competition from Alibaba. In recent years, Alibaba has launched a service called AliExpress (*www.aliexpress.com*) that makes it easier for Chinese-based companies to sell to consumers outside China.

Questions

1. Research the reasons (besides the one listed in the case) why eBay was unsuccessful when it purchased EachNet.
2. eBay has gained a competitive advantage by providing a service for Chinese exporters. Is this a sustainable competitive advantage? Why or why not? Support your answer.
3. What type of e-commerce business model is Alibaba?
4. Discuss different types of payment methods other than PayPal that could be used by eBay's competition Alibaba.
5. What ethical and legal issues could be faced by exporters using eBay? Give a detailed example of each one.

Sources: Compiled from B. Einhorn, "eBay Finds a Secret Door to China," *Bloomberg BusinessWeek*, April 18–24, 2011; L. Chao, "Taobao to Launch Local Deals on Group-Buying Website," *The Wall Street Journal*, February 23, 2011; J. Mangalindan, "Can Groupon Crack the China Puzzle?" *Fortune*, February 23, 2011; G. Epstein, "The Biggest Winner in China in 2015? E-Commerce," *Forbes*, January 4, 2011; H. Wang, "How eBay Failed in China," *Forbes*, September 12, 2010; "eBay Finds It Hard to Topple Alibaba in China," *Forbes*, September 10, 2010; G. Epstein, "eBay Chief Visits His Chinese Conqueror," *Forbes*, September 9, 2010; B. Bao, "How Internet Censorship Is Curbing Innovation in China," *The Atlantic*, April 22, 2013.

[Interactive Case]

Planning E-commerce Applications for Ruby's Club

Go to the Ruby's Club link at the Student Companion website or *WileyPLUS* for information about your current internship assignment. You will evaluate opportunities for e-commerce at Ruby's and build a spreadsheet application that will help Ruby's managers make decisions about e-commerce options.

Chapter 6

Wireless, Mobile Computing, and Mobile Commerce

[LEARNING OBJECTIVES]	[CHAPTER OUTLINE]	[WEB RESOURCES]

1. Describe the four main types of wireless transmission media. Identify at least one advantage and one disadvantage of each type.
2. Discuss the basic purposes of short-range, medium-range, and long-range networks. Explain how businesses can use at least one technology employed by each type of network.
3. Discuss the five major m-commerce applications. Provide a specific example of how each application can benefit a business.
4. Define "pervasive computing." Describe two technologies that underlie this technology. Provide at least one example of how a business can use each one.
5. Identify the four major threats to wireless networks. Explain, with examples, how each one can damage a business.

Student Companion Site

wiley.com/college/rainer

- Student PowerPoints for note taking
- Interactive Case: Ruby's Club Assignments
- Complete glossary

WileyPlus

All of the above and

- E-book
- Mini-lecture by author for each chapter section
- Practice quizzes
- Flash Cards for vocabulary review
- Additional "What's in IT for Me?" cases
- Video interviews with managers
- Lab Manual for Microsoft Office 2010
- How-to Animations for Microsoft Office 2010

What's In IT For Me?
THIS CHAPTER WILL HELP PREPARE YOU TO ...
ACCT
Count and audit inventory
FIN
Manage wireless payment systems
MKT
Manage location-based advertising
POM
Increase productivity in warehouses
HR
Improve employee communications
MIS
Provide a firm's wireless infrastructure

[Case 6.1 The Battle for the Mobile Wallet]

The Problem

Customers today are in more of a hurry than ever before. To satisfy them and keep their business, retailers are looking for strategies to speed up the checkout process and improve the overall customer experience. One strategy is to rely on customers' smart phones as a replacement for all of their credit and debit cards. Instead of swiping a plastic card at the checkout counter, consumers merely wave their phones a few inches above a payment terminal.This process uses a contact-free technology called *near-field communications (NFC)*.

The strategy described in the preceding paragraph, known as the **mobile wallet**, is already being used both in Canada and internationally. Wide adoption of this technology in North America, however, is being hindered by a major battle among large corporations.

In one camp are the established credit card companies such as MasterCard, Visa, and American Express, along with the banks that actually issue the cards to customers. These businesses want to maintain their traditional position at the centre of any payment system and to continue to collect fees from merchants. However, they are facing intense competition from technology companies, such as Google and PayPal, whose goal is to become major players in the new payment system. In addition, Apple and mobile carriers such as Bell, Rogers, and TELUS want to collect fees through control of the phones themselves. Adding to this competitive mix are individual companies, such as Starbucks, that are developing proprietary mobile wallet technologies.

Slavoljub Pantelic/Shutterstock

In the middle, and perhaps playing a deciding role, are the retailers, who have to install terminals that accept mobile payments. Consumer advocates, meanwhile, are concerned that a mobile system will bring higher fees, which would be passed along to customers.

The stakes in this competition are enormous because the small fees generated every time consumers swipe their cards add up to tens of billions of dollars annually.

A Variety of Solutions

Mobile phone carriers. Three large cellular providers in Canada—Bell, Rogers, and TELUS—have a joint venture called *EnStream*. It is a payment network that encompasses credit card companies and card-issuing banks. EnStream (*www.enstream.com*) creates a digital wallet into which customers of card-issuing banks can easily move their accounts.

Credit card issuers. In 2000, RBC (Royal Bank of Canada, *www.rbc.com*) and BMO (Bank of Montreal, *www.bmo.com*) formed a joint venture called Moneris (*www.moneris.com*). Moneris is a payment processor and MasterCard credit card processor, while TD (Toronto Dominion Bank, *www.td.com*) uses Visa. Moneris in turn has made acquisitions that include Ernex Marketing Technologies, which provides loyalty cards and gift cards, and Keycorp Canada Inc., which supports point-of-sale devices. How are mobile credit card apps changing the payment process? They allow consumers to make purchases with the tap of a button, instead of having to enter their credit card number, billing address, and other information each time they make a transaction. For example, a game on a smart phone could allow players to buy add-on features, such as new skins (digital appearances), by clicking on the Visa logo inside the game. A caterer could send a customer a bill by e-mail that they could pay with one click.

Technology companies. Google has its own payment system called *Google Wallet* (*www.google.com/wallet/how-it-works/*). The company claims that it is willing to partner with payment processors to handle purchases made with its smart phones. Interestingly, future models of the iPhone that incorporate NFC may route payments through Apple's iTunes store, which already has more than 200 million accounts tied to credit cards, or with Apple's new EasyPay app. PayPal has developed PayPal X, which has evolved into X-Commerce (*www.x.com*).

Developers (see *http://developer.paypal.com*) can create software for payments using PayPal. For example, if you are at the ballpark and you want to skip the long lines at the concession stand, just download the Yorder (*http://yorder.it*) smart phone app. The app lets sports fans order hot dogs and cold beer from their mobile phones and pay by transferring money from PayPal (*www.paypal.com*) to a nearby food vendor. An alert pops up when the order is ready. PayPal, a unit of eBay, earns about 3 percent on each transaction. The Yorder app is one of more than 5,000 developed by entrepreneurs using PayPal X.

In addition, other services, such as Zong (*www.zong.com*) and Obopay (*www.obopay.com*), are developing applications to make on-line and mobile payments easier.

Individual companies. Starbucks (*www.starbucks.ca*), which was a pioneer in bringing gourmet coffee to the masses, also pioneered ways to pay for those lattes. In January 2011, it announced North America's first major pay-by-phone service. It launched a free bar-code app, allowing customers to hold their phones in front of a scanner at Starbucks cash registers in almost 7,000 of its stores. The money is subtracted from customers' Starbucks accounts, which they can load with credit cards, or, on iPhones, with PayPal funds. Customers can also use the Starbucks app to check their balances, find nearby stores, and earn stars to qualify for free drinks.

Tim Hortons has similarly gone to paperless payments (although it is not considered a mobile wallet). You can use a debit card, credit card, or load money onto your Tim Hortons card for contact-free payments.

The Results

The battle for the transaction fees from your mobile wallet is ongoing, and the results will be several years in arriving. However, the potential for large revenue streams is real, because mobile wallets have clear advantages. For example: Which are you more likely to have with you at any given moment—your phone or your physical wallet? Also, keep in mind that if you lose your phone, it can be located on a map and remotely deactivated. Plus, your phone can be password protected. Your physical wallet, however, does not have such tools.

What We Learned from This Case

Wireless is a term that describes telecommunications in which electromagnetic waves, rather than some form of wire or cable, carry the signal between communicating devices such as computers, smart phones, and iPads. The opening case describes the intense competition among large and small companies for access to the vast sums of money generated by the form of wireless communications called mobile commerce.

Practically all organizations use wireless computing. Therefore, when you begin your career, you likely will be assigned a company smart phone and a wireless computer. Clearly, then, you need to learn about wireless computing not only because you will be using wireless applications, but also because wireless computing is so important to many organizations.

Sources: Compiled from R. Kim, R. Sidel, and S. Raice, "Pay By Phone Dialed Back," *The Wall Street Journal*, May 4, 2011; T. Team, "American Express and Visa Squeeze PayPal's Crown Jewels," *Forbes*, April 4, 2011; A. Efrati and R. Sidel, "Google Sets Role in Mobile Payment," *The Wall Street Journal*, March 28, 2011; T. Bernard and C. Miller, "Swiping Is the Easy Part," *The New York Times*, March 23, 2011; D. Aamoth, "Pay Phone," *Time*, February 21, 2011; D. MacMillan, "Turning Smartphones Into Cash Registers," *Bloomberg BusinessWeek*, February 14–20, 2011; K. Eaton, "The Race Is On to Make NFC Wireless Credit Card Dreams Come True (and Win Market Share)," *Fast Company*, February 2, 2011; M. Hamblen, "NFC: What You Need to Know," *Computerworld*, January 28, 2011; K. Heussner, "Is Your Next Credit Card Your Cell Phone?" *ABC News*, January 26, 2011; S. Greengard, "Mobile Payment, Please," *Baseline Magazine*, January 26, 2011; E. Zemen, "Will Apple, Google Lead Mobile Payment Revolution?" *InformationWeek*, January 25, 2011; B. Ellis, "The End of Credit Cards Is Coming," *CNNMoney*, January 24, 2011; C. Miller, "Now at Starbucks: Buy a Latte by Waving Your Phone," *The New York Times*, January 18, 2011; O. Kharif, "In the Works: A Google Mobile Payment Service?" *Bloomberg BusinessWeek*, January 4, 2011; H. Shaughnessy, "Banking Gets Mobile and Social," *Forbes*, November 22, 2010; J. Galante and P. Eichenbaum, "Card Companies Are Wooing Programmers," *Bloomberg BusinessWeek*, November 22–28, 2010; T. Claburn, "Web 2.0: Google CEO Sees Android Phones Replacing Credit Cards," *InformationWeek*, November 16, 2010; E. Zeman, "Starbucks Mobile Pay Now in NYC," *InformationWeek*, November 1, 2010; *http://yorder.it*, *www.paypal.com*, *http://developer.paypal.com*, *www.moneris.com*, *www.ernex.com*, *www.timhortons.com*, accessed March 6, 2013.

IT's about [small] business

6.1 Tacos, Trucks, and Tweets?

Mark Manguera had a great idea. He thought that Korean barbeque would taste great on a taco. Sound odd? Manguera actually took this idea one step further by planning to sell his concoction from a taco truck like ice cream! But how would he let people know his location so they could find his truck and buy his tacos? The Korean taco from a truck concept involves a number of variables. The location and menu of his Kogi BBQ change daily, and so do the customers. Good communication would be critical to a successful operation.

The answer to Manguera's dilemma was simply to tweet his location. (You learn about Twitter in Chapter 7.) Manguera's family and friends began blogging and tweeting about his tacos. By leveraging Twitter and mobile connectivity via smart phones, Manguera obtained access to all cellular networks and devices that accepted text messages. His story went viral—meaning that it spread rapidly—and it attracted a large number of followers.

Using Twitter to reach customers across mobile networks, Manguera began to share his location and to ask others to forward it. As a result, his truck draws between 300 and 800 people each time it parks. Manguera now operates out of five trucks and one bar in a restaurant. He updates his Twitter feed constantly, informing customers where his trucks are and where they are going. His website provides this information ahead of time and even suggests locations where customers can sit down to enjoy the food.

Mark Manguera's Korean BBQ tacos not only were a hit, but they gave birth to a cultural phenomenon. "Kogi culture," as it is known in Los Angeles, refers to the large crowds of people who congregate around the truck. It brings people out in neighbourhoods where otherwise they would stay indoors. He was even contacted by an entertainment company because his crowds create mini-street parties and have opened the doors to other entrepreneurs.

The street truck movement is gaining ground in Canada, and social media is playing a big role in promotion. As one of many examples, Smoke's Poutinerie, a chain of poutine restaurants across Canada, uses only social media for advertising its mobile trucks, such as posting its locations on Twitter.

Questions

1. Provide specific examples of the advantages that mobile communications provided to Mark Manguera.
2. Which technology, Twitter or mobile communications, enables the other? Support your answer.

Sources: Compiled from "Kogi BBQ—A Combination of Chipotle and Korean Food on Wheels!" *The Howler Online*, January 20, 2011; J. Gelt, "Kogi Korean BBQ, a Taco Truck Brought to You by Twitter," *The Los Angeles Times*, February 11, 2009; *http://kogibbq.com*, accessed March 6, 2013; *http://smokespoutinerie.com*, accessed June 2, 2013.

In your job, you will be involved with customers via wireless transactions, with analyzing and developing mobile commerce applications, and with wireless security. The list goes on.

Simply put, an understanding of wireless technology and mobile commerce applications will make you more valuable to your organization. When you read the What's in IT for Me? section at the end of this chapter, envision yourself performing the activities discussed in your functional area. An understanding of wireless technology can also help you start and grow your own business, as illustrated in IT's About Small Business 6.1.

Before you continue, a distinction needs to be made between the terms "wireless" and "mobile." *Wireless* means exactly what it says: without wires. In contrast, *mobile* is something that changes its location over time. Some wireless networks, such as MiFi (discussed later in this chapter), are also mobile. Others, however, are fixed. For example, microwave towers form fixed wireless networks.

In many situations, the traditional working environment that requires users to come to a wired computer is either ineffective or inefficient. In these situations, the solution is to use computers small enough to carry or wear that can communicate via wireless networks. The ability to communicate anytime and anywhere provides organizations with a strategic advantage by increasing productivity and speed and improving customer service.

Wireless technologies enable individuals and organizations to conduct mobile computing, mobile commerce, and pervasive computing. We will define these terms here, then discuss them in detail later in the chapter. **Mobile computing** involves a real-time, wireless connection between a mobile device and other computing environments, such as the Internet or an intranet. **Mobile commerce**—also known as **m-commerce**—involves e-commerce (EC) transactions that are conducted with a mobile device. **Pervasive computing**, also called

ubiquitous computing, means that virtually every object has processing power with wireless or wired connections to a global network.

Wireless technologies and mobile commerce are spreading rapidly, replacing or supplementing wired computing. In fact, Cisco (*www.cisco.com*) predicted that the volume of mobile devices would exceed the world's population by the end of 2013. The company predicts that the growth rate of wireless data traffic will exceed 66 percent per year until 2017. As you saw in the opening case, a huge battle is underway to provide you with a mobile, digital wallet and to enable you to get rid of your physical wallet altogether, including all of the credit and debit cards you have in it. Billions of dollars are at stake, further highlighting the importance of wireless to individuals and their organizations.

The wireless infrastructure upon which mobile computing is built may reshape the entire IT field. The technologies, applications, and limitations of mobile computing and mobile commerce are the main focus of this chapter. You begin the chapter by learning about wireless devices and wireless transmission media. You continue by examining wireless computer networks and wireless Internet access. You then look at mobile computing and mobile commerce, which are made possible by wireless technologies. Finally, you will turn your attention to pervasive computing and conclude the chapter by familiarizing yourself with a critical component of the wireless environment, namely, wireless security.

6.1 Wireless Technologies

Wireless technologies include both wireless devices, such as smart phones, and wireless transmission media, such as microwave, satellite, and radio. These technologies are fundamentally changing the ways organizations operate.

Individuals find wireless devices convenient and productive to use for several reasons. First, they can make productive use of time that formerly was wasted (for example, the time spent commuting to work on public transportation). Second, because people can take these devices with them, their work locations are becoming much more flexible. Third, wireless technology enables working time to be scheduled around personal and professional obligations.

Wireless Devices

Wireless devices provide three major advantages to users:

- They are small enough to easily carry or wear.
- They have sufficient computing power to perform productive tasks.
- They can communicate wirelessly with the Internet and other devices.

Modern *smart phones* provide capabilities that include cellular telephony, Bluetooth, Wi-Fi, a digital camera for images and video, global positioning system (GPS), an organizer, a scheduler, an address book, a calculator, access to e-mail and short message service (SMS) (sending and receiving short text messages up to 160 characters in length), instant messaging, text messaging, an MP3 music player, a video player, Internet access with a full-function browser, and a QWERTY keyboard.

One downside of smart phones is that people can use them to copy and pass on confidential information. For example, would an executive at Intel want workers snapping pictures of colleagues with the company's secret new technology in the background? Unfortunately, many managers think of these devices as phones, not as digital cameras that can transmit wirelessly. Jamming devices continue to evolve that counter the threat. Some companies, such as Samsung (*www.samsung.com*), have recognized the danger and have banned smart phones from their premises altogether. But regardless of their disadvantages, cell phones, and particularly smart phones, have far greater impact on human society than most of us realize, as you can see in Table 6.1.

The latest version of cell phones—smart phones—are getting smaller and smarter. Example 6.1 talks about how wearable smart phones or computers may be implemented.

Table 6.1

Do Not Underestimate the Power of Cell Phones!

- In January 1982, the first 100 hand-held cell phones, each weighing 1 kilogram, were put into service in Washington, DC. By mid-2009, there was one cell phone for every two humans on earth and by 2011 there were 6 billion (representing more than 85 percent of the world's population at that time). This represents the fastest global diffusion of any technology in human history. Cell phones have transformed the world faster than did electricity, automobiles, refrigeration, credit cards, and television.
- Cell phones have made an even bigger difference in less time in underdeveloped areas where land lines are scarce. Cell phones have become the driving force behind many modernizing economies. They are the first telecommunications technology in history to have more users in the developing world—60 percent of all users—than in the developed nations. As an example, cell phone usage in Africa has been growing at 50 percent annually, faster than any other region.

- Cell phones can heavily influence politics. For example, cell phones played a critical role in the revolutions that erupted across the Middle East in 2011 and in the revolt against sexual abuse in Iran and South Africa in 2013.
- Your cell phone now can be your wallet. As the chapter-opening case demonstrates, there is almost nothing in your wallet that you cannot put into your cell phone; for example, pictures of your spouse and children, credit cards, bus tickets, and many other items.
- In neighbourhoods around Cambridge, England, bicycle couriers monitor air pollution using cell phones equipped with global positioning technology.
- Scientists at Purdue University want to network the United States with millions of cell phones equipped with radiation sensors to detect terrorists trying to assemble dirty bombs.
- In many large cities, cell phones are being used to transmit real-time traffic information, such as automobile speeds, the extent of traffic jams, and expected travel times, and to pay for parking. You can also use a street food app to find the nearest street food vendor.
- And there is more to come! Cell phones, with all their power, have problems such as haphazard sound quality, dropped calls, slow downloads, and annoying delays between speaking and being heard. To help solve these problems, miniature cellular base stations, called *femtocells*, can be used to improve reception. Femtocells work with any cell phone, and they relieve congestion on cell towers and cellular frequencies by creating extra capacity at very low cost. The transmitter is cheap, the broadband connection is free (most houses and offices have existing idle broadband connections), and the low-power signal does not interfere with other frequencies.

Example 6.1

In early 2013, Google announced *Google Glass*, eyeglass-based computing that has a camera and is a fully functioning wireless device that can be used to check the weather from the Internet, and use its camera to record everything that you see. This introduces a new kind of relationship protocol: whenever someone is wearing glasses, you may need to check whether they are recording your conversation before you begin! These glasses are considerably more portable than the first pair invented by Steven Mann (a University of Toronto professor) in 1978, who wore heavy, clunky glasses as a wearable computer and carried the computing equipment to support them in a backpack.

One of the inventions that is facilitating small wearable computers is the development of a watch-sized touch screen by WIMM Labs now called e-paper. Intelligent watches are now available from Pebble, ConnecteDevice, i'm Watch, and Sony, among others, with companies such as Apple, Samsung, Microsoft, LG, and Google rumoured to have some in the works. These watches can function as or interface with your smart phone. They are touch sensitive and may be voice activated.

If the idea of a smaller keyboard does not work for you, how about using your body motions to control your phone? Graduate students conducting research at Toronto's OCAD University used eye movement to control computing devices. A total of 32 movements, including examples like a sideways swipe of the eyes or vertical up and down movement, were used to represent characters. A German team is looking at wearable computers that you attach to your shoe. With a camera and motion sensors, touching your elbow or pinching your finger could be translated into a command sent to your smart phone. If these types of devices are marketed and people like them, then we might see people practising unusual eye movements or strange physical movements. It would make walking down the street a very different experience.

Wireless Transmission Media

Wireless media, or broadcast media, transmit signals without wires. The major types of wireless media are microwave, satellite, radio, and infrared. Table 6.2 lists the advantages and disadvantages of each type.

Microwave. **Microwave transmission** systems transmit data via electromagnetic waves. These systems are used for high-volume, long-distance, line-of-sight communication. *Line-of-sight* means that the transmitter and receiver must be in view of each other. This requirement creates problems because the earth's surface is curved rather than flat. For this reason, microwave towers usually cannot be spaced more than about 50 kilometres apart.

Clearly then, microwave transmissions offer only a limited solution to data communications needs, especially over very long distances. Additionally, microwave transmissions are susceptible to environmental interference during severe weather such as heavy rain or snowstorms. Although long-distance microwave data communications systems are still widely used, they are being replaced by satellite communications systems.

Satellite. **Satellite transmission** systems make use of communication satellites. Currently, there are three types of satellites around the earth: *geostationary (GEO)*, *medium-earth-orbit (MEO)*, and *low-earth-orbit (LEO)*. Each type has a different orbit, with the GEO being farthest from the earth and the LEO the closest. In this section you examine the three types of satellites and then discuss two major satellite applications: global positioning systems and Internet transmission via satellites. Table 6.3 compares and contrasts the three types of satellites.

As with microwave transmission, satellites must receive and transmit data via line-of-sight; however, their enormous *footprint*—the area of the earth's surface reached by a satellite's transmission—overcomes the limitations of microwave data relay stations. The most basic rule governing footprint size is simple: The higher a satellite orbits, the larger its footprint. Thus, medium-earth-orbit satellites have a smaller footprint than do geostationary satellites, and low-earth-orbit satellites have the smallest footprint of all. Figure 6.1 compares the footprints of the three types of satellite.

In contrast to line-of-sight transmission with microwave, satellites use *broadcast* transmission, which sends signals to many receivers at one time. So, even though satellites are line-of-sight like microwave, they are high enough for broadcast transmission, thus overcoming the limitations of microwave.

Types of Orbits. Geostationary earth orbit satellites orbit 35,900 kilometres directly above the equator. These satellites maintain a fixed position above the earth's surface because at their altitude, their orbital period matches the 24-hour rotational period of the earth. For this reason, receivers on the earth do not have to track GEO satellites. GEO satellites are excellent for sending television programs to cable operators and for broadcasting directly to homes.

One major limitation of GEO satellites is that their transmissions take a quarter of a second to send and return. This brief pause, a kind of **propagation delay**, makes two-way telephone conversations difficult. Also, GEO satellites are large and expensive, and they require substantial amounts of power to launch.

Sources: K. Allen, "Touch Your Elbow to Answer Your Phone," *Toronto Star*, p. GT1, GT11, May 12, 2012; A. Ballingall, "The Smartphone Gets Out of Hand," *Toronto Star*, p. B1, B4, February 23, 2013; "Forget QWERTY vs. Touchscreen: Future Smartphones Will Be Controlled with Your Eyes," ITbusiness.ca, April 18, 2013; K. Solomon, "Microsoft Is Also Working on a Smart Watch, Apparently," Techradar.com, April 15, 2013; *http://getpebble.com*, *www.connectedevice.com*, *www.imsmart.com*, *www.sonymobile.com/us/products/accessories/smartwatch/*, accessed April 23, 2013.

Table 6.2

Advantages and Disadvantages of Wireless Media

Channel	Advantages	Disadvantages
Microwave	High bandwidth. Relatively inexpensive.	Must have unobstructed line of sight. Susceptible to environmental interference.
Satellite	High bandwidth. Large coverage area.	Expensive. Must have unobstructed line of sight. Signals experience propagation delay. Must use encryption for security.
Radio	High bandwidth. Signals pass through walls. Inexpensive and easy to install.	Creates electrical interference problems. Susceptible to snooping unless encrypted.
Infrared	Low to medium bandwidth. Used only for short distances.	Must have unobstructed line of sight.

Sources: Compiled from "Juries and the Internet: Justice Online," *The Guardian*, January 3, 2011; "As Jurors Go Online, U.S. Trials Go Off Track," *Reuters*, December 8, 2010.

Medium-earth-orbit satellites are located about 10,354 kilometres above the earth's surface. MEO orbits require more satellites to cover the earth than do GEO orbits because MEO footprints are smaller. MEO satellites have two advantages over GEO satellites: They are less expensive, and they do not have an appreciable propagation delay. Because MEO satellites move with respect to a point on the earth's surface, however, receivers must track these satellites. (Think of a satellite dish slowly turning to remain oriented to an MEO satellite.)

Low-earth-orbit satellites are located 640 to 1,125 kilometres above the earth's surface. Because LEO satellites are much closer to the earth, they have little, if any, propagation delay. Like MEO satellites, however, LEO satellites move with respect to a point on the earth's surface

Table 6.3

Three Basic Types of Telecommunications Satellites

Type	Characteristics	Orbit	Number	Use
GEO	• Satellites remain stationary relative to point on earth. • Few satellites needed for global coverage. • Transmission delay (approximately 0.25 second). • Most expensive to build and launch. • Longest orbital life (many years).	35,900 kilometres	8	TV signal
MEO	• Satellites move relative to point on earth. • Moderate number needed for global coverage. • Require medium-powered transmitters. • Negligible transmission delay. • Less expensive to build and launch. • Moderate orbital life (6–12 years).	10,354 kilometres	10–12	GPS
LEO	• Satellites move rapidly relative to point on earth. • Large number needed for global coverage. • Require only low-power transmitters. • Negligible transmission delay. • Least expensive to build and launch. • Shortest orbital life (as low as 5 years).	640–1,125 kilometres	Many	Telephone

and therefore must be tracked by receivers. LEO satellites are more difficult to track than are MEO satellites because LEO satellites move much more quickly relative to a point on the earth.

Unlike GEO and MEO satellites, LEO satellites can pick up signals from weak transmitters. This characteristic enables satellite telephones to operate via LEO satellites, because they can operate with less power and smaller batteries. Another advantage of LEO satellites is that they consume less power and cost less to launch than do GEO and MEO satellites.

At the same time, however, the footprints of LEO satellites are small, which means that many of them are required to cover the earth. For this reason, a single organization often produces LEO satellites in groups known as *LEO constellations*. Two examples are Iridium and Globalstar.

Iridium (*www.iridium.com*) has placed a LEO constellation in orbit that consists of 66 satellites and 12 in-orbit spare satellites. The company maintains that it provides complete satellite communications coverage of the earth's surface, including the polar regions. Globalstar (*www.globalstar.com*) also has a LEO constellation in orbit.

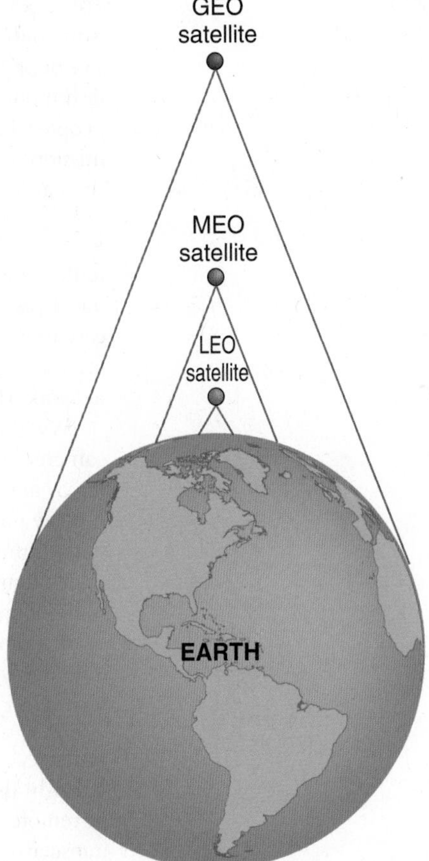

FIGURE 6.1 Comparison of satellite footprints. (*Source:* Drawn by Kelly Rainer)

Global Positioning Systems. The **global positioning system (GPS)** is a wireless system that uses satellites to enable users to determine their position anywhere on the earth. GPS is supported by 24 MEO satellites that are shared worldwide. The exact position of each satellite is always known because the satellite continuously broadcasts its position along with a time signal. By using the known speed of the signals and the distance from three satellites (for two-dimensional location) or four satellites (for three-dimensional location), GPS software can find the location of any receiving station or user within a range of three metres. GPS software also can convert the user's latitude and longitude to an electronic map.

Most of you are probably familiar with GPS in automobiles, which "talks" to drivers when giving directions. Figure 6.2 illustrates two ways for drivers to obtain GPS information in a car: a dashboard navigation system, and a GPS app (TomTom; *www.tomtom.com*) on an iPhone.

Commercial use of GPS for activities such as navigating, mapping, and surveying has become widespread, particularly in remote areas. Cell phones in the United States now must have a GPS embedded in them so that the location of a person making an emergency call (for example, 911) can be detected immediately. For a GPS tutorial, visit *www.trimble.com/gps_tutorial/*.

Three other global positioning systems are either planned or operational. The Russian GPS, called *GLONASS*, was completed in 1995. The system fell into disrepair, however, with the collapse of the Soviet economy. In 2010, GLONASS achieved 100 percent coverage of Russian territory. The European Union GPS, called *Galileo*, has an anticipated completion date of 2015. Finally, China expects to complete its GPS, called *Beidou*, by 2020.

Dashboard GPS

TomTom app on iPhone

FIGURE 6.2 Obtaining GPS information in an automobile. (*Source:* Image Source)

Internet over Satellite (IoS). In many regions of the world, Internet over Satellite (IoS) is the only option available for Internet connections because using cables is either too expensive or physically impossible. IoS enables users to access the Internet via GEO satellites from a dish mounted on the side of their homes. Although IoS makes the Internet available to many people who otherwise could not access it, it has its drawbacks. Not only do GEO satellite transmissions entail a propagation delay, but they can be disrupted by environmental influences such as thunderstorms.

Radio. **Radio transmission** uses radio-wave frequencies to send data directly between transmitters and receivers. Radio transmission has several advantages. To begin with, radio waves travel easily through normal office walls. In addition, radio devices are fairly inexpensive and easy to install. Finally, radio waves can transmit data at high speeds. For these reasons, radio increasingly is being used to connect computers to both peripheral equipment and local area networks (LANs; discussed in Chapter 4).

As with other technologies, however, radio transmission has its drawbacks. First, radio media can create electrical interference problems. Also, radio transmissions are susceptible to snooping by anyone who has similar equipment that operates on the same frequency.

One problem with radio transmission is that when you travel too far away from the source station, the signal breaks up and fades into static. Most radio signals can travel only about 50 or 60 kilometres from their source. *Satellite radio*, however, overcomes this problem. **Satellite radio** offers uninterrupted, near CD-quality music that is beamed to your radio, either at home or in your car, from space. In addition, satellite radio offers a broad spectrum of stations with different types of music, news, and talk. Sirius XM (*www.siriusxm.ca/*) provides satellite radio services in North America. Listeners subscribe to the service for a monthly fee.

Infrared. The final type of wireless transmission is infrared transmission. **Infrared** light is red light that usually is not visible to human eyes. Common applications of infrared light are in remote control units for televisions, VCRs, DVDs, and CD players. In addition, infrared transceivers, like radio transmitters, are used for short-distance connections between computers and peripheral equipment and local area networks. A *transceiver* is a device that can both transmit and receive signals.

before you go on...

1. Describe the most common types of wireless devices.
2. Describe the various types of transmission media.

6.2 Wireless Computer Networks and Internet Access

We have looked at various wireless devices and how they transmit wireless signals. These devices typically form wireless computer networks, and they provide wireless Internet access. Next, we will study wireless networks categorized by their effective distance: short-range, medium-range, and wide-area.

Short-Range Wireless Networks

Short-range wireless networks simplify the task of connecting one device to another by eliminating wires and enabling users to move around while they use the devices. In general, short-range wireless networks have a range of 30 metres or less. In this section we consider three basic short-range networks: Bluetooth, ultra-wideband (UWB), and near-field communications (NFC).

Bluetooth. **Bluetooth** (*www.bluetooth.com*) is an industry specification used to create small personal area networks. Recall from Chapter 4 that a **personal area network (PAN)** is a computer network used for communication among computer devices—for example, telephones, personal digital assistants, and smart phones—located close to one person. Bluetooth 1.0 can link up to eight devices within a 10-metre area with a bandwidth of 700 Kbps (kilobits per second) using low-power, radio-based communication. Bluetooth 2.0 can transmit up to 2.1 Mbps (megabits per second) and at greater power, up to 100 metres. Ericsson, the Scandinavian mobile handset company that developed Bluetooth, named it after the 10th-century Danish king, Harald Blatan (Blatan means "Bluetooth"). It named the standard after him because he unified previously separate islands into the nation of Denmark.

Common applications for Bluetooth are wireless handsets for cell phones and portable music players. Advantages of Bluetooth include low power consumption and the fact that it uses omnidirectional radio waves; that is, radio waves emitted in all directions from a transmitter. For this reason, you do not have to point one Bluetooth device at another to establish a connection.

Ultra-Wideband. **Ultra-wideband (UWB)** is a high-bandwidth wireless technology with transmission speeds in excess of 100 Mbps. This very high speed makes UWB a good choice for applications such as streaming multimedia from, say, a personal computer to a television.

Time Domain (*www.timedomain.com*), a pioneer in ultra-wideband technology, has developed many UWB applications. One interesting application is the PLUS Real-Time Location System (RTLS). An organization can use PLUS to locate multiple people and assets simultaneously. Employees, customers, and/or visitors wear the PLUS Badge Tag. PLUS Asset Tags are placed on equipment and products. PLUS is extremely valuable for health care environments, where real-time location of caregivers (e.g., doctors, nurses, technicians) and mobile equipment (e.g., laptops, monitors) is critical.

Near-Field Communications. **Near-field communications (NFC)** has the smallest range of any short-range wireless network. It is designed to be embedded in mobile devices such as cell phones and credit cards. For example, using NFC, you can swipe your device or card within a few centimetres of point-of-sale terminals to pay for items.

Medium-Range Wireless Networks

Medium-range wireless networks are the familiar wireless local area networks (WLANs). The most common type of medium-range wireless network is Wireless Fidelity, or Wi-Fi. WLANs are useful in a variety of settings, some of which may be challenging.

Wireless Fidelity (Wi-Fi). **Wireless Fidelity** (or **Wi-Fi**) is a medium-range **wireless local area network (WLAN)**, which is basically like a wired LAN, but without the cables. In a typical configuration, a transmitter with an antenna, called a **wireless access point**, connects to a wired LAN or to satellite dishes that provide an Internet connection. Figure 6.3 shows a wireless access point. A wireless access point provides service to a number of users within a small geographical perimeter (up to about 60 metres), known as a **hotspot**. Supporting a larger number of users across a larger geographical area requires multiple wireless access points. To communicate wirelessly, mobile devices, such as laptop PCs, typically have built-in wireless network interface capability.

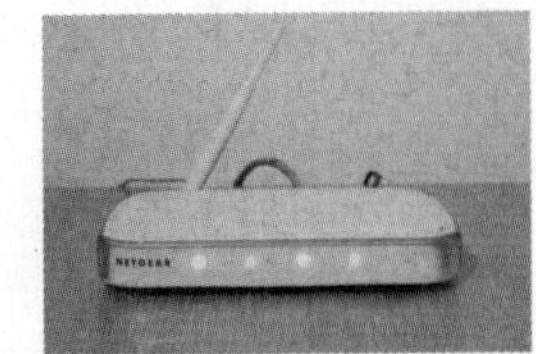

FIGURE 6.3 Wireless access point. (*Source:* @ Pearl Bucknall/ Age Fotostock America, Inc.)

Wi-Fi provides fast and easy Internet or intranet broadband access from public hotspots located at airports, hotels, Internet cafés, universities, conference centres, offices, and homes (see Figure 6.4). Users can access the Internet while walking across the campus, to their office, or through their homes. In addition, users can access Wi-Fi with their laptops, desktops, or PDAs by adding a wireless network card. Most PC and laptop manufacturers incorporate these cards directly into their products.

The Institute of Electrical and Electronics Engineers (IEEE) has established a set of standards for wireless computer networks. The IEEE standard for Wi-Fi is the 802.11 family. There are four standards in this family: 802.11a, 802.11b, 802.11g, and 802.11n.

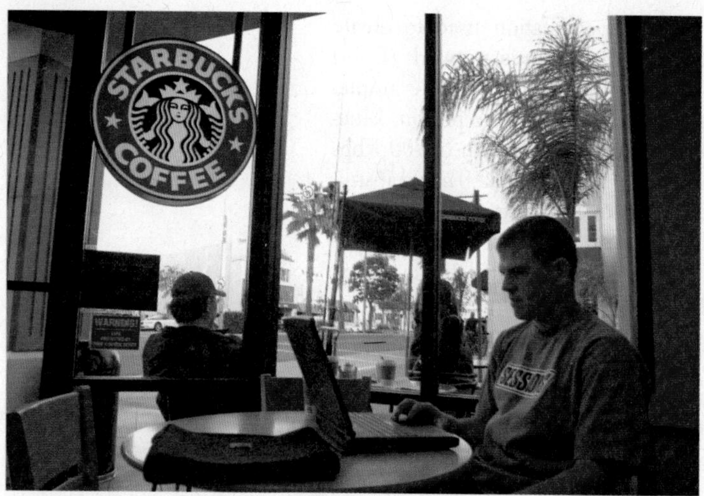

FIGURE 6.4 Starbucks' patrons using Wi-Fi. (*Source:* © Marianna Day Massey/Zuma Press)

Today, many WLANs use the 802.11n standard, which can transmit up to 600 Mbps and has a range of about 250 metres. There are many 802.11n products. One example is Netgear's (*http://ca.netgear.com/*) RangeMax Wireless-N router.

The major benefits of Wi-Fi are its low cost and its ability to provide simple Internet access. It is the greatest facilitator of the *wireless Internet*; that is, the ability to connect to the Internet wirelessly.

Corporations are integrating Wi-Fi into their strategies. For example, Starbucks, McDonalds, Tim Hortons, Indigo, and Second Cup offer customers Wi-Fi in many of their stores, primarily for Internet access.

Although Wi-Fi has become extremely popular, it is not without problems. Three factors are preventing the commercial Wi-Fi market from expanding even further: roaming, security, and cost. Regarding the first factor, currently users cannot roam to and from hotspots that use different Wi-Fi network services. Unless the services are free, users have to log on to separate accounts and, where required, pay a separate fee for each service. (Some Wi-Fi hotspots offer free service, while others charge a fee.)

Lack of security is the second barrier to greater acceptance of Wi-Fi. Because Wi-Fi uses radio waves, it is difficult to shield from intruders.

The final limitation to greater Wi-Fi expansion is its cost. Even though Wi-Fi services are relatively inexpensive, many experts question whether commercial Wi-Fi services can survive when so many free hotspots are available to users.

Wi-Fi Direct. Until late 2010, Wi-Fi required the presence of a wireless antenna at the centre of a hotspot, and ad hoc connections among individual computers or other devices were somewhat limited. Because of these limitations, organizations typically have used Wi-Fi for communications of up to about 250 metres and Bluetooth for shorter, ad hoc connections.

Wi-Fi Direct is a new generation of Wi-Fi. It enables peer-to-peer communications, so devices can connect directly. Wi-Fi Direct enables users to transfer content among devices, even without a wireless antenna. It can connect pairs or groups of devices at Wi-Fi speeds of up to 250 Mbps and at distances of up to 250 metres. Further, devices with Wi-Fi Direct can broadcast their availability to other devices just as Bluetooth devices can. Finally, Wi-Fi Direct is compatible with the billions of Wi-Fi devices currently in use.

Wi-Fi Direct may challenge the dominance of Bluetooth in the area of device-to-device networking. It offers a similar type of connectivity but with greater range and much faster data transfer.

MiFi. MiFi is a small, portable, wireless device that provides users with a permanent Wi-Fi hotspot wherever they go. Thus, users are always connected to the Internet. The range of the MiFi device is about 10 metres. Developed by NovAtel, the MiFi device is also called an *intelligent mobile hotspot*. Accessing Wi-Fi through the MiFi device allows up to five persons to be connected at the same time, sharing the same connection.

MiFi provides broadband Internet connectivity anywhere there is 3G cellular network coverage. MiFi also allows users to use VoIP technology to make free (or cheap) calls, both locally and internationally. One drawback with MiFi is the cost, both for acquiring it and for using it. Some smart phones, such as the iPhones, can be used as a MiFi.

Wireless Mesh Networks. **Mesh networks** use multiple Wi-Fi access points to create a wide area network. Mesh networks could have been discussed in the long-range wireless section, but they appear here because they are essentially a series of interconnected local area networks.

There are many examples of successful mesh-network applications. Consider the following:

- Electric meters now being placed on residential homes can transfer their readings from one to another and eventually to the central office for billing. This eliminates the need for human readers or the need to connect the meters with cables.
- The LEO Iridium constellation operates as a mesh network, with wireless links among adjacent satellites. Calls between satellite phones are routed through the mesh, from one satellite to another across the constellation, without having to go through an earth station. As a result, the signal travels a shorter distance, reducing any transmission lag. In addition, the constellation can operate with fewer earth stations.

Wide-Area Wireless Networks

Wide-area wireless networks connect users to the Internet over a geographically dispersed territory. These networks typically operate over the licensed spectrum. That is, they use portions of the wireless spectrum that are regulated by the government. In contrast, Bluetooth and Wi-Fi operate over the unlicensed spectrum and therefore are more prone to interference and security problems. In general, wide-area wireless network technologies fall into two categories: cellular radio, and wireless broadband.

Cellular Radio. **Cellular telephones** provide two-way radio communications over a cellular network of base stations with seamless handoffs. Cellular telephones differ from cordless telephones, which offer telephone service only within a limited range through a single base station attached to a fixed land line (for example, within a home or an office).

The cell phone communicates with radio antennas, or towers, placed within adjacent geographic areas called *cells* (see Figure 6.5). A telephone message is transmitted to the local cell—that is, the antenna—by the cell phone and then is passed from cell to cell until it

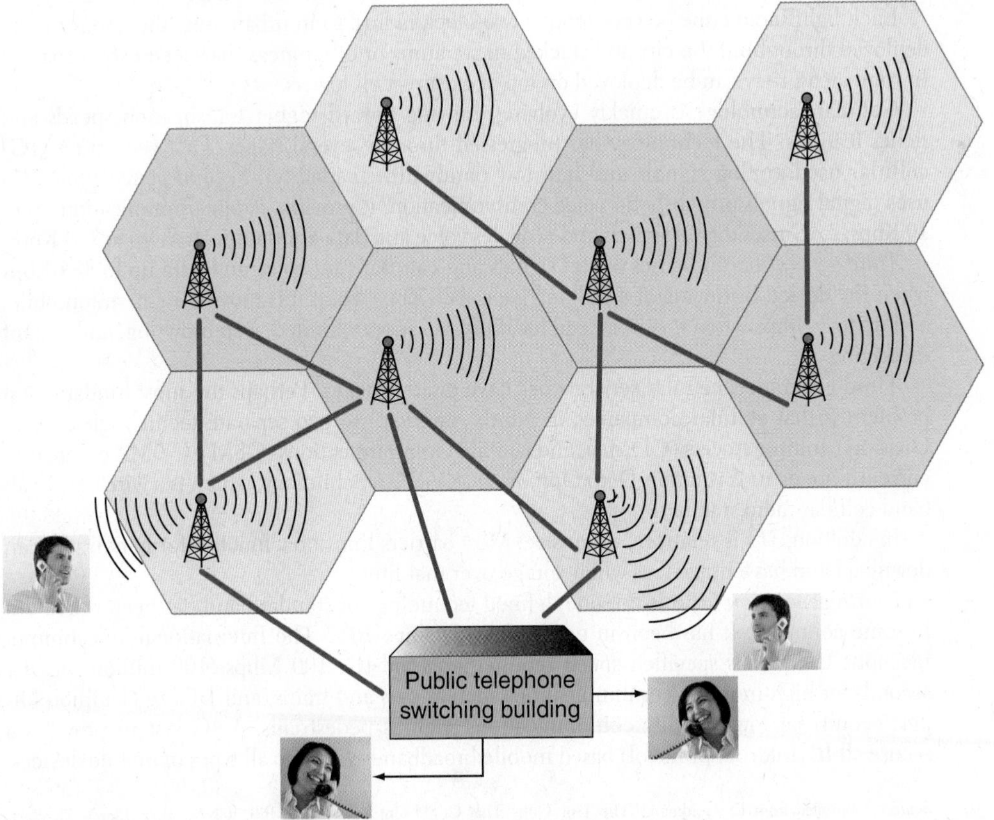

FIGURE 6.5 Smart phone and GPS system. © AP/Wide World Photos Cellular network. (*Sources*: Image Source; © Engine Images-Fotolia.com)

reaches the cell of its destination. At this final cell, the message either is transmitted to the receiving cell phone or is transferred to the public switched telephone system to be transmitted to a wireline telephone. This is why you can use a cell phone to call other cell phones as well as standard wireline phones.

Until early 2011, large cell towers were a "given" for cellular technology. Example 6.2 introduces an exciting new technology from Alcatel-Lucent (*www.alcatel-lucent.com*) that aims to replace these towers.

Example 6.2

The explosion in wireless services and apps is putting enormous pressure on the infrastructure that makes them possible. Despite spending more than $250 billion per year to operate and upgrade its networks, the global wireless industry can't keep up with demand for data usage. By 2020, it's expected that the amount of mobile data usage will grow by 500 times. What might be a saviour is a tiny cube called lightRadio, which combines miniaturization and cloud technology (discussed in Technology Guide 3).

At just 6 centimetres on each side, lightRadio is a cube developed by Alcatel-Lucent that contains all of the necessary components of a cell tower. Engineers removed the heavy power equipment that controls cell towers and moved it to centralized stations. What remains are the essentials inside lightRadio cubes, which are small enough to be set up virtually anywhere, from bus shelters to lamp posts.

lightRadio cubes are also one third more energy efficient than cell towers. They can also be more efficient in terms of maximizing signal power. The cubes emit data about who is using them. Wireless carriers can access these data live and then adjust the antennas' directional beams accordingly. For example, antennas may be pointed in one direction as people are heading to work in the morning and in another direction when they are going home. The cubes are compatible with several generations of networks, able to relay 2G, 3G, and 4G network signals (discussed next).

Each lightRadio cube powers about a two-block radius, so in urban areas the cubes can be deployed throughout the city and stacked in stadiums or other areas that need extra capacity. In rural areas, they can be deployed on top of existing cell towers.

Cellular technology is quickly evolving, moving toward higher transmission speeds and richer features. The technology has progressed through several stages. *First generation (1G)* cellular used analog signals and had low bandwidth (capacity). *Second generation (2G)* uses digital signals primarily for voice communication; it provides data communication up to 10 Kbps. 2.5G uses digital signals and provides voice and data communication up to 144 Kbps. *Third generation* (3G) uses digital signals and can transmit voice and data up to 384 Kbps when the device is moving at a walking pace, 128 Kbps when it is moving in an automobile, and up to 2 Mbps when it is in a fixed location. 3G supports video, web browsing, and instant messaging.

Third-generation cellular service does have disadvantages. Perhaps the most fundamental problem is that cellular companies in North America use two separate technologies: Code Division Multiple Access (CDMA), and Mobile Communications (GSM). CDMA companies currently are using *Evolution-Data Optimized (EV-DO)* technology, which is a wireless broadband cellular radio standard.

In addition, 3G is relatively expensive. Most carriers limit how much information you can download and have usage fees when you go over that limit.

Fourth generation (4G) is not one defined technology or standard and has been rolled out in some countries. It has been in use in Canada since 2012 The International Telecommunications Union has specified speed requirements for 4G: 100 Mbps (100 million bits per second) for high-mobility communications such as cars and trains, and 1 Gbps (1 billion bits per second) for low-mobility communications such as pedestrians. A 4G system provides a secure all-IP (Internet protocol) based mobile broadband system to all types of mobile devices.

Sources: Compiled from D. Goldman, "The Tiny Cube That Could Cut Your Phone Bill," *CNNMoney*, March 21, 2011; C. Babcock, "Alcatel Lucent Shrinks Cell Phone Towers," *InformationWeek*, February 7, 2011; V. C. Silva, "Alcatel-Lucent, China Mobile Launch Co-developed TD-LTE Solution," IDG News Service, *Computerworld*, March 14, 2013; *www.alcatel-lucent.com*, accessed March 6, 2013.

[about business]

6.2 WiMAX Helps the People of Northern Thailand

One of the most exciting business and social applications of technology is improving the lives of people in rural and remote areas. A joint project by Thailand's National Broadcasting and Telecommunications Commission (NBTC) and Mae Fah Luang (MFL) University is a case in point. The project is using WiMAX to deliver broadband communications to schools and villages in a remote region of northern Thailand, where few people have ever used a personal computer or the Internet. The project is part of an e-learning program that also benefits students and teachers.

The NTC and MFL University selected Cisco's Advanced Antenna System (AAS) because it provided increased data transmission volume over greater distances than did its competitors. The AAS uses multiple antennas to send and receive data, which decreases the likelihood that data will be lost. The project required that Cisco provide a minimum of 3 Mbps (3 megabits per second, or 3 million bits per second) upload and download speed. Cisco's actual transmission results were between 4.5 Mbps and 5 Mbps.

After the WiMAX system was deployed, the next phase was to create useful content for students and the communities. MFL University responded by developing an educational program for the surrounding schools. Faculty are responsible for training teachers from the rural schools on how to develop e-books in core subjects such as math, science, English, and social studies. The teachers are initially trained on how to create e-books with just text and images. After several months of training, teachers can enhance their e-books with embedded voice and video using various software applications.

The teachers then return to their respective schools and continue developing educational content, which has been highly successful, according to MFL University faculty members. The e-books are stored on a server farm (discussed in Technology Guide 3) located on the MFL University campus. This enables all the schools to access each other's e-books. The ability of the various village schools to collaborate with one another using the WiMAX technology has helped create a sense of community throughout the region.

Going beyond the schools, the project also provides the information in the e-books to everyone else in the outlying villages (primarily farmers who grow rice, pineapple, coffee, and tea). This is done using a more traditional medium: the radio communication that was standard in the villages before the WiMAX deployment. Now, teachers and school children use the Internet to compile information on important topics such as agriculture and health care. This content is developed into a script that is read by announcers at the radio stations. According to the MFL University staff, this process has been hugely successful. In fact, many villagers are learning to use computers and to access the Internet themselves for the first time in their lives.

What lessons can we learn from the WiMAX project in northern Thailand? First, WiMAX clearly is capable of handling mobile wireless data transmission at a very low total cost of ownership. Second, WiMAX can be implemented faster than wireline solutions.

Questions

1. Provide specific examples of other advantages that WiMAX can deliver to the villagers.
2. Provide specific examples of the advantages of WiMAX compared with wireline communications.

Sources: Compiled from A. Pornwasin, "Thailand Needs to Make Urgent WiMAX Decision," *The Nation*, March 16, 2010; A. Froehlich, "WiMAX Changes Lives in Rural Thailand," *Network World*, May 25–June 1, 2009; *www.mfu.ac.th*, accessed March 6, 2013.

Wireless Broadband or WiMAX. Worldwide Interoperability for Microwave Access, popularly known as *WiMAX*, is the name for IEEE Standard 802.16. WiMAX has a wireless access range of up to 50 kilometres, compared with 100 metres for Wi-Fi. WiMAX also has a data-transfer rate of up to 75 Mbps. It is a secure system, and it offers features such as voice and video. WiMAX antennas can transmit broadband Internet connections to antennas on homes and businesses several kilometres away. The technology can therefore provide long-distance broadband wireless access to rural areas and other locations that are not currently being served, as IT's About Business 6.2 shows.

before you go on...

1. What is Bluetooth? What is a WLAN?
2. Describe Wi-Fi, cellular service, and WIMAX.

6.3 Mobile Computing and Mobile Commerce

In the traditional computing environment, the user's computer is connected with wires to other computers and to networks. Because these networks are linked by wires, they are difficult or even impossible for people on the move to use. In particular, salespeople, repair people, service employees, law enforcement agents, and utility workers can be more effective if they can use IT while in the field or in transit. Thus, mobile computing was designed for workers who travel outside the boundaries of their organizations as well as for anyone travelling outside his or her home.

Recall that mobile computing is a real-time connection between a mobile device and other computing environments, such as the Internet or an intranet. This technology is revolutionizing how people use computers.

Mobile computing has two major characteristics that differentiate it from other forms of computing: mobility and broad reach. *Mobility* means that users carry a device with them and can initiate a real-time contact with other systems from wherever they happen to be. *Broad reach* refers to the fact that users carrying an open mobile device can be reached instantly, even across great distances.

These two characteristics, mobility and broad reach, create five value-added attributes that break the barriers of geography and time: ubiquity, convenience, instant connectivity, personalization, and localization of products and services. A mobile device can provide information and communication regardless of the user's location (*ubiquity*). With an Internet-enabled mobile device, you can access the web, intranets, and other mobile devices quickly and easily, without booting up a PC or placing a call via a modem (*convenience* and *instant connectivity*). A company can customize information and send it to individual consumers as an SMS (*personalization*). Finally, knowing a user's physical location helps a company advertise its products and services (*localization*). Mobile computing provides the foundation for mobile commerce (m-commerce), as you will see next.

Mobile Commerce

In addition to affecting our everyday lives, mobile computing also is transforming the way organizations conduct business. As you saw at the beginning of the chapter, *mobile commerce* (or *m-commerce*) is e-commerce (EC) transactions that are conducted in a wireless environment, especially via the Internet. Like regular EC applications, m-commerce can be transacted via the Internet, private communication lines, smart cards, and other infrastructures. M-commerce creates opportunities for businesses to deliver new services to existing customers and to attract new customers. To see how m-commerce applications are classified by industry, see *www.wirelessresearch.eu*.

The development of m-commerce is driven by the following factors:

- ***Widespread availability of mobile devices.*** At the end of 2011, more than 6 billion cell phones were in use throughout the world. Experts estimate that within a few years most cell phones in developed countries will have Internet access. Further, as discussed earlier in this chapter, cell phones are spreading even more quickly in developing countries. Thus, a potential mass market is developing for mobile computing and m-commerce.
- ***No need for a PC.*** Because users can access the Internet via a smart phone or other wireless device, they do not need a PC to go on-line. Even though the cost of a PC used primarily for Internet access can be less than $300, that amount is still a major expense for the vast majority of people in the world, particularly in developing countries.
- ***The "cell phone culture."*** The widespread use of cell phones is a social phenomenon, especially among young people. The members of the "cell phone culture" will constitute a major force of on-line buyers once they begin to make and spend more money.
- ***Declining prices.*** The price of wireless devices is declining and will continue to decline.

- *Bandwidth improvement.* To properly conduct m-commerce, you need sufficient bandwidth for transmitting text, voice, video, and multimedia. Wi-Fi, 3G cellular technology, and WiMAX provide the necessary bandwidth.

Mobile computing and m-commerce include many applications, which result from the capabilities of various technologies. We examine these applications and their impact on business activities in the next section.

Mobile Commerce Applications

There are a large variety of mobile commerce applications. The most popular applications include location-based applications, financial services, intrabusiness applications, accessing information, and telemetry. The rest of this section examines these various applications and their effects on the ways people live and do business.

Location-Based Applications and Services. M-commerce B2C applications include location-based services and location-based applications. Location-based mobile commerce is called **location-based commerce** or **L-commerce**.

Location-based services provide information that is specific to a given location. For example, a mobile user can: (1) request the nearest business or service, such as an ATM or a restaurant; (2) receive alerts, such as a warning of a traffic jam or an accident; and (3) find a friend. Wireless carriers can provide location-based services such as locating taxis, service personnel, doctors, and rental equipment; scheduling fleets; tracking objects such as packages and train boxcars; finding information such as navigation, weather, traffic, and room schedules; targeting advertising; and automating airport check-ins.

Consider, for example, how location-based advertising can make the marketing process more productive. Marketers can use this technology to integrate the current locations and preferences of mobile users. Then, they can send user-specific advertising messages concerning nearby shops, malls, and restaurants to consumers' wireless devices. IT's About Business 6.3 illustrates how shopping malls are using location-based apps to attract the increasing number of people who shop on-line rather than visit malls.

Financial Services. Mobile financial applications include banking, wireless payments and micropayments, money transfers, wireless wallets, and bill-payment services. The main purpose of mobile financial applications is to make it more convenient for customers to transact business regardless of where they are or what time it is. Harried customers are demanding such convenience.

In many countries, banks increasingly offer mobile access to financial and account information. For example, Bank of Montreal and TD Visa (among others) provide alerts to customers on their digital cell phones about changes in their account information.

Wireless payment systems transform mobile phones into secure, self-contained purchasing tools capable of instantly authorizing payments over the cellular network. For example, TD Canada Trust allows people to transfer money instantly to individuals and to make payments to businesses anywhere in the world with any wireline or mobile phone.

Web shoppers historically have preferred to pay with credit cards. Because credit card companies sometimes charge fees on transactions, however, credit cards are an inefficient way to make very small purchases. The growth of relatively inexpensive digital content such as music (for example, iTunes), ring tones, and downloadable games is increasing the use of micropayments as merchants seek to avoid paying credit card fees on small transactions.

Ultimately, however, the success of micropayment applications will depend on the costs of the transactions. Transaction costs will be small only when the volume of transactions is large. One technology that can increase the volume of transactions is wireless mobile wallets, as you saw in the chapter-opening Case 6.1.

Various companies offer mobile wallet technologies that enable cardholders to make purchases with a single click from their mobile devices. One example is the Nokia wallet. This application securely stores information such as credit card numbers in the customer's Nokia

IT's [about business]

6.3 Location-Based Services at Shopping Malls

The rapid growth of clicks-and-mortar or exclusively on-line retail operations is threatening traditional bricks-and-mortar shopping malls. Many malls are developing their own mobile applications to better compete. Like a portal to a physical instead of digital space, these apps can help shoppers navigate their stores and parking lots, and find sales and special discounts. The mall industry does not expect these efforts to entirely prevent malls from losing more sales to on-line retailers. However, they view the apps as a crucial value-added service for busy shoppers who can easily buy things at the click of a mouse through on-line competitors.

Mall apps are emerging at a time when the malls face a huge challenge. On-line sales still account for just a fraction of overall retail sales, but they are growing rapidly. In fact, they increased about 10 percent in Canada in 2012, reaching a total of $22.3 billion, and they are expected to increase at a compound annual rate of over 13 percent through 2018. Currently, many mall apps are quite rudimentary, doing little more than helping shoppers remember where they parked and providing store directories and movie times. But some apps are offering more attractive services, such as reward points for visiting certain stores. As an example, consider the Simon Property Group, the biggest mall owner in the United States.

The Simon Group offers Shopkick's shopper-rewards app, a form of loyalty program, in about half of its 338 properties. Shopkick is one of the leading mobile apps for shopping, with more than 1 million users. A Shopkick user obtains 60 to 150 Shopkick reward points on average for visiting a participating store. When they have collected 875 points, they can redeem them for a $25 gift certificate from any of the participating retailers.

The Simon Group also is developing its own app to offer group discounts. The company would like the app to emulate Groupon (discussed in Chapter 5). The company's CEO envisions the app as a loyalty program coupled with an offer program for the mall environment. The Simon Group and several retailers, including Target and American Eagle Outfitters, have signed up to offer shoppers' rewards through the app, which is free for the Apple iOS and Android platforms.

Malls in Canada, such as the Scarborough Town Centre, are also creating apps. The mall has a BlackBerry app that provides current promotions about specials and events at the mall, as well as providing locations of all of the stores.

The bottom line? It remains to be seen whether mobile apps will help malls better compete with e-commerce.

Questions

1. Are the advantages of the mall apps discussed in this case enough to entice you to go to a mall? Why or why not? Support your answer.
2. Identify two specific benefits that you would add to mall apps to make them functional enough to attract shoppers to the mall.

Sources: Compiled from K. Hudson, "Malls Test Apps to Aid Shoppers," *The Wall Street Journal*, April 26, 2011; E. Byron, "In-Store Sales Begin at Home," *The Wall Street Journal*, April 25, 2011; E. Morphy, "Don't Be Evil When You Sell, and Other Retail Resolutions," *Forbes*, December 31, 2010; E. Woyke, "A Rewarding Life Through Apps," *Forbes*, October 1, 2010; G. Fowler, "The Green Side of Online Shopping," *The Wall Street Journal*, March 3, 2009; *www.simon.com, www.shopkick.com*, accessed March 7, 2013.

phone for use in making mobile payments. People also can use this information to authenticate transactions by signing them digitally. Microsoft also offers a mobile wallet, Passport, for use in a wireless environment.

In China, SmartPay allows users to use their mobile phones to pay their phone bills and utility bills, buy lottery tickets and airline tickets, and make other purchases. SmartPay launched 172.com (see *www.172.com*), a portal that centralizes the company's mobile, telephone, and Internet-based payment services for consumers. The portal is designed to provide a convenient, centralized source of information for all these transactions.

Intrabusiness Applications. Although business-to-consumer (B2C) m-commerce gets considerable publicity, most of today's m-commerce applications actually are used *within* organizations. In this section you will see how companies use mobile computing to support their employees.

Mobile devices increasingly are becoming an integral part of workflow applications. For example, companies can use nonvoice mobile services to assist in dispatch functions; that is, to assign jobs to mobile employees, along with detailed information about the job. Target areas for mobile delivery and dispatch services include transportation (delivery of food, oil, newspapers, and cargo; courier services; tow trucks; and taxis), utilities (gas, electricity, phone, water), field service (computer, office equipment, home repair), health care (visiting nurses, doctors, social services), and security (patrols, alarm installation). Example 6.3 illustrates an exciting intrabusiness application, telematics, that is being utilized at UPS.

Example 6.3

UPS (*www.ups.com*) was a pioneer in adopting information technology and currently has an IT budget of $1 billion. The company has been using telematics in its trucks for 20 years. *Telematics* is the wireless communication of location-based information and control messages to and from vehicles and other mobile assets. UPS launched a major program in 2009 to capture more data and better utilize them to cut fuel costs, maintain trucks more effectively, and improve safety. UPS employs global positioning systems to obtain data on more than 200 engine measurements, from speed, to number of starts, to oil pressure. It also acquires data on seat belts, cargo doors, and reverse gears in transmissions from sensors located all over the vehicle.

UPS then combines these data with mapping software to provide its managers with a tool for modifying driver behaviours in ways that cut costs, improve safety, and reduce the environmental impact. The company can literally "re-create a driver's day." By analyzing these data, UPS has been able to reduce the need for truck drivers to use reverse gear by 25 percent, thereby diminishing the risk of accidents. UPS also has been able to reduce idling by 15 minutes per driver per day. Although this step might not sound significant, an idling truck in fact burns more than 3.5 litres of gas per hour and generates 20 percent more pollution than a truck running at about 50 kilometres per hour. Therefore, the savings are substantial for both UPS and the environment. Finally, mechanics now make engine repairs based on actual vehicle use rather than according to set schedules. That is, they change a starter based on the number of starts rather than every two years regardless of use.

One of UPS's recent innovations is UPS My Choice (*www.ups.com/mychoice/*), which allows recipients of parcels to manage the receiving process (for example, have the parcel redirected or held at a UPS centre).

Sources: Compiled from E. Sperling, "What's Deep Inside Big Brown's Trucks," *Forbes*, June 7, 2010; C. Murphy, "UPS: Positioned for the Long Haul," *InformationWeek*, January 17, 2009; *www.ups.com*, accessed March 7, 2013.

Accessing Information. Mobile portals and voice portals are designed to aggregate and deliver content in a form that will work within the limited space available on mobile devices. These portals provide information anywhere and anytime to users.

A **mobile portal** aggregates and provides content and services for mobile users. These services include news, sports, and e-mail; entertainment, travel, and restaurant information; community services; and stock trading. The world's best-known mobile portal—i-mode from NTT DOCOMO—has more than 40 million subscribers, primarily in Japan. Major players in Europe are Vodafone, O2, and T-Mobile. Some traditional portals—for example, Yahoo, AOL, and MSN—have mobile portals as well.

A **voice portal** is a website with an audio interface. Voice portals are not websites in the normal sense because they can also be accessed through a standard phone or a cell phone. A phone number connects you to a website, where you can request information verbally. The system finds the information, translates it into a computer-generated voice reply, and tells you what you want to know. Most airlines provide real-time information on flight status this way.

An example of a voice portal is the voice-activated 511 travel-information line developed by Tellme.com that is part of Microsoft. It enables callers to inquire about weather, local restaurants, current traffic, and other handy information. In addition to retrieving information, some sites provide true interaction. For example, iPing (*www.iping.com*) is a reminder and notification service that allows users to enter information via the web and receive reminder calls. This service can even call a group of people to notify them of a meeting or conference call. In Canada, if you dial 411, you can obtain telephone directory information (a paid service charged to your phone number) using a voice-based service.

Telemetry Applications. **Telemetry** is the wireless transmission and receipt of data gathered from remote sensors. Telemetry has numerous mobile computing applications. For example, technicians can use telemetry to identify maintenance problems in equipment. As another example, doctors can monitor patients and control medical equipment from a distance.

Car manufacturers use telemetry applications for remote vehicle diagnosis and preventive maintenance. For instance, drivers of many General Motors cars use the OnStar system (*www.onstar.com*) in numerous ways, as you see in IT's About Business 6.4.

An interesting telemetry application for individuals was an iPhone app called *Find My iPhone*. Find My iPhone was a part of MobileMe, a service from Apple (*www.apple.com*) that synchronizes your e-mail, contacts, and calendars wirelessly across all your devices. Both of these services assign you an address on *www.icloud.com*, a website that gives you access to your information—e-mail, contacts, calendars, photos, and files—from one place on the web. Any changes you make on Me.com are stored in the cloud, so you can see these changes on all your other devices.

Find My iPhone provides several very helpful telemetry functions:

- If you lose your iPhone, there are two ways to see its approximate location on a map: You can sign in to Me.com from any computer, or you can use the Find My iPhone app on another iPhone, iPad, or iPod touch.
- If you have left your iPhone in a location that you remember, you can write a message and display it on your iPhone's screen. The message might say, "Left my iPhone. Please call me at 301-555-1211." Your message appears on your iPhone, even if the screen is locked. And, if the map shows that your iPhone is nearby—perhaps in your office under a pile of papers—you can tell Find My iPhone to play a sound that overrides the volume or silent setting.

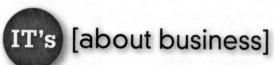

IT's [about business]

6.4 Your Car Becomes a Smart Phone

General Motors (*www.gm.com*) has big ambitions for OnStar (*www.onstar.com*). The company wants to expand the communications service by increasing the number of GM car owners who continue to subscribe after their free six months of service ends. OnStar is the market leader, with 6 million users. More than 4 million of these users pay an average of $240 per year. Add in the mobile-phone minutes from Verizon that OnStar resells, and the GM unit logs more than $1 billion per year in revenue. Its staff of 2,200 agents answers 99.7 percent of emergency calls within one second.

OnStar provides a wide range of features to owners of GM cars. The system can alert owners to most malfunctions in the vehicle and schedule repairs at a dealership. It also can unlock doors remotely and slow down cars if they have been stolen. In addition, it automatically alerts an OnStar operator when an air bag deploys. Drivers also can call OnStar with questions about warning lights that appear on their dashboards.

GM has launched OnStar for its vehicles in China as well, complete with Mandarin-speaking agents. The subscriber base reached 200,000 in February 2011, and is growing by 40,000 per month.

Despite these impressive numbers, GM may have waited too long to keep its competitive advantage. OnStar has earned a reputation for security and safety, thanks to features that alert police if a connected car is stolen or involved in an accident. Ford, however, has jumped ahead of GM in the market for in-car entertainment content. Ford's Sync system plays music on voice command and even reads tweets to drivers. Further, Hyundai Motor has launched a system called *Blue Link* to compete with OnStar for safety and security features.

Questions

1. Explain why OnStar, Sync, and Blue Link are telemetry applications.
2. Provide specific examples of the disadvantages of OnStar, Sync, and Blue Link.

Sources: Compiled from D. Welch, "OnStar Wants to Turn Your Car into a Smartphone," *Bloomberg BusinessWeek*, March 14–20, 2011; "Hyundai Blue Link Tackles OnStar and Sync," *Edmunds Inside Line*, January 5, 2011; *www.gm.com*, *www.onstar.com*, *www.ford.com/technology/sync*, *www.hyundaiusa.com/bluelink/index.aspx*, accessed March 7, 2013.

- If you left your iPhone in a public place, you may want to protect its contents. You can remotely set a four-digit passcode lock to prevent people from using your iPhone, accessing your personal information, or tampering with your settings.
- You can initiate a remote wipe (erase all contents) to restore your iPhone to its factory settings. Then, if you eventually find your iPhone, you can connect it to your computer and use iTunes to restore the data from your most recent backup.
- If you have lost your iPhone and do not have access to a computer, you can download the Find My iPhone app to a friend's iPhone, iPad, or iPod touch and sign in to access all the Find My iPhone features.

before you go on...

1. What are the major drivers of mobile computing?
2. Describe mobile portals and voice portals.
3. Describe wireless financial services.
4. List some of the major intrabusiness wireless applications.

6.4 Pervasive Computing

Pervasive computing, also called *ubiquitous computing*, is a world in which virtually every object has processing power together with wireless or wired connections to a global network. Pervasive computing is invisible, "everywhere computing" that is embedded in the objects around us—the floor, the lights, our cars, the washing machine, our cell phones, our clothes, and so on.

For example, in a *smart home*, your home computer, television, lighting and heating controls, home security system, and many appliances can communicate with one another via a home network. You can control these linked systems through various devices, including your cellular phone, television, home computer, and even your automobile. One of the key elements of a smart home is the *smart appliance*, an Internet-ready appliance that can be controlled by a small hand-held device or a desktop computer via a home network, either wireline or wireless. Two technologies provide the infrastructure for pervasive computing: *radio-frequency identification* (RFID) and *wireless sensor networks* (WSNs).

Radio-Frequency Identification

Radio-frequency identification (RFID) technology allows manufacturers to attach tags with antennas and computer chips to goods and then track their movement through radio signals. RFID was developed to eventually replace barcodes. A typical barcode, known as the *Universal Product Code (UPC)*, is made up of 12 digits that are batched in various groups. The first digit identifies the item type, the next five digits identify the manufacturer, and the next five identify the product. The last digit is a check digit for error detection. Barcodes have worked well, but they have limitations. First, they require line-of-sight to the scanning device, which works well in a store but can pose substantial problems in a manufacturing plant or a warehouse or on a shipping/receiving dock. Second, because barcodes are printed on paper, they can be ripped, soiled, or lost. Third, the barcode identifies the manufacturer and product, but not the actual item. Two systems are being developed to replace barcodes: QR (for "quick response") codes and RFID systems. Figure 6.6 shows a QR code, RFID tag, and barcodes.

A *QR code* is a two-dimensional code, readable by dedicated QR readers and camera phones. QR codes have several advantages over barcodes:

- QR codes can store much more information than barcodes.
- Data types stored in QR codes include numbers, text, URLs, and even Japanese characters.

FIGURE 6.6 QR code, RFID tag, and barcodes.
(*Sources:* © Patrick Duinkerke/iStockphoto; © raphotography/iStockphoto; Media Bakery)

- The size of QR codes is small because they store information horizontally and vertically.
- QR codes are more resistant to damage than are barcodes.
- QR codes can be read from any direction or angle, so the possibility of a failure in reading a QR code is reduced.

RFID systems use tags with embedded microchips, which contain data, and antennas to transmit radio signals over a short distance to RFID readers. The readers pass the data over a network to a computer for processing. The chip in the RFID tag is programmed with information that uniquely identifies an item. It also contains information about the item such as its location and where and when it was made. Figure 6.7 shows an RFID reader and an RFID tag on a pallet.

There are two basic types of RFID tags: active and passive. *Active RFID tags* use internal batteries for power, and they broadcast radio waves to a reader. Because active tags contain batteries, they are more expensive than passive RFID tags and can be read over greater distances. Active tags, therefore, are used for more expensive items. *Passive RFID tags* rely entirely on readers for their power. They are less expensive than active tags and can be read only up to 6 metres. They are generally applied to less-expensive merchandise. Problems with RFID include expense and the comparatively large size of the tags. However, this type of technology was used in an innovative way by the creators of Cat Nav, which attached a device to a cat's collar, monitored by an app linked to a GPS. This meant that the owner could track where the cat is travelling.

Wireless Sensor Networks

Wireless sensor networks (WSNs) are networks of interconnected, battery-powered, wireless sensors called *motes* (analogous to nodes) that are placed into the physical environment. The motes collect data from many points over an extended space. Each mote contains processing, storage, and radio-frequency sensors and antennas. Each mote "wakes up" or activates for a fraction of a second when it has data to transmit. It then relays those data to its nearest neighbour. So, instead of every mote transmitting its data to a remote computer at a base station, the data are moved mote by mote until they reach a central computer, where they can be stored and analyzed. An advantage of a wireless sensor network is that, if one mote fails, another one can pick up the data. This process makes WSNs very efficient and reliable. Also, if the network requires more bandwidth, performance is easily boosted by placing new motes when and where they are required.

The motes provide information that enables a central computer to integrate reports of the same activity from different angles within the network. Therefore, the network can much more accurately determine information such as the direction in which a person is moving, the weight of a vehicle, and the amount of rainfall over a field of crops.

FIGURE 6.7 Small RFID reader and RFID tag.
(*Source:* © Ecken, Dominique/Keystone Pressedienst/Zuma Press)

One kind of wireless sensor network is ZigBee (*www.ZigBee.org*), a set of wireless communications protocols that target applications requiring low data-transmission rates and low power consumption. ZigBee can handle hundreds of devices at once. Its current focus is to wirelessly link sensors that are embedded into industrial controls, medical devices, smoke and intruder alarms, and building and home automation.

A promising application of ZigBee is reading utility meters, such as electricity. ZigBee sensors embedded in these meters would send wireless signals that could be picked up by utility employees driving by your house. The employees would not even have to get out of their trucks to read your meter.

before you go on...

1. Define pervasive computing, RFID, and wireless sensor networks.
2. Provide two specific business uses of RFID technology.

6.5 Wireless Security Issues

Clearly, wireless networks provide numerous benefits for businesses. They present a huge challenge to management, however; namely, their inherent lack of security. Wireless is a broadcast medium, and transmissions can be intercepted by anyone who is close enough and has access to the appropriate equipment. There are four major threats to wireless networks: rogue access points, war driving, eavesdropping, and RF jamming.

A *rogue access point* is an unauthorized access point to a wireless network. The rogue could be someone in your organization who, although meaning no harm, sets up an access point without informing the IT department. In more serious cases the rogue is an "evil twin," someone who wishes to access a wireless network for malicious purposes.

In an evil twin attack, the attacker is in the vicinity with a Wi-Fi-enabled computer and a separate connection to the Internet. Using a hotspotter—a device that detects wireless networks and provides information on them (see *www.canarywireless.com*)—the attacker simulates a wireless access point with the same wireless network name, or SSID, as the one that an authorized user would expect. If the signal is strong enough, users will connect to the attacker's system instead of the real access point. The attacker then can serve the users a web page asking them to provide confidential information such as user names, passwords, and account numbers. In other cases the attacker simply captures wireless transmissions. These attacks are more effective with public hotspots (for example, McDonald's and Starbucks) than in corporate networks.

War driving is the act of locating WLANs while driving (or walking) around a city or elsewhere (see *www.wardriving.com*). To war drive or walk, you simply need a Wi-Fi detector and a wirelessly enabled computer. If a WLAN has a range that extends beyond the building in which it is located, then an unauthorized user might be able to intrude into the network. The intruder then can obtain a free Internet connection and possibly gain access to important data and other resources.

Eavesdropping is efforts by unauthorized users to access data travelling over wireless networks. Finally, in *radio-frequency (RF) jamming*, a person or a device, whether intentionally or unintentionally, interferes with your wireless network transmissions.

As you see, wireless systems can be difficult to secure. IT's About Business 6.5 demonstrates how important protecting wireless networks is at Brigham Young University–Hawaii.

In Technology Guide 5, we discuss various techniques and technologies that you could implement to help you avoid these threats.

before you go on...

1. Describe the four major threats to the security of wireless networks.
2. Which of these threats is the most dangerous for a business? Which is the most dangerous for an individual? Support your answers.

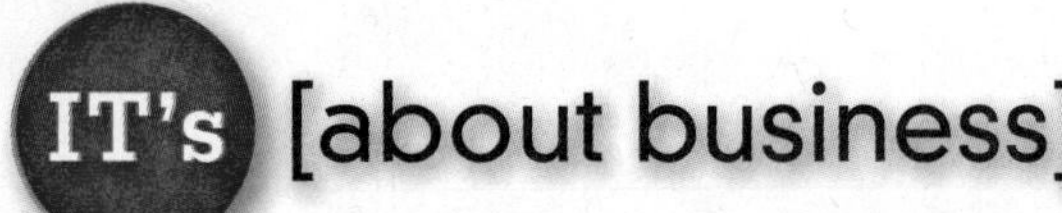

6.5 Protecting an Open Wireless Network at Brigham Young University–Hawaii

Like many campuses, Brigham Young University–Hawaii has an open wireless network. It's used by 2,500 students and 500 faculty and staff. Because it was open, anyone and any computer could connect to the network, and the university was unable to capture important information about the wireless users who were accessing the campus network. The IT team, which consisted of only three people, had no way of knowing who was on the network or how it was being used.

As one specific example, the team realized the importance of identifying users who were using network resources inappropriately. All BYU–Hawaii students are required to sign an honour code of conduct prohibiting various activities, such as downloading inappropriate material. Violators are to be reported to the honour code office. But the IT team had no way to identify users, so reporting violators was almost impossible.

The team decided to add greater authentication (i.e., identification) and authorization, discussed in Chapter 13, to restrict access to campus resources. The challenge was deploying the new system while limiting service disruptions to the users.

Being a Cisco customer, BYU–Hawaii tried to use the Cisco Clean Access solution to authenticate network users. With this system, however, anyone could still connect to the network as a guest, and therefore avoid authentication. The IT team decided to use Avenda (now owned by Aruba Networks, *www.arubanetworks.com/*) because this system works with both wireless networks and wired networks, and it provides virtual private networking for off-campus users.

Avenda automatically provides authorization privileges after a user is authenticated; however, those privileges are limited. That is, once a user is identified, the system provides access only to the systems necessary for that user to do his or her job, a process called *least privilege* (discussed in Chapter 13). To help ease the transition, Avenda has a tool called Quick1X. When a user logged on to the new system for the first time, Quick1X ran a wizard with a pre-configured template to streamline the authentication process.

As a result of implementing the Avenda system, the wireless network is much less open. The IT team now controls and differentiates access to the wireless network. The team also is able to determine users' activities, collect user information, and gather details about network usage and the network's overall performance in only minutes. Also, students and staff have given positive feedback on the new system, which does not require them to re-authenticate their identities when they move from one part of the campus to another.

Questions

1. What are the advantages of the Avenda system to the users?
2. Are there privacy issues associated with the Avenda system for users? If so, provide specific examples.

Sources: Compiled from M. Aughenbaugh and J. Call, "Wireless Networking Case Study," *Baseline Magazine*, April 26, 2011; D. Schaffhauser, "BYU-Hawaii Fences Off Wireless Network," Campustechnology.com, August 19, 2010; *www.byuh.edu*, *www.arubanetworks.com*, accessed March 7, 2013.

What's In IT For Me?

For the Accounting Major

Wireless applications help accountants count and audit inventory. They also expedite the flow of information for cost control. Price management, inventory control, and other accounting-related activities can be improved by the use of wireless technologies.

For the Finance Major

Wireless services can provide banks and other financial institutions with a competitive advantage. For example, wireless electronic payments, including micropayments, are more convenient (any place, any time), as well as less expensive than traditional means of payment. Electronic bill payment from mobile devices is becoming more popular, increasing security and accuracy, expediting cycle time, and reducing processing costs.

For the Marketing Major

Imagine a whole new world of marketing, advertising, and selling, with the potential to increase sales dramatically. Such is the promise of mobile computing. Of special interest for marketing are location-based advertising as well as the new opportunities resulting from pervasive computing and RFIDs. Finally, wireless technology also provides new opportunities in sales force automation, enabling faster and better communications with both customers and for corporate services.

For the **Production/Operations Management Major**

Wireless technologies offer many opportunities to support mobile employees of all kinds. Wearable computers enable off-site employees and repair personnel working in the field to service customers faster, better, and less expensively. Wireless devices also can increase productivity within factories by enhancing communication and collaboration as well as managerial planning and control. In addition, mobile computing technologies can improve safety by providing quicker warning signs and instant messaging to isolated employees.

For the **Human Resources Management Major**

Mobile computing can improve HR training and extend it to any place at any time. Payroll notices can be delivered as SMSs. Finally, wireless devices can make it even more convenient for employees to tailor their own benefits and update their personal data.

For the **MIS Major**

MIS personnel provide the wireless infrastructure that enables all organizational employees to compute and communicate any time, anywhere. This convenience provides exciting, creative, new applications for organizations to cut costs and improve the efficiency and effectiveness of operations (for example, to achieve transparency in supply chains). Unfortunately, as you saw earlier, wireless applications are inherently insecure. This lack of security is a serious problem that MIS personnel must contend with.

[Summary]

1. Describe the four main types of wireless transmission media. Identify at least one advantage and one disadvantage of each type.

Microwave transmission systems are used for high-volume, long-distance, line-of-sight communication. One advantage is the high volume. A disadvantage is that microwave transmissions are susceptible to environmental interference during severe weather such as heavy rain or snowstorms.

Satellite transmission systems make use of communication satellites, and they receive and transmit data via line-of-sight. One advantage is that their enormous footprint—the area of the earth's surface reached by a satellite's transmission—overcomes the limitations of microwave data relay stations. But similar to microwaves, satellite transmissions are susceptible to environmental interference during severe weather.

Radio transmission uses radio-wave frequencies to send data directly between transmitters and receivers. An advantage is that radio waves travel easily through normal office walls. A disadvantage is that radio transmissions are susceptible to snooping by anyone who has similar equipment that operates on the same frequency.

Infrared light is red light that usually is not visible to human eyes. Common applications of infrared light are in remote control units for televisions, VCRs, DVDs, and CD players. An advantage of infrared is that it does not penetrate walls and so does not interfere with other devices in adjoining rooms. A disadvantage is that infrared signals can be easily blocked by furniture.

2. **Discuss the basic purposes of short-range, medium-range, and long-range networks. Explain how businesses can use at least one technology employed by each type of network.**

Short-range wireless networks simplify the task of connecting one device to another, eliminating wires and enabling users to move around while they use the devices. In general, short-range wireless networks have a range of 30 metres or less. Short-range wireless networks include Bluetooth, ultra-wideband, and near-field communications and can be used to attach wireless devices to computing systems.

Medium-range wireless networks include Wireless Fidelity (Wi-Fi) and mesh networks. *Wi-Fi* provides fast and easy Internet or intranet broadband access from public hotspots located at airports, hotels, Internet cafés, universities, conference centres, offices, and homes. *Mesh networks* use multiple Wi-Fi access points to create a wide area network that can be quite large.

Wide-area wireless networks connect users to the Internet over geographically dispersed territory. They include cellular telephones and wireless broadband. *Cellular telephones* provide two-way radio communications over a cellular network of base stations with seamless handoffs. *Wireless broadband* (WiMAX) has a wireless access range of up to 50 kilometres and a data-transfer rate of up to 75 Mbps. WiMAX can provide long-distance broadband wireless access to rural areas and remote business locations.

3. **Discuss the five major m-commerce applications. Provide a specific example of how each application can benefit a business.**

Location-based services provide information specific to a location. For example, a mobile user can (1) request the nearest business or service, such as an ATM or restaurant; (2) receive alerts, such as a warning of a traffic jam or accident; and (3) find a friend. With *location-based advertising*, marketers can integrate the current locations and preferences of mobile users. Then, they can send user-specific advertising messages about nearby shops, malls, and restaurants to wireless devices.

Mobile financial applications include banking, wireless payments and micropayments, money transfers, wireless wallets, and bill-payment services. The bottom line for mobile financial applications is to make it more convenient for customers to transact business regardless of where they are or what time it is.

Intrabusiness applications consist of m-commerce applications that are used within organizations. Companies can use nonvoice mobile services to assist in dispatch functions; that is, to assign jobs to mobile employees, along with detailed information about the job.

Accessing information is facilitated by mobile portals and voice portals designed to aggregate and deliver content in a form that will work within the limited space available on mobile devices. These portals provide information to users anywhere and anytime.

Telemetry is the wireless transmission and receipt of data gathered from remote sensors. Company technicians can use telemetry to identify maintenance problems in equipment. Car manufacturers use telemetry applications for remote vehicle diagnosis and preventive maintenance.

4. **Define "pervasive computing." Describe two technologies that underlie this technology. Provide at least one example of how a business can use each one.**

Pervasive computing is invisible, "everywhere" computing that is embedded in the objects around us. Two technologies provide the infrastructure for pervasive computing: *radio-frequency identification* (*RFID*) and *wireless sensor networks* (*WSNs*).

RFID is the term for technologies that use radio waves to automatically identify the location of individual items equipped with tags that contain embedded microchips. WSNs are networks of interconnected, battery-powered, wireless devices placed in the physical environment to collect data from many points over an extended space.

5. **Identify the four major threats to wireless networks. Explain, with examples, how each one can damage a business.**

The four major threats to wireless networks are rogue access points, war driving, eavesdropping, and radio-frequency jamming. A *rogue access point* is an unauthorized access point to a wireless network. *War driving* is the act of locating WLANs while driving around a city or elsewhere. *Eavesdropping* is efforts by unauthorized users to access data travelling over wireless networks. Unauthorized access using the above three methods can result in unauthorized duplication or destruction of data or programs. *Radio-frequency jamming* occurs when a person or a device, whether intentionally or unintentionally, interferes with wireless network transmissions. This can result in a wireless system going down, disrupting operations.

[Chapter Glossary]

Bluetooth Chip technology that enables short-range connection (data and voice) between wireless devices.

cellular telephones (cell phones) Phones that provide two-way radio communications over a cellular network of base stations with seamless handoffs.

global positioning system (GPS) A wireless system that uses satellites to enable users to determine their position almost anywhere on earth.

hotspot A small geographical perimeter within which a wireless access point provides service to a number of users.

infrared A type of wireless transmission that uses red light not usually visible to human eyes.

location-based commerce (L-commerce) Mobile commerce transactions targeted to individuals in specific locations, at specific times.

mesh network A network composed of motes in the physical environment that "wake up" at intervals to transmit data to their nearest neighbour mote.

microwave transmission A wireless system that uses microwaves for high-volume, long-distance, point-to-point communication.

mobile commerce (m-commerce) Electronic commerce transactions that are conducted with a mobile device.

mobile computing A real-time connection between a mobile device and other computing environments, such as the Internet or an intranet.

mobile portal A portal that aggregates and provides content and services for mobile users.

mobile wallet A technology that allows users to make purchases with a single click from their mobile devices.

near-field communications (NFC) The smallest of the short-range wireless networks, designed to be embedded in mobile devices such as cell phones and credit cards.

personal area network (PAN) A computer network used for communication among computer devices close to one person.

pervasive computing (ubiquitous computing) A computer environment where virtually every object has processing power together with wireless or wired connections to a global network.

propagation delay Any delay in communications due to signal transmission time through a physical medium.

radio-frequency identification (RFID) technology A wireless technology that allows manufacturers to attach tags with antennas and computer chips to goods and then track their movement through radio signals.

radio transmission A wireless transmissions system that uses radio-wave frequencies to send data directly between transmitters and receivers.

satellite radio (digital radio) A wireless system that beams uninterrupted, near CD-quality music to your radio from satellites.

satellite transmission A wireless transmission system that uses satellites for broadcast communications.

telemetry The wireless transmission and receipt of data gathered from remote sensors.

ubiquitous computing (see **pervasive computing**)

ultra-wideband (UWB) A high-bandwidth wireless technology with transmission speeds in excess of 100 Mbps that can be used for applications such as streaming multimedia from, say, a personal computer to a television.

voice portal A website with an audio interface.

wireless Telecommunications in which electromagnetic waves carry the signal between communicating devices.

wireless access point An antenna connecting a mobile device to a wired local area network.

Wireless Fidelity (Wi-Fi) A set of standards for wireless local area networks based on the IEEE 802.11 standard.

wireless local area network (WLAN) A computer network in a limited geographical area that uses wireless transmission for communication.

wireless sensor networks (WSNs) Networks of interconnected, battery-powered, wireless sensors placed in the physical environment.

[Discussion Questions]

1. Discuss how m-commerce can expand the reach of e-business.
2. Discuss how mobile computing can solve some of the problems of the digital divide.
3. List three to four major advantages of wireless commerce to consumers, and explain what benefits it provides to consumers.
4. Discuss the ways in which Wi-Fi is used to support mobile computing and m-commerce. Describe the ways in which Wi-Fi affects the use of cellular phones for m-commerce.
5. You can use location-based tools to help you find your car or the closest gas station. However, some people see location-based tools as an invasion of privacy. Discuss the pros and cons of location-based tools.
6. Discuss the benefits of telemetry in health care for the elderly.
7. Discuss how wireless devices can help people with disabilities.
8. Some experts say that Wi-Fi is "winning the battle" against 3G or 4G cellular service. Others disagree. Discuss both sides of the argument, and support each one.
9. Which of the applications of pervasive computing do you think is likely to gain the greatest market acceptance over the next few years? Why?

[Problem-Solving Activities]

1. Investigate commercial applications of voice portals. Visit several vendors (e.g., *www.microsoft.com/en-us/tellme/*, *www.cisco.com*). What capabilities and applications do these vendors offer?
2. Using a search engine, try to determine whether there are any commercial Wi-Fi hotspots in your area. (Hint: Access *http://v4.jiwire.com/search-hotspot-locations.htm*.)
3. Examine how new data capture devices such as RFID tags help organizations accurately identify and segment their customers for activities such as targeted marketing. Browse the web and develop or locate five potential new applications for RFID technology not listed in this chapter. What issues would arise if a country's laws mandated that such devices be embedded in everyone's body as a national identification system?
4. Investigate commercial uses of GPS. Start with *www.northwestontariomaps.ca*, then go to *www.neigps.com/*. Can some of the consumer-oriented products be used in industry? Prepare a report on your findings.
5. Access *www.bluetooth.com*. Examine the types of products being enhanced with Bluetooth technology. Present two of these products to the class, and explain how they are enhanced by Bluetooth technology.
6. Explore *www.nokia.com*. Prepare a summary of the types of mobile services and applications Nokia currently supports and plans to support in the future.
7. Enter *www.ibm.com*. Search for *wireless e-business*. Research the resulting stories to determine the types of wireless capabilities and applications that IBM's software and hardware supports. Describe some of the ways these applications have helped specific businesses and industries.
8. Research the status of 3G and 4G cellular service by visiting *www.itu.int* and *www.4g.co.uk*. Prepare a report on the status of 3G and 4G based on your findings.
9. Enter *www.onstar.com*. What types of fleet services does OnStar provide? Are these any different from the services OnStar provides to individual car owners?
10. Access *http://en.wikipedia.org/wiki/Internet_of_Things* Read about the Internet of Things. What is it? What types of technologies are necessary to support it? Why is it important?

[Spreadsheet Activity: Mobile Spreadsheets]

Objective: Spreadsheets are powerful tools, but part of their power comes from the user interface. This activity will use on-line demonstrations to allow you to experience spreadsheets in a mobile environment.

Chapter Connection: This activity puts wireless spreadsheets into the palm of your hand. While the demonstrations used here are based on spreadsheet tools, the implications of mobile user interface will apply in many situations. While mobile tools are very useful, they are also limited. This activity will help you see the differences in interacting with spreadsheets based on the method used to connect to them.

Activity: Many on-line tools are available today. Microsoft has an on-line version of its Office suite, though Google is by far the leader in on-line document creation. A single account with Google gives users access to e-mail, calendars, documents, YouTube, and much more. While on-line document creation, editing, and storing offers lots of advantages, there are drawbacks, especially when these tools are used in a mobile environment.

There are three steps to this activity. First, you will create a Microsoft Excel spreadsheet that will track fuel efficiency for your company vehicle. This sheet needs columns for the date, odometer reading, litres pumped, and kilometres per litre. The last column will be calculated based on the difference in the previous and current odometer reading and the number of litres pumped. For this part of the exercise, you need at least five entries to be sure your spreadsheet is working properly.

Once you are satisfied that your spreadsheet is calculating appropriately, create a Google account and log in to Google Drive in a web browser. Upload your spreadsheet, and add five more entries on-line.

Finally, log in to the mobile version of Google Drive on your mobile phone. If you do not have an Internet-enabled phone, search Google for "Opera Mini Demo," and use the demo of Opera's mobile Internet browser. Whether from your phone or the demo browser, add two more entries to your spreadsheet. Keep a detailed diary of your experience, noting which method worked best. Be sure to explain the advantages and disadvantages of each method of accessing and editing the spreadsheet. Finally, open your Google spreadsheet in a browser, and get the URL to share the document. Add this link to your diary, and submit your document to your professor along with your original Excel spreadsheet.

Deliverable: You will submit both an Excel spreadsheet and a Word document. The spreadsheet should have at least five entries that calculate fuel efficiency. The document will be the diary detailing each of the three methods of accessing this spreadsheet.

Discussion Questions

1. What do you think needs to change in the mobile and web-based environments for you to match the traditional Excel experience? Or do they even need to match?
2. Based on your diary thoughts, what improvements can you see that will need to be made in networks, computer interaction devices, storage speeds, and so on for traditional office automation software, such as spreadsheets, to be successful on a smart phone?

[Case Assignment]

Ogly Company produces baking and cooking equipment that is sold around the world and used by restaurants and bakeries. In addition, it produces parts that are sold to distributors who maintain and service the many different types of ovens and fryers. Some distributors are also authorized sales representatives who sell Ogly products.

Ogly sells a large variety of parts by means of its interorganizational information system, based upon an extranet. The company website lists products and their prices. Distributors order the products via the extranet, can check the status of their order, and can also make payments via the secure services offered.

Ogly also has a public portion to its website, which can be searched by the general public. On these web pages, individuals and organizations can locate the distributor nearest them to help them service their existing baking and cooking equipment or buy new equipment. If a customer wants to sell used equipment, they can take it to a distributor, who will have it listed on the Ogly website for resale.

Ogly's website is friendly to small processors (such as smart phones). This means that both a full version of the website is available, as well as a less-memory intensive version that can be used on hand-held devices.

Required

Ogly is considering implementing RFID (radio frequency identification) tagging systems on its inventory. Identify advantages and disadvantages to Ogly of using RFID to track and manage its inventory.

[Team Assignments]

1. Each team should examine a major vendor of mobile devices (Apple, BlackBerry, Samsung, Nokia, Kyocera, Motorola, and so on). Each team will research the capabilities and prices of the devices offered by each company and then make a class presentation, the objective of which is to convince the rest of the class that one should buy that company's products.
2. Each team should explore the commercial applications of m-commerce in one of the following areas: financial services, including banking, stocks, and insurance; marketing and advertising; manufacturing; travel and transportation; human resources management; public services; and health care. Each team will present a report to the class based on their findings. (Start at *www.wirelessresearch.eu*.)

3. For one of the following areas—homes, cars, appliances, or other consumer goods like clothing—have each team investigate how embedded microprocessors are currently being used and will be used in the future to support consumer-centric services. Each team will present a report to the class based on their findings.

[Case 6.2 Mobile Reading with Kobo]

The Business Problem

In the early 2000s, sales of books at Indigo were declining, and the publishing industry was reeling due to the many changes brought by the Internet. Books could be purchased on-line all around the world, and were increasingly available in e-book form. Indigo Books & Music Inc. believed that the future lay in e-books, so it increasingly conducted research and provided books in electronic format. The Shortcovers app was used for this purpose. In 2009, Shortcovers became a separate company called Kobo, now well known in Canada and around the world.

In July 2010, Kobo launched a physical e-reader at Indigo stores. (The original reader was not wireless, while current versions are.) At the time there were many readers (over 100), and Kobo gained market share by becoming a low-cost leader. Such intense price competition caused many e-reader producers to leave the market, leaving fewer readers available. The most popular readers are the Kindle and Kindle Fire sold by Amazon (with about 55 percent of the reader market share as of mid-2012), the Nook by Barnes and Noble (with about 14 percent), and the Apple iPad (with about 12 percent).

Amazon, Barnes and Noble, and Apple have a large user base that buys their books and apps. How is Kobo, a company based in Toronto, going to compete in the world marketplace and succeed?

The IT and Business Solution

We can observe several strategies that Kobo has implemented. The first is rapid and frequent hardware innovation, staying at the low end of the price scale. The Kobo reader hardware has been frequently upgraded and has evolved. From the first black and grey pearl display Kobo in July 2010, numerous versions have been sold. As of April 2013, there were five versions of the Kobo reader available: the Aura, arc, glo, mini, and touch, ranging in price from $79.99 to $199.99 (the colour version). The Kindle had three versions, ranging in price from US$119 to US$399. The Barnes and Noble Nook had two versions, the reader selling at $199 and a tablet selling at $269. Finally, the iPad mini sold for $329 while the regular iPad sold for $499.

A second strategy is the open-standards policy adopted by the company. Rather than using a private book format like Amazon, Kobo's books are sold in epub format, a standard and the most common format used for e-books. As of September 2012, tablet Kobo readers were able to run over 600,000 apps, enabling the company to compete with other Internet appliances (e-readers, smart phones, and tablets).

Kobo also encourages community among its readers. Using social media, readers can find out how many others are reading a particular book, comment about the book, and check out what others are thinking.

But the biggest difference between the Kobo and many other e-readers is that the Kobo is in bookstores, so people who love books can buy their readers in the same place that they go to touch and feel their favourite books. In Canada, Kobo e-readers are sold at Chapters/Indigo. In the United States, they were sold at Borders, which went bankrupt in 2011. The next year, Kobo replaced this connection with an agreement with the American Booksellers Association to sell its hardware. In the United Kingdom, W. H. Smith sells Kobos, while in Italy it is Mondadori, in Hong Kong it is Swinden, and in Japan it is Rakuten, which bought Kobo from Indigo Books & Music in 2012.

The Results

As of the end of 2012, Kobo had over 12 million active readers in over 170 countries. Half of this volume was obtained during 2012 alone. Kobo customers can read Kobo books from other platforms, including BlackBerry, Apple, and Android, which could explain why the company reported an over 500 percent increase in e-gifting (payment of e-books for the use of others) for the December 2012 holiday season.

Questions

1. Explain why it is important for a company like Kobo to continue to innovate its hardware. How has wireless technology contributed to the pace of innovation?
2. Why is Kobo's position on standards (i.e., the use of the epub format) relevant to its success? Why does Kobo provide apps for multiple platforms (i.e., BlackBerry, Apple, and Android)?

Sources: Compiled from interview with Greg Twinney, Chief Operating Officer/Chief Financial Officer of Kobo, March 20, 2013; D. Morel, "The Untold Story of Kobo," *Startupnorth.ca*, November 9, 2011; J. Milliot, "Kindle Share of E-book Reading at 55%, *www.publishersweekly.com*, November 9, 2012; E. Rocha, "Kobo to Launch Revamped Tablet, E-reader Lineup," *Globe and Mail*, September 6, 2012; The Canadian Press, "Kobo Aura HD E-Reader Breaking Into U.S. Market," *Huffington Post*, May 5, 2013; *https://kindle.amazon.com*, *www.kobo.com/ereaders*, *www.barnesandnoble.com/u/nook/379003208/*, *www.apple.com/ca/ipad/*, accessed April 25, 2013.

[Interactive Case]

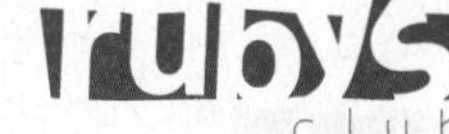

Developing Wireless Solutions for Ruby's Club

Go to the Ruby's Club link at the Student Companion website or *WileyPLUS* for information about your current internship assignment. You will investigate applications of wireless computing that will enhance Ruby's customer experience, and you'll prepare a summary report for Ruby's managers.

Chapter 7

Web 2.0 and Social Networks

[LEARNING OBJECTIVES]

1. Describe the differences between Web 1.0 and Web 2.0, and explain the benefits of three information technologies used by Web 2.0.
2. Identify five prominent Web 2.0 applications, and provide at least one example of how each one can be used in a business setting.
3. Discuss the three categories of Web 2.0 sites, and provide at least one example of how each one can improve business efficiency and profitability.

[CHAPTER OUTLINE]

7.1 Web 2.0 Underlying Technologies
7.2 Web 2.0 Applications
7.3 Categories of Web 2.0 Sites

[WEB RESOURCES]

Student Companion Site
wiley.com/college/rainer

- Student PowerPoints for note taking
- Interactive Case: Ruby's Club Assignments
- Complete glossary

WileyPlus

All of the above and 

- E-book
- Mini-lecture by author for each chapter section
- Practice quizzes
- Flash Cards for vocabulary review
- Additional "What's in IT for Me?" cases
- Video interviews with managers
- Lab Manual for Microsoft Office 2010
- How-to Animations for Microsoft Office 2010

ACCT	FIN	MKT	POM	HR	MIS
Communicate with audit teams	Collaborate with external financial experts	Stay closer to customers	Obtain customer input in new products	Conduct entire range of recruiting activities	Provide IT infrastructure for Web 2.0

[Case 7.1 Social Networks and Crowd-funding]

The Problem

All businesses at one point or another are faced with the problem of raising money. This is definitely the case for new start-up businesses. Did you ever want to become an entrepreneur? To start your own company, one of the first things you will need is money. All businesses from small to large need to find the necessary funds to turn business ideas into products and services.

VLADGRIN/Shutterstock

The Solution

One solution to finding the money that organizations need is the emerging area of social media. Crowdfunding uses websites to allow those in need of cash to raise funds from a large pool of investors or donors. For example, Pursu.it (*http://pursu.it*) is designed to seek funding from sports fans, supporters, and ordinary Canadians to help athletes who otherwise would not have the money to cover their training expenses for the next Olympic games. The website has links to popular social media networks such as Facebook and Twitter and that helps them to reach a large population of potential donors.

The Results

One of the athletes helped by Pursui.it is Larisa Yurkiw, an alpine skier who hoped to represent Canada at the 2014 Winter Olympics in Sochi, Russia. She raised over $20,000 in 60 days though Pursu.it from donors as far away as Switzerland. As of May 2013, Pursu.it athletes had generated more than $111,000, with over 70,000 followers on the website.

Another example of crowdfunding is Kickstarter (*www.kickstarter.com*), a website that helps independent designers and developers create innovative products through the contributions of complete strangers. In 2012, more than 2.2 million people pledged a total of US$320 million to independent projects and entrepreneurs funded through Kickstarter completed more than 18,000 creative projects, mostly video games.

As of mid-2012, there were more than 450 active crowdfunding sites around the world, mostly in North America and Europe, including 17 in Canada. Through these crowdfunding platforms, investors and donors gave almost US$1.5 billion in 2011 to support more than a million causes. It was expected that contributions to crowdsourcing sites would double in 2013 from the previous year.

What We Learned from This Case

The opening case on crowdfunding demonstrates one of the many uses of social networking, which is a key feature of Web 2.0. Organizations today are using Web 2.0 technologies and applications in a variety of innovative ways. You begin this chapter by discussing Web 2.0 technologies and applications. You then will take a look at three widespread categories of Web 2.0 sites.

When you complete this chapter, you will have a thorough understanding of Web 2.0 technologies, applications, and websites and the ways in which modern organizations use them. You also will be familiar with their advantages and disadvantages and the risks and rewards they can bring to your organization. Most of you probably already have pages on social networking sites, so you are familiar with the benefits and drawbacks of such sites. This chapter will enable you to apply this knowledge to your organization's efforts in the Web 2.0 arena. As a result,

Sources: Compiled from Q. Casey, "Crowdfunding Site Pursu.it Gives Olympic Hopefuls Chance to Realize Dreams," *Financial Post*, December 31, 2012; M. Wocks, "Crowd Funding Contributions Expected to Double in 2013: Deloitte," *Financial Post*, January 13, 2013; S. Stanleigh, "Procter & Gamble Bets on Crowdfunding site," *The Globe and Mail*, February 1, 2013; Q. Casey, "Can Crowd Funding Pay Your Tuition Bill?" *http://oncampus.macleans.ca*, April 5, 2013; M. O'Mara, "Kickstarter Received US$320-million in Crowdfunding Pledges in 2012," *National Post*, January 9, 2013.

you will be in a position to contribute to your organization's policies on social networking use while at work. You also will be able to help your organization design its own strategy for social networking.

7.1 Web 2.0 Underlying Technologies

The World Wide Web, which you learned about in Chapter 4, first appeared in 1990. Web 1.0 was the first generation of the web. (We did not use this term in Chapter 4 because there was no need to say "Web 1.0" until Web 2.0 appeared.)

The key developments of Web 1.0 were the creation of websites and the commercialization of the web. Users typically have minimal interaction with Web 1.0 sites. Rather, they passively receive information from those sites.

Web 2.0, although a popular term, has proved difficult to define. According to Tim O'Reilly, a noted blogger (see *www.oreillynet.com/lpt/a/6228*), **Web 2.0** is a loose collection of information technologies and applications, plus the websites that use them. These websites enrich the user's experience by encouraging user participation, social interaction, and collaboration. Unlike Web 1.0 sites, Web 2.0 sites are not so much on-line places to visit as web locations that facilitate information sharing, user-centred design, and collaboration. Web 2.0 sites often harness collective intelligence (for example, wikis); deliver functionality as services, rather than packaged software (for example, web services); and feature remixable applications and data (for example, mashups).

You begin your exploration of Web 2.0 by examining the various Web 2.0 information technologies. Among the most widely used technologies are AJAX, tagging, and really simple syndication (RSS).

AJAX

AJAX is a web development technique that enables portions of web pages to reload with fresh data instead of requiring the entire web page to reload. This process speeds up response time and increases user satisfaction.

Tagging

A **tag** is a keyword or term that describes a piece of information—for example, a blog, a picture, an article, or a video clip. Users typically choose tags that are meaningful to them. Tagging allows users to place information in multiple, overlapping associations rather than in rigid categories. For example, a photo of a car might be tagged with "Corvette," "sports car," and "Chevrolet." Tagging is the basis of *folksonomies*, which are user-generated classifications that use tags to categorize and retrieve web pages, photos, videos, and other web content.

As one example, the website Delicious.com (*http://delicious.com*) provides a system for organizing not just individuals' information but the entire web. Delicious is basically a tagging system, or a place to store links that do not fit in a "Favorites" folder. This system not only collects your links in one place, but it organizes them as well.

One critical feature of Delicious.com is that it has no rules governing how its users create and use tags. Instead, each person designs his or her own rules. Nevertheless, the product of all those individual decisions is well organized. That is, if you conduct a search on Delicious.com for all the pages that are tagged with a particular word, you likely will come up with a very good selection of related web sources.

One specific form of tagging, known as *geotagging*, involves tagging information on maps. For example, Google Maps allows users to add pictures and information, such as restaurant or hotel ratings, to maps. Therefore, the users' experience is enriched because they can see pictures of attractions, reviews, and things to do, all related to the map location they are viewing.

7.1 RSS Survival

A recent decision by Google to discontinue its Google Reader service made some technology observers question the continuity of RSS. Google Reader, up until 2013 when it stopped, was the most widely used RSS reader, yet that didn't deter Google from discontinuing its RSS reader service. By Google discontinuing their Google Reader tool there is the fear that Google users might also stop using it. Or on the other hand, it could mean that Google is developing some alternative tool to replace RSS feeds. Some wonder what the consequences might be for those using RSS technology.

Many people use RSS to disseminate and aggregate content. For example, your favourite newspaper or news agency likely provides RSS feeds. For example, CBC RSS feeds allow you to access CBC content in a variety of ways at your convenience. By using an RSS reader or integrating an RSS feed into your blog or other interface, you can access updated CBC news, sports, entertainment, blogs, and other CBC content in the way that works best for you. CBC's news headline RSS feeds are constantly updated as new stories are published.

What are the other benefits of using RSS technology? For businesses, one benefit is that interested visitors can subscribe to your feed and get a notification each time you publish something new. Also, other websites may want to aggregate your content or publish your new posts to social media sites like Facebook, Twitter, LinkedIn, or Google+.

Perhaps one of the most interesting opportunities for businesses is the possibility to use specialized RSS feeds to communicate new products or services with vendors, affiliates, customers, or members, improving the speed at which you can communicate new opportunities.

Another benefit of an RSS feed is that it can be used as a call to action, which is a prompt for visitors to do something, such as to chat on-line with a sales representative, sign up for a special offer, or subscribe to a newsletter. If a company website doesn't have these calls to action, it can ask visitors to subscribe to its RSS feed. This starts them on the road to what could be a long and happy relationship of one-to-one marketing.

Questions

1. Will RSS technology survive in the future? Why or why not?
2. How could you turn RSS technology into a viable e-commerce business model?
3. Provide specific examples of how RSS technology could be used by a grocery store chain, a hospital, and your university.

Sources: Compiled from M. Allton, "Has Google Killed RSS?" Tech & Gadgets, *www.business2community.com/tech-gadgets*, March 14, 2013; M. Allton, "What Is RSS, and How Does RSS Help My Business?" *www.thesocialmediahat.com*, July 30, 2012; B. Jackson, "Google Reader Dumped Me, But I Can Move On," ITbusiness.ca, March 21, 2013.

Really Simple Syndication

Really simple syndication (RSS) allows you to receive the information you want (customized information), when you want it, without having to surf thousands of websites. RSS allows anyone to syndicate (publish) his or her blog, or any other content, to anyone who has an interest in subscribing. When changes to the content are made, subscribers receive a notification of the changes and an idea of what the new content contains. Subscribers then can click on a link that will take them to the full text of the new content.

As an example, CBC.ca provides RSS feeds for each of its main topic areas, such as world news, sports news, technology news, and entertainment news. CBC uses RSS feeds to allow viewers to download the most current version of shows.

You can find thousands of websites that offer RSS feeds at Syndic8 (*www.syndic8.com*) and NewsIsFree (*www.newsisfree.com*). Figure 7.1 illustrates an RSS feed of new computer textbooks published by Wiley at the time of writing this book.

To use RSS, you need a news reader that displays RSS content feeds from websites you select. Many such readers are available, several of them for free. Most browsers have built-in RSS readers. Recently some have questioned the survival of RSS. IT's About Business 7.1 discusses some of the advantages and features of RSS technologies for users and businesses.

before you go on...

1. Differentiate between Web 1.0 and Web 2.0.
2. Explain how AJAX, tagging, and RSS have made the web more interactive and informative.

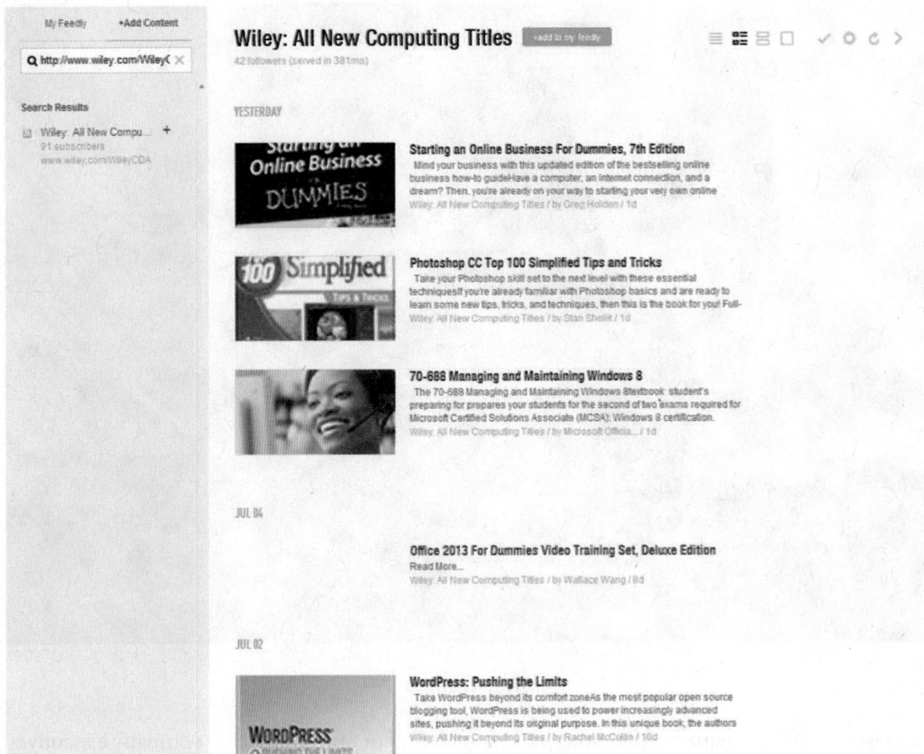

FIGURE 7.1 John Wiley & Sons website (*www.wiley.com*) with RSS toolbar aggregator.

7.2 Web 2.0 Applications

Web 2.0 applications use some or all of the technologies you have just seen. These applications include blogs, wikis, netcasting, printing-on-demand, and crowdsourcing. In this section, you will learn about these applications and the various ways in which business uses them.

Blogs and Blogging

A **weblog** (**blog** for short) is a personal website, open to the public, in which the site creator expresses his or her feelings or opinions via a series of chronological entries. *Bloggers*—people who create and maintain blogs—write stories, convey news, and provide links to other articles and websites that are of interest to them. The simplest method to create a blog is to sign up with a blogging service provider, such as *www.blogger.com* (now owned by Google), *www.xanga.com*, and *www.sixapart.com*. The **blogosphere** is the term for the millions of blogs on the web.

Companies employ blogs in different ways. Some companies listen to the blogosphere for marketing purposes. Others open themselves up to the public for input into their processes and products.

Many companies listen to consumers in the blogosphere who express their views on the companies' products. In marketing, these views are called *consumer-generated media*. Several companies analyze the blogosphere to provide information for their clients in several areas. For example, they help their clients find ways to serve potential markets, ranging from broad-based to niche markets. They also help their clients detect false rumours before these rumours appear in the mainstream media, and they gauge the potency of a marketing push or the popularity of a new product.

Blogs have become influential in the mainstream media as well (Figure 7.2). Many traditional media companies, such as CNN, now use blogs to provide richer versions of the stories

FIGURE 7.2 Community blogs or discussion boards are used in mainstream media. (*Source*: Fancy/Image)

they cover. Further, many corporations maintain blogs. For example, many company executives use Google's Corporate Blog to present their views on their industry and their organization.

Although blogs can be very useful, they also have shortcomings. Perhaps the primary value of blogs is their ability to bring current, breaking news to the public as fast as possible. But in doing so, unfortunately, bloggers sometimes cut corners, and their blogs can be inaccurate. For example, in May 2007, Engadget.com (a technology blog) reported that Apple's iPhone and OS X operating system were going to be delayed. This news caused Apple's stock price to drop by 4 percent in less than 20 minutes. When this report was challenged, Engadget.com retracted it.

Regardless of their various problems, blogs have transformed the ways in which people gather and consume information. In fact, many readers have cancelled their newspaper subscriptions and rely instead on free information from blogs and other on-line sources. In turn, decreasing readership has caused advertisers to withdraw business from traditional newspapers.

Wikis

A **wiki** is a website on which anyone can post material and make changes to already posted material. Wikis have an "edit" link on each page that allows anyone to add, change, or delete material, fostering easy collaboration.

Wikis harness the collective intelligence of Internet users, combining the input of many individuals. Consider the on-line encyclopedia Wikipedia (*www.wikipedia.org*), the largest wiki in existence. Wikipedia contains more than 3.4 million articles in English, which are viewed almost 500 million times every day. Wikipedia's volunteer administrators enforce a neutral point of view and encourage users to delete copy that displays clear bias. Nevertheless, the fundamental question concerning Wikipedia remains: How reliable and accurate are the articles? Many educators do not allow students to cite references from Wikipedia because content can be provided by anyone at any time. Moreover, Wikipedia does not provide any quality assessment or fact checking by experts. This process leads to questions about the authenticity of the content.

The reliability of content on Wikipedia, compared with that of encyclopedias and more specialized sources, is assessed in several ways by outside groups, including statistically, by comparative review, and by analyzing the strengths and weaknesses inherent in the Wikipedia process.

Organizations use wikis in several ways. In project management, for example, wikis provide a central repository for capturing constantly updated product features and specifications, tracking issues, resolving problems, and maintaining project histories. In addition, wikis enable companies to collaborate with customers, suppliers, and other business partners on projects. Wikis also are valuable in knowledge management. For example, companies use wikis to keep enterprise-wide documents, such as guidelines and frequently asked questions, accurate and current.

Netcasting

In many cases, access to blogs and other web resources that consist of written content is often impractical (e.g., when travelling or exercising). Today, however, technologies such as Apple's iPods and other digital music players, which have transformed the way people listen to music while on the go, also enable users to consume information that was previously available only when they accessed the Internet.

Netcasting, including podcasting and videocasting, is the distribution of digital media, primarily audio files (**podcasting**) and video files (**videocasting**), via syndication feeds for playback on digital media players and personal computers. Interestingly, the term "podcasting," derived from combining the words "iPod" and "broadcasting," is a misnomer, because netcasts (or podcasts) can be played on many other devices besides iPods.

Netcasting has become increasingly prevalent, with traditional media organizations now podcasting a wide variety of content, from radio programs to TV shows. In addition to traditional media, educational institutions use netcasts to provide students with access to lectures, lab demonstrations, and sports events. These netcasts enable students to review lectures or prepare for class during their morning and evening commutes or while exercising at the gym. In 2007, Apple launched iTunes U, which offers free content provided by major universities worldwide. Some examples in Canada are Concordia University, the University of British Columbia, and Ryerson University.

Web 2.0 Media

Web 2.0 media sites have a powerful presence on the Internet. These websites allow people to come together and share digital media, such as pictures, audio, and video. **Web 2.0 media** sites provide user-generated media content and promote tagging, rating, commenting, and other interactions among users and their media contributions. Web 2.0 media provide a variety of content, including:

- video (Amazon Video on Demand, YouTube, Hulu, Facebook)
- music (Amazon MP3, Last.fm, Rhapsody, Pandora, Facebook, iTunes)
- photographs (Photobucket, Flickr, Shutterfly, Picasa, Facebook).

Photo-sharing websites combine the features of social networking with photo sharing. IT's About Business 7.2 presents examples of photo-sharing sites.

Printing-on-Demand

Web 2.0 helps users to publish their own material. Traditionally, self-publishing was restricted largely to authors who published original materials (e.g., books). This endeavour was risky, because the author incurred high costs for producing the books and had to sell enough books to recover his or her costs before making a profit.

Today, however, **printing-on-demand**, which is customized printing done in small batches, is becoming increasingly popular. Open-source versions of software for text editing and typesetting are available in word processing programs and on the Internet. Another important innovation is small-book printing machines, which minimize setup and per-print run costs. These technologies have significantly reduced the costs of print-on-demand, making this process very attractive to first-time authors. Leading print-on-demand companies include CreateSpace (*www.createspace.com*), Lulu (*www.lulu.com*), and Blurb (*www.blurb.ca*). Many of these companies also offer distribution services. For example, CreateSpace provides end-to-end service where authors submit their manuscripts and the on-line publisher edits, formats, prints, and sells the work. Publishers provide these services for a sales commission, and the remainder of the revenue from book sales goes to the author.

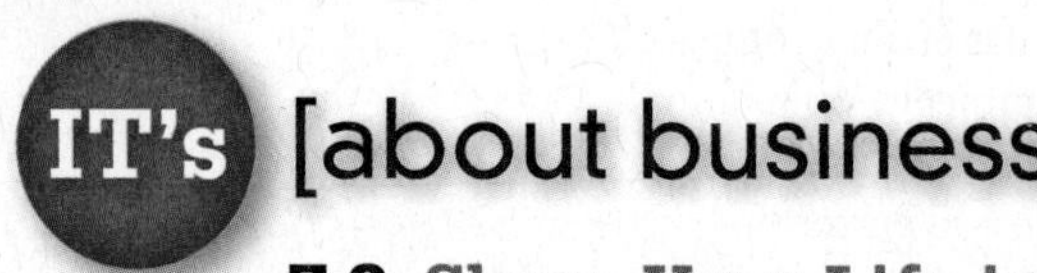

7.2 Share Your Life in Pictures

One of the most popular features of the Internet is photo-sharing services, which have seen explosive growth and constant change. The market began in the late 1990s with photo upload websites such as Ofoto (which became the Kodak Gallery, which closed in 2012) and Shutterfly *(www.shutterfly.com)*, with users mainly uploading photos from their new digital cameras so they could print them. Things changed in 2004, when Flickr *(www.flickr.com)* emerged, allowing serious and amateur photographers to share their photos with others. Yahoo! quickly saw the value in Flickr and purchased it in 2005. Other websites, such as Google's Picasa *(http://picasa.google.com)*, Photobucket *(www.photobucket.com)*, and, more recently, Facebook, provide photo-sharing and photo-editing services.

The more recent overnight photo service/social network success story is Instagram *(www.instagram.com)*. In its first four months, Instagram attracted more than 1.75 million users who collectively were uploading almost 300,000 photos per day.

A big part of Instagram's instant appeal was its ability to add visual effects to pictures taken with members' phones, giving images the classic look of photographs captured on traditional film and developed with chemicals or on Polaroid film. Members' photos can also quickly go viral, as they can post their images to their Instagram accounts or to social networks such as Facebook and Twitter. They also can browse and comment on collections from other photographers. When users post their images, the community provides instant feedback.

Instagram's explosive growth has been spurred not just by nostalgia for the look of analogue photographs, but by the new technology that enables people to take pictures anytime, anywhere, thanks to higher-resolution cameras on smart phones, and faster and more reliable wireless networks that enable people to easily upload their images. Instagram represents a new kind of web start-up that, thanks to platforms such as Apple's App Store, has rapidly become popular before turning into a bricks and mortar company. Just a year after launching, Instagram was snapped up by Facebook for US$1 billion in 2012.

Questions

1. Explain how and why a start-up can survive if it becomes "wildly popular" before it evolves into a real, profit-making business.
2. What are some potential disadvantages to photo-sharing websites such as Instagram?

Sources: Compiled from A. Diana, "Color Labs Offers Location-Based Photo Sharing App," *InformationWeek*, March 24, 2011; B. Stone, "Zero Revenue. Four Staffers. 1.74 Million Users," *Bloomberg BusinessWeek*, February 7–13, 2011; J. Evans, "Collected: What We Know About the Mac App Store," *Computerworld*, January 6, 2011; M. Isaac, "New Social Network Path = iPhone + Instagram + Facebook – 499,999,950 Friends," *Forbes*, November 2010; K. Hill, "10 Reasons Why Facebook Bought Instagram," Forbes.com, April 11, 2012; *www.instagram.com*, accessed March 30, 2011.

Crowdsourcing

Suppose an organization has a problem it needs to solve. Why not offer the problem to a crowd to determine whether their collective knowledge and wisdom can come up with a solution? This process, called **crowdsourcing**, involves taking a job traditionally performed by an employee or a consultant and outsourcing it to an undefined group of people in the form of an open call. Can crowds really outperform experts employed by a company? (See Figure 7.3.) Let's look at some examples where they have done so.

- Tongal (*http://tongal.com*) pays people to create on-line videos for companies such as Mattel and Allstate. Companies typically pay $15,000 to $20,000 for each project they post on Tongal's website. Tongal runs the projects like contests. Instead of a winner-take-all approach, the company breaks up the projects into stages, such as ideas and videos. It rewards the top five ideas with cash. Participants in the video phase are then free to use any of those five ideas to create the video.
- Amazon's Mechanical Turk (*www.amazon.com/mturk*) provides a website where anyone with a task to be completed or a problem to be solved can put it on the site, naming the price for completion or a solution. For performing this role, Amazon takes a small cut of each transaction.

FIGURE 7.3 Crowdsourcing. (*Source:* Scott Maxwell/LuMaxArt/ Shutterstock)

- Pharmaceutical giant Eli Lilly (*www.lilly.com*) has created a website called *InnoCentive* (*www.innocentive.com*), where companies can post scientific problems and everyone can try to solve them.
- Until a few years ago, book publishers had to rely on stock photography for many of the images used in their books. These photos were taken by professional photographers and were quite expensive. Today, high-quality digital cameras cost less than $1,000, and, with available photo editing software, amateur photographers can create images that almost match those of the professionals. The amateurs can upload their pictures to image-sharing websites such as iStockphoto (*www.istockphoto.com*), where interested parties can license and download the images for $1 to $5 per image, which is a fraction of the price of a regular stock photo. Because overhead costs are extremely low, iStockphoto can make a profit while still sharing part of the revenue with the pictures' creators.
- Amazon and Indigo sell the same products, and they receive the same product descriptions and editorial content from their vendors. Amazon, however, has led all bookstores in soliciting user input in the form of user editorial reviews. As a result, most Amazon users go directly to the user reviews when they are deciding whether to buy a book.

The benefits of crowdsourcing to companies include finding large numbers of workers to complete projects quickly, attracting niche expertise, saving money, and making better use of in-house resources. For the workers, crowdsourcing provides unprecedented flexibility to work almost anywhere at any time.

before you go on...

1. Differentiate between blogs and wikis.
2. What is netcasting?
3. Discuss the business benefits of crowdsourcing.

7.3 Categories of Web 2.0 Sites

There are literally thousands of Web 2.0 sites, and each one uses some or all of the Web 2.0 technologies and applications that you have just studied. In this section, you will focus on the three major categories of Web 2.0 sites: social networking, aggregators, and mashups.

Social Networking

Social networking sites allow users to upload their content to the web in the form of text (for example, blogs), voice (for example, podcasts), images, and videos (for example, videocasts). These sites provide an easy, interactive tool for communicating and collaborating with other people on the web. They help users find like-minded people on-line, either to pursue an interest or goal, or just to establish a sense of community with people whom they may never meet in the physical world.

Social networks also are highly valuable business tools. Example 7.1 illustrates how Adagio Teas and other companies use social networking tools to build their business.

Example 7.1

Adagio Teas (*www.adagio.com*) sells premium teas on-line and in stores. The company's website offers many social media features. Almost like a Facebook page for tea lovers, Adagio lets people chat about tea with other customers, post product reviews, read blogs, and keep on top of their orders with tweets.

Unlike most on-line retailers, Adagio does not moderate customer product reviews before they're posted to its website. New reviews are displayed in real time. A customer can post to the site as soon as they place an order and set up an account. The company incorporates the data into its market research, and it decides which teas to offer and which to discontinue based on sales data and customer feedback.

Adagio's site has other features as well. For example, customers can create custom tea blends, which the site then shares with other customers. When a customer buys a custom blend created by someone else, the creator receives points that can be redeemed for a gift certificate. Adagio also harnesses the power of word-of-mouth advertising, awarding points and discounts to customers who send friends a free $5 gift certificate via e-mail, Facebook, and Twitter, once the friends redeem the certificate. Finally, Adagio uses existing social media sites, providing a Facebook "Like" button for all its products, and using Twitter.

One of the most powerful features of most social networks is feeds (or newsfeeds). *Feeds* provide timely updates on the activities of people or topics with which an individual is associated. These feeds are inherently viral. By displaying other peoples' activities on a social network, feeds can rapidly mobilize populations and dramatically spread the adoption of applications. For example, by leveraging feeds, the Toronto-based Facebook group Support the Monks' Protest in Burma was able to attract more than 160,000 members in just 10 days. Feeds also helped the music app iLike acquire 3 million Facebook users just two weeks after its launch.

Feeds are also controversial, however. Many users react negatively to having their on-line activities broadcast publicly. Going further, mismanaged feeds can create public relations fiascos, spur user discontent, and lead to legal actions. For example, Facebook users were outraged when it launched its feeds, and they reacted with a similar backlash when Facebook's Beacon service broadcast user purchases without first explicitly asking the users for permission.

Despite the potential pitfalls, many organizations are finding useful ways to use social networks for specific purposes. For example, employees have organized work groups using publicly available social networking sites because their companies don't offer similar tools. In response, many firms are meeting this demand by implementing secure internal social network platforms that are tailored to company needs. These networks typically replace the traditional employee directory. Social network listings are easy to update and expand, and employees are encouraged to add their own photos, interests, and expertise.

Sources: Compiled from S. Greengard, "Winning Business with Social Media," *Baseline Magazine*, April 6, 2011; J. Stauffer, "The Value of a Strong Alumni Program," *www.cba.org*, accessed June 11, 2013; T. Burgmann and T. Cherry, "Support the Monks via Facebook," *Toronto Star*, September 30, 2007; *www.adagio.com*, accessed April 18, 2011.

Companies such as Deloitte, Dow Chemical, and the Canadian law firm Osler, Hoskin & Harcourt LLP have created social networks for "alumni" who have left the firm or are retired. These networks are useful in maintaining contacts for future business opportunities, rehiring former employees, and recruiting retired staff to serve as contractors. IBM's internal social network makes it easier to locate employee expertise within the company, thereby helping project leaders find needed talent anywhere in the organization.

Well-known social networking sites include:

- *Facebook www.facebook.com*: the most popular social networking website. IT's About Business 7.3 relates the case of Zynga, an on-line gaming website, and how it partnered with Facebook to enable a successful business model.
- *Flickr www.flickr.com*: a photo-sharing website, widely used by bloggers as a photo repository.

IT's [about business]

7.3 On-line Games Are Big Business

Globally, more than 200 million people play social games every month, and their numbers are rapidly increasing. In fact, on-line games have surpassed e-mail as the second-most popular on-line activity, behind social networking.

Not surprisingly, many companies are entering the on-line gaming industry. In July 2010, for example, Disney paid $563 million to purchase the social game developer Playdom (*www.playdom.com*). Meanwhile, Google announced the creation of its Google Game Developer Center, an on-line resource specifically designed to promote Google-related game technology and infrastructure. Why all the interest? The answer is that companies have noticed that 40 percent of Facebook's 600 million users regularly play social games.

One popular Facebook game, Scrabble, is a digital version of the iconic board game that came out in 1948. At the time of writing, Facebook's most popular game was FarmVille, where urban dwellers can try out an imaginary farm, tending to crops and livestock. Facebook members can fulfill countless other virtual fantasies with games, from taking care of fish in Happy Aquarium, throwing parties on Sorority Life, or living the life of a mobster in Mafia Wars.

Even though playing these on-line games is free, Facebook and other gaming sites make money by enticing users to buy add-ons to enhance their gaming experience. For instance, they can pay to be able to move through game levels faster. It's estimated that on-line gamers spent $835 million in 2010.

Consider the case of Zynga (*www.zynga.com*). More than 120 million people play Zynga's on-line social games such as FarmVille and Mafia Wars. In 2012, the company's revenue surpassed $1.2 billion.

As impressive as these numbers are, however, Zynga's success depends on the good graces of Facebook, where almost all of its games are played. In March 2010, Facebook prohibited Zynga and other app creators from promoting games in the "notifications" menu that users see each time they log on. Facebook claimed that users were complaining about spamlike messages that appeared every time one of their game-playing friends performed an action in an on-line game. In fact, 5 million Facebook users organized a protest group that called itself "I Don't Care About Your Farm, Or Your Fish, Or Your Park, Or Your Mafia!"

Zynga claims that the policy change hurt its business by reducing traffic to its games. Nevertheless, Zynga insists that it can help Facebook (and vice versa) because Zynga's games increase the time that users spend on Facebook.

Facebook does receive income from Zynga. Any time a game appears to be a hit, Zynga spends millions of dollars on ads promoting it to Facebook members. In total, Zynga spends between $5 and $8 million per month for banner ads on Facebook, according to neXtup Research (*www.nextupresearch.com*).

How does Zynga make money? Most of its revenues come from users buying the virtual currency of each site in order to purchase add-ons. FarmVille, for example, has Farm Coins. A tractor costs 5,000 Farm Coins, or about $3.30. Zynga used to use a third-party handler such as PayPal, to which it paid less than 10 percent of its revenue. Facebook, however, has developed a service called Facebook Credits that offers a single virtual currency for use on many different apps. In May 2010, Facebook and Zynga agreed to a five-year deal in which Zynga agreed to use Facebook Credits. As a result, Zynga pays Facebook up to 30 percent of every transaction.

Questions

1. From Zynga's perspective, discuss the advantages and disadvantages of the company's close relationship with Facebook.
2. What kinds of actions could Zynga take to minimize its dependence on Facebook? Be specific, and provide examples.

Sources: Compiled from T. Claburn, "Google Gets Gaming," *InformationWeek*, March 3, 2011; A. Diana, "Facebook Makes Credits Sole Legal Currency," *InformationWeek*, January 25, 2011; D. MacMillan, "Inside Zynga's Hit Factory," *Bloomberg BusinessWeek*, November 22–28, 2010; M. Rosenwald, "FarmVille, Other Online Social Games Mean Big Business, and Bonding," *The Washington Post*, August 3, 2010; A. Gonsalves, "Facebook, Zynga Ink Five-Year Deal," *InformationWeek*, May 19, 2010; D. MacMillan, "Zynga and Facebook. It's Complicated," *Bloomberg BusinessWeek*, April 26–May 2, 2010; *www.zynga.com*, accessed March 29, 2011. M. Farokhmanesh, "Zynga 2012 Revenue $1.2B, Up 12 Percent", *www.polygon.com*, February 5, 2013.

- *LinkedIn www.linkedin.com*: a business-oriented social networking site that is valuable for recruiting, sales, and investment. The company makes money from advertising and services. People—primarily the site's 60,000 recruiters—pay an average of $3,600 per year for premium features such as sending messages to LinkedIn members outside their own networks. Corporate members pay fees of up to six figures for access to the network.
- *YouTube www.youtube.com*: a social networking site for video uploads.
- *Twitter http://twitter.com*: allows users to post short updates (called "tweets") on their lives (no more than 140 characters) via the website, instant messaging, or mobile devices. Example 7.2 illustrates the potential power of Twitter.

Example 7.2

The use of social media such as Twitter is becoming more widespread among Canadian farmers. Some use Twitter to inform Canadians where their fruits, vegetables, and dairy products come from; what type of pesticides or herbicides have been used; of if they have used hormones in raising their cattle.

But social media is more than a way to connect and build trust with food-conscious consumers. It is also used to connect with other farmers. For example, the canola growers' association uses Twitter to tell producers about new diseases that have been spotted in a canola field or about meetings that are coming up.

Twitter is also becoming a key business tool for tech-savvy farmers, from marketing products, following commodity prices, and receiving crop information. For example, knowing how a cereal is trading in the U.S. market can have an impact on the decision around when to sell their harvests.

But even more interesting is how farmers can use Twitter to help influence agricultural policy decisions. This is what happened to two Canadian farmers who posted tweets regarding Ontario's Environmental Farm Plan. They were approached by the provincial agriculture minister, who was aware of their tweet and suggested that further discussion was needed. This is possible because many government offices have staffers plugged very firmly into the Twitter world.

Farmers are also using Twitter to share knowledge. For example, if a farmer wants to know how other farmers have gotten along with a particular fertilizer, he or she can pose the question through Twitter and in a matter of minutes someone will answer it. It is this immediacy and brevity that makes Twitter so attractive for busy farmers.

Aggregators

Aggregators are websites that provide collections of content from the web. Well-known aggregator websites include:

- *Bloglines www.bloglines.com*: Collects blogs and news from all over the web and presents the material in one, consistent, updated format.
- *Digg www.digg.com*: Aggregates news in a site that is part news site, part blog, and part forum. Users suggest and rate news stories, which then are ranked based on this feedback.
- *Simply Hired www.simplyhired.ca*: Searches some 4.5 million listings on job and corporate websites and contacts subscribers via an RSS feed or an e-mail alert when a job appears that meets their criteria.

Sources: Compiled from S. Haney, "Twitter Was Made for Farmers – Rick Taillieu," RealAgriculture.com, March 1, 2012; J. Davison, "Tweeting Farmers Bridge Gap between Farm, Table," CBC News, October 20, 2011; A. Finnamore, "Putting Twitter to Work on the Farm," Farm Credit Canada, *www.fcc-fac.ca*, February 15, 2013.

[about business]

7.4 Location, Location, Location

Consider this scenario: At 6 p.m., your smart phone alerts you to your evening's plans. It has already checked your friends' calendars and knows who is free tonight, so it suggests a restaurant that all of you have wanted to try. Your phone notes when a table is available and informs you that three other friends are planning to meet you for dinner.

Harnessing GPS-enabled mobile technology to let users broadcast their location is not a new idea. Google's Latitude (*www.google.com*) and Facebook (*www.facebook.com*) offer location-based, friend-locating apps. Foursquare (*https://foursquare.com*) combines the popularity of location-based apps with games. To entice users to visit certain bars, restaurants, and other venues, Foursquare provides a button they can press when they arrive, or "check in," to earn badges. The person who checks in the most to a certain location in the past 60 days earns the status of "mayor."

Foursquare's business model is simple: Generate as big a user base as possible, and sell national brands and local merchants on the possibilities of marketing to people as they gather to eat, shop, or spend. In mid-2013, over 1 million merchants, including restaurants, bars, and other establishments, used Foursquare to attract customers with promotions.

PepsiCo, Zagat, and more than a dozen other well-known brands have signed paid-partnership deals with Foursquare. PepsiCo teamed up with Foursquare for a charity drive in New York City. Every time someone checked in within the city limits, Pepsi donated 4 cents to a non-profit youth organization called CampInteractive (*www.campinteractive.org*), up to a maximum of $10,000. Pepsi's global director of digital and social media was impressed with the user response on that marketing campaign.

It remains to be seen if Foursquare's check-in feature is enough to build a long-term business. Other websites such as Geoloqi (*http://geoloqi.com*) have implemented rival networks, each with check-in features. In addition, established companies such as Twitter and Yelp have created location-based tools.

Questions

1. What are some possible disadvantages of being a member of Foursquare? Have you joined Foursquare? Why or why not?
2. Analyze the differences between social networking and social location networking, using specific examples.

Sources: Compiled from S. Denning, "Social Location Marketing by Simon Salt," *Forbes*, April 15, 2011; A. Diana, "Foursquare, AMEX Partner on Offer Program at SXSW," *InformationWeek*, March 11, 2011; A. Diana, "Foursquare Value Checks In at $250 Million," *InformationWeek*, January 24, 2011; M. Copeland, "Facebook Is Going Places. Where Will Foursquare Go?" *Fortune*, August 18, 2010; D. Brady, "Social Media's New Mantra: Location, Location, Location," *Bloomberg BusinessWeek*, May 10–16, 2010; G. Moran, "My Smartphone Sent Me," *InformationWeek*, May 6, 2010; *www.foursquare.com*, accessed May 21, 2013.

- *Technorati www.technorati.com*: Contains information on all blogs in the blogosphere. It indicates how many other blogs link to a particular blog, and it ranks blogs by topic.

Mashups

Mashup means to "mix and match" content from other parts of the web. A **mashup** is a website that takes different types of content from other websites and mixes them together to create a new kind of content. The launch of Google Maps is credited with providing the start for mashups. A user can take a map from Google, add his or her own data, and then display a map mashup on his or her website that plots cars for sale, or virtually any other subject. For example, Craigslist has developed a dynamic map of all available apartments in selected cities in the United States and Canada *www.housingmaps.com*.

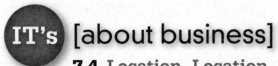

New tools are emerging to build location mashups. For example, the Pipes service from Yahoo! *http://pipes.yahoo.com* lets users drag and drop features from multiple web data sources to visually remix data feeds and create mashups. IT's About Business 7.4 describes the interesting mashup called Foursquare.

before you go on...

1. What are social networks, and how are organizations using them?
2. What are aggregators, and what is their greatest value to Web 2.0 users?
3. Describe mashups, and discuss their business value.

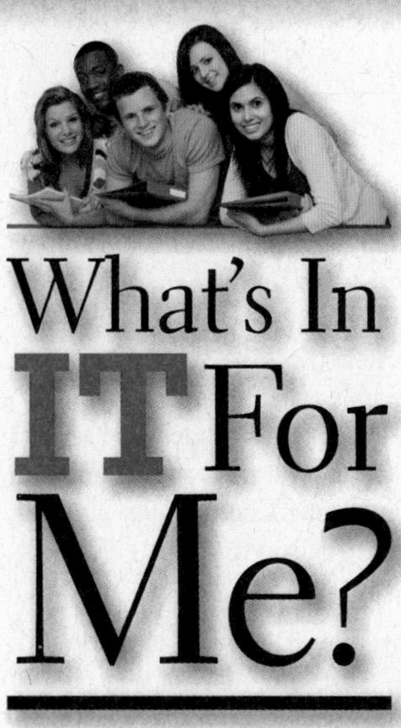

For the **Accounting Major**

Audit teams use social networking technologies internally to stay in touch with team members who are working on multiple projects. These technologies serve as a common channel of communications. For example, an audit team manager can create a group, include his or her team members as subscribers, and then push information regarding projects to all members at once. Externally, these technologies are useful for interfacing with clients and other third parties to whom the firm and its staff provide services.

For the **Finance Major**

Many of the popular social networking sites have users who subscribe to finance-oriented subgroups. Among these users are finance professionals who collaborate and share knowledge as well as nonfinancial professionals who are potential clients.

For the **Marketing Major**

Web 2.0 applications enable marketing professionals to become closer to their customers in various ways, including blogs, wikis, ratings, and recommendations. Marketing professionals now receive almost real-time feedback on products.

For the **Production/Operations Management Major**

Web 2.0 applications allow production personnel to "enlist" business partners and customers in product development activities.

For the **Human Resources Management Major**

Social networks offer tremendous benefits to human resources professionals. HR personnel can perform many of their recruiting activities by accessing such sites as LinkedIn. They also can check out potential new hires by accessing a large number of social networking sites. Internally, HR personnel can use private, internal social networks for employee expertise and experience in order to find the best person for a position or project team.

For the **MIS Major**

The MIS department is responsible for two aspects of Web 2.0 usage: (1) monitoring employee usage of Web 2.0 applications for both time and content while employees are at work; and (2) developing private, internal social networks for company employees and then monitoring the content of these networks.

[Summary]

1. **Describe the differences between Web 1.0 and Web 2.0, and explain the benefits of three information technologies used by Web 2.0.**

Web 1.0 was the first generation of the web. Key developments of Web 1.0 were the creation of websites and the commercialization of the web. Users typically have minimal interaction with Web 1.0 sites, which provide information that users receive passively.

Web 2.0 is a loose collection of information technologies and applications, plus the websites that use them. These websites enrich the user's experience by encouraging user participation, social interaction, and collaboration. Unlike Web 1.0 sites, Web 2.0 sites are not so much on-line places to visit as sites that facilitate information sharing, user-centred design, and collaboration. Web 2.0 sites often harness collective intelligence (for example, wikis); deliver functionality as services rather than packaged software (for example, web services); and feature remixable applications and data (for example, mashups).

AJAX is a web development technique that enables portions of web pages to reload with fresh data instead of requiring the entire web page to reload. This process speeds up response time and increases user satisfaction.

A *tag* is a keyword or term that describes a piece of information (for example, a blog, a picture, an article, or a video clip). Users typically choose tags that are meaningful to them.

Really simple syndication (RSS) allows you to receive the information you want (customized information), when you want it, without having to surf thousands of websites.

2. Identify five prominent Web 2.0 applications, and provide at least one example of how each one can be used in a business setting.

A *weblog* (*blog* for short) is a personal website, open to the public, in which the site creator expresses feelings or opinions with a series of chronological entries. Companies use blogs in different ways. Some companies listen to the blogosphere for marketing purposes. Others open themselves up to the public for input into their processes and products.

A *wiki* is a website on which anyone can post material and make changes to already posted material. Wikis foster easy collaboration, and they harness the collective intelligence of Internet users.

Organizations use wikis in several ways. In project management, for example, wikis provide a central repository for capturing constantly updated product features and specifications, tracking issues, resolving problems, and maintaining project histories. In addition, wikis enable companies to collaborate with customers, suppliers, and other business partners on projects. Wikis also are useful in knowledge management.

Netcasting is the distribution of digital media, such as audio files (*podcasting*) and video files (*videocasting*), via syndication feeds for playback on digital media players and personal computers. Educational institutions use netcasts for providing students with access to lectures, lab demonstrations, and sports events.

Printing-on-demand is customized printing performed in small batches. For example, CreateSpace (owned by Amazon.com) provides end-to-end service where authors submit their manuscripts and the on-line publisher edits, formats, prints, and sells the work. Publishers provide these services for a sales commission, and the remainder of the revenue from book sales goes to the author.

Crowdsourcing is the process of taking a job traditionally performed by an employee or a consultant and outsourcing it to an undefined group of people in the form of an open call.

3. Discuss the three categories of Web 2.0 sites, and provide at least one example of how each can improve business efficiency and profitability.

Social networking websites allow users to upload their content to the web in the form of text (for example, blogs), voice (for example, podcasts), images, and videos (for example, videocasts). Organizations can use social networking to get closer to customers (achieve customer intimacy), business partners, and suppliers.

Aggregators are websites that provide collections of content from the web. Organizations can post job openings on aggregator websites for increased exposure. Organizations also can scan aggregator news sites for information on the organization that is pulled from sites across the web.

A *mashup* is a website that takes different types of content from other websites and mixes them together to create a new kind of content. Many organizations use mashups to deliver valuable information to their customers. Many governments are using mashups to deliver information on housing and health, among other things, to their constituents.

[Chapter Glossary]

aggregator Websites that provide collections of content from the web.

AJAX A web development technique that allows portions of web pages to reload with fresh data rather than requiring the entire web page to reload.

blog (weblog) A personal website, open to the public, in which the site creator expresses feelings or opinions with a series of chronological entries.

blogosphere The millions of blogs on the web.

crowdfunding The process of raising small sums of money

from a large pool of investors or donors using a website and social media.

crowdsourcing The process of taking a job traditionally performed by an employee or consultant and outsourcing it to an undefined group of people in the form of an open call.

mashup Website that takes different types of content from other websites and mixes them together to create a new kind of content.

netcasting The distribution of digital media via syndication feeds for playback on digital media players and personal computers.

podcasting The distribution of digital audio media via syndication feeds for playback on digital media players and personal computers.

printing-on-demand Customized printing done in small batches.

really simple syndication (RSS) A technology that allows users to receive the information they want, when they want it, without having to surf thousands of websites.

social networking sites Websites that allow users to upload their content to the web in the form of text, voice, images, and videos.

tag A keyword or term that describes a piece of information.

videocasting The distribution of digital video media via syndication feeds for playback on digital media players and personal computers.

Web 2.0 A loose collection of information technologies and applications, plus the websites that use them.

Web 2.0 media Any website that provides user-generated media content, and promotes tagging, rating, commenting, and other interactions among users and their media contributions.

weblog (see **blog**)

wiki A website on which anyone can post material and make changes to other material.

[Discussion Questions]

1. How would you describe Web 2.0 to someone who has not taken a course in information systems?
2. If you were the CEO of a company, would you pay attention to blogs about your company? Why or why not? If yes, would you consider some blogs to be more important or more reliable than others? If so, which ones? How would you find blogs relating to your company?
3. Do you have a page on a social networking website? If yes, why? If no, what is keeping you from creating one? Is there any content that you definitely would *not* post on such a page?
4. How can an organization best employ Web 2.0 technologies and applications to benefit their business processes?
5. What factors might cause an individual, an employee, or a company to be cautious in the use of social networks?
6. What risks does a company expose itself to if it leverages feeds? How might the company mitigate these risks?
7. What sorts of restrictions or guidelines should firms place on the use of social networks by employees? Are these Web 2.0 sites a threat to security? Can they tarnish a firm's reputation? If so, how? Can they enhance a firm's reputation? If so, how?

[Problem-Solving Activities]

1. Enter *www.programmableweb.com*, and study the various services that the website offers. Learn how to create mashups, and then propose a mashup of your own. Present your mashup to the class.
2. Go to Amazon's Mechanical Turk website (*www.mturk.com*). View the available HITs. Are there any HITs that you would be interested in for making some extra money? Why or why not?
3. Access ChatRoulette (*www.chatroulette.com*). What is interesting about this social networking site?
4. Using a search engine, look up the most popular or most visited blogs. Pick two, and follow some of the posts. Why do you think these blogs are popular?
5. Research how to be a successful blogger. What is required to become a successful blogger? What time commitment might be needed? How frequently do successful bloggers post?
6. Design a mashup for your university. Include the purpose of the mashup, sources of data, and intended audience.

[Spreadsheet Activity]

Objective: When someone uses the phrase "social network," we generally think of MySpace or Facebook. However, many online tools allow people to collaborate and work together on projects. Google Docs is one of these. This activity will introduce the Google Spreadsheet Survey tool.

Chapter Connection: Although Google Spreadsheets are not social networks like Facebook and MySpace, they are definitely examples of Web 2.0. They allow multiple people to work together and collaborate on many projects. The Google Spreadsheet Survey tool is no exception. It allows for the easy collection and sharing of data.

Activity: Consider the following scenario. You are the marketing officer for "Students for Better Campus Lunches" and have been charged with a campus-wide survey to find out how people feel about the current food offerings and their desires for future possibilities. You decide to use a Google Form because the data are automatically saved in a Google Spreadsheet and will be easy for you to analyze. The following questions have been of these so they will fit a multiple-choice question format. You also may want to have a couple of open-ended questions to allow for comments.

1. How often do you eat on campus?
2. Which meals do you eat?
3. Are you satisfied with the current choices?
4. What cuisines would you like to see more of?
5. What do you think we could do without?
6. Is eating on campus too expensive?
7. Do you have any general recommendations for food on campus?

To complete this exercise, you will need to create a Google account if you do not already have one. Then log in to http://docs.google.com and create a new form.

Go to the Google Docs Web site and watch the tutorials on how to create Google Forms. Or simply search Google for "Google Form Videos" and have a look at the tutorials. Once you have created your form, have some friends complete your survey and have a look at the data in your spreadsheet. Export this spreadsheet as a Microsoft Excel file and submit it to your professor.

Deliverables: The final product will be a workable survey/form built in Google Docs and the spreadsheet that it creates.

Discussion Questions:

1. Discuss the advantages and disadvantages of using this type of tool. For example, how do you know how many times someone completes the survey? Given this lack of control, in how many situations would this truly be useful?
2. If you were to embed a Google Form into another Web page, do you think you should tell people that your form was created on a Google site? Should you explain the security levels available? How much do you want them to know about how easily they could take and retake the survey?

[Case Assignment]

The federal government has many surplus goods, and also seizes goods for a variety of reasons (at the international border, or stolen goods, for example). It recently set up a website called GCSurplus.ca (*www.gcsurplus.ca*; Government of Canada Surplus) where individuals and organizations can bid for and purchase these items. There are hundreds of items listed at GCsurplus.ca, organized into product categories, including automobiles and computer equipment.

Required

a. For each of the following two types of applications, describe the application and explain how the federal government could use the application to support the success of its surplus sales website.
   - Tagging
   - RSS (really simple syndication)

b. For each of the following three types of social networks, describe the application and explain how the federal government could use the application to support the success of its surplus sales website.
   - Social networks
   - Aggregators
   - Mashups

[Team Assignments]

1. Each team will visit a major social networking site. The team will discover features that distinguish its site and present its pros, cons, and distinguishing features to the class.
2. Each team should choose a subject that needs aggregation. The team will set up the plans for an aggregator website to accomplish this goal and present the site to the class.
3. Enter *www.podcasting-tools.com*. Explain how to record a podcast. Each team will create a podcast on some idea in the course and make it available on your class website.
4. Each team will independently take on the following problem: You are an external consulting company with experience in corporate Web 2.0 implementation. Create a PowerPoint presentation that sells Web 2.0 to the company below while addressing the following concerns:
   - The company is a credit card and payment-processing firm that has 100 employees. Many of the employees are not very Internet literate, and most have not heard of Web 2.0. It is believed that there will be resistance by employees to any proposed changes.

- The company's CIO would like to implement Web 2.0 technologies and applications to enhance employee life and perhaps explore new ways of marketing the company's services.

Each team will conduct its research independently and present the results to the class.

[Case 7.2 Marketing with Facebook]

The Problem

The man considered the father of modern advertising, John Wanamaker, said 100 years ago: "Half the money I spend on advertising is wasted; the trouble is, I don't know which half." That mantra held true for nearly a century, until the Internet enabled advertisers to target their audiences and track the results of their investments with a level of precision that Wanamaker could only dream about. Most large websites can tailor ads based on a user's browsing history. For example, Google (*www.google.com*) has developed its brand of targeted advertising so effectively that the company reported some $50 billion in revenues in 2012.

Marketers have long hoped to turn the web into the perfect advertising medium. Pop-ups ads, banners ads, and search ads were steps toward that goal. Facebook, however, is pioneering targeted advertising.

The Solution

Facebook (*www.facebook.com*) has developed a powerful kind of targeted advertising that is more personal, or "social," than any previous type. For example, suppose that you recently became engaged and updated your Facebook status to reflect that fact. You might start seeing ads from local jewellers. Those jewellers likely would have used Facebook's automated ad system to target recently engaged couples living in the area.

Consider David Belden, founder of Residential Solar 101 (*www.residentialsolar101.com*), a San Francisco-based reseller of solar panels. Belden knows exactly who his customer is: male, about 55 years old, and probably with a hybrid car in the driveway. Such details are exactly what Facebook can provide for Belden.

However, ads on Facebook's website (say, for Belden's Residential Solar 101) are located on the far right of the page and are clicked on by fewer than 1 in 1,000 users. In contrast, Google ads, which are triggered by searches for specific topics, can draw clicks from up to 1 in 10 users; however, they also are far more expensive than Facebook ads.

If Facebook's business model was built only on getting users to click through its targeted ads, it would be in the red. But Facebook ads can evolve into conversations among friends, colleagues, and family members, and advertisers want to be involved in these conversations.

The entire premise for Facebook's model of advertising is that advertisements are more valuable when they are reinforced by your friends' behaviours. An ad that enough of your friends like or comment on can move into your main news feed, along with the names of your friends and all the conversations about the ad. The advertiser pays nothing for this movement.

Facebook doesn't promise advertisers that its ads are a call to action. Members are not necessarily going to visit the advertisers' websites and buy something. Instead, the ads build brand awareness, hoping that when you're ready to book a hotel or buy a bag of cookies, you'll remember the conversations about these services and products. If Facebook can entice you to "Like" the brand, even better. It gives the advertiser permission to market to you in your feed.

The Results

Nielsen (*www.nielsen.com*), the marketing research firm, notes that if users discover that their friends "Like" an ad or have commented on it positively or negatively, they are up to 30 percent more likely to recall the ad's message. Consider Nike's (*www.nike.com*) three-minute commercial at the FIFA World Cup in the summer of 2010. Hundreds of millions of people saw the commercial on television; however, Nike had launched the ad on Facebook before it appeared on television.

The commercial quickly went viral, being viewed more than 9 million times by Facebook users sharing and commenting among friends. In just one weekend, Nike doubled its Facebook fans from 1.6 million to 3.1 million. Nike officials said that placing the ad on Facebook cost "a few million dollars"; passing the ad around, however, cost Nike nothing. David Grasso, Nike's chief marketing officer, noted that Facebook for Nike was what TV was for marketers in the 1960s. Facebook now is an integral part of Nike's marketing strategy.

Ford, 7-Eleven, and McDonald's have unveiled products on their Facebook pages, in some cases using their fan groups to help design those items in advance. Starbucks offers coupons and free pastries to its 14 million fans. Other brands use Facebook to pursue what they describe as their products' "service mission." For example, Tim Hortons' more than 1.4 million fans talk about what the iconic coffee chain means to them, and Special K's page provides nutritional tips. Coca-Cola, which has more than 12 million Facebook fans, also relies and focuses on Facebook.

And the bottom line for Facebook? The company reported revenue of $5 billion in 2012 and was valued at $61.5 billion in May 2013.

Even though Facebook's bottom line looks good, the company's success is creating competition. Google is adding a feature to its web searches that enables users to recommend useful search results to friends. This process could lead Google to rank websites based on what users and their friends find useful rather than using only Google's PageRank algorithm. Google's social search effort is called "+1" or "plus one." "Plus one" came after Google's previous attempt to create a viable social-networking service, called Google Buzz, fizzled. Google and Facebook increasingly appear to be on a collision course for on-line advertising dollars.

Questions

1. Describe the advantages enjoyed by advertisers who place ads on Facebook.
2. Discuss disadvantages that users may encounter when advertisers target them on Facebook.
3. Who should be responsible for the use of social networks in a business? The marketing department or the IT department? Justify your answer.
4. Could the use of social networks confer a company a competitive advantage over the long run? Justify your answer.
5. What aspects of a company's IT infrastructure does one need to consider when building a social network website or linking to an existing social network website?

Sources: Compiled from A. Efrati, "Google Wants Search to Be More Social," *The Wall Street Journal*, March 31, 2011; T. Team, "Squint Your Eyes and Facebook Looks Like a $55 Billion Biz," *Forbes*, February 16, 2011; B. Stone, "Sell Your Friends," *Bloomberg BusinessWeek*, September 27–October 3, 2010; A. Ostrow, "Spending a Lot on Facebook," *Forbes*, August 31, 2010; T. Bradley, "Facebook Set to Challenge Google Ad Empire," *CIO*, March 22, 2010; AFP, "Google 2012 Revenue Hits $50 Billion, Profits up," Dawn.com, January 23, 2013; M. Gorman, "Facebook Finishes 2012 on a High Note: Q4 Revenue $1.585 Billion, $64 Million in Net Income," Engadget.com, January 30, 2013; M. Oliveira, Canadian Press, "Business Turning Facebook into Marketing Network," *The Globe and Mail*, August 23, 2012; *www.facebook.com*, accessed June 12, 2013.

Chapter 8

Information Systems within the Organization

[LEARNING OBJECTIVES]

1. Explain the purposes of transaction processing systems. Provide at least one example of how businesses use these systems.
2. Define functional area information systems. Provide an example of the support they provide for each functional area of the organization.
3. Explain the purpose of enterprise resource planning systems. Identify four advantages and four drawbacks to implementing an ERP system.
4. Discuss the three major types of reports generated by functional area information systems and enterprise resource planning systems. Provide an example of each type.

[CHAPTER OUTLINE]

8.1 Transaction Processing Systems
8.2 Functional Area Information Systems
8.3 Enterprise Resource Planning Systems
8.4 Reports

[WEB RESOURCES]

Student Companion Site
wiley.com/college/rainer

- Student PowerPoints for note taking
- Interactive Case: Ruby's Club Assignments
- Complete glossary

WileyPLUS

All of the above and

- E-book
- Mini-lecture by author for each chapter section
- Practice quizzes
- Flash Cards for vocabulary review
- Additional "What's in IT for Me?" cases
- Video interviews with managers
- Lab Manual for Microsoft Office 2010
- How-to Animations for Microsoft Office 2010

What's In IT For Me?
THIS CHAPTER WILL HELP PREPARE YOU TO ...
ACCT
Prepare annual budget
FIN
Analyze cash flows
MKT
Understand customers' needs, wants
POM
Manage materials handling
HR
Manage recruiting
MIS
Supervise the firm's information systems

[Case 8.1 Helping Baseball Hitters with It]

The Problem

There is probably no professional sport that relies more heavily on statistics than baseball. Analysts have spent decades applying scientific principles to measure player performance in everything from the number of a batter's stolen bases to a pitcher's ratio of ground balls allowed to fly balls allowed. The last remaining nonscientific frontier in baseball is fielding, or defence. John Dewan, the owner of Baseball Info Solutions (BIS; *www.baseballinfosolutions.com*), has made fielding statistics his latest mission.

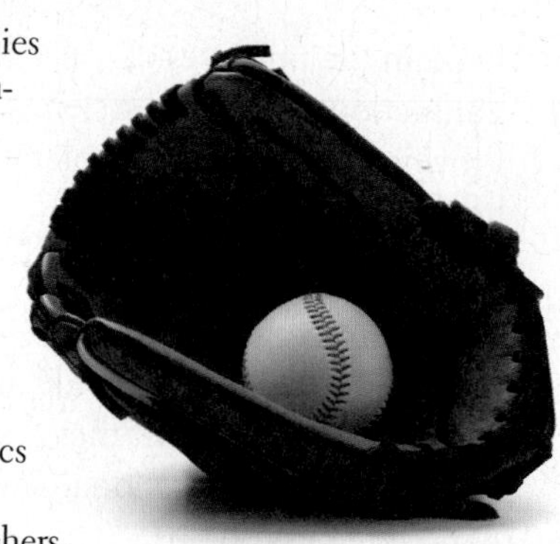

Fotoline/Shutterstock

While there's little left to measure for hitters and pitchers, when it comes to fielders, however, the existing metrics only evaluate about 5 percent of what they do. Scorekeepers have traditionally captured a fielder's work only after he gets to the ball. The usual fielding metric, the fielding average, merely records how many plays a fielder makes successfully. This is not true of other players. For example, when a shortstop catches a grounder but does not throw it to first in time to make the out, he gets an error.

Dewan looked for a better way to assess fielding in baseball. He created a whole new statistic: the ultimate zone rating. It measures how well a fielder plays in one of 3,000 zones on the field. Dewan counts how often fielders made outs on balls hit into each zone, and compares that against the average of all fielders at that position. A centre fielder, for instance, who made a catch on a ball that 70 percent of major leaguers would also catch was given an ultimate zone rating of 0.3. Dewan then converted the zone rating into the number of runs saved by a fielder's play.

BIS employs about 20 video scouts to compile all these numbers. They watch videos of every game at least three times. They record data on every batted ball: its direction, distance, speed, and type. Major league teams pay to see these numbers.

The BIS data, however, are not perfect. For example, they do not indicate where a fielder was standing when the ball was hit. In addition, the data are susceptible to human error, and could be off by 15 to 20 feet (4.5 to 6 metres) on some plays. Dewan estimated that BIS and its video scouts could measure only 60 percent of a fielder's ability.

The Solution

Enter Sportvision (*www.sportvision.com*), a leader in sports broadcasting technology. Sportvision created Fieldf/x, a motion-capture, or optical tracking, system that helps eliminate human error and the need to be in the right place at the right time. Sportvision claims that Fieldf/x is accurate to within one foot (30 centimetres).

Fieldf/x uses four cameras placed high above the field to track players and the ball, and to log their movements. The system collects movement data and produces valuable information such as a fielder's reaction time, his path to the ball, the base runner's speed, and the arc of a fly ball. The system generates more than 2.5 million records per game, or 2 terabytes of data. When installed at all Major League Baseball parks, Fieldf/x will create a digital catalogue of virtually every movement of every fielder at every game.

The Results

In mid-2011, Fieldf/x was in place at San Francisco's AT&T Park, and it was installed in four more parks by October 2012. The goal was to install the system in every major league park in the United States by the end of 2013. Tom Tippett, the director of baseball information services for the Boston Red Sox, is responsible for gathering and analyzing data to put together a winning team in Boston. He asserts that Fieldf/x will essentially make all other fielding statistics irrelevant.

Ultimately, Fieldf/x will generate new baseball metrics, such as degree-of-difficulty fielding ratings. Fieldf/x also will make coaching more precise; for example, coaches will be able to better position their fielders, depending on the hitter and the pitch being thrown (e.g., fast ball versus slow curve ball). Finally, the system will enhance the process by which clubs evaluate—and pay—their players.

What We Learned from This Case

The opening case illustrates the astonishing variety of information systems (ISs) that you will learn about in this chapter. Information systems are everywhere, and they affect organizations in countless ways. Who would have thought that an IS could help a large organization like professional baseball become more like a science?

Information systems also have an impact on small organizations, as IT's About Small and Big Business 8.1 shows. It illustrates how tightly integrated all the topics in this text are. Pizza Pizza is using an app to save costs (by having customers do transaction processing) while also connecting to its customers.

IT's about [small and big] business

8.1 Pizza Pizza's Customer App

Although Pizza Pizza (*www.pizzapizza.ca*) appears to be a large chain, each store is individually owned by a franchisee who operates the franchise. This means that each Pizza Pizza store is a small business that receives support such as marketing and information technology from the head office. Pizza Pizza stores must compete with other pizza chains across Canada as well as with other takeout products, such as submarine sandwiches, chicken, and hamburgers. Pizza Pizza prides itself on providing good quality food with innovative recipes. It must also be convenient and fun for its customers.

Pizza Pizza engaged Plastic Mobile to create an iPhone app for the company in 2011. It selected the iPhone because they only needed to use one platform to reach many people. The app is free and fun: you can design your own pizza and place an order. It's also pleasing on the eyes—so pleasing that it won several design awards, including one from the Canadian Marketing Association. Apple featured it as a new app for one week, and over 100,000 people ordered pizza using the app in the first week. As of January 2013, this had increased to over 250,000 orders placed, with over three quarters of a million transactions (such as payments) completed with the app.

Not only is the app convenient for customers and brings in more sales, but franchise owners have another benefit. Transactions that are done via the app do not have to be keyed by Pizza Pizza employees, reducing costs and saving the potential for error, such as entering the wrong order details.

Pizza Pizza is continuing to use apps to innovate and draw customers. For example, it has enabled students from some universities to pay for their pizza with their student meal plan cards. This shows how e-payment systems can work seamlessly with the smart phone as the intermediary. It has also provided version of the app for iPads and iPods.

Such success has drawn the competition into the pizza app arena. Late in 2011 another franchise pizza chain, Domino's, created an app that would allow users to play a game (preparing pizzas and responding to orders) in addition to being able to order their own pizzas.

Questions

1. What are the advantages and disadvantages of customer entry of pizza orders?
2. What are some of the features that you would want on a pizza app? How would these features result in costs or benefits for Pizza Pizza?

Sources: Compiled from G. Ng, "Pizza Pizza iOS App Surpasses 250K Downloads, New iPad Version Available," iPhoneinCanada.ca, January 13, 2013; A. Shilton, "Convenience Is Key for Pizza Pizza's New App," *The Globe and Mail*, April 4, 2011; B. Jackson, "Plastic Mobile Delivers Pizza Pizza iPad," ITbusiness.ca, January 17, 2013.

Sources: Compiled from I. Boudway, "Running the Numbers," *Bloomberg BusinessWeek*, April 4–10, 2011; J. Dubow, "New System Tries to Measure Pitchers Command," *Forbes*, April 1, 2011; K. Bhasin, "FIELDf/x: The Amazing Tracking Technology That's About to Change Baseball Forever," *Business Insider*, March 31, 2011; J. Letzing, "In Baseball, It Pays to Be a Data Nerd," *The Wall Street Journal*, October 22, 2012; *www.sportvision.com*, accessed March 14, 2013.

You need to have a working knowledge of information systems within your organization for a variety of reasons. First, your job will require you to access corporate data that are largely supplied by your firm's transaction processing systems and enterprise resource planning systems. Second, you will have a great deal of input into the format and content of the reports that you receive from these systems. Third, you will use the information in these reports to perform your job more productively.

This chapter will show you the various information systems within the organization. You begin by considering transaction processing systems, the most fundamental information systems within organizations. You continue with the functional area management information systems, and then proceed to the enterprise resource planning systems.

A *transaction processing system (TPS)* supports the monitoring, collection, storage, and processing of data generated by each of the organization's basic business transactions. For example, when you check out at Walmart, one transaction occurs each time the cashier swipes an item across the bar code reader. The TPS collects data continuously, in *real time*—that is, as soon as the data are generated—and it provides the input data for the corporate databases. The TPSs are critical to the success of any enterprise because they support core operations.

Each department or functional area within an organization has its own application programs, or information systems. Each of these *functional area information systems* supports a particular functional area in the organization. For example, there are ISs for accounting, finance, production/operations management (POM), marketing, and human resources.

Enterprise resource planning (ERP) systems are designed to correct a lack of communication among the functional area ISs. ERP systems resolve this problem by tightly integrating the functional area ISs via a common database. For this reason, experts credit ERP systems with greatly increasing organizational productivity.

8.1 Transaction Processing Systems

Millions (sometimes billions) of transactions occur in large organizations every day. A **transaction** is any business event that generates data worth being captured and stored in a database. Examples of transactions are a product manufactured, a service sold, a person hired, and a payroll cheque generated.

In the modern business world, **transaction processing systems (TPSs)** are inputs for functional area information systems and business intelligence systems, as well as for business operations such as customer relationship management, knowledge management, and e-commerce. TPSs have to efficiently handle data both in high volumes and during large variations in volume (for example, during peak times). In addition, they must avoid errors and downtime, record results accurately and securely, and maintain privacy and security. Figure 8.1 shows how TPSs manage data. Consider these examples of how TPSs manage the complexities of transactional data:

- When multiple persons or application programs can access the database at the same time, the database has to be protected from errors resulting from overlapping updates. The most common error is that the results of one of the updates may be lost or incomplete.

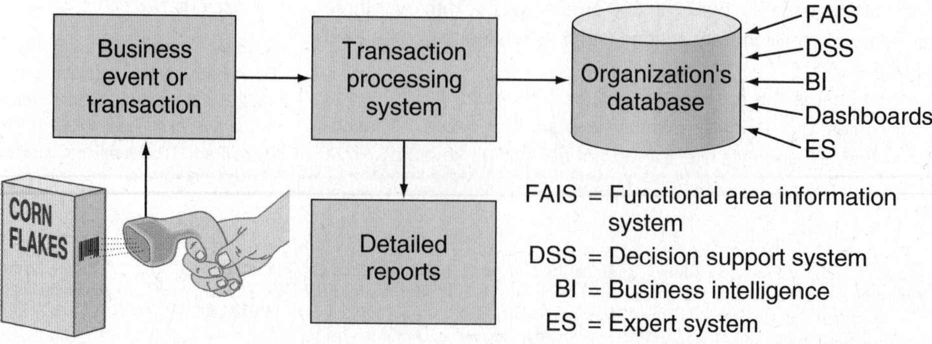

FIGURE 8.1 How transaction processing systems manage data.

- When a transaction involves more than one computer, the database and all users must be protected against inconsistencies arising from the failure of any component at any time. For example, an error that occurs at some point in an ATM withdrawal can enable the customer to receive cash although the bank's computer indicates that he did not. (Conversely, the customer might not receive cash although the bank's computer indicates that he did.)
- A transaction must be reversible in its entirety if it turns out to be in error. For example, it is necessary to reverse a sales transaction when a purchased item is returned.
- It is important to preserve an audit trail of transaction flow. An audit trail is legally required for most transactions.

These and similar issues explain why organizations spend millions of dollars on expensive mainframe computers. In today's business environment, firms must have dependable and reliable computers with the capacity to handle the organization's transaction processing loads.

Regardless of the type of data processed, the TPS functions tend to be standard, whether they occur in a manufacturing firm, a service firm, or a government organization. First, people or sensors collect the data, which are entered into the computer via any input device. Generally speaking, because of the large volumes of data involved, organizations automate TPS data entry as much as possible, a process called *source data automation*.

Next, the system processes the data in one of two basic ways: batch processing and on-line transaction processing. In **batch processing**, data are collected from transactions as they occur and are placed in groups or *batches*. The system then prepares and processes the batches periodically (say, every night).

In **on-line transaction processing (OLTP)**, business transactions are processed on-line as soon as they occur. For example, when you pay for an item at a store, the system records the sale by reducing the inventory on hand by one unit, increasing sales figures for the item by one unit, and increasing the store's cash position by the amount you paid. The system performs these tasks in real time by means of on-line technologies.

before you go on...

1. Define TPS.
2. List the key functions of a TPS.

8.2 Functional Area Information Systems

A **functional area information system (FAIS)** provides support for the various functional areas in an organization by increasing each area's internal efficiency and effectiveness. FAISs often convey information in a variety of reports, as you will see in Section 8.4. Figure 8.1 shows how FAISs access data from the corporate databases. Typical FAISs support accounting and finance, marketing, production/operations (POM), and human resources management. The following sections show you the support that functional area information systems provide for these functional areas.

Information Systems for Accounting and Finance

A primary mission of the accounting and finance functional areas is to manage money flows into, within, and out of organizations. This mission is broad because money is involved in all organizational functions. Therefore, accounting and finance information systems are diverse and comprehensive. In this section you focus on certain selected activities of the accounting/finance functional area.

Financial Planning and Budgeting. Managing financial assets is a major task in financial planning and budgeting. Managers must plan for both acquiring and utilizing resources.

- **Financial and economic forecasting.** Knowing the availability and cost of money is key for successful financial planning. Cash flow projections are particularly important because they inform organizations what funds they need, when they need them, and how they will acquire them.

  Funds for operating organizations come from multiple sources, including shareholders' investments, bond sales, bank loans, sales of products and services, and income from investments. Decisions concerning funding for ongoing operations and for capital investment can be supported by decision support systems, business intelligence applications (discussed in Chapter 10), and expert systems (discussed in Technology Guide 4). In addition, numerous software packages are available for conducting economic and financial forecasting. Many of these packages can be downloaded from the Internet, some of them for free.
- **Budgeting.** An essential part of the accounting/finance function, the annual budget allocates the organization's financial resources among participants and activities. The budget enables management to distribute resources in the way that best supports the organization's mission and goals.

  Several software packages are available that support budget preparation and control, and facilitate communication among participants in the budget process. These packages can reduce the time involved in the budget process. Further, they can automatically monitor exceptions for patterns and trends.

Managing Financial Transactions. Many accounting/finance software packages are integrated with other functional areas. For example, Sage 50 by Sage (formerly called Simply Accounting or Peachtree software) (*http://na.sage.com/Accounting*) offers a sales ledger, purchase ledger, cash book, sales order processing, invoicing, stock control, fixed assets register, and more.

Companies involved in electronic commerce need to access customers' financial data (e.g., credit line), inventory levels, and manufacturing databases (e.g., to see available capacity, to place orders). For example, Microsoft Dynamics AX (formerly Great Plains Software; *www.microsoft.com/en-ca/dynamics/erp-ax-overview.aspx*) offers 50 modules that meet the most common financial, project, distribution, manufacturing, and e-business needs.

Organizations, business processes, and business activities operate with, and manage, financial transactions. Consider these examples:

- **Global stock exchanges.** Financial markets operate in global, 24/7/365, distributed electronic stock exchanges that use the Internet both to buy and sell stocks and to broadcast real-time stock prices.
- **Multiple currency management.** Global trade involves financial transactions in different currencies. The conversion ratios of these currencies are constantly in flux. Using financial data from different countries, financial and accounting systems convert any and all currencies in seconds. Reports based on these data, which used to take days to generate, now take seconds to produce. These systems manage multiple languages as well.
- **Virtual close.** Traditionally, companies closed their books (accounting records) quarterly, usually to meet regulatory requirements. Today, many companies want to be able to close their books at any time, on very short notice. Information systems enable firms to close the books quickly in a process called a *virtual close*. This process provides almost real-time information on the organization's financial health.
- **Expense management automation.** Expense management automation systems automate the data entry and processing of travel and entertainment expenses. These web-based applications enable companies to quickly and consistently collect expense information, enforce company policies and contracts, and reduce unplanned purchases as well as airline and hotel services. They also allow companies to reimburse their employees more quickly, because expense approvals are not delayed by poor documentation.

Investment Management. Organizations invest large amounts of money in stocks, bonds, real estate, and other assets. Managing these investments is a complex task, for several reasons. First, there are literally thousands of investment alternatives, which are dispersed throughout the world. In addition, these investments are subject to complex regulations and tax laws, which vary from one location to another.

Investment decisions require managers to evaluate financial and economic reports provided by diverse institutions, including federal and provincial agencies, universities, research institutions, and financial services firms. In addition, thousands of websites provide financial data, often for free.

To monitor, interpret, and analyze the huge amounts of on-line financial data, financial analysts employ two major types of IT tools: (1) Internet search engines, and (2) business intelligence and decision support software.

Control and Auditing. One major reason why organizations go out of business is their inability to forecast and/or secure a sufficient cash flow. Underestimating expenses, overspending, engaging in fraud, and mismanaging financial statements can lead to disaster. Consequently, it is essential that organizations effectively control their finances and financial statements. Let's examine some of the most common forms of financial control.

- **Budgetary control.** Once an organization has finalized its annual budget, it divides those amounts into monthly allocations. Managers at various levels monitor departmental expenditures and compare them against the budget and the operational progress of the corporate plans.
- **Internal auditing.** The Institute of Internal Auditors (*http://na.theiia.org*) explains that internal auditors should be independent of management by reporting to the audit committee of the board of directors. Then, these internal auditors can evaluate the controls at the organization and evaluate the organization's risk assessment and governance processes. These employees can also prepare for periodic external audits by outside public accounting firms.
- **Financial ratio analysis.** Another major accounting/finance function is to monitor the company's financial health by assessing a set of financial ratios. Included here are liquidity ratios (the availability of cash to pay debt); activity ratios (how quickly a firm converts non-cash assets to cash assets); debt ratios (the firm's ability to repay long-term debt); and profitability ratios (the firm's use of its assets and control of its expenses to generate an acceptable rate of return).

Information Systems for Marketing

It is impossible to overestimate the importance of customers to any organization. Therefore, any successful organization must understand its customers' needs and wants and then develop its marketing and advertising strategies around them. Information systems provide numerous types of support to the marketing function. In fact, customer-centric organizations are so important that half of Chapter 9 (Customer Relationship Management and Supply Chain Management) is devoted to this topic.

Information Systems for Production/Operations Management

The production and operations management (POM) function in an organization is responsible for the processes that transform inputs into useful outputs as well as for the overall operation of the business. Because POM processes are many and varied, we discuss only four of them here: in-house logistics and materials management, planning production and operation, computer-integrated manufacturing (CIM), and product life cycle management (PLM).

The POM function is also responsible for managing the organization's supply chain. Because supply chain management is vital to the success of modern organizations, the second half of Chapter 9 covers this topic in detail.

In-House Logistics and Materials Management. Logistics management deals with ordering, purchasing, inbound logistics (receiving), and outbound logistics (shipping) activities. Related activities include inventory management and quality control.

Inventory Management. As the name suggests, inventory management determines how much inventory to maintain. Both excessive inventory and insufficient inventory create problems. Overstocking can be expensive, due to storage costs and the costs of spoilage and obsolescence. However, keeping insufficient inventory is also expensive, due to last-minute orders and lost sales.

Operations personnel make two basic decisions: when to order, and how much to order. Inventory models, such as the economic order quantity model, support these decisions. There are many commercial inventory software packages that automate the application of these models.

Many large companies allow their suppliers to monitor their inventory levels and ship products as they are needed. This strategy, called *vendor-managed inventory*, eliminates the need for the company to submit purchasing orders.

Quality Control. Quality control systems are used by manufacturing units to obtain information about the quality of incoming material and parts, as well as that of in-process semifinished products and finished products. Such systems record all inspection results and compare them with established metrics. These systems also generate periodic reports containing information about quality; for example, the percentage of defects and the percentage of necessary rework. Quality control data, collected by web-based sensors, can be interpreted in real time, or can be stored in a database for future analysis.

Planning Production and Operations. In many firms, POM planning is supported by IT. POM planning has evolved from material requirements planning, to manufacturing resource planning, to enterprise resource planning. We briefly discuss material requirements planning and manufacturing resource planning here, and we examine enterprise resource planning in detail later in this chapter.

Inventory systems that use an economic order quantity approach are designed for items for which demand is completely independent; for example, the number of identical personal computers a computer manufacturer will sell. In manufacturing operations, however, the demand for some items is interdependent. Consider, for example, a company that makes three types of chairs, all of which use the same screws and bolts. In this case, the demand for screws and bolts depends on the total demand for all three types of chairs and their shipment schedules. The planning process that integrates production, purchasing, and inventory management of interdependent items is called *material requirements planning (MRP)*.

MRP deals only with production scheduling and inventories. More complex planning, however, involves allocating related resources, such as money and labour, as well. For these cases, more complex, integrated software, called *manufacturing resource planning (MRP II)*, is available. MRP II integrates a firm's production, inventory management, purchasing, financing, and labour activities. Thus, MRP II adds functions to a regular MRP system. In fact, MRP II has evolved into enterprise resource planning.

Computer-Integrated Manufacturing. **Computer-integrated manufacturing** (**CIM**; also called *digital manufacturing*) is an approach that integrates various automated factory systems. CIM has three basic goals: (1) to simplify all manufacturing technologies and techniques, (2) to automate as many of the manufacturing processes as possible, and (3) to integrate and coordinate all aspects of design, manufacturing, and related functions via computer systems.

Product Life Cycle Management. Even within a single organization, designing and developing new products can be expensive and time consuming. When multiple organizations are involved, the process can become very complex. *Product life cycle management (PLM)* is a business strategy that enables manufacturers to share product-related data that support both product design and development and supply chain operations. PLM applies web-based collaborative technologies to product development. By integrating formerly disparate functions, such as a manufacturing process and the logistics that support it, PLM enables these functions to collaborate, essentially forming a single team that manages the product from its inception to its completion.

Information Systems for Human Resource Management

Initially, human resource information system (HRIS) applications dealt primarily with transaction processing systems, such as managing benefits and keeping records of vacation days. As organizational systems have moved to intranets and the web, however, so have HRIS applications.

Many HRIS applications are delivered via an HR portal. For example, numerous organizations use their web portals to advertise job openings and conduct on-line hiring and training. In this section, you will see how organizations use IT to perform some key HR functions: recruitment, HR maintenance and development, and HR planning and management.

Recruitment.

Recruitment involves finding and evaluating potential employees, and then deciding which ones to hire. Some companies are flooded with viable applicants; others have difficulty finding the right people. IT can be helpful in both cases. In addition, IT can assist in related activities such as testing and screening job applicants.

Millions of resumés are available on-line, so it is not surprising that companies are trying to find appropriate candidates on the web, usually with the help of specialized search engines. Companies also advertise hundreds of thousands of jobs on the web. On-line recruiting can reach more candidates, which may bring in better applicants. In addition, on-line recruitment usually costs less than traditional recruiting methods such as advertising in newspapers or in trade journals.

Human Resources Maintenance and Development.

After employees are recruited, they become part of the corporate human resources pool, which means they must be evaluated and developed. IT provides support for these activities.

Most employees are evaluated periodically by their immediate supervisors, and sometimes by peers or subordinates. Evaluations are typically digitized and are used to support many decisions, ranging from rewards, to transfers, to layoffs.

IT also plays an important role in training and retraining. Some of the most innovative developments are taking place in the areas of intelligent computer-aided instruction and the application of multimedia support for instructional activities. For example, companies conduct much of their corporate training over their intranet or via the web.

Human Resources Planning and Management.

Managing human resources in large organizations requires extensive planning and detailed strategy. Following are three areas where IT can provide support.

- **Payroll and employees' records.** The HR department is responsible for payroll preparation. This process is typically automated, with paycheques being printed or money being transferred electronically into employees' bank accounts.
- **Benefits administration.** Employees are rewarded with wages, bonuses, and other benefits for their work contributions to their organizations. Benefits include health and dental care, pension contributions, wellness centres, and child care centres.

Managing benefits is a complex task, due to the multiple options offered and organizations' tendency to allow employees to choose and trade off their benefits. In many organizations, employees can access the company portal to self-register for specific benefits.

- **Employee relationship management.** In their efforts to better manage employees, companies are developing *employee relationship management (ERM)* applications. A typical ERM application is a call centre for employees' problems.

Table 8.1 provides an overview of the activities that functional area information systems support. Figure 8.2 diagrams many of the information systems that support these five functional areas.

Table 8.1

Activities Supported by Functional Area Information Systems

Activities Supported by Functional Area Information Systems
Accounting and Finance
Financial planning—availability and cost of money
Budgeting—allocating financial resources among participants and activities
Capital budgeting—financing of asset acquisitions
Managing financial transactions
Handling multiple currencies
Virtual close—ability to close books at any time on short notice
Investment management—managing organizational investments in stocks, bonds, real estate, and other investment vehicles
Budgetary control—monitoring expenditures and comparing against budget
Auditing—evaluating controls and corporate governance
Payroll—processing paycheques
Marketing and Sales
Customer relations—knowing who customers are and treating them like royalty
Customer profiles and preferences
Sales force automation—using software to automate the business tasks of sales, thereby improving the productivity of salespeople
Production/Operations and Logistics
Inventory management—how much inventory to order, how much inventory to keep, and when to order new inventory
Quality control—controlling for defects in incoming material and defects in goods produced
Materials requirements planning (MRP)—planning process that integrates production, purchasing, and inventory management of interdependent items
Manufacturing resource planning (MRP II)—planning process that integrates an enterprise's production, inventory management, purchasing, financing, and labour activities
Just-in-time systems (JIT)—principle of production and inventory control in which materials and parts arrive precisely when and where they are needed for production
Computer-integrated manufacturing—manufacturing approach that integrates several computerized systems, such as computer-assisted design, computer-assisted manufacturing, MRP, and JIT
Product life cycle management—business strategy that enables manufacturers to collaborate on product design and development efforts, using the web
Human Resource Management
Recruitment—finding employees, testing them, and deciding which ones to hire
Performance evaluation—periodic evaluation by superiors
Training
Employee records
Benefits administration—medical, retirement, disability, unemployment, and others

	ACCOUNTING	FINANCE	HUMAN RESOURCES	PRODUCTION/ OPERATIONS	MARKETING
STRATEGIC	Profitability Planning	Financial Planning	Employment Planning, Outsourcing	Product Life Cycle Management	Sales Forecasting, Advertising Planning
TACTICAL	Auditing, Budgeting	Investment Management	Benefits Administration, Performance Evaluation	Quality Control, Inventory Management	Customer Relations, Sales Force Automation
OPERATIONAL	Payroll, Accounts Payable, Accounts Receivable	Manage Cash, Manage Financial Transactions	Maintain Employee Records	Order Fulfillment, Order Processing	Set Pricing, Profile Customers

FIGURE 8.2 Examples of information systems supporting the functional areas.

before you go on...

1. What is a functional area information system? List its major characteristics.
2. How do information systems benefit the finance and accounting functional area?
3. Explain how POM personnel use information systems to perform their jobs more effectively and efficiently.
4. What are the most important HRIS applications?

8.3 Enterprise Resource Planning Systems

In the sections on business processes in Chapter 2, you learned that the functional area information systems were developed independently of one another, resulting in *information silos*. These silos did not communicate well with one another, and this lack of communication and integration made organizations less efficient. This inefficiency was particularly evident in business processes that involve more than one functional area.

An **enterprise resource planning (ERP) system** adopts a business process view of the overall organization to integrate the planning, management, and use of all of an organization's resources, employing a common software platform and database. Recall from Chapter 2 that a *business process* is a set of related steps or procedures designed to produce a specific outcome.

The major objectives of ERP systems are to tightly integrate the functional areas of the organization, enabling information to flow seamlessly across them. This means that changes in one functional area will be immediately reflected in all other pertinent functional areas. In essence, ERP systems provide the information necessary to control the business processes of the organization.

It is important to understand that ERP systems evolved out of FAISs. That is, ERP systems function much the same as FAISs and produce the same reports. ERP systems simply integrate the functions of the various FAISs.

Although some companies have developed their own ERP systems, most organizations use commercially available ERP software. The leading ERP software vendor is SAP (*www.sap.com/canada/index.epx*), which features its SAP R/3 package. Other major vendors include Oracle (*www.oracle.com/ca-en/index.html*) and PeopleSoft, now an Oracle company. For up-to-date information on ERP software, visit *http://erp.ittoolbox.com*.

Although it can be difficult to implement ERP systems because they are large and complicated, many companies have done so successfully. IT's About Business 8.2 recounts a successful SAP deployment at Airgas.

Evolution of ERP Systems

ERP systems originally were deployed to facilitate business processes associated with manufacturing, such as raw materials management, inventory control, order entry, and distribution. These early ERP systems, however, did not extend to other functional areas, such as sales and marketing. They also did not include any customer relationship management capabilities that would enable organizations to capture customer-specific information. Further, they did not provide web-enabled customer service or order fulfillment.

Over time, ERP systems evolved to include administrative, sales, marketing, and human resources processes. Companies now employ systems with an enterprise-wide approach to ERP that use the web and connect all facets of the value chain. Such systems are called ERP II.

IT's [about business]

8.2 SAP at Airgas

Airgas (*www.airgas.com*), which sells medical, industrial, and specialized gases and related equipment, implemented a "highly customized" version of SAP that the company lauded as a huge success. Airgas chose approximately 300 subject-matter experts from the 14,000-person company to identify which new functionalities were required in the SAP system. These experts worked side-by-side with a 120-member, full-time project team composed of Deloitte consultants and Airgas executives.

In July 2010, Airgas switched over its hard-goods supply chain operation to SAP. The supply chain touches nearly every area of Airgas. As of March 2013, the company had 70 percent of its information systems functional on SAP. At that time, it expected to have saved up to $125 million by the end of 2013, thanks to improved sales, better price management, and leaner operating costs. Airgas expects to find additional benefits as the project continues to move forward.

Questions

1. What actions can a company such as Airgas take to help ensure the successful implementation of ERP software such as SAP?
2. What benefits could a company such as Airgas expect to receive from its deployment of SAP?

Sources: Compiled from C. Kanaracus, "Gas Distributor Says Its SAP Project Expected to Succeed," *Computerworld*, August 31, 2010; C. Gutierrez, "Air Products Makes Latest Bid for Airgas," *Forbes*, September 7, 2010; "Airgas Hints at 4Q13 Guidance Miss – Analyst Blog," Zacks.com, March 22, 2013; *www.nasdaq.com*; *www.airgas.com*, accessed March 14, 2013.

ERP II Systems

ERP II systems are interorganizational ERP systems that provide web-enabled links between a company's key business systems—such as inventory and production—and its customers, suppliers, distributors, and others. These links integrate internal-facing ERP applications with the external-focused applications of supply chain management and customer relationship management. Figure 8.3 illustrates the organization and functions of an ERP II system.

The various functions of ERP II systems are now delivered as e-business suites. The major ERP vendors have developed modular, web-enabled software suites that integrate ERP, customer relationship management, supply chain management, procurement, decision support, enterprise portals, and other business applications and functions. An example is Oracle's E-Business Suite. The goal of such a system is to enable companies to operate most of their business processes using a single web-enabled system of integrated software rather than separate e-business applications.

ERP II systems include a variety of modules, which are divided into core ERP modules—financial management, operations management, and human resource management—and extended ERP modules—customer relationship management, supply chain management, business intelligence, and e-business. A system that does not have the core ERP modules cannot be called an ERP system; the extended ERP modules, in contrast, are optional. Table 8.2 describes each of these modules.

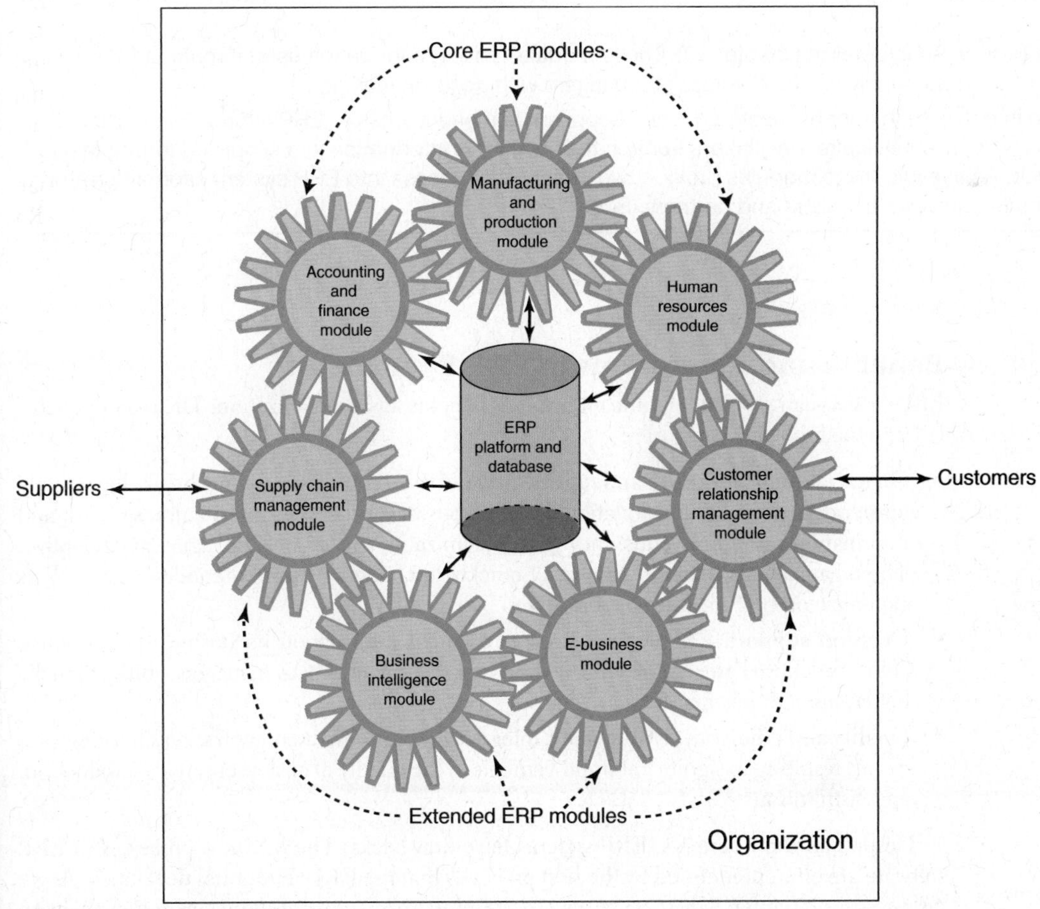

FIGURE 8.3 ERP II system.

Table 8.2

Core ERP Modules

Financial management. These modules support accounting, financial reporting, performance management, and corporate governance. They manage accounting data and financial processes such as general ledger, accounts payable, accounts receivable, fixed assets, cash management and forecasting, product-cost accounting, cost-centre accounting, asset accounting, tax accounting, credit management, budgeting, and asset management.

Operations management. These modules manage the various aspects of production planning and execution such as demand forecasting, procurement, inventory management, materials purchasing, shipping, production planning, production scheduling, materials requirements planning, quality control, distribution, transportation, and plant and equipment maintenance.

Human resource management. These modules support personnel administration (including workforce planning, employee recruitment, assignment tracking, personnel planning and development, and performance management and reviews), time accounting, payroll, compensation, benefits accounting, and regulatory requirements.

Extended ERP Modules

Customer relationship management (discussed in detail in Chapter 9). These modules support all aspects of a customer's relationship with the organization. They help the organization increase customer loyalty and retention and thus improve its profitability. They also provide an integrated view of customer data and interactions, enabling organizations to be more responsive to customer needs.

Supply chain management (discussed in detail in Chapter 9). These modules manage the information flows between and among stages in a supply chain to maximize supply chain efficiency and effectiveness. They help organizations plan, schedule, control, and optimize the supply chain, from the acquisition of raw materials to the receipt of finished goods by customers.

Business intelligence (discussed in detail in Chapter 10). These modules collect information used throughout the organization, organize it, and apply analytical tools to assist managers with decision making.

E-business (discussed in detail in Chapter 5). Customers and suppliers demand access to ERP information including order status, inventory levels, and invoice reconciliation. Further, they want this information in a simplified format that can be accessed via the web. As a result, these modules provide two channels of access into ERP system information—one for customers (B2C) and the other for suppliers and partners (B2B).

Benefits and Limitations of ERP Systems

ERP systems can generate significant business benefits for an organization. The major benefits fall into the following categories:

- **Organizational flexibility and agility.** As you have seen, ERP systems break down many former departmental and functional silos of business processes, information systems, and information resources. Thus, they make organizations more flexible, agile, and adaptive. The organizations therefore can react quickly to changing business conditions as well as capitalize on new business opportunities.
- **Decision support.** ERP systems provide essential information on business performance across functional areas. This information significantly improves managers' ability to make better, more timely decisions.
- **Quality and efficiency.** ERP systems integrate and improve an organization's business processes, resulting in significant improvements in the quality of customer service, production, and distribution.

Despite all their benefits, ERP systems have drawbacks. The business processes in ERP software are often predefined by the best practices that the ERP vendor has developed. As we discussed in Chapter 3, *best practices* are the most successful solutions or problem-solving methods for achieving a business objective. As a result, companies may need to change existing business processes to fit the predefined business processes of the software. For companies with well-established procedures, this requirement can be a huge problem. Note that best practices, by definition, are appropriate for *most* organizations. Organizations differ, however; therefore a "best practice" might not be the "best" one for your company.

In addition, ERP systems can be extremely complex, expensive, and time consuming to implement. In fact, the costs and risks of failure in implementing a new ERP system are substantial. Quite a few companies have experienced costly ERP implementation failures, resulting in large losses in revenue, profits, and market share when core business processes and information systems failed or did not work properly. In many cases, orders and shipments were lost, inventory changes were not recorded correctly, and unreliable inventory levels caused major stock outs to occur. Companies such as Hershey Foods, Nike, and A-DEC sustained losses totalling hundreds of millions of dollars. In the case of FoxMeyer Drugs, a \$5-billion pharmaceutical wholesaler in the United States, a failed ERP implementation caused the company to file for bankruptcy protection.

In almost every ERP implementation failure, the company's business managers and IT professionals underestimated the complexity of the planning, development, and training required to prepare for a new ERP system that would fundamentally change the firm's business processes and information systems. Failing to involve affected employees in the planning and development phases and in change management processes, and trying to do too much too fast in the conversion process, were typical causes of unsuccessful ERP projects. Insufficient training in the new work tasks required by the ERP system and failure to convert data properly and test the new system also contributed to unsuccessful implementations. Case 8.2 at the end of the chapter highlights many of the difficulties involved in implementing and maintaining ERP systems.

Enterprise Application Integration

For some organizations, ERP systems are not appropriate. This is particularly true for companies (whether manufacturing or nonmanufacturing) that find the process of converting from their existing system too difficult, time consuming, or expensive.

Such companies, however, still may have isolated information systems that need to be connected. To accomplish this task, these companies may use enterprise application integration. An **enterprise application integration (EAI) system** integrates existing systems by providing software, called *middleware*, that connects applications together. In essence, the EAI system allows existing applications to communicate and share data, thereby enabling organizations to use these applications while eliminating many of the problems caused by isolated information systems.

before you go on...

1. Define ERP, and describes its functionalities.
2. What are ERP II systems?
3. Differentiate between core ERP modules and extended ERP modules.
4. List some drawbacks of ERP software.

8.4 Reports

Various information systems produce reports: transaction processing systems, functional area information systems, ERP systems, customer relationship management systems, business intelligence systems, and others. We discuss reports here because they are so closely associated with FAISs and ERP systems. The important point, however, is that *all* information systems produce reports. These reports generally fall into three categories: routine, ad hoc (on-demand), and exception.

Routine reports are produced at scheduled intervals. They range from hourly quality control reports to daily reports on absenteeism rates. Although routine reports are extremely valuable to an organization, managers frequently need special information that is not included in routine reports; and, at other times, they need information normally included in routine reports, but at different times. ("I need a report today; one for the last three days, not the whole week.") Such nonroutine reports are called **ad hoc (on-demand) reports**. Ad hoc reports also can be characterized by the following types of information they may include:

- **Drill-down reports** display a greater level of detail. For example, a manager might examine sales by region and then "drill down" for more detail by looking at sales by store and then by salesperson.
- **Key-indicator reports** summarize the performance of critical activities. For example, a chief financial officer might want to monitor cash flow and cash on hand.
- **Comparative reports** may compare, for example, performances of different business units or of a single unit during different time periods.

Finally, some managers prefer **exception reports**. Exception reports include only information that falls outside certain threshold standards. To implement *management by exception*, management first creates performance standards. The company then sets up systems to monitor performance (via incoming data about business transactions such as expenditures), compare actual performance with the standards, and identify exceptions to the standards. The system alerts managers to the exceptions via exception reports.

Let's use sales as an example. First, management establishes sales quotas. The company then implements an FAIS that collects and analyzes all of the sales data. An exception report would identify only those cases where sales fell outside an established threshold; for example, more than 20 percent short of the quota. It would *not* report expenditures that fell *within* the accepted range of standards. By leaving out all "acceptable" performances, exception reports save managers time, helping them focus on problem areas.

before you go on...

1. Compare and contrast the three major types of reports.
2. Compare and contrast the three types of on-demand ad hoc reports.

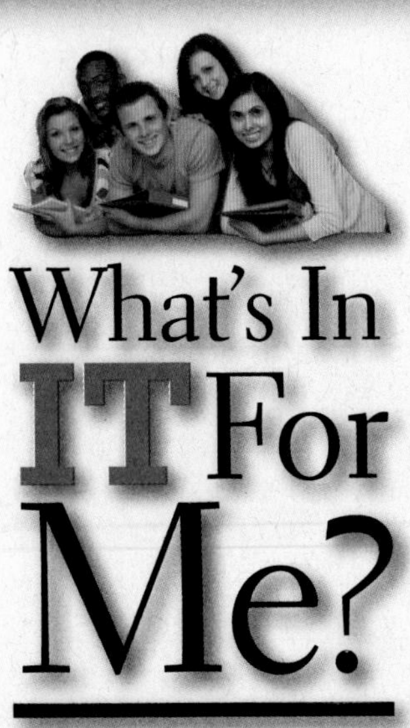

For the Accounting Major

Understanding the functions and outputs of TPSs is a major concern of any accountant. Accountants must also understand the various activities of all functional areas and how they are interconnected. Accounting information systems are a central component in any ERP package. In fact, all large public accounting firms actively consult with clients on ERP implementations, using specially trained accounting majors.

For the Finance Major

IT helps financial analysts and managers perform their tasks better. Of particular importance is analyzing cash flows and securing the financing required for smooth operations. Further, financial applications can support such activities as risk analysis, investment management, and global transactions involving different currencies and fiscal regulations.

Finance activities and modelling are key components of ERP systems. Flows of funds (payments), at the core of most supply chains, must be executed efficiently and effectively. Financial arrangements are especially important along global supply chains, where currency conventions and financial regulations must be considered.

For the Marketing Major

Marketing and sales expenses are usually targets in a cost-reduction program. Also, sales force automation not only improves salespeople's productivity (and thus reduces costs) but also improves customer service.

For the Production/Operations Management Major

Managing production tasks, materials handling, and inventories in short time intervals, at a low cost, and with high quality is critical for competitiveness. These activities can be achieved only if they are properly supported by IT. In addition, IT can greatly enhance interaction with other functional areas, especially sales. Collaboration in design, manufacturing, and logistics requires knowledge of how modern information systems can be connected.

For the Human Resources Management Major

Human resources managers can increase their efficiency and effectiveness by using IT for some of their routine functions. Human resources personnel need to understand how information flows between the HR department and the other functional areas. Finally, the integration of functional areas via ERP systems has a major impact on skill requirements and scarcity of employees, which are related to the tasks performed by the HRM department.

For the MIS Major

The MIS function is responsible for the most fundamental information systems in organizations, the transaction processing systems. The TPSs provide the data for the databases. All the other information systems, in turn, use these data. MIS personnel develop applications that support all levels of the organization (from clerical to executive) and all functional areas. The applications also enable the firm to do business with its partners.

[Summary]

1. Explain the purposes of transaction processing systems. Provide at least one example of how businesses use these systems.

TPSs monitor, store, collect, and process data generated from all business transactions. These data provide the inputs into the organization's database. An example is the recording of sales transactions upon purchase of items.

2. Define functional area information systems. Provide an example of the support they provide for each functional area of the organization.

The major business functional areas are production/operations management, marketing, accounting/finance, and human resources management. Table 8.1 provides an overview of the many activities in each functional area supported by FAISs.

3. Explain the purpose of enterprise resource planning systems. Identify four advantages and four drawbacks to implementing an ERP system.

Enterprise resource planning (ERP) systems integrate the planning, management, and use of all of the organization's resources. The major objective of ERP systems is to tightly integrate the functional areas of the organization. This integration enables information to flow seamlessly across the various functional areas.

4. Discuss the three major types of reports generated by functional area information systems and enterprise resource planning systems. Provide an example of each type.

Routine reports are produced at scheduled intervals. They range from hourly quality control reports to daily reports on absenteeism rates.

Nonroutine reports are called *ad hoc (on-demand) reports*. For example, a chief financial officer might want to monitor cash flow and cash on hand.

Exception reports include only information that falls outside certain threshold standards. An exception report might identify only those cases where sales fell outside an established threshold; for example, more than 20 percent short of the quota.

[Chapter Glossary]

ad hoc (on-demand) reports Nonroutine reports that often contain special information that is not included in routine reports.

batch processing TPS that processes data in batches at fixed periodic intervals.

comparative reports Reports that compare performances of different business units or time periods.

computer-integrated manufacturing (CIM) An information system that integrates various automated factory systems.

drill-down reports Reports that show a greater level of detail than is included in routine reports.

enterprise application integration (EAI) system A system that integrates existing systems by providing layers of software that connect applications together.

enterprise resource planning (ERP) system Information system that takes a business process view of the overall organization to integrate the planning, management, and use of all of an organization's resources, employing a common software platform and database.

ERP II systems Interorganizational ERP systems that provide web-enabled links between a company's key business systems (such as inventory and production) and its customers, suppliers, distributors, and others.

exception reports Reports that include only information that exceeds certain threshold standards.

functional area information system (FAIS) A system that provides information to managers (usually mid-level) in the functional areas, in order to support managerial tasks of planning, organizing, and controlling operations.

key-indicator reports Reports that summarize the performance of critical activities.

on-line transaction processing (OLTP) Transaction processing system that processes data after transactions occur, frequently in real time.

routine reports Reports produced at scheduled intervals.

transaction Any business event that generates data worth capturing and storing in a database.

transaction processing system (TPS) Information system that supports routine, core business transactions.

[Discussion Questions]

1. Consider the chapter-opening Case 8.1. What are the advantages that Fieldf/x provides for the owners of professional baseball teams? What are the advantages that Fieldf/x provides for professional baseball players? Are there disadvantages for the players? Support your answers.
2. Why is it logical to organize IT applications by functional areas?
3. Describe the role of a TPS in a service organization.
4. Describe the relationship between TPS and FAIS.
5. Discuss how IT facilitates the budgeting process.
6. How can the Internet support investment decisions?
7. Describe the benefits of integrated accounting software packages.
8. Discuss the role that IT plays in support of auditing.
9. Investigate the role of the web in human resources management.
10. What is the relationship between information silos and enterprise resource planning?

[Problem-Solving Activities]

1. Finding a job on the Internet is challenging, because there are almost too many places to look. Visit the following sites: *www.careerbuilder.com*, *www.craigslist.org*, *www.linkedin.com*, *www.careermag.com*, and *www.monster.ca*. What does each of these sites provide you as a job seeker?

2. Enter *www.sas.com* and access revenue optimization there. Explain how the software helps in optimizing prices.
3. Enter *www.eleapsoftware.com* and review the product that helps with on-line training (training systems). What are the most attractive features of this product?
4. Enter *www.microsoft.com/en-us/dynamics/erp-try-sl-demos.aspx*. View three of the demos in different functional areas of your choice. Prepare a report on each product's capabilities.
5. Examine the capabilities of the following financial software package: Financial Analyzer (from Oracle). Look for similar packages and prepare a report comparing the capabilities of the software packages.
6. Surf the Net to find free accounting software (try *http://download.cnet.com*, *www.rkom.com*, *www.tucows.com*, *www.passtheshareware.com*, and *www.freeware-guide.com*). Download the software and try it. Compare the ease of use and usefulness of each software package.
7. Examine the capabilities of the following financial software packages: Financial Analyzer (from *www.oracle.com*), and Financial Management (from *www.sas.com*). Prepare a report comparing the capabilities of the software packages.
8. Find Sage 50 Accounting 2013 (formerly Simply Accounting) from Sage Software (*http://na.sage.com/Accounting*). Why is this product recommended for small businesses?
9. Enter *www.halogensoftware.com* and *www.successfactors.com*. Examine and compare their software products.
10. Enter *www.asuresoftware.com/products/asureforce* and find the support it provides to human resources management activities. View the demos and prepare a report on the capabilities of the products.

[Spreadsheet Activity: Regression in Excel]

Objective: Microsoft Excel is powerful for more than just keeping up with numbers. With the right add-ins, you can run elaborate statistical analyses. This activity will introduce simple regression within Microsoft Excel.

Chapter Connection: Transaction processing systems are just the beginning. They provide data to many systems throughout an organization. Ultimately, the data they provide are used to plan and forecast for years ahead. This activity ties the spreadsheet tool to the data found in the various systems within the organization.

Activity: Imagine that you are an intern for a local restaurant/bar/club (the focus tends to change as it gets later in the evening). You have been asked to help the owners with a serious problem—managing their supply chain.

Forecasting has always been a problem for them. One week they are booming and another week, things are dead. Really, they expect as much because they are in a university town. But there are weekends when people should be in town and the establishment is not busy and weekends that everyone should be gone and the place is packed.

The owners have put together a spreadsheet for you to use to help them understand their demand and how to better match their food and drink supplies to what the demand will be. For restaurant owners, there is nothing worse than telling customers that the kitchen is out of the daily special or throwing away unsold goods that spoiled. They need better forecasting.

Please go to *www.wiley.com/go/rainer/spreadsheet* and click on the videos for Chapter 8.

One describes an "Add-In" you may have to install for Excel to run a regression and the other is about regression analysis itself. You will use this tool in Excel to help your employers better understand the situation they are in. Ultimately, you will complete your analysis to determine which variables have the most statistically significant impact on their demand. Finally, you will write a short memo to your employers (your professor) explaining your findings in a way they can understand.

The spreadsheet you will download has many 1's and 0's in it. A "1" means an event was "true." For example, under "Jazz" a "1" would mean that jazz was the genre of music playing that night in the club. A "0" would mean that jazz was not playing that night.

Most of the variables are considered independent variables. This means that whether or not jazz was playing is not dependent on any other variables. You use these independent factors to help understand the *dependent* variables that you are most concerned about—cover sales, food sales, and drink sales.

Deliverable: Your work will include a spreadsheet that includes the regression analysis as well as a Word document that shows the interpretation of that analysis. The Word document will also (based on the interpretation) offer suggestions that will help the employers understand their demand and better schedule their food and drink purchases.

[Case Assignment]

Sweety Snacks Limited is a coffee shop chain that has hundreds of locations around the world. Recently, it has been experiencing slumping sales due to the recession, and decided to close some of its stores. The remaining stores have been asked to pay closer attention to their sales and inventory, as well as try to reduce costs, by using the information available from their computer-based information systems.

Required

a. Describe three ways that enterprise systems (also known as ERP or enterprise resource planning systems) could benefit the company.

b. Describe two limitations of enterprise systems to the company.

[Team Assignments]

1. Divide the class into groups. Each group member will represent a major functional area: accounting/finance, sales/marketing, production/operations management, or human resources. Each group will find and describe several examples of processes that require the integration of functional information systems in a company of their choice. Each group also will show the interfaces to the other functional areas.
2. Each group is to investigate an HRM software vendor (Oracle, PeopleSoft [now owned by Oracle], SAP, Lawson Software, and others). The group should prepare a list of all HRM functionalities supported by the software. Then, each group will make a presentation to convince the class that its vendor is the best.
3. Each group in the class will be assigned to a major ERP vendor such as SAP, Oracle, Lawson Software, and others. Members of the groups will investigate topics such as: (a) web connections, (b) use of business intelligence tools, (c) relationship to customer relationship management and to electronic commerce, and (d) major capabilities by the specific vendor. Each group will prepare a presentation for the class, trying to convince the class why the group's software is best for a local company known to you (for example, a supermarket chain).

[Case 8.2 Difficulties in Managing Enterprise Resource Planning Systems]

Companies initially installed ERP systems to make sense of their complicated operations. In doing so, they were able to operate better and faster than their competition, at least until the competition caught up. In many of these companies, ERP systems are still essential; however, they no longer provide a competitive advantage. Further, they are not helping bring in new revenue, and managing them is consuming an increasing share of the company's IT budget. The companies, however, are not getting rid of ERP systems because they are still needed to manage the supply chain, financial information, and employee data. Nevertheless, ERP systems are causing problems for many organizations.

The First Problem: Lack of Flexibility

Kennametal (*www.kennametal.com*), a $2-billion manufacturer of construction tools, has spent more than $10 million on SAP maintenance contracts since 1998. Throughout this entire period, however, the company has been unable to take advantage of any upgrades in the SAP software. The reason is that, over the years, Kennametal made more than 6,000 customizations to its SAP system. Consequently, the company could not implement any new capabilities that SAP built into its software. The firm's SAP implementation was simply too customized: The time and effort needed to install and test the upgrades outweighed any benefits. In late 2009, Kennametal inquired about the costs of hiring consultants to assist with an SAP reimplementation. The company was shocked by the estimates, which ranged from $15 million to $54 million. Kennametal's CIO charged that not only SAP, but all the major ERP packages, are "old and inflexible, and the vendors cannot build flexibility into their packages."

A Potential Solution

Even if Kennametal could afford to pay $54 million for consultants to help the company upgrade to the latest version of its SAP software, the CIO would not want to spend this much money. Instead, he plans to turn Kennametal's old ERP strategy upside down by installing a generic version of SAP. Kennametal's CIO and CEO are more willing to change the company's internal business processes to match the way SAP works than to modify the SAP software to match Kennametal's business processes.

Kennametal also wants to perform the implementation itself. The company consulted IBM about requirements definitions and to identify business processes that must be reworked to conform to SAP's procedures. In fact, Kennametal had originally planned to implement at least 90 percent of the SAP software unmodified.

Haworth (*www.haworth.com*), a $1.7-billion office furniture manufacturer, is another company that decided to make no customer changes to the core SAP code. The company uses tools from iRise (*www.irise.com*) to visually plan its SAP rollouts in its major offices on four continents. The iRise tools will simulate how the finished SAP system will look to employees, to get them accustomed to the changes before the actual rollout. The company also uses a sales compensation application from Vertex (*www.vertex.com*) because SAP does not support the complicated, multitiered compensation model that Haworth uses to pay its salespeople.

The Result

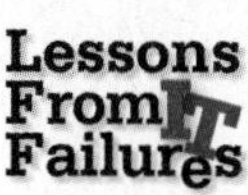

Implementing the core code of an ERP system without any significant modifications minimized both the costs of the system and the time devoted to the system for Kennametal and Haworth. There is a trade-off, however. Both companies had to spend time and money reworking their business processes to meet the procedures established by their ERP systems.

The Second Problem: High Maintenance Fees

Dana Holding Corporation (*www.dana.com*) is an $8.1-billion auto parts supplier. Dana's CIO discovered that 90 percent of the fees the company paid to maintain its ERP system were pure profit for the ERP vendor. When the auto market hit tough times, Dana wanted its ERP vendor to work with the company to reduce maintenance fees, but the vendor objected. To persuade Dana that its maintenance fees were justifiable, the vendor analyzed Dana's use of its support. The analysis concluded that Dana made 21,000 requests to the vendor over a nine-month period. Dana countered that 98 percent of the requests did not involve human interaction, but were automated look-ups on the vendor's knowledge base.

Dana's Solution

Dana stopped making maintenance payments to its ERP vendor. The risks to any company that decides to stop paying maintenance fees include incurring penalties assessed by the vendor for breaking a contract and being left without technical support in an emergency. Dana's lawyers studied the contracts with the vendor and felt comfortable that the firm would not be violating any terms by terminating the payments. Then, Dana's IT team explored ways to obtain support for its ERP system through other avenues. They found many alternatives, including on-line user forums, books, and consultants.

The Result

One result of the move away from provider support is that Dana's IT group has to be more knowledgeable about the company's ERP system to be able to fix whatever goes wrong. Dana's CIO notes, however, that there have been no technology disasters with the ERP system because it is mature and reliable. Further, eliminating maintenance saves money because Dana is no longer paying for a service of questionable value.

Questions

1. Describe what it means for an ERP system to be inflexible.
2. Describe the pros and cons of tailoring your organization's business processes to align with the procedures in an ERP system.

Sources: Compiled from K. Nash, "ERP: How and Why You Need to Manage It Differently," *CIO*, January 27, 2010; *www.kennametal.com*, *www.sap.com*, *www.haworth.com*, *www.dana.com*, accessed March 14, 2013.

[Interactive Case]

Improving Transaction Processing for Ruby's Club

Go to the Ruby's Club link at the Student Companion website or *WileyPLUS* for information about your current internship assignment. You will outline a plan to help Ruby's managers effectively collect and analyze their organizational data.

Chapter 9

Customer Relationship Management and Supply Chain Management

[LEARNING OBJECTIVES]

1. Define "customer relationship management" and "collaborative CRM," and identify the primary functions of both processes.
2. Describe the two major components of operational CRM systems, list three applications used in each component, and provide at least one example of how businesses use each application.
3. Define "analytical CRM systems," and describe four purposes for which businesses use these systems.
4. Define "mobile CRM systems," "on-demand CRM systems," and "open-source CRM systems," and identify one main advantage and one main drawback of each.
5. Define "supply chain," and describe the three components and the three flows of a supply chain.
6. Identify two major challenges in setting accurate inventory levels throughout the supply chain, and describe three popular strategies to solve supply chain problems.
7. Define "electronic data interchange (EDI)," "extranet," and "portal," and explain how each of these applications helps support supply chain management.

[CHAPTER OUTLINE]

[WEB RESOURCES]

Student Companion Site

wiley.com/college/rainer

- Student PowerPoints for note taking
- Interactive Case: Ruby's Club Assignments
- Complete glossary

WileyPlus

WILEY PLUS

All of the above and

- E-book
- Mini-lecture by author for each chapter section
- Practice quizzes
- Flash Cards for vocabulary review
- Additional "What's in IT for Me?" cases
- Video interviews with managers
- Lab Manual for Microsoft Office 2010
- How-to Animations for Microsoft Office 2010

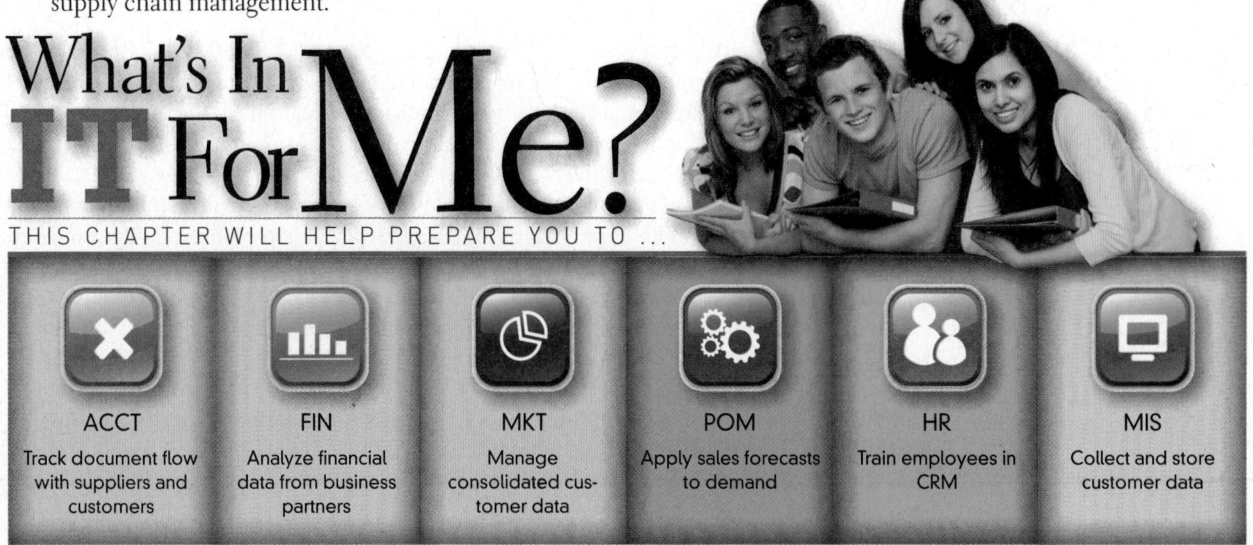

What's In IT For Me?
THIS CHAPTER WILL HELP PREPARE YOU TO ...
ACCT
Track document flow with suppliers and customers
FIN
Analyze financial data from business partners
MKT
Manage consolidated customer data
POM
Apply sales forecasts to demand
HR
Train employees in CRM
MIS
Collect and store customer data

[Case 9.1 The Next Step in Customer Relationship Management]

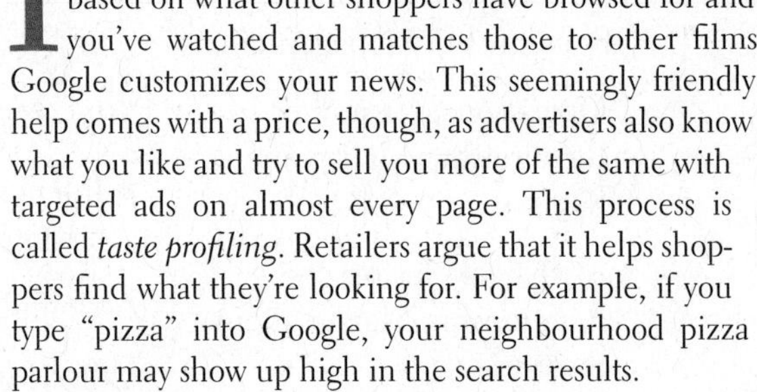

It's hard to remain anonymous on the Internet. Many websites track what you buy or look at and remember your tastes. For example, Amazon.com suggests books you might like based on what other shoppers have browsed for and purchased. Netflix knows the movies you've watched and matches those to other films. Google customizes your news. This seemingly friendly help comes with a price, though, as advertisers also know what you like and try to sell you more of the same with targeted ads on almost every page. This process is called *taste profiling*. Retailers argue that it helps shoppers find what they're looking for. For example, if you type "pizza" into Google, your neighbourhood pizza parlour may show up high in the search results.

Maxx-Studio/Shutterstock

If taste profiling wasn't personalized enough, how about *persuasion profiling*? This technique goes well beyond suggesting content that you might enjoy. It actually figures out how you think.

For some time, on-line retailers have used algorithms to guess what products people might want based on their previous purchases. But persuasion profiling tries to guess what will persuade you to buy something. The research indicates that different people respond to different approaches, or pitches. For example, in an on-line bookstore, different pitches might look like this:

- Appeal to Authority: "Another famous author says that you will like this book."
- Social Proof: "All your friends on Facebook are buying this book."
- High Need for Cognition: Smart, subtle points that require some thinking to realize, such as: "*The Hunger Games* is the *Inferno* of children's literature."
- Hit over the Head: A simple message such as: "*The Hunger Games* is a fun, fast read!"

Researchers can track which pitch is the most persuasive for each person. By using the best pitch, a retailer can boost the effectiveness of recommendations by 30 to 40 percent. That effectiveness holds true no matter what product people are shopping for. So once an advertiser determines the optimal pitch for you, they can use the same pitch to sell you clothes as they do books.

As you have probably have figured out by now, your persuasion profile would be worth quite a lot of money to many companies. The information about what pitches you respond to could become a valuable commodity that companies would buy and sell. If a site figures out that you respond best to limited-time offers of deep discounts, you might find banner ads on every site urging you to buy in the next 10 minutes at half off.

Persuasion profiling can provide many benefits. Consider DirectLife (*www.directlife.philips.com*), a wearable coaching device manufactured by Philips that uses human coaches to determine which arguments motivate a particular individual to eat a healthier diet and exercise more regularly. While the device is called DirectLife, it has to work indirectly; that is, it can't be too overt or it won't be as effective.

Many companies that use persuasion profiling don't have your well-being in mind. Instead of tapping into your motivation to eat healthy, for example, persuasion profiling could capitalize on your political fears by having a candidate target you with ads on your Facebook page claiming that all your friends are voting for him or her.

To prevent advertisers from pouncing on your personal psychological weak spots, you should watch for signs of persuasion profiling and view all marketing arguments with a grain of salt.

Persuasion profiling can cause another problem. *Micro-profiling*, or micro-personalization, can encase individuals in a silent, subtle bubble, isolating them from discoveries and insights that fall outside their usual tastes and interests. This bubble is invisible, so users are unaware of how their Internet and the websites they visit differ from what other people see. In fact, several years ago, when users searched a particular topic, everyone would get the same result. Today, different people who Google the same topic can get different results. These different results are based on the enormous amount of data (through search, Gmail, Maps, and other services) that Google maintains on its users.

What We Learned from This Case

In Chapter 8, you learned about information systems that supported organizational activities within the organization. In this chapter, you study information systems that support organizational activities that extend outside the organization to customers (customer relationship management systems; CRM) and suppliers (supply chain management systems; SCM). Both of these systems are critical to the success of modern businesses. Accordingly, the first half of this chapter is devoted to CRM and CRM systems, and the last half to SCM and SCM systems.

The chapter-opening Case 9.1 provides a specific example of the evolving nature of the business-customer relationship. As personal technology usage changes, so too must the methods that businesses use to interface with their customers. Organizations increasingly are emphasizing a customer-centric approach to their business practices because they know that sustainable value is found in long-term customer relationships that extend beyond any given day's business transaction. The chapter-closing Case 9.2 addresses the critical importance of effectively managing a complex, global supply chain.

Customer relationship management is not just for large organizations. CRM is essential for small organizations as well.

At this point, however, you may be asking yourself: Why should I learn about CRM and SCM? As you will see in this chapter, customers and suppliers are supremely important to *all* organizations. Regardless of the job you perform, you will have an impact, whether direct or indirect, on managing your firm's customers and suppliers. When you read the What's in IT For Me? section at the end of the chapter, you will learn about opportunities in which you can make immediate contributions on your first job. Therefore, it is important that you gain a working knowledge of CRM, CRM systems, SCM, and SCM systems.

9.1 Defining Customer Relationship Management

Before the supermarket, the mall, and the automobile, people purchased goods at their neighbourhood store. The owners and employees recognized customers by name and knew their preferences and wants. For their part, customers remained loyal to the store and made repeated purchases. Over time, however, this personal customer relationship became impersonal as people moved from farms to cities, consumers became mobile, and supermarkets and department stores achieved economies of scale through mass marketing. Although prices were lower and products were more uniform in quality, the relationship with customers became nameless and impersonal.

The customer relationship has become even more impersonal with the rapid growth of the Internet and the World Wide Web. In today's hypercompetitive marketplace, customers are increasingly powerful; if they are dissatisfied with a product and/or a service from one organization, a competitor is often just one mouse click away. Further, as more and more customers shop on the web, an enterprise does not even have the opportunity to make a good first impression *in person*.

Customer relationship management (CRM) returns to personal marketing. That is, rather than market to a mass of people or companies, businesses market to each customer individually. By employing this approach, businesses can use information about each customer—for example, previous purchases, needs, and wants—to create offers that customers are more likely to accept. That is, the CRM approach is designed to achieve *customer intimacy*. This CRM approach is enabled by information technology in the form of various CRM systems and applications.

Customer relationship management is not only about the software. Sometimes the problem with managing relationships is simply time and information. Old systems may contain needed information, but the information may take too long to access and may not be usable across

Sources: D. Gross, "What the Internet Is Hiding from You," CNN.com, May 19, 2011; E. Pariser, "Mind Reading," *Wired*, May 2011.

a variety of applications. The result is reduced time to spend with customers. Thus, companies can implement a CRM tool that manages e-mail distribution, scheduling, billing, and customer information. This tool enables them to find everything they need in one place so they can focus on what their business is really about: providing their customers with excellent service.

Customer relationship management (CRM) is a customer-focused and customer-driven organizational strategy. That is, organizations concentrate on assessing customers' requirements for products and services and then providing high-quality, responsive service. CRM is not a process or a technology per se; rather, it is a customer-centric way of thinking and acting. The focus of organizations today has shifted from conducting business transactions to managing customer relationships. In general, organizations recognize that customers are the core of a successful enterprise, and the success of the enterprise depends on effectively managing relationships with them.

CRM builds sustainable long-term customer relationships that create value for the company as well as for the customer. That is, CRM helps companies acquire new customers, retain existing profitable customers, and grow relationships with existing customers. This last CRM function is particularly important because repeat customers are the largest generator of revenue for an enterprise. Also, organizations have long understood that getting back a customer who has switched to a competitor is vastly more expensive than keeping that customer satisfied in the first place.

Figure 9.1 depicts the CRM process. The process begins with marketing efforts, where the organization solicits prospects from a target population of potential customers. A certain number of these prospects will make a purchase, thus becoming customers. Of the organization's customers, a certain number will become repeat customers. The organization then segments its repeat customers into low-value and high-value repeat customers. An organization's overall goal is to maximize the *lifetime value* of a customer, which is that customer's potential revenue stream over a number of years.

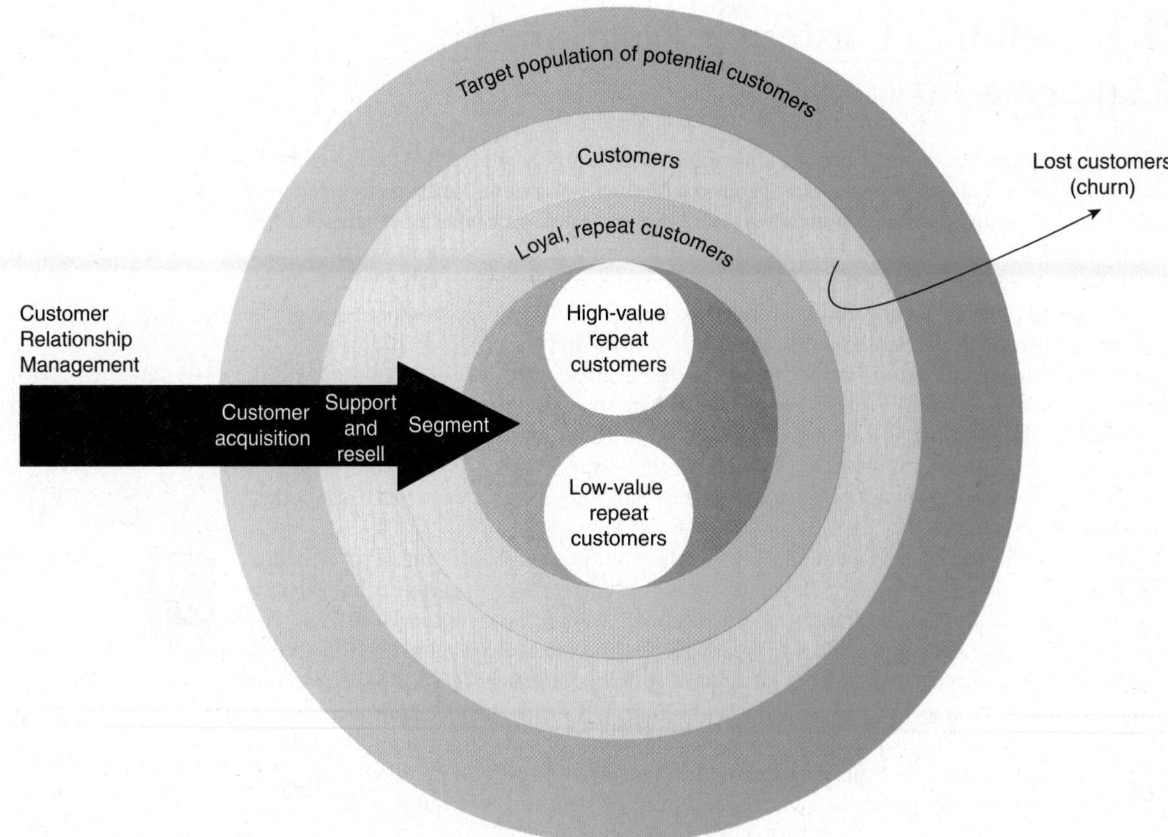

FIGURE 9.1 The customer relationship management process.

The organization inevitably will lose a certain percentage of customers, a process called *customer churn*. The optimal result of the organization's CRM efforts is to maximize the number of high-value repeat customers while minimizing customer churn.

CRM is basically a simple idea: Treat different customers differently, because their needs differ and their value to the company also may differ. A successful CRM strategy not only improves customer satisfaction, but it makes the company's sales and service employees more productive, which in turn generates increased profits. In fact, researchers at the National Quality Research Center at the University of Michigan found that a 1 percent increase in customer satisfaction can lead to as much as a 300 percent increase in a company's market capitalization, defined as the number of shares of the company's stock outstanding multiplied by the price per share of the stock. Put simply, a minor increase in customer satisfaction can lead to a major increase in a company's overall value.

Up to this point, we have been looking at an organization's CRM strategy. It is important to distinguish between a CRM *strategy* and CRM *systems*. Basically, CRM systems are information systems designed to support an organization's CRM strategy. For organizations to pursue excellent relationships with their customers, they need to employ CRM systems that provide the infrastructure needed to support those relationships. Because customer service and support are essential to a successful business, organizations must place a great deal of emphasis on both their CRM strategy and their CRM systems.

Broadly speaking, CRM systems lie on a continuum, from low-end CRM systems—designed for enterprises with many small customers—to high-end CRM systems—for enterprises with a few large customers. CRM systems can also link to social networking sites. IT's About Small Business 9.1 illustrates the case of P.F. Chang's restaurants and how they used Twitter to score a customer-relationship coup. As you study the cases and examples in this chapter, consider where on the continuum a particular CRM system would fall.

IT's about [small] business

9.1 An Instantaneous CRM Effort

While sitting in a P.F. Chang's China Bistro restaurant (*www.pfchangs.com*) in Florida, a woman tweeted that her lettuce-wrap appetizer was delicious. An employee at P.F. Chang's headquarters in Scottsdale, Arizona, spotted the tweet. He alerted a manager, who immediately called the Florida restaurant. Using the customer's profile picture, the restaurant manager identified the woman and had a server thank her for her support by presenting her free lettuce wraps and a dessert.

P.F. Chang's was being social media savvy, not only reinforcing the woman's enthusiasm, but likely setting off a chain of word-of-mouth advertising among her friends and co-workers. The restaurant gets additional exposure for its social media coup when the case is mentioned in IT and marketing conferences as a good example of intuitive branding. In addition to rewarding happy customers, the chain, with more than 200 restaurants across the United States, systematically monitors what customers are saying on social networking sites such as Facebook, Twitter, and TripAdvisor and makes improvements when patrons have been unhappy, say with service or cold food. For example, the chain moved its takeout order-taking function to a call centre so hostesses in the restaurants could focus on greeting customers on location instead of answering the phone.

In the case of P.F. Chang's, social media presented an easy opportunity to make the most of the customer experience and to demonstrate to the organization that there is "gold" in tweets. Regardless of whether organizations have a social media strategy, customers are on Twitter and Facebook, telling the world how they feel about companies, their products, and their services. Whether it is a Facebook group begging Trader Joe's (*www.traderjoes.com*) to open a grocery store in a certain geographic location or a blogger complaining about a washing machine to a million followers, companies ignore social media at their peril.

Questions

1. Provide two examples of specific actions a company could take to use social media in its CRM efforts.
2. Should all organizations include a social media component in their CRM strategy? Why or why not? Support your answer.

Sources: Compiled from W. Schuchart, "How P.F. Chang's Turned a Plate of Lettuce Wraps into a Twitter Win," *IT Knowledge Exchange*, March 16, 2011; J. Schectman, "P.F. Chang's Adds Social Media to Its Menu," *CIO Journal*, November 9, 2012; *www.pfchangs.com*, accessed June 15, 2013.

Although CRM varies according to circumstances, all successful CRM policies share two basic elements. First, the company must identify the many types of customer touch points. Second, it needs to consolidate data about each customer. Let's examine these two elements in more detail.

Customer Touch Points

Organizations must recognize the numerous and diverse interactions that they have with their customers. These various types of interactions are referred to as **customer touch points**. Traditional customer touch points include telephone contact, direct mailings, and actual physical interactions with customers during their visits to a store. Organizational CRM systems, however, must manage many additional customer touch points that occur through the use of popular personal technologies. These touch points include e-mail, websites, and communications via smart phones (see Figure 9.2).

Data Consolidation

Data consolidation also is critical to an organization's CRM efforts. Customer data must be managed effectively by the organization's CRM systems. In the past, customer data were located in isolated systems in different functional areas across the business (for example, in separate databases in the finance, sales, logistics, and marketing departments). Even if all of these data related to the same customer, they were difficult to share across the various functional areas.

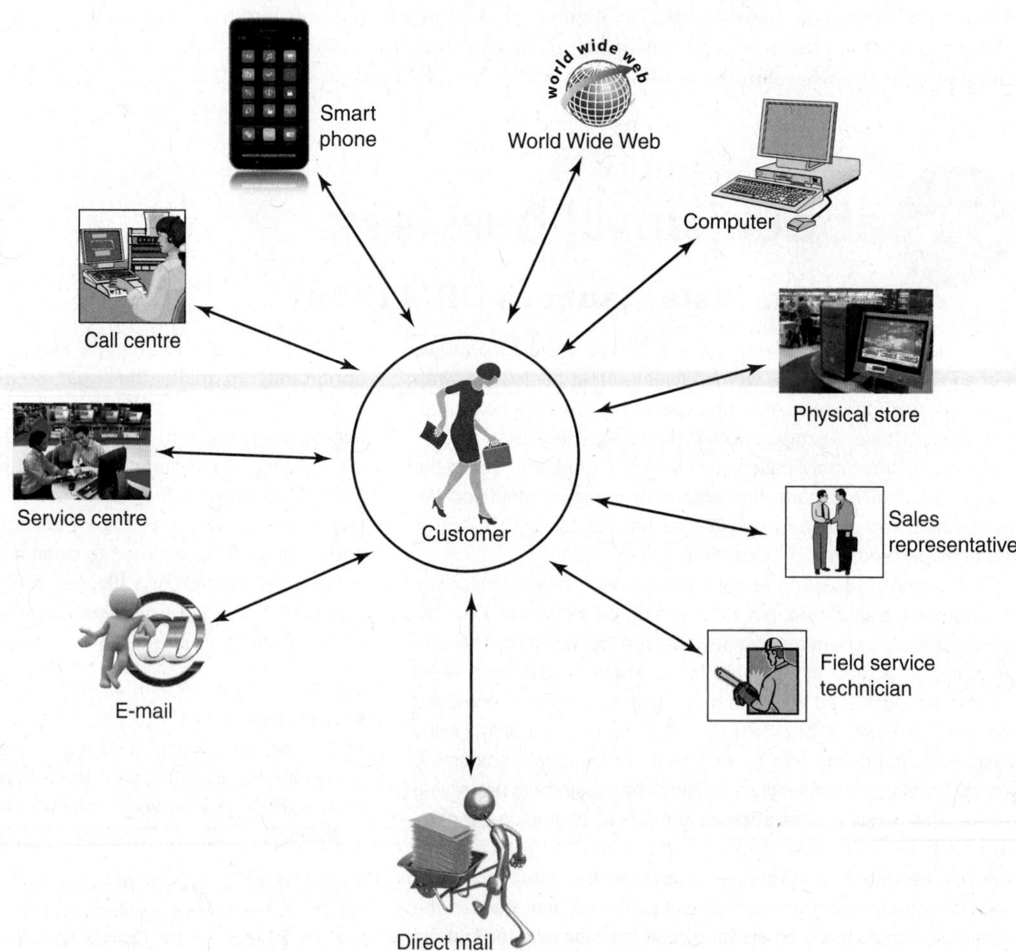

FIGURE 9.2 Customer touch points. (*Sources*: Oleksiy Mark/Shutterstock; Media Bakery).

As you saw in Chapter 3, modern, interconnected systems built around a data warehouse now make all customer-related data available to every unit of the business. This complete data set on each customer is called a *360-degree view* of that customer. By accessing this 360-degree view, a company can enhance its relationship with its customers and ultimately make more productive and profitable decisions.

Data consolidation and the 360-degree view of the customer enable the organization's functional areas to readily share information about customers. This information sharing leads to collaborative CRM. **Collaborative CRM systems** provide effective and efficient interactive communication with the customer throughout the entire organization. That is, collaborative CRM systems integrate communications between the organization and its customers in all aspects of marketing, sales, and customer support. Collaborative CRM systems also enable customers to provide direct feedback to the organization. As you read in Chapter 7, Web 2.0 applications such as blogs and wikis are very important to companies that value customer input into their product and service offerings, as well as into new product development.

The main CRM software vendors include Salesforce.com, SAP, Oracle, and Microsoft. A comparison of some of these vendors can be found by visiting *www.crmlandmark.com* and searching for "compare CRM." Typically a CRM system in an organization contains two major components: operational CRM systems and analytical CRM systems. You will learn about these components in the next two sections.

before you go on...

1. What is the definition of "customer relationship management"?
2. Why is CRM so important to any organization?
3. Define and provide examples of customer touch points.

9.2 Operational Customer Relationship Management Systems

Operational CRM systems support front-office business processes. Front-office processes are those that directly interact with customers; that is, sales, marketing, and service. The two major components of operational CRM systems are customer-facing applications and customer-touching applications.

Customer-Facing Applications

In **customer-facing CRM applications**, an organization's sales, field service, and customer interaction centre representatives interact directly with customers. These applications include customer service and support, sales force automation, marketing, and campaign management.

Customer Service and Support. Customer service and support include systems that automate service requests, complaints, product returns, and requests for information. Today, organizations have implemented **customer interaction centres (CIC)**, where organizational representatives use multiple channels such as the web, telephone, fax, and face-to-face interactions to communicate with customers. The CIC manages several different types of customer interaction.

One of the most well-known customer interaction centres is the *call centre*, a centralized office set up to receive and transmit a large volume of requests by telephone. Call centres enable companies to respond to a large variety of questions, including product support and complaints. IT's About Business 9.2 demonstrates how CRM software can help companies significantly improve the operations in their call centres and their CRM efforts overall.

Organizations use the CIC to create a call list for the sales team, whose members contact sales prospects. This type of interaction is called *outbound telesales*. In these interactions, the customer and the sales team collaborate in discussing products and services that can satisfy customers' needs and generate sales.

Customers can communicate directly with the CIC to initiate a sales order, inquire about products and services before placing an order, and obtain information about a transaction that they have already made. These interactions are referred to as *inbound teleservice*. Teleservice representatives respond to requests either by using service instructions found in an organizational knowledge base or by noting incidents that can be addressed only by field service technicians.

The CIC also provides the information help desk. The help desk assists customers with their questions concerning products or services, and it also processes customer complaints. Complaints generate follow-up activities such as quality-control checks, delivery of replacement parts or products, service calls, generation of credit memos, and product returns.

New technologies are extending the traditional CIC's functionality to include e-mail and web interaction. For example, Epicor (*www.epicor.com*) provides software solutions that combine web channels, such as automated e-mail reply, and web knowledge bases. The information the software provides is available to CIC representatives and field service personnel. Another recent technology, live chat, allows customers to connect to a company representative and conduct an instant messaging session. The advantage of live chat over a telephone conversation is the ability to show documents and photos (see *www.livechatinc.com* and *www.websitealive.com*). Some companies conduct the chat with a computer using natural language processing rather than with a real person.

Sales Force Automation. **Sales force automation (SFA)** is the component of an operational CRM system that automatically records all of the components in a sales transaction process. SFA systems include a *contact management system*, which tracks all contacts that have been made with a customer, the purpose of each contact, and any follow-up that might be necessary. This system eliminates duplicated contacts and redundancy, which in turn reduces the risk of irritating customers. SFA also includes a *sales lead tracking system*, which lists potential customers or customers who have purchased related products.

Other elements of an SFA system can include a *sales forecasting system*, which is a mathematical technique for estimating future sales, and a *product knowledge system*, which is a comprehensive source of information regarding products and services. More-developed SFA systems also have on-line product-building features, called *configurators*, that enable customers to model the product to meet their specific needs. For example, you can customize your own running shoe at NikeID (*http://nikeid.nike.com*). Finally, many of the current SFA systems enable the salesperson in the field to connect remotely via web-based interfaces that can be displayed on smart phones.

Marketing. Thus far, you have focused primarily on how sales and customer service personnel can benefit from CRM systems; however, CRM systems have many important applications for an organization's marketing department as well. For example, they enable marketers to identify and target their best customers, to manage marketing campaigns, and to generate quality leads for the sales teams. Additionally, CRM marketing applications can sift through volumes of customer data—a process known as data mining—to develop a *purchasing profile*—a snapshot of a consumer's buying habits that may lead to additional sales through cross selling, up selling, and bundling. IT's About Business 9.2 relates how up selling and cross selling was enabled by a CRM system.

Cross selling is the marketing of additional related products to customers based on a previous purchase. This sales approach has been used very successfully by the world's largest on-line retailer, Amazon.com. For example, if you have purchased several books on Amazon, the next time you visit the website, Amazon will recommend other similar books you might like to purchase.

Up selling is a sales strategy in which the business provides to customers the opportunity to purchase higher-value related products or services in place of, or along with, the consumer's initial product or service selection. For example, if a customer goes into an electronics store to

IT's [about business]

9.2 Chinatrust Philippines CRM Effort

Chinatrust Philippines Commercial Bank Corporation (*www.chinatrust.com.ph*) is a subsidiary of Chinatrust Commercial Bank, one of the 200 biggest banks in the world in terms of capital. It is also the most-awarded banking institution in Taiwan. It specializes in the personal loan business including mortgages, a business that has been experiencing steady growth and intensifying competition. Part of its CRM strategy is a call centre from which customers are contacted and serviced.

However, the data from these call centres was collected manually and analyzed using Microsoft Excel, a business process that was prone to inaccuracies, delays, and increasing costs. For example, Chinatrust Philippines did not have reliable data on call volumes, service levels, or abandoned calls. The bank responded to all calls with live agents, and did not use automated voice response. In addition, the bank could not track customers' transaction history and therefore could not perform market segmentation and related up- and cross-selling activities.

As the number of its personal loan products was rapidly increasing, the company embarked on process integration and automation in customer relationship management (CRM) and its contact centre to help it acquire and retain customers more effectively. With the new CRM system, Chinatrust Philippines can now record all customer interactions. Sales agents can access and analyze customers' transaction history, and can use appropriate strategies for targeting customers more effectively, including up selling and cross selling. Since the new CRM system integrates directly with the call centre, call agents have access to customer data at their fingertips and can use the interactive voice response system to automate routine tasks, saving their time for more complicated requests. Also, the CRM software's real-time monitoring capabilities allow the bank to keep track of service performance indicators including call volume and productivity of telesales.

The results of the new CRM system were quick to appear. In the first year after the implementation, call service levels (calls answered within 10 seconds) were drastically improved from 35 percent to 85 percent. The company also expected to increase revenue from its personal loan business by 10 percent year over year while maintaining the same number of sales agents.

Questions

1. To what extent is technology important in a call centre?
2. Why is historical transaction data so important in CRM?
3. Why is the integration between communication technology and the CRM so important for effective CRM?

Sources: Compiled from "Chinatrust (Philippines) Commercial Bank Increasing Customer Service Quality with SAP® Software," SAP case study, January 2011, *www.sap.com*; *www.chinatrust.com.ph*, accessed May 20, 2013.

---

buy a new television, a salesperson may show him a pricey 1080i HD LCD television next to a non-HD television in the hope of selling the more expensive set (assuming that the customer is willing to pay more for a sharper picture). Other common examples of up selling are warranties on electronics merchandise and the purchase of a carwash after buying gas at the gas station.

Finally, **bundling** is a form of cross selling in which a business sells a group of products or services together at a price lower than their combined individual prices. For example, your cable company might bundle basic cable TV, broadband Internet access, and local telephone service at a lower price than what you would pay for each service separately.

Campaign Management. **Campaign management applications** help organizations plan campaigns that send the right messages to the right people through the right channels. Organizations manage their customers very carefully to avoid targeting people who have opted out of receiving marketing communications. Further, companies use these applications to personalize individual messages for each particular customer.

Customer-Touching Applications

Corporations have used manual CRM systems for many years. The term "electronic CRM" (or "e-CRM") appeared in the mid-1990s, when organizations began using the Internet, the web, and other electronic touch points (e.g., e-mail, point-of-sale terminals) to manage customer relationships. In contrast with customer-facing applications, where customers deal directly with a company representative, customers interact directly with these technologies and applications. Such applications are called **customer-touching CRM applications** or **electronic CRM (e-CRM) applications**. Customers typically can use these applications to help themselves. There are many types of e-CRM applications. We now present some of the major ones.

Search and Comparison Capabilities. It is often difficult for customers to find what they want from the vast array of products and services available on the web. To assist customers, many on-line stores and malls offer search and comparison capabilities, as do independent comparison websites (see *www.mysimon.com*).

Technical and Other Information and Services. Many organizations offer personalized experiences to induce customers to make purchases or to remain loyal. For example, websites often allow customers to download product manuals. One example is General Electric's website (*www.ge.com*), which provides detailed technical and maintenance information and sells replacement parts to customers who need to repair outdated home appliances. Another example is Goodyear's website (*www.goodyear.com*), which provides information about tires and their use.

In addition, customers now can view account balances or check the shipping status of orders at any time from their computers or smart phones. If you order books from Amazon, for example, you can look up the anticipated arrival date. Following this model, many other companies provide similar services (see *www.fedex.com* and *www.ups.com*).

Customized Products and Services. Another customer-touching service that many on-line vendors use is mass customization, a process in which customers can configure their own products. For example, Dell Computer (*www.dell.ca*) allows customers to configure their own computer systems. The Gap (*www.gapcanada.ca*) allows customers to "mix and match" an entire wardrobe. Websites such as Hitsquad (*www.hitsquad.com*) allow customers to pick individual music titles from a library and customize a CD, a feature that traditional music stores do not offer.

Personalized Web Pages. Many organizations permit their customers to create personalized web pages. Customers use these pages to record purchases and preferences, as well as problems and requests. For example, American Airlines generates personalized web pages for each of approximately 800,000 registered travel-planning customers.

FAQs. Frequently asked questions (FAQs) are a simple tool for answering repetitive customer queries. Customers may find the information they need by using this tool, thereby not needing to communicate with an actual person.

E-mail and Automated Response. The most popular tool for customer service is e-mail. Inexpensive and fast, e-mail is used not only to answer inquiries from customers but also to disseminate information, send alerts and product information, and conduct correspondence on any topic.

Loyalty Programs. **Loyalty programs** recognize customers who repeatedly use a vendor's products or services. Loyalty programs are appropriate when two conditions are met: a high frequency of repeat purchases, and little product customization for each customer.

The purpose of loyalty programs is not to reward past behaviour, but to influence future behaviour. Note that the most profitable customers are not necessarily those whose behaviour can be influenced the most easily. As one example, most major airlines provide some "elite" benefits to anyone who flies a certain distance with them and their partners over the course of a year regardless of how much they spend. The reason is that, although first-class passengers are far more profitable than discount seekers, they also are less influenced by loyalty programs. Discount flyers respond much more enthusiastically to the benefits of frequent flyer programs. Therefore, airlines award more benefits to discount flyers than to first-class flyers (relative to their spending).

Perhaps the best-known loyalty programs are the airlines' frequent flyer programs. In addition, gas stations and supermarkets use similar programs to reward frequent shoppers. Loyalty programs use a database or data warehouse to keep a record of the points (or miles) a customer has accrued and the rewards to which he or she is entitled. The programs then use analytical tools to mine the data and learn about customer behaviour.

Operational CRM systems benefit organizations by allowing them to do the following:

- Provide efficient, personalized marketing, sales, and service.
- Get a 360-degree view of each customer.
- Give sales and service employees access to a complete history of customer interaction with the organization, regardless of the touch point.

- Improve sales and account management by optimizing the information shared by multiple employees and by streamlining existing processes (for example, taking orders using mobile devices).
- Form individualized relationships with customers, with the aim of improving customer satisfaction and maximizing profits.
- Identify the most profitable customers, and provide them the highest level of service.
- Provide employees with the information and processes necessary to know their customers.
- Understand and identify customer needs, and effectively build relationships among the company, its customer base, and its distribution partners.

before you go on...

1. Differentiate between customer-facing applications and customer-touching applications.
2. Provide examples of cross selling, up selling, and bundling (other than the examples presented in the text).

9.3 Analytical Customer Relationship Management Systems

Whereas operational CRM systems support front-office business processes, **analytical CRM systems** provide business intelligence by analyzing customer behaviour and perceptions. For example, analytical CRM systems typically provide information on customer requests and transactions, as well as on customer responses to the organization's marketing, sales, and service initiatives. These systems also create statistical models of customer behaviour and the value of customer relationships over time, as well as forecasts about acquiring, retaining, and losing customers. Figure 9.3 illustrates the relationship between operational CRM systems and analytical CRM systems.

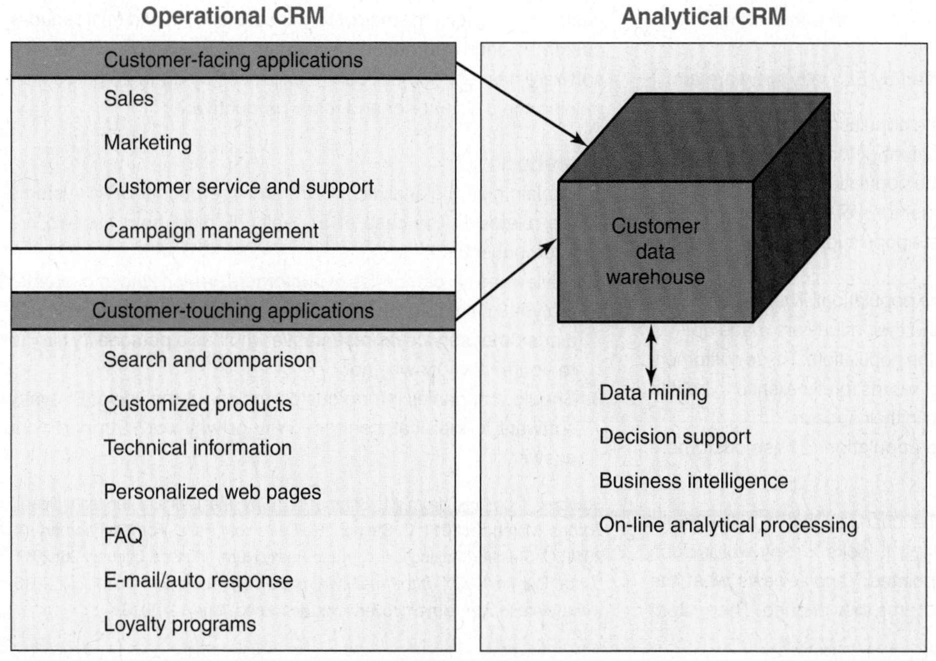

FIGURE 9.3 The relationship between operational CRM and analytical CRM.

Important technologies in analytical CRM systems include data warehouses, data mining, decision support, and other business intelligence technologies (discussed in Chapter 10). After these systems have completed their various analyses, they supply information to the organization in the form of reports and digital dashboards.

Analytical CRM systems analyze customer data for a variety of purposes, including:

- Designing and executing targeted marketing campaigns
- Increasing customer acquisition, cross selling, and up selling
- Providing input into decisions relating to products and services (e.g., pricing and product development)
- Providing financial forecasting and customer profitability analysis.

IT's About Business 9.3 presents the case of a call centre using analytical CRM to match callers with the appropriate customer support representative.

IT's [about business]

9.3 Refining the Call Centre

Call centres are expensive. An average call centre seat (representative) costs about $50,000 per year to maintain. The biggest companies, such as AT&T, with 100,000 seats, spend billions of dollars to placate irritated customers. ELoyalty from TeleTech Holdings (*www.teletech.com/eloyalty/overview/*) provides complex software that not only can define a specific complaint, but also can analyze a caller's personality.

ELoyalty has analyzed 600 million conversations, and its 1,000 servers store 600 terabytes of customer data. (By way of comparison, as of early 2013, all the English-language articles on Wikipedia took up 10 terabytes of storage.) Based on this analysis, the software categorizes people into one of six personality types, looking for telltale phrases that provide clues as to what the customer's specific complaint might be. It then routes callers to the service representative most qualified to handle that combination of problem and personality.

The six personality types identified by ELoyalty software are:

- Emotions-driven (30 percent of the population): These customers forge relationships with agents before getting into the problem.
- Thoughts-driven (25 percent of the population): These customers want facts and analysis and are not fond of small talk.
- Reactions-driven (20 percent of the population): These customers either love something or hate it.
- Opinions-driven (10 percent of the population): These customers' language is full of imperatives, and their minds are made up.
- Reflections-driven (10 percent of the population): These customers are introverts who live in their own worlds, prefer silence to banter, and often skip personal pronouns in their speech.
- Actions-driven (5 percent of the population): These customers want movement and progress.

ELoyalty assesses the chances that a caller might want to cancel their service. It looks for key words such as "cancel" and "disappointed," and reviews what the caller said and did the last time they phoned. The system can also assess how important a customer is, based on factors such as how fast they pay their bills and how large the bills are in the first place. Customers who spend more each month get a higher priority than those who use services less frequently.

Research revealed that when callers were paired with a representative with a similar personality, their calls averaged just over 5 minutes, and the parties reached a satisfactory resolution 92 percent of the time. In contrast, when customers spoke with a representative with a different type of personality from themselves, calls averaged nearly 10 minutes, and the parties reached resolution only 47 percent of the time.

Pairing callers with like-minded representatives offers four benefits to companies: (1) it saves them a great deal of money; (2) it enables company representatives to resolve issues for more customers; (3) it increases customer satisfaction; and (4) it reduces customer churn (turnover). According to ELoyalty's clients, the software has reduced call centre expenses by up to 20 percent by making the calls shorter and more productive.

Questions

1. Explain how the analytical CRM and operational CRM systems are related in the case of ELoyalty. Explain how the two are interconnected.
2. Review the six categories of customers. Which kind of customer are you? Do you think it would be advantageous to speak with a customer service representative who has a personality similar to yours? Why or why not?
3. Should companies inform customers about the use of ELoyalty software in their call centres? Why or why not? Support your answer.

Sources: Compiled from M. Schroeck, "Why the Call Center Isn't Dead," *Forbes*, March 15, 2011; C. Steiner, "He Feels Your Pain," *Forbes*, February 14, 2011; C. Steiner, "Making Call Centers Really Hum," *Forbes*, January 26, 2011; "Data Dumps/FAQ," *http://meta.wikimedia.org*, accessed June 15, 2013; *www.teletech.com/eloyalty/overview/*, accessed June 14, 2013.

before you go on...

1. What is the relationship between operational CRM systems and analytical CRM systems?
2. What are some of the functions of analytical CRM systems?

9.4 Other Types of Customer Relationship Management Systems

Now that you have examined operational and analytical CRM systems, the focus shifts to other types of CRM systems. Three exciting developments in this area are on-demand CRM systems, mobile CRM systems, and open-source CRM systems.

On-Demand CRM Systems

Customer relationship management systems may be implemented as either *on-premise* or *on-demand.* Traditionally, organizations used on-premise CRM systems, meaning that they purchased the systems from a vendor and then installed them on site. This arrangement was expensive, time consuming, and inflexible. Some organizations, particularly smaller ones, could not justify the cost of these systems.

On-demand CRM systems became a solution for the drawbacks of on-premise CRM systems. An **on-demand CRM system** is one that is hosted by an external vendor in the vendor's data centre. This arrangement spares the organization the costs associated with purchasing the system. In addition, because the vendor creates and maintains the system, the organization's employees need to know only how to access and use it. The concept of on-demand is also known as *utility computing* (see Technology Guide 3) or *software-as-a-service* (SaaS; see Chapter 11).

Despite their benefits, on-demand CRM systems have potential problems. First, the vendor could prove to be unreliable or go out of business, in which case the company would have no CRM functionality at all. Second, hosted software is difficult or impossible to modify, and only the vendor can upgrade it. Third, vendor-hosted CRM software may be difficult to integrate with the organization's existing software. Finally, giving strategic customer data to vendors always carries risks.

Salesforce (*www.salesforce.com*) is the best-known on-demand CRM vendor. The goal of Salesforce is to provide a new business model that allows companies to rent the CRM software instead of buying it. The secret to Salesforce's success appears to be that CRM has common requirements across many customers.

One Salesforce customer is Häagen-Dazs Shoppe (*www.haagendazs.com*). Häagen-Dazs estimated that it would have had to spend $65,000 for a custom-designed database to remain in close contact with its retail franchises. Rather than spend this amount, the company spent an initial $20,000 to establish service with Salesforce. It now pays $125 per month for 20 users to remotely monitor, via the web or a smart phone, all the Häagen-Dazs franchises across the United States.

Other vendors also offer on-demand CRM software. Example 9.1 demonstrates the advantages that McKesson Corporation gained from deploying Oracle's CRM On Demand application.

Example 9.1

The McKesson Corporation (*www.mckesson.com*) specializes in the distribution of branded, generic, and over-the-counter pharmaceuticals and products.

McKesson wanted a CRM system that would enable it to perform the following functions:

- Make sales activities and customer accounts more visible to the corporation.
- Standardize and automate sales and CRM processes.
- Track reported problems, inconsistent processes, and resolution time.

In addition, the system had to be easy to use.

McKesson ultimately implemented Oracle's CRM On Demand application to standardize the sales and marketing systems across all of its product lines. The new system enabled the company to consolidate reporting across product lines, and it provided the necessary flexibility to accommodate multiple sales processes. Further, it allowed the organization to monitor and track issues that arose in the resolution process.

In essence, Oracle's CRM On Demand application provided McKesson with a 360-degree view of customer account information across the entire organization, which has proved to be very useful. In addition, McKesson was able to deploy the system in less than 90 days.

Mobile CRM Systems

A **mobile CRM system** is an interactive system that enables an organization to conduct communications related to sales, marketing, and customer service activities through a mobile medium for the purpose of building and maintaining relationships with its customers. Simply put, mobile CRM systems involve interacting directly with consumers through portable devices such as smart phones. Many forward-thinking companies believe that mobile CRM systems have tremendous potential to create personalized customer relationships that may be accessed anywhere and at any time. In fact, the potential opportunities provided through mobile marketing appear so rich that many companies already have identified mobile CRM systems as a cornerstone of their future marketing activities. Example 9.2 shows how retailer Harry Rosen implemented CRM.

Example 9.2

Harry Rosen Inc. (*www.harryrosen.com*) is a Canadian retail chain store that sells high-end men's clothing in 15 stores across the country, with more than 700 sales associates. Since its beginnings 60 years ago, Harry Rosen has been committed to providing excellent customer service. In order to do so, the company relies on a one-on-one sales approach where customers are encouraged to book an appointment with a sales associate who will help them make purchasing decisions, for both off-the-rack and custom-tailored garments. Once the appointment is scheduled, the sales associate prepares for the meeting by consulting any customer information that they already collected such as the customer's body measurements and purchase history.

However, this system suffered from a number of problems. For example, sometimes during the appointment with the customer, the sales associate would have to leave the customer to access the information on a workstation at the other end of the store. Also, sales associates were not able to help customers by locating merchandise in another store, showing them what other patterns or fabrics were available to order, or letting them know when particular merchandise would be available in the store. In addition, the system would not work with customers who did not make an appointment.

It was clear that for top-notch customer service, some changes needed to be made, starting with sales associates being able to access real-time information from other stores as well as a new way to assist customers who did not make an appointment.

Sources: Compiled from "McKesson Specialty: Oracle Customer Snapshot," *www.oracle.com*, accessed March 27, 2009; "McKesson Specialty Standardizes Sales and Marketing Processes and Increases Customer Visibility," *www.techrepublic.com*, accessed March 26, 2009; T. Berk, "Siebel Upgrade Lifts McKesson's Sales Efficiency and Performance," Oracle Customer Experience Blog, July 26, 2012, *https://blogs.oracle.com*.

Harry Rosen realized that customer relationship management software could help solve some of its problems. After researching several options, the company selected the SalesLogix CRM system (*www.saleslogix.com*). The system combined applications for web deployment, mobile devices, and system integration capabilities.

The company acquired new mobile devices and launched a customized application on pocket PCs to provide sales associates with quick access to customer data and product preferences, such as how often a customer shops, average purchase price, and brands most often purchased. The devices also allow them to look up inventory across the company's locations in real time, know when a new shipment of merchandise will arrive, and schedule tasks such as suit tailoring—all while still on the sales floor.

Open-Source CRM Systems

As explained in Technology Guide 2, the source code for open-source software is available at no cost. **Open-source CRM systems**, therefore, are CRM systems whose source code is available to developers and users.

Open-source CRM systems provide the same features or functions as other CRM software, and they may be implemented either on-premise or on-demand. Leading open-source CRM vendors include SugarCRM (*www.sugarcrm.com*), Concursive (*www.concursive.com*), and vtiger (*www.vtiger.com*).

The benefits of open-source CRM systems include favourable pricing and a wide variety of applications. In addition, these systems are easy to customize. This is an attractive feature for organizations that need CRM software designed for their specific needs. Finally, updates and bug (software error) fixes for open-source CRM systems are rapidly distributed, and extensive support information is available free of charge.

Like all software, however, open-source CRM systems have certain risks. The most serious risk involves quality control. Because open-source CRM systems are created by a large community of unpaid developers, there sometimes is no central authority responsible for overseeing the quality of the product. Further, for best results, companies must have the same information technology platform in place as that on which the open-source CRM system was developed.

before you go on...

1. Define on-demand CRM.
2. Define mobile CRM.
3. Define open-source CRM.

9.5 Supply Chains

Modern organizations are increasingly concentrating on their core competencies and on becoming more flexible and agile. To accomplish these objectives, they rely on other companies to supply necessary goods and services, rather than on companies that they themselves own. Organizations recognize that these suppliers can perform these activities more efficiently and effectively than they can. This trend toward relying on an increasing number of suppliers

Sources: Compiled from "Sage CRM SalesLogix for Harry Rosen," *www.erpko.com*, April 27, 2010; "Harry Rosen Inc. Wins Gartner & 1to1 Media CRM Excellence Award Supported by Sage SalesLogix System," Sage news release, March 14, 2012; "Harry Rosen Inc. Wins Saugatuck Technology Beacon Award for Customer Experience Strategy Supported by Sage SalesLogix Mobile," Sage news release, November 14, 2012; *www.harryrosen.com*, accessed June 14, 2013.

has led to the concept of supply chains. A **supply chain** is the flow of materials, information, money, and services from raw material suppliers, through factories and warehouses, to the end customers. A supply chain also includes the *organizations* and *processes* that create and deliver products, information, and services to end customers.

Supply chains improve trust and collaboration among supply chain partners, thus improving supply chain visibility and inventory velocity. **Supply chain visibility** is the ability for all organizations in a supply chain to access or view relevant data on purchased materials as these materials move through their suppliers' production processes and transportation networks to their receiving docks. In addition, organizations can access or view relevant data on outbound goods as they are manufactured, assembled, or stored in inventory and then shipped through their transportation networks to their customers' receiving docks. The sooner a company can deliver products and services after receiving the materials required to make them—that is, the higher the *inventory velocity*—the more satisfied the company's customers will be.

Supply chains are a vital component of the overall strategies of many modern organizations. To utilize supply chains efficiently, a business must be tightly integrated with its suppliers, business partners, distributors, and customers. A critical component of this integration is the use of information systems to facilitate the exchange of information among the participants in the supply chain.

You might ask, "Why do I need to study supply chain management?" The answer is that supply chains are critical to modern organizations. Therefore, regardless of your position within an organization, you will be involved with some aspect of your company's supply chain.

The Structure and Components of Supply Chains

The term *supply chain* comes from a picture of how the partnering organizations are linked together. Figure 9.4 illustrates a typical supply chain. (Recall that Figure 1.5 also illustrated a supply chain, in a slightly different way.) Note that the supply chain involves three segments:

1. *Upstream*, where sourcing or procurement from external suppliers occurs.

   In this segment, supply chain (SC) managers select suppliers to deliver the goods and services the company needs to produce their product or service. Further, SC managers develop the pricing, delivery, and payment processes between a company and its suppliers. Included here are processes for managing inventory, receiving and verifying shipments, transferring goods to manufacturing facilities, and authorizing payments to suppliers.
2. *Internal*, where packaging, assembly, or manufacturing takes place.

   SC managers schedule the activities necessary for production, testing, packaging, and preparing goods for delivery. SC managers also monitor quality levels, production output, and worker productivity.

3. *Downstream*, where distribution takes place, frequently by external distributors.

   In this segment, SC managers coordinate the receipt of orders from customers, develop a network of warehouses, select carriers to deliver products to customers, and develop invoicing systems to receive payments from customers.

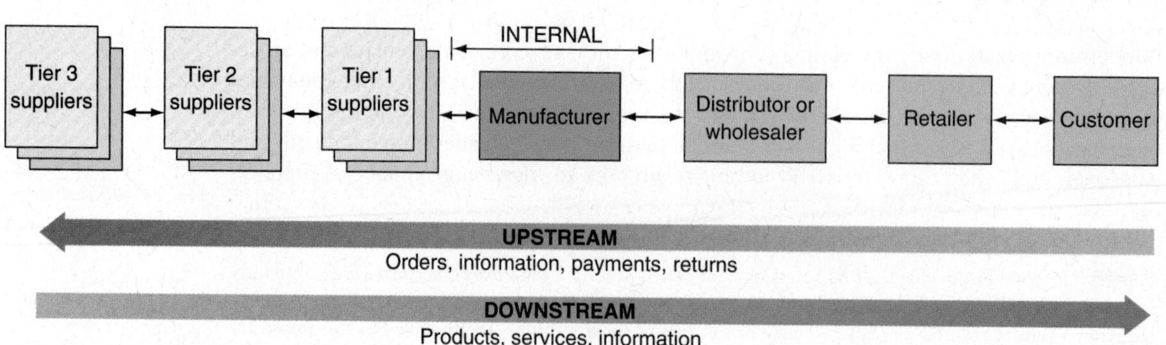

FIGURE 9.4 Generic supply chain.

The flow of information and goods can be bidirectional. For example, damaged or unwanted products can be returned, a process known as *reverse logistics*. In the retail clothing industry, for example, reverse logistics would involve clothing that customers return, either because the item had defects or because the customer did not like the item.

Tiers of Suppliers. Figure 9.4 shows several tiers of suppliers. As the diagram indicates, a supplier may have one or more subsuppliers, a subsupplier may have its own subsupplier(s), and so on. For an automobile manufacturer, for example, Tier 3 suppliers produce basic products such as glass, plastic, and rubber; Tier 2 suppliers use these inputs to make windshields, tires, and plastic mouldings; and Tier 1 suppliers produce integrated components such as dashboards and seat assemblies.

The Flows in the Supply Chain. There are typically three flows in the supply chain: material, information, and financial. *Material flows* are the physical products, raw materials, supplies, and so forth that flow along the chain. Material flows also include *reverse* flows (or reverse logistics)—returned products, recycled products, and disposal of materials or products. A supply chain thus involves a *product life cycle* approach, from "dirt to dust."

Information flows consist of data related to demand, shipments, orders, returns, and schedules, as well as changes in any of these data. Finally, *financial flows* involve money transfers, payments, credit card information and authorization, payment schedules, e-payments, and credit-related data.

Significantly, different supply chains have different numbers and types of flows. For example, in service industries there may be no physical flow of materials, but frequently there is a flow of information, often in the form of documents (physical or electronic copies). In fact, the digitization of software, music, and other content may create a supply chain without any physical flow. Notice, however, that in such a case, there are two types of information flows: one that replaces materials flow (for example, digitized software), and another that provides the supporting information (orders, billing, and so on). To manage the supply chain, an organization must coordinate all of the above flows among all of the parties involved in the chain.

before you go on...

1. What is a supply chain?
2. Describe the three segments of a supply chain.
3. Describe the flows in a supply chain.

9.6 Supply Chain Management

The function of **supply chain management (SCM)** is to plan, organize, and optimize the various activities performed along the supply chain. Like other functional areas, SCM uses information systems. The goal of SCM systems is to reduce the problems, or friction, along the supply chain. Friction can involve increased time, costs, and inventories as well as decreased customer satisfaction. SCM systems, therefore, reduce uncertainty and risks by decreasing inventory levels and cycle time while improving business processes and customer service. All of these benefits make the organization more profitable and competitive.

Significantly, SCM systems are a type of interorganizational information system. In an **interorganizational information system (IOS)**, information flows among two or more organizations. By connecting the information systems of business partners, IOSs enable the partners to perform a number of tasks:

- Reduce the costs of routine business transactions.
- Improve the quality of the information flow by reducing or eliminating errors.
- Compress the cycle time involved in fulfilling business transactions.

- Eliminate paper processing and its associated inefficiencies and costs.
- Make the transfer and processing of information easier for users.

The Push Model versus the Pull Model

Many supply chain management systems use the push model. In the **push model**, also known as *make-to-stock*, the production process begins with a forecast, which is simply an educated guess as to customer demand. The forecast must predict which products customers will want as well as the quantity of each product. The company then produces the amount of products in the forecast, typically by using mass production, and sells, or "pushes," those products to consumers.

Unfortunately, these forecasts are often incorrect. Consider, for example, an automobile manufacturer that wants to produce a new car. Marketing managers conduct extensive research, including customer surveys and analyses of competitors' cars, and then provide the results to forecasters. If the forecasters' predictions are too high—that is, if they predict that a certain number of the new car will be sold, but actual customer demand falls below this amount—then the automaker has excess cars in inventory and will incur large carrying costs. Further, the company will probably have to sell the excess cars at a discount.

From the opposite perspective, if the forecasters' predictions are too low—that is, they predict that so many new cars will be sold, but the actual customer demand turns out to be more than this number—the automaker probably will have to run extra shifts to meet the demand and thus will incur large overtime costs. Further, the company risks losing business to competitors if the car that customers want is not available. Using the push model in supply chain management can cause problems, as you will see in the next section.

To avoid the uncertainties associated with the push model, many companies now employ the pull model of supply chain management, using web-enabled information flows. In the **pull model**, also known as *make-to-order*, the production process begins with a customer order. Therefore, companies make only what customers want, a process closely aligned with mass customization.

A prominent example of a company that uses the pull model is Dell Computer. Dell's production process begins with a customer order. This order not only specifies the type of computer the customer wants, but it also alerts each Dell supplier as to the parts of the order for which that supplier is responsible. That way, Dell's suppliers ship only the parts Dell needs to produce the computer.

Not all companies can use the pull model. Automobiles, for example, are far more complicated and more expensive to manufacture than are computers, so automobile companies require longer lead times to produce new models. Automobile companies do use the pull model, but only for specific automobiles that some customers order.

Problems along the Supply Chain

As you saw earlier, friction can develop within a supply chain. One major consequence of ineffective supply chains is poor customer service. In some cases, supply chains do not deliver products or services when and where customers—either individuals or businesses—need them. In other cases, the supply chain provides poor-quality products. Other problems associated with supply chain friction are high inventory costs and loss of revenues.

The problems along the supply chain arise primarily from two sources: (1) uncertainties, and (2) the need to coordinate multiple activities, internal units, and business partners. A major source of supply chain uncertainties is the *demand forecast*. Demand for a product can be influenced by numerous factors such as competition, prices, weather conditions, technological developments, overall economic conditions, and customers' general confidence. Another uncertainty is delivery times, which depend on factors ranging from production machine failures to road construction and traffic jams. In addition, quality problems in materials and parts can create production delays, which also generate supply chain problems.

One major challenge that managers face in setting accurate inventory levels throughout the supply chain is known as the *bullwhip effect*. The **bullwhip effect** is erratic shifts in orders

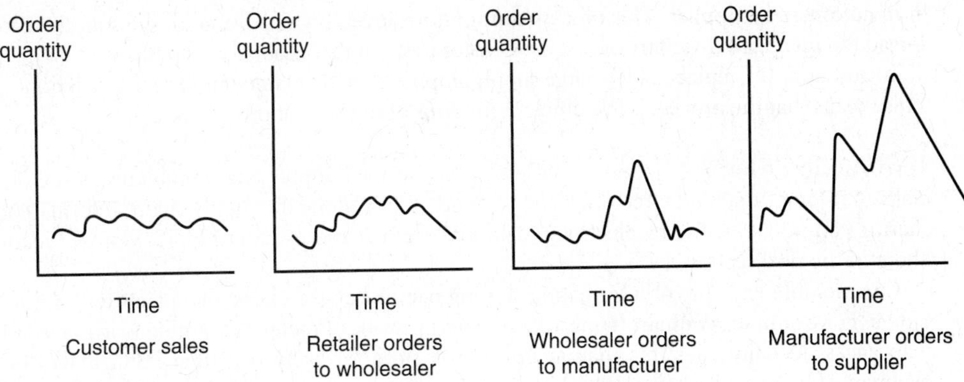

FIGURE 9.5 The bullwhip effect.

up and down the supply chain (see Figure 9.5). Basically, the variables that affect customer demand can become magnified when viewed through the eyes of managers at each link in the supply chain. If each distinct entity that makes ordering and inventory decisions places its interests above those of the chain, then stockpiling can occur at as many as seven or eight locations along the chain. Research has shown that in some cases such hoarding has led to as much as a 100-day supply of inventory that is waiting "just in case," versus the 10- to 20-day supply at hand under normal circumstances.

Solutions to Supply Chain Problems

Supply chain problems can be very costly. Therefore, organizations are motivated to find innovative solutions. During the oil crises of the 1970s, for example, Ryder Systems, a large trucking company, purchased a refinery to control the upstream part of the supply chain and to ensure sufficient gasoline for its trucks. Ryder's decision to purchase a refinery is an example of vertical integration. **Vertical integration** is a business strategy in which a company purchases its upstream suppliers to ensure that its essential supplies are available as soon as they are needed. Ryder later sold the refinery because it could not manage a business it did not understand and because oil became more plentiful.

Ryder's decision to vertically integrate was not the best method for managing its supply chain. In the remainder of this section, you will look at some other possible solutions to supply chain problems, many of which are supported by IT.

Using Inventories to Solve Supply Chain Problems. Undoubtedly, the most common solution to supply chain problems is *building inventories* as insurance against supply chain uncertainties. As you have learned, costs are associated with holding too much inventory. Thus, companies strive to optimize and control inventories with the support of information technology. For example, Loblaw Companies Limited (*www.loblaw.ca*) implemented a warehouse management system to get all of its 25 distribution centres across Canada operating on one system and to standardize the processes of transferring merchandize from suppliers to distribution centres and from distribution centres to its grocery stores. This resulted in a reduction in inventory and increased inventory turnover, resulting in savings of up to $5 million annually and bringing fresher products to store shelves.

A well-known initiative to optimize and control inventories is the **just-in-time (JIT) inventory system**, which attempts to minimize inventories. That is, in a manufacturing process, JIT systems deliver the precise number of parts, called *work-in-process* inventory, to be assembled into a finished product at precisely the right time.

Although JIT offers many benefits, it has certain drawbacks as well. To begin with, suppliers are expected to respond instantaneously to requests. As a result, they have to carry more inventory than they otherwise would. The inventory has not gone away in JIT; rather, it has just shifted from customer to supplier. This process can improve inventory size overall if the supplier can spread the increased inventory over several customers, but that is not always possible.

In addition, JIT replaces a few large supply shipments with a large number of smaller ones. This means that the process is less efficient in terms of transportation.

Information Sharing. Another common way to solve supply chain problems, and especially to improve demand forecasts, is *sharing information* along the supply chain. Information sharing can be facilitated by electronic data interchange and extranets, topics you will learn about in the next section.

One notable example of information sharing occurs between large manufacturers and retailers. For example, Walmart (*www.walmart.com*) provides Procter & Gamble (*www.pg.com*) with access to daily sales information from every store for every item that P&G makes for Walmart. This access enables P&G to manage the *inventory replenishment* for Walmart's stores. By monitoring inventory levels, P&G knows when inventories fall below the threshold for each product at any Walmart store. These data trigger an immediate shipment.

Information sharing between Walmart and P&G is executed automatically. It is part of a vendor-managed inventory strategy. **Vendor-managed inventory (VMI)** occurs when the supplier, rather than the retailer, manages the entire inventory process for a particular product or group of products. Significantly, P&G has similar agreements with other major retailers. The benefit for P&G is accurate and timely information on consumer demand for its products. Thus, P&G can plan production more accurately, minimizing the bullwhip effect.

before you go on...

1. Differentiate between the push model and the pull model.
2. Describe various problems that can occur along the supply chain.
3. Discuss possible solutions to problems along the supply chain.

9.7 Information Technology Support for Supply Chain Management

Clearly, SCM systems are essential to the successful operation of many businesses. According to the market research firm Gartner, the major SCM software vendors include SAP, Oracle, JDA Software, Ariba (now part of SAP), and Manhattan Associates. These systems—and IOSs in general—rely on various forms of IT to resolve problems.

Three technologies, in particular, provide support for IOSs and SCM systems: electronic data interchange, extranets, and web services. You will learn about web services in Technology Guide 3. In this section you examine the other two technologies.

Electronic Data Interchange (EDI)

Electronic data interchange (EDI) is a communication standard that enables business partners to exchange routine documents, such as purchasing orders, electronically. EDI formats these documents according to agreed-upon standards (for example, data formats). It then transmits messages over the Internet using a converter, called a *translator*.

EDI provides many benefits not available with a manual delivery system. To begin with, it minimizes data entry errors, because each entry is checked by the computer. In addition, the length of the message can be shorter, and messages are secured. EDI also reduces cycle time, increases productivity, enhances customer service, and minimizes paper usage and storage. Figure 9.6 contrasts the process of fulfilling a purchase order with and without EDI. These

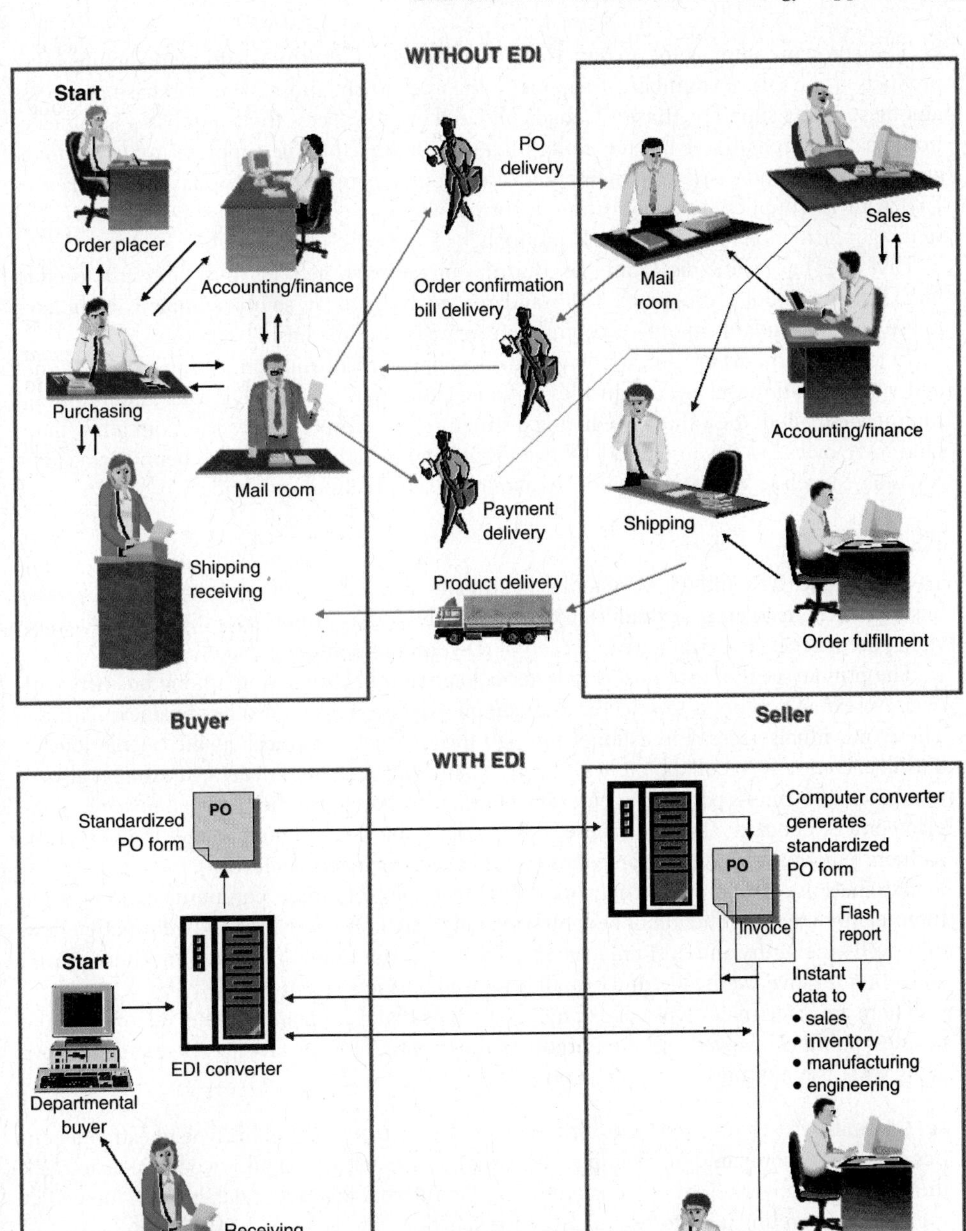

FIGURE 9.6 Comparing purchase order (PO) fulfillment with and without EDI. (*Source:* Drawn by E. Turban)

benefits are quick to realize when a company has a large number of suppliers, such as in the case of Baxter Canada in Example 9.3.

Example 9.3

Baxter Canada, a subsidiary of Baxter International Inc., manufactures a wide arrange of medical supplies that are used by hospitals, kidney dialysis clinics, nursing homes, rehabilitation centres, doctors' offices, clinical and medical research laboratories, and by patients at home under physician supervision.

The company sources the materials and components that it needs to manufacture these products from a large number of suppliers. In order to streamline the purchasing process among so many suppliers, Baxter Canada allows them to process their purchases using electronic data interchange (EDI) technology that can be linked to the suppliers' materials management information system or their enterprise resource planning system. Baxter Canada uses EDI with its suppliers to support transactions such as invoicing, processing payments, and sending information about prices and products.

EDI does have some disadvantages. Business processes sometimes must be restructured to fit EDI requirements. Also, many EDI standards are in use today, so one company might have to use several standards in order to communicate with multiple business partners.

In today's world, where virtually every business has a broadband connection to the Internet and where multi-megabyte design files, product photographs, and PDF sales brochures are routinely e-mailed, the value of reducing a structured e-commerce message from a few thousand XML bytes to a few hundred EDI bytes is negligible. As a result, EDI is being replaced by XML-based web services. (You will learn about XML in Technology Guide 3.)

Extranets

To implement IOSs and SCM systems, a company must connect the intranets of its various business partners to create extranets. Extranets link business partners over the Internet by providing them access to certain areas of each other's corporate intranets (see Figure 9.7).

The primary goal of extranets is to foster collaboration between and among business partners. An extranet is open to selected B2B suppliers, customers, and other business partners. These individuals access the extranet through the Internet. Extranets enable people located outside a company to collaborate with the company's internal employees. An extranet also allows external business partners to enter the corporate intranet, via the Internet, to access data, place orders, check the status of those orders, communicate, and collaborate. It also enables partners to perform self-service activities such as checking inventory levels.

Extranets use virtual private network (VPN) technology to make communication over the Internet more secure. The major benefits of extranets are faster processes and information flow, improved order entry and customer service, lower costs (for example, communications, travel, and administrative overhead), and overall improved business effectiveness.

There are three major types of extranets. The type that a company chooses depends on the business partners involved and the purpose of the supply chain. Each type is presented below, along with its major business applications.

A Company and Its Dealers, Customers, or Suppliers.

This type of extranet centres on a single company. An example is the FedEx extranet, which allows customers to track the status of a delivery. To do so, customers use the Internet to access a database on the FedEx intranet. By enabling a customer to check the location of a package, FedEx saves the cost of having a human operator perform that task over the phone.

Sometimes extranets are part of corporate portals. As you saw in Chapter 4, corporate portals offer a single point of access through a web browser to critical business information in an organization. In the context of business-to-business supply chain management, these portals enable companies and their suppliers to collaborate very closely.

There are two basic types of corporate portals: procurement (sourcing) portals for a company's suppliers (upstream in the supply chain), and distribution portals for a company's customers (downstream in the supply chain). **Procurement portals** automate the business processes involved in purchasing or procuring products between a single buyer and multiple suppliers. For example, Boeing has deployed a procurement portal called the Boeing Supplier Portal (*www.boeingsuppliers.com*) through which it conducts business with its suppliers. **Distribution portals** automate the business processes involved in selling or distributing products from a single supplier to multiple buyers. For example, Dell services its business customers through its distribution portal at *http://premier.dell.com.*

Sources: Compiled from *www.123edi.com*, *www.baxter.ca*, accessed May 24, 2013.

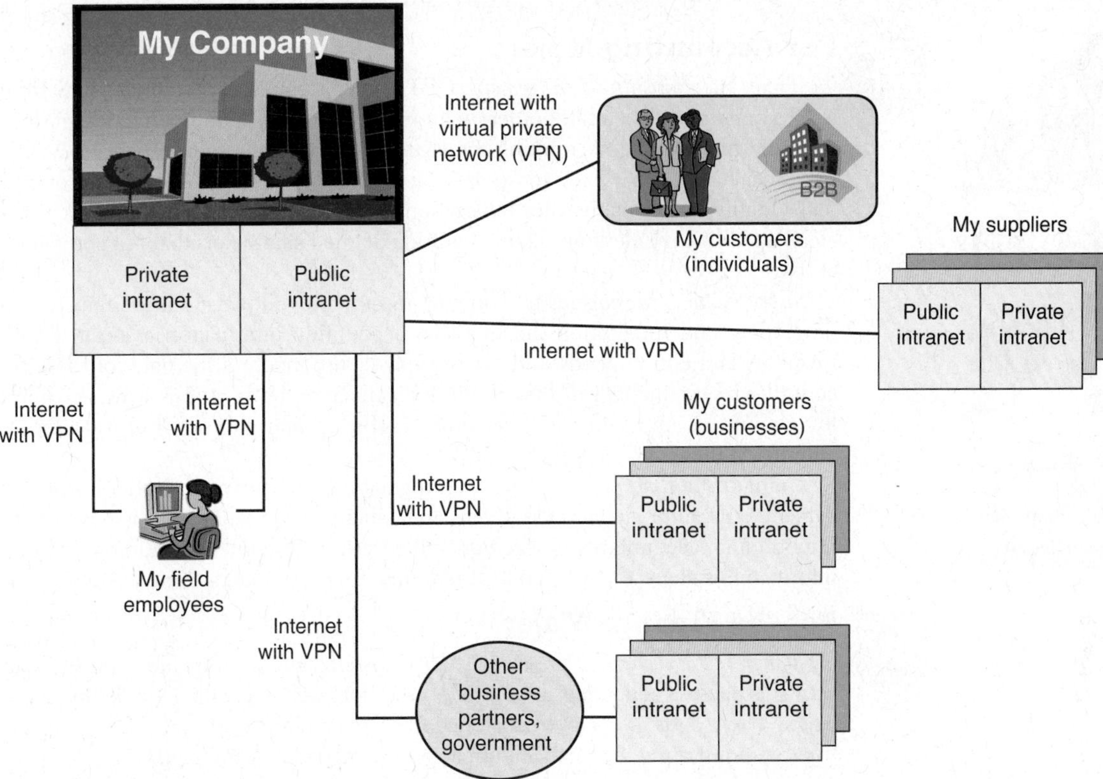

FIGURE 9.7 The structure of an extranet.

An Industry's Extranet. Just as a single company can set up an extranet, the major players in an industry can team up to create an extranet that will benefit all of them. For example, ANXeBusiness (*www.anx.com*) enables companies to collaborate effectively through a network that provides a secure global medium for B2B information exchange. The ANX Network is used for mission-critical business transactions by leading international organizations in aerospace, automotive, chemical, electronics, financial services, health care, logistics, manufacturing, transportation, and related industries. The network offers customers a reliable extranet and VPN services.

Joint Ventures and Other Business Partnerships. In this type of extranet, the partners in a joint venture use the extranet as a vehicle for communications and collaboration. An example is Bank of America's (*www.bankofamerica.com*) extranet for commercial loans. The partners involved in making these loans include a lender, a loan broker, and a title company. The extranet connects lenders, loan applicants, and the loan organizer, Bank of America. A similar case is Lending Tree (*www.lendingtree.com*), a company that provides mortgage quotes and also sells mortgages on-line. Lending Tree uses an extranet for its business partners (for example, the lenders).

before you go on...

1. Define EDI, and list its major benefits and limitations.
2. Define an extranet, and explain its infrastructure.
3. List and briefly define the major types of extranets.
4. Differentiate between procurement portals and distribution portals.

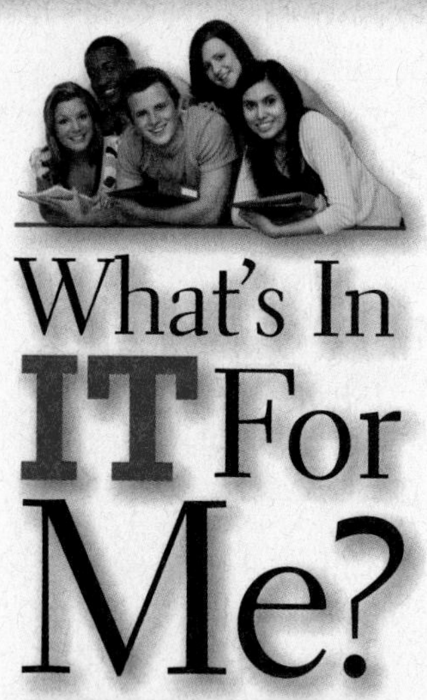

For Accounting Majors

Customer Relationship Management. CRM systems can track document flow from a sales opportunity, to a sales order, to an invoice, to an accounting document, thus enabling finance and accounting managers to monitor the entire flow. CRM systems that track sales quotes and orders can be used to incorporate process controls that identify questionable sales transactions. CRM systems can provide exception-alert capabilities to identify instances outside defined parameters that put companies at risk.

Supply Chain Management. The cost accountant will play an important role in developing and monitoring the financial accounting information associated with inventory and cost of goods sold. In a supply chain, much of the data for these accounting requirements will flow into the organization from various partners within the chain. It is up to the chief accountant—the comptroller or CFO—to prepare and review these data.

Going further, accounting rules and regulations and the cross-border transfer of data are critical for global trade. IOSs can facilitate such trade. Other issues that are important for accountants are taxation and government reports. In addition, creating information systems that rely on EDI requires the attention of accountants.

For the Finance Major

Customer Relationship Management. CRM systems allow companies to track marketing expenses, collecting appropriate costs for each individual marketing campaign. These costs then can be matched to corporate initiatives and financial objectives, demonstrating the financial impact of the marketing campaign.

Pricing is another key area that impacts financial reporting. For example, what discounts are available? When can a price be overridden? Who approves discounts? CRM systems can put controls into place for these issues.

Supply Chain Management. In a supply chain, the finance major will be responsible for analyzing the data created and shared among supply chain partners. In many instances, the financial analyst will recommend actions to improve supply chain efficiencies and cash flow. This may benefit all the partners in the chain. These recommendations will be based on financial models that incorporate key assumptions such as supply chain partner agreements for pricing. Through the use of extensive financial modelling, the financial analyst helps to manage liquidity in the supply chain.

Many finance-related issues exist in implementing IOSs. For one thing, establishing EDI and extranet relationships involves structuring payment agreements. Global supply chains may involve complex financial arrangements, which may have legal implications.

For the Marketing Major

Customer Relationship Management. CRM systems are an integral part of every marketing professional's work activities. CRM systems contain the consolidated customer data that provide the foundation for making informed marketing decisions. Using these data, marketers develop well-timed and targeted sales campaigns with customized product mixes and established price points that enhance potential sales opportunities and therefore increase revenue. CRM systems also support the development of forecasting models for future sales to existing clients through the use of historical data captured from previous transactions.

Supply Chain Management. A tremendous amount of useful sales information can be derived from supply chain partners through the supporting information systems. For example, many of the customer support activities take place in the downstream portion of the supply chain. For the marketing manager, an understanding of how the downstream activities of the supply chain relate to prior chain operations is critical.

Further, a tremendous amount of data is fed from the supply chain supporting information systems into the CRM systems that are used by marketers. The information and a complete understanding of its genesis are vital for mixed-model marketing programs.

For the **Production/Operations Management Major**

Customer Relationship Management. Production is heavily involved in the acquisition of raw materials, conversion, and distribution of finished goods. However, all of these activities are driven by sales. Increases or decreases in the demand for goods result in a corresponding increase or decrease in a company's need for raw materials. Integral to a company's demand is forecasting future sales, an important part of CRM systems. Sales forecasts are created from the historical data stored in CRM systems.

This information is critically important to a production manager who is placing orders for manufacturing processes. Without an accurate future sales forecast, production managers may face inventory problems. The use of CRM systems for production and operational support is critical to efficiently managing the resources of the company.

Supply Chain Management. The production/operations management major plays a major role in the supply chain development process. In many organizations, the production/operations management staff may even lead the supply chain integration process because of their extensive knowledge of the manufacturing components of the organization. Because they are in charge of procurement, production, materials control, and logistical handling, a comprehensive understanding of the techniques of SCM is vital for the production/operations staff.

The downstream segment of supply chains is where marketing, distribution channels, and customer service are conducted. An understanding of how downstream activities are related to the other segments is critical. Supply chain problems can reduce customer satisfaction and negate marketing efforts. It is essential, then, that marketing professionals understand the nature of such problems and their solutions. Also, learning about CRM, its options, and its implementation is important for designing effective customer services and advertising.

As competition intensifies globally, finding new global markets becomes critical. Use of IOSs provides an opportunity to improve marketing and sales. Understanding the capabilities of these technologies as well as their implementation issues will enable the marketing department to excel.

For the **Human Resources Major**

Customer Relationship Management. Companies trying to enhance their customer relationships must recognize that employees who interact with customers are critical to the success of CRM strategies. Essentially, the success of CRM is based on the employees' desire and ability to promote the company and its CRM initiatives. In fact, research analysts have found that customer loyalty is based largely on employees' capabilities and their commitment to the company.

As a result, human resource managers know that a company that desires valued customer relationships needs valued relationships with its employees. Therefore, HR managers are implementing programs to increase employee satisfaction and are training employees to execute CRM strategies.

Supply Chain Management. Supply chains require interactions among the employees of partners in the chain. These interactions are the responsibility of the human resources manager. The HR manager must be able to address supply chain issues that relate to staffing, job descriptions, job rotations, and accountability. All of these areas are complex within a supply chain and require the HR function to understand the relationship among partners as well as the movement of resources.

Preparing and training employees to work with business partners (frequently in foreign countries) requires knowledge about how IOSs operate. Sensitivity to cultural differences and extensive communication and collaboration can be facilitated with IT.

For the MIS Major

Customer Relationship Management. The IT function in the enterprise is responsible for the corporate databases and data warehouse, as well as the correctness and completeness of the data in them. That is, the IT department provides the data used in a 360-degree view of the customer. Further, IT personnel provide the technologies underlying the customer interaction centre.

Supply Chain Management. The MIS staff will be instrumental in the design and support of information systems—both internal organizational and interorganizational—that will underpin the business processes that are part of the supply chain. In this capacity, the MIS staff must have a concise knowledge of the business, the systems, and the points of intersection between the two.

[Summary]

1. Define "customer relationship management" and "collaborative CRM," and identify the primary functions of both processes.

Customer relationship management (CRM) is an organizational strategy that is customer focused and customer driven. That is, organizations concentrate on assessing customers' requirements for products and services and then providing high-quality, responsive service. CRM functions include acquiring new customers, retaining existing customers, and growing relationships with existing customers.

Collaborative CRM is an organizational CRM strategy where data consolidation and the 360-degree view of the customer enable the organization's functional areas to readily share information about customers. The functions of collaborative CRM include integrating communications between the organization and its customers in all aspects of marketing, sales, and customer support processes, and enabling customers to provide direct feedback to the organization.

2. Describe the two major components of operational CRM systems, list three applications used in each component, and provide at least one example of how businesses use each application.

Operational CRM systems support the front-office business processes that interact directly with customers (i.e., sales, marketing, and service). The two major components of operational CRM systems are customer-facing applications and customer-touching applications.

Customer-facing CRM applications include customer service and support, sales force automation, marketing, and campaign management. *Customer-touching applications* include search and comparison capabilities, technical and other information and services, customized products and services, personalized web pages, FAQs, e-mail and automated response, and loyalty programs.

3. Define "analytical CRM systems," and describe four purposes for which businesses use these systems.

Analytical CRM systems analyze customer behaviour and perceptions in order to provide business intelligence. Organizations use analytical systems for many purposes, including designing and executing targeted marketing campaigns; increasing customer acquisition, cross selling, and up selling; providing input into decisions relating to products and services (e.g., pricing, and product development); and providing financial forecasting and customer profitability analysis.

4. **Define "mobile CRM systems," "on-demand CRM systems," and "open-source CRM systems," and identify one main advantage and one main drawback of each.**

   Mobile CRM systems are interactive systems where communications related to sales, marketing, and customer service activities are conducted through a mobile medium for the purpose of building and maintaining customer relationships between an organization and its customers. Advantages of mobile CRM systems include convenience for customers and the chance to build a truly personal relationship with customers. A drawback could be difficulty in maintaining customer expectations; that is, the company must be extremely responsive to customer needs in a mobile, near-real-time environment.

   On-demand CRM systems are those hosted by an external vendor in the vendor's data centre. Advantages of on-demand CRM systems include lower costs and a need for employees to know only how to access and use the software. Drawbacks include possibly unreliable vendors, difficulty in modifying the software, and difficulty in integrating vendor-hosted CRM software with the organization's existing software.

   Open-source CRM systems are those whose source code is available to developers and users. The benefits of open-source CRM systems include favourable pricing, a wide variety of applications, easy customization, rapid updates and bug (software error) fixes, and extensive free support information. The major drawback of open-source CRM systems is quality control.

5. **Define "supply chain," and describe the three components and the three flows of a supply chain.**

   A *supply chain* is the flow of materials, information, money, and services from raw material suppliers, through factories and warehouses, to the end customers. A supply chain involves three segments: upstream, where sourcing or procurement from external suppliers occurs; internal, where packaging, assembly, or manufacturing takes place; and downstream, where distribution takes place, frequently by external distributors.

   There are three flows in the supply chain: *material flows*, which are the physical products, raw materials, supplies, and so forth; *information flows*, which consist of data related to demand, shipments, orders, returns, and schedules, as well as changes in any of these data; and *financial flows*, which involve money transfers, payments, credit card information and authorization, payment schedules, e-payments, and credit-related data.

6. **Identify two major challenges in setting accurate inventory levels throughout the supply chain, and describe three popular strategies to solve supply chain problems.**

   Two major challenges in setting accurate inventory levels throughout a supply chain are the *demand forecast* and the *bullwhip effect*. Demand for a product can be influenced by numerous factors such as competition, prices, weather conditions, technological developments, economic conditions, and customers' general confidence. The *bullwhip effect* is erratic shifts in orders up and down the supply chain.

   The most common solution to supply chain problems is *building inventories* as insurance against supply chain uncertainties. Another solution is the *just-in-time (JIT)* inventory system, which delivers the precise number of parts, called *work-in-process inventory*, to be assembled into a finished product at precisely the right time. The third possible solution is *vendor-managed inventory (VMI)*, which occurs when the vendor, rather than the retailer, manages the entire inventory process for a particular product or group of products.

7. Define "electronic data interchange (EDI)," "extranet," and "portal," and explain how each of these applications helps support supply chain management.

Electronic data interchange (EDI) is a communication standard that enables the electronic transfer of routine documents, such as purchasing orders, between business partners.

Extranets are networks that link business partners over the Internet by providing them access to certain areas of each other's corporate intranets. The main goal of extranets is to foster collaboration among business partners.

Corporate portals offer a single point of access through a web browser to critical business information in an organization. In the context of business-to-business supply chain management, these portals enable companies and their suppliers to collaborate very closely.

[Chapter Glossary]

analytical CRM system CRM system that analyzes customer behaviour and perceptions in order to provide actionable business intelligence.

bullwhip effect Erratic shifts in orders up and down the supply chain.

bundling A form of cross selling where an enterprise sells a group of products or services together at a lower price than the combined individual price of the products.

campaign management applications CRM applications that help organizations plan marketing campaigns that send the right messages to the right people through the right channels.

collaborative CRM system A CRM system where communications between the organization and its customers are integrated across all aspects of marketing, sales, and customer support processes.

cross selling The practice of marketing additional related products to customers based on a previous purchase.

customer-facing CRM applications Areas where customers directly interact with the organization, including customer service and support, sales force automation, marketing, and campaign management.

customer interaction centre (CIC) A CRM operation where organizational representatives use multiple communication channels to interact with customers in functions such as inbound teleservice and outbound telesales.

customer relationship management (CRM) A customer-focused and customer-driven organizational strategy that concentrates on addressing customers' requirements for products and services, and then providing high-quality, responsive service.

customer-touching CRM applications (electronic CRM or **e-CRM)** Applications and technologies with which customers interact and typically help themselves.

customer touch point Any interaction between a customer and an organization.

distribution portals Corporate portals that automate the business processes involved in selling or distributing products from a single supplier to multiple buyers.

electronic CRM (e-CRM) (see **customer-touching CRM applications**)

electronic data interchange (EDI) A communication standard that enables the electronic transfer of routine documents between business partners.

interorganizational information system (IOS) An information system that supports information flow among two or more organizations.

just-in-time (JIT) inventory system A system in which a supplier delivers the precise number of parts to be assembled into a finished product at precisely the right time.

loyalty program Program that offers rewards to customers to influence future behaviour.

mobile CRM system An interactive CRM system where communications related to sales, marketing, and customer service activities are conducted through a mobile medium for the purpose of building and maintaining customer relationships between an organization and its customers.

on-demand CRM system A CRM system that is hosted by an external vendor in the vendor's data centre.

open-source CRM system CRM software whose source code is available to developers and users.

operational CRM system The component of CRM that supports the front-office business processes that directly interact with customers (i.e., sales, marketing, and service).

procurement portals Corporate portals that automate the business processes involved in purchasing or procuring products between a single buyer and multiple suppliers.

pull model A business model in which the production process begins with a customer order and companies make only what customers want, a process closely aligned with mass customization.

push model A business model in which the production process begins with a forecast, which predicts the products that customers will want as well as the quantity of each product. The company then produces the amount of products in the forecast, typically by using mass production, and sells, or "pushes," those products to consumers.

sales force automation (SFA) The component of an operational CRM system that automatically records all the aspects in a sales transaction process.

supply chain The coordinated movement of resources from organizations through conversion to the end consumer.

supply chain management (SCM) An activity in which the leadership of an organization provides extensive oversight for the partnerships and processes that compose the supply chain and leverages these relationships to provide an operational advantage.

supply chain visibility The ability of all organizations in a supply chain to access or view relevant data on purchased materials as these materials move through their suppliers' production processes.

up selling A sales strategy where the organizational representative provides to customers the opportunity to purchase higher-value related products or services in place of, or along with, the consumer's initial product or service selection.

vendor-managed inventory (VMI) An inventory strategy where the supplier monitors a vendor's inventory for a product or group of products and replenishes products when needed.

vertical integration Strategy of integrating the upstream part of the supply chain with the internal part, typically by purchasing upstream suppliers, in order to ensure timely availability of supplies.

[Discussion Questions]

1. How do customer relationship management systems help organizations achieve customer intimacy?
2. What is the relationship between data consolidation and CRM systems?
3. Discuss the relationship between CRM and customer privacy.
4. Distinguish between operational CRM systems and analytical CRM systems.
5. Differentiate between customer-facing CRM applications and customer-touching CRM applications.
6. Explain why web-based customer interaction centres are critical for successful CRM systems.
7. Why are companies so interested in e-CRM applications?
8. Discuss why it is difficult to justify CRM applications.
9. You are the CIO of a small company with a rapidly growing customer base. Which CRM system would you use: an on-premise CRM system, an on-demand CRM system, or an open-source CRM system? Remember that open-source CRM systems may be implemented either on-premise or on-demand. Discuss the pros and cons of each type of CRM system for your business.
10. Refer to the example concerning the CRM efforts of Chinatrust Philippines. Where on the CRM continuum (low-end to high-end) does the company's CRM strategy fit? Explain your answer.
11. List and explain the important components of a supply chain.
12. Explain how a supply chain approach may be part of a company's overall strategy.
13. Explain the important role that information systems play in supporting a supply chain strategy.
14. Would Rolls-Royce Motorcars (*www.rolls-roycemotorcars.com*) use a push model or a pull model in its supply chain? Support your answer.
15. Why is planning so important in supply chain management?

[Problem-Solving Activities]

1. Access *www.ups.com* and *www.fedex.com*. Examine some of the IT-supported customer services and tools provided by the two companies. Compare and contrast the customer support provided on the two companies' websites.
2. Enter *www.anntaylor.com*, *www.hermes.com*, and *www.tiffany.com*. Compare and contrast the customer service activities offered by these companies on their websites. Do you see marked similarities? Differences?
3. Access your university's website. Investigate how your university provides for customer relationship management. (Hint: First decide who your university's customers are.)
4. Access *www.sugarcrm.com* and take the interactive tour. Prepare a report on SugarCRM's functionality to the class.
5. Access *www.ups.com* and *www.fedex.com*. Examine some of the IT-supported customer services and tools provided by the two companies. Write a report on how the two companies contribute to supply chain improvements.
6. Enter *www.supply-chain.org*, *www.cio.com*, and *www.google.com*, and search for recent information on IT developments in supply chain management.
7. GXS (*www.gxs.com*) is one of the largest providers of EDI services worldwide. Review what EDI products it provides and prepare a report. Would a small company be able to implement these solutions? Prepare a report with your analysis.

[Spreadsheet Activity 1: Mail Merge as CRM]

Objective: Customer relationship management (CRM) is very important in today's market. Competition is reaching new frontiers with global companies doing business in rural areas that have traditionally been served by small mom-and-pop companies. How, exactly, can these smaller companies survive without the complex CRM tools available to the "big-box" companies? Although some tools are free (open-source), they do not come with customer support or instruction manuals. It is good to be aware of some of the tasks that CRM tools can help with that can also be accomplished in an Excel spreadsheet. This activity will walk you through the steps of automating and customizing customer engagement based on recent activity.

Chapter Connection: CRM is an excellent use of technology. It is probably easy for you to understand because you are often on the "receiving" end of this particular system. However, you also experience many of its flaws because you receive invitations and coupons that you do not use. This money ends up being wasted because it did not bring its target customer into the store. This activity teaches you how to use a simple spreadsheet to create your own basic CRM. Although it is a very basic function and a poor example of a CRM solution, it does show how simple tools such as Excel and Word can be used to create helpful systems.

Activity: A year ago, Dustin was very busy in his shop. That was before Walmart opened its Tire & Lube Express. Now a lot of Dustin's customers have switched to Walmart for the convenience of having their vehicle serviced while they shop. However, Dustin has an idea. He has created a spreadsheet of data from all customers who have brought their car to him on a regular basis. He wants to contact them with a personal letter to try to win back their service. Dustin wants to thank his customers for past business and draw on their hometown emotions to pull them back to him in spite of Walmart's convenience and lower price. Although he cannot afford an expensive CRM tool, he does remember something about Microsoft Excel having a mail merge feature that would allow him to rapidly produce customized letters for the mail.

Visit *www.wiley.com/go/rainer/spreadsheet* and click on the first link provided for Chapter 9. This will take you to Microsoft's website and an explanation of how the mail merge process works. It is a simple process and it is explained in just a couple of pages. Once you feel comfortable with the concept, visit *www.wiley.com/go/rainer/spreadsheet* again and click on the second link provided. Here you can download the files required for Chapter 9. There will be an Excel spreadsheet and the Word document that Dustin plans to mail out. Your activity is to connect the two such that the letters will be automatically created for multiple customers at one time. After you connect the files, produce a batch of letters ready to send out to customers.

Deliverable: Submit your spreadsheet and Word document, which are linked such that your work can be checked. Your instructor will choose how many letters need to be submitted.

Discussion Questions

1. CRM does not have to be complicated; it is simply an effort to reach out to the customer to develop and/or maintain loyalty. As such, simple tools like Excel's mail merge tool can be used to touch customers on a personal basis. In what other ways could this tool be used in place of a more complex and more expensive CRM?
2. What do you think should be the determining factor regarding the type of CRM to use? Given that simple Excel tools can be used to reach customers, why would a company spend lots of time and energy implementing a system that may not reach more customers than the Excel tools would? What creates the "breaking point" of when things need to change?

[Spreadsheet Activity 2: Project Management in Excel]

Objective: Supply chain management is a vital operation for organizations—so much so that if one supplier fails to do its job, the entire operation may be shut down. Microsoft Excel is often used to assist in this basic planning. Logic and algebra can be applied in a spreadsheet to make simple calculations that apply within the supply chain scenario.

Chapter Connection: At one time, Dell Computer realized it had almost perfected the assembly process within its plant. The only way to improve its product was to improve the entire supply chain. So Dell began working with its suppliers to streamline its processes. Although its supply chain system is too complex for a spreadsheet, the principle applies to many situations.

This activity will take a simpler scenario and introduce the concept of planning for the supply chain and using spreadsheet tools to improve the process.

Activity: Mr. Stephens works in construction. Specifically, he builds custom homes. He always gets complaints about his work being late, even though his customers are generally happy with the final product. To try to deal with the complaints and to give his customers a better understanding of when their home will be complete, he wants to build a spreadsheet that will lay out the entire process of building the home, specify the amount of time each part will take, and build in time for bad weather, corrections, and other issues that always arise.

Mr. Stephens compiled the following data for his next construction job. Although he ultimately wants to create a universal spreadsheet, for now he just wants to work on the concept and get it to work for this next job. Use the data and build him a spreadsheet that has the job description in one column and other columns for start date, earliest end date, and latest end date. Unless otherwise noted, these steps are performed in order, and one cannot begin until the previous step is completed.

1. Groundwork will take 3 to 4 days.
2. Footers will take 2 to 3 days.
3. Block work for crawl space will take 7 to 10 days.
4. Foundation will take 3 to 4 days. Lumber should be ordered a week in advance.
5. Remaining frame will take 2 to 3 weeks. Home should be dried-in at this time.
6. Exterior oriented strand board (OSB) and house wrap will take 7 to 10 days.
7. Electrical work may begin at this point. It will take 8 to 12 days to complete the rough-in wiring for the home.
8. Rough-in plumbing work may begin when the exterior OSB is complete. Rough-in plumbing will take 5 to 7 days.
9. Insulation and drywall may go up at this time when both electrical and plumbing are roughed in. It will take 17 to 21 days to complete the installation of the exterior and interior walls' insulation as well as the drywall work.
10. Cabinetry and final electrical work may begin at this point. Cabinetry will take 1 to 3 days, and the finish work on electrical items will take 7 to 10 days. Cabinets should be ordered a month in advance.
11. The final plumbing work may begin when the cabinets are complete and will take 3 to 5 days to complete.
12. All work on the rest of the house may begin at this time. Paint, trim, and flooring typically take 2 to 3 weeks.

Given this description from Mr. Stephens, build a spreadsheet that will allow him to demonstrate to his customers how long it takes to build a home. Use a start date of May 1 and allow two weeks for weather delays. Given this information, determine the projected end date if everything finishes as early as possible and the projected end date if everything takes as long as possible.

Deliverable: Submit your spreadsheet along with a Word document that answers the questions listed below.

Discussion Questions

1. Supply chain management is extremely important in today's business environment. Look up some supply chain management tools and compare them with your Excel activity. Discuss the advantages and disadvantages of these systems. What do they provide that the spreadsheet example does not?
2. Given that some refer to supply chains as a web rather than a chain, what type of problems do you see arising from a parent company's need to share information with so many others at the same time? Also, what complications arise from the suppliers needing to share information? Which company should determine the platform and methods of sharing data?

[Case Assignments]

BLOSS is a retailer of jeans and casual clothing. It operates over 80 retail and factory stores in Canada, over 300 in-store shops in other retailers, and sells merchandise in over 40 countries worldwide. In order to support its operating activities, BLOSS implemented an information system for its suppliers and independent retailers in Canada and 55 other countries called Apparel Buying Network. The company can use the Apparel Buying Network to purchase direct items such as trim, fabric, and finished goods and indirect items such as office and maintenance supplies. Store buyers can order merchandise directly from BLOSS by entering their purchases on a private website called ApparelBuy.com, which is integrated with the firm's core order processing system.

BLOSS also maintains a public website for retail customers called BLOSS.com, which offers product catalogues and merchandise ordering on-line. This e-commerce site generates as many sales as one of the BLOSS flagship stores. BLOSS established BabyBLOSS.com and BLOSSKids.com as e-commerce sites for retailing infants' and children's clothing and accessories. BLOSS is also using Internet technology to streamline its internal business processes. BLOSSExpress is an internal private network based on Internet technology that is used for purchasing from suppliers, reviewing architectural plans for new stores, making travel arrangements, and broadcasting messages to managers about operating instructions and company and industry trends.

Required

a. Provide three specific examples of customer-touching applications that BLOSS could use in relation to its website BLOSS.com.
b. Describe analytical CRM and explain how BLOSS could use it.
c. Provide two examples of how BLOSS could use mobile CRM.
d. Define EDI and provide three examples of how BLOSS could use EDI with its suppliers.
e. According to the material discussed in the chapter, which type of SCM system would you consider the Apparel Buying Network to be? What about BLOSSExpress? Justify your answer.

[Team Assignments]

1. Assign each group to an open-source CRM vendor. Each group should examine the vendor, its products, and the capabilities of those products and make a presentation to the class detailing how its vendor's product is superior to the other open-source CRM products. See SugarCRM (*www.sugarcrm.com*), Concursive (*www.concursive.com*), vtiger (*www.vtiger.com*), SplendidCRM Software (*www.splendidcrm.com*), Compiere (*www.compiere.com*), Hipergate (*http://sourceforge.net/projects/hipergate/*), and openCRX (*www.opencrx.com*).

2. Assign each group to an on-demand CRM vendor. Each group should examine each vendor, its products, and the capabilities of those products and make a presentation to the class detailing how its vendor's product is superior to the other on-demand CRM products. See Salesforce (*www.salesforce.com*), Oracle (*http://crmondemand.oracle.com*), Aplicor (*www.aplicor.com*), NetSuite (*www.netsuite.com*), SalesNexus (*www.salesnexus.com*), SageCRM (*www.sagecrm.com*), Commence (*www.commence.com*), and eSalesTrack (*www.esalestrack.com*).
3. Create groups to investigate the major CRM applications and their vendors.
   - Sales force automation (Microsoft Dynamics, Oracle, FrontRange Solutions, Maximizer Software)
   - Call centres (LivePerson, Cisco, Oracle)
   - Marketing automation (SalesNexus, Marketo, Chordiant [now part of Pegasystems], Infor, Consona, Pivotal, Oracle)
   - Customer service (Oracle, Amazon, Dell, Sage)

   Start with *www.searchcrm.com* and *www.customerthink.com* (to ask questions about CRM solutions). Have each group present arguments to convince the class members to use the product(s) the group investigated.
4. Assign each group in the class to a major supply chain management vendor, such as SAP, Oracle, and IBM. Each group will investigate topics such as (a) the products, (b) major capabilities, (c) relationship to customer relationship management, and (d) customer success stories. Each group will prepare a presentation for the class, trying to convince the class why that group's software product is best.
5. Have each team locate several organizations that use IOSs, including one with a global reach. You should contact the companies to find out what IOS technology support they use (for example, an EDI, an extranet, etc.) and what issues they faced in implementation. Prepare a report.

[Case 9.2 **IT Helps Cannondale Manage Its Complex Supply Chain**]

The Problem

Cannondale (*www.cannondale.com*), a division of Montreal-based Dorel Industries, is a pioneer in the engineering and manufacturing of high-end bicycles, apparel, footwear, and accessories for independent dealers and distributors in more than 66 countries. Cannondale designs, develops, and produces bicycles at its factory in Bedford, Pennsylvania, and it operates subsidiaries in Holland, Switzerland, Japan, and Australia. As a leading custom bicycle manufacturer with an extensive and impressive customer list, including Olympic athletes, professional racing teams, and Tour de France competitors, Cannondale realizes that meeting customer demands and expectations is critical to its success.

Cannondale produces more than 100 different bicycle models annually, 60 percent of which are newly introduced lines. Because Cannondale is an international company that works in a cyclical business affected by market and weather conditions, the firm is faced with highly complex and volatile consumer demand. In addition to constantly shifting demand and a rapidly changing product portfolio, Cannondale has a global supply chain that must integrate global manufacturing, assembly, and sales and distribution sites.

Cannondale manufactures both make-to-order and make-to-stock models. Consequently, the company needs to manage a range of product batch sizes, sometimes including one-of-a-kind orders. A typical bicycle requires a 150-day lead time with a four-week manufacturing window, and some bicycles have more than 250 parts in their bills of materials (BOMs). (A bill of materials specifies the raw materials, assemblies, components, and parts needed to manufacture a final product, along with the quantities of each.) Cannondale has to manage more than 1 million BOMs and more than 200,000 individual parts. Adding to Cannondale's manufacturing complexity, some of these parts are supplied by specialty vendors who require long lead times and have only limited production capacity. This complexity significantly challenged Cannondale's capacity to quickly deliver complex and custom products that meet its customers' high expectations.

In order to manage parts availability and varying customer demands, Cannondale's manufacturing operations need to be highly flexible. Therefore, the company needed a global system that allowed managers to access all plant inventory levels and supply schedules to better manage shifts in product and customer demand.

Cannondale had been using a legacy material requirements planning system (MRP II) that generated weekly reports. Because Cannondale's manufacturing environment is so dynamic, however, by Tuesday afternoon Monday's reports were so outdated that they were useless. The supply chain team had to substitute parts in order to meet demand, causing an ever-increasing parts flow problem. Cannondale's primary objective was to find an IT solution that would improve the accuracy of the company's parts flow, support the company's need for flexibility, and operate within the confines of its existing business systems—all at an affordable cost.

The Solution

Cannondale selected the Kinaxis RapidResponse (*www.kinaxis.com*) system for its integrated demand and supply planning and monitoring. RapidResponse provides users with necessary information in minutes, as opposed to eight hours with the previous system. RapidResponse generates accurate and detailed supply chain information with an easy-to-use spreadsheet user interface, employing data supplied from the company's existing MRP II systems.

RapidResponse has transformed Cannondale's entire supply chain. Buyers, planners, master schedulers, sourcers (people who procure products), product managers, customer service personnel, and financial managers use the system for sales reporting, forecasting, monitoring daily inventory availability, and providing production schedule information to the MRP II and order-processing systems. Supply chain participants located around the world now can instantly simulate, share, and score what-if scenarios to evaluate and select the actions they need to take to respond to changing supply and demand conditions.

Company managers now receive up-to-date visibility of global operations. In addition, the management team uses RapidResponse daily to examine the company's manufacturing backlog. Having access to current information enables the team to compare old forecasts with new ones.

The Results

Today, Cannondale responds to customer orders quickly, and it has significantly reduced its inventory, together with its associated costs. In addition, the company has benefitted from higher inventory turns, reductions in safety stock (extra inventory held to avoid shortages), improvement in cycle times, reduced lead times, and more accurate promise dates. As a result, customer satisfaction has improved. All of these benefits have provided Cannondale with a competitive advantage in a highly competitive industry.

Questions

1. Describe Cannondale's complex manufacturing environment, and identify some of the problems that this environment created.
2. Describe the RapidResponse system's impact on Cannondale's global supply chain management.
3. Draw a diagram of Cannondale's supply chain, including the physical flow, information flow, and financial flow.
4. Provide two examples describing other types of IT solutions to support the supply chain that Cannondale could use.

Sources: Compiled from B. Ferrari, "Kinaxis RapidResponse—Much More Than a Planning Application," *Supply Chain Matters*, January 8, 2010; Kinaxis Corporation, "Cannondale Improves Customer Response Times While Reducing Inventory Using RapidResponse," *Kinaxis Customer Spotlight*, 2010; A. Ackerman, "Cannondale's Supply Chain Is Built for Speed," *Consumer Goods Technology*, October 15, 2008; *www.kinaxis.com*, *www.cannondale.com*, accessed May 24, 2013.

[Interactive Cases]

Planning CRM Solutions for Ruby's Club

Go to the Ruby's Club link at the Student Companion website or *WileyPLUS* for information about your current internship assignment. You will investigate how CRM can help retain customers at Ruby's Club.

Creating Supply Chain Management Solutions for Ruby's Club

Go to the Ruby's Club link at the Student Companion website or *WileyPLUS* for information about your current internship assignment. You will help Ruby's managers build a better forecast for purchasing food and drinks using past data.

Chapter 10

Business Intelligence

[LEARNING OBJECTIVES]	[CHAPTER OUTLINE]	[WEB RESOURCES]

1. Identify the phases in the decision-making process, and use a decision-support framework to demonstrate how technology supports managerial decision making.
2. Describe and provide examples of the three different ways in which organizations use business intelligence (BI).
3. Specify the BI applications available to users for data analysis, and provide examples of how each one might be used to solve a business problem at your university.
4. Describe three BI applications that present the results of data analyses to users, and offer examples of how businesses and government agencies can use each of these technologies.
5. Describe corporate performance management, and provide an example of how your university could use CPM.

Student Companion Site

wiley.com/college/rainer

- Student PowerPoints for note taking
- Interactive Case: Ruby's Club Assignments
- Complete glossary

WileyPlus

All of the above and

- E-book
- Mini-lecture by author for each chapter section
- Practice quizzes
- Flash Cards for vocabulary review
- Additional "What's in IT for Me?" cases
- Video interviews with managers
- Lab Manual for Microsoft Office 2010
- How-to Animations for Microsoft Office 2010

What's In IT For Me?
THIS CHAPTER WILL HELP PREPARE YOU TO ...
ACCT
Uncover fraudulent transactions
FIN
Make stock market investment decisions
MKT
Allocate advertising budgets
POM
Schedule production activities
HR
Control job applicant process
MIS
Provide information in dashboards

[Case 10.1 Quality Assurance at Daimler AG]

The Business Problem

German automaker Daimler AG's (*www.daimler.com*) divisions include Mercedes-Benz Cars, Daimler Trucks, Mercedes-Benz Vans, Daimler Buses, and Daimler Financial Services. The central tenet of Daimler's strategy is quality assurance, meaning that the company guarantees complete customer satisfaction. Daimler collects quality assurance data from the vehicles themselves, from garage service centres, and from related operations. In the past, the company relied on a variety of data stored in separate databases: warranty and billing information, diagnostic data downloaded from on-board vehicle systems, and performance data gathered during service checks.

Alperium/Shutterstock

Dating back to the 1980s, Daimler's warranty data were housed on its Quality Information System (QUIS), a mainframe-based platform. Employees used QUIS to conduct analysis, but data in the system were also accessed by users from many departments using a variety of tools, creating an enormous demand for information. But because the information was accessed from a variety of tools, it was used inconsistently. Further, the users found the existing tools inadequate to meet user analysis requirements.

At the same time, the diagnostic and warranty data were located in different information silos, so they could not be evaluated together. Consequently, the organization was unable to take full advantage of the data. In addition, the diagnosis database had reached the limits of its capacity.

The IT Solution

The obvious solution to this problem was to combine the various data sources into a single enterprise data warehouse. Over a three-year period, Daimler consolidated its data on a data warehouse, making these data available to users through a shared interface. The new system is called *Advanced Quality Analysis (AQUA)*.

The company intended AQUA to provide support for two strategic goals: (1) to increase customer satisfaction and (2) to reduce costs. By creating a "single version of the truth"—a global, standardized perspective on all vehicle-related data—the new system could enable Daimler to better analyze both product and diagnostic effectiveness, as well as to ensure the quality of maintenance and repairs. Additionally, sophisticated real-time analyses on AQUA would improve the existing early-warning systems, which detect the possible failure of a vehicular component such as the brakes. Finally, eliminating the existing, old systems would reduce IT operating costs.

The Results

Since the implementation of the new system, users have been receiving warranty and customer satisfaction reports via AQUA. Daimler used these data to implement an enhanced early-warning system that reports problems much faster than did the previous system. AQUA has also enabled Daimler to implement the "First Fixed Visit" tool, which identifies recurring repairs based on data collected in dealership service operations. Daimler maps those repairs back to its manufacturing processes so that the company can make improvements in those processes.

After Daimler integrated its data-mining tool into AQUA, the company no longer needed to copy data from one database to another. This arrangement dramatically lowered follow-on costs. By eliminating problems in the production stage, Daimler can avoid future warranty and goodwill costs. (If customers are not satisfied with their cars or with Daimler maintenance, the company loses goodwill.)

Another feature of the new system, the AQUA Miner, provides a step-by-step approach to identifying the individual features that contribute to a high rate of part defects. Basically, the engineer selects a specific series type (of car) and then chooses failure codes suspected of contributing to a particular defect. AQUA Miner then identifies subgroups of vehicles where such defects appear more frequently than in the remainder of the vehicle fleet.

Along with warranty and goodwill data, AQUA Miner also analyzes data on each vehicle's electronic control unit, such as revolutions per minute, vibration behaviour, and temperature. These analyses help uncover the causes of defects based on actual driving experience. Daimler uses these data to improve the design of future vehicle models.

For the first time, Daimler has a data source that provides all quality-related information across its complete range of components and model lines. Developers and engineers use these data to analyze thousands of variables, such as the repair frequency of all components. AQUA warns the engineers of any significant deviations from accepted standards, and it provides warnings up to two weeks faster than did the previous system. As a result, Daimler can pinpoint potential problems in vehicles that have been on the road for as briefly as one month, and it can adjust its production processes to eliminate these problems. This process is reducing long-term warranty costs.

AQUA has enabled Daimler to achieve deeper insights into how to optimize its production processes. Defects can be detected more quickly, resolved, and eliminated from future models. AQUA supports Daimler's strategic goals of quality leadership, customer satisfaction, and profitability.

What We Learned from This Case

The Daimler case illustrates the importance and far-reaching nature of business intelligence applications. **Business intelligence (BI)** is a broad category of applications, technologies, and processes for gathering, storing, accessing, and analyzing data to help business users make better decisions. BI applications enable decision makers to quickly ascertain the status of a business enterprise by examining key information. Daimler managers needed current, timely, and accurate information that their old system could not provide. Implementing the BI applications generated significant benefits throughout the company, supporting important decisions about Daimler's overall business goal: the highest levels of customer satisfaction.

This chapter describes information systems that support *decision making*. It begins by reviewing the manager's job and the nature of modern managerial decisions. This discussion will help you to understand why managers need computerized support. You then learn about the concepts of business intelligence for supporting individuals, groups, and entire organizations.

It is impossible to overstate the importance of business intelligence to you. Recall from Chapter 1 that the essential goal of information systems is to provide the right information to the right person, in the right amount, at the right time, in the right format. In essence, BI achieves this goal. BI systems provide business intelligence that you can act on in a timely fashion.

It is also impossible to overstate the importance of your input into the BI process within an organization, for several reasons. First, you (the user community) will decide what data should be stored in your organization's data warehouse. You will then work closely with the MIS department to obtain these data.

Further, you will use your organization's BI applications, probably from your first day on the job. With some BI applications, such as data mining and decision support systems (DSS), you will decide how you want to analyze the data (user-driven analysis). With other BI applications, such as dashboards, you will decide which data you want to see and in which format. Again, you will work closely with your MIS department to ensure that these applications meet your needs.

Much of this chapter is concerned with large-scale BI applications. You should keep in mind, however, that smaller organizations, and even individual users, can implement small-scale BI applications as well. For example, Excel spreadsheets provide some BI functions, as do SQL queries of a database.

The most popular BI tool by far is Microsoft Excel. For years, BI vendors "fought" against the use of Excel. Eventually, however, they decided to "join it" by designing their software so

Sources: Compiled from S. DeCarlo, "The World's Biggest Companies," *Forbes*, April 20, 2011; H. Elliot, "Daimler's Dieter Zetsche: Sales Are Not Our No. 1 Priority," *Forbes*, January 11, 2011; A. Dullaghan, "Daimler Drives High Performance," *Teradata Magazine*, v. 11, no. 1, 2011; *www.daimler.com*, accessed May 25, 2013.

that it interfaces with Excel. How does this process work? Essentially, users download plug-ins that add functionality (e.g., the ability to list the top 10 percent of customers, based on sales) to Excel. This process can be thought of as creating "Excel on steroids." Excel then connects to the vendor's application server—which provides additional data-analysis capabilities—which in turn connects to a backend database, such as a data mart or warehouse. This arrangement gives Excel users the functionality and access to data typical of sophisticated BI products, while allowing them to work with a familiar client—Excel.

Microsoft has made similar changes to its product line. Specifically, Excel now can be used with MS SQL Server (a database product), and it can be used in advanced BI applications, such as dashboards and data mining/predictive analysis.

After you finish this chapter, you will have a basic understanding of decision making, the business intelligence process, and BI applications in organizations today. This knowledge will enable you to immediately and confidently provide input into your organization's BI processes and applications. Further, the hands-on exercises in this chapter will familiarize you with the actual use of BI software. These exercises will enable you to use your organization's BI applications to effectively analyze data and thus make better decisions. Enjoy!

10.1 Managers and Decision Making

Management is a process by which an organization achieves its goals through the use of resources (people, money, materials, and information). These resources are considered to be *inputs*. Achieving the organization's goals is the *output* of the process. Managers oversee this process in an attempt to optimize it. A manager's success often is measured by the ratio between the inputs and outputs for which he or she is responsible. This ratio is an indication of the organization's **productivity**.

The Manager's Job and Decision Making

To appreciate how information systems support managers, you first must understand the manager's job. Managers do many things, depending on their position in the organization, the type and size of the organization, the organization's policies and culture, and the personalities of the managers themselves. Despite these variations, however, all managers perform three basic roles (Mintzberg, 1973):

1. ***Interpersonal roles***—figurehead, leader, liaison
2. ***Informational roles***—monitor, disseminator, spokesperson, analyzer
3. ***Decisional roles***—entrepreneur, disturbance handler, resource allocator, negotiator

Early information systems primarily supported the informational roles. In recent years, information systems have been developed that support all three roles. In this chapter, you will focus on the support that IT can provide for decisional roles.

A **decision** is a choice among two or more alternatives that individuals and groups make. Decisions are diverse and are made continuously. Decision making is a systematic process. Economist Herbert Simon (1977) described decision making as composed of three major phases: intelligence, design, and choice. Once the choice is made, the decision is implemented. Figure 10.1 illustrates this process, indicating which tasks are included in each phase. Note that there is a continuous flow of information from intelligence, to design, to choice (bold lines), but at any phase there may be a return to a previous phase (broken lines).

This model of decision making is quite general. Undoubtedly, you have made decisions where you did not construct a model of the situation, validate your model with test data, or conduct a sensitivity analysis. The model we present here is intended to encompass all of the conditions that might occur when making a decision. For some decisions, some steps or phases may be minimal, implicit (understood), or absent.

The decision-making process starts with the *intelligence phase*, in which managers examine a situation and identify and define the problem or opportunity. In the *design phase*,

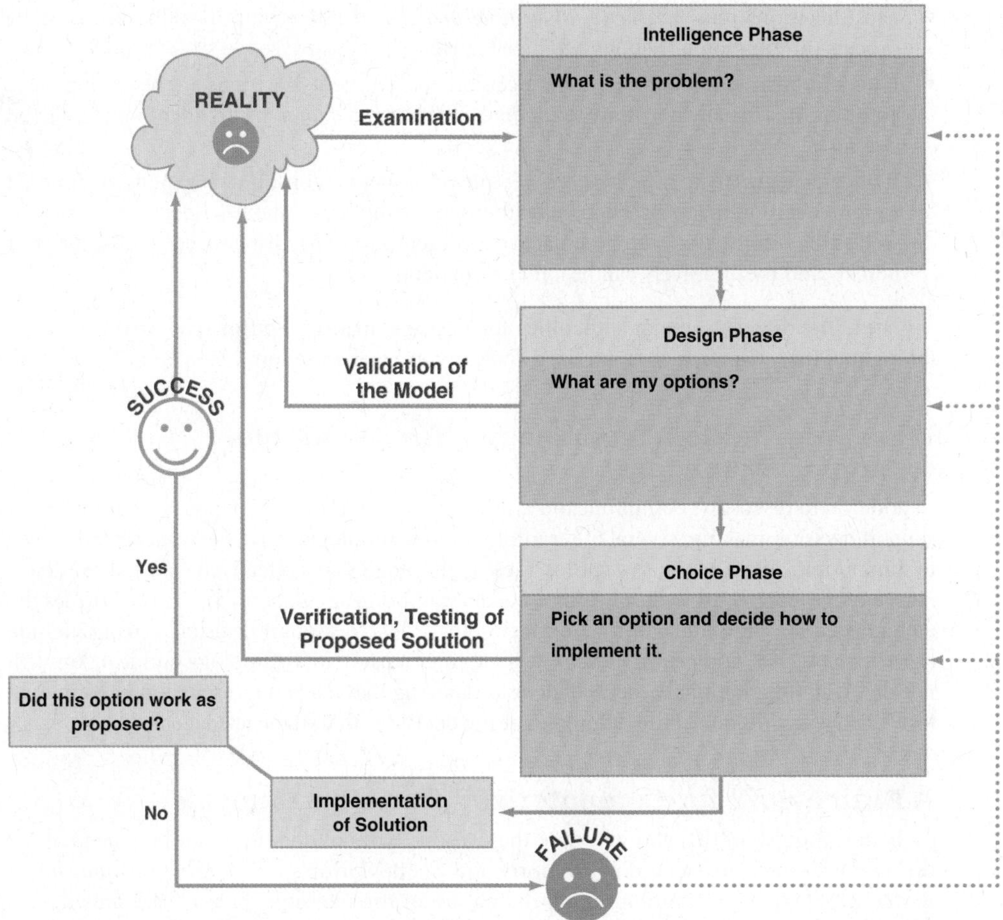

FIGURE 10.1 The process and phases in decision making.

decision makers construct a model for the situation. They do this by making assumptions that simplify reality and by expressing the relationships among all the relevant variables. Managers then validate the model by using test data. Finally, decision makers set criteria for evaluating all of the potential solutions that are proposed. The *choice phase* involves selecting a solution or course of action that seems best suited to resolve the problem. This solution (the decision) is then implemented. Implementation is successful if the proposed solution solves the problem or seizes the opportunity. If the solution fails, then the process returns to the previous phases. Computer-based decision support assists managers in the decision-making process.

Why Managers Need IT Support

Making good decisions is very difficult without solid information. Information is vital for each phase and activity in the decision-making process. Even when information is available, however, decision making is difficult due to the following trends:

- The *number of alternatives* is constantly *increasing*, due to innovations in technology, improved communications, the development of global markets, and the use of the Internet and e-business. A key to good decision making is to explore and compare many relevant alternatives. The more alternatives that exist, the more a decision maker needs computer-assisted searches and comparisons.

- Most decisions must be made *under time pressure*. It often is not possible to manually process information fast enough to be effective.
- Due to increased uncertainty in the decision environment, decisions are becoming more complex. It is usually necessary to *conduct a sophisticated analysis* in order to make a good decision.
- It often is necessary to rapidly access remote information, consult with experts, or conduct a group decision-making session, all without incurring large expenses. Decision makers, as well as the information, can be situated in different locations. Bringing everything together quickly and inexpensively can be a major challenge.

These trends create major difficulties for decision makers. Fortunately, as you will see throughout this chapter, a computerized analysis can be of enormous help.

What Information Technologies Are Available to Support Managers?

In addition to discovery, communication, and collaboration tools (Chapter 4) that indirectly support decision making, several other information technologies have been successfully used to support managers. As you saw earlier, these technologies are collectively referred to as *business intelligence (BI)*. BI is closely linked to data warehousing (Chapter 3), which provides the data needed for BI. Other information technology tools to support decision making include *expert systems* (ES) and *neural networks* which are discussed in Technology Guide 4. You will now learn about additional aspects of decision making that place our discussion of BI in context. First, you will look at the different types of decisions that managers face.

A Framework for Computerized Decision Analysis

To better understand BI, you will note that various types of decisions can be placed along two major dimensions according to Gorry and Scott-Morton's (1971) *Sloan Management Review article*: problem structure and the nature of the decision. Figure 10.2 provides an overview of decision making along these two dimensions.

Problem Structure. The first dimension is *problem structure*, where decision-making processes fall along a continuum ranging from highly structured to highly unstructured (see the far-left column in Figure 10.2). *Structured decisions* deal with routine and repetitive problems for which standard solutions exist, such as inventory control. In a structured decision, the first three phases of the decision process—intelligence, design, and choice—are laid out in a particular sequence, and the procedures for obtaining the best (or at least a good enough) solution are known. Two basic criteria used to evaluate proposed solutions are minimizing costs and maximizing profits. These types of decisions are candidates for decision automation.

At the other extreme of complexity are *unstructured decisions*. These are intended to deal with "fuzzy," complex problems for which there are no cut-and-dried solutions. An unstructured decision is one in which there is no standardized procedure for carrying out any of the three phases. In making such a decision, human intuition and judgement often play an important role. Typical unstructured decisions include planning new service offerings, hiring an executive, and choosing a set of research and development (R&D) projects for the coming year. Although BI cannot make unstructured decisions, it can provide information that assists decision makers.

Located between structured and unstructured decisions are *semi-structured* decisions, in which only some of the decision process phases are structured. Semi-structured decisions require a combination of standard solution procedures and individual judgement. Examples of semi-structured decisions are evaluating employees, setting marketing budgets for consumer products, performing capital acquisition analysis, and trading bonds.

		Nature of Decision		
Type of Decision	**Operational Control**	**Management Control**	**Strategic Planning**	**Support Needed**
Structured	1 Accounts receivable, order entry	2 Budget analysis, short-term forecasting, personnel reports, make-or-buy analysis	3 Financial management (investment), warehouse location, distribution systems	Management science
Semi-structured	4 Production scheduling, inventory control	5 Credit evaluation, budget preparation, plant layout, project scheduling, reward systems design	6 Building new plant, mergers and acquisitions, new product planning, compensation planning, quality assurance planning	Decision support systems (DSS)
Unstructured	7 Selecting a cover for a magazine, buying software, approving loans	8 Negotiating, recruiting an executive, buying hardware, lobbying	9 R & D planning, new technology development, social responsibility planning	BI, DSS Expert systems (ES) neural networks
Support Needed	Management science	Management science, DSS, Business intelligence (BI), ES	Business intelligence (BI), ES, neural networks	

FIGURE 10.2 Decision support framework. Technology is used to support the decisions shown in the column at the far right and in the bottom row.

The Nature of Decisions. The second dimension of decision support deals with the *nature of decisions*. All managerial decisions fall into one of three broad categories:

1. *Operational control*—executing specific tasks efficiently and effectively
2. *Management control*—acquiring and using resources efficiently in accomplishing organizational goals
3. *Strategic planning*—the long-range goals and policies for growth and resource allocation

These categories are displayed along the top row of Figure 10.2.

Note that strategic decisions define the context in which management control decisions are made. In turn, management control decisions define the context in which operational control decisions are made.

The Decision Matrix. The three primary classes of problem structure and the three broad categories of the nature of decisions can be combined in a decision-support matrix that consists of nine cells, as diagrammed in Figure 10.2. Lower-level managers usually perform tasks in cells 1, 2, and 4 (shaded in blue). The tasks in cells 3, 5, and 7 (shaded in orange) are usually the responsibility of middle managers and professional staff. Finally, tasks in cells 6, 8, and 9 (shaded in yellow) are generally carried out by senior executives.

Computer Support for Structured Decisions. Business intelligence applications might be used for the nine cells in the matrix, although structured and some semi-structured decisions, especially of the operational and management control type, have been supported by computers since the 1950s. Decisions of this type are made in all functional areas, but particularly in finance and operations management.

Problems that lower-level managers encounter on a regular basis typically have a high level of structure. Examples are capital budgeting (for example, replacement of equipment), allocating resources, distributing merchandise, and controlling inventory. For each type of structured decision, prescribed solutions have been developed, which often include mathematical formulas. This approach is called *management science* or *operations research*, and it also is executed with the aid of computers.

before you go on...

1. Describe the decision-making process proposed by Simon.
2. You are registering for classes next semester. Apply the decision-making process to your decision about how many and which courses to take. Is your decision structured, semi-structured, or unstructured?
3. Consider your decision-making process when registering for classes next semester. Explain how information technology supports (or does not support) each phase of this process.

10.2 What Is Business Intelligence?

To provide users with access to corporate data, many organizations are implementing data warehouses and data marts, which you learned about in Chapter 3. Users analyze the data in warehouses and marts using a wide variety of BI tools. Many vendors offer integrated packages of these tools under the overall label of *business intelligence (BI) software*. Major BI software vendors include SAS (*www.sas.com*), Oracle's Hyperion (*www.hyperion.com*), SAP's Business Objects (*www.businessobjects.com*), Information Builders (*www.informationbuilders.com*), IBM's SPSS (*www.spss.com*), and Cognos (*www-01.ibm.com/software/analytics/cognos*).

As you have seen, BI is vital to modern decision making and organizational performance. Let's consider in greater detail the technical foundation for BI and the wide variety of ways that BI can be used.

The phrase *business intelligence* is relatively new. Business and IT analyst Howard Dresner coined the term in 1989 while he was an analyst at Gartner, a leading IT market research firm. The expression is especially popular in industry, where it is used as an umbrella term that encompasses all decision support applications.

BI encompasses not only applications, but also technologies and processes. It includes both "getting data in" (to a data mart or warehouse) and "getting data out" (through BI applications).

In addition, a significant change is taking place within the BI environment. In the past, organizations used BI only to support management. Today, however, BI applications are increasingly available to front-line personnel (e.g., call centre operators), suppliers, customers, and even regulators. These groups rely on BI to provide them with the most current information.

The Scope of Business Intelligence

The use of BI in organizations varies considerably. In smaller organizations, BI may be limited to Excel spreadsheets. In larger ones, BI often is enterprise-wide, and it includes applications such as data mining and predictive analytics, dashboards, and data visualization. It is important to recognize that the importance of BI to organizations continues to grow.

Not all organizations use BI in the same way. For example, some organizations employ only one or a few applications, while others use enterprise-wide BI. In this section you will examine three specific BI targets that represent different levels of change:

- The development of one or a few related BI applications
- The development of infrastructure to support enterprise-wide BI
- Support for organizational transformation

These targets differ in terms of their focus; scope; level of sponsorship, commitment, and required resources; technical architecture; impact on personnel and business processes; and benefits.

The Development of One or a Few Related BI Applications. This BI target often is a point solution for a departmental need, such as campaign management in marketing. Sponsorship, approval, funding, impacts, and benefits typically occur at the departmental level. For this target, organizations usually create a data mart to store the necessary data. Organizations must be careful that the data mart—an "independent" application—does not become a "data silo" that stores data that are inconsistent with, and cannot be integrated with, data used elsewhere in the organization.

One example of this type of BI use in the human resources department is Adelaide Brighton Cement, an Australian company with over 1,300 employees that provides cement to construction, engineering, and infrastructure industries. Its employees operate in a production environment defined by heavy machinery and high temperatures—a risky combination unless thorough safety measures are implemented. The company needed a better system to monitor safety throughout the entire plant and decided to implement a hosted BI system. Previously reports were generated only once a month; in contrast, the new BI system alerts plant managers any time a new incident occurs. They can also drill down into reports to find more detailed information.

The Development of Infrastructure to Support Enterprise-Wide BI. This BI target supports current and future BI needs. A crucial component of BI at this level is an enterprise data warehouse. Because it is an enterprise-wide initiative, senior management often provides sponsorship, approval, and funding. In addition, the impacts and benefits are felt throughout the organization.

An example of this target is the 3M corporation. Traditionally, 3M's various divisions had operated independently, using separate decision support platforms. Not only was this arrangement costly, but it prevented 3M from integrating the data and presenting a "single face" to its customers. Thus, for example, sales representatives did not know whether or how business customers were interacting with other 3M divisions. The solution was to develop an enterprise data warehouse that enabled 3M to operate as an integrated company. As an added benefit, the cost of implementing this system was covered by savings resulting from the consolidation of the various platforms.

Support for Organizational Transformation. BI is also used to fundamentally transform the ways in which a company competes in the marketplace. BI supports a new business model, and it enables the business strategy. Because of the scope and importance of these changes, critical elements such as sponsorship, approval, and funding originate at the highest organizational levels. The impact on personnel and processes can be significant, and the benefits are organization-wide. The example of Kelley Blue Book in IT's About Small Business 10.1 provides a clear illustration of how BI can support organizational transformation.

In Chapter 3, you studied the basics of data warehouses and data marts. In this section, you have seen how important data warehouses and marts are to the different ways that organizations use BI. In the next section, you will learn how the user community can analyze the data in warehouses and marts, how the results of these analyses are presented to users, and how organizations can use the results of these analyses.

before you go on...

1. Define BI.
2. Discuss the breadth of support provided by BI applications to organizational employees.
3. Identify and discuss the three basic targets of BI.

10.3 Business Intelligence Applications for Data Analysis

A good strategy to study the ways in which organizations use business intelligence applications is to consider how the users analyze data, how the results of their analyses are presented to them, and how managers and executives implement these results. Recall from Chapter 3 that the data are stored in a data warehouse or data mart. The user community analyzes these data using a variety of BI applications. The results of these analyses can be presented to users via other BI applications. Finally, managers and executives put the overall results to good use. You will become familiar with data analysis, presentation, and use in depth in the next three sections.

A variety of BI applications for analyzing data are available. They include multidimensional analysis (also called *on-line analytical processing*, or *OLAP*), data mining, and decision support systems.

Multidimensional Analysis or On-Line Analytical Processing (OLAP)

Some BI applications include **on-line analytical processing (OLAP)**, also referred to as **multidimensional analysis** capabilities. OLAP involves "slicing and dicing" data stored in a dimensional format, drilling down in the data to greater detail, and aggregating the data.

Consider our example from Chapter 3. Recall Figure 3.11 showing the data cube. The product is on the x-axis, geography is on the y-axis, and time is on the z-axis. Now, suppose you want to know how many nuts the company sold in the West region in 2011. You would slice and dice the cube, using *nuts* as the specific measure for product, *West* as the measure for geography, and *2011* as the measure for time. The value or values that remain in the cell(s) after our slicing and dicing is (are) the answer to our question. As an example of drilling down, you also might want to know how many nuts were sold in January 2011. Alternatively, you might want to know how many nuts were sold during from 2011 to 2013, which is an example of aggregation, also called "rollup."

Data Mining

Data mining is the process of searching for valuable business information in a large database, data warehouse, or data mart. Data mining can perform two basic operations: (1) predicting trends and behaviours; and (2) identifying previously unknown patterns. BI applications typically provide users with a view of what has happened; data mining helps to explain why it is happening, and it predicts what will happen in the future.

Regarding the first operation, data mining automates the process of finding predictive information in large databases. Questions that traditionally required extensive hands-on analysis now can be answered directly and quickly from the data. For example, *targeted marketing* uses predictive information. Data mining can use data from past promotional mailings to identify those people who are most likely to respond favourably to future mailings. Another business problem that uses predictive information is the forecasting of bankruptcy and different forms of default.

Data mining can also identify previously hidden patterns in a single step. For example, it can analyze retail sales data to discover seemingly unrelated products that people often purchase together. The classic example is beer and diapers. Data mining found that young men tend to buy beer and diapers at the same time when shopping at convenience stores in the United States.

One significant pattern-discovery operation is detecting fraudulent credit card transactions. After you use your credit card for a time, a pattern emerges of the typical ways you use your card—the places in which you use your card, the amounts you spend, and so on. If your card is stolen and used fraudulently, the usage often becomes different from your pattern. Data mining tools can discern this difference and bring the issue to your attention.

Numerous data mining applications are used in business and in other fields. IT's About Small Business 10.1 provides the example of Kelley Blue Book and its use of data analytics. According to a Gartner report (*www.gartner.com*), most Fortune 1000 companies worldwide currently use data mining, as the following representative examples illustrate. Note that in most cases the purpose of data mining is to identify a business opportunity in order to create a sustainable competitive advantage, just as in the case of Kelley Blue Book.

- *Retailing and sales*—predicting sales, preventing theft and fraud, and determining correct inventory levels and distribution schedules among outlets. For example, retailers such as AAFES (stores on U.S. military bases) use Fraud Watch from SAP (*www.sap.com*) to combat fraud by employees in their stores.

IT's about [small] business

10.1 Data Analytics Helps Kelley Blue Book Remain Competitive

Since 1926, Kelley Blue Book (*www.kbb.com*) essentially has been a publishing company known for its guide to used and new car values. In the 2000s, however, Blue Book sales began to decline, and the company needed to devise new strategies to generate revenue and compete with new on-line rivals, such as Cars.com, Edmunds.com, and Autos.MSN.com. As Kelley analyzed its situation, it concluded that data and information were the company's products, not just by-products. That is, Kelley realized that it was actually an "information company."

Kelley already possessed vast amounts of data on new and used cars. The company turned to data analytics to use those data more effectively. The first step was to update the company's data management infrastructure. Until that time, the company's appraisers had collected information by hand, recorded it in notebooks, and faxed it back to headquarters, where it was keyed into a database system.

Before Kelley could complete this update, it had to determine what data it actually had. To achieve this objective, the company performed an audit of its data, including both clickstream data collected from its website and third-party data.

Kelley invested in a data warehouse to collect, integrate, and house the data. In addition, it purchased business intelligence and data analytics software from MicroStrategy (*www.microstrategy.com*) and the SAS Institute (*www.sas.com*) in order to analyze its warehouse data more efficiently and effectively.

The next step was to determine how Kelley could use data analytics to improve its existing services. Kelley discovered, for example, that by using the software to integrate third-party data, it could refine its car value estimates on its website more quickly and accurately than ever before.

Kelley also developed applications to make money with its new data analytics capabilities. For instance, the company created an application designed to help car owners determine the best time to sell. This application uses historical data to estimate when a particular car make and model will need significant repairs. Thus, if a particular type of car usually needs a new water pump at a certain mileage mark, the owner may want to sell it before reaching that mark.

Kelley was also considering adding a widget to its website that forecasts likely car prices over a three-month period. This application helps potential buyers make their purchases when prices may be lowest. Another application under development would help buyers understand how much negotiating room they have with dealers based on recent sales of similar cars in the same geographic region.

The bottom line is that data analytics has enabled Kelley to provide more rapid and accurate quotes. In addition, data analytics is helping Kelley develop new sources of revenue, which are essential if the company is to remain competitive with the on-line companies.

Questions

1. Provide specific examples of other revenue-generating applications that Kelley could develop from its data-mining application.
2. Analyze this case in terms of the three phases of the decision-making model (intelligence, design, and choice).
3. Provide additional examples of data mining analyses that Kelley Blue Book could perform.
4. Analyze the interrelationship between data management technology, business intelligence/data analytics, and strategy using the case of Kelley Blue Book.

Sources: Compiled from L. Davidson, "Seller Beware: Don't Give Away the Store When Selling," *Forbes*, February 3, 2011; J. Kelly, "Data Analytics Software, Data Management Transforms Kelley Blue Book," *Search Business Analytics*, November 16, 2010; R. O'Regan, "How Kelley Blue Book Uses Web Analytics to Fuel Its Ad-Supported Model," *www.emediavitals.com*, October 6, 2010; H. Elliot, "The Easiest Cars to Bargain For," *Forbes*, August 10, 2010; *www.kbb.com*, *www.microstrategy.com*, *www.sas.com*, accessed April 5, 2011.

- *Banking*—forecasting levels of bad loans and fraudulent credit card use, predicting credit card spending by new customers, and determining which kinds of customers will best respond to (and qualify for) new loan offers
- *Manufacturing and production*—predicting machinery failures, and finding key factors that help optimize manufacturing capacity
- *Insurance*—forecasting claim amounts and medical coverage costs, classifying the most important elements that affect medical coverage, and predicting which customers will buy new insurance policies
- *Police work*—tracking crime patterns, locations, and criminal behaviour; identifying attributes to assist in solving criminal cases
- *Health care*—correlating demographics of patients with critical illnesses, and developing better insights on how to identify and treat symptoms and their causes
- *Marketing*—classifying customer demographics that can be used to predict which customers will respond to a mailing or buy a particular product

Decision Support Systems

Decision support systems (DSSs) combine models and data in an attempt to analyze semi-structured and some unstructured problems with extensive user involvement. **Models** are simplified representations, or abstractions, of reality. DSSs enable business managers and analysts to access data interactively, to manipulate these data, and to conduct appropriate analyses.

Decision support systems can both enhance learning and contribute to all levels of decision making. DSSs also employ mathematical models. Finally, they have the related capabilities of sensitivity analysis, what-if analysis, and goal-seeking analysis, which you will learn about next. You should keep in mind that these three types of analysis are useful for any type of decision support application; Excel, for example, supports them.

Sensitivity Analysis. *Sensitivity analysis* is the study of the impact that changes in one or more parts of a decision-making model have on other parts. Most sensitivity analyses examine the impact that changes in input variables have on output variables.

Most models include two types of input variables: decision variables and environmental variables. "What is our reorder point for these raw materials?" is a decision variable (internal to the organization). "What will the rate of inflation be?" is an environmental variable (external to the organization). The output in this example would be the total cost of raw materials. The point of a sensitivity analysis is usually to determine the impact of environmental variables on the result of the analysis.

Sensitivity analysis is extremely valuable because it enables the system to adapt to changing conditions and to the varying requirements of different decision-making situations. It provides a better understanding of the model as well as the problem that the model purports to describe.

What-If Analysis. A model builder must make predictions and assumptions regarding the input data, many of which are based on the assessment of uncertain futures. The results depend on the accuracy of these assumptions, which can be highly subjective. *What-if analysis* attempts to predict the impact of a change in the assumptions (input data) on the proposed solution. For example, *what* will happen to the total inventory cost *if* the originally assumed cost of carrying inventories is not 10 percent but 12 percent? In a well-designed BI system, managers themselves can interactively ask the computer these types of questions as often as they need to.

Goal-Seeking Analysis. *Goal-seeking analysis* represents a "backward" solution approach. It attempts to find the value of the inputs necessary to achieve a desired level of output. For example, let's say that an initial BI analysis predicted a profit of $2 million. Management might want to know what sales volume would be necessary to generate a profit of $3 million. To find out, they would perform a goal-seeking analysis.

The managers, however, cannot simply press a button that says "increase sales." Some action(s) will be needed to make the sales increase possible. The action(s) could be to lower prices, to increase research and development, to provide a higher commission rate for the sales force, to increase advertising, or to implement some combination of these actions. Whatever the action is, it will cost money, and the goal-seeking analysis must take this into account.

before you go on...

1. Describe multidimensional analysis, and construct a data cube with information from IT's About Small Business 10.1. (Hint: You must decide which three business dimensions you would like to analyze in your data cube.)
2. What are the two basic operations of data mining?
3. What is the purpose of decision support systems?

10.4 Business Intelligence Applications for Presenting Results

The results of the types of data analyses you just learned about can be presented with dashboards and data visualization technologies. Today, users are increasingly relying on data that are real time or almost real time. Therefore, you also study real-time BI in this section.

Dashboards

Dashboards evolved from executive information systems, which were information systems designed specifically for the information needs of top executives. As you saw in this chapter's opening case, however, today all employees, business partners, and customers can use digital dashboards.

A dashboard provides easy access to timely information and direct access to management reports. It is user friendly, is supported by graphics, and, most importantly, enables managers to examine exception reports and drill down into detailed data. Table 10.1 summarizes the various capabilities common to many dashboards. Moreover, some of the capabilities discussed in this section are now part of many BI products, as illustrated in Figure 10.3.

Table 10.1 The Capabilities of Dashboards

Capability	Description
Drill-down	The ability to go to details, at several levels; it can be done by a series of menus or by clicking on a drillable portion of the screen.
Critical success factors (CSFs)	The factors most critical for the success of business. These can be organizational, by industry, departmental, or for individual workers.
Key performance indicators (KPIs)	The specific measures of CSFs.
Status access	The latest data available on KPI or some other metric, often in real time.
Trend analysis	Short-, medium-, and long-term trend of KPIs or metrics, which are projected using forecasting methods.
Exception reporting	Reports that highlight deviations larger than certain thresholds. Reports may include only deviations.

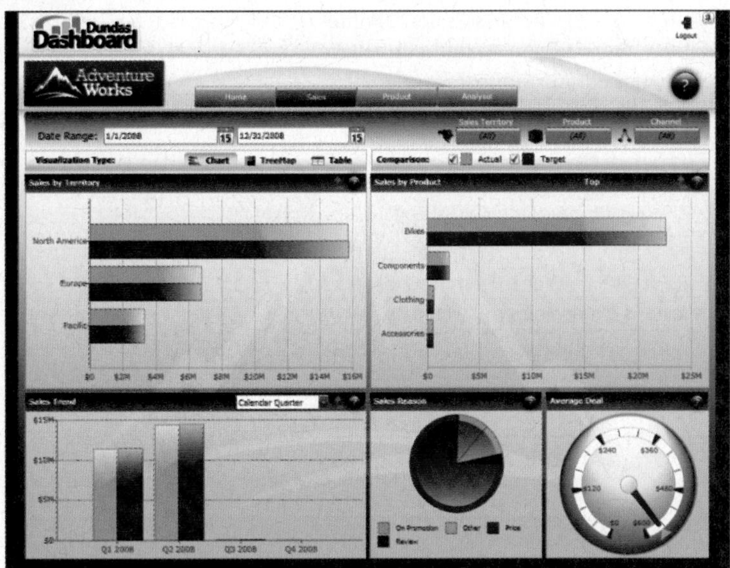

FIGURE 10.3 Sample performance dashboard. (*Source:* Image courtesy of Dundas Data Visualization, Inc. - www.dundas.com)

One outstanding example of a dashboard is the Bloomberg Terminal. Bloomberg LP (*www.bloomberg.com*), a privately held company, provides a subscription service that sells financial data, software to analyze these data, trading tools, and news (electronic, print, TV, and radio). All of this information is accessible through a colour-coded Bloomberg keyboard that displays the desired information on a computer screen, either the user's or one that Bloomberg provides. Users can also set up their own computers to access the service without a Bloomberg keyboard. The subscription service plus the keyboard is called the Bloomberg Terminal. It literally represents a do-it-yourself dashboard, because users can customize their information feeds as well as the look and feel of those feeds (see Figure 10.4).

In another example, Figure 10.5 shows a human resources dashboard/scorecard developed by iDashboards (*www.idashboards.com*), one of the leading BI software vendors. At a glance, users can see employee productivity, hours, team, department, and division performance in graphical, tabular, summary, and detailed form. The selector box to the left enables the user to easily change between specific analysts to compare their performance.

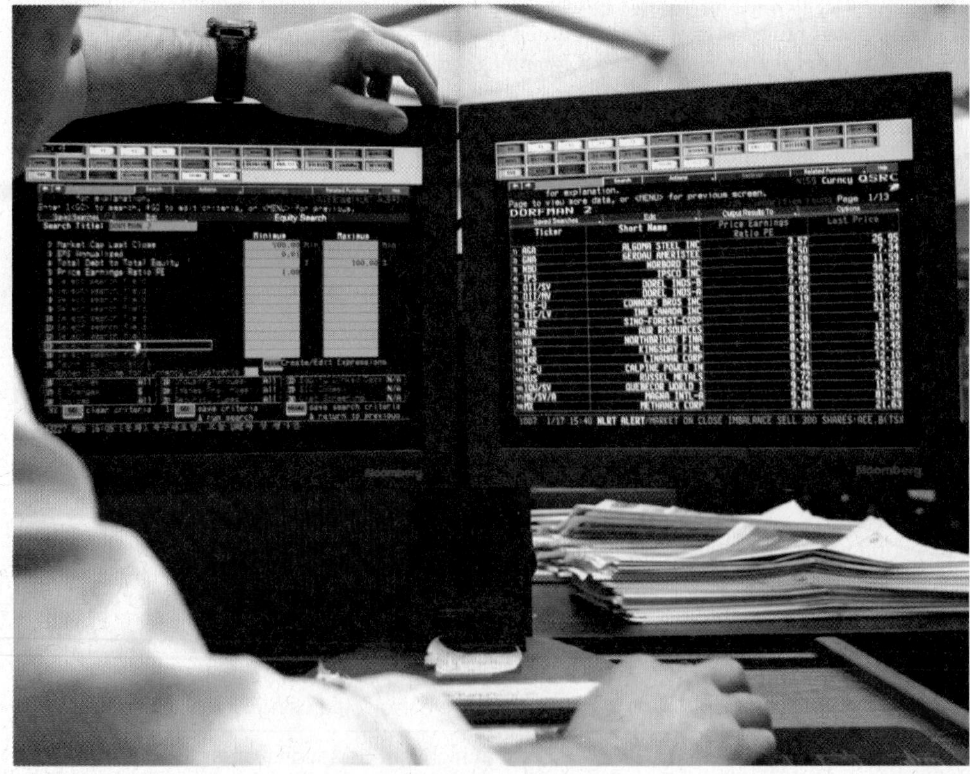

FIGURE 10.4 A Bloomberg terminal. (*Source:* Carlos Osario/Zuma Press)

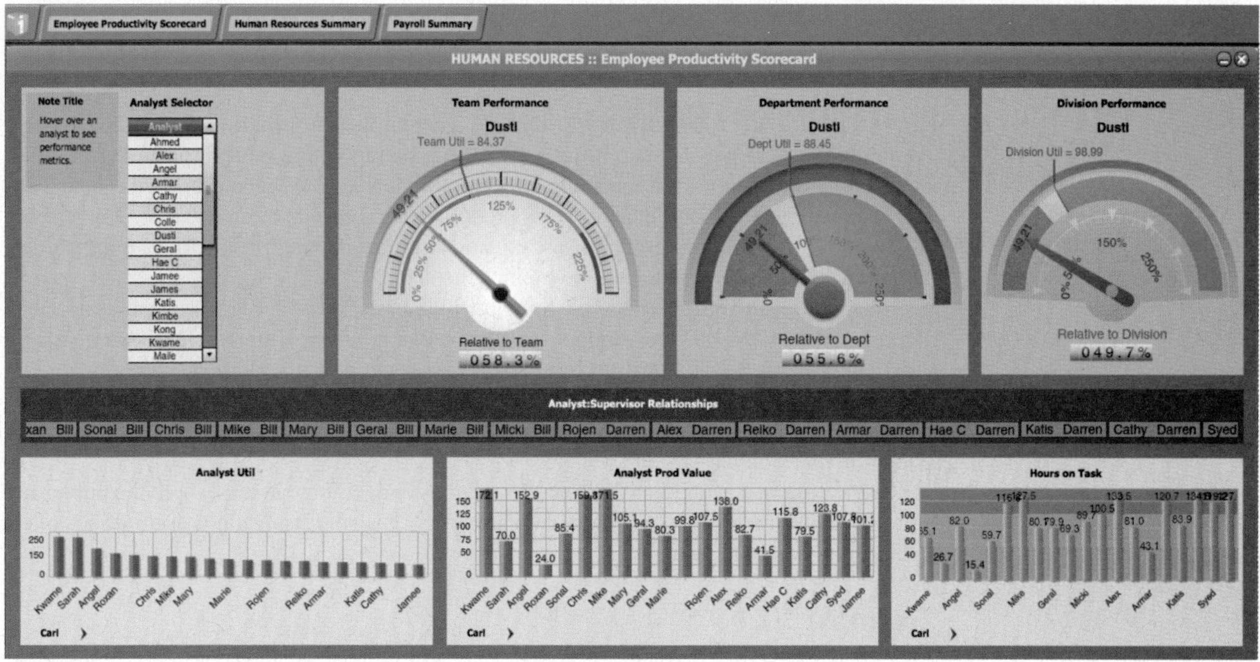

FIGURE 10.5 A human resources dashboard/scorecard. (*Source:* www.iDashboards.com)

A unique and interesting application of dashboards to support the informational needs of executives is the management cockpit. Essentially, a management cockpit is a strategic management room containing an elaborate set of dashboards that enable top-level decision makers to pilot their businesses better. The goal is to create an environment that encourages more efficient management meetings and boosts team performance via effective communication. To help achieve this goal, the dashboard graphically displays key performance indicators and information relating to critical success factors on the walls of a meeting room called the *management cockpit room* (see Figure 10.6). The cockpit-like arrangement of instrument panels and displays helps managers visualize how all the different factors in the business interrelate.

Within the room, the four walls are designated by colour: black, red, blue, and white. The black wall displays the principal success factors and financial indicators. The red wall measures market performance. The blue wall projects the performance of internal processes and employees. Finally, the white wall indicates the status of strategic projects. The flight deck, a six-screen, high-end PC, enables executives to drill down to detailed information. External information needed for competitive analyses can easily be imported into the room.

Board members and other executives hold meetings in the management cockpit room. Managers also meet there with the comptroller to discuss current business issues. The management cockpit can implement various what-if scenarios for this purpose. It also provides a common basis for information and communication. Finally, it supports efforts to translate a corporate strategy into concrete activities by identifying performance indicators.

FIGURE 10.6 Management cockpit. (*Source:* The Management Cockpit is a registered trademark of SAP, created by Professor Patrick M. Georges)

Data Visualization Technologies

After data have been processed, they can be presented to users in visual formats such as text, graphics, and tables. This process, known as data visualization, makes IT applications more attractive and understandable to users.

Data visualization is becoming increasingly popular on the web for decision support. A variety of visualization methods and software packages that support decision making are available. Two particularly valuable applications are geographic information systems and reality mining.

Geographic Information Systems. A **geographic information system (GIS)** is a computer-based system for capturing, integrating, manipulating, and displaying data using digitized maps. Its most distinguishing characteristic is that every record or digital object has an identified geographical location. This process, called *geocoding*, enables users to generate information for planning, problem solving, and decision making. In addition, the graphical format makes it easy for managers to visualize the data.

Today, relatively inexpensive, fully functional PC-based GIS packages are readily available. Representative GIS software vendors are ESRI (*www.esri.com*), Intergraph (*www.intergraph.com*), and Pitney Bowes Location Intelligence (*www.pb.com*). In addition, both government sources and private vendors provide diversified commercial GIS data. Some of these GIS packages are free; for example ArcGIS Explorer Desktop from *www.esri.ca* and downloadable GIS data from *http://data.geocomm.com*.

There are countless applications of GISs to improve decision making in both the public and private sectors. Example 10.1 shows how a group of Canada's First Nations uses GIS to collect data about traditional values.

Example 10.1

One of the most challenging decisions that First Nations across Canada must make is whether to allow resource extraction on their traditional lands, and if so, under what conditions. They are turning to business intelligence software to help them make those decisions. The Matawa First Nations, representing nine nations in Northern Ontario, for example, recently adopted a geographic information system (GIS) technology from software vendor ESRI Canada. The GIS collects and stores data on their traditional values, such traditional hunting areas, archaeological sites, former Aboriginal settlements, and burial grounds.

Having GIS information gives both the Matawa First Nations and mining companies a better understanding of their joint challenges regarding potential claims on Aboriginal territory, and in developing a project. At the negotiating table, both sides need data to support their points of view and to help them make decisions. Mining companies want a reasonable return on their investment, including exploration costs, and want a mine that will be economically viable for years to come. First Nations want to be compensated for the use of their resources, while protecting the environment and their traditional uses of the land. The Matawa First Nations hired their own GIS/data specialist to use the GIS technology, whereas previously they had to hire a consultant to make sense of the vast amounts of data regarding natural resources or rely on data collected by other sources, such as governments.

Elsewhere across Canada, other examples of using ESRI software include public utilities, mapping underground pipes that move water from treatment plants to taps that are leaking, and the health field, where a GIS system monitors disease outbreaks and provides real-time surveillance information to the public and also serves as a dashboard for centralizing environmental health indicators such as temperature and humidity.

Reality Mining. One important emerging trend is the integration of GISs and global positioning systems (GPSs, discussed in Chapter 6). Using GISs and GPSs together can produce an interesting new type of technology called *reality mining*. **Reality mining** allows analysts to extract information from the usage patterns of mobile phones and other wireless devices.

Real-Time BI

Until recently, BI has focused on the use of historical data. This focus has changed with the emergence of technology for capturing, storing, and using real-time data. Real-time BI enables

Source: Compiled from L. Kelly, "First Nation Using GIS Data to Map Cultural Values," *Northern Ontario Business*, November 22, 2012; "Matawa First Nations Recognized for Leveraging GIS to Map Out Territories and Cultural Values for Environmental Planning," Esri Canada User Conference, May 8, 2013; *www.esri.com*, accessed May 25, 2013.

users to employ multidimensional analysis, data mining, and decision support systems to analyze data in real time. In addition, it helps organizations to make decisions and to interact with customers in new ways. It also influences how workers can be monitored and rewarded. Example 10.2 shows how Canadian Blood Services uses real-time BI to see current demand of blood in Canada and to forecast future demand.

Example 10.2

Canadian Blood Services uses real-time BI to see current demand of blood in Canada and to be able to and forecast future demand. Canadian Blood Services is the sole blood supplier across Canada, except for Québec. One of its main activities is the collection of blood from blood donors. They typically collect about 1 million blood donations at 20,000 clinics across Canada. These donations must be specifically coded based on blood type, ethnicity, antibodies, and more. Mistakes are not an option.

Canadian Blood Services keeps track of six distinct metrics using its BI software, including blood inventory levels, donor appointment cancellation rates, donor no-show rates, blood collection volume, and other. Keeping track of these indicators might signal a change in supply, which is critical for hospitals across Canada who are the main customers of Canadian Blood Services. These indicators are updated in real-time instead of once or twice a week as it used to be. Figure 10.7 shows a screenshot of Canadian Blood Services real-time BI dashboard.

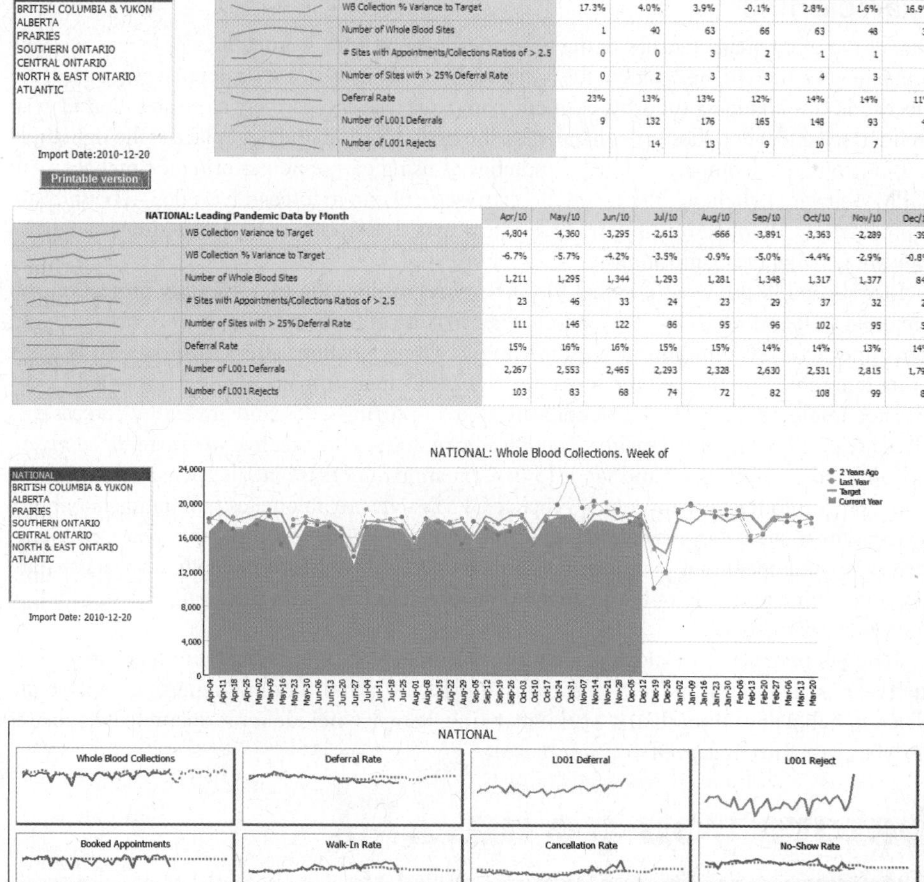

NATIONAL: Leading Pandemic Indicators	2010-12-12	2010-12-13	2010-12-14	2010-12-15	2010-12-16	2010-12-17	2010-12-18
WB Collection Variance to Target	14	114	153	-3	100	37	293
WB Collection % Variance to Target	17.3%	4.0%	3.9%	-0.1%	2.8%	1.6%	16.9%
Number of Whole Blood Sites	1	40	63	66	63	48	35
# Sites with Appointments/Collections Ratios of > 2.5	0	0	3	2	1	1	1
Number of Sites with > 25% Deferral Rate	0	2	3	3	4	3	0
Deferral Rate	23%	13%	13%	12%	14%	14%	11%
Number of L001 Deferrals	9	132	176	165	148	93	42
Number of L001 Rejects		14	13	9	10	7	1

NATIONAL: Leading Pandemic Data by Month	Apr/10	May/10	Jun/10	Jul/10	Aug/10	Sep/10	Oct/10	Nov/10	Dec/10
WB Collection Variance to Target	-4,804	-4,360	-3,295	-2,613	-666	-3,891	-3,363	-2,289	-397
WB Collection % Variance to Target	-6.7%	-5.7%	-4.2%	-3.5%	-0.9%	-5.0%	-4.4%	-2.9%	-0.8%
Number of Whole Blood Sites	1,211	1,295	1,344	1,293	1,281	1,348	1,317	1,377	842
# Sites with Appointments/Collections Ratios of > 2.5	23	46	33	24	23	29	37	32	29
Number of Sites with > 25% Deferral Rate	111	146	122	86	95	96	102	95	54
Deferral Rate	15%	16%	16%	15%	15%	14%	14%	13%	14%
Number of L001 Deferrals	2,267	2,553	2,465	2,293	2,328	2,630	2,531	2,815	1,796
Number of L001 Rejects	103	83	68	74	72	82	108	99	88

FIGURE 10.7 Canadian Blood Services real-time BI dashboard.

Sources: Compiled from: Brian Jackson, "Business Intelligence a Life Line for Canadian Blood Services," ITbusiness.ca, July 19, 2010; Canadian Blood Services, *www.blood.ca*, accessed May 27, 2013.

before you go on...

1. What is a dashboard? Why are dashboards so valuable to employees?
2. Explain the difference between geographic information systems and reality mining, and provide examples of how each of these technologies can be used by businesses and government agencies.
3. What is real-time BI, and why is this technology valuable to an organization's managers and executives?

10.5 Business Intelligence in Action: Corporate Performance Management

Corporate performance management (CPM) is the monitoring and managing of an organization's performance according to *key performance indicators* (KPIs) such as revenue, return on investment (ROI), overhead, and operational costs. For on-line businesses, CPM includes additional factors such as the number of page views, server load, network traffic, and transactions per second. BI applications allow managers and analysts to analyze data to obtain valuable information and insights concerning the organization's KPIs. Example 10.3 demonstrates how a cosmetics company uses corporate performance management software.

Example 10.3

One of the main characteristics of the cosmetics industry is its seasonality. For example, many companies see their highest sales in the holiday season, as cosmetics are a popular gift. In order to succeed in this changing industry, cosmetic companies have to pay very close attention to what products sell and when those sales happen, so the right stock is in the right place at the right time.

One cosmetics company, LUSH Cosmetics, is using corporate performance management (CPM) software to help with its inventory management and to forecast cash flow. The software is provided by Prophix, an Ontario-based firm that specializes in BI and business analytics software for smaller organizations.

LUSH used to use what it called the "best guess format," basing inventory projections on what sold well and what didn't the year before, making sales forecasting hit and miss. It would sometimes have $1.5 million in inventory in the wrong locations after Christmas. "It is really difficult to sell Santa-themed products after the 25th!" the company's IT director noted.

After implementing the CPM software and improving sales and inventory forecasting, LUSH realized $500,000 in savings in not-lost inventory in the first five weeks, reduced inventory on hand by seven days, and saw a 15 percent annual increase in sales per store.

In addition to tracking inventory, Prophix CPM's software automates non-transactional processes in the finance department, including budgeting, monthly reporting, mid-year forecasting, scorecards, and operations planning. It also includes dashboards and in-depth analysis capabilities, and automates many of the financial processes associated with preparing and distributing budgeting information.

Tangible benefits of this type of software can include shorter budget and reporting cycles such as a three-month budget cycle cut to three weeks, and monthly reporting being completed in half a day rather than a week. Intangible benefits include more accurate data, better analytics, and thus improved decision making.

before you go on...

1. What is corporate performance management?
2. How do BI applications contribute to corporate performance management?

Source: Compiled from L. Greiner, "Prophix Software Shows Corporate Performance Management Goes Beyond Annual Budget," ITbusiness.ca, June 25, 2012; "LUSH Cosmetics Uses Prophix Software to Predict Customer Purchasing Patterns," Prophix case study, February 7, 2013; *www.prophix.com*, accessed May 25, 2013.

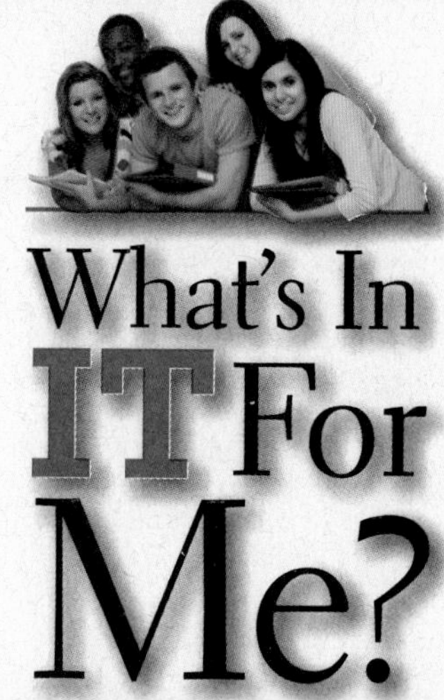

For the **Accounting Major**

BI is used extensively in auditing to uncover irregularities. It also is used to uncover and prevent fraud. Accountants use BI for many of their duties, ranging from risk analysis to cost control.

For the **Finance Major**

People have been using computers for decades to solve financial problems. Innovative BI applications have been created for activities such as making stock market decisions, refinancing bonds, assessing debt risks, analyzing financial conditions, predicting business failures, forecasting financial trends, and investing in global markets.

For the **Marketing Major**

Marketing personnel use BI in many applications, such as planning and executing marketing campaigns, allocating advertising budgets, and evaluating alternative routings of salespeople. New marketing approaches such as targeted marketing and database marketing depend heavily on IT in general, and on data warehouses and business intelligence applications in particular.

For the **Production/Operations Management Major**

BI supports complex operations and production decisions, such as inventory control, production planning, and supply chain integration.

For the **Human Resources Management Major**

Human resources personnel use BI for many of their activities. For example, BI applications can be used to find resumés of applicants posted on the web and sort them to match needed skills and to support management succession planning.

For the **MIS Major**

MIS provides the data infrastructure used in BI. MIS personnel are also involved in building, deploying, and supporting BI applications.

[Summary]

1. Identify the phases in the decision-making process, and use a decision-support framework to demonstrate how technology supports managerial decision making.

When making a decision, either organizational or personal, the decision maker goes through a three-step process: intelligence, design, and choice. When the choice is made, the decision is implemented.

Several information technologies have been successfully used to directly support managers. Collectively, they are referred to as *business intelligence information systems.* Figure 10.2 provides a matrix that shows how technology supports the various types of decisions that managers must make.

2. Describe and provide examples of the three different ways in which organizations use business intelligence (BI).

There are three major ways that organizations use BI:

- The development of one or a few related BI applications: This BI target often is a point solution for a departmental need, such as campaign management in marketing. A data mart usually is created to store necessary data.
- The development of infrastructure to support enterprise-wide BI: This target supports current and future BI needs. A critical component is an enterprise data warehouse.

- Support for organizational transformation: With this target, BI is used to fundamentally change how a company competes in the marketplace. BI supports a new business model and enables the business strategy.

3. **Specify the BI applications available to users for data analysis, and provide examples of how each one might be used to solve a business problem at your university.**

Users have a variety of BI applications available to help them analyze data. These applications include multidimensional analysis, data mining, and decision support systems.

Multidimensional data analysis, also called *on-line analytical processing (OLAP)*, involves "slicing and dicing" data stored in a dimensional format, drilling down to greater data detail, and aggregating data. Data mining is the process of searching for valuable business information in a large database, data warehouse, or data mart. Decision support systems (DSS) combine models and data in an attempt to analyze semi-structured and some unstructured problems with extensive user involvement. (We leave it to you to provide examples of using each application at your university.)

4. **Describe three BI applications that present the results of data analyses to users, and offer examples of how businesses and government agencies can use each of these technologies.**

A dashboard provides easy access to timely information and direct access to management reports. A geographic information system (GIS) is a computer-based system for capturing, integrating, manipulating, and displaying data using digitized maps. Reality mining analyzes information extracted from the usage patterns of mobile phones and other wireless devices. (Examples of how these technologies might be used by businesses and government agencies, we leave to you.)

5. **Describe corporate performance management, and provide an example of how your university could use CPM.**

Corporate performance management (CPM) is involved with monitoring and managing an organization's performance according to key performance indicators (KPIs) such as revenue, return on investment (ROI), overhead, and operational costs. (We leave it to you to supply an example of how your university might use CPM.)

[Chapter Glossary]

business intelligence (BI) A broad category of applications, technologies, and processes for gathering, storing, accessing, and analyzing data to help business users make better decisions.

corporate performance management (CPM) The area of business intelligence involved with monitoring and managing an organization's performance, according to key performance indicators (KPIs) such as revenue, return on investment (ROI), overhead, and operational costs.

dashboard A BI application that provides rapid access to timely information and direct access to management reports.

data mining The process of searching for valuable business information in a large database, data warehouse, or data mart.

decision A choice that individuals and groups make among two or more alternatives.

decision support systems (DSSs) Business intelligence systems that combine models and data in an attempt to solve semi-structured and some unstructured problems with extensive user involvement.

geographic information system (GIS) A computer-based system for capturing, integrating, manipulating, and displaying data using digitized maps.

management A process by which organizational goals are achieved through the use of resources.

model A simplified representation, or abstraction, of reality in decision making.

multidimensional data analysis (see **on-line analytical processing (OLAP)**)

on-line analytical processing (OLAP) (multidimensional data analysis) A set of capabilities for "slicing and dicing" data using dimensions and measures associated with the data.

productivity The ratio between the inputs to a process and the outputs from that process.

reality mining Process that allows analysts to extract information from the usage patterns of mobile phones and other wireless devices.

[Discussion Questions]

1. Your company is considering opening a new factory in China. List several typical activities involved in each phase of the decision (intelligence, design, and choice).
2. Recall that data mining found that young men in the United States tend to buy beer and diapers at the same time when they shop at convenience stores. Now that you know this relationship exists, can you provide a rationale for it?
3. Chipotle is one of the fastest-growing restaurant companies in the United States. Chipotle continues to offer a focused menu of burritos, tacos, burrito bowls (a burrito without the tortilla) and salads made from fresh, high-quality raw ingredients, prepared using classic cooking methods and served in a distinctive atmosphere. One of the main decisions that Chipotle's operations managers often need to make is about menu changes (e.g., dishes to add, remove or change) for Chipotle's 1,400 restaurants. Describe how the intelligence phase of Simon's decision-making process would apply to this decision and explain the role that information systems would play in this phase of the decision-making process. How can the use of BI assist the company in this endeavour?
4. Discuss the strategic benefits of BI systems.
5. Will BI replace business analysts? (Hint: See W. McKnight, "Business Intelligence: Will Business Intelligence Replace the Business Analyst?" *DMReview*, February 2005.)

[Problem-Solving Activities]

1. The city of London (England) charges an entrance fee for automobiles and trucks into the city centre. About 1,000 digital cameras photograph the licence plate of every vehicle passing by. Computers read the plate numbers and match them against records in a database of cars for which the fee has been paid for that day. If the computer does not find a match, the car owner receives a citation by mail. Examine the issues pertaining to how this process is accomplished, the mistakes it can make, and the consequences of those mistakes. Also, examine how well the system is working by checking press reports. Finally, relate the process to business intelligence.
2. Using your favourite web search engine find the answers to the following questions:
   a. What technology components are required to implement business intelligence systems?
   b. Who are the potential users of BI? What would each type of user attempt to achieve?
   c. What are the people, organizational, and management requirements in order to implement a business intelligence system in a company?
3. Enter *www.fico.com*, and find products for fraud detection and risk analysis. Prepare a report.
4. Access *www.ted.com/index.php/talks/view/id/92* to find the video of Hans Rosling's presentation. Comment on his data visualization techniques.
5. Enter *www.visualmining.com*. Explore the relationship between visualization and business intelligence. See how business intelligence is related to dashboards.
6. Access *http://businessintelligence.ittoolbox.com*. Identify all types of business intelligence software. Join a discussion group about topics discussed in this chapter. Prepare a report.
7. Visit the sites of some GIS vendors (such as *www.mapinfo.com*, *www.esri.ca*, or *www.autodesk.com*). Download a demo. What are some of the most important capabilities and applications?

[Spreadsheet Activity: Linking Sheets with Formulas]

Objective: The objective of this activity is to help you understand that while spreadsheets are powerful, an interconnected workbook is even more so. You will learn how to write formulas that use information contained in different pages to help tie the workbook together.

Chapter Connection: Even though spreadsheets are antiquated and often not able to keep up with the vast amounts of data needed to run an organization, spreadsheets still occupy an important place in most organizations. This activity brings business intelligence to smaller organizations.

Activity: As you have seen, business intelligence is a huge concept. It can, however, also apply in much smaller ways to everyday business. Business intelligence can help small organizations in tremendous ways. Consider the following example.

Ted is a 45-year-old full-time accountant. He loves his job and has had quite a successful career. He also takes great pride in working with his hands. Specifically, he has always enjoyed working with wood and making small rocking horses for children. For years he just made these for family and friends, but lately he has decided to start selling his work. The accountant side of him has kept detailed records of his inventory, costs, sales, hours, profits, losses, and so on. Now it is time to take his workbook and create business intelligence out of it.

Ted's spreadsheet contains some basic information but no formulas. Notes describe what he has done and the decisions he wants to make. You can download the spreadsheet from *www.wiley.com/go/rainer/spreadsheet* (look for Chapter 10 links). Specifically, Ted wants to know how much he has invested in each rocking horse. His time, materials, advertising, and other costs will definitely make a difference in his final price. Keep in mind that the point of this spreadsheet is to provide business intelligence. Although spreadsheet skills are required, they are the means to the end of helping Ted set appropriate prices.

Deliverable: The final product will be a spreadsheet with Ted's data calculated to provide business intelligence in a small business scenario.

Discussion Questions

1. How does algebra play a role in writing formulas?
2. What happens to your data if you build a formula off of a previously incorrect formula?
3. If formulas are set up to predict or forecast (such as in regression), how many scenarios could be calculated?

[Case Assignment]

Insurance companies and credit card providers are concerned with preventing fraud and theft. To do so, they often use advanced information systems.

Insurance companies are diversified companies that sell a wide variety of products. Often, they discontinue products and then decide to add new ones. For example, individuals may be subject to mortgage fraud, where an individual may have identity theft occur and an unauthorized mortgage is placed against his or her property. To help protect individuals, some insurance companies are starting to sell title insurance. The insurance would cover the costs associated with the individual removing the unauthorized mortgage from his or her records.

Required

a. For each of the following BI systems, describe how it functions, and explain how an insurance company could use the system.
   - OLAP
   - GIS
   - DSS
   - CPM
b. The Arviat Insurance Company is thinking of offering title insurance as one of its products. Describe the three phases of Simon's decision-making model (intelligence, design, and choice). For each of these three phases, provide an example of how information systems could be used during the phase to help the insurance company decide whether or not it should offer title insurance as one of its products.

[Team Assignments]

1. Using data mining, it is possible not only to capture information that has been buried in distant courthouses, but also to manipulate and index it. This process can benefit law enforcement but invade privacy. In 1996, Lexis-Nexis, the on-line information service, was accused of permitting access to sensitive information on individuals. The company argued that it was unfairly targeted because it provided only basic residential data for lawyers and law enforcement personnel. Should Lexis-Nexis be prohibited from providing access to such information? Debate the issue.

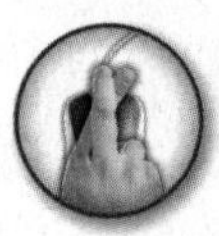

2. Each group will use a search engine of their choice to find combined GIS/GPS applications as well as look at various vendor sites to find success stories. (For GPS vendors, look at *http://biz.yahoo.com* (directory) and Google.) Each group will make a presentation of five applications and their benefits.
3. Each group will access a leading business intelligence vendor's website (for example, MicroStrategy, Oracle, Hyperion, Microsoft, SAS, SPSS, Cognos, and Business Objects). Each group will present a report on a vendor, highlighting each vendor's BI capabilities.

[Case 10.2 **Norfolk Southern**]

The Business Problem

Norfolk Southern is one of four large freight railroads in the United States. Each day, the company moves approximately 500 freight trains across 21,000 route miles (34,000 km) in 22 eastern U.S. states, as well as Ontario. Norfolk Southern manages more than $26 billion in assets and employs more than 30,000 people.

For more than a century, the railroad industry was heavily regulated, and Norfolk Southern and its predecessor railroads made money by managing their costs. Managers focused on optimizing the use of railcars to get the maximum production out of their fixed assets. Then, in 1980, the industry was partially deregulated, which opened up opportunities for mergers and allowed companies to charge rates based on service and to enter into contracts with customers. On-time delivery became an important factor in the industry.

Over time, Norfolk Southern responded to these industry changes by becoming a "scheduled railroad." Simply put, the company developed a fixed set of train schedules for cars to go between trains and yards. In this way, managers could predict when they could deliver a shipment to a customer.

Norfolk Southern had always used a variety of sophisticated systems to run its business. Becoming a scheduled railroad, however, required new systems that would use statistical models to determine the best routes and connections to optimize railroad performance and then apply the models to create the plan that would actually run the railroad operations. These new systems were called *TOP*, short for Thoroughbred Operating Plan. The railroad deployed TOP in 1992.

Norfolk Southern realized that in addition to implementing TOP, it had to monitor and measure its performance against the TOP plan. Norfolk Southern's numerous information systems generate millions of records about freight, railcars, train GPS information, train fuel levels, revenue information, crew management, and historical tracking records. Unfortunately, the company was not able to tap these data without jeopardizing the system's performance.

The IT Solution

In 1995, the company invested in a 1-terabyte data warehouse in which the data are easy to access (using a web browser) and can be manipulated for decision support. The warehouse data are collected from source systems that run the company. After the data are moved from the source systems' databases to the warehouse, users can access and use the data without affecting company operations.

In 2002, the data warehouse became a critical component of TOP. Norfolk Southern built a TOP dashboard application that pulls data from the data warehouse and then graphically depicts actual performance against the trip plan for both train performance and connection performance. The application uses visualization technology so that field managers can more easily interpret the large volumes of data (e.g., 160,000 weekly connections across the network).

Norfolk Southern has an enterprise data warehouse, which means that data placed in the warehouse become available across the company, not just for a single application or a single department. Although the company uses train and connection performance data primarily for the TOP application, it can use those data for many other purposes as well. For example, the marketing department has developed an application called *accessNS* for Norfolk Southern customers who want visibility into the company's extensive transportation network. Customers usually want to know where their shipments are "right now," and sometimes they also want historical information: Where did my shipment come from? How long did it take to arrive? What were the problems along the route?

The accessNS app enables more than 14,500 users from 8,000 customer organizations to log in and access predefined and customer reports about their accounts at any time. Users can access current data, which are updated hourly, and can also review data from the past three years. The app also provides alerts and RSS feeds. In fact, accessNS pushes 4,500 reports to users daily. The self-service nature of accessNS has allowed Norfolk Southern to provide customers the information they want while reducing the number of people needed for customer service. Without accessNS, approximately 47 people would be needed to support the current level of customer reporting.

Departments across the company—from engineering and strategic planning to accounting and human resources—use the enterprise data warehouse. One especially creative internal application was developed by human resources. The department needed to determine where to locate its field offices in order to best meet the needs of Norfolk Southern's approximately 30,000 employees. By combining employee demographic data (e.g., postal codes) with geospatial data traditionally used by the engineering group, HR was able to visually map out the employee population density, making it much easier to optimize the location of service offices.

The Results

The Norfolk Southern data warehouse has evolved into a 34-terabyte system that manages a voluminous amount of information on the company's vast network of railroads and shipping services. Norfolk Southern uses the data warehouse to analyze trends, develop forecasting schedules, archive records, and facilitate customer self-service. The data warehouse provides information to more than 3,000 employees and 14,000 external customers and stakeholders. The number of missed connections has decreased by 60 percent since the application was implemented. Further, the amount of time it takes to unload a railcar, reload it, and attach it to another train has decreased by an entire day, which translates into millions of dollars in annual savings.

Norfolk Southern was the first railroad to offer self-service business intelligence, and this innovation served as an example that other railroads have followed. The company was also one of the first railroads to provide a large variety of historical data to external customers.

Questions

1. Provide one example applied to Norfolk Southern of the use of BI as "one or a few related BI applications" and another example of the use of BI as "the development of infrastructure to support enterprise-wide BI."
2. Would all three types of uses of BI applications require the same data management technologies? Why or why not? Could all three types of BI usage be implemented without having to make changes to management styles within the company? Why or why not?
3. Describe other BI applications for data analysis that Norfolk Southern could develop using the data warehouse. (Hint: Remember that a railroad has to track trains, railcars, people, and cargo.)
4. Describe two BI applications for presenting results that Norfolk Southern could benefit from.
5. Provide two examples of how corporate performance management could be used at Norfolk Southern.
6. What is the importance of allowing external parties to access data in Norfolk Southern's data warehouse? What are the risks and rewards of allowing such access?

Source: Used with permission of Professors Barbara Wixom (University of Virginia), Hugh Watson (University of Georgia), and Jeff Hoffer (University of Dayton); *www.nscorp.com*, accessed May 27, 2013.

[Interactive Case]

Developing Managerial Support Systems for Ruby's Club

Go to the Ruby's Club link at the Student Companion website or *WileyPLUS* for information about your current internship assignment. You will analyze and recommend managerial support systems to help the club's managers better understand their monthly goals and how to achieve them.

Chapter 11

Acquiring Information Systems and Applications

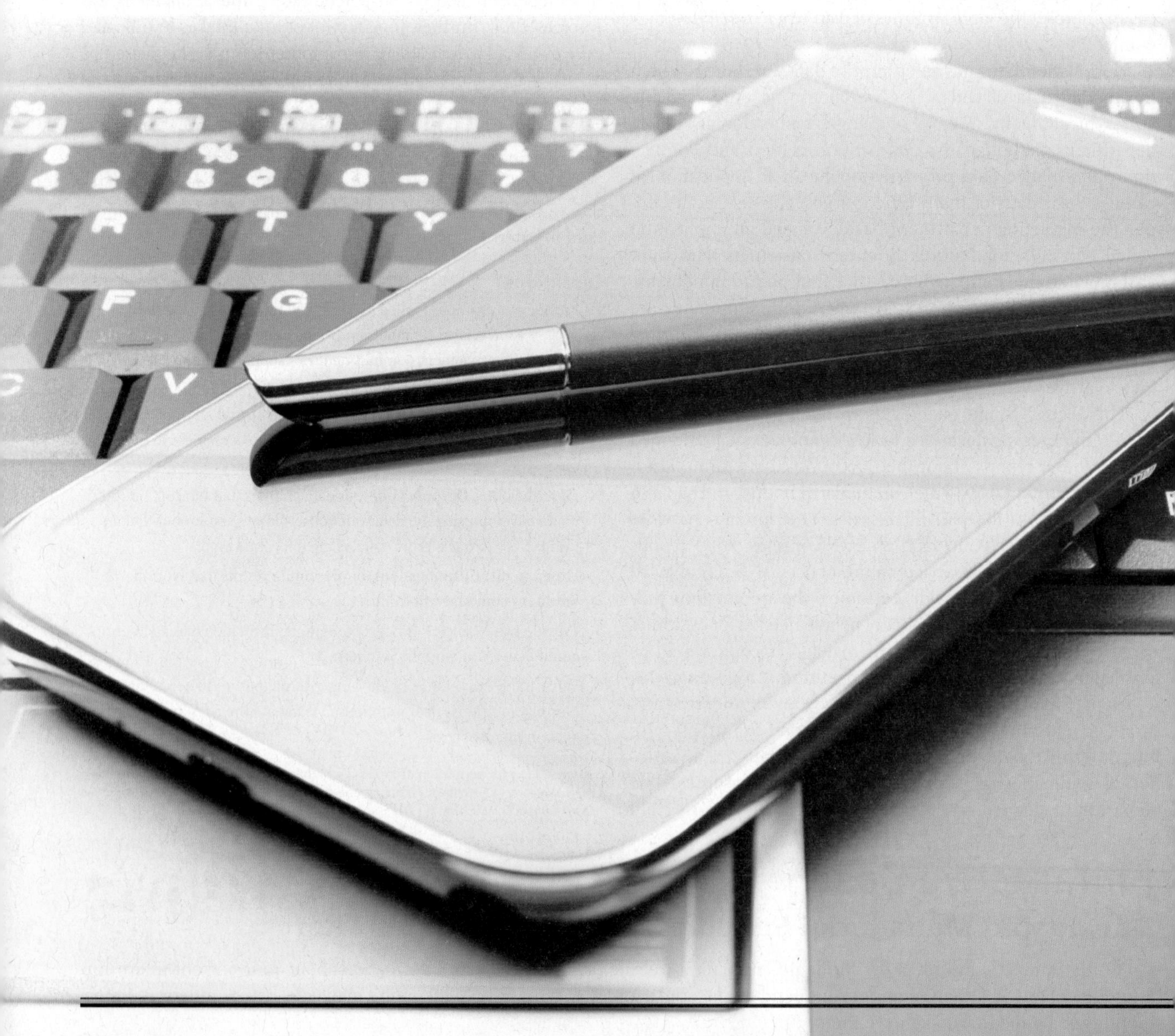

[LEARNING OBJECTIVES]

1. Define an IT strategic plan. Identify the three objectives it must meet. Describe the four common approaches to cost-benefit analysis.
2. Discuss the four business decisions that companies must make when they acquire new applications.
3. Identify the six processes involved in the systems development life cycle. Explain the primary tasks and the importance of each process.
4. Describe four alternative development methods and four tools that augment development methods. Identify at least one advantage and one disadvantage of each method and tool.
5. Analyze the process of vendor and software selection.

[CHAPTER OUTLINE]

11.1 Planning for and Justifying IT Applications
11.2 Strategies for Acquiring IT Applications
11.3 The Traditional Systems Development Life Cycle
11.4 Alternative Methods and Tools for Systems Development
11.5 Vendor and Software Selection

[WEB RESOURCES]

Student Companion Site
wiley.com/college/rainer

- Student PowerPoints for note taking
- Interactive Case: Ruby's Club Assignments
- Complete glossary

WileyPlus

All of the above and

- E-book
- Mini-lecture by author for each chapter section
- Practice quizzes
- Flash Cards for vocabulary review
- Additional "What's in IT for Me?" cases
- Video interviews with managers
- Lab Manual for Microsoft Office 2010
- How-to Animations for Microsoft Office 2010

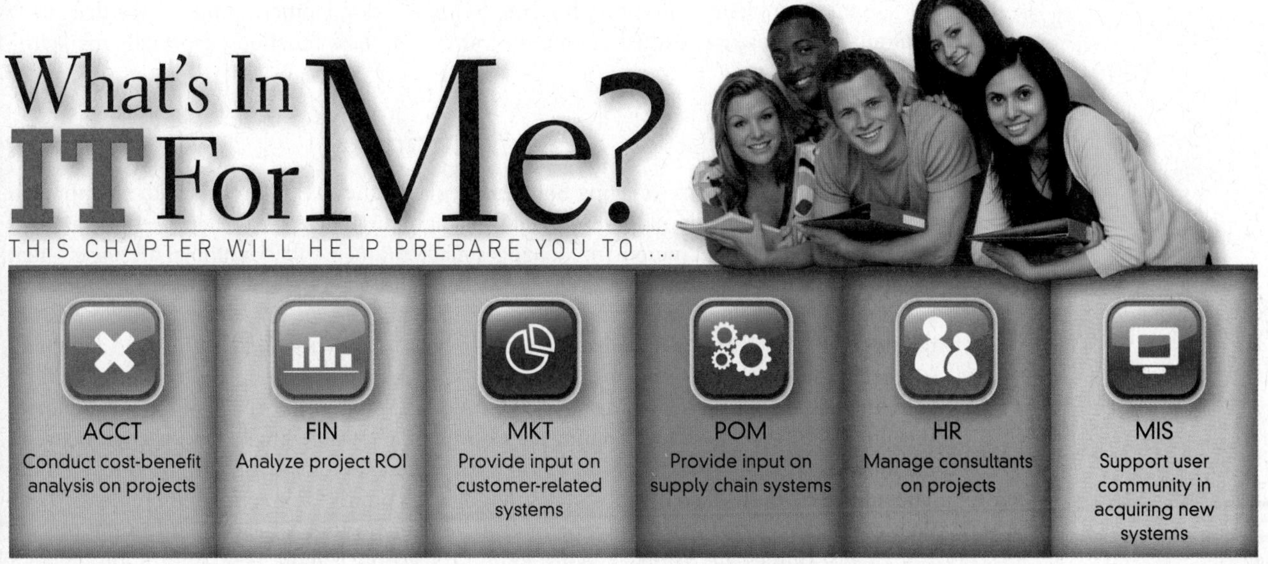

What's In IT For Me?
THIS CHAPTER WILL HELP PREPARE YOU TO ...
ACCT
Conduct cost-benefit analysis on projects
FIN
Analyze project ROI
MKT
Provide input on customer-related systems
POM
Provide input on supply chain systems
HR
Manage consultants on projects
MIS
Support user community in acquiring new systems

[Case 11.1 GE Healthcare Switches from Systems Development Life Cycle to Agile Development]

The Business Problem

It's difficult enough for small and medium-sized enterprises to adapt new software to change their business processes. But what do you do when you're a multibillion-dollar business? That was the problem facing GE Healthcare (*www.gehealthcare.com*), a $17-billion business unit of multinational giant General Electric (*www.ge.com*). GE Healthcare manufactures more than a dozen types of high-tech medical equipment, ranging from high-definition CT scanners to diagnostic pharmaceutical devices. These products are developed by the company's Imaging Solutions unit, which has some 375 engineers. Unfortunately, this unit was experiencing several difficulties.

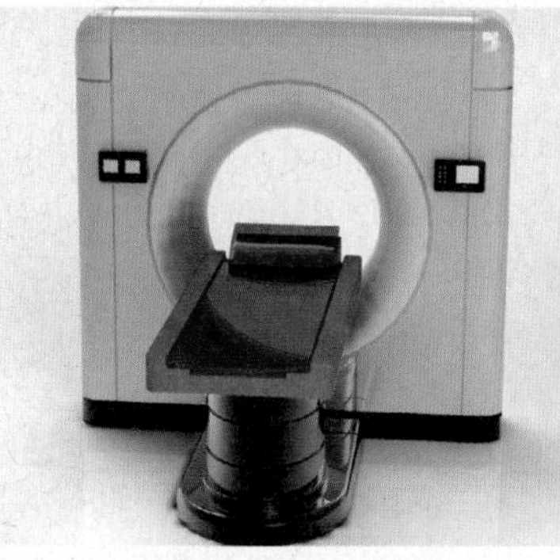

Dariush M./Shutterstock

First, Imaging Solutions' traditional systems development life cycle (SDLC; discussed in detail in the chapter) was too long, taking from 18 to 24 months. To compensate for these significant delays, the unit tried to appease customers by adding features that were never part of the products' original design. This often made matters worse, increasing the scope of projects, causing further delays, and increasing project cycle time even more. By the time a product was ready for market, the original user requirements were sometimes out of date.

Second, Imaging Solutions' SDLC approach followed a long and regimented process. It began with investigation, systems analysis, and systems design. Next, the unit would conduct a formal design review. Only after the unit received the various approvals for the design would it begin programming the new product.

The programming phase usually lasted several months, after which the development team released the product into a test environment for user feedback. This stage usually was the first time that the users saw the new product. After accumulating and incorporating the users' input, the team continued testing before implementing the new product.

Because users did not have input until late in the project cycle, the company could not incorporate user-requested modifications until quite late in the project development. Any significant errors that users identified could require the team to change the design completely or, in effect, to start over. This approach wasted a great deal of time and effort, and it further delayed the project.

The third problem confronting Imaging Solutions' development projects was that many communication barriers existed among the various business functions, especially marketing and engineering.

The Solution

To address these problems, Imaging Solutions replaced the SDLC process with an approach to software and product development called agile development. Agile development is based on iterations—frequent and incremental changes made through collaboration at all stages—that usually result in shorter product cycles. Imaging Solutions implemented a scrum initiative based on agile development. *Scrum* (discussed in detail later in this chapter) maximizes the development team's ability to deliver iterations quickly and to respond effectively to additional user requirements as they emerge. The agile development of scrum, in contrast to the SDLC, adds functionality in a series of phases and then tests the product after each phase is completed. Imaging Solutions hoped that adopting agile development would break down barriers between the functional areas so that everyone would work together to release the right product on time. The unit particularly liked the idea of developing each product in a series of increments. They then could demonstrate each increment's functionality to users at each point in the process and receive immediate feedback. This approach was much more economical and efficient than receiving feedback when the system was almost complete.

Imaging Solutions launched its move to agile development with a single development team. The unit staffed a strong cross-functional team and defined a manageable four-month pilot project substantial enough that the team could learn scrum skills while still delivering a valuable product. The team also established clear success criteria for evaluating whether goals had been achieved.

The Results

The pilot project was delivered successfully with the correct features and functionality. However, the release was delayed by one month, so Imaging Solutions was working to make further improvements in the predictability of delivery.

Imaging Solutions learned important lessons from the pilot project. The products it makes are highly regulated, meaning that engineers need to identify, plan for, and meet many additional quality and regulatory steps. These steps must be part of the iterations, and they can't be skipped over or done as quickly as some agile development projects. Operating in a regulated industry required the unit to use a hybrid development process that involved more initial planning and testing than would be used by other agile organizations.

Following the pilot project, Imaging Solutions formed 10 scrum teams of seven to nine people each, including one team consisting of unit leaders. Every two weeks, the teams conduct their increment reviews together on Wednesday morning and hold planning meetings for the next increment on Wednesday afternoon. This process ensures that teams share their knowledge, and it also provides visibility into what is going on outside any team's activities.

The scrum teams need to be managed closely so they work together when needed but otherwise stay out of each other's way. Imaging Solutions discovered that it needs to identify these cross-team dependencies early. The unit implemented software from Rally called Agile ALM (*www.rallydev.com*) to track cross-team dependencies and to generate real-time status updates on the progress of each increment.

Ever since Imaging Solutions implemented the new methodology, the various development teams have begun to share user stories and tasks. Further, the teams that complete their own tasks early now assist other teams.

To obtain maximum benefits from the agile process, Imaging Solutions had to transform its culture by modifying the roles of managers and individual contributors on scrum teams. For example, managers now avoid a command-and-control style, where work is done by order, and instead concentrate on putting together empowered teams.

Imaging Solutions is still rolling out agile development, using it for about 60 percent of its new products as of 2012, and aiming to use it eventually for most of its products.

Imaging Solutions is seeing positive results. One of its first projects using agile was completed in 12 months instead of the usual 18 to 24 months. Obtaining user feedback early and often enables the unit to prioritize features correctly. In one case, the system helped a team identify a clinical workflow of which they were previously unaware.

What We Learned from This Case

The GE Healthcare case highlights several problems with systems development that employs the traditional systems development life cycle. The case also emphasizes the importance of early, frequent user input into the systems development process, which the agile development methodology encourages. GE Healthcare is a huge, complex, multibillion-dollar enterprise; but acquiring information systems in smaller organizations is a complicated process as well. IT's About Small Business 11.1 illustrates how ShopMyClothes.com deals with some it its technology issues.

Even for small businesses, information system upgrades present a complex problem. Small organizations must select vendors based on a number of factors, specifically (1) the ability of the vendor's product(s) to meet the organization's current business needs, (2) the viability of the vendor as a whole (i.e., you do not want to sign a contract with someone who might go into bankruptcy), and (3) the relationship between the two companies. After the organization has selected a vendor, the two parties must decide on the contract and clear it with their lawyers. Finally, the organization must acquire the hardware to support the new software. Even for a small business, these decisions are very important because of the lasting impact of the investment: the right information systems may not "make or break" the organization, but they can definitely help it become more competitive.

IT's about [small] business

11.1 ShopMyClothes: High Fashion Sales

What do you do with your used clothing? Give them to places like Value Village or the Salvation Army? If you spend hundreds of dollars for clothing and it is still in good shape, you might want to consider selling them at ShopMyClothes.com. This website was started by Torontonian Jonathan Elias, who had too many clothes and wanted to sell some of them. He created an easy-to-use website so that people can post clothes for sale without haggling (which he believes is a major selling feature of his website). The site earns its revenue from advertising.

To ensure quality control over the thousands of clothing items that are posted, each item is individually checked before posting. However, the company had high website development and maintenance costs, due to the complexity of the platform it used, Microsoft's .NET Framework, which is described as "cumbersome." Microsoft claims that this platform is easy to use and provides the flexibility of object-oriented programming. ShopMyClothes.com dealt with the high costs by moving from having totally local programming to outsourcing much of its programming to India and having local programming available on a standby basis. To get a functioning website after many delays, the company had to fire its previous contract programmer.

Questions

1. Would acquiring a new information system for a small organization be a longer or shorter process than acquiring one for a large organization? Why or why not? Support your answer.
2. How does the selection of an underlying technology platform (such as Microsoft .NET) affect programming choices?

Sources: Compiled from S. Findlay, "Cracking Code in the Name of High Fashion," *Toronto Star*, January 14, 2013, p. B3, C. Wong, "ShopMyClothes Sees Big Dollar Signs in Used Designer Duds," ITbusiness.ca, January 10, 2012; M. Johne, "Connecting Fashionistas with a Shared Love Bargains," *Globe and Mail*, October 31, 2011; C. Sliwa, "Pros & Cons: .Net vs. J2EE," Computerworld.com, May 20, 2002, accessed May 1, 2013.

Competitive organizations move quickly to acquire new information technologies or modify existing ones when they need to improve efficiencies and gain strategic advantage. Today, however, acquisition goes beyond building new systems in-house, and IT resources go beyond software and hardware. The old model in which firms built their own systems is being replaced with a broader perspective of IT resource acquisition that provides companies multiple options. Thus, companies now must decide which IT tasks will remain in-house, and even whether the entire IT resource should be provided and managed by outside organizations. Regardless of which approach an organization chooses, however, it must be able to manage IT projects adeptly.

In this chapter you learn about the process of acquiring IT resources from a managerial perspective. This means from *your* perspective, because you will be closely involved in all aspects of acquiring information systems and applications in your organization. In fact, when "users" are mentioned in this chapter, we are talking about you. You will also study and learn how to evaluate the available options for acquiring IT resources. Finally, you will learn how organizations plan and justify the acquisition of new information systems.

11.1 Planning for and Justifying IT Applications

Organizations must analyze the need for applications, justifying each purchase in terms of costs and benefits. The need for information systems is usually related to organizational planning and to the analysis of the organization's performance vis-à-vis its competitors. The cost-benefit

Sources: Compiled from J. Hammond, "Customer-Centric Development: It's Now or Never for IT Shops," *InformationWeek*, April 26, 2011; S. Denning, "Six Common Mistakes That Salesforce.com Didn't Make," *Forbes*, April 18, 2011; A. Deitsch and R. Hughes, "GE Healthcare Goes Agile, "*InformationWeek*, December 6, 2010; J. Vijayan, "The Grill: John Burke, "*Computerworld*, September 13, 2010; J. Kobelius, "Agile Data Warehousing: Do You Scrum?" *InformationWeek*, July 21, 2010; R. King, "GE Becomes More Agile," *The CIO Report*, *Wall Street Journal*, May 30, 2012; *www.ge.com*, *www.gehealthcare.com*, *www.rallydev.com*, accessed March 17, 2013.

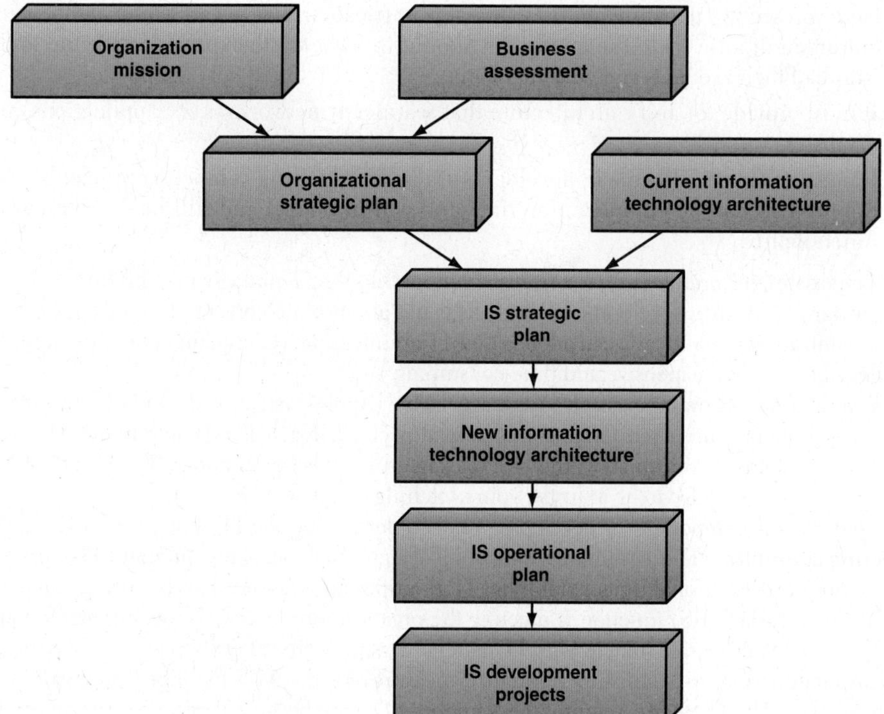

FIGURE 11.1 The information system (IS) planning process.

justification must determine whether investing in a specific IT application is preferable to spending the funds on alternative projects. This chapter focuses on the formal processes of large organizations. Smaller organizations employ less formal processes, or no processes at all. At the very least, decision makers in small organizations should consider each step for planning changes to their information systems (ISs).

IT Planning

The planning process for new IT applications begins with analyzing the *organizational strategic plan*, which is illustrated in Figure 11.1. The organization's strategic plan identifies the firm's overall mission, the goals that follow from that mission, and the broad steps required to reach these goals. The strategic planning process modifies the organization's objectives and resources to match its changing markets and opportunities.

The organizational strategic plan and the existing IT architecture provide the inputs in developing the IT strategic plan. The *IT architecture* describes how an organization should use its information resources to accomplish its mission. This encompasses both the technical and the managerial aspects of information resources. The technical aspects include hardware and operating systems, networking, data management systems, and applications software. The managerial aspects specify how the IT department will be managed, how the functional area managers will be involved, and how IT decisions will be made.

The **IT strategic plan** is a set of long-range goals that describe the IT infrastructure and identify the major IT initiatives needed to achieve the organization's goals. The IT strategic plan must meet three objectives:

1. It must be aligned with the organization's strategic plan. This alignment is critical because the organization's ISs have to support the organization's strategies. (Recall the discussion of organizational strategies and information systems in Chapter 2.)

   Consider the example of Hudson's Bay versus Walmart. An application that improves customer service at a small cost would probably be considered favourably at The Bay, but it would be rejected at Walmart. The reason is that the application would align with The Bay's customer service strategy. It would not fit in well, however, with Walmart's low-cost strategy.

Here you see two department stores, the same application, and the same cost and benefits, but different answers to the question, "Should we develop the application?" due to the nature of their products and customer base.

2. It must provide for an IT architecture that seamlessly networks users, applications, and databases.
3. It must efficiently allocate IS development resources among competing projects so that the projects can be completed on time and within budget and still have the required functionality.

The existing IT architecture is a necessary input into the IT strategic plan because it acts as a constraint on future development efforts. It is not an absolute constraint, however, because the organization theoretically can adopt a new IT architecture. (Companies prefer to avoid this strategy because it is expensive and time-consuming.)

Consider the following example: You have a Mac (Apple) system, and you need a new software application. You search for, and find several packages for, both Macintosh and Microsoft Windows systems. Unfortunately, the best package runs only on Windows. How much better would this package have to be to justify your switching to a new system?

One critical component in developing and implementing the IT strategic plan is the **IT steering committee**. This committee, consisting of a group of managers and staff who represent the various organizational units, establishes IT priorities and ensures that the management information system (MIS) function is meeting the organization's needs. The committee's major tasks are to link corporate strategy with IT strategy, to approve the allocation of resources for the MIS function, and to establish performance measures for the MIS function and ensure that they are met. The IT steering committee is important to you because it ensures that you get the information systems and applications that you need to do your job.

After a company has agreed on an IT strategic plan, it next develops the *IS operational plan*. This plan consists of a clear set of projects that the IS department and the functional area managers will execute in support of the IT strategic plan. A typical IS operational plan contains the following elements:

- *Mission*—The mission of the IS function (derived from the IT strategy).
- *IS environment*—A summary of the information needs of the functional areas and of the organization as a whole.
- *Objectives of the IS function*—The best current estimate of the goals of the IS function.
- *Constraints on the IS function*—Technological, financial, personnel, and other resource limitations on the IS function.
- *Application portfolio*—A prioritized inventory of present applications and a detailed plan of projects to be developed or continued during the current year.
- *Resource allocation and project management*—A listing of who is going to do what, how, and when.

Evaluating and Justifying IT Investment: Benefits, Costs, and Issues

Developing an IT plan is the first step in the acquisition process. Because all companies have limited resources, they must justify investing resources in some areas, including IT, rather than in others. Essentially, justifying IT investment involves calculating the costs, assessing the benefits (values), and comparing the two. This comparison is frequently referred to as *cost-benefit analysis*. Cost-benefit analysis is not a simple task.

Assessing the Costs. Placing a dollar value on the cost of IT investments is not as simple as it sounds. One major challenge that companies face is allocating fixed costs among different IT projects. *Fixed costs* are those costs that remain the same regardless of any change in the activity level. For IT, fixed costs include costs for infrastructure, IT services, and IT management. The salary of the IT director, for example, is fixed, and adding one more project will not change it.

Another complication is that a system's costs do not end after it is installed; rather, costs for maintaining, debugging, and improving the system can accumulate over many years. This is a critical point because organizations sometimes fail to anticipate these costs when they make the initial investment.

A dramatic example of unanticipated expenses was the Year 2000 (Y2K) reprogramming projects, which cost organizations worldwide billions of dollars. In the 1960s, computer memory was very expensive. To save money, programmers coded the "year" in the date field as 19_ _ instead of _ _ _ _. With the "1" and the "9" hard-coded in the computer program, only the last two digits varied, so computer programs needed less memory. The problem with this approach, however, was that when the year 2000 rolled around, computers would display the year as 1900. This programming technique could have caused serious problems with financial applications, insurance applications, and countless other apps.

This Y2K example illustrates the point that database design choices tend to impact the organization for a long time. As the 21st century approached, no one still used hardware or software from the 1960s (other than in a few legacy applications). Database design choices made in the 1960s, however, often were still in effect.

Assessing the Benefits. Evaluating the benefits of IT projects is typically even more complex than calculating the costs. Benefits may be harder to quantify, especially because they may be intangible (for example, improved customer or partner relations or improved decision making). As an employee, you probably will be asked for input about the intangible benefits that an IS provides for you.

The fact that organizations use IT for multiple purposes complicates benefit analysis. To obtain a return from an IT investment, the company must implement the technology successfully. In reality, many systems are not implemented on time, within budget, or with all the features originally envisioned for them. If the proposed system is "cutting edge," there may be no historical basis for identifying the types of financial payback the company can expect. Companies may actually implement the technology at one or more locations to verify that the technology functions effectively and is accepted by consumers. For example, Walmart tested the use of iPhones for scanning of products as they are placed into bags. Consumers still had to pay for the purchases at a self-checkout counter. The test was conducted in a store near Walmart's headquarters in the U.S. This type of a test helps a company confirm how a technology will function, and to solidify the estimates of costs and benefits.

Conducting the Cost-Benefit Analysis. After a company has assessed the costs and benefits of IT investments, it must compare them. You have studied, or will study, cost-benefit analyses in more detail in your finance courses. The point here is that real-world business problems do not come in neatly wrapped packages labelled "finance problem" or "IS problem"; rather, business problems span multiple functional areas.

There is no uniform strategy for conducting a cost-benefit analysis. An organization can perform this task in several ways. Here you see four common approaches: (1) net present value, (2) return on investment, (3) breakeven analysis, and (4) the business case approach.

- Analysts use the *net present value (NPV)* method to convert future values of benefits to their present-value equivalents by "discounting" them at the organization's cost of funds. They then can compare the present value of the future benefits with the cost required to achieve those benefits to determine whether the benefits exceed the costs.
- *Return on investment (ROI)* measures management's effectiveness in generating profits with its available assets. ROI is calculated by dividing the net income that a project generates by the average assets invested in the project. ROI is a percentage, and the higher the percentage return, the better.
- *Breakeven analysis* determines the point at which the cumulative dollar value of the benefits from a project equals the investment made in the project.
- In the *business case approach*, system developers write a business case to justify funding one or more specific applications or projects. You will be a major source of input when business cases are developed because these cases describe what you do, how you do it, and how a new system could better support you.

before you go on...

1. What are some problems associated with assessing the costs of IT?
2. What difficulties accompany the intangible benefits from IT?
3. Describe the NPV, ROI, breakeven analysis, and business case approaches.

11.2 Strategies for Acquiring IT Applications

After a company has justified an IT investment, it must then decide how to pursue it. As with cost-benefit analyses, there are several options for acquiring IT applications. When contemplating which option to choose, companies must make a series of business decisions. The fundamental decisions are:

- *How much computer code does the company want to write?*

  A company can choose a totally prewritten application (to write no computer code); to customize a prewritten application (to write some computer code); or to custom-write an entire application (write all new computer code).
- *How will the company pay for the application?*

  Once the company has decided how much computer code to write, it must decide how to pay for it. In the case of prewritten or customized prewritten software, the company can buy or lease the applications. For totally custom applications, it can use internal funding.
- *Where will the application run?*

  The next decision is whether to run the application on the company's platform or on someone else's. In other words, it can employ either a software-as-a-service vendor or an application service provider. (We examine these options later in the chapter.) Some applications require unique decisions. For example, Carrie Underwood decided to wear a garment that had a projection screen (so that images could be projected onto the dress) to her Grammy performance in February 2013. The garment was actually an application system developed by Montreal's Groupe J.S. International (*www.jsgroup.com*). This meant that software and hardware to run the application had to be available at the awards ceremony location where the recording and broadcasting took place.
- *Where will the application originate?*

  Prewritten applications can be open-source software or they can come from a vendor. The company may choose to customize prewritten open-source applications or prewritten proprietary applications from vendors. Further, it may customize applications in-house or outsource the customization. Finally, it can write totally custom applications in-house or outsource this process.

In the following sections, you will see more detail on the various ways in which companies can acquire applications. As a general rule, an organization should consider all feasible acquisition methods in the light of its business requirements.

Purchase a Prewritten Application

Many commercial software packages contain the standard features required by IT applications. Therefore, purchasing an existing package can be a cost-effective and time-saving strategy compared with developing a custom application in-house. Nevertheless, a company should carefully consider and plan the buy option to ensure that the selected package addresses the company's current and future needs; otherwise, the package can quickly become obsolete. But before a company can perform this process, it must decide which features a suitable package must include.

In reality, a single software package rarely satisfies all of an organization's needs. Therefore, a company sometimes must purchase multiple packages to fulfill different needs, then

Table 11.1

Advantages and Limitations of the "Buy" Option

Advantages
Many different types of off-the-shelf software are available.
Software can be tried out.
The company can save much time by buying rather than building.
The company can know what it is getting before it invests in the product.
The company is not the first and only user.
Purchased software may eliminate the need to hire personnel specifically dedicated to a project.
Disadvantages
Software may not exactly meet the company's needs.
Software may be difficult or impossible to modify, or it may require huge business process changes to implement.
The company will not have control over software improvements and new versions.
Purchased software can be difficult to integrate with existing systems.
Vendors may discontinue a product or go out of business.
Software is controlled by another company with its own priorities and business considerations.
There may be a lack of intimate knowledge in the purchasing company about how and why the software works.

integrate these packages with one another as well as with its existing software. Table 11.1 summarizes the advantages and limitations of the buy option.

Customize a Prewritten Application

Customizing existing software is an especially attractive option if the software vendor allows the company to modify the application to meet its needs. This option, however, may not be attractive if customization is the only method of flexibly addressing those needs. It also is not the best strategy if the software is either very expensive or likely to become obsolete quickly. Further, customizing a prewritten application, particularly a large, complex one, can be extremely difficult. IT's About Business 11.2 recounts a disastrous effort by eHealth Ontario, which attempted to develop a diabetes registry.

Lease the Applications

Compared with the buy option and the option to develop applications in-house, the lease option can save a company both time and money. Of course, leased packages (like purchased packages) may not exactly fit the company's application requirements. As previously noted, however, vendor software generally includes the features most commonly needed by organizations in a given industry. Again, the company will decide which features are necessary.

It is common for interested companies to apply the 80/20 rule when evaluating vendor software. Simply put, if the software meets 80 percent of the company's needs, the company should seriously consider changing its business processes so that the remaining 20 percent are met as well. Often this is a better long-term solution than modifying the vendor software. Otherwise, the company will have to customize its software every time the vendor releases an updated application.

Leasing can be especially attractive to small and medium-size enterprises (SMEs) that cannot afford major investments in IT software. Large companies also may prefer to lease packages in order to test potential IT solutions before making major investments. As well, a company without sufficient IT personnel skilled in developing custom IT applications may choose to lease instead of developing software in-house. Even the companies that employ in-house experts may not be able to wait for strategic applications to be developed in-house. They therefore lease (or buy) applications from external resources to establish a quicker presence in the market.

IT's [about business]

11.2 A Disastrous Development Project: Hidden Costs

eHealth Ontario (*www.ehealthontario.on.ca*), an independent agency of the Ontario Ministry of Health and Long-Term Care, is responsible for the development of electronic health records in the province of Ontario. As part of this process, it contracted in mid-2010 with CGI Information Systems and Management Consultants Inc. (*www.cgi.com*) for the development of a diabetes registry, aimed at recording and tracking information about Ontarians with diabetes.

While the diabetes registry project was being developed, eHealth successfully coordinated the development of a platform to manage electronic medical records (EMRs) for the province's residents. A group of 13 different software developers was involved in that project. As of September 2012, about 9,000 Ontario physicians were using EMRs.

By 2012, there no longer seemed to be a need for a dedicated diabetes registry, since EMRs could be used to exchange information about all of an individual's medical conditions, including diabetes. Perhaps that is why eHealth Ontario cancelled the diabetes registry when it was not developed on time. It was supposed to be completed by June 30, 2011, and was still not functional in September 2012.

When the eHealth board of directors announced that the CGI contract had been cancelled, it stated that taxpayers would be shielded from the cost, since the $46.2-million contract had a clause that no payments would be made to CGI unless the system was completed. This meant that CGI was out of pocket $10- to $15 million, representing the amount of money it had so far put into

the contract for design, testing, and programming. But amid the fanfare about "no loss to taxpayers," the Ontario government at the time did not disclose that there were other costs associated with the contract that also had been paid for.

Only in the provincial auditor general's report later in 2012 was it revealed that the province had spent $24 million on the project outside of the CGI contract. This shows that external consulting costs are only a fraction of the costs associated with systems development projects. It is also uncertain whether CGI would sue eHealth with respect to the cancelled contract.

Questions

1. Debate the potential lawsuit from the point of view of eHealth and CGI.
2. Discuss the advantages and disadvantages of a long-term outsourcing contract for the development of software.

Sources: Compiled from R. Ferguson and R. Benzie, "EHealth Diabetes Registry Faxes Axe," *Toronto Star*, September 15, 2012, p. A1, A26; "eHealth Ontario Cancels Diabetes Registry," CBCNews.ca, September 18, 2012; R. Ferguson, "Scrapped Diabetes Registry Cost $24M," *Toronto Star*, December 13, 2012, p. A6; R. Ferguson, "Dalton McGuinty Admits eHealth Troubles Continued with Diabetes Registry," *Toronto Star*, September 17, 2012; "CGI Signs $46 Million, Six-Year Contract with eHealth Ontario for a Diabetes Registry and Portal Solution," CGI news release, August 9, 2010; *www.ehealthontario.on.ca*, accessed June 20, 2013.

Leasing can be executed in one of three ways. The first way is to lease the application from a software developer and install and run it on the company's platform. The vendor can assist with the installation and frequently will offer to contract for the support and maintenance of the system. Many conventional applications are leased this way.

The other two options involve leasing an application and running it on the vendor's platform. Organizations can accomplish this process by using an application service provider or a software-as-a-service (SaaS) vendor.

Application Service Providers and Software-as-a-Service Vendors

An **application service provider (ASP)** is an agent or a vendor who assembles the software needed by enterprises and packages the software with services such as development, operations, and maintenance. The customer then accesses these applications via the Internet. Figure 11.2 illustrates the operation of an ASP. Note that the ASP hosts an application and a database for each customer.

Software-as-a-service (SaaS) is a method of delivering software in which a vendor hosts the applications and provides them as a service to customers over a network, typically the Internet. Customers do not own the software; rather, they pay for using it. SaaS eliminates the need for customers to install and run applications on their own computers. Therefore, SaaS customers save the expense (money, time, IT staff) of buying, operating, and maintaining the software. For

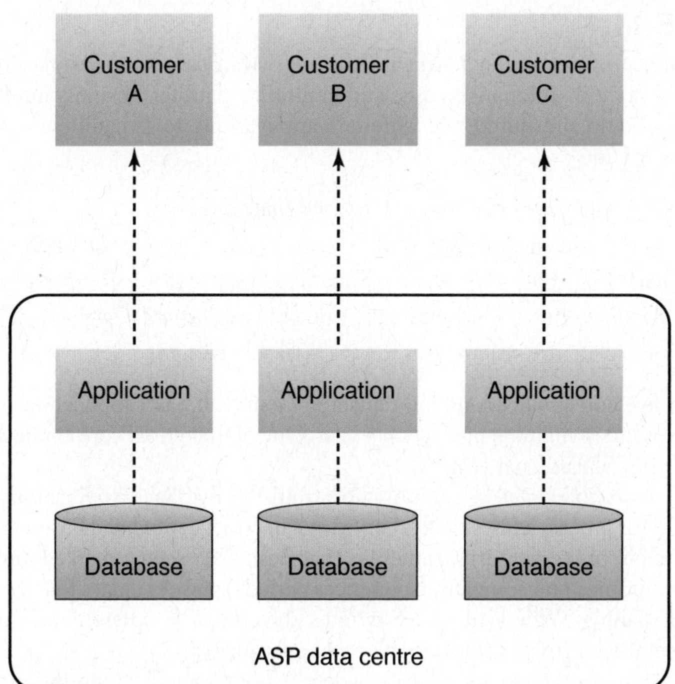

FIGURE 11.2 Operation of an application service provider (ASP).

example, Salesforce (*www.salesforce.com*), a well-known SaaS provider for customer relationship management (CRM) software, provides these advantages for its customers. Figure 11.3 displays the operation of a SaaS vendor. Note that the vendor hosts an application that multiple customers can use. Further, the vendor hosts a database that is partitioned for each customer to protect the privacy and security of each customer's data.

Software-as-a-service can provide advantages to an organization. Example 11.1 illustrates how Bosley Medical Institute made effective use of SaaS.

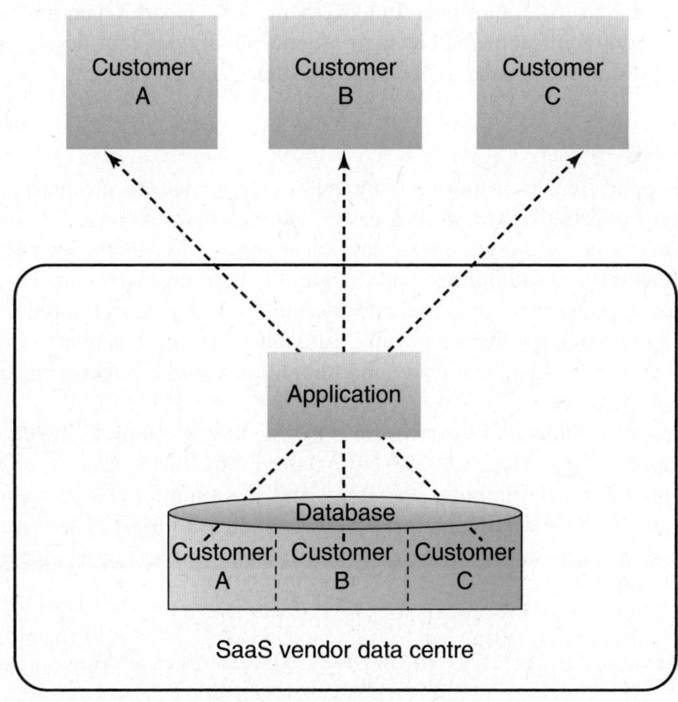

FIGURE 11.3 Operation of a software-as-a-service (SaaS) vendor.

EXAMPLE 11.1

Hair restoration provider Bosley Medical Institute (*www.bosley.com*) wanted to consolidate applications, reduce maintenance costs, and centralize data for business intelligence. The company decided to outsource five different applications to five different software-as-a-service (SaaS) vendors:

- Its scheduling system went to TimeTrade (*www.timetrade.com*).
- Its address verification application went to Acme Data (*www.acmedata.net*).
- Its direct marketing application went to Silverpop Systems (*www.silverpop.com*).
- Its inbound call centre system went to inContact (*www.incontact.com*).
- Its outbound call centre system went to Five9 (*www.five9.com*).

By retiring five core applications and replacing them with SaaS applications, Bosley is saving 20 to 30 percent in maintenance fees per year. One of the retired core applications by itself was costing Bosley $20,000 per year.

Bosley's IT team integrated the information from the five SaaS applications into its own CRM system. This process addressed the company's need for centralized business intelligence.

Another benefit of the new arrangement is that Bosley has seen a marked improvement in its application uptime. The company experiences periodic power outages that disrupt inbound and outbound dialling. With its new SaaS systems, the company representatives can still make and receive calls by logging on from wherever they are located.

This shows that when companies decide where to obtain applications, they are not limited to one vendor. Recall that in general, for prewritten applications, they can use open-source software or obtain the software from a vendor. For customized prewritten applications, they can customize open-source software or customize vendor software. For totally custom applications, they can write the software in-house or outsource the process.

Open-Source Software

Organizations obtain a licence to implement an open-source software product and either use it as is, customize it, or develop applications with it. Unless the company is one of the few that want to tinker with their source code, open-source applications are basically the same as proprietary applications except for licensing, payment, and support. Open-source is really an alternative source of applications rather than a conceptually different development option. (Open-source software is discussed in Technology Guide 2.)

Outsourcing

Acquiring IT applications from outside contractors or external organizations is called **outsourcing**. Keep in mind that outsourcing can be used in many situations. Companies may choose this strategy in certain circumstances. For example, they might want to experiment with new IT technologies without making a substantial upfront investment. They also might use outsourcing to protect their internal networks and to gain access to outside experts. One disadvantage of outsourcing is that a company's valuable corporate data may be under the control of the outsourcing vendor. There are other disadvantages with outsourcing, as IT's About Business 11.3 demonstrates.

Several types of vendors offer services for creating and operating IT systems, including e-commerce applications. Many software companies, from IBM to Oracle, offer a range of outsourcing services for developing, operating, and maintaining IT applications. IT outsourcers, such as EDS (now HP Enterprise Services), offer a variety of services. Also, large public accounting firms and management consultants—for example, Accenture—offer outsourcing services.

Sources: Compiled from C. Torode, "SaaS Applications Help Bosley Consolidate Apps, Cut Maintenance Costs," SearchCIO.com, January 13, 2010; *www.bosley.com*, accessed May 11, 2011.

IT's [about business]

11.3 Presto Card Scope Creep and Cost Escalation

Many transit systems around the world are moving from paper tickets and passes to electronic cards, to make fare payment more convenient for passengers and more cost-effective for the operators. But the development and implementation of the cards does not always go smoothly, as the case of the Presto card in Ontario shows.

Metrolinx (*www.metrolinx.com*) is an agency of the Government of Ontario, created to improve the integration of all modes of transport in the Greater Toronto and Hamilton area. In 2006, Metrolinx used a competitive process to sign a $250-million contract with consultants Accenture (*www.accenture.com*) to develop and operate the Presto card, a magnetic stripe card fare payment system. The card would be used by transit riders on GO Transit (the Government of Ontario's bus and train system in the Greater Toronto Area), and other transit systems, such as Oakville Transit and Burlington Transit. Absent from this contractual process were the cities of Toronto and Ottawa. At the time that Metrolinx signed the contract for Presto, the Toronto Transit Commission (TTC) and Ottawa's OC Transpo were going through their own processes to acquire their own transit card systems.

The Presto card system was implemented in late 2010 for its original participants, but as it rolled out for additional systems, by the end of 2012 the costs had escalated to $700 million! How did that happen?

Requirements had expanded and changed. As technology changed, Metrolinx decided that some system changes were required and that payment of fares should be possible not just by cash, but by using debit card, credit card, or smart phone. This is called an "open fare" concept. Accenture was given untendered contract additions for these enhanced capabilities. The biggest additional cost was the "open fare" subsystems, which were priced at $344 million. This additional cost was criticized by the Ontario Auditor General in December 2012, who stated that it should have gone for competitive bid as well, which could have lowered the cost of that enhancement.

One additional set of costs was consulting fees to manage the project, at $4.2 million. Apparently, Metrolinx staff were supposed to manage the project, but had also given this process to the consulting agency, Accenture. The Ontario Auditor General felt that Accenture could have been penalized according to its contract terms for not delivering the system on time. (It was due in October 2010 to go live, but in fact went live several months later.)

Given that other organizations have failed to implement transit card systems successfully, this delay looks better than failure. For example, in November 2012 the city of Calgary cancelled its contract for its own electronic fare system. Calgary had been working for two years with a Spanish company called Telvent, hoping to automate the fare systems for its light rail transit (LRT).

Even though it was late, the Presto card was successfully implemented in the original Ontario transit systems. That may have been what convinced the TTC and OC Transpo to join in with Presto. Toronto took part only after placing a cap on the amount it would pay as part of the project ($47 million in development costs), as well as placing a fixed percentage for usage (5.25 percent of fare revenues). The City of Ottawa chipped in $25 million toward the Presto card's development costs. But the launch of the card for OC Transpo was delayed by several months due to technical glitches, including the inability of card readers in buses to recognize the cards, resulting in Metrolinx refunding Ottawa $3 million of its contributions.

Transit riders did not immediately flock to use the Presto card. For example, GO Transit riders only switched to the card in big numbers when the system cancelled its monthly passes and discounted booklets of 10-trip tickets.

Questions

1. How can organizations like Metrolinx manage "scope creep" (the increase of a project's scope or functions after the project has started)? Do you think that the "open fare" system should have gone out to competitive bid? Why or why not?
2. What actions should Metrolinx have taken to manage the Presto card implementation rather than allowing Accenture to do so?

Sources: T. Kalinowski, "Presto Card Costs Soar to $700 Million," *Toronto Star*, December 13, 2012, p. A1, A6, G. Nesci, "Presto Card Fare System Will Cost $700 Million to Implement, Says Ontario's Auditor General," *National Post*, December 12, 2013, J. Lorinc, "System Builder of Presto Fare Card Had Poor Track Record," *The Globe and Mail*, December 18, 2012; D. Reevely, "Presto Ready to Go, OC Transpo Says," *Ottawa Citizen*, April 11, 2013; GO Transit, "How to Use PRESTO on GO Transit," April 2011, *www2.prestocard.ca/en-US/*, accessed May 3, 2013.

The trend to outsource is rising, and so is the trend to relocate these operations offshore, particularly in India and China. *Offshoring* can save money, but it includes risks as well. The risks depend on which services are being offshored. If a company is offshoring application development, the major risk is poor communication between users and developers.

Custom Development

Companies may also decide to custom-build an application. They can either perform this operation in-house or outsource the process. Although custom development is usually more time consuming and costly than buying or leasing, the results often fit better with the organization's specific requirements.

The development process for a new system starts when the MIS steering committee (discussed earlier in the chapter), having received suggestions, decides the idea is worth looking into. These suggestions come from users (you, in the near future). Understanding this process will help you get the systems that you will need. Not understanding this process will reduce your chances, because other people who do understand it will make suggestions that use up available resources.

As the company goes through the development process, the mindset changes. In systems investigation, the organization is trying to decide whether to build something: everyone knows that it either may or may not be built. In later stages of the development process, the organization is fully committed to building the application, and although a project can be cancelled at any time, this change in attitude is still important.

The basic backbone methodology for custom development is the systems development life cycle (SDLC), which you will study in the next section. In Section 11.4, you examine the methodologies that complement the SDLC: prototyping, joint application development, integrated computer-assisted systems development tools, and rapid application development. You also consider four other methodologies: agile development, end-user development, component-based development, and object-oriented development.

before you go on...

1. Describe the four fundamental business decisions that organizations must make when acquiring information systems.
2. Discuss each of the seven development methods in this section with regard to the four business decisions that organizations must make.

11.3 The Traditional Systems Development Life Cycle

The **systems development life cycle (SDLC)** is the traditional systems development method that organizations use for large-scale IT projects. The SDLC is a structured framework that consists of sequential processes by which information systems are developed. For our purposes, we define six processes, each of which consists of clearly defined tasks (see Figure 11.4):

- Systems investigation
- Systems analysis
- Systems design
- Programming and testing
- Implementation
- Operation and maintenance

Other models for the SDLC may contain more or fewer than the six stages presented here. The flow of tasks, however, remains largely the same. When problems occur in any phase of the SDLC, developers often must go back to previous phases.

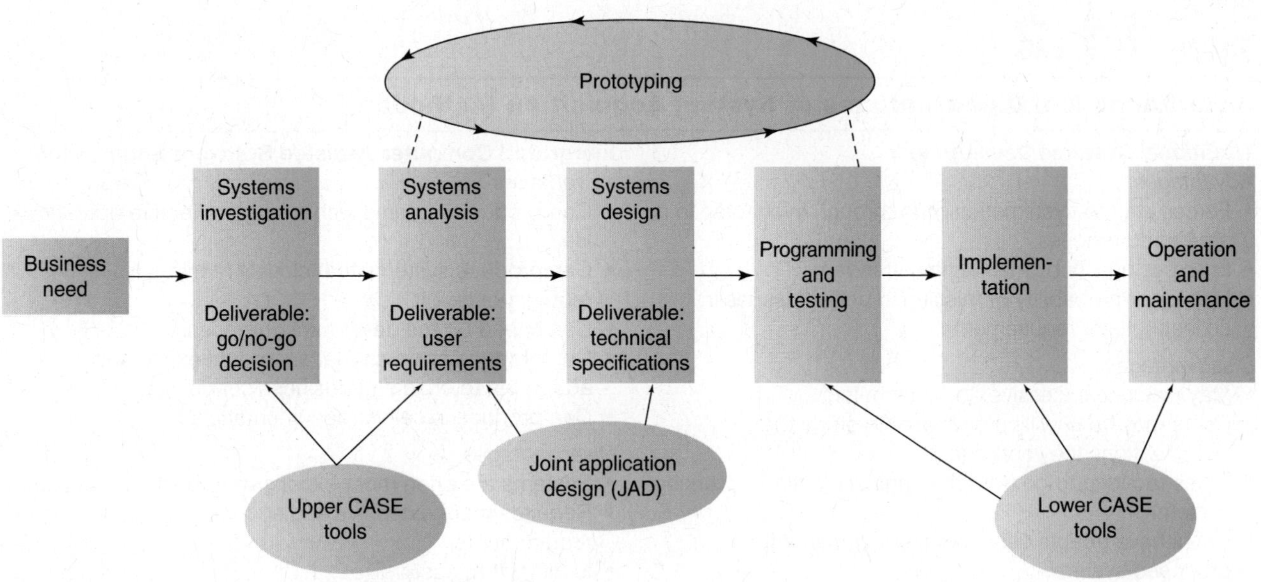

FIGURE 11.4 A six-stage systems development life cycle (SDLC) with supporting tools, including computer-aided software engineering (CASE).

Systems development projects produce desired results through team efforts. Development teams typically include users, systems analysts, programmers, and technical specialists. *Users* are employees from all functional areas and levels of the organization who interact with the system, either directly or indirectly. **Systems analysts** are information system professionals who specialize in analyzing and designing information systems. **Programmers** are information system professionals who either modify existing computer programs or write new ones to satisfy user requirements. **Technical specialists** are experts on a specific type of technology, such as databases or telecommunications. Finally, the **systems stakeholders** include everyone who is affected by changes in a company's information systems; for example, users and managers. All stakeholders typically are involved in systems development at various times and in varying degrees. Figure 11.5 indicates that users have high involvement in the early stages of the SDLC, lower involvement in the programming and testing stage, and higher involvement in the later stages. Table 11.2 discusses the advantages and disadvantages of the SDLC.

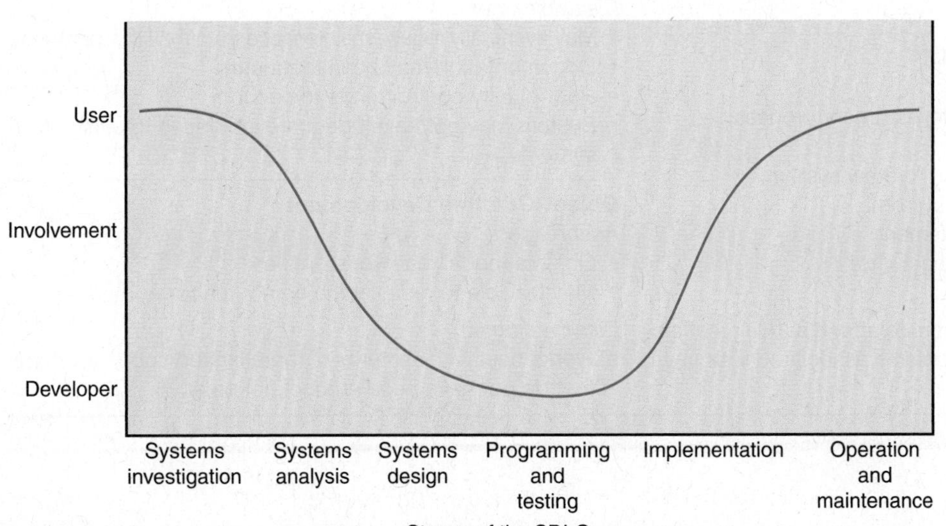

FIGURE 11.5 Comparison of user and developer involvement over the SDLC.

Table 11.2

Advantages and Disadvantages of System Acquisition Methods

Traditional Systems Development

Advantages

- Forces staff to systematically go through every step in a structured process.
- Enforces quality by maintaining standards.
- Has lower probability of missing important issues in collecting user requirements.

Disadvantages

- May produce excessive documentation.
- Users may be unwilling or unable to study the specifications they approve.
- Takes too long to go from the original ideas to a working system.
- Users have trouble describing requirements for a proposed system.

Prototyping

Advantages

- Helps clarify user requirements.
- Helps verify the feasibility of the design.
- Promotes genuine user participation.
- Promotes close working relationship between systems developers and users.
- Works well for ill-defined problems.
- May produce part of the final system.

Disadvantages

- May encourage inadequate problem analysis.
- Not practical with a large number of users.
- Users may not give up the prototype when the system is completed.
- May generate confusion about whether the system is complete and maintainable.
- System may be built quickly, which may result in lower quality.

Joint Application Design (JAD)

Advantages

- Involves many users in the development process.
- Saves time.
- Provides greater user support for new system.
- Improves quality of the new system.
- New system is easier to implement.
- New system has lower training costs.

Disadvantages

- It can be difficult to get all users to attend a JAD meeting.
- JAD approach has all the problems associated with any group meeting.

Integrated Computer-Assisted Software Engineering

Advantages

- Can produce systems with a longer effective operational life.
- Can produce systems that closely meet user requirements.
- Can speed up the development process.
- Can produce systems that are more flexible and adaptable to changing business conditions.
- Can produce excellent documentation.

Disadvantages

- Systems are often more expensive to build and maintain.
- Requires more extensive and accurate definition of user requirements.
- Is difficult to customize.

Rapid Application Development

Advantages

- Can speed up systems development.
- Users are intensively involved from the start.
- Improves the process of rewriting legacy applications.

Disadvantages

- Produces functional components of final systems, but not final systems.

End-User Development

Advantages

- Bypasses the IS department and avoids delays.
- User controls the application and can change it as needed.
- Directly meets user requirements.
- There is increased user acceptance of new system.
- Frees up IT resources.
- May create lower-quality systems.

Disadvantages

- May eventually require maintenance from the IS department.
- Documentation may be inadequate.
- Poor quality control tends to occur.
- System may not have adequate interfaces to existing systems.

Object-Oriented Development

Advantages

- Objects model real-world entities.
- May be able to reuse some computer code.

Disadvantages

- Works best with systems of more limited scope (systems that do not have huge numbers of objects).

Systems Investigation

The initial stage in a traditional SDLC is systems investigation. Systems development professionals agree that the more time they invest in (1) understanding the business problem to be solved, (2) specifying the technical options for the systems, and (3) anticipating the problems they are likely to encounter during development, the greater the chances of success. For these reasons, systems investigation addresses the *business problem* (or business opportunity) by means of the feasibility study.

The main task in the systems investigation stage is the feasibility study. Organizations have three basic solutions to any business problem relating to an information system: (1) do nothing and continue to use the existing system unchanged, (2) modify or enhance the existing system, or (3) develop a new system. The **feasibility study** analyzes which of these three solutions best fits the particular business problem. It also provides a rough assessment of the project's technical, economic, and behavioural feasibility.

- *Technical feasibility* determines whether the company can develop and/or acquire the hardware, software, and communications components needed to solve the business problem. Technical feasibility also determines whether the organization can use its existing technology to achieve the project's performance objectives.
- *Economic feasibility* determines whether the project is an acceptable financial risk and, if so, whether the organization has the necessary time and money to successfully complete the project. You have already learned about the methods commonly used to determine economic feasibility: NPV, ROI, breakeven analysis, and the business case approach.
- *Behavioural feasibility* addresses the human issues of the systems development project. Clearly, you will be heavily involved in this aspect of the feasibility study.

After the feasibility analysis is completed, a "go/no-go" decision is reached by the steering committee, if there is one, or by top management in the absence of a committee. The go/no-go decision does not depend solely on the feasibility analysis. Organizations often have more feasible projects than they can fund. Therefore, the firm must prioritize the feasible projects and pursue those with the highest priority. Unfunded feasible projects may not be presented to the IT department at all. These projects therefore contribute to the *hidden backlog*, which are projects of which the IT department is not aware.

If the decision is "no-go," either the project is put on the shelf until conditions are more favourable or it is discarded. If the decision is "go," the project proceeds and the systems analysis phase begins.

Systems Analysis

Once a development project has the necessary approvals from all participants, the systems analysis stage begins. **Systems analysis** is the examination of the business problem that the organization plans to solve with an information system.

The main purpose of the systems analysis stage is to gather information about the existing system in order to determine the requirements for an enhanced system or a new system. The end product of this stage, known as a *deliverable*, is a set of *system requirements*.

Perhaps the most difficult task in systems analysis is identifying the specific requirements that the system must satisfy. These requirements often are called *user requirements*, because users (meaning you) provide them. When the systems developers have accumulated the user requirements for the new system, they proceed to the systems design stage.

Systems Design

Systems design describes how the system will resolve the business problem. The deliverable of the systems design phase is a set of *technical system specifications*, which specifies the following:

- System outputs, inputs, calculations or processing, and user interfaces
- Hardware, software, databases, telecommunications, personnel, and procedures
- A blueprint of how these components are integrated

The system specifications, when approved by all participants, are "frozen"; that is, they should not be changed. Adding functions after the project has been initiated causes **scope creep**, which endangers the project's budget and schedule. Because scope creep is expensive, successful project managers place controls on changes requested by users. These controls help to prevent runaway projects, such as the Presto card in IT's About Business 11.3.

Programming and Testing

If the organization decides to construct the software in-house, then programming begins. **Programming** involves translating the design specifications into computer code. This process can be lengthy and time consuming, because writing computer code is as much an art as a science. Large systems development projects can require hundreds of thousands of lines of computer code and hundreds of computer programmers. These large-scale projects employ programming teams, which often include functional area users, who help the programmers focus on the business problem.

Thorough and continuous testing occurs throughout the programming stage. Testing is the process that checks to see whether the computer code will produce the expected and desired results. It is also intended to detect errors, or bugs, in the computer code.

Implementation

Implementation (or *deployment*) is the process of converting from the old system to the new system. The conversion process involves organizational change. Both end users and the MIS department need to work together to manage organizational change. Organizations use three major conversion strategies: direct, pilot, and phased.

In a **direct conversion**, the old system is cut off and the new system is turned on at a certain point in time. This type of conversion is the least expensive. It is also the riskiest, because if the new system does not work as planned, there is no support from the old system. Consequently, few systems are implemented using direct conversion.

A **pilot conversion** introduces the new system in one part of the organization, such as in one plant or one functional area. The new system runs for a period of time and then is assessed. If the assessment confirms that the system is working properly, the system is implemented in other parts of the organization.

Finally, a **phased conversion** introduces components of the new system, such as individual modules, in stages. Each module is assessed. If it works properly, other modules are introduced until the entire new system is operational. Large organizations commonly combine the pilot and phased approaches; that is, they execute a phased conversion using a pilot group for each phase.

A fourth strategy is *parallel conversion*, in which the old and new systems operate simultaneously for a time. This strategy is seldom used today. One reason for this is that parallel conversion is totally impractical when both the old and new systems are on-line. Imagine that you are finishing an order on Amazon.com, only to be told, "Before your order can be entered here, you must provide all the same information again, in a different form, and on a different set of screens." The results would be disastrous for Amazon. A variation, called a "historic parallel," is used in which real transactions are run through the new system and the results compared with the old system before the new systems are moved in for live usage.

Operation and Maintenance

The new system, after it is implemented, will operate for a period of time, until (like the old system it replaced) it no longer meets its objectives or business needs change. Once the new system's operations are stabilized, the company performs audits to assess the system's capabilities and to determine whether it is being used correctly.

Systems require several types of maintenance. The first type is *debugging* the program, a process that continues throughout the life of the system. The second is *updating* the system to accommodate changes in business conditions. An example is adjusting to new governmental regulations, such as changes in tax rates. These corrections and upgrades usually do not add any new functions. Instead, they simply help the system to continue meeting its objectives. In contrast, the third type of maintenance *adds new functions* to the existing system.

before you go on...

1. Describe a feasibility study.
2. What is the difference between systems analysis and systems design?
3. Describe structured programming.
4. What are the four conversion methods?

11.4 Alternative Methods and Tools for Systems Development

There are multiple alternative methods for systems development. These methods include joint application design, rapid application development, agile development, and end-user development.

Joint Application Design

Joint application design (JAD) is a group-based tool for collecting user requirements and creating system designs. It is used most often within the systems analysis and systems design stages of the SDLC. JAD involves a group meeting attended by the analysts and all of the users. It is a group decision-making process that can be conducted manually or via the computer. During this meeting, all users jointly define and agree on the systems requirements. This process saves a tremendous amount of time. Table 11.2 lists the advantages and disadvantages of the JAD process.

Rapid Application Development

Rapid application development (RAD) is a systems development method that can combine JAD, prototyping, and ICASE tools (discussed later in this section) to rapidly produce a high-quality system. In the first RAD stage, developers use JAD sessions to collect system requirements. This strategy ensures that users are intensively involved early on. The development process in RAD is iterative, similar to prototyping; that is, requirements, designs, and the system itself are developed and then undergo a series, or sequence, of improvements. RAD uses ICASE tools to quickly structure requirements and develop prototypes. As the prototypes are developed and refined, users review them in additional JAD sessions. RAD produces the functional components of a final system rather than prototypes. Table 11.2 highlights the advantages and disadvantages of the RAD process.

Agile Development

Agile development is a software development methodology that delivers functionality in rapid iterations, which usually are measured in weeks. To be successful, this methodology requires frequent communication, development, testing, and delivery. Agile development focuses on rapid development and frequent user contact to create software that addresses the needs of business users. This software does not have to include every possible feature the user will require. Rather, it must meet only the user's more important and immediate needs. It can be updated later to introduce additional functions as they become necessary. The core tenet of agile development is to do only what you have to do to be successful right now.

One type of agile development uses the *scrum approach*. A key principle of scrum is that during a project users can change their minds about what they want and need. Scrum acknowledges that a development problem cannot be fully understood or defined from the start. Therefore, scrum focuses on maximizing the development team's ability to deliver iterations quickly and to respond effectively to additional user requirements as they emerge.

Scrum contains sets of practices and predefined roles. The primary roles are:

- The *Scrum Master*: maintains the processes (typically replaces a project manager)
- The *Product Owner*: represents the business users and any other stakeholders in the project
- The *Team*: a cross-functional group of about seven people who perform the actual analysis, design, coding, implementation, testing, etc.

Scrum works as follows: During each sprint—typically a two- to four-week period—the team creates a potentially shippable product increment, such as working and tested software. The set of features that go into each sprint come from the product backlog, which is a prioritized set of high-level work requirements to be completed.

The sprint planning meeting determines which backlog items will be addressed during a sprint. During this meeting, the product owner informs the team about the items in the product backlog that he or she wants completed. The team then determines how many of these projects they can commit to during the next sprint, and they record this information in the sprint backlog.

During a sprint, no one is allowed to change the sprint backlog, which means that the requirements are frozen for the sprint. Each sprint must end on time. If the requirements are not completed for any reason, they are left out and returned to the product backlog. After each sprint is completed, the team demonstrates how to use the software.

End-User Development

End-user development is an approach in which the organization's end users develop their own applications with little or no formal assistance from the IT department. Table 11.2 lists the advantages and disadvantages of end-user development.

Tools for Systems Development

Several tools can be used with various systems development methods. These tools include prototyping, integrated computer-assisted software engineering (ICASE), component-based development, and object-oriented development.

Prototyping. The **prototyping** approach defines an initial list of user requirements, builds a model of the system, and then refines the system in several iterations based on users' feedback. Developers do not try to obtain a complete set of user specifications for the system at the outset, and they do not develop the system all at once. Instead, they quickly develop a smaller version of the system known as a **prototype**. A prototype can take two forms. In some cases it contains only the components of the new system that are of most interest to the users. In other cases it is a small-scale working model of the entire system.

Users make suggestions for improving the prototype, based on their experiences with it. The developers then review the prototype with the users and use their suggestions to refine the prototype. This process continues through several iterations until the users approve the system or it becomes apparent that the system cannot meet the users' needs. If the system is viable, the developers can use the prototype to build the full system. One typical use of prototyping is to develop screens that a user will see and interact with. Table 11.2 describes the advantages and disadvantages of the prototyping approach.

There is a practical problem with prototyping: A prototype usually looks more complete than it is. It may not use the real database, it usually does not have the necessary error checking, and it almost never includes the necessary security features. Users who review a prototype that resembles the finished system may not recognize these problems. Consequently, they might have unrealistic expectations about how close the actual system is to completion.

Integrated Computer-Assisted Software Engineering Tools. **Computer-aided software engineering (CASE)** is a group of tools that automate many of the tasks in the SDLC. The tools used to automate the early stages of the SDLC (systems investigation, analysis, and design) are called *upper* CASE tools. The tools used to automate later stages in the SDLC (programming, testing, operation, and maintenance) are called *lower* CASE tools. CASE tools that provide links between upper CASE and lower CASE tools are called **integrated CASE (ICASE) tools**. Table 11.2 lists the advantages and disadvantages of ICASE tools.

Component-Based Development. **Component-based development** uses standard components to build applications. Components are reusable applications that generally have one specific function, such as a shopping cart, user authentication, or a catalogue. Component-based development is closely linked with the idea of web services and service-oriented architectures, which we examine in Technology Guide 3.

Many start-up companies are pursuing the idea of component-based application development, or less programming and more assembly. An example of these companies is Ning (*www.ning.com*), which allows organizations to create, customize, and share their own social network.

Object-Oriented Development. **Object-oriented development** is based on a different view of computer systems than the perception that characterizes traditional development approaches. Traditional approaches can produce a system that performs the original task but may not be suited for handling other tasks. This observation applies even when these other tasks involve the same real-world entities. For example, a billing system will handle billing but probably cannot be adapted to handle mailings for the marketing department or to generate leads for the sales force. This is true even though the billing, marketing, and sales functions all use similar data, including customer names, addresses, and purchases. In contrast, an *object-oriented (OO) system* begins not with the task to be performed, but with the aspects of the real world that must be modelled to perform that task. Therefore, in the above example, if the firm has a good model of its customers and its interactions with them, it can use this model equally well for billings, mailings, and sales leads.

The development process for an object-oriented system begins with a feasibility study and an analysis of the existing system. Systems developers identify the *objects* in the new system—the fundamental elements in OO analysis and design. Each object represents a tangible, real-world entity, such as a customer, bank account, student, or course. Objects have *properties*, or *data values*. For example, a customer has an identification number, a name, an address, account number(s), and so on. Objects also contain the *operations* (also referred to as *behaviours*) that can be performed on their properties. For example, operations that can be performed on the customer object may include "obtain-account-balance," "open-account," "withdraw-funds," and so on.

This approach enables object-oriented analysts to define all the relevant objects needed for the new system, including their properties and operations. The analysts then model how the objects interact to meet the objectives of the new system. In some cases, analysts can reuse existing objects from other applications (or from a library of objects) in the new system. This process saves the analysts the time they otherwise would spend coding these objects. In most cases, however, even with object reuse, some coding will be necessary to customize the objects and their interactions for the new system.

You have studied many methods that can be used to acquire new systems. Table 11.2 provides an overview of the advantages and disadvantages of these methods.

before you go on...

1. Describe the tools that augment the traditional SDLC.
2. Describe the alternate methods that can be used for systems development other than the SDLC.

11.5 Vendor and Software Selection

Few organizations, especially SMEs, have the time, financial resources, or technical expertise required to develop today's complex IT or e-business systems. As a result, business firms increasingly rely on outside vendors to provide software, hardware, and technical expertise. Consequently, selecting and managing these vendors and their software offerings has become a major aspect of developing an IT application. The following six steps are useful in selecting a software vendor and an application package.

Step 1: Identify potential vendors. Companies can identify potential software application vendors through various sources:

- Software catalogues
- Lists provided by hardware vendors
- Technical and trade journals
- Consultants and industry analysts experienced in the application area
- Peers in other companies
- Web searches

These sources often yield so many vendors and packages that the company must use some evaluation criteria to eliminate all but the most promising ones from further consideration. For example, it can eliminate vendors that are too small or have a questionable reputation. Also, it can eliminate packages that do not have the required features or are not compatible with the company's existing hardware and/or software.

Step 2: Determine the evaluation criteria. The most difficult and crucial task in evaluating a vendor and a software package is to select a detailed set of evaluation criteria. Some areas in which a customer should develop detailed criteria are:

- Characteristics of the vendor
- Functional requirements of the system
- Technical requirements that the software must satisfy
- Amount and quality of documentation provided
- Vendor support of the package

These criteria should be set out in a **request for proposal (RFP)**. An RFP is a document that is sent to potential vendors inviting them to submit a proposal that describes their software package and explains how it would meet the company's needs. The RFP provides the vendors with information about the objectives and requirements of the system. Specifically, it describes the environment in which the system will be used, the general criteria that the company will use to evaluate the proposals, and the conditions for submitting proposals. The RFP also may request a list of current users of the package whom the company may contact. Finally, the RFP can require the vendor to demonstrate the package at the company's facilities using specified inputs and data files.

Step 3: Evaluate vendors and packages. The responses to an RFP generate massive volumes of information that the company must evaluate. The goal of this evaluation is to determine the gaps between the company's needs (as specified by the requirements) and the capabilities of the vendors and their application packages. Often, the company gives the vendors and packages an overall score by (1) assigning an importance weight to each of the criteria, (2) ranking the vendors on each of the weighted criteria (say 1 to 10), and then (3) multiplying the ranks by the associated weights. The company then can shorten the list of potential suppliers to include only those vendors that achieved the highest overall scores.

Step 4: Choose the vendor and package. Once the company has shortened the list of potential suppliers, it can begin negotiations with these vendors to determine how their packages might be modified to remove any discrepancies with the company's IT needs. Thus, one of the most important factors in the decision is the additional development effort that may be required to tailor the system to the company's needs or to integrate it into the company's computing environment. The company also must consider the opinions of both the users and the IT personnel who will have to support the system.

Companies typically use several common methods for selecting software. For a list of general criteria, see Table 11.3.

Step 5: Negotiate a contract. The contract with the software vendor is very important. It specifies both the price of the software and the type and amount of support that the vendor agrees to provide. The contract will be the only recourse if either the system or the vendor does not perform as expected. It is essential, then, that the contract directly refer to the proposal, because this is the vehicle that the vendor used to document the functionality supported in its system. Further, if the vendor is modifying the software to tailor it to the company's needs, the contract must include detailed specifications (essentially the requirements) of the modifications. Finally, the contract should describe in detail the acceptance tests that the software package must pass.

Because contracts are legal documents, they can be quite tricky. For this reason, companies might need the services of experienced contract negotiators and lawyers. Many organizations employ software-purchasing specialists who assist in negotiations and write or approve the contract. These specialists should be involved in the selection process from the start.

Table 11.3

Criteria for Selecting a Software Application Package
Functionality (Does the package do what the organization needs?)
Cost and financial terms
Upgrade policy and cost
Vendor's reputation and availability for help
Vendor's success stories (Visit its website, contact clients.)
System flexibility
Ease of Internet interface
Availability and quality of documentation
Necessary hardware and networking resources
Required training (Check if provided by vendor.)
Security
Speed of learning for developers and users
Graphical presentation
Data handling
System-required hardware

Step 6: Establish a service-level agreement. Service-level agreements (SLAs) are formal agreements that specify how work is to be divided between the company and its vendors. These specifications are based on a set of agreed-upon milestones, quality checks, and what-if situations. They describe how quality checks will be made and what is to be done in case of disputes. SLAs accomplish these goals by (1) defining the responsibilities of both parties, (2) providing a framework for designing support services, and (3) allowing the company to retain as much control as possible over its own systems. SLAs deal with such issues as performance, availability, backup and recovery, upgrades, and hardware and software ownership. For example, the SLA might specify that the ASP have its system available to the customer 99.9 percent of the time.

before you go on...

1. List the major steps of selection of a vendor and a software package.
2. Describe a request for proposal (RFP).
3. Explain why SLAs play an important role in systems development.

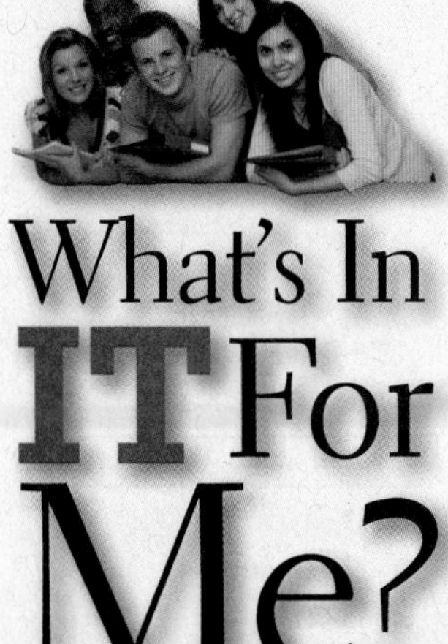

What's In IT For Me?

For the Accounting Major

Accounting personnel help perform the cost-benefit analyses on proposed projects. They also may monitor ongoing project costs to keep them within budget. Accounting personnel undoubtedly will find themselves involved with systems development at various points throughout their careers.

For the Finance Major

Finance personnel frequently are involved with the financial issues that accompany any large-scale systems development project (for example, budgeting). They also are involved in cost-benefit and risk analyses. To perform these tasks, they need to stay abreast of the emerging techniques used to determine project costs and ROI. Finally, because they must manage vast amounts of information, finance departments also are common recipients of new systems.

For the Marketing Major

In most organizations, marketing, like finance, involves massive amounts of data and information. Like finance, then, marketing is also a hotbed of systems development. Marketing personnel will increasingly find themselves participating on systems development teams. Such involvement increasingly means helping to develop systems, especially web-based systems that reach out directly from the organization to its customers.

For the Production/Operations Management Major

Participation on development teams is a common role for production/operations people as well. Manufacturing is becoming increasingly computerized and integrated with other allied systems, from design, to logistics, to customer support. Production systems frequently interface with marketing, finance, and human resources. In addition, they may be part of a larger, enterprise-wide system. Also, many end users in POM either develop their own systems or collaborate with IT personnel on specific applications.

For the Human Resources Management Major

The human resources department is closely involved with several aspects of the systems acquisitions process. Acquiring new systems may require hiring new employees, changing job descriptions, or terminating employees. Human resources performs all of these tasks. Further, if the organization hires consultants for the development project or outsources it, the human resources department may handle the contracts with these suppliers.

For the MIS Major

Regardless of the approach that the organization adopts for acquiring new systems, the MIS department spearheads it. If the organization chooses either to buy or to lease the application, the MIS department leads in examining the offerings of the various vendors and in negotiating with the vendors. If the organization chooses to develop the application in-house, the process falls to the MIS department. MIS analysts work closely with users to develop their information requirements. MIS programmers then write the computer code, test it, and implement the new system.

[Summary]

1. Define an IT strategic plan. Identify the three objectives it must meet. Describe the four common approaches to cost-benefit analysis.

The *IT strategic plan* is a set of long-range goals that describe the IT infrastructure and identify the major IT initiatives needed to achieve the organization's goals. The IT strategic plan must meet three objectives:

- It must be aligned with the organization's strategic plan.
- It must provide for an IT architecture that enables users, applications, and databases to be seamlessly networked and integrated.
- It must efficiently allocate IS development resources among competing projects so the projects can be completed on time and within budget and have the required functionality.

The four common approaches to cost-benefit analysis are:

The *net present value (NPV)* method converts future values of benefits to their present-value equivalents by "discounting" them at the organization's cost of funds. The firm then can compare the present value of the future benefits with the costs required to achieve those benefits to determine whether the benefits exceed the costs.

Return on investment (ROI) measures management's effectiveness in generating profits with its available assets. ROI is calculated by dividing net income attributable to a project by the average assets invested in the project. ROI is a percentage, and the higher the percentage return, the better.

Breakeven analysis determines the point at which the cumulative dollar value of the benefits from a project equals the investment made in the project.

In the *business case approach*, system developers write a business case to justify funding one or more specific applications or projects.

2. Discuss the four business decisions that companies must make when they acquire new applications.

How much computer code does the company want to write?

A company can choose to use a totally prewritten application (to write no computer code); to customize a prewritten application (to write some computer code); or to custom write an entire application (write all new computer code).

How will the company pay for the application?

Once the company has decided how much computer code to write, it must decide on how to pay for it. In the case of either prewritten or customized prewritten software, companies can buy the applications or lease them. For totally custom applications, companies can use internal funding.

Where will the application run?

The company now must decide where to run the application. The company may run the application on its own platform or on someone else's (using either a software-as-a-service vendor or an application service provider).

Where will the application originate?

Prewritten applications can be open-source software or can come from a vendor. Companies may choose to customize prewritten open-source applications or prewritten proprietary applications from vendors. Companies may customize applications in-house or outsource the customization. Lastly, they can write totally custom applications in-house or outsource the process.

3. Identify the six processes involved in the systems development life cycle. Explain the primary tasks and importance of each process.

The six processes are:

Systems investigation: addresses the business problem (or business opportunity) by means of the feasibility study; the main task in the systems investigation stage is the feasibility study.

Systems analysis: examines the business problem that the organization plans to solve with an information system; the main purpose is to gather information about the existing system in order to determine the requirements for the new system; the end product of this stage, known as a "deliverable," is a set of system requirements.

Systems design: describes how the system will resolve the business problem; the deliverable is a set of technical system specifications.

Programming and testing: programming translates the design specifications into computer code; testing checks to see whether the computer code will produce the expected and desired results and detects errors, or bugs, in the computer code; the deliverable is the new application.

Implementation: converts from the old system to the new system via three major conversion strategies: direct, pilot, and phased; the deliverable is a properly working application.

Operation and maintenance: performs various types of maintenance, including debugging, updating, and adding new functions when needed.

4. Describe four alternative development methods and four tools that augment development methods. Identify at least one advantage and one disadvantage of each method and tool.

Alternative Methods

Joint application design (JAD) is a group-based tool for collecting user requirements and creating system designs.

Rapid application development (RAD) is a systems development method that can combine JAD, prototyping, and ICASE tools to rapidly produce a high-quality system.

Agile development is a software development methodology that delivers functionality in rapid iterations, which usually are measured in weeks.

End-user development is the development by an organization's end users of their own applications with little or no formal assistance from the IT department.

The Tools

The *prototyping* approach defines an initial list of user requirements, builds a model of the system, and then improves the system in several iterations based on users' feedback.

Integrated computer-aided software engineering (ICASE) combines upper CASE tools (used to automate systems investigation, analysis, and design) and lower CASE tools (used to automate programming, testing, operation, and maintenance).

Component-based development uses standard components to build applications. Components are reusable applications that generally have one specific function, such as a shopping cart, user authentication, or a catalogue.

Object-oriented development begins with the aspects of the real world that must be modelled to perform that task. Systems developers identify the *objects* in the new system. Each object represents a tangible, real-world entity, such as a customer, bank account, student, or course. Objects have *properties*, or *data values*. Objects also contain the *operations* that can be performed on their properties.

Table 11.2 shows advantages and disadvantages of alternative methods and tools.

5. Analyze the process of vendor and software selection.

The process of vendor and software selection is composed of six steps: identify potential vendors, determine evaluation criteria, evaluate vendors and packages, choose the vendor and package, negotiate a contract, and establish service-level agreements.

[Chapter Glossary]

agile development A software development methodology that delivers functionality in rapid iterations, measured in weeks, requiring frequent communication, development, testing, and delivery.

application portfolio The set of recommended applications resulting from the planning and justification process in application development.

application service provider (ASP) An agent or vendor who assembles the software needed by enterprises and packages it with outsourced development, operations, maintenance, and other services.

component-based development A software development methodology that uses standard components to build applications.

computer-aided software engineering (CASE) Development approach that uses specialized tools to automate many of the tasks in the SDLC; upper CASE tools automate the early stages of the SDLC, and lower CASE tools automate the later stages.

direct conversion Implementation process in which the old system is cut off and the new system is turned on at a certain point in time.

end-user development An approach in which the organization's end users develop their own applications with little or no formal assistance from the IT department.

feasibility study Investigation that gauges the probability of success of a proposed project and provides a rough assessment of the project's feasibility.

implementation The process of converting from an old computer system to a new one.

integrated CASE (ICASE) tools CASE tools that provide links between upper CASE and lower CASE tools.

IT steering committee A committee, consisting of a group of managers and staff representing various organizational units, that establishes IT priorities and ensures that the management information system (MIS) function is meeting the needs of the enterprise.

IT strategic plan A set of long-range goals that describe the IT infrastructure and major IT initiatives needed to achieve the goals of the organization.

joint application design (JAD) A group-based tool for collecting user requirements and creating system designs.

object-oriented development A systems development methodology that begins with aspects of the real world that must be modelled to perform a task.

outsourcing Use of outside contractors or external organizations to acquire IT services.

phased conversion Implementation process that introduces components of the new system in stages, until the entire new system is operational.

pilot conversion Implementation process that introduces the new system in one part of the organization on a trial basis; when the new system is working properly, it is introduced in other parts of the organization.

programmers IS professionals who modify existing computer programs or write new computer programs to satisfy user requirements.

programming The translation of a system's design specifications into computer code.

prototype A small-scale working model of an entire system or a model that contains only the components of the new system that are of most interest to the users.

prototyping Approach that defines an initial list of user requirements, builds a prototype system, and then improves the system in several iterations based on users' feedback.

rapid application development (RAD) A development method that uses special tools and an iterative approach to rapidly produce a high-quality system.

request for proposal (RFP) Document that is sent to potential vendors inviting them to submit a proposal describing their software package and how it would meet the company's needs.

scope creep The addition of functions to an information system after the project has begun.

service-level agreements (SLAs) Formal agreements regarding the division of work between a company and its vendors.

software-as-a-service (SaaS) A method of delivering software in which a vendor hosts the applications and provides them as a service to customers over a network, typically the Internet.

systems analysis The examination of the business problem that the organization plans to solve with an information system.

systems analysts IS professionals who specialize in analyzing and designing information systems.

systems design A description of how the new system will provide a solution to the business problem.

systems development life cycle (SDLC) Traditional structured framework, used for large IT projects, that consists of sequential processes by which information systems are developed.

systems stakeholders All people who are affected by changes in information systems.

[Discussion Questions]

1. Discuss the advantages of a lease option over a buy option.
2. Why is it important for all business managers to understand the issues of IT resource acquisition?
3. Why is it important for everyone in business organizations to have a basic understanding of the systems development process?
4. Should prototyping be used on every systems development project? Why or why not?
5. Discuss the various types of feasibility studies. Why are all of them needed?
6. Discuss the issue of assessing intangible benefits and the proposed solutions.
7. Discuss the reasons why end-user-developed information systems can be of poor quality. What can be done to improve this situation?

[Problem-Solving Activities]

1. Access *www.ecommerce-guide.com*. Find the product review area. Read reviews of three software payment solutions. Assess them as possible components.
2. Use an Internet search engine to obtain information on CASE and ICASE tools. Select several vendors, and compare and contrast their offerings.
3. Access *www.ning.com*. Observe how the site provides components for you to use to build applications. Build a small application.
4. Enter *www.ibm.com/software*. Find its WebSphere product. Read recent customers' success stories. What makes this software so popular?
5. Enter the websites of the GartnerGroup (*www.gartner.com*), the Yankee Group (*www.yankeegroup.com*), and Computing Canada (*www.itbusiness.ca*). Search for recent material about ASPs and outsourcing, and prepare a report on your findings.
6. StoreFront (*www.storefront.net*) is a vendor of e-business software. At its site, the company provides demonstrations illustrating the types of storefronts that it can create for shoppers. The site also provides demonstrations of how the company's software is used to create a store.
   a. Run the StoreFront demonstration to see how this is done.
   b. What features does StoreFront provide?
   c. Does StoreFront support smaller or larger stores?
   d. What other products does StoreFront offer for creating on-line stores? What types of stores do these products support?

[Spreadsheet Activity: If-Then Statements]

Objective: This activity will introduce the "if-then" statement within the context of making a decision. It will help you take criteria from a situation and build them into a spreadsheet.

Chapter Connection: Acquiring an information system is always an easy task, right? Wrong! Sometimes the method of acquiring the system is as complex as the system itself. Although most situations would require a much more complicated decision support system, in this situation a spreadsheet can help make the decision by using formulas to narrow down the top contenders and provide a score/ranking for the companies under consideration.

Activity: It is time for your university to upgrade its website. This decision is very important because it will affect current and potential students, faculty, and the community at large.

The university has graded 50 different vendors on 10 criteria and allocated a weight to each. The 10 criteria and their weights are given below.

1. Customizability (15 percent)
2. Expandability (15 percent)
3. Faculty tutorials (5 percent)
4. Student tutorials (5 percent)
5. Mobile access (10 percent)
6. Video support (10 percent)
7. File system (5 percent)
8. Course migration (15 percent)
9. Faculty user interface (10 percent)
10. Student user interface (10 percent)

Visit *www.wiley.com/go/rainer/spreadsheet*, download the spreadsheet provided for Chapter 11, and then create two formulas. One will calculate a final grade based on the weights provided above and the work already done by the university. Once you have the final grade, you will then create an if-then formula to find those vendors that rank worthy of an "A" and those that "fail" to meet the stated criteria. If you are not familiar with if-then statements, please see the Help material in Microsoft Excel under the formulas area of the program. Basically, your statement will say "If the score is greater than a 90, then say 'Yes,' otherwise, 'No.'"

Deliverable: Prepare a written summary of your findings. Is there a clear winner? Or does it depend on what the university favours in the rankings?

Discussion Questions

1. Acquisition of information systems is a complicated affair. Decisions to build in-house, outsource, or purchase off-the-shelf software can sometimes be the greatest asset or the Achilles heel of a company. Given the complexity, what roles can a spreadsheet play in this process other than the one illustrated by this case?
2. Implementation strategies vary as much as the acquisition decision. Considering products like the Google Spreadsheet Flow Chart, how can spreadsheets assist with the planning of software implementation?

[Case Assignment]

Great West Canadian Bank (GWC) comprises a group of companies that employs over 3,000 people in 108 locations. GWC has grown by acquiring other smaller banks and financial service organizations. To reduce costs and improve information systems services, the organization has several projects planned for the coming year.

The first of these projects is server consolidation. Some of the bank's servers are at a main data centre in Edmonton, while many others are distributed in regional banking centres as part of the branch network. The bank plans on reducing the number of locations with servers from 15 to 3 over the next year. As part of this project, the bank will be implementing an enterprise storage system and improving the way it manages data access and sharing among the bank branches.

GWC is also looking to improve turnaround and provide greater consistency in its loan and credit approval processes. Loan applications are currently recorded manually or using standard word processing templates. The printed version of the loan application document is then sent to a central credit risk group for approval, often resulting in delays of two to six days before a loan is approved or declined. By automating this process and integrating the credit-granting process with external credit checks and an expert system-based credit evaluation system, the bank hopes to reduce time for credit granting and reduce credit losses. Rather than sending paper documents for credit approval, the bank will use an expanded intranet to provide access to internal documents by authorized employees.

Required

a. The new credit-granting system will likely be custom-developed. The bank would like to engage in best practices during the acquisition and development of this software. Describe three activities that the bank needs to complete within each of the following two phases of the traditional systems development life cycle.
   - Systems investigation
   - Systems design
b. Describe two conversion strategies that would be suitable for the bank to use in the implementation of the new credit-granting system. For each conversion method strategy, describe an advantage associated with that conversion strategy.

[Team Assignments]

1. Assessing the functionality of an application is a part of the planning process (Step 1). Select three to five websites catering to the same type of buyer (for instance, several websites that offer CDs or computer hardware), and divide the sites among the teams. Each team will assess the functionality of its assigned website by preparing an analysis of the different sorts of functions provided by the sites. In addition, the team should compare the strong and weak points of each site from the buyer's perspective.
2. Divide the class into groups, with each group visiting a local company (include your university). At each firm, study the systems acquisition process. Find out the methodology or methodologies used by each organization and the type

of application each methodology applies. Prepare a report and present it to the class.

3. As a group, design an information system for a start-up business of your choice. Describe your chosen IT resource acquisition strategy, and justify your choices of hardware, software, telecommunications support, and other aspects of a proposed system.

[Case 11.2 A Tale of Two Software Upgrades]

The Problem

Two airlines—WestJet (*www.westjet.com*) and JetBlue (*www.jetblue.com*)—had been using a reservation system designed for start-up airlines with reasonably simple reservation requirements. As the two airlines moved from start-up regional airlines—WestJet based in western Canada, and JetBlue serving the eastern United States—to becoming national and international airlines, they needed more computing power to deal with increasing numbers of customers. They also wanted their IT systems to have additional capabilities, such as tapping into the databases of prices and seat availabilities of other airlines with whom they wished to cooperate. It was also important to have increasing levels of automation to deal with irregular events, such as snow storms or hurricanes, which can cause numerous flight cancellations.

The Solution

WestJet and JetBlue independently selected a system offered by Sabre Holdings (*www.sabre.com*), a provider of airline reservation systems (SabreSonic; *www.sabreairlinesolutions.com*). Sabre provides technology to 300 airlines, and it owns Travelocity (*www.travelocity.ca*) and other on-line travel agencies. JetBlue reported that the new system cost about $40 million, including $25 million in capital spending and $15 million in one-time operating expenses. WestJet did not disclose how much its system cost.

In addition to selling seats and collecting passenger payments, the Sabre system controls much of the passenger experience: shopping on the airline's website, interacting with reservation agents, using airport kiosks, selecting seats, checking bags, boarding at the gate, and rebooking and obtaining refunds for cancellations. To perform these functions, the Sabre system has to integrate with the airline's other information systems. Due to its large customer base, Sabre also continuously improves its systems. For example, since 2011 it has had a Reaccommodation module, which allows for automated rescheduling of customers due to flight cancellations.

Two Different Results

WestJet, with 88 planes at the time, switched to Sabre after it had shifted to a lighter winter schedule and cancelled some flights. One imposing challenge was the overnight transition of 840,000 files—transactions of customers who already had purchased tickets—from WestJet's old reservations system to the Sabre system. The process did not go well because the migration required WestJet agents to go through complex steps to process the data.

Despite months of planning, when WestJet made its conversion, its website crashed repeatedly, and its call centre was overwhelmed. Making matters worse, WestJet did not reduce the number of passengers on the flights operating after the transition to the new system, nor did it inform customers of its upgrade plans until the day of the switch.

WestJet's customer loyalty scores dropped as a result of long waits and booking difficulties. The airline sent apology letters, offered flight credits to some customers, and bolstered its call centre with temporary staffers located in India. Two months after the conversion, the airline installed a "virtual hold" in its call centres so callers would be promised a response within a certain time. A virtual hold offers callers the option for a call back rather than waiting on hold.

The bottom line for WestJet? After several months, the airline was able to fulfill its plans to cooperate with international airlines on some of its routes.

In contrast, JetBlue, with 151 aircraft, decided to make its switch on a Friday night, because Saturday traffic tends to be low. The airline trimmed its schedule that weekend and sold abnormally low numbers of seats on the remaining flights. JetBlue also developed a backup website that it used twice for a few hours during the transition.

JetBlue also contracted for 500 outside reservations agents. After the transition, in which 900,000 passenger records were moved to Sabre, JetBlue routed basic calls to the temporary workers, freeing up its own call staff to manage more complex tasks. The extra agents stayed in place for two months.

JetBlue still experienced some problems. Call wait times increased, and not all of its airport kiosks and ticket printers became operational right away. Despite these problems, however, JetBlue contends that migrating to Sabre was an important factor in the airline's decision to cooperate on some routes in and out of Boston and New York with American Airlines. Also, when Hurricane Irene hit in 2011, affecting the northeastern coast of the U.S., with hundreds of flights cancelled, the airline was able to reallocate customers to alternative flights without overburdening its employees.

Questions

1. Explain why WestJet and JetBlue decided to upgrade their reservation systems.
2. Compare and contrast the software upgrade processes of WestJet and JetBlue.

Sources: Compiled from "JetBlue: Class of 2011 Yearbook," *Computerworld*, 2011; B. Evans, "Global CIO: WestJet's IT Nightmare and the Power of Customers," *Information-Week*, April 16, 2010; S. Carey, "Two Paths to Software Upgrade," *The Wall Street Journal*, April 13, 2010; "JetBlue Airways: 2010 Winner Profile," *CIO*, 2010; "Sabre Enhances JetBlue Performance," September 22, 2011, BreakingTravelNews.com; *www.westjet.com*, *www.jetblue.com*, *www.sabre.com*, accessed March 18, 2013.

[Interactive Case]

Acquiring Systems for Ruby's Club

Go to the Ruby's Club link at the Student Companion website or *WileyPLUS* for information about your current internship assignment. You will help the club's managers make decisions about purchasing, outsourcing, or building new systems for Ruby's.

Chapter 12

Ethics and Privacy

[LEARNING OBJECTIVES]	[CHAPTER OUTLINE]	[WEB RESOURCES]

1. Define ethics, list and describe the three fundamental tenets of ethics, and describe the four categories of ethical issues related to information technology.
2. Identify three places that store personal data and, for each one, discuss at least one potential threat to the privacy of the data stored there.

Student Companion Site

wiley.com/college/rainer

- Student PowerPoints for note taking
- Complete glossary

WileyPlus

All of the above and

- E-book
- Mini-lecture by author for each chapter section
- Practice quizzes
- Flash Cards for vocabulary review
- Additional "What's in IT for Me?" cases
- Video interviews with managers
- Lab Manual for Microsoft Office 2010
- How-to Animations for Microsoft Office 2010

What's In IT For Me?
THIS CHAPTER WILL HELP PREPARE YOU TO ...
ACCT
Ensure correctness of confidential data
FIN
Adhere to regulations
MKT
Ensure privacy of customer data
POM
Monitor labour laws
HR
Monitor appropriate use of IT in the workplace
MIS
Monitor correct use of sensitive company data

[Case 12.1 What to Do About WikiLeaks?]

The Problem (?)

Whistleblowers—employees with insider knowledge of an organization—can capture huge amounts of incriminating documents on a laptop, memory stick, or portable hard drive. They can send the information through personal e-mail accounts or on-line drop sites, or they can simply submit it directly to WikiLeaks (*www.wikileaks.org*).

FSTOP/Image Source

WikiLeaks was officially unveiled in December 2006. Julian Assange, one of the founders, was reportedly inspired by the leak of the Pentagon Papers (documents leaked pertaining to the Vietnam War). Assange intended WikiLeaks to serve as a dropbox for anyone, anywhere, who disagreed with any organization's activities or secrets. According to its website, WikiLeaks focuses on material of ethical, political, and historical significance. In its first year, the organization's database expanded to 1.2 million documents. In addition, WikiLeaks receives approximately 10,000 new documents every day. Since its inception, WikiLeaks has had significant impacts on both businesses and governments. We discuss several examples below.

In January 2008, WikiLeaks posted documents alleging that the Swiss bank Julius Baer (*www.juliusbaer.com*) hid its clients' profits from even the Swiss government by concealing them in what seemed to be shell companies in the Cayman Islands. The bank sued WikiLeaks, claiming that the site stole data from its clients and published it. By the time Baer dropped the lawsuit, it had been subject to considerable negative publicity surrounding the case.

In October 2008, Iceland's Kaupthing Bank collapsed, saddling the country with $128 billion in debts. Nearly a year later, Icelandic national broadcaster RUV aired a story stating that a legal injunction had prevented the network from airing an exposé on the bank. Instead, the network suggested that viewers who wanted to see the material should visit WikiLeaks. On the site was a summary of Kaupthing's loans, detailing more than $6 billion funnelled from the bank to its owners and companies they owned, often with little or no collateral. WikiLeaks promptly became a household name in Iceland.

WikiLeaks's ability to effect change continued when, in 2009, it published incriminating documents from a pharmaceutical trade group. It appeared as if the group's lobbyists were receiving confidential documents from, and exerting influence over, a World Health Organization (WHO, *www.who.int*) project to fund drug research in the developing world. The WHO terminated the project, in part due to the attention it received from the WikiLeaks publicity.

In September 2009, commodities company Trafigura (*www.trafigura.com*) requested an injunction from the courts preventing the British media from mentioning a damaging internal report. The report indicated that the company had dumped tonnes of toxic waste in the Ivory Coast that sickened 100,000 local inhabitants. Although Trafigura could prevent the official media from reporting this story, it could not stop WikiLeaks from publishing the information. The public became aware of the transgression, and Trafigura eventually had to pay out more than $200 million in settlements.

As consequential as these business leaks were, probably the most controversial WikiLeaks exposé involved the U.S. government. From November 2009 to April 2010, U.S. Army Private First Class Bradley Manning downloaded hundreds of thousands of diplomatic cables to a CD at an outpost in Iraq. He then passed the information to WikiLeaks. In doing so, Manning violated a U.S. law that criminalizes unauthorized computer downloads. Beginning on November 28, 2010, WikiLeaks published the contents of more than 250,000 diplomatic cables, the largest unauthorized release of contemporary classified information in history. Among these cables were 11,000 documents marked "secret." The U.S. government defines a secret document as a document that, if released, would cause "serious damage to national security."

WikiLeaks continues to be active, employing sophisticated data analysis techniques to examine increasingly large databases of "secret" information. In December 2011 it released "The Spy Files," which talk about a mass collection of e-mails and telephone conversations around the world. In February 2012 it revealed "The GI Files," focused on a global private intelligence-gathering organization called Stratfor. July 2012 saw the release of the "Syria Files," with over 2.4 million e-mails focused around Syria's internal wars.

The problem, then, boils down to this: How can governments, organizations, and even individuals prevent future disclosures? Is it possible to accomplish this task, given that the sources of WikiLeaks's information often appear to be internal?

The Solution (?)

In the initial moments after the U.S. State Department cables were released, unknown hackers tried to shut down WikiLeaks by exposing its website to denial-of-service attacks (discussed in Chapter 13). It is unclear whether the hackers were working on behalf of the U.S. government, but they seemed to endorse the government's claims that the disclosures threatened national security.

WikiLeaks's supporters retaliated with anonymous "hacktivism," attacking the websites of companies such as Amazon, which had thrown WikiLeaks off its servers, and MasterCard and PayPal, which had frozen the organization's accounts and prevented its supporters from donating to the cause.

Ultimately, all attempts to stifle WikiLeaks have proved futile. When the organization is blocked from one host server, it simply jumps to another. Further, the number of mirror websites—essentially clones of WikiLeaks's main content pages—had mushroomed to 1,300 by the end of 2010. These sites continue to mirror materials published by WikiLeaks.

Prior to the 9/11 terrorist attacks, the U.S. State Department had operated its own internal cable system and encrypted documents to ensure security. After the attacks, the State Department system was merged into a new digital records system controlled by the Department of Defense. Since the WikiLeaks disclosures, the State Department has temporarily severed its connection to the new system while it takes steps to prevent future unauthorized downloads.

In other attempts at thwarting WikiLeaks, governments and companies have turned to cyber security. Since 2007, every major security software vendor (for example, McAfee, *www.mcafee.com*, Symantec, *www.symantec.com*, and Trend Micro, *www.trendmicro.com*) has spent hundreds of millions of dollars to acquire companies in the data leak prevention (DLP) industry. These companies produce software that locates and tags sensitive information and then guards against its being stolen or illegally duplicated. Unfortunately, to date, DLP software has not been effective.

The failure of DLP software has prompted organizations to turn to *network forensics*, which is the process of constantly collecting every digital "fingerprint" on an organization's servers to trace and identify an intruder who has broken into the system. Although this software gathers data and makes them easily available, it does not identify the culprit.

The Results

How can organizations and governments respond to WikiLeaks? Lawsuits will not work, because WikiLeaks, as a mere conduit for documents, is legally protected in the United States. Moreover, even if a company or a government somehow won a judgement against WikiLeaks, that would not shut down the organization, because its assets are spread all over the world.

In fact, WikiLeaks has a nation-size ally—Iceland. Since WikiLeaks discovered the corrupt loans that helped destroy Iceland's biggest bank, the country has set out to become the conduit for a global flood of leaks. Birgitta Jónsdóttir, a member of Iceland's parliament, created the Icelandic Modern Media Institute (IMMI, *https://immi.is*) in 2010. This initiative seeks to bring to Iceland all the laws that support protecting anonymous sources, freedom of information, and transparency from around the world. It would then set up a Nobel-style international award for activities supporting free expression. IMMI would also make Iceland the world's friendliest legal base for whistleblowers. As of December 2012, Iceland had passed several laws and regulations that move toward implementing IMMI, but the initiative was not fully functional at that time due to its complexity.

Should WikiLeaks falter, other websites around the world are ready to take its place. For example, GreenLeaks (*http://greenmela.com/Green/ViewAll_Leaks.aspx*) is a website for whistleblowers on environmental issues. Perhaps the most controversial site is Anonymous, the hacker collective.

What is the best protection against unauthorized leaks? Icelandic WikiLeaks staffer Kristinn Hrafnsson suggested, rather drily, that companies—and perhaps governments to some extent—reform their practices to avoid being targeted.

What We Learned from This Case

The WikiLeaks case addresses the two major issues you will study in this chapter: ethics and privacy. Both issues are closely related to IT and raise significant questions. For example, are WikiLeaks's actions ethical? Does WikiLeaks violate the privacy of governments, organizations, and individuals? The answers to these questions are not straightforward. In fact, IT has made finding answers to these questions even more difficult.

You will encounter numerous ethical and privacy issues in your career, many of which will involve IT in some manner. This chapter will give you insights into how to respond to these issues. Further, it will help you make immediate contributions to your company's code of ethics and its privacy policies. You will also be able to provide meaningful input concerning the potential ethical and privacy impacts of your organization's information systems on people within and outside the organization.

For example, suppose your organization decides to adopt Web 2.0 technologies (discussed in Chapter 7) to include business partners and customers in new product development. You will be able to analyze the potential privacy and ethical implications of implementing these technologies.

All organizations, large and small, must be concerned with ethics. IT's About Small Business 12.1 discusses the difficult issues associated with cyber harassment.

Small business owners face a very difficult situation when their employees have access to sensitive customer information. There is a delicate balance between access to information and its appropriate use and the temptation for workers to be nosey and curious about what they can find. This balance is best maintained by hiring honest and trustworthy employees who abide by the organization's code of ethics. Ultimately this leads to another question: Does the small business even have a code of ethics to fall back on in this type of situation?

12.1 Ethical Issues

Ethics are the principles of right and wrong that individuals use to make choices that guide their behaviour. Deciding what is right or wrong is not always easy or clear cut. Fortunately, there are many frameworks that can help us make ethical decisions.

Ethical Frameworks

There are many approaches, or frameworks, to developing ethical standards. Here we consider four widely used approaches: the utilitarian approach, the rights approach, the fairness approach, and the common good approach. There are many other approaches, but these four are representative.

Sources: Compiled from R. Somaiya, "Former WikiLeaks Colleagues Forming New Web Site, OpenLeaks," *The New York Times*, February 6, 2011; A. Greenberg, "WikiLeaks' StepChildren," *Forbes*, January 17, 2011; M. Calabresi, "Winning the Info War," *Time*, December 20, 2010; A. Greenberg, "WikiLeaks' Julian Assange," *Forbes*, December 20, 2010; J. Dougherty and E. Labott, "The Sweep: WikiLeaks Stirs Anarchy Online," CNN.com, December 15, 2010; E. Robinson, "In WikiLeaks Aftermath, An Assault on Free Speech," *The Washington Post*, December 14, 2010; M. Calabresi, "The War on Secrecy," *Time*, December 13, 2010; I. Shapira and J. Warrick, "WikiLeaks' Advocates Are Wreaking 'Hacktivism'," *The Washington Post*, December 12, 2010; F. Rashid, "WikiLeaks, Anonymous Force Change to Federal Government's Security Approach," *eWeek*, December 12, 2010; E. Mills, "Report: Ex-WikiLeakers to Launch New OpenLeaks Site," CNET.com, December 10, 2010; G. Keizer, "Pro-WikiLeaks Cyber Army Gains Strength; Thousands Join DDos Attacks," *Computerworld*, December 9, 2010; J. Warrick and R. Pegoraro, "WikiLeaks Avoids Shutdown as Supporters Worldwide Go on the Offensive," *The Washington Post*, December 8, 2010; F. Rashid, "PayPal, PostFinance Hit by DoS Attacks, Counter-Attack in Progress," *eWeek*, December 6, 2010; "Holder: 'Significant' Actions Taken in WikiLeaks Investigation," CNN.com, December 6, 2010; "WikiLeaks Back Online After Being Dropped by U.S. Domain Name Provider," CNN.com, December 3, 2010; "WikiLeaks Reports Another Electronic Disruption," CNN.com, November 30, 2010; "Feds Open Criminal Investigation into WikiLeaks Disclosures," CNN.com, November 29, 2010; A. Greenberg, "WikiLeaks' Julian Assange Wants to Spill Your Corporate Secrets," Forbes.com, November 29, 2010; L. Fadel, "Army Intelligence Analyst Charged in WikiLeaks Case," *The Washington Post*, July 7, 2010; G. Goodale, "WikiLeaks Q&A with Daniel Ellsberg, the Man Behind the Pentagon Papers," *The Christian Science Monitor*, July 29, 2010, accessed May 12, 2011, *www.wikileaks.org*, accessed May 13, 2013.

IT's about [small] business

12.1 The Nightmare of Cyber-Harassment

Elayna Katz was having a meal at the Mambo Nuevo Latino restaurant in Ottawa. Apparently, ingredients that she requested to be removed from her order were included, substitutions were made without being disclosed, and she was billed for two meals after she had returned one of them. On top of that, service was poor. After leaving the restaurant, Katz posted two negative reviews about her experience on a restaurant review website. Then, the nightmare began.

It is alleged that the owner of the restaurant, Marisol Simoes, began a two-year defamatory campaign against Katz, posting comments about her sanity, emotions, and appearance on chat rooms and other on-line media. The owner apparently also gathered and used confidential information to impersonate Katz, causing Katz severe embarrassment and stress by sending sexualized messages to Katz's co-workers and superiors at her work.

What is positive is that Katz's employer supported her, providing added security at her place of work, such as requiring that all individuals who wanted to see her make an appointment. Katz went to the police and had the case investigated and prosecuted. As a result, Simoes was charged with libel and found guilty in November 2012. The restaurant owner was subsequently sentenced to 90 days in jail, and ordered to take anger management courses and perform a specified number of hours of community work.

However, Simoes was released after five days, since she provided bail and launched an appeal. At the time of writing, the results of the appeal were unavailable.

Questions

1. What should the restaurant owner have done when she found out about the negative review? Support your answer.
2. What actions could Elayna Katz have taken during the process of being cyber-harassed?

Source: D. Graham, "Revenge Is Not a Sweet Dish," *Toronto Star*, November 7, 2012, pp. E1, E7; D. Graham, "Ottawa Restaurateur Is Found Guilty of Defaming Citizen Reviewer," *Toronto Star*, November 7, 2012; "Marisol Simoes Jailed: Co-owner of Kinki and Mambo in Ottawa Gets 90 Days for Defamation," *Huffington Post*, November 16, 2012; T. Spears, "Cyber Bullying Restaurateur Marisol Simoes Released on Bail," *Ottawa Sun*, November 21, 2012.

The *utilitarian approach* states that an ethical action is the one that provides the most good or does the least harm. The ethical corporate action would be the one that produces the greatest good and does the least harm for all affected parties—customers, employees, shareholders, the community, and the environment.

The *rights approach* maintains that an ethical action is the one that best protects and respects the moral rights of the affected parties. Moral rights can include the rights to make one's own choices about what kind of life to lead, to be told the truth, to be free from emotional injury, and to have a degree of privacy. Which of these rights people are actually entitled to—and under what circumstances—is widely debated. Nevertheless, most people acknowledge that individuals are entitled to some moral rights. An ethical organizational action would be one that protects and respects the moral rights of customers, employees, shareholders, business partners, and even competitors.

The *fairness approach* posits that ethical actions treat all human beings equally or, if unequally, then fairly, based on some defensible standard. For example, most people might believe it is fair to pay people higher salaries if they work harder or if they contribute a greater amount to the firm. However, there is less certainty regarding CEO salaries that are hundreds or thousands of times larger than those of other employees. Many people question whether this huge disparity of wages is based on a defensible standard or is the result of an imbalance of power and hence is unfair.

Finally, the *common good approach* highlights the interlocking relationships that underlie all societies. This approach argues that respect and compassion for all others is the basis for ethical actions. It emphasizes the common conditions that are important to the welfare of everyone. These conditions can include a system of laws, effective police and fire departments, health care, a public educational system, and even public recreation areas.

These four standards are used to develop general frameworks for ethics (or ethical decision making). Two such frameworks are shown in Table 12.1: a generic "traditional" approach, and the GVV (giving voice to values) approach.

Table 12.1

Traditional and GVV Approaches: Steps to Take and Questions to Ask When Resolving Ethical Issues

Traditional Approach	Giving Voice to Values (GVV) Approach
1. Recognize an ethical issue • Could this decision or situation damage someone or some group? • Does this decision involve a choice between a good and a bad alternative? • Is this issue about more than what is legal? If so, how?	1. Identify an ethical issue • What are the different issues that give rise to the ethical issue? • What are the values of the individuals or organizations underlying the ethical issue(s)? • Is there a possibility of action to resolve the ethical issue?
2. Get the facts • What are the relevant facts of the situation? • Do I know enough to make a decision? • Which individuals and/or groups have an important stake in the outcome? • Have I consulted all relevant persons and groups?	2. Purpose and choice • What personal choices do I have in reacting to this ethical issue? • What is my most appropriate professional choice, being guided by professional rules, and what would be a "good" choice?
3. Evaluate alternative actions • Which option will produce the most good and do the least harm? (the utilitarian approach) • Which option best respects the rights of all stakeholders? (the rights approach) • Which option treats people equally or proportionately? (the fairness approach) • Which option best serves the community as a whole, and not just some members? (the common good approach)	3. Stakeholder analysis • Who is affected by the ethical issue? • How are they affected, if I do give voice to resolving the issue? • How are they affected, if I do not give voice to resolving the issue? • How can I connect with the stakeholders to best deal with the ethical issue?
4. Make a decision and test it • Considering all the approaches, which option best addresses the situation? • How can I implement my decision with the greatest care and attention to the concerns of all stakeholders? • After acting on my decision, how did it turn out, and what did I learn from this specific situation?	4. Powerful response • Who is my audience? • What types of things could I say to provide a response to the ethical issue? • What are some *inhibiting arguments* that would prevent me from acting? • What could I say in response to the inhibiting arguments (called an *enabling argument*)? • What external arguments (called *levers*) support my enabling arguments? • What external research supports or refutes my arguments?
	5. Scripting and coaching • What words (script) could I use when talking about the ethical issue? (Consider both positive and negative responses.) • Who can I practise with? • How would I approach my audience to provide the best opportunity for discussing the ethical issue?

Using the traditional ethical framework provides a tool for deciding the nature of an action response that you can take. The GVV approach provides tools for dealing with the ethical issue in a cooperative way. We now focus specifically on ethics in a corporate environment.

Ethics in the Corporate Environment

Many companies and professional organizations develop their own codes of ethics. A **code of ethics** is a collection of principles intended to guide decision making by members of the organization. For example, the Association for Computing Machinery (*www.acm.org*), an organization of computing professionals, has a thoughtful code of ethics for its members (see *www.acm.org/about/code-of-ethics*).

Keep in mind that different codes of ethics are not always consistent with one another. Therefore, an individual might be expected to conform to multiple codes. For example, a person who is a member of two large professional computing-related organizations may be simultaneously required by one organization to comply with all applicable laws and by the other organization to refuse to obey unjust laws.

Fundamental tenets of ethics include responsibility, accountability, and liability. **Responsibility** means that you accept the consequences of your decisions and actions. **Accountability** involves determining who is responsible for actions that were taken. **Liability** is a legal concept that gives individuals the right to recover the damages done to them by other individuals, organizations, or systems.

Before you go any further, it is very important that you realize that what is *unethical* is not necessarily *illegal*. For example, a bank's decision to foreclose on a home can be technically legal, but it can raise many ethical questions. In many instances, then, an individual or organization faced with an ethical decision is not considering whether to break the law. As the foreclosure example illustrates, however, ethical decisions can have serious consequences for individuals, organizations, and society at large.

Unfortunately, we have seen a large number of extremely poor ethical decisions, not to mention outright criminal behaviour. Three of the most highly publicized scandals in the United States occurred at Enron Corporation (now Enron Creditors Recovery Corporation), WorldCom (now MCI Inc.), and Tyco International. At each company, executives were convicted of various types of fraud using illegal accounting practices. These illegal acts resulted, at least in part, in the passage of the Sarbanes Oxley Act in 2002 in the United States. This law requires that public companies implement stricter financial controls and that, to ensure accountability, executives must personally certify financial reports. Similar problems occurred in Canada at companies like Nortel and Hollinger International. In Canada, Bill 198, the Budget Measures Act, imposes similar requirements of management.

Improvements in information technologies have generated a new set of ethical problems. Computing processing power doubles about every two years, meaning that organizations are more dependent than ever on their information systems. Organizations can store increasing amounts of data at decreasing cost, enabling them to store more data on individuals for longer periods of time. Computer networks, particularly the Internet, enable organizations to collect, integrate, and distribute enormous amounts of information on individuals, groups, and institutions. As a result, ethical problems are arising concerning the appropriate collection and use of customer information, personal privacy, and the protection of intellectual property, as IT's About Business 12.2 illustrates.

Ethics and Information Technology

All employees have a responsibility to encourage ethical uses of information and information technology. Many of the business decisions you will face at work will have an ethical dimension. Consider the following decisions that you might have to make:

- Should organizations monitor employees' web surfing and e-mail?
- Should organizations sell customer information to other companies?
- Should organizations audit employees' computers for unauthorized software or illegally downloaded music or video files?

The diversity and ever-expanding use of IT applications have created a variety of ethical issues. These issues fall into four general categories: privacy, accuracy, property, and accessibility.

1. *Privacy issues* involve collecting, storing, and disseminating information about individuals.
2. *Accuracy issues* involve the authenticity, fidelity, and accuracy of information that is collected and processed.
3. *Property issues* involve the ownership and value of information.
4. *Accessibility issues* revolve around who should have access to information and whether a fee should be paid for this access.

[about business]

12.2 Big Brother Is Watching You

People today live with a degree of surveillance that would have been unimaginable just a few generations ago. For example, surveillance cameras track you at airports, subways, banks, and other public venues. In addition, inexpensive digital sensors are now everywhere. They are incorporated into laptop webcams, video-game motion sensors, smart phone cameras, utility meters, passports, and employee ID cards. You could find yourself photographed by Google or Microsoft as you walk down the street as they update their mapping services.

Several developments are helping to increase the monitoring of human activity, including low-cost digital cameras, motion sensors, and biometric readers. In addition, the cost of storing digital data is decreasing. The result is an explosion of sensor data collection and storage.

In addition, technology to analyze the increasing amounts of digital sensor data is becoming more efficient and less expensive. For instance, Affectiva (*www.affectiva.com*) recently introduced biometric wristbands that monitor tiny changes in sweat-gland activity to gauge emotional reactions. Marketing consultants are using the bands to discover what pleases or frustrates shoppers.

At a recent International Consumer Electronics Show, Intel and Microsoft introduced an in-store digital billboard that can memorize your face. These billboards can keep track of the products you are interested in based on purchases or your browsing behaviour. One marketing analyst has predicted that your experience in every store will soon be customized.

Clearly, privacy concerns must be addressed, particularly with the capacity of databases to share data and therefore to put together the pieces of a puzzle that can identify us in surprising ways. For example, lawyers in the U.S. have begun to use bridge toll records to establish travel patterns of spouses in divorce proceedings. Police looking to issue traffic tickets can now correlate photos, taken by cameras located at intersections, with vehicle ownership records.

One of the most troubling privacy problems involves a practice advocated by Google and Facebook. These companies are using facial-recognition software—Google Picasa and Facebook Photo Albums—in their popular on-line photo-editing and sharing services. Both companies encourage users to assign names to people in photos, a practice referred to as *photo tagging.* Facial-recognition software then indexes facial features. Once an individual in a photo is tagged, the software looks for similar facial features in untagged photos. This process allows the user to quickly group photos in which the tagged person appears. Significantly, the individual is not aware of this process.

Once you are tagged in a photo, that photo could be used to search for matches across the entire Internet or in private databases, including databases fed by surveillance cameras. The technology could be used by a car dealer who takes a picture of you when you step on the car lot. The dealer could then quickly profile you on the web to gain an edge in making a sale. Even worse, a stranger in a restaurant could photograph you with a smart phone and then go on-line to profile you. One privacy lawyer says that losing the right to anonymity would have a chilling effect on where you go, whom you meet, and how you live your life. Also, once the data are in your smart phone, they can be searched by police.

Another problem arises with smart phones equipped with global positioning system (GPS) sensors. These sensors routinely *geotag* photos and videos, embedding images with the longitude and latitude of the location shown in the image. You could be inadvertently supplying criminals with useful intelligence by posting personal images on social networks or photo-sharing websites. These actions would show the criminals exactly where you live.

Questions

1. Apply the general framework for ethical decision making to the practices of photo tagging and geotagging.
2. Discuss and provide examples of the benefits and the drawbacks of photo tagging and geotagging.
3. Are users responsible for their loss of privacy if they do not know that their photos can be tagged and that they can be located with GPS sensors?

Sources: Compiled from Autopia Blog, "Cellphone Networks and the Future of Traffic," *Wired*, March 2, 2011; "Hello, Big Brother: Digital Sensors Are Watching Us," *USA Today*, January 26, 2011; B. Acohido, "Helpful Digital Sensors," *USA Today*, January 25, 2011; D. Priest and W. Arkin, "Top Secret America," *The Washington Post,* December 20, 2010; P. Elmer-DeWitt, "How the iPhone Spills Your Secrets," *Fortune*, December 18, 2010; T. Carmody, "The Internet of Cars: New R&D For Mobile Traffic Sensors," *Wired,* September 29, 2010; T. Harbert, "Beeps, Blips, and IT: Making Sense of Sensor Data," *Computerworld*, June 24, 2008; *www.eff.org,* accessed March 17, 2011.

Table 12.2

Categories and Questions for Ethical Issues

Privacy Issues
What information about oneself should an individual be required to reveal to others?
What kind of surveillance can an employer use on its employees?
What types of personal information can people keep to themselves and not be forced to reveal to others?
What information about individuals should be kept in databases, and how secure is the information there?
Accuracy Issues
Who is responsible for the authenticity, integrity, and accuracy of the information collected?
How can we ensure that the information will be processed properly and presented accurately to users?
How can we ensure that errors in databases, data transmissions, and data processing are accidental and not intentional?
Who is to be held accountable for errors in information, and how should the injured parties be compensated?
Property Issues
Who owns the information?
What are the just and fair prices for its exchange?
How should we handle software piracy (copying copyrighted software)?
Under what circumstances can one use proprietary databases?
Can corporate computers be used for private purposes?
How should experts who contribute their knowledge to create expert systems be compensated?
How should access to information channels be allocated?
Accessibility Issues
Who is allowed to access information?
How much should companies charge for permitting access to information?
How can access to computers be provided for employees with disabilities?
Who will be provided with equipment needed for accessing information?
What information does a person or an organization have a right to obtain, under what conditions, and with what safeguards?

Table 12.2 lists representative questions and issues for each of these categories. In addition, On-line Ethics Cases presents 14 ethics scenarios for you to consider. These scenarios will provide a context for you to consider situations that involve ethical or unethical behaviour.

Many of the issues and scenarios discussed in this chapter, such as photo tagging and geo-tagging, involve privacy as well as ethics. In the next section, you will learn about privacy issues in more detail.

before you go on...

1. What does a code of ethics contain?
2. Describe three fundamental tenets of ethics.

12.2 Privacy

In general, **privacy** is the right to be left alone and to be free of unreasonable personal intrusions. **Information privacy** is the right to determine when, and to what extent, information about you can be gathered and/or communicated to others. Privacy rights apply to individuals, groups, and institutions.

The definition of privacy can be interpreted quite broadly. However, court decisions in many countries have followed two rules fairly closely:

1. The right of privacy is not absolute. Privacy must be balanced against the needs of society.
2. The public's right to know supersedes the individual's right of privacy.

These two rules illustrate why determining and enforcing privacy regulations can be difficult. The right to privacy is recognized today in all Canadian provinces and by the federal government, through privacy legislation.

Rapid advances in information technologies have made it much easier to collect, store, and integrate data on individuals in large databases. On an average day, data about you are generated in many ways: surveillance cameras on toll roads, in public places, and at work; credit card transactions; telephone calls (land line and cellular); banking transactions; queries to search engines; and government records (including police records). These data can be integrated to produce a **digital dossier**, which is an electronic profile of you and your habits. The process of forming a digital dossier is called **profiling**.

Data aggregators in the United States, such as LexisNexis (*www.lexisnexis.com*) and Acxiom (*www.acxiom.com*), are good examples of profiling. These companies collect public data such as real estate records and published telephone numbers, in addition to nonpublic information such as social security numbers (and social insurance numbers in Canada); financial data; and police, criminal, and motor vehicle records. Statistics Canada (*www.statcan.gc.ca*), Canada's national statistics agency, provides aggregated information about businesses and individuals.

Data aggregators then integrate these data to form digital dossiers on most adults in North America. They sell these dossiers to law enforcement agencies and companies that conduct background checks on potential employees. They also sell the dossiers to companies that want to know their customers better, a process called *customer intimacy*.

However, data on individuals can be used in more controversial ways. For example, a map in California identifies the addresses of donors who supported Proposition 8, the referendum that outlawed same-sex marriage in California (see *www.eightmaps.com*). Gay activists created the map by combining Google's satellite mapping technology with publicly available campaign records that listed Proposition 8 donors who contributed $100 or more. These donors are outraged, claiming that the map invades their privacy and could expose them to retribution.

Electronic Surveillance

Electronic surveillance is rapidly increasing, particularly with the emergence of new technologies. Electronic surveillance is conducted by employers, the government, and other institutions.

In general, employees have very limited legal protection against surveillance by employers. The law supports the right of employers to read their employees' e-mail and other electronic documents and to monitor their employees' Internet use. Today many organizations are monitoring employees' Internet usage. Organizations also use software to block connections to inappropriate websites, a practice called *URL filtering*. Organizations are installing monitoring and filtering software to enhance security by stopping malicious software and to improve employee productivity by discouraging employees from wasting time.

In one organization, the chief information officer (CIO) monitored about 13,000 employees for three months to determine the type of traffic they engaged in on the network. He then forwarded the data to the chief executive officer (CEO) and the heads of the human resources and legal departments. These executives were shocked at the questionable websites the employees were visiting, as well as the amount of time they were spending on those sites. The executives quickly made the decision to implement a URL filtering product.

Surveillance is also a concern for private individuals regardless of whether it is conducted by corporations, government bodies, or criminals. As a country, we are still struggling to define the appropriate balance between personal privacy and electronic surveillance, especially when threats to national security are involved.

Personal Information in Databases

Information is being kept about individuals in many databases. Perhaps the most visible locations of such records are credit-reporting agencies. Other institutions that store personal information include banks and financial institutions; cable TV, telephone, and utilities companies; employers; mortgage companies; hospitals; schools and universities; retail establishments; government agencies (Canada Revenue Agency, your province, your municipality); and many others.

There are several concerns about the information you provide to these record keepers. Some of the major concerns are:

- Do you know where the records are?
- Are the records accurate?
- Can you change inaccurate data?
- How long will it take to make a change?
- Under what circumstances will personal data be released?
- How are the data used?
- To whom are the data given or sold?
- How secure are the data against access by unauthorized people?

Information on Internet Bulletin Boards, Newsgroups, and Social Networking Sites

Every day we see more and more *electronic bulletin boards*, *newsgroups*, *electronic discussions* such as chat rooms, and *social networking sites* (discussed in Chapter 7). These sites appear on the Internet, within corporate intranets, and on blogs. As you saw in Chapter 7, a *blog*, short for "weblog," is an informal, personal journal that is frequently updated and intended for general public reading. How does society keep owners of bulletin boards from disseminating information that may be offensive to readers or simply untrue? This is a difficult problem because it involves the conflict between freedom of speech on the one hand and privacy on the other.

Social networking sites also can present serious privacy concerns. IT's About Business 12.3 takes a look at Facebook's problems with its privacy policies.

Privacy Codes and Policies

Privacy policies or **privacy codes** are an organization's guidelines for protecting the privacy of its customers, clients, and employees. In many corporations, senior management has begun to understand that when they collect vast amounts of personal information, they must protect it. In addition, many organizations give their customers some voice in how their information is used by providing them with opt-out choices. The **opt-out model** of informed consent permits the company to collect personal information until the customer specifically requests that the data not be collected. You can see an example of this by looking at the American Express privacy statement (*www.americanexpress.com*). At the end of the privacy statement there is a box where users need to click if they do not want to receive targeted advertising from the credit card company. This means that everyone automatically will receive those types of e-mails unless they request not to.

Privacy advocates prefer the **opt-in model** of informed consent, which prohibits an organization from collecting any personal information unless the customer specifically authorizes it. Although the opt-out model is a common approach, Canada's privacy commissioner (*www.priv.gc.ca*) states that consent should be sought, which is the opt-in model. Canada's anti-spam legislation, Bill C-28, requires that organizations use the opt-in model for the sending of e-mails.

IT's [about business]

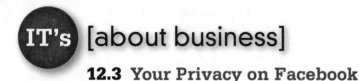

12.3 Your Privacy on Facebook

In December 2009, Facebook (*www.facebook.com*) adopted a new privacy policy that declared certain information, including lists of friends, be publicly available, with no privacy settings. Previously, Facebook users could restrict access to this information. As a result of this change, users who had set their list of friends as private were forced to make the list public without even being informed. Further, the option to make the list private again was removed. For example, a user whose Family and Relationships information was set to be viewable by Friends Only would default to being viewable by Everyone (publicly viewable). Therefore, information such as the gender of your partner, relationship status, and family relations became viewable even to people who did not have a Facebook account. Facebook CEO Mark Zuckerberg justified this policy by asserting that privacy is no longer a social norm.

To compound this issue, the new Facebook policy can also expose endorsements of various organizations and groups that you make when you click the "Like" button. In addition, Facebook's "Instant Personalization" shares some of your data, without your advance permission, with other websites.

The results of this change? The Facebook privacy policy was protested by many people as well as privacy organizations such as the Electronic Frontier Foundation (*www.eff.org*). The policy had political implications as well; for example, Iranian dissidents began deleting their Facebook accounts so that the government could not track their contacts.

In another instance, four college students decided to build a social network that would not force people to surrender their privacy. They used an on-line website called Kickstarter (*www.kickstarter.com*), which helps creative people find support, to raise $10,000. When they introduced their software, called Diaspora (*http://diasporaproject.org*), in May 2010, they made the source code openly available. Users can employ this software to set up personal servers, create their own information hubs, and control the information they share. The Diaspora "crew" attracted more than 2,000 followers of "joindiaspora" on Twitter in just a few weeks.

Facebook responded by rolling back requirements that some content be public, such as promotional pages that users respond to, or "Like," in Facebook language. Facebook is also providing a virtual one-click "off switch" that lets users block all access to their information from third-party applications and websites. Further, instead of being forced to make public every status update and photo for "friends" or other individuals, users can put information such as employment history and vacation videos into buckets designated either for friends, friends of friends, or everyone on the Internet.

Facebook privacy practices seem to be constantly in the news. Searches of the Office of the Privacy Commissioner of Canada (*www.priv.gc.ca*) reveal hundreds of references to Facebook, since that office has engaged in numerous actions against the company. Facebook continues to innovate, however. For example, in January 2013 it provided a Graph Search feature, and in April 2013 it launched Facebook Home software for Android users. Every new product announcement is greeted by privacy concerns, while Facebook's view is that users still have the ability to tailor their privacy settings while having better services available.

Questions

1. Why does Facebook change its privacy policies in response to government or user pressures?
2. Research the functions of Facebook Graph Search and discuss whether it affects privacy.
3. Research the functions of Facebook Home software and discuss whether it affects privacy.
4. Discuss the trade-offs between conveniently sharing information and protecting privacy.

Sources: Compiled from J. Angwin and G. Fowler, "Microsoft, Facebook Offer New Approaches to Boost Web Privacy," *The Wall Street Journal*, February 26–27, 2011; C. Kang, "Facebook CEO Announces Revamped Privacy Settings," *The Washington Post*, May 27, 2010; M. Wagner, "Who Trusts Facebook Now?" *Computerworld Blogs*, May 27, 2010; J. Perez, "Facebook Earns Praise for Privacy Changes," *Computerworld*, May 26, 2010; S. Gaudin, "Amid Backlash, Facebook Unveils Simpler Privacy Controls," *Computerworld*, May 26, 2010; S. Gaudin, "Facebook CEO Says Mistakes Made, Privacy Changes Coming," *Computerworld*, May 24, 2010; R. Pegoraro, "Facebook Meets the 'Unlike' Button," *Washington Post*, May 17, 2010; J. Sutter, "Some Quitting Facebook As Privacy Concerns Escalate," CNN.com, May 13, 2010; J. Dwyer, "Four Nerds and a Cry to Arms Against Facebook," *The New York Times*, May 11, 2010; B. Johnson, "Privacy No Longer a Social Norm, Says Facebook Founder," *The Guardian*, January 11, 2010, F. Y. Rashid, "Facebook Home Raises Security, Privacy Concerns," PCMag.com, April 6, 2013; E. Burns, "Facebook's Graph Search Turns Up Privacy Issues," TechNewsWorld.com, January 19, 2013.

This means that organizations need to have data collection processes so that they can keep records of which customers have agreed to receive e-mails, and which ones have not. Details about the requirements of the law are available at *www.fightspam.gc.ca*.

One privacy tool currently available to consumers is the Platform for Privacy Preferences (P3P, see *www.w3.org/TR/P3P/*). It was developed by the World Wide Web Consortium, a group that creates standards for the web. P3P automatically communicates privacy policies between an electronic commerce website and visitors to that site. P3P enables visitors to determine the types of personal data that can be extracted by the websites they visit. It also allows visitors to compare a website's privacy policy with the visitors' preferences or with other standards, such as the Canadian Standards Association (CSA) Model Code for the Protection of Personal Information (*www.csa.ca/cm/ca/en/privacy-code*) or the European Union Directive on Data Protection.

Canada's privacy legislation is called the Personal Information Protection and Electronic Documents Act (PIPEDA). It became effective January 1, 2004. The legislation applies to businesses and other organizations, such as non-profit organizations. PIPEDA is based upon the principles in the Canadian Standards Association Model Code. As part of the legislation, organizations are required to establish a privacy policy, as well as procedures to ensure that the policy is adhered to.

Table 12.3 provides a sampling of privacy policy guidelines. The last section of Table 12.3, "Data Confidentiality," refers to security, as you will see in Chapter 13. All the good privacy intentions in the world are useless unless they are supported and enforced by effective security measures.

International Aspects of Privacy

As the number of on-line users increases globally, governments throughout the world have enacted a large number of inconsistent privacy and security laws. This highly complex global legal framework is creating regulatory problems for companies. Approximately 50 countries have some form of data-protection laws. Many of these laws conflict with those of other countries, or they require specific security measures. Other countries have no privacy laws at all.

Table 12.3

Privacy Policy Guidelines: A Sampler

Data Collection

- Data should be collected on individuals only for the purpose of accomplishing a legitimate business objective.
- Data should be adequate, relevant, and not excessive in relation to the business objective.
- Individuals must give their consent before data pertaining to them can be gathered. Such consent may be implied from the individual's actions (e.g., applications for credit, insurance, or employment).

Data Accuracy

- Sensitive data gathered on individuals should be verified before the data are entered into the database.
- Data should be kept current, where and when necessary.
- The file should be made available so that the individual can ensure the data are correct.
- In any disagreement about the accuracy of the data, the individual's version should be noted and included with any disclosure of the file.

Data Confidentiality

- Computer security procedures should be implemented to ensure against unauthorized disclosure of data. These procedures should include physical, technical, and administrative security measures.
- Third parties should not be given access to data without the individual's knowledge or permission, except as required by law.
- Disclosures of data, other than the most routine, should be noted and maintained for as long as the data are maintained.
- Data should not be disclosed for reasons incompatible with the business objective for which they are collected.

The absence of consistent or uniform standards for privacy and security obstructs the flow of information among countries, which is called *transborder data flows*. The European Union (EU), for one, has taken steps to overcome this problem. In 1998 the European Community Commission (ECC) issued guidelines to all its member countries regarding the rights of individuals to access information about themselves. The EU data-protection laws are stricter than North American laws and therefore could create problems for multinational corporations that operate in Europe, which could face lawsuits for privacy violation.

The transfer of data into and out of a nation without the knowledge of either the authorities or the individuals involved raises a number of privacy issues. Whose laws have jurisdiction when records are stored in a different country for reprocessing or retransmission purposes? For example, if data are transmitted by a Polish company through a U.S. satellite to a British corporation, which country's privacy laws control the data, and when? Questions like these will become more complicated and frequent as time goes on. Governments must make an effort to develop laws and standards to cope with rapidly changing information technologies in order to solve some of these privacy issues.

before you go on...

1. Describe the issue of privacy as it is affected by IT.
2. Discuss how privacy issues can impact transborder data flows.

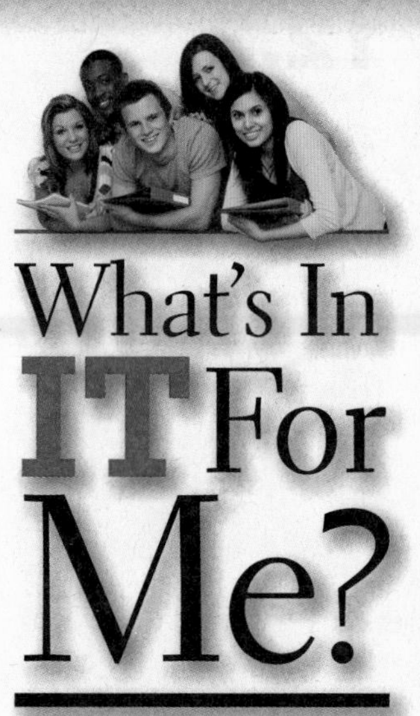

For the Accounting Major

Public companies, their accountants, and their auditors have significant ethical responsibilities. Accountants now are being held professionally and personally responsible for increasing the transparency of transactions and assuring compliance with Canadian privacy legislation (PIPEDA).

For the Finance Major

As a result of global and national regulatory requirements, financial managers must follow strict ethical guidelines. They are responsible for full, fair, accurate, timely, and understandable disclosure in all financial reports and documents that their companies submit to regulatory authorities. Further, financial managers are responsible for compliance with all applicable governmental laws, rules, and regulations.

For the Marketing Major

Marketing professionals have new opportunities to collect data on their customers; for example, through business-to-consumer electronic commerce (discussed in Chapter 5). Business ethics clearly mandate that these data should be used only within the company and should not be sold to anyone else. Marketers do not want to be sued for invasion of privacy over data collected for the marketing database.

Customers expect their data to be properly secured. However, profit-motivated criminals want that data. Therefore, marketing managers must analyze the risks of their operations. Failure to protect private corporate and customer data will cause significant public relations problems and outrage customers. Customer relationship management operations (discussed in Chapter 9) and the tracking of customers' on-line buying habits can expose unencrypted data to misuse or result in privacy violations.

For the **Production/Operations Management Major**

POM professionals decide whether to outsource (or offshore) manufacturing operations. In some cases, these operations are sent overseas to countries that do not have strict labour laws. This situation raises serious ethical questions. For example, is it ethical to hire employees in countries with poor working conditions in order to reduce labour costs?

For the **Human Resources Management Major**

Ethics is critically important to HR managers. HR policies explain the appropriate use of information technologies in the workplace. Questions such as the following can arise: Can employees use the Internet, e-mail, or chat systems for personal purposes while at work? Is it ethical to monitor employees? If so, how? How much? How often? HR managers must formulate and enforce such policies while at the same time maintaining trusting relationships between employees and management.

For the **MIS Major**

Ethics might be more important for MIS personnel than for anyone else in the organization, because these individuals have control of the information assets. They also have control over a huge amount of the employees' personal information. As a result, the MIS function must be held to the highest ethical standards. In fact, as you will see in Case 12.2 about Terry Childs, a former network administrator for the City of San Francisco, regardless of what he actually did, what one thinks of what he did, and whether his conviction was justified, a person in his situation has the opportunity to behave improperly, and shouldn't.

[Summary]

1. Define ethics, list and describe the three fundamental tenets of ethics, and describe the four categories of ethical issues related to information technology.

Ethics are the principles of right and wrong that individuals use to make choices that guide their behaviour.

Fundamental tenets of ethics include responsibility, accountability, and liability. Responsibility means that you accept the consequences of your decisions and actions. Accountability involves determining who is responsible for actions that were taken. Liability is a legal concept that gives individuals the right to recover the damages done to them by other individuals, organizations, or systems.

The major ethical issues related to IT are privacy, accuracy, property (including intellectual property), and access to information. Privacy may be violated when data are held in databases or transmitted over networks. Privacy policies that address issues of data collection, data accuracy, and data confidentiality can help organizations avoid legal problems.

2. Identify three places that store personal data and, for each one, discuss at least one potential threat to the privacy of the data stored there.

Privacy is the right to be left alone and to be free of unreasonable personal intrusions. Threats to privacy include advances in information technologies, electronic surveillance, personal information in databases, Internet bulletin boards, newsgroups, and social networking sites. The privacy threat in Internet bulletin boards, newsgroups, and social networking sites is that you might post too much personal information that many unknown people can see.

[Chapter Glossary]

accountability A tenet of ethics that involves determining who is responsible for actions that were taken.

code of ethics A collection of principles intended to guide decision making by members of an organization.

digital dossier An electronic description of an individual and his or her habits.

electronic surveillance Tracking people's activities with the aid of computers.

ethics The principles of right and wrong that individuals use to make choices to guide their behaviours.

information privacy The right to determine when, and to what extent, personal information can be gathered by and/or communicated to others.

liability A legal concept that gives individuals the right to recover the damages done to them by other individuals, organizations, or systems.

opt-in model A model of informed consent in which a business is prohibited from collecting any personal information unless the customer specifically authorizes it.

opt-out model A model of informed consent that permits a company to collect personal information until the customer specifically requests that the data not be collected.

privacy The right to be left alone and to be free of unreasonable personal intrusions.

privacy codes (see **privacy policies**)

privacy policies (privacy codes) An organization's guidelines for protecting the privacy of customers, clients, and employees.

profiling The process of forming a digital dossier.

responsibility A tenet of ethics in which you accept the consequences of your decisions and actions.

[Discussion Questions]

1. In January 2013, a student at Dawson College in Montreal was expelled after finding a security flaw in the college's information systems and reporting it to the information technology department. It seems that the student was expelled after checking whether the security flaw was still present, which means that he hacked into the college's systems. What do you think: Should the student have been expelled? What is the line between "checking whether a security flaw is still present" and hacking?
2. Frank Abagnale, the criminal played by Leonardo DiCaprio in the motion picture *Catch Me If You Can*, ended up in prison. After he left prison, however, he worked as a consultant to many companies on matters of fraud.
   a. Why do these companies hire the perpetrators (if caught) as consultants? Is this a good idea?
   b. You are the CEO of a company. Discuss the ethical implications of hiring Frank Abagnale as a consultant.

[Problem-Solving Activities]

1. An information security manager routinely monitored the web surfing among her company's employees. She discovered that many employees were visiting the "sinful six" websites. (Note: The "sinful six" are websites with material related to pornography, gambling, hate, illegal activities, tastelessness, and violence.) She then prepared a list of the employees and their surfing histories and gave the list to management. Some managers punished their employees. Some employees, in turn, objected to the monitoring, claiming that they should have a right to privacy.
   a. Is monitoring of web surfing by managers ethical? (It is legal.) Support your answer.
   b. Is employee web surfing on the "sinful six" ethical? Support your answer.
   c. Is the security manager's submission of the list of abusers to management ethical? Why or why not?
   d. Is punishing the abusers ethical? Why or why not? If yes, then what types of punishment are acceptable?
   e. What should the company do in this situation? (Note: There are a variety of possibilities here.)
2. Access the Computer Ethics Institute's "Ten Commandments of Computer Ethics" at *www.cpsr.org/issues/ethics/cei*. Study these rules and decide whether any others should be added.
3. Access the Association for Computing Machinery's code of ethics for its members (*www.acm.org/about/code-of-ethics*). Discuss the major points of this code. Is this code complete? Why or why not? Support your answer.

4. Access *www.eightmaps.com*. Is the use of data on this website illegal? Unethical? Support your answer.
5. The Electronic Frontier Foundation (*www.eff.org*) has a mission of protecting rights and promoting freedom in the "electronic frontier." Review the organization's suggestions about how to protect your on-line privacy, and summarize what you can do to protect yourself.
6. Access your university's guidelines for ethical computer and Internet use. Are there limitations as to the types of websites that you can visit and the types of material you can view? Are you allowed to change the programs on the lab computers? Are you allowed to download software from the lab computers for your personal use? Are there rules governing the personal use of computers and e-mail?
7. Access *www.albion.com/netiquette/corerules.html*. What do you think of this code of ethics? Should it be expanded? Is it too general?
8. Access *www.cookiecentral.com*. Does this site provide information that helps you protect your privacy? If so, then explain how.
9. Do you believe that a university should be allowed to monitor e-mail sent and received on university computers? Why or why not? Support your answer.

[Spreadsheet Activity: Protecting Information in a Spreadsheet]

Objective: You will learn how to lock and protect spreadsheets to keep private information protected. You will also learn the difference between a "protected" spreadsheet and a secure database.

Chapter Connection: Ethics are a difficult subject in information systems. The tighter you keep a system, the less useful it is. However, the more freely you allow people to access data, the more privacy issues you have on your hands. The object of this exercise is to help establish the necessary balance between privacy and data usefulness.

Activity: Recently, a drumming club on campus made plans to host a party and took reservations for T-shirt orders. One of the members was an MIS student who had set up a Google Survey for the orders and had exported all of the data into a spreadsheet. The data included name, address, shirt size, address, phone number, and so on. The university has asked the drumming club to keep these data confidential due to problems in the past.

Specifically, a year earlier, the same data were stored in an unsecured spreadsheet that was e-mailed among some of the club members. One of the male club members took some of the information and used it to exploit and make fun of a physically larger woman. To ensure that this does not happen again, the university is asking the club to show evidence that the spreadsheet is locked and will only be seen by those approved to deliver the T-shirts.

As a member of those approved by the university to manage this information, your job is to take the data collected by the Google Survey and move private information to the private page and lock it so that it cannot be used to exploit any member of the club. You will need to use your own judgement to determine which information needs to be moved to the private, locked page of the spreadsheet.

Go to *www.wiley.com/go/rainer/spreadsheet* to download the Excel file you will need. Then watch the accompanying video to learn how to make a spreadsheet secure.

Deliverable: The final product will be a spreadsheet with a single page of data divided between a secure page and an "open" page.

Discussion Questions

1. How can a spreadsheet be helpful if it is so easy to secure and hack?
2. Are Google spreadsheets more secure than Excel spreadsheets?
3. If a sheet needs to be "very hidden," then why not go ahead and delete it?

[Case Assignment]

Sweety Snacks Limited is a coffee shop chain that has hundreds of locations around the world. Recently, it has been experiencing slumping sales due to the recession and so has decided to close some of its stores. The remaining stores have been asked to pay closer attention to their sales and inventory, as well as try to reduce costs, by using the information available from its computer-based information systems.

Required

a. Describe three ways that enterprise systems (also known as ERP or enterprise resource planning systems) could benefit the company using data analysis.

b. Describe two limitations of enterprise systems to the company and why they would increase costs.

[Team Assignments]

Access *www.ftc.gov/sentinel* to learn how law enforcement agencies around the world work together to fight consumer fraud. Each team should obtain current statistics on one of the top five consumer complaint categories and prepare a report. Are any categories growing faster than others? Are any categories more prevalent in certain parts of the world?

[Case 12.2 You Be the Judge]

Terry Childs worked in San Francisco's information technology department for five years as a highly valued network administrator. Childs, who holds a Cisco Certified Internet-work Expert certification, the highest level of certification offered by Cisco, built San Francisco's new multimillion-dollar computer network, the FiberWAN. He handled most of the implementation, including the acquisition, configuration, and installation of all the routers and switches that compose the network. The FiberWAN contains essential city information, such as officials' e-mails, city payroll files, confidential law enforcement documents, and jail inmates' booking information.

On July 13, 2008, Childs was arrested and charged with four felony counts of computer tampering. Authorities accused him of commandeering the FiberWAN by creating passwords that granted him exclusive access to the system. In addition to refusing to give city officials the passwords necessary to access the FiberWAN, Childs has been accused of other actions. Authorities allege that he implemented a tracing system to monitor what administrators were saying and doing. Authorities also discovered dial-up and digital subscriber line (DSL) modems (discussed in Chapter 4) that would enable an unauthorized user to connect to the FiberWAN. They also found that he had placed a command on several network devices to erase critical configuration data in the event that anyone tried to restore administrative access to the devices. Further, he allegedly collected pages of user names and passwords, including his supervisor's, to use their network login information. He was also charged with downloading terabytes of city data to a personal encrypted storage device. The extent of Childs's activities was not known until a June 2008 computer audit.

Childs had been disciplined on the job in the months leading up to his arrest, and his supervisors had tried to fire him. Those attempts were unsuccessful, in part because of his exclusive knowledge of the city's FiberWAN.

After his arrest, Childs kept the necessary passwords to himself for 10 days, and then gave them to the mayor of San Francisco in a secret meeting in the city jail. What was he thinking? Had he become a rogue employee? His lawyer paints a different picture of the man and his situation.

Childs seems to have taken his job very seriously, to the point of arrogance. He worked very hard, including evenings and weekends, and rarely took vacations. Because the FiberWAN was so complex and Childs did not involve any of the other network engineers in his unit, he was the only person who fully understood the network's configuration. He apparently trusted no one but himself with the details of the network, including its configuration and login information.

Childs had a poor relationship with his superiors, who were all managerially oriented rather than technically oriented. He considered his direct supervisor to be intrusive, incompetent, and obstructive, and he believed the managers above him had no real concept of the FiberWAN. In fact, he felt that his superiors were more interested in office politics than in getting anything done. He also complained that he was overworked and that many of his colleagues were incompetent freeloaders.

Childs's lawyer maintained that his client had been the victim of a "bad faith" effort to force him out of his post by incompetent city officials whose meddling was jeopardizing the network that Childs had built. He further charged that in the past, Childs's supervisors and co-workers had damaged the FiberWAN themselves, hindered Childs's ability to maintain the system, and shown complete indifference to maintaining it themselves.

Childs was the only person in the department capable of operating the FiberWAN. Despite this fact, the department had established no policies as to the appropriate person to whom Childs could give the passwords. Childs maintains that none of the persons who requested the passwords from him was qualified to have them.

Childs's lawyer raised the question: "How could the department say his performance was poor when he had been doing what no one else was able or willing to do?" Interestingly, the FiberWAN continued to run smoothly while Childs was holding the passwords.

On April 27, 2010, after nearly three days of deliberation, a jury convicted Childs of one count of felony computer tampering for withholding passwords to the city's FiberWAN network. The judge later sentenced Childs to four years in prison.

As of mid-2011, San Francisco officials said that they had paid Cisco contractors almost $200,000 to fix the problems with the FiberWAN. The city retained a security consulting firm, Secure DNA (*www.secure-dna.com*), to conduct a vulnerability assessment of its network. It also set aside a further $800,000 to address potential ongoing problems. In May 2011, Childs was released from jail but was ordered to pay nearly $1.5 million in restitution for his actions.

Questions

1. Do you agree with the jury that Childs is guilty of computer tampering?
   a. Discuss the case from the perspective of the prosecutor of the City of San Francisco.
   b. Discuss the case from the perspective of Childs's defence lawyer.
2. A single point of failure is a component of a system that, if it fails, will prevent the entire system from functioning. For this reason, a single point of failure is clearly undesirable, whether it is a person, a network, or an application. Is Childs an example of a single point of failure? Why or why not? If he is guilty, then how should the City of San Francisco (or any organization) protect itself from such a person?

Sources: Compiled from R. McMillan, "Network Admin Terry Childs Gets 4-Year Sentence," *Bloomberg BusinessWeek*, August 7, 2010; J. Niccolai, "Terry Childs Is Denied Motion for Retrial," *PC World*, July 30, 2010; J. Vijayan, "After Verdict, Debate Rages in Terry Childs' Case," *Computerworld*, April 28, 2010; P. Venezia, "Slouching toward Justice for Terry Childs," *InfoWorld*, March 1, 2010; J. Van Derbeken, "S.F. Officials Locked Out of Computer Network," SFGate.com, July 15, 2008; Z. Church, "San Francisco IT Hack Story Looks a Bit Too Much Like *Chinatown*," SearchCIO-Midmarket.com, July 16, 2008; P. Venezia, "Why San Francisco's Network Admin Went Rogue," *InfoWorld*, July 18, 2008; J. Van Derbeken, "Lawyer Says Client Was Protecting City's Code," SFGate.com, July 23, 2008; R. McMillan and P. Venezia, "San Francisco's Mayor Gets Back Keys to the Network," *Network World*, July 23, 2008; R. McMillan, "Parts of San Francisco Network Still Locked Out," *Network World*, July 23, 2008; J. Vijayan, "City Missed Steps to Avoid Network Lockout," *Computerworld*, July 28, 2008; A. Surdin, "San Francisco Case Shows Vulnerability of Data Networks," *Washington Post*, August 11, 2008; R. McMillan, "San Francisco Hunts for Mystery Device on City Network," *Computerworld*, September 11, 2008; B. Egelko, "S.F. Computer Engineer to Stand Trial," SFGate.com, December 27, 2008; "Former City IT Worker Who Shut Down SF Computer System Fined $1.5 Million," KTVU.com, May 17, 2011.

Chapter 13

Information Security and Controls

[LEARNING OBJECTIVES]

1. Identify the five factors that contribute to the increasing vulnerability of information resources, and provide a specific example of each one.
2. Compare and contrast human mistakes and social engineering, and provide a specific example of each one.
3. Discuss the 10 types of deliberate software attacks.
4. Define the three risk mitigation strategies, and provide an example of each one in the context of owning a home.
5. Identify the types of controls that organizations can use to protect their information resources, and provide an example of each one.

[CHAPTER OUTLINE]

13.1 Introduction to Information Security

13.2 Unintentional Threats to Information Systems

13.3 Deliberate Threats to Information Systems

13.4 What Organizations Are Doing to Protect Information Resources

13.5 Information Security Controls

[WEB RESOURCES]

Student Companion Site

wiley.com/college/rainer

- Student PowerPoints for note taking
- Interactive Case: Ruby's Club Assignments
- Complete glossary

WileyPlus

All of the above and

- E-book
- Mini-lecture by author for each chapter section
- Practice quizzes
- Flash Cards for vocabulary review
- Additional "What's in IT for Me?" cases
- Video interviews with managers
- Lab Manual for Microsoft Office 2010
- How-to Animations for Microsoft Office 2010

What's In IT For Me?
THIS CHAPTER WILL HELP PREPARE YOU TO ...
ACCT
Ensure compliance with regulations
FIN
Manage investment risk
MKT
Secure customer data
POM
Ensure information security with supply chain partners
HR
Secure sensitive employee data
MIS
Provide security infrastructure for firms

[Case 13.1 Cyber-Criminals Use Social Networks for Targeted Attacks]

The Problem

Each infected personal computer in a corporate network represents a potential point of access to valuable intellectual property, such as customer information, patents, and strategic documents. The attackers who breached Google and 30 other technology, media, defence, and financial companies from mid- to late 2009 were after these kinds of information. Dubbed Operation Aurora by cyber security company McAfee (*www.mcafee.com*), the attacks were likely initiated by fake friendly messages sent to specific employees at the targeted companies. These types of attacks continue, with perpetrators sending e-mails about your bank accounts or credit cards "being compromised" so that you provide your passwords. How do more targeted attacks work? Consider the following example.

karen roach/Shutterstock

Karim works for a large multinational financial company. Somehow, attackers gained access to Karim's Facebook account, logged into it, grabbed his contact list of about 50 friends, and began manually reviewing messages and postings on his profile page. The attackers noted discussions about a recent company picnic, and they sent individual messages to Karim's co-workers.

One of Karim's co-workers, Weiling, received a Facebook message apparently from Karim, asking her to look at some pictures from a company picnic. She had, in fact, attended the picnic with Karim. When she clicked on the accompanying web link, she expected to see Karim's pictures. The message, however, had come from the attackers and the link carried malicious software, known as malware.

When Weiling clicked on the link, she unknowingly downloaded a keystroke logger, which is a program designed to save everything she typed at her keyboard and, once per hour, to send a text file of all her keystrokes to a free Gmail account controlled by the attackers. (The keystroke logger was available free on the Internet.) The attackers reviewed Weiling's hourly keystroke reports, and they noted when she logged into a virtual private network (VPN) account to access her company's network. Having achieved access to Weiling's user name and password, the attackers were able to log on to the financial firm's network, where they obtained access to the company's servers and all of the sensitive information they contained. The attackers also took control of Weiling's computer without her knowing it. Her computer essentially had become a zombie computer, under the control of the attackers.

Successful breaches such as the above example illustrate another way in which cyber-criminals—criminals who use the Internet—attack their targets. Cyber-criminals aggressively take advantage of an unanticipated gap in corporate defences: the use of social networks in corporate settings. Attackers increasingly are using the personal information provided by individuals who communicate on social networks such as Facebook and Twitter. These networks provide a rich repository of information that cyber-criminals can use to more precisely target individual corporate employees through phishing attacks. A phishing attack is an attack that acquires sensitive information by masquerading as an authentic e-mail. In fact, phishing attacks now are so precisely targeted that they have a new name: *spear phishing*.

In addition to copying and/or stealing sensitive personal and corporate information, attackers combine many zombie computers into botnets, which can contain millions of computers. The attackers then use these botnets to execute cyber-crimes.

In just four weeks in early 2010, cyber thieves known as the Kneber gang stole 3,644 user names and passwords for Facebook accounts from individuals in more than 2,000 companies. Stolen credentials like these flow into hacking websites, where a batch of 1,000 Facebook user name and password pairs, guaranteed to be valid, can sell for $75 to $200 on the black market, depending on the number of friends tied to the accounts. Botnet attacks continue, and are frequently described in the media. For example, in December 2012 it was discovered that a gang using botnets controlled by the Zeus virus stole an estimated 36 million euros ($47 million). The time period covered by the attacks was not stated, but it was estimated that more than 30,000 banking customers were affected. Another example of malicious software is the Koobface worm (its name is an anagram of Facebook), which targets users of social networking websites, including Facebook, Twitter, MySpace, hi5, Bebo, and Friendster. Kaspersky Labs (*www.kaspersky.ca*), a security firm, estimates that 500,000 Koobface-controlled personal computers are active on the Internet on any given day.

An Attempted Solution

Facebook, the dominant social network and therefore the biggest target, is partnering with Microsoft and security firm McAfee to help filter malicious programs. A Facebook spokesperson claimed that this process should keep compromised accounts to a minimum. He added that Facebook is "constantly working to improve complex systems that quickly detect and block suspicious activity, delete malicious links, and help people restore access to their accounts."

The Results

Unfortunately, attackers continue to exploit vulnerabilities in social networking websites. Many owners of infected zombie computers do not know that their computers are compromised. The best solution to this problem is for all users of social networks to be extremely careful of what information they post on their pages. Further, all computer users should be very careful when clicking on any link in an e-mail, and if they do decide to click on a link, its source should be one that they can trust.

What We Learned from This Case

The lessons that you can learn from the security problems with social networks address the major topic discussed in this chapter: information security. Information security is closely related to information technology, and it raises many significant questions. For example, do social networking sites show due diligence in protecting sensitive, classified information? Are security breaches of social networking sites caused by members' carelessness, by the sites' poor security, or by some combination of these factors? How should social networks protect their members more effectively? Does better protection on social networking sites involve technology, policy, or both? The most important question raised by the opening case, however, is whether it is possible to secure the Internet. The answer to this question impacts each and every one of us.

As you learn about information security in the context of information technology, you will acquire a better understanding of these issues, their importance, their relationships, and their trade-offs. Keep in mind that the issues involved in information security impact individuals and small organizations, as well as large companies. IT's About Small Business 13.1 shows how a lack of data backup affects a small business.

Sources: Compiled from "Information Security Experts at Facebook Fix Vulnerability Discovered by Indiana University Students," *EzineMark.com*, February 3, 2011; R. McMillan, "Five 2010 Stories That Nobody Predicted," *CIO*, January 3, 2011; T. Eston, "Social Networks' Threat to Security," *InformationWeek*, October 30, 2010; M. Schwartz, "Americans Maximize Social Network Security," *InformationWeek*, October 27, 2010; A. Freed, "Enterprise Information Security and Social Networks," *Infosec Island*, October 25, 2010; M. Schwartz, "Social Networks Pose Security Risks to SMBs," *InformationWeek*, September 14, 2010; A. Diana, "Employees Flout Social Network Security Policies," *InformationWeek*, July 23, 2010; M. Schwartz, "Social Network Security Policies Lacking," *InformationWeek*, June 28, 2010; "Facebook Fixes Bug That Exposed Private Chats," *CIO*, May 5, 2010; N. Roiter, "Tweet This: Social Network Security Is Risky Business," *Computerworld*, March 4, 2010; B. Acohido, "An Invitation to Crime," *USA Today*, March 4, 2010; Admin, "Hacking a Corporate Network with Facebook," *Information Security Resources*, January 12, 2010, M. J. Schwartz, "Zeus Botnet Eurograbber Steals $47 Million," *InformationWeek*, December 5, 2012.

IT's about [small] business

13.1 Thomas Tax Service

When Dwight Thomas tried to boot up his computer one morning, he realized he had a major problem. The tax service he operates relied completely on the QuickBooks (*http://quickbooks.intuit.com*) program to maintain all of his customers' financial information. After multiple attempts to resurrect his computer, he called a local computer repair service. The technician determined that the motherboard was bad, and he would require a $5,000 minimum charge to restore Dwight's data. And the worst part of it all? Dwight had no backup. So he purchased a new computer and began the long and arduous process of manually restoring his data from his paper files.

After this incident, Dwight put a backup plan in place. Each of his three employees received a USB drive to back up their QuickBooks files. Dwight also purchased a fireproof safe. Each Friday, he takes the USB drives out of the safe and all the employees back up their files, using the built-in backup system in QuickBooks. Dwight keeps the three most recent backups. When the employees back up each Friday, QuickBooks erases the oldest backup and creates a new one. Therefore, two safe backups can still be accessed if there is a problem when the new backup is being created. While this process seems simple, it is much more effective than not having a backup at all. Given the nature of Dwight's small business, his system is enough to keep his business going in spite of any computer failure.

Recently, Dwight had another computer failure. Fortunately, the problem turned out to be only a few corrupted files that were quickly repaired by the local technician for $40. However, Dwight had peace of mind knowing that if he had to start over from scratch with a new computer, he could easily restore his data and continue his business operations.

Questions

1. Why did Dwight restore his data manually by himself?
2. What are the advantages and disadvantages of Dwight's backup plan?

Source: Compiled from author interview with Dwight Thomas, owner of Thomas Tax Service.

A solid backup plan is critical to information availability. As you consider this case, think about your personal data—pictures, videos, schoolwork, financial information, or any digital files that you would like to have if you lost your computer. A duplicate backup is easy to keep, but you have to be diligent about backing up your essential files. For a small business, this process is even more important, because any loss of data could mean lost customers and lost revenue.

In addition to potential availability problems, unfortunately, information technologies can be misused, often with devastating consequences. Consider the following scenarios:

- Individuals can have their identities stolen.
- Organizations can have customer information stolen, leading to financial losses, erosion of customer confidence, and legal action.
- Countries face the threat of *cyberterrorism* and *cyberwarfare*, terms for Internet-based attacks.

In fact, the misuse of information technologies has come to the forefront of any discussion of IT. For example, the Ponemon Institute (*www.ponemon.org*), a research firm, found that in 2012 each security breach cost organizations an average of $8.9 million, up from $8.4 million the year before. The study measured the direct costs of a data breach, such as hiring forensic experts, notifying customers, setting up telephone hotlines to field queries from concerned or affected customers, offering free credit monitoring, and giving discounts for future products and services. The study also measured more intangible costs of a breach, such as the loss of business from increased customer turnover—called *customer churn*—and decreases in customer trust. The study further concluded that employee negligence caused many of the data breaches. This finding confirms that organizational employees are a weak link in information security. It is therefore very important for you to learn about information security so that you will be better prepared when you enter the workforce.

13.1 Introduction to Information Security

Information security consists of the processes and policies designed to protect an organization's information and information systems (IS) from unauthorized access, use, disclosure, disruption, modification, or destruction.

Organizations collect huge amounts of information and employ numerous information systems that are subject to myriad threats. A **threat** to an information resource is any danger to which a system may be exposed. An information resource's **vulnerability** is the possibility that the system will be harmed by a threat.

Today, five key factors are contributing to the increasing vulnerability of organizational information resources, making it much more difficult to secure them:

- The modern interconnected, interdependent, wirelessly networked business environment
- Smaller, faster, cheaper computers and storage devices
- Decreasing skills necessary to be a computer hacker
- International organized crime taking over cyber-crime
- Lack of management support

The first factor is the evolution of the IT resource from mainframe-only to today's highly complex, interconnected, interdependent, wirelessly networked business environment. The Internet now enables millions of computers and computer networks to communicate freely and seamlessly with one another. Organizations and individuals are exposed to a world of untrusted networks and potential attackers. A *trusted network*, in general, is any network within your organization. An *untrusted network*, in general, is any network external to your organization. In addition, wireless technologies enable employees to compute, communicate, and access the Internet anywhere and anytime. Significantly, wireless is an inherently non-secure broadcast communications medium.

The second factor reflects the fact that modern computers and storage devices (e.g., thumb drives or flash drives) continue to become smaller, faster, cheaper, and more portable, with greater storage capacity. These characteristics make it much easier to steal or lose a computer or storage device that contains huge amounts of sensitive information. Also, far more people are able to afford powerful computers and connect inexpensively to the Internet, thus raising the potential of an attack on information assets.

The third factor is that the computing skills necessary to be a hacker are *decreasing*. The reason is that the Internet contains information and computer programs called *scripts* that users with few skills can download and use to attack any information system connected to the Internet. (Security experts can also use these scripts for legitimate purposes, such as testing the security of various systems.)

The fourth factor is that international organized crime is taking over cyber-crime. **Cyber-crime** is illegal activity conducted over computer networks, particularly the Internet. According to iDefense (a division of VeriSign [*www.verisigninc.com*] that specializes in providing security information to governments and Fortune 500 companies), groups of well-organized criminal organizations have taken control of a global billion-dollar crime network. The network, powered by skillful hackers, targets known software security weaknesses. These crimes are typically non-violent, but quite lucrative. For example, the losses from armed robberies average hundreds of dollars, and those from white-collar crimes average tens of thousands of dollars. In contrast, losses from computer crimes average hundreds of thousands of dollars. Also, computer crimes can be committed from anywhere in the world, at any time, effectively providing an international safe haven for cyber-criminals. Computer-based crimes cause billions of dollars in damages to businesses each year, including the costs to repair information systems and the costs of lost business.

The fifth, and final, factor is lack of management support. For the entire organization to take security policies and procedures seriously, senior managers must set the tone. Ultimately, however, lower-level managers may be even more important. These managers are in close contact with employees every day and thus are in a better position to determine whether employees are following security procedures.

before you go on...

1. Define "information security."
2. Differentiate among a threat, an exposure, and a vulnerability.
3. Why are the skills needed to be a hacker decreasing?

13.2 Unintentional Threats to Information Systems

Information systems are vulnerable to many potential hazards and threats, as you can see in Figure 13.1. The two major categories of threats are unintentional threats and deliberate threats. This section discusses unintentional threats, and the next section addresses deliberate threats.

Unintentional threats are acts performed without malicious intent that nevertheless represent a serious threat to information security. A major category of unintentional threats is human error.

Human Errors

Organizational employees span the breadth and depth of the organization, from mail clerks to the CEO, and across all functional areas. There are two important points to be made about employees. First, the higher the level of employee, the greater the threat he or she poses to information security. This is true because higher-level employees typically have greater access to corporate data and enjoy greater privileges on organizational information systems. Second, employees in two areas of the organization pose especially significant threats to information security: human resources and information systems (IS). Human resources employees generally have access to sensitive personal information about all employees. Likewise, IS employees not only have access to sensitive organizational data, but they often control the means to create, store, transmit, and modify that data.

Other employees include contract labour, consultants, and janitors and security guards. Contract labour, such as temporary hires, may be overlooked in information security arrangements. However, these employees often have access to the company's network, information systems, and information assets. Consultants, although technically not employees, perform work for the company. Depending on the nature of their work, they may also have access to the company's network, information systems, and information assets.

Finally, janitors and guards are the most frequently ignored people in information security systems. Companies frequently outsource their security and janitorial services. As with contractors, then, these individuals work for the company although they technically are not employees. Moreover, they are usually present when most—if not all—other employees have gone home. They typically have keys to every office, and nobody questions their presence in even the most sensitive parts of the building. In fact, an article from *2600: The Hacker Quarterly* described how to get a job as a janitor for the purpose of gaining physical access to an organization.

Human errors or mistakes by employees pose a large problem as the result of laziness, carelessness, or a lack of awareness concerning information security. This lack of awareness comes from poor education and training efforts by the organization. Human mistakes manifest themselves in many different ways, as shown in Table 13.1.

The human errors that you have just studied, although unintentional, are committed entirely by the employee. However, employees also can make unintentional mistakes as a result of actions by an attacker. Attackers often employ social engineering to induce individuals to make unintentional mistakes and disclose sensitive information.

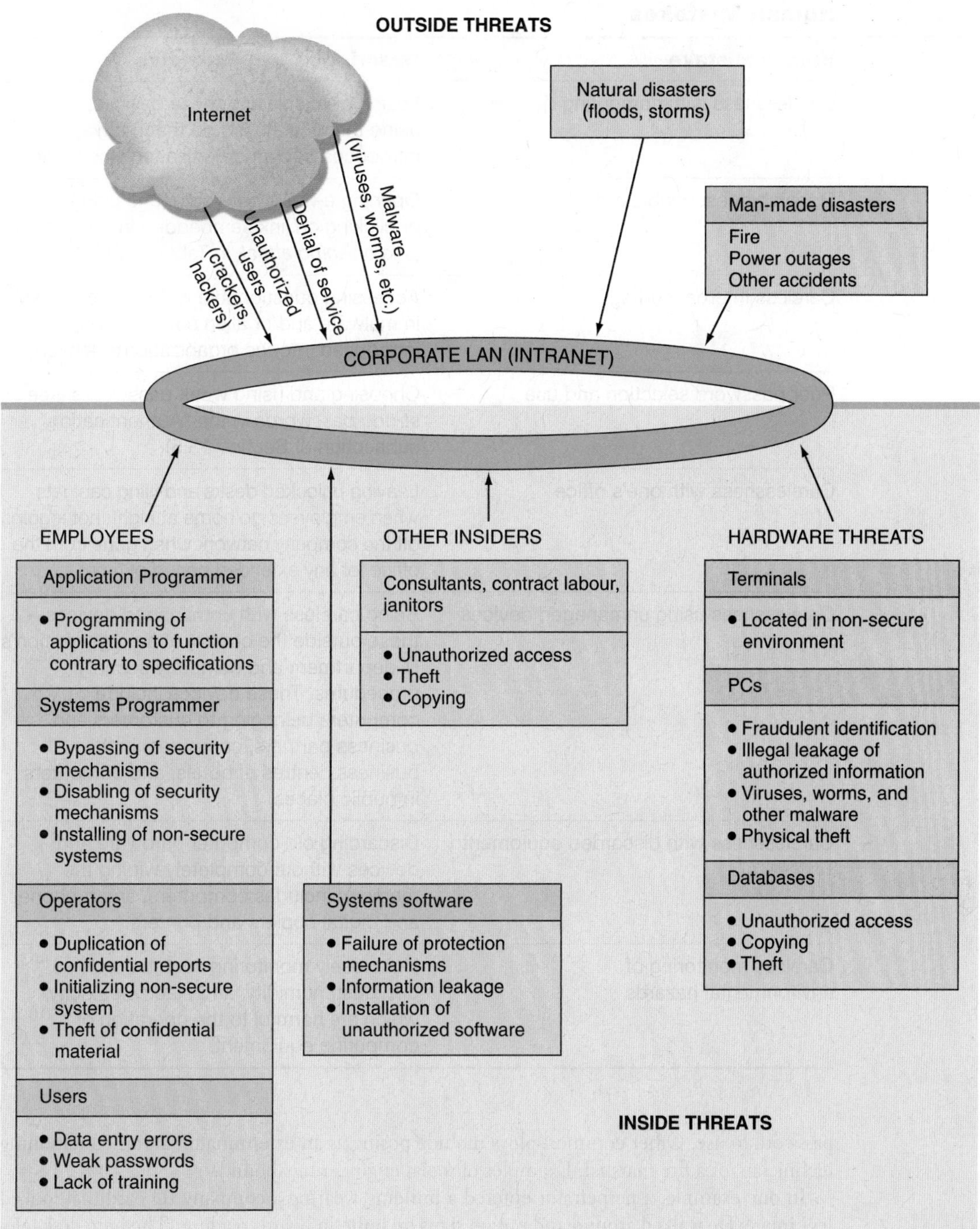

FIGURE 13.1 Security threats.

Social Engineering

Social engineering is an attack in which the perpetrator uses social skills to trick or manipulate a legitimate employee into providing confidential company information such as passwords. The most common example of social engineering occurs when the attacker impersonates someone else on the telephone, such as a company manager or an information systems employee. The attacker claims he forgot his password and asks the legitimate employee to give him a

TABLE 13.1 Human Mistakes

Human Mistake	Description and Examples
Carelessness with computing devices	Losing or misplacing these devices, or using them carelessly so that malware is introduced into an organization's network.
Opening questionable e-mails	Opening e-mails from someone unknown, or clicking on links embedded in e-mails (see *phishing attack* in Table 13.2).
Careless Internet surfing	Accessing questionable websites; can result in malware and/or alien software being introduced into the organization's network.
Poor password selection and use	Choosing and using weak passwords (see *strong passwords* in the "Authentication" subsection of Section 13.5).
Carelessness with one's office	Leaving unlocked desks and filing cabinets when employees go home at night; not logging off the company network when gone from the office for any extended period of time.
Carelessness using unmanaged devices	Being careless with unmanaged devices—those outside the control of an organization's IT department and company security procedures. These devices include computers belonging to customers and business partners, computers in the business centres of hotels, and computers in public places.
Carelessness with discarded equipment	Discarding old computer hardware and devices without completely wiping the memory; includes computers, smart phones, and digital copiers and printers.
Careless monitoring of environmental hazards	Not closely monitoring such hazards as dirt, dust, humidity, and static electricity, which are harmful to the operation of computing equipment.

password to use. Other common ploys include posing as an exterminator, an air-conditioning technician, or a fire marshal. Examples of social engineering abound.

In one example, a perpetrator entered a building wearing a company ID card that looked legitimate. He walked around and put up signs on bulletin boards reading "The help desk telephone number has been changed. The new number is 555-1234." He then exited the building and began receiving calls from legitimate employees thinking they were calling the company help desk. Naturally, the first thing the perpetrator asked for was user name and password. He now had the information necessary to access the company's information systems.

Two other social engineering techniques are tailgating and shoulder surfing. *Tailgating* is a technique designed to allow the perpetrator to enter restricted areas that are controlled with locks or card entry. The perpetrator follows closely behind a legitimate employee and, when the employee gains entry, the attacker asks him or her to "hold the door." *Shoulder surfing* occurs when a perpetrator watches an employee's computer screen over the employee's shoulder. This technique is particularly successful in public areas such as in airports and on commuter trains and airplanes.

before you go on...

1. What is an unintentional threat to an information system?

2. Provide examples of social engineering attacks other than the ones just discussed.

13.3 Deliberate Threats to Information Systems

There are many types of deliberate threats to information systems. We provide a list of 10 common types for your convenience.

- Espionage or trespass
- Information extortion
- Sabotage or vandalism
- Theft of equipment or information
- Identity theft
- Compromises to intellectual property
- Software attacks
- Alien software
- Supervisory control and data acquisition (SCADA) attacks
- Cyberterrorism and cyberwarfare

Espionage or Trespass

Espionage or trespass occurs when an unauthorized individual attempts to gain illegal access to organizational information. It is important to distinguish between competitive intelligence and industrial espionage. Competitive intelligence consists of legal information-gathering techniques, such as studying a company's website and press releases, attending trade shows, and so on. In contrast, industrial espionage crosses the legal boundary, involving things such as theft of confidential data.

Information Extortion

Information extortion occurs when an attacker either threatens to steal or actually steals information from a company. The perpetrator demands payment for not stealing the information, for returning stolen information, or for agreeing not to disclose the information.

Sabotage or Vandalism

Sabotage and vandalism are deliberate acts that involve defacing an organization's website, possibly damaging the organization's image and causing its customers to lose faith in the organization. One form of on-line vandalism is a "hacktivist" or "cyberactivist" operation. These are cases of high-tech civil disobedience to protest the operations, policies, or actions of an organization or government agency.

Theft of Equipment or Information

Computing devices and storage devices are becoming smaller yet more powerful with vastly increased storage (for example, laptops, smart phones, digital cameras, thumb drives, and iPods). As a result, these devices are becoming easier to steal and easier for attackers to use to steal information.

Table 13.1 points out that one type of human mistake is carelessness with laptops. In fact, many laptops have been stolen due to such carelessness. The cost of a stolen laptop includes: the loss of data; the loss of intellectual property; laptop replacement, legal and regulatory costs; investigation fees; and lost productivity.

One form of theft, known as *dumpster diving*, involves the practice of rummaging through commercial or residential garbage to find information that has been discarded. Paper files, letters, memos, photographs, IDs, passwords, credit cards, and other forms of information can be found in dumpsters. Unfortunately, many people never consider that the sensitive items they throw in the garbage may be recovered. Such information, when recovered, can be used for fraudulent purposes.

Dumpster diving is not necessarily theft, because the legality of this act varies. Where dumpsters are located on private premises, it is likely illegal. However, these laws are enforced with varying degrees of rigour.

Identity Theft

Identity theft is the deliberate assumption of another person's identity, usually to gain access to his or her financial information or to frame him or her for a crime. Techniques for illegally obtaining personal information include:

- stealing mail or dumpster diving;
- stealing personal information in computer databases;
- infiltrating organizations that store large amounts of personal information (e.g., data aggregators such as Acxiom) (*www.acxiom.com*); and
- impersonating a trusted organization in an electronic communication (phishing).

The Office of the Privacy Commissioner of Canada provides instructions for businesses and individuals to help reduce their risk of identity theft (see *www.privcom.gc.ca/id/business_e.cfm*). Additional information and articles are also available at the Better Business Bureau website (*www.bbb.org/canada*). The department stated that it would send letters to all affected individuals, letting them know the actions that they could take to prevent identity theft.

Recovering from identity theft is costly, time consuming, and difficult. Victims also report problems in obtaining credit and obtaining or holding a job, as well as adverse effects on insurance or credit rates. In addition, victims state that it is often difficult to remove negative information from their records, such as their credit reports.

Your personal information can be compromised in other ways. For example, the nature of your identity can be uncovered just by examining your searches in a search engine. The ability to analyze all searches made by a single user can enable a criminal to identify who the user is and what he or she is doing. Human error is also a common cause of risks associated with identity theft. There are frequent accounts of laptops or equipment being lost or stolen. For example, in February 2013 it was reported that a hard drive belonging to Human Resources and Skills Development Canada could not be located. The hard drive had held student loan information on close to 600,000 Canadians. Student loan information would include personal details such as name, address, birth date, social insurance number, and banking information.

Compromises to Intellectual Property

Protecting intellectual property is a vital issue for people who make their livelihood in knowledge fields. **Intellectual property** is the property created by individuals or corporations that is protected under *trade secret*, *patent*, and *copyright* laws.

A **trade secret** is an intellectual work, such as a business plan, that is a company secret and is not based on public information. An example is the Coca-Cola formula. A **patent** is an official document that grants the holder exclusive rights on an invention or a process for 20 years. **Copyright** is a statutory grant that provides the creators or owners of intellectual property with ownership of the property, for the life of the creator plus 50 years. Owners are entitled to collect fees from anyone who wants to copy the property. It is important to note that these are definitions under Canadian law. There is some international standardization of copyrights and patents, but it is far from total. Therefore, there will be differences between Canadian law and other countries' laws.

The most common intellectual property related to IT deals with software. However, copyright law does not protect fundamental concepts, functions, and general features of software such as pull-down menus, colours, and icons. Under copyright law, copying a software program without making payment to the owner—including giving a disk to a friend to install on his or her computer—is a copyright violation. Not surprisingly, this practice, called **piracy**, is a major problem for software vendors. The global trade in pirated software amounts to hundreds of billions of dollars.

Table 13.2

Types of Software Attacks

Types of Software Attacks	Description
(1) Remote attacks requiring user action	
Virus	Segment of computer code that performs malicious actions by attaching to another computer program.
Worm	Segment of computer code that performs malicious actions and will replicate, or spread, by itself (without requiring another computer program).
Phishing attack	Attack that uses deception to acquire sensitive personal information by masquerading as official-looking e-mails or instant messages.
Spear phishing attack	Attack that targets large groups of people. The perpetrators find out as much information as they can about an individual, tailoring their phishing attacks to improve their chances of obtaining sensitive, personal information.
(2) Remote attacks needing no user action	
Denial-of-service attack	Attack in which the attacker sends so many information requests to a target computer system that the target cannot handle them successfully and typically crashes (ceases to function).
Distributed denial-of-service (DDoS) attack	Attack in which an attacker first takes over many computers, typically by using malicious software. These computers are called *zombies* or *bots*. The attacker uses these bots—which form a *botnet*—to deliver a coordinated stream of information requests to a target computer, causing it to crash.
(3) Attacks by a programmer developing a system	
Trojan horse	Software programs that hide in other computer programs and reveal their designed behaviour only when they are activated.
Back door	Typically a password, known only to the attacker, that allows him or her to access a computer system at will, without having to go through any security procedures (also called a *trap door*).
Logic bomb	Segment of computer code that is embedded within an organization's existing computer programs and is designed to activate and perform a destructive action under specific conditions, such as at a certain time or date.

The Canadian Alliance Against Software Theft (CAAST) is an organization representing the commercial software industry that promotes legal software and conducts research on software piracy in an attempt to eliminate it. CAAST is affiliated with the Business Software Alliance (BSA; see *www2.bsa.org*). In a 2012 survey of almost 15,000 computer users in 33 countries, over 57 percent of those surveyed said that they had used illegally copied software. The BSA estimated that the "shadow market"—the sales of pirated software—was equal to about $63.4 billion in 2011.

Software Attacks

Software attacks have evolved from the early years of the computer era, when attackers used malicious software to infect as many computers worldwide as possible, to the profit-driven, web-based attacks of today. Modern cyber-criminals use sophisticated, blended malware attacks, typically via the web, to make money. Table 13.2 displays a variety of software attacks. These attacks are grouped into three categories: remote attacks requiring user action, remote attacks requiring no user action, and software attacks by programmers during the development of a system. IT's About Business 13.2 provides an example of a software attack.

Source: http://globalstudy.bsa.org/2011/downloads/study_pdf/2011_BSA_Piracy_Study-InBrief.pdf

IT's [about business]

13.2 Virus Attack Hits the University of Exeter

In January 2010, the University of Exeter (*www.exeter.ac.uk*), located in southwestern England, became the target of a massive virus attack. The university has 16,000 students on three campuses, two in Exeter and one in Cornwall. The virus attack, which exploited computers running Microsoft Windows Vista Service Pack 2, caused the university to temporarily take its entire network off-line. University officials maintained that this measure was necessary in order to scan and repair all of the university's computers. The university also scanned personal computers used by students who had connected to the university's network. In addition, the Cornwall campus was isolated from the main campuses in Exeter to avoid spreading the virus.

The virus wreaked havoc for university faculty. The interactive teaching boards in all classrooms became inoperable, so professors could not use PowerPoint presentations or access the Internet in class. Also, the university's voice over Internet protocol (VoIP) telephone system was disrupted.

The attack also affected the students. Perhaps the most serious problem was that they lost access to the university's Virtual Learning Environment (VLE). Consequently, students who had assignments or papers due could not access on-line versions of their work stored in the VLE. In fact, students could not access *any* data stored in the VLE. The university faculty promised to make allowances for students and granted short-term deadline extensions. Interestingly, computers in student residence halls were the last to be added back to the operational university network.

It took three days to clean infected computers and bring the network back into operation. As of May 2011, no one had identified the perpetrators or determined how they managed to infect the university network. However, an internal university e-mail suggested that appropriate patches for the security software had not been applied in a timely fashion, making the system vulnerable to attack. Around the same time (February 2011), several Canadian government departments (Defence Research and Development Canada, Department of Finance Canada, and the Treasury Board of Canada Secretariat) shut down their computer systems while they dealt with hacker attacks.

Questions

1. What other actions could the university have taken to prevent the attack?
2. What actions should the university now perform to prevent future attacks?

Sources: Compiled from "University of Exeter Shuts Down Its Network Because of the Attack of a Virus," *Dedicated 2-viruses*, January 21, 2010; L. Constatin, "Mystery Computer Virus Hits UK University," *Softpedia.com*, January 21, 2010; J. Leyden, "Exeter Uni Goes Offline to Fight Mystery Malware," *The Register*, January 21, 2010; Z. Whittaker, "Virus Attack Hits Vista Machines, Cripples University Network," *ZDNet.com*, January 20, 2010; "University of Exeter Malware Outbreak," *Ja.net*, January 20, 2010; G. Weston, "Foreign Hackers Attack Canadian Government," *CBC.ca*, February 16, 2011; *www.exeter.ac.uk*, accessed May 5, 2013.

Alien Software

Many personal computers have alien software, or *pestware*, running on them that the owners do not know about. **Alien software** is clandestine software that is installed on your computer through duplicitous methods. It typically is not as malicious as viruses, worms, or Trojan horses, but it does use up valuable system resources. In addition, it can report on your web surfing habits and other personal behaviour.

The vast majority of pestware is **adware**—software that causes pop-up advertisements to appear on your screen. Adware is common because it works. According to advertising agencies, for every 100 people who close a pop-up ad, 3 click on it. This "hit rate" is extremely high for Internet advertising.

Spyware is software that collects personal information about users without their consent. Two common types of spyware are keystroke loggers and screen scrapers.

In the chapter-opening Case 13.1, you saw an example of a keystroke logger. Keystroke loggers, also called *keyloggers*, record both your individual keystrokes and your Internet web browsing history. The purposes range from criminal—for example, theft of passwords and sensitive personal information such as credit card numbers—to annoying—for example, recording your Internet search history for targeted advertising.

Companies have attempted to counter keyloggers by switching to other forms of identifying users. For example, at some point all of us have been forced to look at wavy, distorted letters and type them correctly into a box. That string of letters is called a *CAPTCHA*, and it is a test.

The point of CAPTCHA is that computers cannot (yet) accurately read those distorted letters. Therefore, the fact that you can transcribe them means that you are probably not a software program run by an unauthorized person, such as a spammer. As a result, attackers have turned to *screen scrapers*, or *screen grabbers*. This software records a continuous "movie" of a screen's contents rather than simply recording keystrokes.

Spamware is pestware that uses your computer as a launch pad for spammers. **Spam** is unsolicited e-mail, usually advertising for products and services. When your computer is infected with spamware, e-mails from spammers are sent to everyone in your e-mail address book, but they appear to come from you.

Not only is spam a nuisance, but it wastes time and money. Spam costs companies around the world billions of dollars per year. These costs come from productivity losses, clogged e-mail systems, additional storage, user support, and anti-spam software. Spam can also carry viruses and worms, making it even more dangerous.

Cookies are small amounts of information that websites store on your computer, temporarily or more or less permanently. In many cases, cookies are useful and innocuous. For example, some cookies are passwords and user IDs that you do not want to retype every time you access the website that issued the cookie. Cookies are also necessary for on-line shopping because merchants use them for your shopping carts.

Tracking cookies, however, can be used to track your path through a website, the time you spend there, what links you click on, and other details that the company wants to record, usually for marketing purposes. Tracking cookies can also combine this information with your name, purchases, credit card information, and other personal data to develop an intrusive profile of your spending habits.

Most cookies can be read only by the party that created them. However, some companies that manage on-line banner advertising are, in essence, cookie-sharing rings. These companies can track information such as which pages you load and which ads you click on. They then share this information with their client websites, which may number in the thousands. For a cookie demonstration, see *http://privacy.net/cookie-tracking-demo/*.

Supervisory Control and Data Acquisition (SCADA) Attacks

SCADA is a large-scale, distributed measurement and control system. SCADA systems are used to monitor or to control chemical, physical, and transport processes such as those used in oil refineries, water and sewage treatment plants, electrical generators, and nuclear power plants. Essentially, SCADA systems provide a link between the physical world and the electronic world.

SCADA systems consist of multiple sensors, a master computer, and communications infrastructure. The sensors connect to physical equipment. They read status data such as the open/closed status of a switch or a valve, as well as measurements such as pressure, flow, voltage, and current. They control the equipment by sending signals to it, such as opening or closing a switch or valve or setting the speed of a pump.

The sensors are connected in a network, and each sensor typically has an Internet address (Internet protocol, or IP, address, discussed in Chapter 4). If attackers gain access to the network, they can cause serious damage, such as disrupting the power grid over a large area or upsetting the operations of a large chemical or nuclear plant. Such actions could have catastrophic results, as you can see in IT's About Business 13.3.

Cyberterrorism and Cyberwarfare

Cyberterrorism and **cyberwarfare** are malicious acts in which attackers use a target's computer systems, particularly via the Internet, to cause physical, real-world harm or severe disruption, usually to carry out a political agenda. These actions range from gathering data to attacking critical infrastructure (via SCADA systems). We treat the two types of attacks as synonymous here, even though cyberterrorism typically is carried out by individuals or groups whereas cyberwarfare is carried out by nation states. IT's About Business 13.3 describes how worms and viruses can affect countries' computer systems. Attacks that are directed at national or international infrastructure are also in this category, as discussed in Example 13.1.

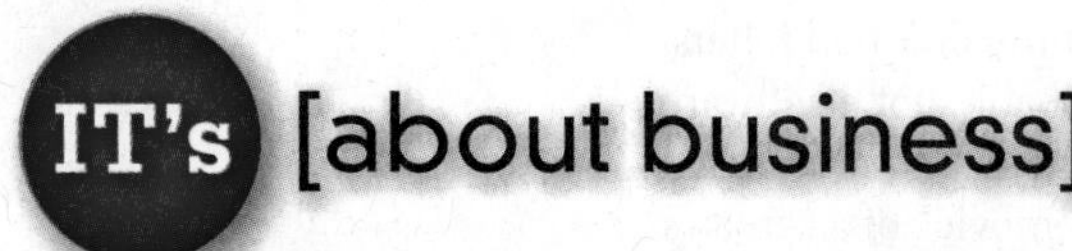

13.3 The Stuxnet Worm

Stuxnet, discovered in July 2010, is a worm that targets industrial supervisory control and data acquisition (SCADA) systems. In particular, Stuxnet targets Siemens SCADA systems that are configured to control and monitor specific industrial processes. In fact, security experts around the world suspect that the worm's target was the uranium enrichment industrial infrastructure in Iran. On November 29, 2010, Iran confirmed that its nuclear program had been damaged by Stuxnet. Therefore, the worm may have damaged Iran's nuclear facilities in Natanz and eventually delayed the start-up of the Bushehr nuclear power plant.

Whoever constructed the Stuxnet worm must have possessed an in-depth knowledge of nuclear industrial processes. The worm fakes the sensor signals that control industrial processes so that an infected system does not shut down when it behaves abnormally. The worm appears to have impaired Iran's computer-controlled uranium centrifuges, which mysteriously lost 30 percent of their production capacity, thereby delaying any plans to produce a nuclear weapon. Stuxnet changes the speed of the motors that spin the centrifuges from very high to very low, and then back again. This process stops the uranium from being enriched and also damages the motors themselves. At the same time, however, the worm adjusts the user interface for the centrifuge control systems to make it appear that the centrifuges are operating normally. Therefore, the system does not shut down as it normally would when it malfunctions.

After infecting Iran's nuclear facilities, Stuxnet spread rapidly throughout the country, affecting more than 30,000 Internet protocol addresses. This problem was compounded by the worm's ability to mutate, meaning that new versions of the worm continue to spread.

As of this printing, no one knows who created the worm, and no one has taken credit for creating it. Security experts from Symantec (*www.symantec.com/en/ca/*), a leading vendor of information security systems, suspect that the group that developed Stuxnet was well funded, consisted of five to 10 people, and took six months to create the worm. According to the *New York Times*, experts studying Stuxnet have concluded that the worm is so complex that only a nation state would have the capabilities to produce it.

Stuxnet heralds a frightening new era in cyberwarfare. China, Russia, the United States, and other nations have been quietly engaging in cyberwarfare for several years, but this worm represents a major technological escalation. One security expert has warned that nation states construct worms such as Stuxnet when their only other option is to go to war.

Viruses continue to evolve. In February 2013 another new type of virus that takes over computer systems attacked European governments. The virus went in via a security hole in Adobe software, affecting the Czech Republic, Romania, and other European countries.

Questions

1. Describe the implications of the precisely targeted nature of the Stuxnet attack.
2. Analyze the statement: "Nations use malware such as the Stuxnet worm when their only alternative is to go to war."

Sources: Compiled from M. Schwartz, "Stuxnet Iran Attack Launched from 10 Machines," *InformationWeek*, February 14, 2011; G. Keizer, "Stuxnet Struck Five Targets in Iran, Say Researchers," *Computerworld*, February 11, 2011; M. Schwartz, "Symantec Finds Stuxnet Targets Iranian Nuclear Enrichment," *InformationWeek*, November 16, 2010; "Stuxnet: Declaring Cyberwarfare on Iran," *The Week*, October 8, 2010; E. Messmer, "Is Stuxnet an Israeli-Invented Attack Against Iran?", *NetworkWorld*, September 30, 2010; T. Claburn, "Iran Denies Stuxnet Worm Hurt Nuclear Plant," *InformationWeek*, September 27, 2010; D. Goodin, "SCADA Worm a Nation-State Search-and-Destroy Weapon," *The Register*, September 22, 2010; M. Clayton, "Stuxnet Malware: Is 'Weapon' Out to Destroy . . . Iran's Bushehr Nuclear Plant?", *The Christian Science Monitor*, September 21, 2010; J. Kirk, "Eset Discovers Second Variation of Stuxnet Worm," *NetworkWorld*, July 20, 2010; J. Finkle, "Hackers Target European Governments," *Toronto Star*, February 28, 2013, p. B2; *www.symantec.com*, accessed May 5, 2013.

EXAMPLE 13.1

In March 2013, a massive *distributed denial-of-service (DDoS)* attack targeted Spamhaus and other anti-spam organizations. At the same time, though, DDoS attacks appeared to be taking place against other organizations, such as stock-trading Internet exchanges around the world (based in London, Germany, Amsterdam, and Hong Kong). There were concerns that the high volume of traffic (over 300 gigabits per second) would affect the Internet's ability to function. The attack spanned at least 10 days, starting on March 18, with a second wave on March 22. It was reported that over 30,000 servers were involved in the attack. This particular DDoS received significant attention because it did not seem to be caused by unleashing a botnet. The media stated that this may have been the "largest ever" DDoS attack, made possible by problems with domain name resolvers (Internet service provider processes that translate domain names into an IP address) that allowed information packets to be sent that masqueraded

Sources: Compiled from K. Allen, "Online Spam Fight Becomes Largest-Ever Snarl Attack," *Toronto Star*, March 28, 2013, p. A25; J. Leyden, "Biggest DDoS in History FAILS to Slash Interweb Arteries," *The Register*, March 28, 2013; S. Hanford, "Chronology of a DDoS: SpamHaus," March 28, 2013, *http://blogs.cisco.com/security*, accessed May 18, 2013.

as coming from the target site. The DDoS escalates when the target site's systems respond to these messages, magnifying the effect of the information blockage.

The good thing is that there are now strategies for dealing with such high volumes of traffic, so that organizations do not go down for extended periods of time (or not at all). During this DDoS attack, apparently Internet traffic slowed, but did not stop. The problems with the domain name system resolvers have been corrected, so that this particular type of attack cannot be replicated.

before you go on...

1. How do DDoS attacks affect organizations?
2. What are the three types of software attacks?
3. Explain how hardware and software problems can be exploited by hackers.

13.4 What Organizations Are Doing to Protect Information Resources

Why is it so difficult to stop cyber-criminals? Table 13.3 illustrates the many major difficulties involved in protecting information. Because organizing an appropriate defence system is so important to the entire enterprise, it is one of the major responsibilities of any prudent CIO as well as of the functional managers who control information resources. In fact, IT security is the business of *everyone* in an organization. As explained in Chapter 12, governments assist with such processes by implementing legislation, such as the anti-spam legislation that was passed in Canada in 2010.

Another reason why information resources are difficult to protect is that the on-line commerce industry is not particularly willing to install safeguards that would make completing transactions more difficult or complicated. As one example, merchant systems could demand passwords or personal identification numbers for all credit card transactions, as they do for chip cards at retail outlets. However, these requirements might discourage people from shopping on-line. For credit card companies, it is cheaper to block a stolen credit card and move on than to invest time and money on a prosecution.

Table 13.3

The Difficulties in Protecting Information Resources
Hundreds of potential threats exist.
Computing resources may be situated in many locations.
Many individuals control or have access to information assets.
Computer networks can be located outside the organization, making them difficult to protect.
Rapid technological changes make some controls obsolete as soon as they are installed.
Many computer crimes are undetected for a long period of time, so it is difficult to learn from experience.
People tend to violate security procedures because the procedures are inconvenient.
The amount of computer knowledge necessary to commit computer crimes is usually minimal. As a matter of fact, a potential criminal can learn hacking, for free, on the Internet.
The costs of preventing hazards can be very high. Therefore, most organizations simply cannot afford to protect themselves against all possible hazards.
It is difficult to conduct a cost-benefit justification for controls before an attack occurs because the impact of a hypothetical attack is unknown.

Despite these difficulties, the information security industry is battling back. Companies are developing software and services that deliver early warnings of trouble on the Internet. Unlike traditional antivirus software, which is reactive, early-warning systems are proactive, scanning the web for new viruses and alerting companies to the danger.

Organizations spend a great deal of time and money protecting their information resources. Before doing so, they perform risk management.

A **risk** is the probability that a threat will impact an information resource. The goal of **risk management** is to identify, control, and minimize the impact of threats. In other words, risk management seeks to reduce risk to acceptable levels. Risk management consists of three processes: risk analysis, risk mitigation, and controls evaluation.

Organizations perform risk analyses to ensure that their IS security programs are cost effective. **Risk analysis** involves three steps: (1) assessing the value of each asset being protected, (2) estimating the probability that each asset will be compromised, and (3) comparing the probable costs of the asset's being compromised with the costs of protecting that asset. The organization then considers how to mitigate the risk.

In **risk mitigation**, the organization takes concrete actions against risks. Risk mitigation has two functions: (1) implementing controls to prevent identified threats from occurring, and (2) developing a means of recovery should the threat become a reality. There are several risk mitigation strategies that organizations can adopt. The three most common are risk acceptance, risk limitation, and risk transference.

- **Risk acceptance:** Accept the potential risk, continue operating with no controls, and absorb any damages that occur.
- **Risk limitation:** Limit the risk by implementing controls that minimize the impact of the threat.
- **Risk transference:** Transfer the risk by using other means to compensate for the loss, such as by purchasing insurance.

Finally, in controls evaluation, the organization identifies security deficiencies and calculates the cost of implementing. If the costs of implementing a control are greater than the value of the asset being protected, the control is not cost effective. In the next section, you will study the various controls that organizations use to protect their information resources.

before you go on...

1. Describe several reasons why it is difficult to protect information resources.
2. Compare and contrast risk management and risk analysis.

13.5 Information Security Controls

The purpose of **controls** is to safeguard assets, optimize the use of the organization's resources, and prevent or detect errors or fraud. Organizations protect their systems using "layers" of control systems. First comes the control environment, and then general controls, followed by application controls. The **control environment** encompasses management attitudes toward controls, as evidenced by management actions, as well as by stated policies and procedures that address ethical issues and the quality of supervision. **General controls** apply to more than one functional area. For example, passwords are general controls. Controls specific to one application, such as payroll, are **application controls**. A typical payroll application control would be the approval of payroll wage rates.

Information systems security encompasses all of the types of controls, as organizations need to have security policies and procedures, to protect all applications using physical and software controls such as antivirus or firewalls, and to protect individual applications with controls over how information is entered and managed.

Because it is so important to the entire enterprise, organizing an appropriate defence system is one of the major activities of any prudent CIO and of the functional managers who control information resources. As a matter of fact, IT security is the business of *everyone* in an organization. Table 3.5 lists the major difficulties involved in protecting information.

Controls that protect information assets are called defence mechanisms or *countermeasures*. *Security controls* are designed to protect all of the components of an information system, including data, software, hardware, and networks.

Controls are intended to prevent accidental hazards, deter intentional acts, detect problems as early as possible, enhance damage recovery, and correct problems. Before we discuss controls in more detail, we emphasize that the most effective control is user education and training, leading to increased awareness of the vital importance of information security on the part of every organizational employee.

We will look at three categories of general controls: physical controls, access controls, and communications controls. Figure 13.2 illustrates these controls. Then, we will look at examples of application controls.

Physical Controls

Physical controls prevent unauthorized individuals from gaining access to a company's facilities. Common physical controls include walls, doors, fencing, gates, locks, badges, guards, and alarm systems. More sophisticated physical controls include pressure sensors, temperature sensors, and motion detectors. One shortcoming of physical controls is that they can be inconvenient to employees.

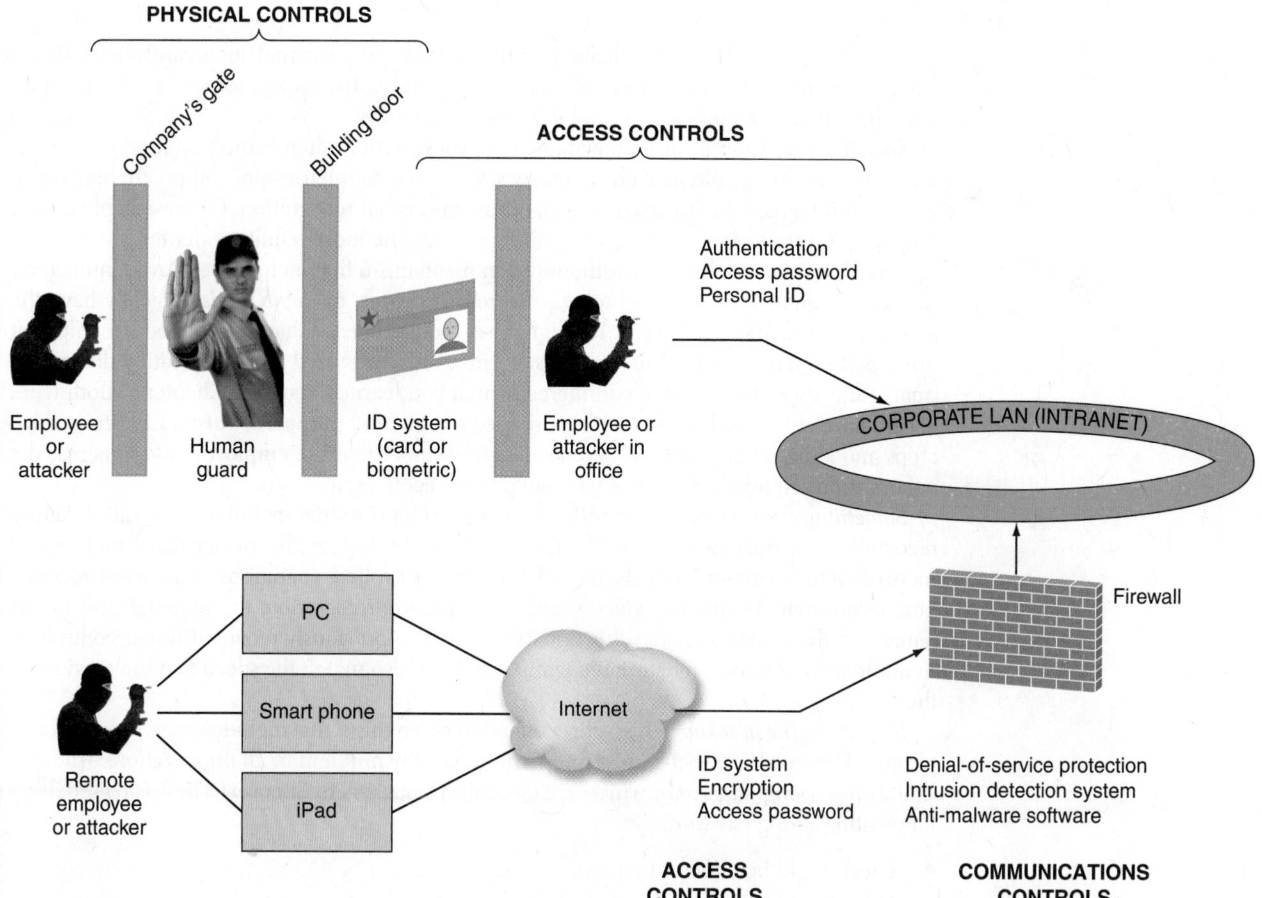

FIGURE 13.2 Where defence mechanisms are located. (*Sources:* © Sergey Titov/iStockphoto; © fatihoca/iStockphoto)

Guards deserve special mention because they have very difficult jobs for at least two reasons. First, their jobs are boring and repetitive and generally do not pay well. Second, if guards perform their jobs thoroughly, the other employees harass them, particularly if they slow up the process of entering the facility.

Organizations also implement physical security measures in combination with access controls (discussed next) that limit computer users to acceptable login times and locations. These controls may limit the number of unsuccessful login attempts, and require all employees to log off their computers when they leave for the day. In addition, they set the employees' computers to automatically log the user off after a certain period of disuse.

Access Controls

Access controls restrict unauthorized individuals from using information resources. Access controls can be physical controls or logical controls. Both types restrict unauthorized individuals from using information resources. **Logical controls** are implemented by software. For example, access control programs limit users to acceptable login times and acceptable login locations. These controls can limit the number of unsuccessful login attempts and they require everyone to log off their computers when they leave for the day. In addition, computers are set to automatically log the user off after a certain period of disuse.

Access controls involve two major functions: authentication and authorization. **Authentication** confirms the identity of the person requiring access. After the person is authenticated (identified), the next step is authorization. **Authorization** determines which actions, rights, or privileges the person has, based on his or her verified identity. Good control systems limit authorization to only those tasks needed to accomplish a person's job.

Authentication.

To authenticate (identify) authorized personnel, an organization can use one or more of the following types of methods: something the user is, something the user has, something the user does, and/or something the user knows.

Something the user is, also known as **biometrics**, is an authentication method that examines a person's innate physical characteristics. Common biometric applications are fingerprint scans, palm scans, retina scans, iris recognition, and facial recognition. Of these applications, fingerprints, retina scans, and iris recognition provide the most definitive identification.

Something the user has is an authentication mechanism that includes regular identification (ID) cards, smart ID cards, and tokens. *Regular ID cards*, or *dumb cards*, typically have the person's picture and often his or her signature. *Smart ID cards* have an embedded chip that stores pertinent information about the user. (Smart ID cards used for identification differ from smart cards used in electronic commerce, which you learned about in Chapter 5. Both types of card have embedded chips, but they are used for different purposes.) *Tokens* have embedded chips and a digital display that presents a login number that the employees use to access the organization's network. The number changes with each login.

Something the user does is an authentication mechanism that includes voice and signature recognition. In *voice recognition*, the user speaks a phrase (e.g., his or her name and department) that has been previously recorded under controlled conditions. The voice recognition system matches the two voice signals. In *signature recognition*, the user signs his or her name and the system matches this signature with one previously recorded under controlled, monitored conditions. Signature recognition systems also match the speed and the pressure of the signature.

Something the user knows is an authentication mechanism that includes passwords and passphrases. **Passwords** present a huge information security problem in all organizations. All users should use *strong passwords*, which are difficult for hackers to discover. The basic guidelines for creating strong passwords are:

- They should be difficult to guess.
- They should be long rather than short.
- They should have uppercase letters, lowercase letters, numbers, and special characters.

- They should not be recognizable words.
- They should not be the name of anything or anyone familiar, such as family names or names of pets.
- They should not be a recognizable string of numbers, such as a Social Insurance Number or a birthday.

Unfortunately, strong passwords are more difficult to remember than weak ones. Consequently, employees frequently write them down, which defeats their purpose. The ideal solution to this dilemma is to create a strong password that is also easy to remember. To achieve this objective, many people use passphrases.

A *passphrase* is a series of characters that is longer than a password but is still easy to memorize. Examples of passphrases are "maytheforcebewithyoualways," "goaheadmakemyday," and "livelongandprosper." A passphrase can serve as a password itself, or it can help you create a strong password. You can turn a passphrase into a strong password in this manner. Using the middle passphrase above, take the first letter of each word. You will have "gammd". Then capitalize every other letter to create "GaMmD". Finally, add special characters and numbers to create "9GaMmD//*". You now have a strong password that you can remember.

To identify authorized users more efficiently and effectively, organizations frequently implement more than one type of authentication, a strategy known as *multifactor authentication*. This system is particularly important when users log in from remote locations.

Single-factor authentication, which is notoriously weak, commonly consists simply of a password. Two-factor authentication consists of a password plus one type of biometric identification (e.g., a fingerprint). Three-factor authentication is any combination of three authentication methods. In most cases, the more factors the system uses, the more reliable it is. However, stronger authentication is also more expensive and, as with strong passwords, it can be irritating to users.

Authorization. After users have been properly authenticated, the rights and privileges they have on the organization's systems are established in a process called *authorization*. A **privilege** (also known as user profile) is a collection of related computer system operations that a user is authorized to perform. Companies typically base authorization policies on the principle of **least privilege**, which posits that users be granted the privilege for an activity only if there is a justifiable need for them to perform that activity. As IT's About Business 13.4 illustrates, granting rights and privileges to users can be complicated.

Communications Controls

Communications controls (also called **network controls**) secure the movement of data across networks. Communications controls consist of firewalls, anti-malware systems, whitelisting and blacklisting, encryption, virtual private networks (VPNs), secure socket layer (SSL), and employee monitoring systems.

Firewalls. A **firewall** is a system that prevents a specific type of information from moving between untrusted networks, such as the Internet, and private networks, such as your company's network. Put simply, firewalls prevent unauthorized Internet users from accessing private networks. All messages entering or leaving your company's network pass through a firewall. The firewall examines each message and blocks those that do not meet specified security rules.

Firewalls range from simple, for home use, to very complex for organizational use. Figure 13.3a illustrates a basic firewall for a home computer. In this case, the firewall is implemented as software on the home computer. Figure 13.3b shows an organization that has implemented an external firewall, which faces the Internet, and an internal firewall, which faces the company network. Corporate firewalls typically consist of software running on a computer dedicated to the task. A **demilitarized zone (DMZ)** is located between the two firewalls. Messages

13.4 Information Security at City National Bank and Trust

City National Bank and Trust in the U.S. (*www.cnbok.com*) has 32 branches throughout Oklahoma, and it is continuing to expand the scope of its operations. Many of the bank's new branches are located in Walmart stores. In addition to its new branches, the bank implemented CityNET, its on-line banking service. CityNET is designed to make banking easy for its customers wherever they are. The bank also implemented services for improved customer convenience, including banking by phone and access to its statewide ATM system. During this expansion, the bank doubled the number of employees and quadrupled the size of its network.

The bank's rapid growth in branches and customer service offerings, coupled with the global increase in malicious software, has placed the bank's networks and its employees at much greater risk. The security risks also reflect the fact that growing numbers of employees need access to the web.

Before the bank expanded, it had adequate controls in place to prevent employees from installing software. In addition, the bank strictly controlled the number of users who had access to the web. It also conducted scans to identify which websites those employees were visiting and to determine whether malware inadvertently had been downloaded. However, the IT group could prevent and remove such malware intrusions with antivirus software only on desktops, not at the gateway to the bank's network.

The IT group was also wasting too much time repeatedly making minor changes in the bank's security policies. These changes included accepting a sender as friendly and blocking or adding a specific website. In short, the bank needed to replace its existing piecemeal system with an enterprise security solution. The bank selected M86 Security (now owned by Trustwave) (*www.trustwave.com*) for its strong content-filtering capabilities and its capability to dynamically set and modify security policies. Within weeks, the security system was protecting the bank from e-mail-based and web-based malware and offensive content.

The bank quickly applied policy-based standards throughout its network. For example, it configured the system to block e-mail messages with attached batch, executable, and .zip files. Another policy prevented employees from downloading potentially dangerous files and accessing offensive websites. With this level of control, the IT group can apply basic security policies to all employees and feel secure that employees cannot accidentally download malware.

The M86 Security system also helps the bank comply with U.S. Sarbanes-Oxley legislation, requiring adequate controls over data. For example, the IT group can sample information to make certain that customers' confidential information, such as credit card numbers, is not leaving the company unencrypted.

The bank occasionally receives malware threats that it does not recognize. In these cases, it scans the threat and sends it to the M86 Security content system. This system subjects the threat to the bank's security policies. Threats that do not clear all of the bank's policies are automatically quarantined.

The bank's e-mail policies also are stringent. The bank grants access to external e-mail only when there is a business justification, an example of the principle of least privilege. This policy leaves 60 percent of the bank's employees with only internal e-mail access.

The M86 Security system also provides excellent dynamic website categorization. If an employee accesses a website that has not already been classified as pornographic, the security system scans all the content on the website and looks for characteristics that would indicate that the site is pornographic. If the site has those characteristics, access to it is blocked immediately and the site is blacklisted, meaning it cannot be accessed via the company's system.

Questions

1. Why is it so important for organizations to establish enterprise-wide security policies?
2. Are the bank's e-mail policies too stringent? Why or why not? Support your answer.

Sources: Compiled from T. Austin, "How Banks Are Fighting Fraud," *Bank Info Security*, February 1, 2011; M. Meason, "Bank Protects More Than Money," *Baseline Magazine*, May 19, 2009; "Information Security Policies Are Your First Line of Defense," *BankersOnline.com*, April 20, 2009; T. Claburn, "Most Bank Sites Are Insecure," *InformationWeek*, July 23, 2008; *www.cnbok.com*, accessed February 6, 2011; *www.trustwave.com/*, accessed May 5, 2013.

from the Internet must first pass through the external firewall. If they conform to the defined security rules, they are then sent to company servers located in the DMZ. These servers typically handle web page requests and e-mail. Any messages designated for the company's internal network (for example, its intranet) must pass through the internal firewall, again with its own defined security rules, to gain access to the company's private network.

The danger from viruses and worms is so severe that many organizations are placing firewalls at strategic points *inside* their private networks. In this way, if a virus or worm does get through both the external and internal firewalls, then the internal damage may be contained.

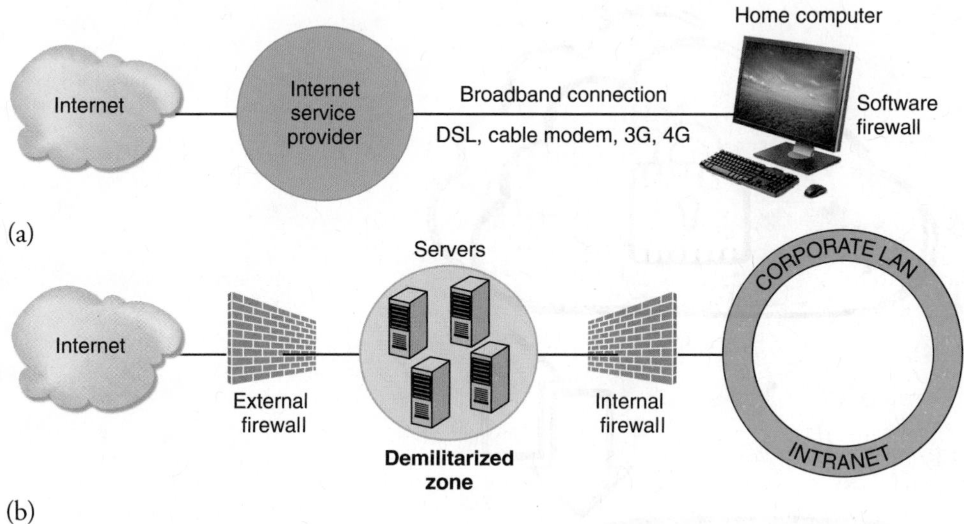

FIGURE 13.3 (a) Basic firewall for home computer.
(b) Organization with two firewalls and demilitarized zone. (*Source:* Dmitry Rukhlenko-Fotolia.com)

Anti-malware Systems.

Anti-malware systems, also called *antivirus*, or *AV*, software, are software packages that attempt to identify and eliminate viruses and worms (known as **malware**) and other malicious software. This software is implemented at the organizational level by the information systems department. There are currently hundreds of AV software packages available. Among the best known are Norton AntiVirus (*www.symantec.com/en/ca/*), McAfee VirusScan (*www.mcafee.com/ca/*), and Trend Micro PC-cillin (*www.trendmicro.ca*).

Anti-malware systems are generally reactive. Whereas firewalls filter network traffic according to categories of activities likely to cause problems, anti-malware systems filter traffic according to a database of specific problems. These systems create definitions, or signatures, of various types of malware and then update these signatures in their products. The anti-malware software then examines suspicious computer code to see if it matches a known signature. If a match is found, the software will remove the code. For this reason organizations update their malware definitions often, using on-line updates.

Because malware is such a serious problem, the leading vendors are rapidly developing anti-malware systems that function proactively as well as reactively. These systems evaluate behaviour rather than relying entirely on signature matching. In theory, therefore, it is possible to catch malware before it can infect systems.

Whitelisting and Blacklisting.

A report by the Yankee Group (*www.yankeegroup.com*), a technology research and consulting firm, stated that 99 percent of organizations had anti-malware systems installed, but 62 percent still suffered malware attacks. As we have seen, anti-malware systems are usually reactive, and malware continues to infect companies.

One solution to this problem is **whitelisting**. Whitelisting is a process in which a company identifies the software that it will allow to run on its computers. Whitelisting permits acceptable software to run and either prevents any other software from running or lets new software run in a quarantined environment until the company can verify its validity.

Whereas whitelisting allows nothing to run unless it is on the whitelist, **blacklisting** allows everything to run unless it is on the blacklist. A blacklist, then, states which types of software are not allowed to run in the company environment. For example, a company might blacklist peer-to-peer file sharing on its systems. In addition to software, people, devices, and websites can also be whitelisted and blacklisted.

FIGURE 13.4 The power of encryption. (*Source:* ©vasilki/gettyimages)

Encryption. Organizations that do not have a secure channel for sending information use encryption to stop unauthorized eavesdroppers. **Encryption** is the process of converting an original message into a form that cannot be read by anyone except the intended receiver. This "locks" the information from view (see Figure 13.4).

All encryption systems use a key, which is the code that scrambles and then decodes the messages. The majority of encryption systems use public-key encryption. **Public-key encryption**—also known as *asymmetric encryption*—uses two different keys: a public key and a private key. Both keys are created simultaneously using the same mathematical formula or algorithm. Because the two keys are mathematically related, the data encrypted with one key can be decrypted by using the other key. The public key is publicly available in a directory that all parties can access. The private key is kept secret, never shared with anyone, and never sent across the Internet. In this system, if Weiling, for example, wants to send a message to Karim, she first obtains Karim's public key, which she uses to encrypt (scramble) her message. When Karim receives Weiling's message, he uses his private key to decrypt (unscramble) it.

Public key systems also show that a message is authentic. That is, if you encrypt a message using your private key, you have electronically "signed" it. A recipient can verify that the message came from you by using your public key to decrypt it.

Although this arrangement is adequate for personal information, organizations doing business over the Internet require a more complex system. In such cases, a third party, called a **certificate authority**, acts as a trusted intermediary between companies. The certificate authority issues digital certificates and verifies the integrity of the certificates. A **digital certificate** is an electronic document attached to a file that certifies that the file is from the organization it claims

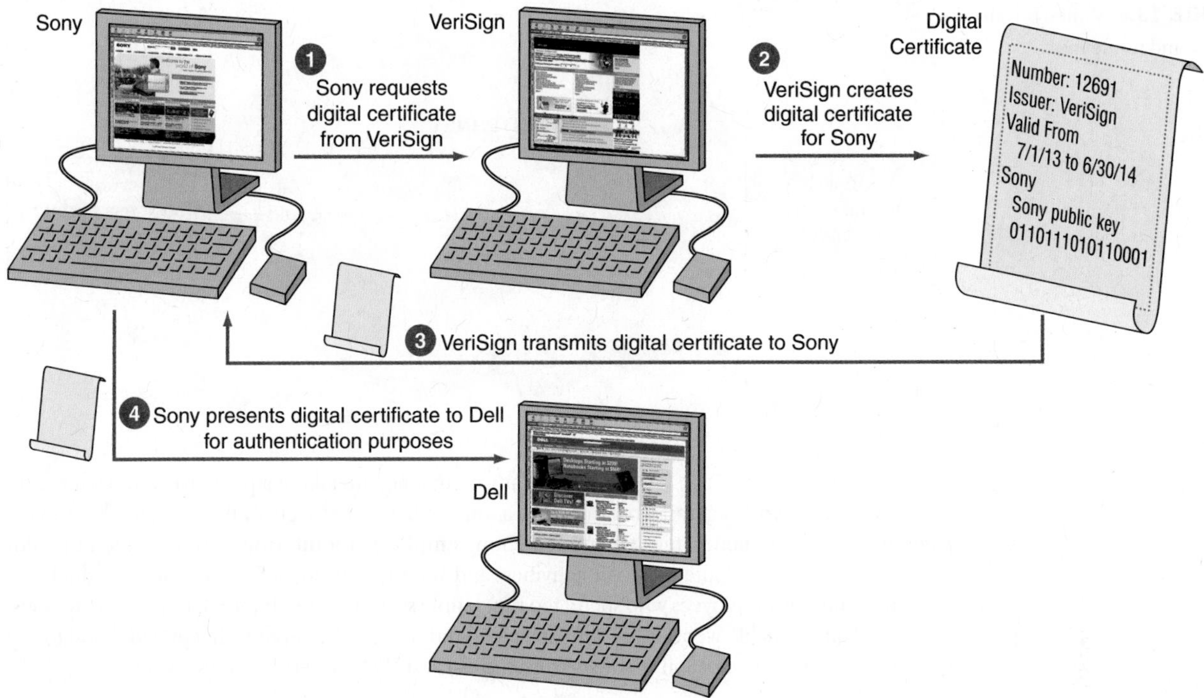

FIGURE 13.5 How digital certificates work. Sony and Dell, business partners, use a digital certificate from VeriSign for authentication.

to be from and has not been modified from its original format. As you can see in Figure 13.5, Sony requests a digital certificate from VeriSign, a certificate authority, and uses this certificate when it conducts business with Dell. Note that the digital certificate contains an identification number, the issuer, validity dates, and the requester's public key. For examples of certificate authorities, see *www.entrust.com*, *www.verisign.com*, *www.secude.com*, and *www.thawte.com*.

Virtual Private Networking. A **virtual private network (VPN)** is a private network that uses a public network (usually the Internet) to connect users. VPNs essentially integrate the global connectivity of the Internet with the security of a private network and thereby extend the reach of the organization's networks. VPNs are called *virtual* because they have no separate physical existence. They use the public Internet as their infrastructure. They are created by using logins, encryption, and other techniques to enhance the user's **privacy**—the right to be left alone and to be free of unreasonable personal intrusion.

VPNs have several advantages. First, they allow remote users to access the company network. Second, they provide flexibility. That is, mobile users can access the organization's network from properly configured remote devices. Third, organizations can impose their security policies through VPNs. For example, an organization may dictate that only corporate e-mail applications are available to users when they connect from unmanaged devices.

To provide secure transmissions, VPNs use a process called tunnelling. **Tunnelling** encrypts each data packet to be sent and places each encrypted packet inside another packet. In this manner, the packet can travel across the Internet with confidentiality, authentication, and integrity. Figure 13.6 illustrates a VPN and tunnelling.

Secure Socket Layer (SSL). **Secure socket layer,** now called **transport layer security (TLS),** is an encryption standard used for secure transactions such as credit card purchases and on-line banking. TLS encrypts and decrypts data between a web server and a browser end to end.

TLS is indicated by a URL that begins with "https" rather than "http," and it often displays a small padlock icon in the browser's status bar. Using a padlock icon to indicate a secure connection and placing this icon in a browser's status bar are artifacts of specific browsers. Other browsers use different icons (e.g., a key that is either broken or whole). The important thing to remember is that browsers usually provide visual confirmation of a secure connection.

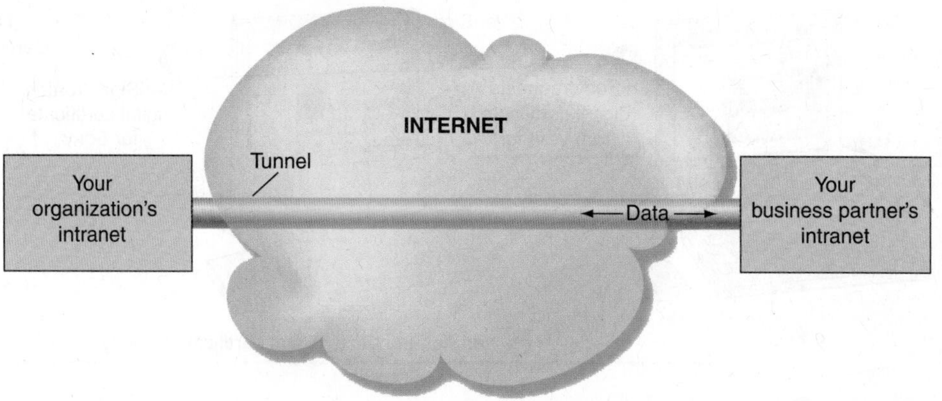

FIGURE 13.6 Virtual private network and tunneling.

Employee Monitoring Systems. Many companies are taking a proactive approach to protecting their networks against what they view as one of their major security threats, namely, employee mistakes. These companies are implementing **employee monitoring systems,** which monitor their employees' computers, e-mail activities, and Internet surfing activities. These products are useful to identify employees who spend too much time surfing on the Internet for personal reasons, who visit questionable websites, or who download music illegally. Vendors that provide monitoring software include SpectorSoft (*www.spectorsoft.com*) and Websense (*www.websense.com*).

Application Controls. **Application controls**, as their name suggests, are security countermeasures that protect specific applications. Application controls fall into three major categories: input controls, processing controls, and output controls.

Input controls are programmed routines that edit input data for errors before they are processed. For example, social insurance numbers should not contain any alphabetical characters.

Processing controls are programmed routines that perform actions that are part of the record-keeping of the organization, reconcile and check transactions, or monitor the operation of applications. Processing controls, for example, might match entered quantities of goods received in the shipping area to amounts ordered on authorized purchase orders. Processing controls also balance the total number of transactions processed with the total number of transactions input or output.

Finally, output controls are programmed routines that edit output data for errors, or help to ensure that output is provided only to authorized individuals. An example of output controls is documentation specifying that authorized recipients have received their reports, paycheques, or other critical documents.

Business Continuity Planning, Backup, and Recovery

An important strategy for organizations is to be prepared for any eventuality. A critical element in any security system is a business continuity plan, also known as a disaster recovery plan.

Business continuity is the chain of events linking planning to protection and recovery. The purpose of the business continuity plan is to keep the business operating after a disaster occurs. The plan prepares for, reacts to, and recovers from events that affect the security of information assets, and the subsequent restoration to normal business operations. The plan ensures that critical business functions continue.

In the event of a major disaster, organizations can employ several strategies for business continuity. These strategies include hot sites, warm sites, cold sites, and off-site data storage. A **hot site** is a fully configured computer facility, with all services, communications links, and physical plant operations. A hot site duplicates computing resources, peripherals, telephone systems, applications, and work stations. A **warm site** provides many of the same services and options as the hot site. However, a warm site typically does not include the actual applications the company needs. A warm site does include computing equipment such as servers, but it often does not include user work stations. A **cold site** provides only rudimentary services and facilities, such as a building or room with heating, air conditioning, and humidity control. This type of site provides no computer hardware or user work stations. Hot sites reduce risk to the greatest extent, but they are the most expensive option. Conversely, cold sites reduce risk the least, but they are the least expensive option. In addition to hot, warm, and cold sites, organizations also use off-site data storage services. Off-site data storage is a service that allows companies to store valuable data in a secure location geographically distant from the company's data centre.

Information Systems Auditing

Companies implement security controls to ensure that information systems work properly. These controls can be installed in the original system, or they can be added after a system is in operation. Installing controls is necessary but not sufficient to provide adequate security. In addition, people responsible for security need to answer questions such as:

- Are all controls installed as intended?
- Are the controls effective?
- Has any breach of security occurred?
- If so, what actions are required to prevent future breaches?

These questions must be answered by independent and unbiased observers. Such observers perform the task of *information systems auditing*. An audit involves the accumulation and evaluation of evidence that is used to prepare a report about the information or controls that are being examined, using established criteria and standards. In an IS environment, an **audit** is an examination of information systems, their inputs, outputs, and processing.

Types of Auditors and Audits. There are several types of auditors. External auditors, also referred to as independent auditors, work at a public accounting firm, auditing primarily financial statements. Government auditors work for the provincial or federal auditors general offices. Canada Revenue Agency auditors audit compliance with tax legislation. Internal auditors work for specific organizations, and may have the Certified Internal Auditor (CIA) designation. Specialist auditors can be from a variety of fields. Information systems auditors, for example, may work for any of the above organizations, and may have a Certified Information Systems Auditor (CISA) designation.

IS auditing is usually conducted as part of the controls evaluation for the financial statement audit or as part of *internal auditing*, which looks at the efficiency or effectiveness of systems.

IS auditing is a broad topic, so we present only its essentials here. Auditing focuses on topics such as operations, data integrity, software applications, security and privacy, budgets and expenditures, cost control, and productivity. Guidelines are available to assist auditors in their jobs, such as those from the Institute of Internal Auditors (*www.theiia.org*) or the Information Systems Audit and Control Association (*www.isaca.org*).

How Does the Auditor Decide on Audits? IS auditors conduct their work using a risk-based approach. They consider the likelihood of errors or fraud, or the risk of organizations not following their procedures. Then they design procedures to test compliance or the percentages of errors. Information systems audits could be part of the evaluation of controls for a financial statement audit, which are required by law for organizations that sell shares to the public, or for publicly accountable organizations such as registered charities.

Internal auditors conduct their audits based on a plan approved by management. This plan may look at areas where there are high risks of theft, such as an electronic commerce system, or at new systems development projects where there is an elevated potential for error, such as a new point-of-sale system. Where legislation is relatively new, such as privacy legislation, auditors could conduct a privacy audit to evaluate whether the organization is in compliance with the legislation.

Auditors could use computers in the actual conduct of their audit, by using software to create reports or by creating test data that are run through systems to evaluate their functioning.

before you go on...

1. Differentiate between authentication and authorization. Which of these processes is always performed first?
2. Compare and contrast whitelisting and blacklisting.
3. Describe the major types of controls for information systems.
4. What is information systems auditing?
5. What is the purpose of a disaster recovery plan?

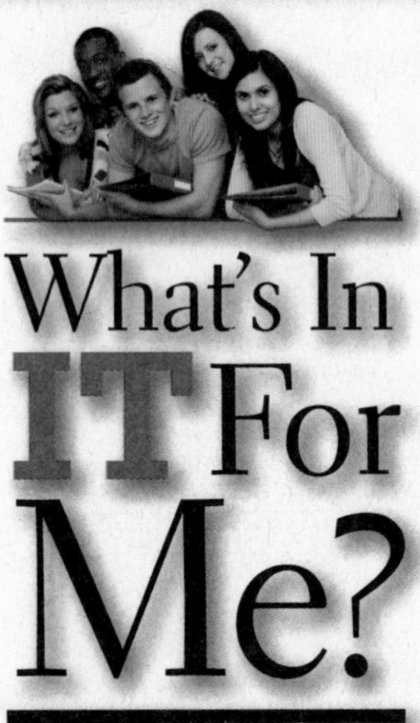

What's In IT For Me?

For the Accounting Major

Public companies, their accountants, and their auditors have significant information security responsibilities. Accountants are now being held professionally responsible for reducing risk, assuring compliance, reducing the risk of fraud, and increasing the transparency of transactions according to generally accepted accounting principles (GAAP). Regulatory agencies require information security, fraud prevention and detection, and internal controls over financial reporting and over the privacy of information. Forensic accounting, a combination of accounting and information security, is one of the most rapidly growing areas in accounting today.

For the Finance Major

Because information security is essential to the success of organizations today, it is no longer just the concern of the CIO. As a result of global regulatory requirements, responsibility for information security lies with the CEO and CFO. Consequently, all aspects of the security audit, including the security of information and information systems, are a key concern for financial managers.

In addition, CFOs and treasurers are increasingly involved with investments in information technology. They know that a security breach of any kind can have devastating financial effects on a company. Banking and financial institutions are prime targets for computer criminals. A related problem is fraud involving stocks and bonds that are sold over the Internet. Finance personnel must be aware of both the hazards and the available controls associated with these activities.

For the Marketing Major

Marketing professionals have new opportunities to collect data on their customers, such as through business-to-consumer electronic commerce. Customers expect their data to be properly secured. However, profit-motivated criminals want those data. Therefore, marketing managers must analyze the risk of their operations. Failure to protect corporate and customer data will cause significant public relations problems, make customers angry, maybe lead to lawsuits, and maybe result in losing customers to competitors. CRM operations and the tracking of customers' on-line buying habits can expose data to misuse (if they are not encrypted) or result in privacy violations.

For the Production/Operations Management Major

Every process in a company's operations—inventory purchasing, receiving, quality control, production, and shipping—can be disrupted by an IT security breach. Any weak link in supply chain management or enterprise resource management systems puts the entire chain at risk. Companies may be held liable for IT security failures that impact other companies.

For the Human Resources Management Major

HR managers have responsibilities to secure confidential employee data. In addition, they must ensure that all employees explicitly verify that they understand the company's information security policies and procedures.

For the MIS Major

The MIS function provides the security infrastructure that protects the organization's information assets. This function is critical to the success of the organization, even though it is almost invisible until an attack succeeds. All application development, network deployment, and introduction of new information technologies have to be guided by IT security considerations. MIS personnel must customize the risk exposure security model to help the company identify security risks and prepare responses to security incidents and disasters.

Senior executives of publicly held companies look to the MIS function for help in detecting significant deficiencies or material weaknesses in internal controls and remediating them. Other functional areas also look to the MIS function to help them meet their security responsibilities.

[Summary]

1. Identify the five factors that contribute to the increasing vulnerability of information resources, and provide a specific example of each one.

The five factors are:

- Today's interconnected, interdependent, wirelessly networked business environment
  Example: The Internet
- Smaller, faster, cheaper computers and storage devices
  Examples: Netbooks, thumb drives, iPads
- Decreasing skills necessary to be a computer hacker
  Example: Information system hacking programs circulating on the Internet
- International organized crime taking over cyber-crime
  Example: Organized crime has formed transnational cyber-crime cartels. Because it is difficult to know exactly where cyber attacks originate, these cartels are extremely hard to bring to justice.
- Lack of management support
  Example: Suppose that your company spent $10 million on information security countermeasures last year and experienced no successful attacks on information resources. Short-sighted management might conclude that the company could spend less during the next year and obtain the same results. Bad idea.

2. Compare and contrast human mistakes and social engineering, and provide a specific example of each one.

Human mistakes are unintentional errors. However, employees can also make unintentional mistakes as a result of actions by an attacker, such as social engineering. *Social engineering* is an attack where the perpetrator uses social skills to trick or manipulate a legitimate employee into providing confidential company information.

An example of a human mistake is tailgating. An example of social engineering is when an attacker calls an employee on the phone and impersonates someone in the company.

3. Discuss the 10 types of deliberate attacks.

The 10 types of deliberate attacks are:

Espionage or trespass occurs when an unauthorized individual attempts to gain illegal access to organizational information.

Information extortion occurs when an attacker either threatens to steal or actually steals information from a company. The perpetrator demands payment for not stealing the information, for returning stolen information, or for agreeing not to disclose the information.

Sabotage and vandalism are deliberate acts that involve defacing an organization's website, possibly causing the organization to lose its image and experience a loss of confidence by its customers.

Theft of equipment and information is becoming a larger problem because computing devices and storage devices are becoming smaller yet more powerful with vastly increased storage, making these devices easier and more valuable to steal.

Identity theft is the deliberate assumption of another person's identity, usually to gain access to his or her financial information or to frame him or her for a crime.

Protecting intellectual property is a vital issue for people who make their livelihood in knowledge fields. Protecting intellectual property is particularly difficult when that property is in digital form.

Software attacks occur when malicious software penetrates an organization's computer system. Today, these attacks are typically profit-driven and web-based.

Alien software is clandestine software that is installed on your computer through duplicitous methods. It typically is not as malicious as viruses, worms, or Trojan horses, but it does use up valuable system resources.

Supervisory control and data acquisition (SCADA) is a large-scale, distributed measurement and control system. SCADA systems are used to monitor or control chemical, physical, and transport processes. A *SCADA attack* attempts to compromise such a system in order to cause damage to the real-world processes that the system controls.

With both *cyberterrorism* and *cyberwarfare*, attackers use a target's computer systems, particularly via the Internet, to cause physical, real-world harm or severe disruption, usually to carry out a political agenda.

4. Define the three risk mitigation strategies, and provide an example of each one in the context of owning a home.

The three risk mitigation strategies are:

Risk acceptance, where the organization accepts the potential risk, continues operating with no controls, and absorbs any damages that occur. If you own a home, you may decide not to insure it. Thus, you are practising risk acceptance. Clearly, this is a bad idea.

Risk limitation, where the organization limits the risk by implementing controls that minimize the impact of threats. As a homeowner, you practise risk limitation by putting in an alarm system or cutting down weak trees near your house.

Risk transference, where the organization transfers the risk by using other means to compensate for the loss, such as by purchasing insurance. The vast majority of homeowners practise risk transference by purchasing insurance on their houses and other possessions.

5. Identify the types of controls that organizations can use to protect their information resources, and provide an example of each one.

Information systems are protected with a wide variety of controls such as security procedures, physical guards, and detection software. Management is responsible for the control environment, the attitudes, and the policies used as a framework to establish controls. General controls include controls for the prevention, deterrence, detection, damage control, recovery, and correction of information systems. The major types of general controls include physical controls (such as security guards or locks), logical controls (such as passwords or automated calculations), access controls (such as multifactor authentication), and communications controls (such as firewalls). Application controls include input, processing, and output controls.

Preparation for disaster recovery specifically addresses how to avoid, plan for, and quickly recover from a disaster. Information systems auditing is a specialization that helps financial, internal, government, or tax auditors evaluate or assess controls or compliance with procedures or legislation. A detailed internal and external IT audit may involve hundreds of issues and can be supported by both software and checklists.

[Chapter Glossary]

access controls Controls that restrict unauthorized individuals from using information resources and are concerned with user identification.

adware Alien software designed to help pop-up advertisements appear on your screen.

alien software Clandestine software that is installed on your computer through duplicitous methods.

anti-malware systems (antivirus software) Software packages that attempt to identify and eliminate viruses, worms, and other malicious software.

application controls Controls that apply to input, processing or output for a particular functional information system.

audit In an IS environment, an examination of information systems, their inputs, outputs, and processing.

authentication A process that determines the identity of the person requiring access.

authorization A process that determines which actions, rights, or privileges the person has, based on verified identity.

back door (trap door) A password, known only to the attacker, that allows the attacker to access the system without having to go through any security procedures.

biometrics The science and technology of authentication (i.e., establishing the identity of an individual) by measuring the subject's physiologic or behavioural characteristics.

blacklisting A process in which a company identifies certain types of software that are not allowed to run in the company environment.

certificate authority A third party that acts as a trusted intermediary between computers (and companies) by issuing digital certificates and verifying the worth and integrity of the certificates.

cold site A backup location that provides only rudimentary services and facilities.

communications controls (network controls) Controls that deal with the movement of data across networks.

control environment Controls that affect mutliple functional information systems or the entire organization and include management attitudes towards controls.

controls Defence mechanisms (also called *countermeasures*): actions used to safeguard assets, optimize the use of the organization's resources, and prevent or detect errors or fraud.

cookie Small amounts of information that websites store on your computer, temporarily or more or less permanently.

copyright A grant that provides the creator of intellectual property with ownership of it for a specified period of time, currently the life of the creator plus 50 years.

cyber-crime Illegal activities executed on the Internet.

cyberterrorism A premeditated, politically motivated attack against information, computer systems, computer programs, and data that results in physical attacks against noncombatant targets by subnational groups or clandestine agents.

cyberwarfare War in which a country's information systems could be paralyzed from a massive attack by destructive software.

demilitarized zone (DMZ) A separate organizational local area network that is located between an organization's internal network and an external network, usually the Internet.

denial-of-service attack A cyber attack in which an attacker sends a flood of data packets to the target computer, with the aim of overloading its resources.

digital certificate An electronic document attached to a file certifying that this file is from the organization it claims to be from and has not been modified from its original format or content.

distributed denial-of-service (DDoS) attack A denial-of-service attack that sends a flood of data packets from many compromised computers simultaneously.

employee monitoring systems Systems that monitor employees' computers, e-mail activities, and Internet surfing activities.

encryption The process of converting an original message into a form that cannot be read by anyone except the intended receiver.

firewall A system (either hardware, software, or a combination of both) that prevents a specific type of information from moving between untrusted networks, such as the Internet, and private networks, such as your company's network.

general controls Automated controls that affect multiple information systems, such as access controls.

hot sites A fully configured computer facility, with all information resources and services, communications links, and physical plant operations, that duplicates your company's computing resources and provides near real-time recovery of IT operations.

identity theft Crime in which someone uses the personal information of others to create a false identity and then uses it for some fraud.

information security Protecting an organization's information and information systems from unauthorized access, use, disclosure, disruption, modification, or destruction.

intellectual property The intangible property created by individuals or corporations, which is protected under trade secret, patent, and copyright laws.

least privilege A principle that users be granted the privilege for some activity only if there is a justifiable need to grant this authorization.

logic bombs Segments of computer code embedded within an organization's existing computer programs.

logical controls Those that are implemented by software.

malware Malicious software such as viruses and worms.

network controls (see **communications controls**)

password A private combination of characters that only the user should know.

patent A document that grants the holder exclusive rights on an invention or process for a specified period of time, currently 20 years.

phishing attack An attack that uses deception to fraudulently acquire sensitive personal information by masquerading as an official-looking e-mail.

physical controls Controls that restrict unauthorized individuals from gaining access to a company's computer facilities.

piracy Copying a software program (other than freeware, demo software, etc.) without making payment to the owner.

privacy The right to be left alone and to be free of unreasonable personal intrusion.

privilege A collection of related computer system operations that can be performed by users of the system.

public-key encryption (also called *asymmetric encryption*) A type of encryption that uses two different keys, a public key and a private key.

risk The likelihood that a threat will occur.

risk acceptance A strategy in which the organization accepts the potential risk, continues to operate with no controls, and absorbs any damages that occur.

risk analysis The process by which an organization assesses the value of each asset being protected, estimates the probability that each asset might be compromised, and compares the probable costs of each being compromised with the costs of protecting it.

risk limitation A strategy in which the organization limits its risk by implementing controls that minimize the impact of a threat.

risk management A process that identifies, controls, and minimizes the impact of threats, in an effort to reduce risk to manageable levels.

risk mitigation A process whereby the organization takes concrete actions against risks, such as implementing controls and developing a disaster recovery plan.

risk transference A process in which the organization transfers the risk by using other means to compensate for a loss, such as by purchasing insurance.

secure socket layer (SSL) (transport layer security) An encryption standard used for secure transactions such as credit card purchases and on-line banking.

social engineering Getting around security systems by tricking computer users inside a company into revealing sensitive information or gaining unauthorized access privileges.

spam Unsolicited e-mail.

spamware Alien software that uses your computer as a launch platform for spammers.

spear phishing attack Phishing attacks that use specific personal information.

spyware Alien software that can record your keystrokes and/or capture your passwords.

threat Any danger to which an information resource may be exposed.

trade secret Intellectual work, such as a business plan, that is a company secret and is not based on public information.

transport layer security (TLS) (see **secure socket layer**)

trap door (see **back door**)

Trojan horse A software program containing a hidden function that presents a security risk.

tunnelling A process that encrypts each data packet to be sent and places each encrypted packet inside another packet.

virtual private network (VPN) A private network that uses a public network (usually the Internet) to securely connect users by using encryption.

viruses Malicious software that can attach itself to (or "infect") other computer programs without the owner of the program being aware of the infection.

vulnerability The possibility that an information resource will be harmed by a threat.

warm site A site that provides many of the same services and options of the hot site, but does not include the company's applications.

whitelisting A process in which a company identifies acceptable software and permits it to run, and either prevents anything else from running or lets new software run in a quarantined environment until the company can verify its validity.

worms Destructive programs that replicate themselves without requiring another program to provide a safe environment for replication.

[Discussion Questions]

1. Why are computer systems so vulnerable?
2. Why should information security be a prime concern to management?
3. Is security a technical issue? A business issue? Both? Support your answer.
4. Compare information security in an organization with insuring a house.
5. Why are authentication and authorization important to e-commerce?
6. Why is cross-border cyber-crime expanding rapidly? Discuss possible solutions.
7. Discuss why legislation is having an impact on information security.
8. What types of user authentication are used at your university and/or place of work? Do these measures seem to be effective? What if a higher level of authentication were implemented? Would it be worth it, or would it decrease productivity?
9. Why are federal authorities so worried about SCADA attacks?

[Problem-Solving Activities]

1. A critical problem is assessing how far a company is legally obligated to go in order to secure personal data. Because there is no such thing as perfect security (i.e., there is always more that you can do), resolving this question can significantly affect cost.
   a. When are security measures that a company implements sufficient to comply with its obligations?
   b. Is there any way for a company to know if its security measures are sufficient? Can you devise a method for any organization to determine if its security measures are sufficient?
2. Enter *www.scambusters.org*. Find out what the organization does. Learn about e-mail scams and website scams. Report your findings.
3. Visit *www.international.gc.ca/crime/cyber_crime-criminalite.aspx* (Foreign Affairs and International Trade Canada's page on cyber-crime). Read the section on "Domestic Initiatives" and write a report on accomplishments to date using the links found in this section.
4. Enter *www.alltrustnetworks.com* and other vendors of biometrics. Find the devices they make that can be used to control access into information systems. Prepare a list of products and major capabilities of each vendor.
5. Software piracy is a global problem. Access the following websites: *http://ww2.bsa.org* and *www.microsoft.com/en-us/piracy/*. What can organizations do to mitigate this problem? Are some organizations dealing with the problem better than others?
6. Investigate the Sony PlayStation Network hack that occurred in April 2011.
   - What type of attack was it?
   - Was the success of the attack due to technology problems at Sony, management problems at Sony, or a combination of both? Provide specific examples to support your answer.
   - Which Sony controls failed?
   - Could the hack have been prevented? If so, how?
   - Discuss Sony's response to the hack.
   - Describe the damages that Sony incurred from the hack.

[Spreadsheet Activity: Risk Analysis with a Spreadsheet]

Objective: This activity will bring together the ideas of security and formula writing in a spreadsheet. Upon completion, you will be able to take data presented in written form, translate them into numbers, create formulas, and then rank security issues based on the spreadsheet you create.

Chapter Connection: Security issues are not all created equal. Some are frequent and inexpensive to overcome; others are rare and costly. Intentional and unintentional threats must be dealt with. But as a network manager, how do you know what deserves the most resources? Given that you never know where the next threat will come from, how will you allocate resources? This activity will bring this discussion to a spreadsheet and help you apply your math and spreadsheet skills to this real-world situation.

Activity: Consider the following situation. You are the network manager at a local credit union. A number of security issues must be dealt with. However, like everyone else, you have limited resources. You only have $10,000 in your budget to allocate to security. This money can be spent on hardware, software, training, or anything else you deem worthy of this money. Here is a list of potential threats.

- *Malware:* If malware ends up installed on a computer in the system, it could easily spread to the other machines without anyone knowing it is there. The expense of repairing the machines and restoring data are minimal when compared with the cost of rebuilding trust in the customer. Estimated total cost of marketing and repairing customer trust: $25,000. Probability of occurring: 35 percent. Cost of preventive maintenance and training: $3,500.
- *Careless employees:* Rowena has to run to the restroom. Because she trusts everyone she works with, she walks away from her computer without locking it. When she is away from her desk and her computer is unlocked, Michel walks in. No one thinks anything about Michel on Rowena's computer because he is the local "computer guru" even though he is a janitor. While Rowena is away and Michel is on her computer, he transfers a total of $7,500 from over 150 accounts by running a script in the computer system. When Rowena returns, she sees Michel on the computer and thanks him for watching it, laughing about how she accidentally left it unlocked. Probability of occurring: 5 percent. Cost of preventive maintenance and training: $2,000.
- *Cloud computing:* Financial institutions such as credit unions rely on many software packages to accomplish their goals. Not the least of these are the many packages run by the administrative office. These are accessed over the Internet, and private data are transferred back and forth. A hacker who is able to hack into the local system would by default have access to the cloud. The cost of this is monumental. Customer data from across the system would be compromised. Having a backup of all data is imperative. Keeping employees trained on

using the system, avoiding social engineering, changing passwords, and other issues are paramount to help protect the administrative office and the local office. Total potential loss: $2.5 million. Probability of occurrence: 2.5 percent. Cost of preventive maintenance and training: $7,000.

- *Fire:* This is always a threat. If a fire breaks out, it could be devastating. Loss of technology equipment alone would run close to $20,000. Loss of records (if not stored off-site) would be almost unrecoverable. However, the chance of fire is relatively low. At a 2 percent chance of fire, this is a minimal concern. The cost of preventive maintenance is not cheap. Sprinklers have to be inspected, fire retardant material must be tested, and fire extinguishers must be replaced. Total preventive maintenance cost is $1,500. However, the total potential loss is a devastating $250,000.

Most people agree that risk (R) is equal to the consequence (C) multiplied by the probability of occurrence (P): $R = C \times P$. Create a spreadsheet that calculates this formula. Then use your estimated risk to figure the return on security investment (ROSI) that most consider to be equal to risk avoided (R; hopefully it will be avoided by the investment) divided by the cost of preventive maintenance (PM). $ROSI = R \div PM$. This number represents the "impact" of an investment and can be used to help determine how to create a budget so that the return is maximized. The higher the number, the more of the risk is covered by the investment. Use this number to prioritize where to make security investments. Because your budget is only $10,000, you will need to determine where to spend your money. According to this scenario, total coverage would cost $14,000. Use the ROSI to recommend a budget. Also provide your spreadsheet for justification of the budget.

Deliverable: The final product will be a spreadsheet formula, ranking, and presentation of a suggested budget.

Discussion Questions

1. Discuss the advantages and disadvantages of building a formula once and copying it to multiple rows or columns.
2. Discuss the importance of taking verbal or written clues and being able to build a spreadsheet. Is a spreadsheet the ultimate combination of math and business?
3. Given that no one has unlimited resources, is it possible to ever cover all the bases and ensure security? What type of agreement must there be between the business and the consumer for this situation to exist and be acceptable?

[Case Assignment]

In 2006, a fire broke out in an office tower of Place Alexis Nihon, Montreal, across from the Forum, a community gathering centre. The building had stores and restaurants on the main level and a subway platform below. The fire department condemned the building and tenants were unable to retrieve anything from their offices for nearly two weeks. Fully 60 percent of the companies in this building did not survive more than six months, declaring bankruptcy or simply shutting down.

Required

a. You are the IT manager of a company in this building. Your company sells directly to consumers through salespeople. What control measures should you use to prepare for such a disaster? What steps should you have taken after the disaster to minimize its impact on your company?

b. Normally, employees use the computer for processing sales orders, customer billing and employee payroll, inventory monitoring, purchase orders, and payments to suppliers. What application programs would need to be recovered first? What application recoveries could wait until the situation was less critical? Justify your answers.

c. The fire was a blow to the company but also an opportunity to make improvements to prevent future disasters. Identify four other types of disasters and their impacts. Also describe controls that could be implemented to prevent or reduce the impact of each potential disaster.

[Team Assignments]

1. Access *www.ftc.gov/sentinel* and *www.publicsafety.gc.ca/prg/ns/cybr-scrty* to learn more about how law enforcement agencies around the world work together to fight consumer fraud and establish effective cyber security. Each team should obtain current statistics on one of the top five consumer complaint categories and prepare a report. Are any categories growing faster than others? Are any categories more prevalent in certain parts of the world?
2. Read the article "Why You Might Need to Rethink Your Internet Security—Now" at *www.entrepreneur.com/article/224007*. Each team should download a product that addresses security concerns and discuss its pros and cons for the class.

[Case 11.2 Who Is Minding the Security Store?]

The Problem

On April 21, 2010, computers in companies, hospitals, and schools around the world became trapped in a cycle of repeatedly rebooting themselves after an antivirus program from security vendor McAfee (*www.mcafee.com/ca/*) identified a normal Windows file as a virus. Computers running Windows XP Service Pack 3 in combination with McAfee VirusScan 8.7 were affected. The repercussions were widespread.

- In Rhode Island, about one in three hospitals had to postpone elective surgeries and stop treating emergency-room patients who were not experiencing traumas such as gunshot wounds.
- In Kentucky, state police officers had to shut down the computers in their patrol cars while technicians worked on the problem.
- In Winnipeg, a senior security administrator with the Wawanesa Mutual Insurance Company posted on the McAfee support forum that the virus was causing "ridiculous" problems with that company's computers.

McAfee's policy is to update its corporate customers on a daily basis. The April 21, 2010, update was intended to detect and destroy a minor threat, the "W32/wecorl.a" virus. However, the update incorrectly identified the critical "svchost.exe" file in Windows XP Service Pack 3 as malicious software and then quarantined it. In some cases, the update actually deleted the file. Without "svchost.exe", a Windows personal computer will not boot (start up) correctly.

When users applied the McAfee update and then rebooted their computers, the computers crashed and rebooted repeatedly. Most of these computers lost all network capability as well. Adding to these problems, some computers became unable to recognize their own USB drives. This problem turned out to be a major one, because recovery required users to reinstall svchost.exe, a process that could be done more easily by walking a flash drive from one crippled computer to the next.

The Solution

Because virtually all the affected personal computers were unable to connect to a network, corporate IT personnel had to manually fix each machine. Of course, this process became much more difficult if the affected computers could not recognize their own USB drives.

Later that day, McAfee placed a document on its website that specified the necessary recovery steps. The following day the company made available a semiautomated tool that had to be run on affected computers after entering Windows' Safe Mode.

The Results

McAfee took two days (until April 23, 2010) to post a list of frequently asked questions (FAQ) concerning the update disaster on its website. Late on April 23, McAfee's home page contained a link to a blog post by McAfee's Barry McPherson that attempted to minimize the issue. (Interestingly, McPherson was McAfee's executive vice president of support and customer service, not its CEO.) McPherson pledged that McAfee would improve its quality assurance processes to see that this problem did not reoccur.

Most large McAfee customers had their computers up and running in two days or less. However, a number of small businesses that did not have IT departments were still trying to fix their computers several days later.

Perhaps modern organizations are somewhat to blame for this problem. Today, organizations are pushing for more rapid updates to their antivirus software to minimize their exposure time to new malware threats. Antivirus vendors have responded to these pressures by speeding up the delivery of their software updates in an attempt to match the pace of new malware development by hackers. These rapid updates can cause security vendors to make mistakes in their quality control procedures, which apparently is what happened to McAfee.

Questions

1. Discuss McAfee's handling of the update disaster. Should McAfee have done anything differently? If so, what? Support your answer.
2. What should organizations do to prevent such problems in the future?

Sources: Compiled from G. Keizer, "McAfee Apologizes for Crippling PCs with Bad Update," *Computerworld*, April 23, 2010; "McAfee Antivirus Program Goes Berserk, Freezes PCs," *The Economic Times*, April 22, 2010; A. Kingsley-Hughes, "McAfee Issues Fix, and Apology, for Hosed XP SP3 PCs," *ZDNET.com*, April 22, 2010; G. Keizer, "The McAfee Update Mess Explained," *PC World*, April 22, 2010; E. Bott, "McAfee Admits 'Inadequate' Quality Control Caused PC Meltdown," *ZDNET.com*, April 22, 2010; S. Choney, "Some Still Recovering from McAfee PC Problem," *MSNBC.com*, April 22, 2010; "McAfee Program Goes Berserk, Reboots PCs," *MSNBC.com*, April 21, 2010; G. Keizer, "McAfee Antivirus Update Halts Corporate PCs," *Computerworld*, April 21, 2010.

[Interactive Case]

Developing Information Security Measures for Ruby's Club

ruby's club

Go to the Ruby's Club link at the Student Companion website or *WileyPLUS* for information about your current internship assignment. You will investigate security policies at other clubs, make suggestions for Ruby's information security system, and build security measures into the spreadsheet that currently maintains member information.

Technology Guide 1

Hardware

[LEARNING OBJECTIVES]

1. Identify the major hardware components of a computer system.
2. Discuss the strategic issues that link hardware design to business strategy.
3. Describe the hierarchy of computers according to power and their respective roles.
4. Differentiate the various types of input and output technologies and their uses.
5. Describe the design and functioning of the central processing unit.
6. Distinguish between primary and secondary storage along the dimensions of speed, cost, and capacity.

[CHAPTER OUTLINE]

[WEB RESOURCES]

Student Companion Site

wiley.com/college/rainer

- Student PowerPoints for note taking
- Interactive Case: Ruby's Club Assignments
- Complete glossary

WileyPlus

All of the above and

- E-book
- Mini-lecture by author for each chapter section
- Practice quizzes
- Flash Cards for vocabulary review
- Additional "What's in IT for Me?" cases
- Video interviews with managers
- Lab Manual for Microsoft Office 2010
- How-to Animations for Microsoft Office 2010

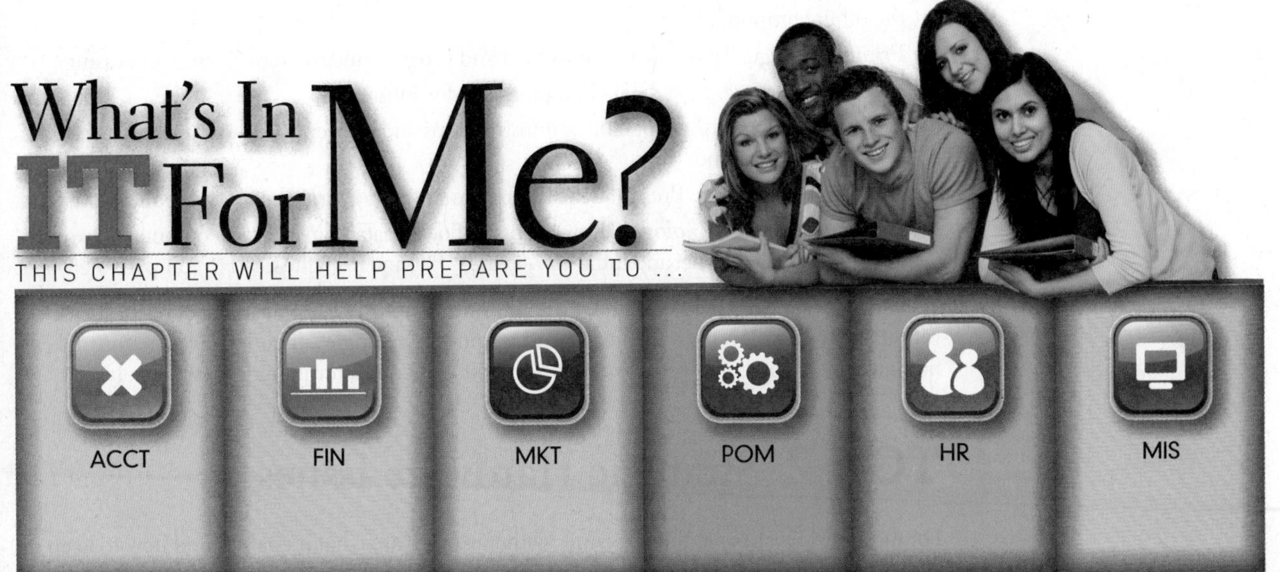

As you begin this Technology Guide, you might be wondering: Why do I have to know anything about hardware? There are several reasons why it is beneficial to know the basics of hardware. First, regardless of your major (and your future functional area in an organization), you will be using different types of hardware throughout your career. Second, you will provide input concerning the hardware you will use. In this capacity, you will be answering many questions, such as "Is the current hardware performing adequately for our needs? If not, what types of problems are we experiencing?" Third, you also will provide input when your functional area or organization decides to upgrade or replace its hardware. Finally, in some organizations, the hardware budget is allocated to functional areas or departments. In such cases, you might be making hardware decisions (at least locally) yourself.

This Technology Guide will help you better understand the computer hardware decisions your organization must make as well as your personal computing decisions. Many of the design principles presented here apply to computers of all sizes, from enterprise-wide systems to personal computers. In addition, the dynamics of innovation and cost discussed in this guide can affect personal as well as corporate hardware decisions.

TG 1.1 Introduction

Recall from Chapter 1 that *hardware* is the physical equipment used for the input, processing, output, and storage activities of a computer system. Decisions about hardware focus on three interrelated factors: appropriateness for the task, speed, and cost. The incredibly rapid rate of innovation within the computer industry complicates hardware decisions because computer technologies become obsolete more quickly than other organizational technologies.

In general, hardware is becoming smaller, faster, cheaper, and more powerful over time. In fact, these trends are so rapid that often it is difficult for companies to know when to purchase (or upgrade) hardware, because if they delay hardware purchases, they likely will be able to buy more powerful hardware for the same amount of money in the future. This means that buying more powerful hardware for the same amount of money in the future is a trade-off: An organization that delays purchasing computer hardware forgoes the benefits of the new technology it could buy today until the future purchase date arrives.

Hardware consists of the following:

- ***Central processing unit (CPU).*** Manipulates the data and controls the tasks performed by the other components.
- ***Primary storage.*** Temporarily stores data and program instructions during processing.
- ***Secondary storage.*** Stores data and programs for future use.
- ***Input technologies.*** Accept data and instructions and convert them to a form that the computer can understand.
- ***Output technologies.*** Present data and information in a form that people can understand.
- ***Communication technologies.*** Provide for the flow of data from external computer networks—for example, the Internet and intranets—to the CPU, and from the CPU to computer networks.

The next section discusses strategic hardware issues. The following sections address the various types of computers and input and output technologies. The last two sections takes a nuts-and-bolts look at the central processing unit and computer memory respectively.

TG 1.2 Strategic Hardware Issues

For most business people the key issues with hardware are what it enables and how to keep up with rapid price/performance increases. In many industries, exploiting computer hardware is essential to achieving competitive advantage. Successful hardware exploitation comes from thoughtful consideration of the following questions:

- How will the organization keep up with the rapid price and performance advancements in hardware? For example, how often should the organization upgrade its computers and storage systems? Will upgrades increase personal and organizational productivity? If so, then how can the organization measure such increases?
- How should the organization determine the need for new hardware infrastructures, such as server farms, virtualization, grid computing, and utility computing? (See Technology Guide 3 for a discussion of these infrastructures.)
- Portable computers and advanced communications technologies enable employees to work from home or almost any other location. Will these new work styles benefit employees and the organization? How do organizations manage such new work styles?

before you go on...

1. Define "hardware," and list the major hardware components.
2. Decisions about hardware focus on what three strategic factors?

TG 1.3 Computer Hierarchy

The traditional standard for comparing classes of computers is processing power. This section presents each class of computers, from the most powerful to the least powerful. It describes both the computers themselves and their roles in modern organizations.

Supercomputers

The term **supercomputer** does not refer to a specific technology. Rather, it indicates the fastest computers available at any given time. Some of the most recent supercomputers include Cray's Titan and IBM's Blue Gene.

Because supercomputers are costly as well as fast, large organizations generally use them to execute computationally demanding tasks involving large data sets. In contrast to mainframes, which specialize in transaction processing and business applications, supercomputers typically run military and scientific applications. For example, the University of Toronto and the University of Manitoba both have recently acquired supercomputers for research purposes. Environment Canada, the government agency in charge of producing the weather forecasts for the country, also operates two of the largest supercomputers in Canada. Although these machines cost millions of dollars, they are also being used for commercial applications where huge amounts of data must be analyzed. For example, large banks employ supercomputers to calculate the risks and returns of various investment strategies, and health care organizations use them to analyze giant databases of patient data to determine optimal treatments for various diseases.

Mainframe Computers

Although mainframe computers are increasingly being viewed as just another type of server (albeit at the high end of the performance and reliability scales), they remain a distinct class of systems differentiated by hardware and software features. **Mainframes** remain popular in large enterprises for extensive computing applications that are accessed by thousands of users simultaneously. Examples of mainframe applications are airline reservation systems, corporate payroll programs, website transaction processing systems (e.g., Amazon and eBay), and student grade calculation and reporting.

Today's mainframes perform at teraflop speeds (trillions of floating point operations per second) and can handle millions of transactions per day. In addition, mainframes provide a secure, robust environment in which to run strategic, mission-critical applications.

Midrange Computers

Larger midrange computers, called **minicomputers**, are relatively small, inexpensive, and compact computers that perform the same functions as mainframe computers, but to a more limited extent. In fact, the lines between minicomputers and mainframes have blurred in both price and performance. Minicomputers are a type of **server**; that is, a computer that supports computer networks and enables users to share files, software, peripheral devices, and other resources. Note that mainframes are a type of server as well, because they provide support for entire enterprise networks.

Microcomputers

Microcomputers—also called *micros, personal computers,* or *PCs*—are the smallest and least expensive category of general-purpose computers. A PC is frequently defined as a computer that uses the Microsoft Windows operating system. In fact, however, a variety of PCs are available, many of which do not use Windows. One well-known example is the Apple Macintosh, which uses the OS X operating system. The major categories of microcomputers are desktops, thin clients, notebooks and laptops, netbooks, and tablets.

Desktop PCs.

The *desktop personal computer* is the familiar microcomputer system that has been a standard tool for business and the home. (Desktops are being replaced with portable devices such as laptops, netbooks, and tablets.) A desktop generally includes a central processing unit (CPU)—which you will learn about later—and a separate but connected monitor and keyboard. Modern desktop computers have gigabytes of primary storage, rewriteable CD-ROM and DVD drives, and up to a few terabytes of secondary storage.

Thin-Client Systems.

Before we address thin-client systems, we need to differentiate between clients and servers. Servers are computers that provide a variety of services for clients, including running networks, processing websites, processing e-mail, and many other functions. *Clients* typically are computers on which users perform their own tasks, such as word processing, spreadsheets, and others.

Thin-client systems are desktop computer systems that do not offer the full functionality of a PC. Compared with a PC, or **fat client**, thin clients are less complex, particularly because they don't have locally installed software. When thin clients need to run an application, they access it from a server over a network rather than from a local disk drive. For example, a thin client would not have Microsoft Office installed on it.

Thus, thin clients are easier and less expensive to operate and support than PCs. The benefits of thin clients include fast application deployment; centralized management; lower cost of ownership; and easier installation, management, maintenance, and support. The main disadvantage of thin clients is that, if the network fails, users can do very little on their computers. Users who have fat clients, in contrast, can still perform some functions when the network fails because the necessary software, such as Microsoft Office, is installed on their computers.

Laptop and Notebook Computers.

Laptop and **notebook computers** are small, lightweight microcomputers that fit easily into a briefcase (Figure TG 1.1). Notebooks and laptops are designed to be as convenient and easy to transport as possible. Just as importantly, they provide users with access to processing power and data outside an office environment. At the same time, they cost more than desktops for similar functionality.

Laptop computer

Netbook

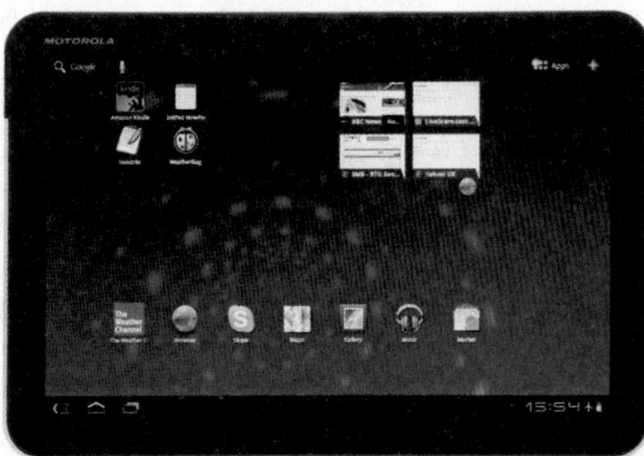

Motorola Xoom tablet

Apple iPad tablet

FIGURE TG 1.1 Laptop, notebook, and tablet computers. (*Source:* © Dragonian/iStockphoto; © Såndor Kelemen/iStockphoto; © PhotoEdit/Alamy Limited; © Oleksiy Maksymenko/Alamy Limited)

Netbooks. A **netbook** is a very small, lightweight, portable computer that is energy efficient and relatively inexpensive (Figure TG 1.1). Netbooks are generally optimized for Internet-based services such as web browsing and e-mailing.

Tablet Computers. A **tablet computer**, or simply a **tablet**, is a complete computer contained entirely in a flat touchscreen that users operate via a stylus, a digital pen, or their fingertip instead of a keyboard or mouse (Figure TG 1.1). Examples of tablets are the Apple iPad (*www.apple.ca/ipad*), the HP Slate (*www.hp.com*), the Toshiba Excite (*www.toshiba.ca*), and the Motorola Xoom (*www.motorola.ca*).

before you go on...

1. Explain the computer hierarchy from the largest to the smallest computers.

TG 1.4 Input and Output Technologies

Input technologies enable people and other technologies to enter data into a computer. The two main types of input devices are human data-entry devices and source-data automation devices. *Human data-entry* devices, as their name implies, require a certain amount of human effort to input data. Examples are keyboard, mouse, pointing stick, trackball, joystick, touchscreen, stylus, and voice recognition.

An interesting development in input/output technologies is voice recognition applications such as Apple's Siri. This application allows users to simply speak to their phone and receive intelligent feedback. As this method of interaction develops, it will transform how and where we use computers as there will be far less need for traditional input/output devices. For example, a group of Toronto-based entrepreneurs have decided to develop a voice-activated computing device named Ubi. This device would be the size of a smart phone, and would plug into an electrical outlet and connect to the web via Wi-Fi.

In contrast, *source-data automation* devices input data with minimal human intervention. These technologies speed up data collection, reduce errors, and gather data at the source of a transaction or other event. Barcode readers, ATMs, and radio frequency identification are examples of source-data automation. Table TG 1.1 describes the various input devices.

Table TG 1.1

Input Devices

Input Device	Description
Human Data-Entry Devices	
Keyboards	Most common input device (for text and numerical data).
Mouse	Hand-held device used to point cursor at a point on the screen, such as an icon; user clicks mouse button, instructing computer to take some action.
Optical mouse	Mouse is not connected to computer by a cable; mouse uses camera chip to take images of the surface it passes over, comparing successive images to determine its position.
Trackball	User rotates a ball built into top of device to move cursor (rather than moving entire device such as a mouse).
Pointing stick	Small button-like device; cursor moves in the direction of the pressure you place on the stick. Located between keys near centre of keyboard.
Touchpad (also called a *trackpad*)	User moves cursor by sliding finger across a sensitized pad and then can tap pad when cursor is in desired position to instruct computer to take action (also called *glide-and-tap pad*).
Graphics tablet	A device that can be used in place of, or in conjunction with, a mouse or trackball; has a flat surface for drawing and a pen or stylus that is programmed to work with the tablet.
Joystick	Device that moves cursor to desired place on screen; commonly used in workstations that display dynamic graphics and in video games.
Touchscreen	Users instruct computer to take some action by touching a particular part of the screen; commonly used in information kiosks such as bank ATMs. Touchscreens now have gesture controls for browsing through photographs, moving objects around on a screen, flicking to turn the page of a book, and playing video games.
Stylus	Pen-style device that allows user either to touch parts of a predetermined menu of options or to handwrite information into the computer; works with touch-sensitive screens.
Digital pen	Mobile device that digitally captures everything you write; built-in screen confirms that what you write has been saved; also captures sketches, figures, etc. with on-board flash memory.

Table TG 1.1 (Continued)

Input Device	Description
Wii	A video game console by Nintendo. A distinguishing feature of the Wii is its wireless controller, which can be used as a hand-held pointing device and can detect movement in three dimensions.
Microsoft Kinect	Enables users to control and interact with the Xbox 360 without the need to touch a game controller, through a natural user interface using gestures and spoken commands.
Web camera (webcam)	A real-time video camera whose images can be accessed via the web or instant messaging.
Voice recognition	Microphone converts analog voice sounds to digital input for computer; critical technology for physically challenged people who cannot use other input devices.
Source-Data Automation Input Devices	
Magnetic stripe reader	Device that reads data from a magnetic stripe, usually on the back of a plastic card (for example, credit or debit card).
Barcode scanners	Devices that scan black-and-white barcode lines printed on merchandise labels.
Optical mark reader	Scanner for detecting presence of dark marks on predetermined grid, such as multiple-choice test answer sheets.
Magnetic ink character reader	Reads magnetic ink printed on cheques that identifies the bank, chequing account, and cheque number.
Optical character recognition	Software that converts text into digital form for input into computer.
Sensors	Collect data directly from the environment and input data directly into computer (for example, temperature sensor or a wind sensor).
Cameras	Digital cameras capture images and convert them to digital files.
Radio frequency identification (RFID)	Uses active or passive tags (transmitters) to wirelessly transmit product information to electronic readers.
Source-Data Automation Computer Devices	
Automated teller machine (ATM)	Computer device that includes several input and output devices including a magnetic stripe reader; human input via a keyboard; and output via a monitor, printer, and cash dispenser.
Point-of-sale terminals (POS)	Computerized cash registers that combine a number of different input and output devices such as touchscreen technology and barcode scanners to input data, and output devices such as a monitor and printer.

The output generated by a computer can be transmitted to the user via multiple output devices and media. These devices include monitors, printers, plotters, and voice. Table TG 1.2 describes the various output devices.

Multimedia technology is the computer-based integration of text, sound, still images, animation, and digitized motion video. It typically represents a collection of various input and output technologies. Multimedia merges the capabilities of computers with televisions, VCRs, CD players, DVD players, video and audio recording equipment, and music and gaming technologies. High-quality multimedia processing requires powerful microprocessors and extensive memory capacity, including both primary and secondary storage (discussed later in the guide).

Table TG 1.2

Output Devices

Output Device	Description
Monitors	
Cathode ray tubes	Video display screens on which an electron beam illuminates pixels.
Liquid crystal display (LCDs)	Flat displays that have liquid crystals between two polarizers to form characters and images on a backlit screen.
Flexible displays	Thin, plastic, bendable computer screens.
Organic light-emitting diodes (OLEDs)	Displays that are brighter, thinner, lighter, cheaper, and faster and that take less power to run than LCDs.
Retinal scanning displays	Displays that project image directly onto a viewer's retina; used in medicine, air traffic control, and controlling industrial machines.
Heads-up displays	Any transparent display that presents data without requiring that the user look away from his or her usual viewpoint.
Printers	
Laser	Use laser beams to write information on photosensitive drums; produce high-resolution text and graphics.
Inkjet	Shoot fine streams of coloured ink onto paper; usually less expensive to buy than laser printers, but can be more expensive to operate; can offer resolution quality equal to that of laser printers.
Thermal	Produce a printed image by selectively heating coated thermal paper; when the paper passes over the thermal print head, the coating turns black in the areas where it is heated, producing an image.
Plotters	Use computer-directed pens for creating high-quality images, blueprints, schematics, drawings of new products, etc.
Voice output	A software function that, used in a speaker/headset, can output sounds of any type.
Electronic book reader	A wireless, portable reading device with access to books, blogs, newspapers, and magazines. On-board storage holds hundreds of books. Some examples are Amazon's Kindle and Indigo's Kobo.
Pocket projector	Hand-held device that provides an alternative display method to alleviate the problem of tiny display screens in hand-held devices. Pocket projectors will project digital images onto any viewing surface. One kind of pocket projector is the *pico projector*, a very small projector incorporated into portable devices, such as cameras and smart phones.

before you go on...

1. Distinguish between human data-input devices and source-data automation.

TG 1.5 The Central Processing Unit

The **central processing unit (CPU)** performs the actual computation or "number crunching" inside any computer. The CPU is a **microprocessor**—for example, Intel's Core i3, i5, and i7 chips, with more to come—made up of millions of microscopic transistors embedded in a circuit on a silicon wafer or *chip*. Hence, microprocessors are commonly referred to as "chips."

As shown in Figure TG 1.2, the microprocessor has different parts, which perform different functions. The **control unit** sequentially accesses program instructions, decodes them, and controls the flow of data to and from the arithmetic-logic unit, the registers, the caches, primary storage, secondary storage, and various output devices. The **arithmetic-logic unit (ALU)** performs mathematic calculations and makes logical comparisons. The **registers** are high-speed storage areas that store very small amounts of data and instructions for short periods of time.

How the CPU Works

Inputs enter the CPU and are stored until they are needed. At that point, they are retrieved and processed, and the output is stored and then delivered somewhere. Figure TG 1.3 illustrates this process, which works as follows.

1. The inputs consist of data and brief instructions about what to do with the data. These instructions come into the CPU from random access memory (RAM). Data can be entered by the user through the keyboard, for example, or read from a data file in another part of the computer. The inputs are stored in registers until they are sent to the next step in the processing.

   Data and instructions travel in the chip via electrical pathways called *buses*. The size of the bus—analogous to the width of a highway—determines how much information can flow at any time.
2. The control unit directs the flow of data and instructions within the chip and get decoded into binary code.
3. The ALU receives the data and instructions from the registers and performs the desired computation. These data and instructions have been translated into **binary form**; that is, only 0s and 1s. A "0" or a "1" is called a **bit**. The CPU can process only binary data. All types of data, such as letters, decimal numbers, photographs, and music, can be represented in binary form and then be processed by the CPU.

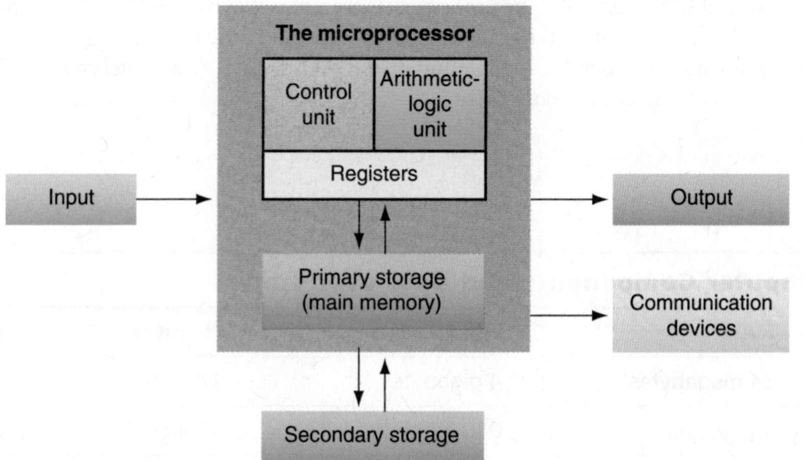

FIGURE TG 1.2 Parts of a microprocessor.

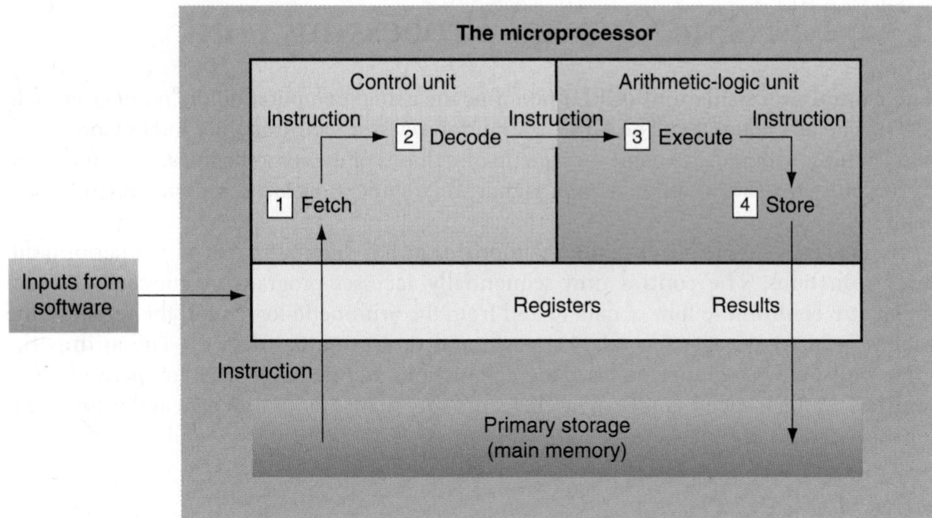

FIGURE TG 1.3 How the CPU works.

4. The data in their original form and the instructions are sent to storage registers, and then are sent back to a storage place outside the chip, such as the computer's hard drive (discussed below). Meanwhile, the transformed data go to another register and on to other parts of the computer (for example, to the monitor for display or to storage).

This cycle of processing, known as a *machine instruction cycle*, occurs billions of times per second.

Advances in Microprocessor Design

Innovations in chip designs are coming at an increasingly faster rate, as described by **Moore's Law**. In 1965, Gordon Moore, a co-founder of Intel Corporation, predicted that microprocessor complexity would double approximately every two years. His prediction has been amazingly accurate. These increased speeds and performance have also reduced computing costs, as you can see in Table TG 1.3.

The advances predicted from Moore's Law arise primarily from the following innovations:

- Increasingly miniaturized transistors.
- Multiple processors placed on a single chip. Chips with more than one processor are called *multicore* chips. For example, the Cell chip, produced by a consortium of Sony, Toshiba, and IBM, contains nine processors. Computers that use the Cell chip display very rich graphics. The Cell chip is also used in TV sets and home theatres that can download and show large numbers of high-definition programs. Intel (*www.intel.com*) and AMD (*www.amd.com*) offer multicore chips.

Table TG 1.3

Comparison of Personal Computer Components and Cost over Time

Year	Chip	RAM	Hard Drive	Monitor	Cost
1997	Pentium II	64 megabytes	4 gigabytes	17-inch	$4,000
2007	Dual-core	1 gigabyte	250 gigabytes	19-inch	$1,700
2013	Core i7	8 gigabytes	750 gigabytes	22-inch	$1,400

TG 1.6 Computer Memory

The amount and type of memory that a computer possesses largely determines its general utility. A computer's memory also determines the types of programs the computer can run, the work it can perform, its speed, and its cost. There are two basic categories of computer memory. The first is *primary storage*. It is called "primary" because it stores small amounts of data and information that the CPU will use immediately. The second category is *secondary storage*, which stores much larger amounts of data and information—an entire software program, for example—for extended periods of time.

Memory Capacity

Recall that CPUs process only binary units—0s and 1s—which are translated through computer languages. A particular combination of bits represents a certain alphanumeric character or a simple mathematical operation. Eight bits are needed to represent any given character. This 8-bit string is known as a **byte**. The storage capacity of a computer is measured in bytes. Bits typically are used as units of measure only for telecommunications capacity, as in how many million bits per second can be transmitted through a particular medium.

The hierarchy of terms used to describe memory capacity is as follows:

- ***Kilobyte.*** *Kilo* means 1 thousand, so a kilobyte (KB) is approximately 1,000 bytes. Actually, a kilobyte is 1,024 bytes. Computer designers find it convenient to work with powers of 2. When 2 is raised to the 10th power, the result is 1,024. This number is close enough to 1,000 that people use the standard prefix "kilo," which means exactly 1,000 in familiar units such as the kilogram or kilometre.
- ***Megabyte.*** *Mega* means 1 million, so a megabyte (MB) is approximately 1 million bytes.
- ***Gigabyte.*** *Giga* means 1 billion, so a gigabyte (GB) is approximately 1 billion bytes.
- ***Terabyte.*** A terabyte is approximately 1 trillion bytes. The storage capacity of modern personal computers can be several terabytes.
- ***Petabyte.*** A petabyte is approximately 1,000 terabytes.
- ***Exabyte.*** An exabyte is approximately 1,000 petabytes.
- ***Zettabyte.*** A zettabyte is approximately 1,000 exabytes.

To get a feel for these amounts, consider the following example: A computer that has 1 terabyte of storage capacity on its hard drive (a type of secondary storage) can store approximately 1 trillion bytes of data. The average page of text contains about 2,000 bytes, so the hard drive could store approximately 500 million pages, or 1 million books like this one.

Primary Storage

Primary storage, or **main memory**, as it is sometimes called, stores three types of information for very brief periods of time: (1) data to be processed by the CPU, (2) instructions for the CPU on how to process the data, and (3) operating system programs that manage various aspects of the computer's operation. Primary storage takes place in chips mounted on the computer's main circuit board, called the *motherboard*, which are located as close as physically possible to the CPU chip. As with the CPU, all of the data and instructions in primary storage have been translated into binary code.

There are four main types of primary storage: (1) register, (2) cache memory, (3) random access memory (RAM), and (4) read-only memory (ROM). You learn about each type below.

Registers are part of the CPU. They have the least capacity, storing extremely limited amounts of instructions and data only immediately before and after processing.

Cache memory is a type of high-speed memory that a processor can access more rapidly than main memory (RAM). Cache memory enables the computer to temporarily store frequently used blocks of data. Blocks used less often remain in RAM until they are transferred to cache; blocks used infrequently remain in secondary storage. Cache memory is physically located closer to the CPU than is RAM. Because the instructions travel a shorter distance to the CPU, cache is faster than RAM.

Random access memory (RAM) is the part of primary storage that holds a software program and small amounts of data for processing. When a software program (such as Microsoft Word) is started on your computer, the entire program is transferred from secondary storage into RAM. As you use the program, small parts of its instructions and data are sent into the registers and then to the CPU. Compared with the registers, RAM stores more information and is located farther away from the CPU. Compared with secondary storage, however, RAM stores less information and is much closer to the CPU.

RAM is temporary and, in most cases, is *volatile*. That is, RAM chips lose their contents if the current is lost or turned off, as occurs in a power surge, a brownout, or electrical noise generated by lightning or nearby machines.

Most of us have lost data at some time due to a computer "crash" or a power failure. The data lost are whatever was in RAM, cache, or the registers at the time, because these types of memory are volatile. Therefore, greater security is needed when certain types of critical data or instructions are stored. Cautious computer users frequently save data to nonvolatile memory (secondary storage). In addition, most modern software applications have autosave functions. Programs stored in secondary storage, although temporarily copied into RAM when they are being used, remain intact because only a copy is lost, not the original.

Read-only memory (ROM) is the place—actually, a type of chip—where certain critical instructions are safeguarded. ROM is nonvolatile, so it retains instructions when the power to the computer is turned off. The "read-only" designation means that instructions in ROM can only be read, not changed. An example of ROM is the initial instructions needed to start or "boot" the computer.

Secondary Storage

Secondary storage is designed to store large amounts of data for extended periods of time. Secondary storage has the following characteristics:

- It is nonvolatile.
- More time is needed to retrieve data from secondary storage than from RAM.
- It is cheaper than primary storage (see Figure TG 1.4).
- It consists of a variety of media, each with its own technology, as you will see next.

One storage device, **magnetic tape**, is kept on a large open reel or in a smaller cartridge or cassette. Although this is an old technology, it remains popular because it is the cheapest storage medium, and it can handle enormous amounts of data. As a result, many organizations use magnetic tape for archival storage. The downside is that it is the slowest method for retrieving

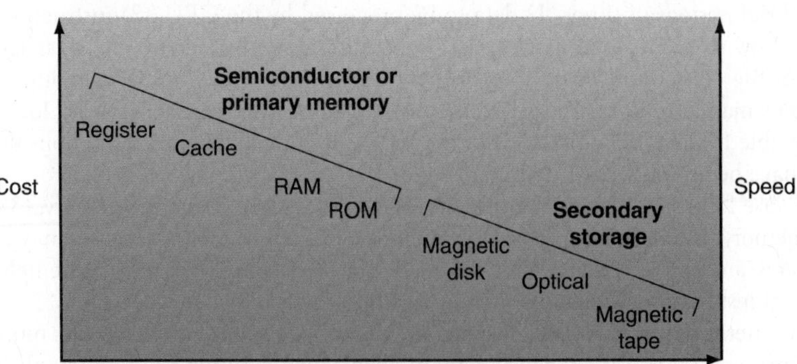

FIGURE TG 1.4 Primary memory compared with secondary storage.

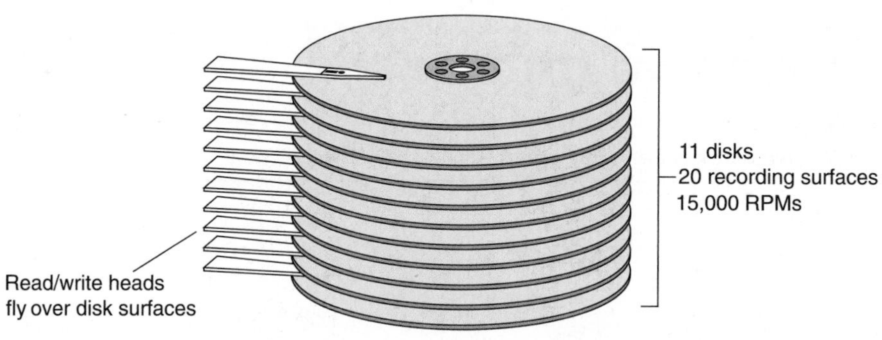

FIGURE TG 1.5
Read/write heads.

data, because all the data are placed on the tape sequentially. *Sequential access* means that the system might have to run through most of the tape before the desired piece of data appears.

Magnetic disks, called **hard drives** or *fixed disk drives*, are the most commonly used mass storage devices because of their low cost, high speed, and large storage capacity. Hard disk drives read from, and write to, stacks of rotating (at up to 15,000 RPM) magnetic disk platters mounted in rigid enclosures and sealed against environmental and atmospheric contamination (see Figure TG 1.5). These disks are permanently mounted in a unit that may be internal or external to the computer.

Solid state drives (SSDs), which serve the same purpose as hard drives, store data in memory chips. Whereas hard drives have moving parts, SSDs do not. SSDs use the same interface to the computer's CPU as hard drives, and therefore are a seamless replacement for hard drives. SSDs offer many advantages over hard drives. They use less power, are silent and faster, and produce about one third the heat of a hard drive. The major disadvantage of SSDs is that they cost more than hard drives.

Unlike magnetic media, **optical storage devices** do not store data via magnetism. Rather, a laser reads the surface of a reflective plastic platter. Optical disk drives are slower than magnetic hard drives, but they are less susceptible to damage from contamination, and they are less fragile.

In addition, optical disks can store a great deal of information on a routine basis as well as when combined with storage systems. Common types of optical disks include compact disk read-only memory (CD-ROM), and digital video disk (DVD).

Compact disk, read-only memory (CD-ROM) storage devices feature high capacity, low cost, and high durability. Because a CD-ROM is a read-only medium, however, it cannot be written on. A CD-R can be written to, but once this is done, the data written on it cannot be changed later. That is, CD-R is writeable (which CD-ROM is not) but is not rewriteable. In some applications, not being rewriteable is an advantage because it prevents some types of accidental data destruction. Compact disk, rewritable (CD-RW) adds rewritability to the recordable compact disk market.

The **digital video disk (DVD)** is a five-inch disk that can store about 135 minutes of digital video. DVDs can also perform as computer storage disks, providing storage capabilities of 17 gigabytes. DVD players can read current CD-ROMs, but current CD-ROM players cannot read DVDs. The access speed of a DVD drive is faster than that of a typical CD-ROM drive.

Flash memory devices (or *memory cards*) are nonvolatile electronic storage devices that contain no moving parts and use 30 times less battery power than hard drives. Flash devices are also smaller and more durable than hard drives. The trade-off is that flash devices store less data than do hard drives. Flash devices are used with digital cameras, hand-held and laptop computers, telephones, music players, and video game consoles.

One popular flash memory device is the **thumb drive**, also called *memory stick*, *jump drive*, or *flash drive*. These devices fit into universal serial bus (USB) ports on personal computers and other devices, and they can store many gigabytes. Thumb drives have replaced magnetic floppy disks for portable storage (see Figure TG 1.6).

FIGURE TG 1.6 Thumb drive.
(*Source*: © laggerbomber-Fotolia.com)

before you go on...

1. Briefly describe how a microprocessor functions.
2. Distinguish between primary storage and secondary storage.

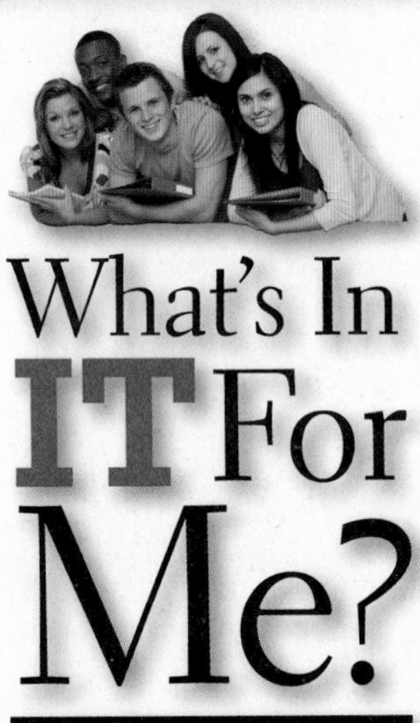

For all Business Majors

Practically all professional jobs in business today require computer literacy and skills for personal productivity. Going further, all industries use computer technology for various forms of competitive advantage.

Clearly, the design of computer hardware has a profound impact for businesspeople. It is clear also that personal and organizational success can depend on an understanding of hardware design as well as of where it is going and the opportunities and challenges that hardware innovations will bring. Because these innovations are occurring so rapidly, hardware decisions at both the individual and organizational levels are difficult.

At the *individual level*, most people who want to upgrade an existing home or office computer system or are contemplating their first computer purchase face the decision of *when* to buy as much as of *what* to buy and at what cost. These same issues plague information system (IS) professionals at the *organizational level* as well, but the issues are more complex and more costly. Most organizations have many different computer systems in place at the same time. Innovations may come to different classes of computers at different times or rates. Therefore, managers must decide whether hardware *legacy systems* still have a productive role in the IS architecture or should be replaced. A legacy system is an old computer system or application that continues to be used, typically because it still functions for the users' needs, even though newer technology is available.

IS management at the corporate level is one of the most challenging careers today, due in no small part to the constant innovation in computer hardware. A career in this field may not be your objective, but you will benefit from becoming familiar with this area. After all, the people who equip you with the right computing hardware are very important allies in your success.

[Summary]

1. **Identify the major hardware components of a computer system.**

   Modern computer systems have six major components: the central processing unit (CPU), primary storage, secondary storage, input technologies, output technologies, and communications technologies.

2. **Discuss the strategic issues that link hardware design to business strategy.**

   Strategic issues linking hardware design to business strategy include: How do organizations keep up with the rapid price/performance advancements in hardware? How often should an organization upgrade its computers and storage systems? How can organizations measure benefits gained from price/performance improvements in hardware?

3. **Describe the hierarchy of computers according to power and their respective roles.**

Supercomputers are the most powerful computers, designed to handle the maximum computational demands of science and the military. Mainframes, although not as powerful as supercomputers, are powerful enough for large organizations to use for centralized data processing and large databases. Minicomputers are smaller and less powerful versions of mainframes that are often devoted to managing specific subsystems. Desktop personal computers (PCs) are the common, well-known personal and business computers. Laptop or notebook computers are small, easily transportable PCs. Tablet computers (or tablets) are complete computers contained entirely in a flat touchscreen that uses a stylus, digital pen, or fingertip as an input device instead of a keyboard or mouse.

4. **Differentiate the various types of input and output technologies and their uses.**

Principal human data-entry input technologies include the keyboard, mouse, optical mouse, trackball, touchpad, joystick, touchscreen, stylus, and voice-recognition systems. Principal source-data automation input devices are barcode scanners, optical mark readers, magnetic ink character readers, optical character readers, sensors, cameras, and radio frequency identification. Common output technologies include various types of monitors, impact and nonimpact printers, plotters, and voice output.

5. **Describe the design and functioning of the central processing unit.**

The CPU is made up of the arithmetic-logic unit (ALU), which performs the calculations; the registers, which store minute amounts of data and instructions immediately before and after processing; and the control unit, which controls the flow of information on the microprocessor chip. After processing, the data in their original form and the instructions are sent back to a storage place outside the chip.

Microprocessor designs aim to increase processing speed by minimizing the physical distance that the data (as electrical impulses) must travel, increasing the number of transistors on the chip, increasing the number of CPUs on the chip, and using three-dimensional chip architecture.

6. **Distinguish between primary and secondary storage along the dimensions of speed, cost, and capacity.**

There are four types of primary storage: registers, cache memory, random access memory (RAM), and read-only memory (ROM). Secondary storage includes magnetic media (tapes; hard drives; and thumb, or flash, drives) and optical media (CD-ROM, DVD).

Primary storage has much less capacity than secondary storage, and it is faster and more expensive per byte stored. It is also located much closer to the CPU. Sequential-access secondary storage media such as magnetic tape are much slower and less expensive than hard drives and optical media.

[Technology Guide Glossary]

arithmetic-logic unit (ALU) Portion of the CPU that performs mathematic calculations and makes logical comparisons.

binary form The form in which data and instructions can be read by the CPU—only 0s and 1s.

bits Short for "binary digits" (0s and 1s), the only data that a CPU can process.

byte An 8-bit string of data, needed to represent any one alphanumeric character or simple mathematical operation.

cache memory A type of primary storage where the computer can temporarily store often-used blocks of data, and which a processor can access more rapidly than main memory (RAM).

central processing unit (CPU) Hardware that performs the actual computation or "number crunching" inside any computer.

compact disk, read-only memory (CD-ROM) A form of secondary storage that can be only read, not written on.

control unit Portion of the CPU that controls the flow of information.

digital video disk (DVD) An optical storage device used to store digital video or computer data.

fat clients Desktop computer systems that offer full functionality.

flash memory devices Electronic storage devices that are compact and portable, require little power, and contain no moving parts.

hard drives A form of secondary storage that reads from, and writes to, stacks of rotating magnetic disk platters mounted in rigid, sealed enclosures.

laptop computers (notebook computers) Small, easily transportable, lightweight microcomputers.

magnetic disks A form of secondary storage on a magnetized disk divided into tracks and sectors that provide addresses for various pieces of data; also called *hard disks.*

magnetic tape A secondary storage medium on a large open reel or in a smaller cartridge or cassette.

mainframe Relatively large computer used in large enterprises for extensive computing applications that are accessed by thousands of users.

main memory (see **primary storage**)

microcomputers The smallest and least expensive category of general-purpose computers; also called *micros*, *personal computers*, or *PCs*.

microprocessor The CPU, made up of millions of transistors embedded in a circuit on a silicon wafer or chip.

minicomputers Relatively small, inexpensive, and compact midrange computers that perform the same functions as mainframe computers, but to a more limited extent.

Moore's Law Prediction by Gordon Moore, an Intel co-founder, that microprocessor complexity would double approximately every two years.

multimedia technology Computer-based integration of text, sound, still images, animation, and digitized full-motion video.

netbook A very small, lightweight, low-cost, energy-efficient, portable computer, typically optimized for Internet-based services such as web browsing and e-mailing.

notebook computer (see **laptop computer**)

optical storage devices A form of secondary storage in which a laser reads the surface of a reflective plastic platter.

primary storage (main memory) High-speed storage located directly on the motherboard that stores data to be processed by the CPU, instructions telling the CPU how to process the data, and operating system programs.

random access memory (RAM) The part of primary storage that holds a software program and small amounts of data brought from secondary storage.

read-only memory (ROM) A type of primary storage in which certain critical instructions are safeguarded; the storage is nonvolatile and retains instructions when power to the computer is turned off.

registers High-speed storage areas in the CPU that store very small amounts of data and instructions for short periods of time.

secondary storage Technology that can store large amounts of data for extended periods of time.

server Smaller midrange computers that support networks, enabling users to share files, software, and other network devices.

supercomputer Computers with the most processing power available; used primarily in scientific and military work for computationally demanding tasks on large data sets.

tablet computer (tablet) A complete computer contained entirely in a flat touchscreen that users operate via a stylus, digital pen, or fingertip instead of a keyboard or mouse.

thin-client systems Desktop computer systems that do not offer the full functionality of a PC.

thumb drive Storage device that fits into the USB port of a personal computer and is used for portable storage.

[Discussion Questions]

1. What factors affect the speed of a microprocessor?
2. If you were the CIO of a firm, what factors would you consider when selecting secondary storage media for your company's records (files)?
3. Given that Moore's Law has proved itself over the past two decades, speculate on what chip capabilities will be in 10 years. What might your desktop PC be able to do?
4. If you were the CIO of a firm, how would you explain the workings, benefits, and limitations of using thin clients as opposed to fat clients?

[Problem-Solving Activities]

1. Access the websites of the major chip manufacturers, for example, Intel (*www.intel.com*), Motorola (*www.motorola.com*), and Advanced Micro Devices (*www.amd.com*), and obtain the latest information regarding new and planned chips. Compare performance and costs across these vendors. Be sure to take a close look at the various multicore chips (e.g., read about the Cell chip on Wikipedia).
2. Access "The Journey Inside" on Intel's website (*www.intel.com/content/www/us/en/education/k12/the-journey-inside.html*). Prepare a presentation of each step in the machine instruction cycle.

Technology Guide 2

Software

[LEARNING OBJECTIVES]

1. Discuss the major software issues that confront modern organizations.
2. Analyze the advantages and disadvantages of open-source software.
3. Differentiate between the two major types of software and describe the general functions of the operating system.
4. Identify the major types of application software.

[CHAPTER OUTLINE]

[WEB RESOURCES]

Student Companion Site

wiley.com/college/rainer

- Student PowerPoints for note taking
- Interactive Case: Ruby's Club Assignments
- Complete glossary

WileyPlus

All of the above and WILEY PLUS

- E-book
- Mini-lecture by author for each chapter section
- Practice quizzes
- Flash Cards for vocabulary review
- Additional "What's in IT for Me?" cases
- Video interviews with managers
- Lab Manual for Microsoft Office 2010
- How-to Animations for Microsoft Office 2010

As you begin this Technology Guide, you might be wondering, "Why do I have to know anything about software?" There are several reasons why you need to know the basics of software. First, regardless of your major (and the functional area in which you will work), you will use different types of software throughout your career. Second, you will provide input concerning the software you will use. In this capacity, you will be required to answer many questions, such as "Does my software help me do my job?" "Is this software easy to use?" "Do I need more functionality and, if so, what functionality would be most helpful to me?" Third, you will also provide input when your functional area or organization upgrades or replaces its software. Finally, some organizations allocate the software budget to functional areas or departments. In such cases, you might be responsible for making software decisions (at least locally) yourself.

TG 2.1 Introduction

Computer hardware is only as effective as the instructions you give it, and those instructions are contained in **software**. The importance of computer software cannot be overestimated. The first software applications for computers in business were developed in the early 1950s. At that time, software was less costly. Today, software comprises a much larger percentage of the cost of modern computer systems because the price of hardware has dramatically decreased, while both the complexity and the price of software have dramatically increased.

We will begin our examination of software by defining some fundamental concepts. Software consists of **computer programs**, which are sequences of instructions for the computer. The process of writing or *coding* programs is called *programming*. Individuals who perform this task are called *programmers*.

Computer programs include **documentation**, which is a written description of the functions of the program. Documentation helps the user operate the computer system and it helps other programmers understand what the program does and how it accomplishes its purpose. Documentation is vital to the business organization. Without it, if a key programmer or user leaves, the knowledge of how to use the program or how it is designed may be lost as well.

The ever-increasing complexity of software has also increased the potential for errors, or *bugs*. Large applications today may contain millions of lines of computer code, written by hundreds of people over the course of several years. The potential for errors is huge, and testing and *debugging* software is expensive and time consuming. In spite of these overall trends—increasing complexity, cost, and numbers of defects—software has become an everyday feature of our business and personal lives.

A computer can do nothing until it is instructed by software. Computer hardware, by design, is general purpose. Software enables the user to instruct the hardware to perform specific functions that provide business value. There are two major types of software: systems software and application software. Figure TG 2.1 illustrates the relationship among hardware, systems software, and application software.

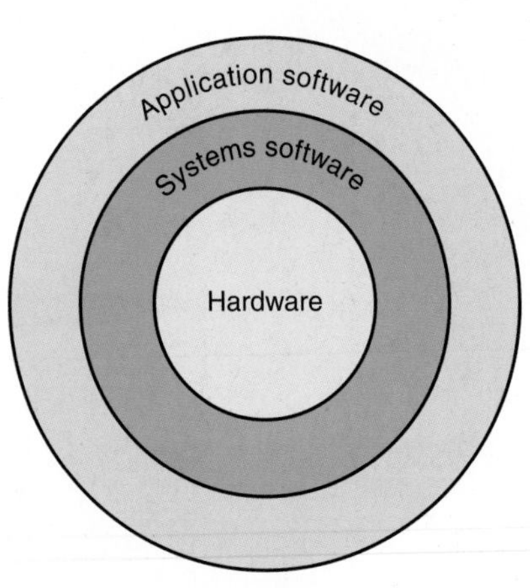

FIGURE TG 2.1 Systems software serves as an intermediary between hardware and functional applications.

Systems software is a set of instructions that serves primarily as an intermediary between computer hardware and application programs. Systems software enables computer systems to perform self-regulatory functions by loading itself when the computer is first turned on and providing commonly used sets of instructions for all applications. *Systems programming* is both the creation and the maintenance of systems software.

Application software is a set of computer instructions that provide more specific functionality to a user. This functionality may be broad, such as general word processing, or narrow, such as an organization's payroll program. Essentially, an application program applies a computer to a certain need. *Application programming* is the creation, modification, and improvement of application software. Application software may be proprietary or off-the-shelf. As you will see, modern organizations use many different software applications.

TG 2.2 Software Issues

The importance of software in computer systems has brought new issues to the forefront for organizational managers. These issues include software defects (bugs), licensing, open systems, and open-source software.

Software Defects

All too often, computer program code is inefficient, poorly designed, and riddled with errors. The Software Engineering Institute (SEI) at Carnegie Mellon University in Pittsburgh defines good software as usable, reliable, defect free, cost effective, and maintainable. As dependence on computers and networks increases, the risks associated with software defects are getting worse.

The SEI maintains that, on average, professional programmers make between 100 and 150 errors in every 1,000 lines of code they write. Fortunately, the software industry recognizes this problem and is taking initial steps to resolve it. For example, by adopting the SEI Capability Maturity Model (CMM), software developers are able to produce error-free software code efficiently and on schedule. Instead of 1 error in every 10 lines of code, CMM-certified companies now make 1 error in every 1,000 lines of code. One critical step in creating error-free software is better design and planning at the beginning of the development process (discussed in Chapter 11).

Software Licensing

Many people routinely copy proprietary software, but making copies without the manufacturer's explicit permission is illegal. The Business Software Alliance (BSA) (*www.bsa.org*) has calculated that software piracy costs software vendors around the world billions of dollars annually. The BSA, a non-profit trade association dedicated to promoting a safe and legal digital world, collects, investigates, and acts on software piracy tips. Most tips come from current and past employees of offending companies.

To protect their investment, software vendors must prevent their products from being copied and distributed by individuals and other software companies. A company can copyright its software, which grants the company the exclusive legal right to reproduce, publish, and sell that software.

The number of desktop computers continues to grow, and businesses continue to decentralize, so information system managers are finding it increasingly difficult to supervise their software assets. In fact, in a recent survey, 70 percent of chief information officers (CIOs) were "not confident" that their companies are in compliance with software licensing agreements. For example, one medium-size company was fined $10,000 for unknowingly using Microsoft Exchange mailbox licences that had not been purchased. Worse, the company was also fined $100,000 for not having the necessary licences for Autodesk, Inc.'s AutoCAD design software.

Open Systems

The **open systems** concept is a group of computing products that work together. In an open system, the same operating system with compatible software is installed on all computers that interact within an organization. A complementary approach is to employ application software that will run across all computer platforms. Where hardware, operating systems, and application software are designed as open systems, users can purchase the best software, called *best of breed*, for a job without worrying whether it will run on particular hardware.

Open-Source Software

Within the software industry, the trend is away from proprietary software and toward open-source software. **Proprietary software** is purchased software that has restrictions on its use, copying, and modification. Companies developing such software spend money and time researching and developing their products, which are then sold in the marketplace. The proprietary nature of this software means that the company keeps the source code—the actual computer instructions—private (as Coca-Cola does with its formula).

In contrast, the source code for **open-source software** is available at no cost to developers or users. Open-source software is distributed with licence terms that ensure that its source code will always be available.

Open-source software is produced by worldwide "communities" of developers who write and maintain the code. Inside each community, however, only a small group of developers, called *core developers*, is allowed to modify the code directly. All the other developers must submit their suggested changes to the core developers.

There are advantages to implementing open-source software in an organization. According to OpenSource (*www.opensource.org*), open-source development produces high-quality, reliable, low-cost software. This software is also flexible, meaning that the code can be changed to meet users' needs. In many cases, open-source software is more reliable than commercial software. Because the code is available to many developers, more bugs are discovered early and quickly, and they are fixed immediately. Technical support for open-source software is also available from firms that offer products derived from the software. An example is Red Hat (*www.redhat.com*), a major Linux vendor that supplies solutions to problems associated with open-source technology. Firms such as Red Hat provide education, training, and technical support, for a fee.

Open-source software also has disadvantages, however. The biggest is that companies that use open-source software depend on the continued goodwill of an army of volunteers for enhancements, bug fixes, and so on, even if there is a contract for support. Some companies will not accept this risk, although as a practical matter the support community for Linux, Apache, or Firefox is not likely to disappear. Further, organizations without in-house technical experts will have to purchase maintenance-support contracts from a third party. In addition, open-source software poses questions concerning ease of use, the time and expense needed to train users, and compatibility with existing systems either within or outside the organization.

There are many examples of open-source software, including the GNU (GNU's Not UNIX) suite of software (*www.gnu.org*) developed by the Free Software Foundation (*www.fsf.org*); the Linux operating system (see, for example, LinuxMint *www.linuxmint.com* or Ubuntu *www.ubuntu.com*); Apache web server (*www.apache.org*); sendmail SMTP (Send Mail Transport Protocol) e-mail server (*www.sendmail.org*); the Firefox browser from Mozilla (*www.mozilla.com*); Office suite Open Office (*www.openoffice.org/*) *and LibreOffice* (*www.libreoffice.org/*); and learning platform *Moodle* (*https://moodle.org/*). In fact, more than 150,000 open-source projects are underway at SourceForge (*www.sourceforge.net*), the popular open-source hosting site.

Even popular IT business solutions such as database management, ERP, and CRM systems are also available open-source. The following are some examples: MySQL (*www.mysql.com*) open-source database management software; Open Bravo *ERP* (*www.openbravo.com/*); and SugarCRM (*www.sugarcrm.com*) for certain customer relationship management tasks.

before you go on...

1. What does this statement mean: "Hardware is useless without software?"
2. What is open-source software, and what are its advantages? Can you think of any disadvantages?

TG 2.3 Systems Software

As you saw earlier, the programs in systems software control and support the computer system and its information-processing activities. Systems software also helps users and IT personnel program, test, and debug their own computer programs. Systems software programs support application software by directing the computer's basic functions. For example, when the computer is turned on, the initialization program (a systems program) prepares and readies all devices for processing. The major type of systems software with which we are concerned is the operating system.

The **operating system (OS)** is the "director" of your computer system's operations. It supervises the overall operation of the computer by monitoring the computer's status, scheduling operations, and managing input and output processes. Well-known desktop operating systems include Microsoft Windows (*www.microsoft.com*), Apple Mac OS X (*www.apple.com*), and open-source Linux (*www.linux.org/*). When a new version with new features is released, the developers often give the new version a new designation. For example, the latest version of Windows is Windows 8, and the latest version of OS X is Mountain Lion or OS X 10.8.

The operating system also provides an interface between the user and the hardware. This user interface hides the complexity of the hardware from the user. That is, you do not have to know how the hardware actually operates; you simply have to know what the hardware will do and what you need to do to obtain the desired results.

The ease or difficulty of the interaction between the user and the computer is determined to a large extent by the graphical user interface. The **graphical user interface (GUI)** allows users to exercise direct control of the hardware through manipulation of visible objects (such as icons) and actions that replace complex commands. Microsoft Windows provides a widely recognized GUI.

The next generation of GUI technology incorporates features such as virtual reality, head-mounted displays, speech input (user commands) and output, pen and gesture recognition, animation, multimedia, artificial intelligence, and cellular/wireless communication capabilities. The new interfaces, called *natural user interfaces* (NUIs), will combine social, haptic, and touch-enabled gesture-control interfaces.

A **social interface** guides the user through computer applications by using cartoonlike characters, graphics, animation, and voice commands. The cartoonlike characters can be puppets, narrators, guides, inhabitants, or avatars (computer-generated humanlike figures). Social interfaces are hard to create without being corny. For example, the assistant "Clippy," an animated paperclip, was so annoying to users of Microsoft Office 97 that the feature was eliminated from Office 2003 onwards.

Touch-enabled gesture-control interfaces enable users to browse through photos, "toss" objects around a screen, "flick" to turn the pages of a book, play video games, and watch movies. Tablet PCs and smart phones make use of this type of interface and some examples include Google's Android, Apple's iPad and iPhone, as well as Microsoft's Surface.

before you go on...

1. Describe the functions of the operating system.

TG 2.4 Application Software

As you saw earlier, application software consists of instructions that direct a computer system to perform specific information-processing activities and also provide functionality for users. Because there are so many different uses for computers, the number of application software programs is correspondingly large.

Application software may be developed in-house by the organization's information systems personnel, or it may be commissioned from a software vendor. Alternatively, the software can be purchased, leased, or rented from a vendor that develops applications and sells them to many organizations. We called this type of software "off-the-shelf" software and it may be a standard package, or it may be customizable. Special-purpose programs or "packages" can be tailored for a specific purpose, such as inventory control or payroll. The word **package** refers to a computer program (or group of programs) that has been developed by a vendor and is available for purchase in a prepackaged form.

General-purpose, off-the-shelf application programs designed to help individual users increase their productivity are referred to as **personal application software**. Some of the major types of personal application software are listed in Table TG 2.1. *Software suites* combine some of these applications and integrate their functions. Microsoft Office is a well-known example of a software suite.

Table TG 2.1

Personal Application Software

Category of Personal Application Software	Major Functions	Examples
Spreadsheet	Uses rows and columns to manipulate primarily numerical data; useful for analyzing financial information and for what-if and goal-seeking analyses.	Microsoft Excel; Corel Quattro Pro; Apple iWork Numbers
Word Processing	Allows users to manipulate primarily text with many writing and editing features.	Microsoft Word; Apple iWork Pages
Desktop Publishing	Extends word processing software to allow production of finished, camera-ready documents, which may contain photographs, diagrams, and other images combined with text in different fonts.	Microsoft® Publisher; QuarkXPress; Adobe InDesign
Data Management	Allows users to store, retrieve, and manipulate related data.	Microsoft Access; FileMaker Pro
Presentation	Allows users to create and edit graphically rich information to appear on electronic slides.	Microsoft PowerPoint; Apple iWork Keynote
Graphics	Allows users to create, store, and display or print charts, graphs, maps, and drawings.	Adobe Photoshop; Corel DRAW
Personal Information Management	Allows users to create and maintain calendars, appointments, to-do lists, and business contacts.	IBM Lotus Notes; Microsoft Outlook
Personal Finance	Allows users to maintain chequebooks, track investments, monitor credit cards, and bank and pay bills electronically.	Quicken; Microsoft Money Plus Sunset
Web Authoring	Allows users to design websites and publish them on the web.	Microsoft Expression Web; Adobe Dreamweaver
Communications	Allows users to communicate with other people over any distance.	Novell Groupwise

Speech-recognition software is an input technology, rather than strictly an application, that can feed systems software and application software. **Speech-recognition software**, also called *voice recognition*, recognizes and interprets human speech, either one word at a time (discrete speech) or in a conversational stream (continuous speech). Advances in processing power, new software algorithms, and better microphones have enabled developers to design extremely accurate voice recognition software. Experts predict that, in the near future, voice-recognition systems will be built into almost every device, appliance, and machine that people use. Applications for voice recognition technology abound. Consider these examples:

- Call centres are using the technology. The average call costs $5 if it is handled by an employee, but only 50 cents with a self-service, speech-enabled system. The on-line brokerage firm E-Trade Financial uses Tellme (*www.tellme.com*) to field about 50,000 calls per day, thereby saving at least $30 million annually.

- Vocera Communications (*www.vocera.com*) has developed a communicator badge that combines voice recognition with wireless technologies. Among its first customers were medical workers, who used the badge to search through hospital directories for the right person to handle a patient problem or to find medical records.

before you go on...

1. What are the differences between systems software and application software?

SOFTWARE

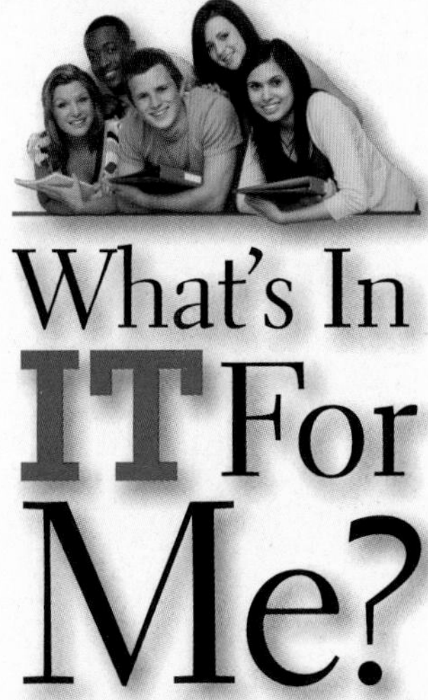

For the Accounting Major

Accounting application software performs the organization's accounting functions, which are repetitive and performed in high volumes. Each business transaction (e.g., a person hired, a paycheque produced, an item sold) produces data that must be captured. Accounting applications capture these data and then manipulate them as necessary. Accounting applications adhere to relatively standardized procedures, handle detailed data, and have a historical focus (i.e., what happened in the past).

For the Finance Major

Financial application software provides information about the firm's financial status to persons and groups inside and outside the firm. Financial applications include forecasting, funds management, and control applications. Forecasting applications predict and project the firm's future activity in the economic environment. Funds management applications use cash flow models to analyze expected cash flows. Control applications enable managers to monitor their financial performance, typically by providing information about the budgeting process and performance ratios.

For the Marketing Major

Marketing application software helps management solve problems that involve marketing the firm's products. Marketing software includes marketing research and marketing intelligence applications. Marketing applications provide information about the firm's products and competitors, its distribution system, its advertising and personal selling activities, and its pricing strategies. Overall, marketing applications help managers develop strategies that combine the four major elements of marketing: product, promotion, place, and price.

For the Production/Operations Management Major

Managers use production/operations management (POM) applications software for production planning and as part of the physical production system. POM applications include production, inventory, quality, and cost software. These applications help management operate manufacturing facilities and logistics. Materials requirements planning (MRP) software also is widely used in manufacturing. This software identifies which materials will be needed, how much will be needed, and the dates on which they will be needed. This information enables managers to be proactive.

For the **Human Resources Management Major**

Human resources management application software provides information concerning recruiting and hiring, education and training, maintaining the employee database, termination, and administering benefits. HRM applications include workforce planning, recruiting, workforce management, compensation, benefits, and environmental reporting subsystems (e.g., employment equity records and analysis, union enrollment, toxic substances, and grievances).

For the **MIS Major**

If your company decides to develop its own software, the MIS function is responsible for managing this activity. If the company decides to buy software, the MIS function deals with software vendors in analyzing their products. The MIS function also is responsible for upgrading software as vendors release new versions.

[Summary]

1. **Discuss the major software issues that confront modern organizations.**

Computer program code often contains errors. The industry recognizes the enormous problem of software defects, but only initial steps are being taken to resolve it. Software licensing is yet another issue for organizations and individuals. Copying proprietary software is illegal. Software vendors copyright their software to protect it from being copied. As a result, companies must license vendor-developed software to use it.

2. **Analyze the advantages and disadvantages of open-source software.**

The advantages of open-source software include high quality, reliability, flexibility (code can be changed to meet users' needs), and low cost. Open-source software can be more reliable than commercial software. Because the code is available to many developers, more bugs are discovered early and quickly and are fixed immediately. Disadvantages include the cost of maintenance support contracts, concerns about ease of use, the time and expense needed to train users, and the lack of compatibility with existing systems both inside and outside the organization.

3. **Differentiate between the two major types of software and describe the general functions of the operating system.**

Software consists of computer programs (coded instructions) that control the functions of computer hardware. There are two main categories of software: systems software and application software. Systems software manages the hardware resources of the computer system; it functions between the hardware and the application software. The major type of systems software is the operating system. Application software enables users to perform specific tasks and information-processing activities. Application software may be proprietary or open source.

Operating systems manage the actual computer resources (i.e., the hardware). They schedule and process applications (jobs); manage and protect memory; manage the input and output functions and hardware; manage data and files; and provide security, fault tolerance, and graphical user interfaces.

4. **Identify the major types of application software.**

The major types of application software are spreadsheet, data management, word processing, desktop publishing, graphics, multimedia, communications, speech recognition, and groupware. Software suites combine several types of application software (e.g., word processing, spreadsheet, and data management) into an integrated package.

[Technology Guide Glossary]

application software The class of computer instructions that directs a computer system to perform specific processing activities and provide functionality for users.

computer programs The sequences of instructions for the computer, which comprise software.

documentation Written description of the functions of a software program.

graphical user interface (GUI) System software that allows users to have direct control of the hardware by manipulating visible objects (such as icons) and actions, which replace command syntax.

open-source software Software made available in source-code form at no cost to developers.

open systems Computing products that work together by using the same operating system with compatible software on all the computers that interact in an organization.

operating system (OS) The main system control program, which supervises the overall operations of the computer, allocates CPU time and main memory to programs, and provides an interface between the user and the hardware.

package A computer program developed by a vendor and available for purchase in prepackaged form.

personal application software General-purpose, off-the-shelf application programs that support general types of processing, rather than being linked to any specific business function.

proprietary software Software that has been developed by a company and has restrictions on its use, copying, and modification.

social interface A user interface that guides the user through computer applications by using cartoonlike characters, graphics, animation, and voice commands.

software A set of computer programs that enable the hardware to process data.

speech-recognition software Software that recognizes and interprets human speech, either one word at a time (discrete speech) or in a stream (continuous speech).

systems software The class of computer instructions that serve primarily as an intermediary between computer hardware and application programs; provides important self-regulatory functions for computer systems.

[Discussion Question]

1. You are the CIO of your company, and you have to develop an application of strategic importance to your firm. What are the advantages and disadvantages of using open-source software?
2. What are the implications for the users if a company decides to switch from its current proprietary operating system to an open-source operating system?
3. What would be the costs and benefits associated with this decision? Make a table outlining the costs and benefits of an open-source operating system.
4. Would you consider the following software solutions to be systems software or application software? Justify your answer.
   a. ERP
   b. Database management system
   c. Accounting software
   d. Customer relationship management
5. What would be the implications if a company allows users to choose the type of operating system (for example, Windows, Macintosh, or Linux) they want in their work computers? Explore both the benefits/advantages and costs/disadvantages.

[Problem-Solving Activities]

1. A great deal of free software is available over the Internet. Go to *www.pcmag.com/article2/0,2817,2381591,00.asp*, and observe all the software available for free. Choose a software program, and download it to your computer. Prepare a brief discussion about the software for your class.
2. Enter the IBM website (*www.ibm.com*) and perform a search on the term "software." Click on the drop box for Products and notice how many software products IBM produces. Is IBM only a hardware company?
3. Compare the following proprietary software packages with their open-source software counterparts. Prepare your comparison for the class.

Proprietary	Open Source
Microsoft Office	Google Docs, OpenOffice
Adobe Photoshop	Google Picasa

4. Compare the Microsoft Surface interface with Oblong Industries' g-speak spatial operating environment. Demonstrate examples of both interfaces to the class. What are the advantages and disadvantages of each?

Technology Guide 3

Emerging Types of Enterprise Computing

[LEARNING OBJECTIVES]

1. Describe the evolution of IT infrastructure.
2. Describe a server farm.
3. Define "virtualization," and discuss its advantages.
4. Define "grid computing," and discuss its advantages.
5. Define "utility computing," and discuss its advantages.
6. Define "cloud computing," and analyze its advantages and disadvantages.
7. Define and discuss "web services" and "service-oriented architecture."

[CHAPTER OUTLINE]

[WEB RESOURCES]

Student Companion Site

wiley.com/college/rainer

- Student PowerPoints for note taking
- Complete glossary

WileyPlus

All of the above and 

- E-book
- Mini-lecture by author for each chapter section
- Practice quizzes
- Flash Cards for vocabulary review
- Additional "What's in IT for Me?" cases
- Video interviews with managers
- Lab Manual for Microsoft Office 2010
- How-to Animations for Microsoft Office 2010

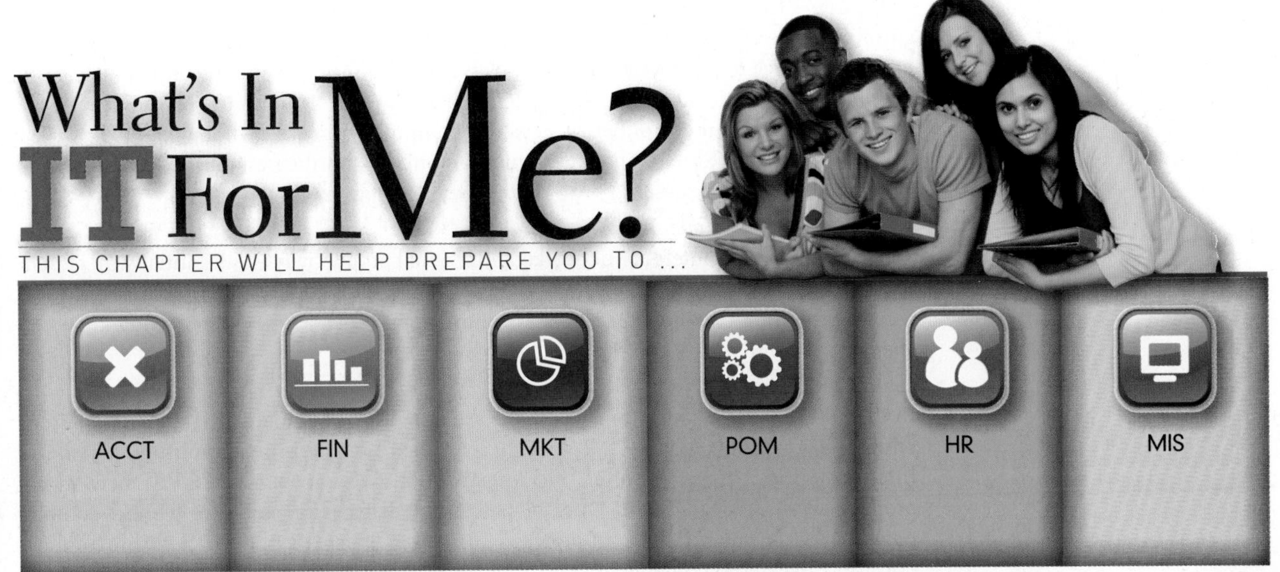

Because the overall goal of this book is to make you an informed user of information technology, we devote this Technology Guide to a vital and cutting-edge topic: emerging systems of enterprise computing. A working knowledge of the topics discussed here will enhance your appreciation of what technology can and cannot do for a business. In addition, it will enable you to make an immediate contribution by analyzing how your organization manages its information technology assets.

You will be using these computing resources yourself in your career, and you also will provide input into your department's or organization's decisions on how best to use them. Finally, these resources—particularly cloud computing—can be extremely valuable if you decide to start your own business.

TG 3.1 Introduction

You were introduced to the concept of IT infrastructure in Chapter 1. Recall that an organization's *IT infrastructure* consists of IT components—hardware, software, networks, and databases—and IT services—developing information systems, managing security and risk, and managing data. (Review Figure 1.3 here.) The organization's IT infrastructure is the foundation for all of the information systems that the organization uses.

Modern IT infrastructure has evolved through several stages since the early 1950s, when firms first began to apply information technology to business applications. These stages are:

- *Stand-alone mainframe*
  Organizations initially used mainframe computers in their engineering and accounting departments. The mainframe typically was housed in a secure area, and only MIS personnel had access to it.
- *Mainframe and dumb terminals*
  Forcing users to go to wherever the mainframe was located was time consuming and inefficient. As a result, firms began placing so-called dumb terminals—essentially electronic typewriters with little processing power—in user departments. This arrangement enabled users to input computer programs into the mainframe from their departments, a process called *remote job entry*.
- *Stand-alone personal computers*
  In the late 1970s, the first personal computers appeared. The IBM PC's debut in 1981 legitimized the entire personal computer market. Users began bringing personal computers to the workplace to improve their productivity (for example, by using spreadsheet and word processing applications). These computers initially were not supported by the firm's MIS department. When the number of personal computers increased dramatically, however, organizations decided to support personal computers, and they established policies as to which personal computers and software they would support.
- *Local area networks (client/server computing)*
  When personal computers are networked, individual productivity is substantially increased. For this reason, organizations began to connect personal computers into local area networks (LANs), and then connected these LANs to the mainframe, a type of processing known as *client/server computing*.
- *Enterprise computing*
  In the early 1990s, organizations began to use networking standards to integrate different kinds of networks throughout the firm, thereby creating enterprise computing. When the Internet became widespread after 1995, organizations began using the TCP/IP networking protocol to integrate different types of networks. All types of hardware were eventually networked, from mainframes, to personal computers, to smart phones. Software applications and data now could flow seamlessly throughout the enterprise and between and among organizations.

- *Cloud computing and mobile computing*
  Today, organizations can use the power of cloud computing. As you will see in this Technology Guide, cloud computing provides access to a shared pool of computing resources (including computers, storage, applications, and services) over a network, typically the Internet.

Keep in mind that the computing resources in each stage can be cumulative. For instance, in addition to all the other types of computing resources, most large firms still use mainframe computers as large servers to manage operations that involve millions of transactions per day. They also employ mainframes to operate corporate websites.

TG 3.2 Server Farms

A company that does not have enough computer processing power to meet its needs can simply buy more servers. Recall that a *server* is a computer that supports networks, enabling users to share files, software, and network devices. The problem then becomes where to install all the servers and how to manage them. As a solution, some companies are building massive data centres called **server farms**, which contain hundreds or thousands of networked computer servers (see Figure TG 3.1).

The huge number of servers in a server farm provides redundancy and fault tolerance. This means that if one computer on the grid fails, the application it was running is automatically "rolled over" to another computer. Server farms require massive amounts of electrical power, air conditioning, backup generators, and security, and must be located fairly close to fibre optic communications links.

Locations satisfying these requirements are difficult to find; however, the access to cheap, clean, and reliable energy and the ability to provide "free cooling" is making Canada a very attractive place to build and operate server farms and data centres. Free cooling is a technology

FIGURE TG 3.1 Server farm. (*Source:* Media Bakery)

that uses cold air from outside to cool off the rooms where servers are located. A company can save as much as 50 percent of the costs associated with cooling by using free cooling. Several businesses are already benefiting from free cooling, including IBM (*www.ibm.com*), the Bank of Montreal (*www.bmo.com*), and TD Canada Trust (*www.tdcanadatrust.com*)—all of which operate data centres in Barrie, Ontario. Other businesses such as Fujitsu Canada (*www.fujitsu.com/ca/*) and even Facebook (*www.facebook.com*) are also planning to open new data centre facilities in Canada and take advantage of what Canada has to offer.

TG 3.3 Virtualization

According to Gartner Inc. (*www.gartner.com*), a research firm, typical utilization rates on servers range from 5 to 10 percent; that is, most of the time, organizations use only a small percentage of their total computing capacity. One reason for this low rate is that most organizations buy a new server every time they implement a new application. CIOs tolerate this inefficiency to ensure that they can supply enough computing resources to users, when needed. Also, because server prices have dropped more than 80 percent in the last decade, it is easier and cheaper to buy another server than to increase use of existing servers. Virtualization, however, has changed this situation.

Virtualization is a system in which servers do not have to be dedicated to particular tasks. **Server virtualization** uses software-based partitions to create multiple virtual servers—called *virtual machines*—on a single physical server. This arrangement enables multiple applications to run on a single physical server, with each application running within its own software environment. Organizations that employ virtualization enjoy many benefits, including the following:

- A lower number of physical servers generates cost savings in equipment, energy, space in the data centre, cooling, personnel, and maintenance.
- Virtualization enhances an organization's agility by enabling it to quickly modify its systems in response to changing demands.
- The IT department can shift its focus from the technology itself to the services that the technology can provide.

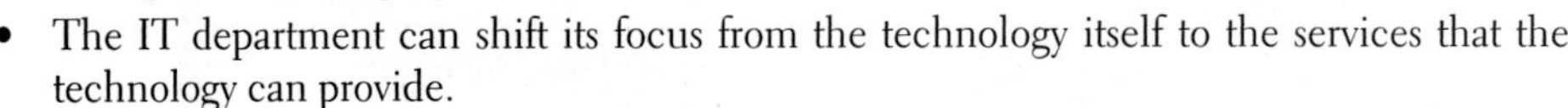

Example TG 3.1, involving MaximumASP, illustrates the benefits of virtualization.

Example TG 3.1

MaximumASP is a web-hosting company based in Louisville, Kentucky. Its 35 employees host more than 48,000 domains for customers located in more than 60 countries. MaximumASP prides itself on its innovative offerings and its dedication to customer service. Unfortunately, the company's rapid expansion resulted in a proliferation of servers that required increasing amounts of resources to manage. This situation adversely affected the company's bottom line. Further, adding servers pulled staff away from researching new services, which diminished the company's agility and innovation.

In many parts of the world, web hosting has become extremely competitive and even commoditized; that is, customers see web hosting as an interchangeable service to buy based on the lowest price. The CIO for MaximumASP notes that there is tremendous market pressure to develop new products, but pricing tends to be commoditized. To offer new services, MaximumASP had to add new servers, which increased the company's costs.

MaximumASP added hundreds of new servers every year, each of which took roughly four hours to deploy. The company spent so much time deploying new servers that it no longer could respond quickly to its customers' needs or its competitors' moves. MaximumASP also wanted to reduce not only the rising cost of physical servers but also their related real estate and power costs, since the company was spending thousands of dollars every year on new hardware, software licences, and electrical power. Finally, the firm was concerned that if it continued to deploy more servers, it would outgrow its Louisville data centre and have to build another one. Funding new servers each year was especially inefficient because most of the company's existing servers operated at a very low capacity, often 5 percent or less.

MaximumASP decided to implement Microsoft's server virtualization technology, and the results have been remarkable. The company was able to set up between 5 and 10 virtual machines on each physical server, which saved $350,000 in hardware costs alone. In addition, the technology enabled MaximumASP to utilize its data centre floor space much more efficiently, thereby eliminating the need for building a new data centre. Further, average server utilization increased dramatically, from 5 percent to 65 percent.

And the bottom line? MaximumASP used virtualization to expand its product offerings, enhance its business agility, and improve its customer service, while actually lowering its operating costs.

TG 3.4 Grid Computing

Grid computing combines the unused processing resources of many geographically dispersed computers in a network to form a virtual supercomputer. Grid computing usually targets scientific or technical problems that require a large amount of computer processing and access to large amounts of data. Applications that run on a grid computing system are divided among multiple servers in the grid, with each server processing a particular component of the application. After processing has been completed, the results from the application must be reassembled from the participating servers.

Grid computing provides many benefits to organizations. Specifically, it:

- Enables organizations to use computing resources more efficiently. Applications can run on the organization's otherwise unused computer capacity.
- Enables applications to run faster.
- Provides fault tolerance and redundancy. Further, because there is no single point of failure, the failure of one computer will not stop an application from executing.
- Makes it easy to "scale up" (add computers) to meet the processing demands of complex applications.
- Makes it easy to "scale down" (remove computers) when extensive processing is not needed.

Example TG 3.2 illustrates how Digital Dimension uses grid computing to its advantage.

Example TG 3.2

Most blockbuster movies today rely on some kind of special effects created by computer. Grid computing is ideal for such intense and demanding applications.

Montreal-based Digital Dimension (*www.digitaldimension.com*) is an award-winning studio that specializes in high-end visual effects, three-dimensional animation, and motion graphics for the film and television industries. The studio has provided the effects in many popular movies and television shows, including *Clash of the Titans*, *The Last Samurai*, *LOST*, and *Alias*. It has won six Emmy awards for its work and three Visual Effects Society awards.

As Digital Dimension's business grew, so did the complexity of its IT infrastructure. Creating special effects in action movies, for example, requires a tonne of computing power. The company acquired a lot of expensive hardware and specialized software. Often, the studio's graphics software packages would only work on computers set up with specific applications. When the studio was working on a multitude of projects with different requirements and

Sources: Compiled from "MaximumASP," *Microsoft Virtualization Case Study*, 2011; *www.maximumasp.com*, accessed May 31, 2013.

deadlines, managing all the studio's applications was becoming cumbersome. Scheduling staff and computing resources to get jobs done on time was difficult.

In order to get the additional computing resources needed to meet heavy application processing demands, the company decided to implement a grid computing solution from Digipede Technologies (*www.digipede.net*). This has provided Digital Dimension with the ability to manage multiple applications without having to acquire additional computers.

TG 3.5 Utility Computing

In **utility computing**, a service provider makes computing resources and infrastructure management available to a customer as needed. The provider then charges the customer for specific usage rather than a flat rate. Utility computing is also called *subscription computing* and *on-demand computing*. Utility computing enables companies to efficiently meet fluctuating demands for computing power by lowering the cost of owning hardware infrastructure.

before you go on...

1. What are the main stages in the development of IT infrastructure?
2. Describe server farm
3. Describe virtualization
4. Describe grid computing
5. Describe utility computing

TG 3.6 Cloud Computing

Every year, companies spend billions of dollars on IT infrastructure and expert staffs to build and maintain complex information systems. Software licensing (discussed in Technology Guide 2), hardware integration, power and cooling, and staff training and salaries add up to a large amount of money for an infrastructure that often is not used to its full capacity. Enter cloud computing.

In **cloud computing**, tasks are performed by computers that are physically removed from the user. Users access computers in the cloud over a network, in particular the Internet. The cloud is composed of the computers, the software on those computers, and the network connections among those computers. The computers in the cloud typically are located in data centres, or server farms, which can be located anywhere in the world and accessed from anywhere in the world (see Figure TG 3.2).

A cloud can be private or public. A *public cloud* is maintained by an external cloud service provider (such as Amazon Web Services), accessed through the Internet, and available to the general public. A *private cloud* is a proprietary data centre that integrates servers, storage, networks, data, and applications as a set of services that users share inside a company. Both public and private clouds are able to allocate storage, computing power, applications, and other resources on an as-needed basis.

The primary advantage of cloud computing is that it dramatically lowers infrastructure costs. The disadvantages consist of privacy, security, and reliability concerns. Example TG 3.3

Sources: Compiled from "Digital Dimension Increases Capacity with the Digipede Network," Digipede Customer Case Study, 2011; *www.digipede.net*, *www.digitaldimension.com*, accessed May 31, 2013.

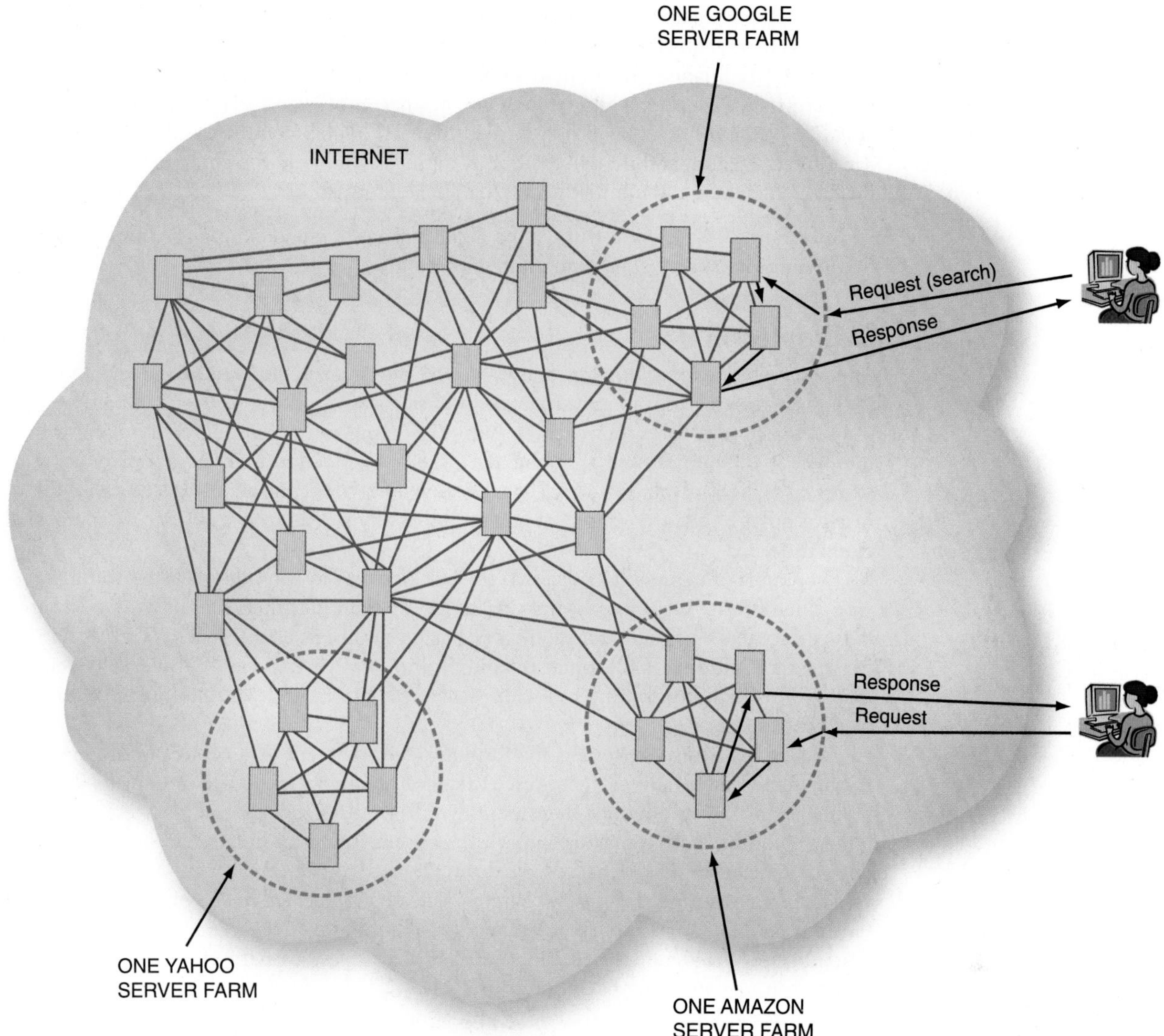

FIGURE TG 3.2 Organizational server farms in relation to the Internet.

relates the case of a well-known brewer that has embraced cloud computing in order to support the expansion of its business.

Example TG 3.3

Molson Coors Brewing Company (*www.molsoncoors.com*) is a multinational brewery with more than 65 leading beer brands, including Canadian, Molson, and Coors. It operates in 30 countries through its five subsidiaries. In recent years the company has experienced a tremendous amount of growth through a number of acquisitions, mainly in international markets such as Europe. One of those recent acquisitions was the central and eastern European brewery giant StarBev, with over 4,100 employees, and brewing operations in the Czech Republic, Serbia, Croatia, Romania, Bulgaria, Hungary, and Montenegro.

This massive expansion brought added pressure to Molson's IT infrastructure. In response, the company recently announced that it will be using Hewlett Packard's (HP) cloud platform to manage its finance and human resources systems. If the experience is successful, the company might consider adding some more business processes to HP's cloud platform. These cloud computing services will be provided from HP global centres based in Canada, Costa Rica, India, Poland, and the United States, and it should help the company to reduce costs, increase efficiency, and improve access to critical information.

In Example TG 3.4, you will see the disadvantages of cloud computing from the perspective of Amazon.com, a cloud computing provider.

Example TG 3.4

Amazon Web Services (*http://aws.amazon.com*), the Amazon cloud, is designed with backups to the backups' backups to prevent hosted websites and applications from failing. Despite all of these safety measures, however, in April 2011, Amazon's cloud crashed, taking with it a number of different websites, including Quora (*www.quora.com*), FourSquare (*www.foursquare.com*), parts of the *New York Times* (*www.nytimes.com*), and about 70 other websites. The massive outage raised questions about the reliability of Amazon Web Services and of the cloud itself.

Thousands of companies use Amazon Web Services to run their websites through a service called Elastic Compute Cloud (EC2). Rather than host their sites on their own servers, these customers essentially rent some of Amazon's unused server capacity. EC2 is hosted in five regions: Virginia, California, Ireland, Tokyo, and Singapore. Within each region are multiple "availability zones," and within each availability zone are multiple "locations" or data centres.

Amazon assured its customers that its network of different data centres would protect the system from isolated failures. It promised to keep customers' sites up and running 99.95 percent of the year or it would reduce their monthly bills by 10 percent. Based on these claims, customers could be down a maximum of just 4.4 hours in a year. In fact, during the April 2011 outage, some customers' websites were down for days.

The crash occurred at Amazon's Virginia data centre, located in one of the company's East Coast availability zones. Amazon blamed the failure on a "networking event" that caused a domino effect across other availability zones in that region, which in turn caused many of its storage volumes to create backups of themselves. That process filled up Amazon's available storage capacity and prevented some websites from accessing their data. Amazon did not reveal what the "networking event" was.

Websites like Quora were able to come back on-line in read-only mode, meaning that users could not post new content for many hours. Many experts blamed Amazon's customers themselves, saying that they should have spread out the processing for their hosted websites among multiple geographical regions to take full advantage of Amazon's backup systems.

Amazon's cloud came down again in June, October, and December 2012. GoDaddy's cloud (*www.godaddy.com*) crashed in September 2012. Facebook, CloudFlare (*www.cloudflare.com*), Google Drive (*https://drive.google.com*), and Microsoft's (*www.windowsazure.com*) clouds all failed in the first quarter of 2013.

Some companies have been able to mitigate the risk of IT failure by not putting all their cloud computing "eggs" in the same basket. This was the case of Voices.com, a Canadian company based in London, Ontario. Voices.com uses Amazon Web Services for its on-line database, where it stores audio files of more than 25,000 voice actors for such studios as DreamWorks and networks that include NBC, ABC, and the History Channel. At the time of Amazon's cloud failure, Voices.com kept about 20 terabytes of voice files with Amazon. When the Amazon cloud came down, Voices.com was also using other cloud computing providers in different parts of its business: Google Docs and Google Apps for its office applications and

Sources: Compiled from "HP Helps Molson Coors Move to Cloud," HP press release, *www.hp.ca*, March 11, 2013; C. Boodoosingh, "Molson Coors Taps HP for Cloud Hosting Services," Digitalhome.ca, March 18, 2013.

Gmail as its e-mail platform. This diversification strategy proved to be very effective for Voices.com, which was able to access its audio files stored on Amazon servers within the next 90 minutes after the failure happened, compared with the several days that it took some of the other Amazon customers.

Cloud computing consists of three different types of services:

- *Cloud infrastructure as a service:* Customers use processing, storage, networking, and other computing resources from cloud service providers to operate their information systems. Amazon, for example, sells the spare capacity of its vast IT infrastructure to its customers in a cloud environment. These services include its Simple Storage Service (S3) for storing customers' data, and its Elastic Compute Cloud (EC2) service for operating their applications. Customers pay only for the amount of storage and computing they use.
- *Cloud platform as a service:* Customers use IT infrastructure and programming tools hosted by the cloud service provider to develop their own applications. For instance, IBM provides a Smart Business Application Development and Test service for software development and testing on the IBM cloud. Also, Salesforce.com allows developers to build applications on the Salesforce cloud.
- *Cloud software as a service:* Customers use software that is hosted by a cloud service provider on the provider's hardware and delivered to customers over a network. You learned about software-as-a-service in Chapter 11.

TG 3.7 Emerging Software Trends

Today, several emerging software trends are having a significant impact on organizations. Among the major trends are open-source software, software-as-a-service, web services, and service-oriented architecture. We discussed the first two trends in Technology Guide 2 and Chapter 11, respectively. In this section we examine web services and service-oriented architecture.

Web Services

Web services are applications delivered over the Internet that MIS professionals can select and combine through almost any device, from personal computers to mobile phones. By using a set of shared standards, or protocols, these applications enable different systems to "talk" with one another—that is, to share data and services—without requiring human beings to translate the conversations.

Web services have great potential because they can be used in a variety of environments (for example, over the Internet, on an intranet inside a corporate firewall, or on an extranet set up by business partners). Or a web service that checks a consumer's credit could be used with a service that processes a mortgage application or a credit card application.

Web services perform a wide variety of tasks, from automating business processes, to integrating components of an enterprise-wide system, to streamlining on-line buying and selling.

They provide numerous benefits for organizations, including the following:

- The organization can use the existing Internet infrastructure without having to implement any new technologies.
- Organizational personnel can access remote or local data without having to understand the complexities of this process.
- The organization can create new applications quickly and easily.

Sources: Compiled from C. Brooks, "A Crack in the Cloud: Why the Amazon Outage Caught So Many by Surprise," *Search-CloudComputing.com*, April 27, 2011; D. Goldman, "Why Amazon's Cloud Titanic Went Down," *CNN Money*, April 22, 2011; J. Brodkin, "Amazon EC2 Outage Calls 'Availability Zones' into Question," *CIO*, April 21, 2011; N. Arellano, "Firm Averts Amazon Cloud Crash by 'Spreading Out the Risk,'" ITBusiness.ca, April 26, 2011; B. Wachtel, "The Cloud Crashed – Again: Understanding 'The Cloud,'" *http://wisdomforawiredworld.com, April 23, 2013; http://aws.amazon.com*, accessed May 21, 2011.

Web services are based on four key protocols: XML, SOAP, WSDL, and UDDI. You will learn about each one below.

Extensible markup language (XML) makes it easier to exchange data among a variety of applications and to validate and interpret these data. XML is a more powerful and flexible markup language than *hypertext markup language (HTML)*, a page-description language for specifying how text, graphics, video, and sound are placed on a web page. Whereas HTML is limited to describing how data should be presented in the form of web pages, XML can perform presentation, communication, and storage of data. For example, in XML a number is not simply a number. The XML tag specifies whether the number represents a price, a date, or a postal code. Consider the following example of XML, which identifies the contact information for Jane Smith.

```
<contact-info>
<name>Jane Smith</name>
<company>Bell Canada</company>
<phone>(416) 555-4567</phone>
</contact-info>
```

Simple object access protocol (SOAP) is a set of rules that define how messages can be exchanged among different network systems and applications through the use of XML. These rules establish a common protocol that enables different web services to interoperate. For example, Visual Basic clients can use SOAP to access a Java server. SOAP runs on all hardware and software systems.

The *web services description language (WSDL)* is used to create the XML document that describes the tasks performed by the various web services. Tools such as VisualStudio.NET automate the process of accessing the WSDL, reading it, and coding the application to reference the specific web service.

Universal description, discovery, and integration (UDDI) allows MIS professionals to search for needed web services by creating public or private searchable directories of these services. In other words, UDDI is the registry of descriptions of web services.

Service-Oriented Architecture

A **service-oriented architecture (SOA)** is an IT architecture that makes it possible to construct business applications using web services. Software vendor Epicor (*www.epicor.com*) provides an ERP (enterprise resource planning) system developed on a SOA. This allows a company to make quick changes to Epicor's ERP system (for example, when a new ERP module needs to be added or updated). SOA is an example of an IT architecture that allows for plug-and-play software deployments.

Take the example of TD Canada Trust. Through a number of recent mergers and acquisitions, it has ended up with several disparate technology applications running on a variety of platforms. TD Canada Trust looked at SOA and web services in an effort to take the legacy systems from the companies it acquired and integrate them with its own system.

before you go on...

1. Define "cloud computing."
2. Discuss the advantages and disadvantages of cloud computing.
3. Describe the function of web services.
4. Describe the function of service-oriented architectures.

For all Business Majors

As with hardware (Technology Guide 1), the design of enterprise IT architectures has profound impacts for business people. Personal and organizational success can depend on an understanding of these architectures and a commitment to knowing the opportunities and challenges they will bring.

At the organizational level, server farms, virtualization, and grid/utility/cloud computing make the IT function more efficient and effective, save the organization money, and contribute to the environment because they are "green" technologies. Web services and SOA make the organization more flexible when deploying new IT applications.

At the individual level, you will be only peripherally concerned with server farms, virtualization, grid computing, utility computing, web services, and SOA. If you want to be an entrepreneur, you most likely will be involved with cloud computing (see "IT's About Business 1.2, "Build Your Own Multinational Company" in Chapter 1).

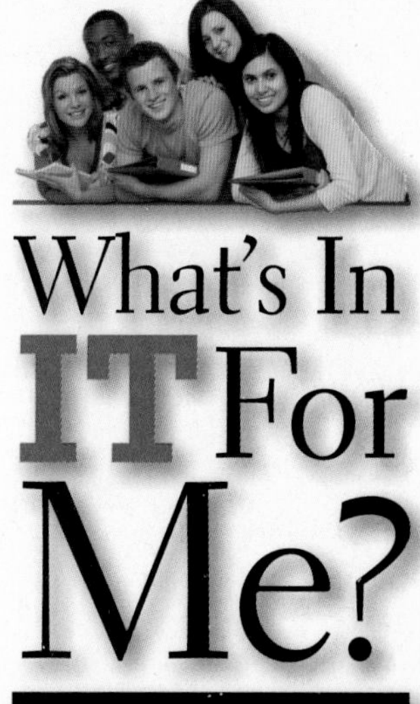

[Summary]

1. **Describe the evolution of IT infrastructure.**

   The IT infrastructure in organizations has evolved through these stages:
   - The stand-alone mainframe
   - Mainframe and dumb terminals
   - Stand-alone personal computers
   - Local area networks (client/server computing)
   - Enterprise computing
   - Cloud computing and mobile computing

2. **Describe a server farm.**

   Server farms are massive data centres, which may contain hundreds or thousands of networked computer servers.

3. **Define "virtualization," and discuss its advantages.**

   Server virtualization is a technology that typically is used in server farms. This technology divides physical servers into several software-based partitions. These partitions allow one physical server to run multiple applications, with each application having its own partition. The benefits of virtualization include:
   - A lower number of physical servers leads to cost savings in equipment, energy, space in the data centre, cooling, personnel, and maintenance.
   - Organizational agility is enhanced.
   - The focus of the information technology department can shift from the technology itself to the services that the technology can provide.

4. **Define "grid computing," and discuss its advantages.**

   Grid computing combines the unused processing resources of many geographically dispersed computers in a network to form a virtual supercomputer.

   Grid computing provides many benefits to organizations. Specifically, it:
   - Enables more efficient use of computing resources: Applications can run on the otherwise unused capacity of the organization's computers.

- Enables applications to run faster.
- Provides fault tolerance and redundancy: If one computer on the grid fails, the application running on it is automatically "rolled over" to another computer. Further, because there is no single point of failure, the failure of one computer will not stop an application from executing.
- Makes it easy to "scale up" (add computers) to meet the processing demands of complex applications.
- Makes it easy to "scale down" (remove computers) when extensive processing is not needed.

5. **Define "utility computing," and discuss its advantages.**

   In utility computing, a service provider makes computing resources and infrastructure management available to a customer as needed. Utility computing enables companies to efficiently meet fluctuating demands for computing power by lowering the cost of owning hardware infrastructure.

6. **Define "cloud computing," and analyze its advantages and disadvantages.**

   With cloud computing, tasks are performed by computers physically removed from the user and accessed over a network, in particular the Internet. The advantages of cloud computing include much lower infrastructure costs; disadvantages include privacy, security, and reliability concerns.

7. **Define and discuss "web services" and "service-oriented architecture."**

   Web services are applications delivered over the Internet that MIS professionals can select and combine through almost any device, from personal computers to mobile phones. A service-oriented architecture makes it possible for MIS professionals to construct business applications using web services.

[Technology Guide Glossary]

cloud computing A technology in which tasks are performed by computers physically removed from the user and accessed over a network, in particular, the Internet.

grid computing A technology that combines the unused processing resources of many geographically dispersed computers in a network to form a virtual supercomputer.

server farm A massive data centre, which may contain hundreds or thousands of networked computer servers.

server virtualization A technology that uses software-based partitions to create multiple virtual servers (called *virtual machines*) on a single physical server.

service-oriented architecture (SOA) An IT architecture that makes it possible to construct business applications using web services.

utility computing A technology in which a service provider makes computing resources and infrastructure management available to a customer as needed.

web services Applications delivered over the Internet that users can select and combine through almost any device, from personal computers to mobile phones.

[Discussion Questions]

1. What is the value of server farms and virtualization to any large organization?
2. If you were the chief information officer (CIO) of a firm, how would you explain the workings, benefits, and limitations of cloud computing?
3. What is the value of cloud computing to a small organization?
4. What is the value of cloud computing to an entrepreneur who is starting a business?

[Problem-Solving Activity]

1. Investigate the status of cloud computing by researching the offerings of these leading vendors. Produce a table highlighting the differences among the vendors.
   - Dell (see, e.g., *www.dell.com/learn/us/en/555/dell-cloud-computing?c=us&l=en&s=biz*)
   - Oracle (see, e.g., *www.oracle.com/technetwork/topics/cloud/whatsnew/index.html*)
   - IBM (see, e.g., *www.ibm.com/cloud-computing/*)
   - Amazon (see, e.g., *http://aws.amazon.com*)
   - Microsoft (see, e.g., *www.windowsazure.com*)
   - Google (see, e.g., *https://cloud.google.com/products/compute-engine*)

Technology Guide

Intelligent Systems

[LEARNING OBJECTIVES]

1. Differentiate between artificial intelligence and human intelligence.
2. Define "expert systems," and provide examples of their use.
3. Define "neural networks," and provide examples of their use.
4. Define "fuzzy logic," and provide examples of its use.
5. Define "genetic algorithms," and provide examples of their use.
6. Define "intelligent agents," and provide examples of their use.

[CHAPTER OUTLINE]

[WEB RESOURCES]

Student Companion Site

wiley.com/college/rainer

- Student PowerPoints for note taking
- Complete glossary

WileyPlus

All of the above and 

- E-book
- Mini-lecture by author for each chapter section
- Practice quizzes
- Flash Cards for vocabulary review
- Additional "What's in IT for Me?" cases
- Video interviews with managers
- Lab Manual for Microsoft Office 2010
- How-to Animations for Microsoft Office 2010

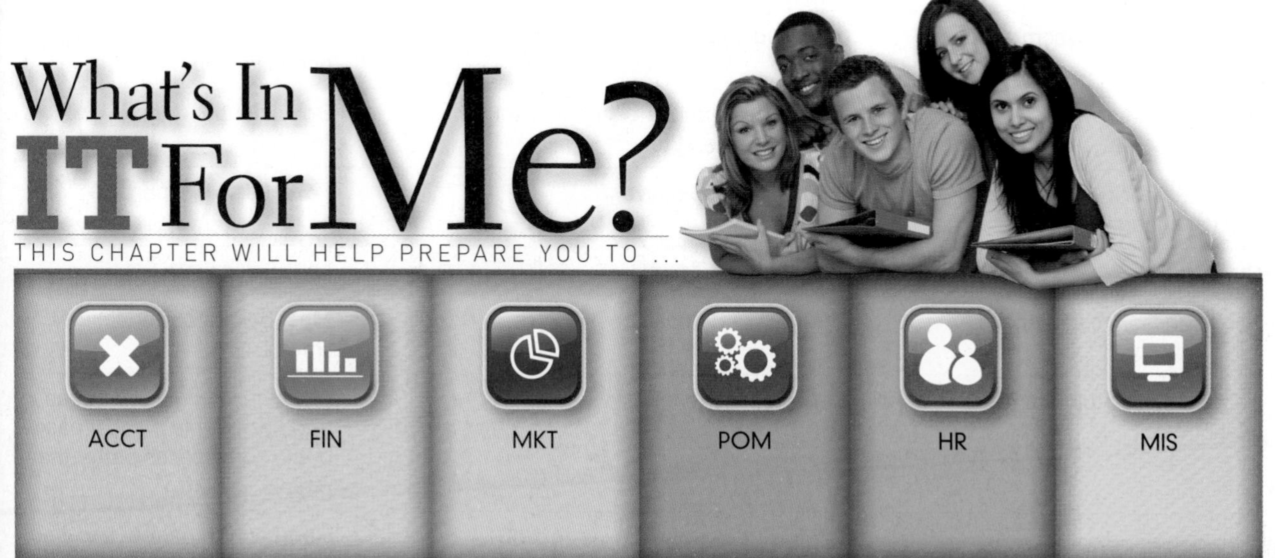

TG 4.1 Introduction

This Technology Guide focuses on information systems that can make decisions by themselves. These systems are called *intelligent systems*. The major categories of intelligent systems are expert systems, neural networks, fuzzy logic, genetic algorithms, and intelligent agents. You will learn about each of these systems in the following sections.

The term **intelligent systems** describes the various commercial applications of artificial intelligence. **Artificial intelligence (AI)** is a subfield of computer science that studies the thought processes of humans and recreates the effects of those processes via machines, such as computers and robots.

One well-publicized definition of AI is "behaviour by a machine that, if performed by a human being, would be considered *intelligent*." This definition raises the question, "What is *intelligent behaviour*?" The following capabilities are considered to be signs of human intelligence: learning or understanding from experience, making sense of ambiguous or contradictory messages, and responding quickly and successfully to new situations.

The ultimate goal of AI is to build machines that mimic human intelligence. A widely used test to determine whether a computer exhibits intelligent behaviour was designed by Alan Turing, a British AI pioneer. The **Turing test** proposes a scenario in which a man and a computer both pretend to be women (or men), and a human interviewer has to identify which is the real human. Based on this standard, the intelligent systems exemplified in commercial AI products are far from exhibiting any significant intelligence.

We can better understand the potential value of AI by contrasting it with natural (human) intelligence. AI has several important commercial advantages over natural intelligence, but it also displays some limitations, as outlined in Table TG 4.1.

Table TG 4.1

Comparison of the Capabilities of Natural vs. Artificial Intelligence

Capabilities	Natural Intelligence	Artificial Intelligence
Preservation of knowledge	Perishable from an organizational point of view	Permanent
Duplication and dissemination of knowledge	Difficult, expensive, takes time	Easy, fast, and inexpensive once in a computer
Total cost of knowledge	Can be erratic and inconsistent, incomplete at times	Consistent and thorough
Documentability of process and knowledge	Difficult, expensive	Fairly easy, inexpensive
Creativity	Can be very high	Low, uninspired
Use of sensory experiences	Direct and rich in possibilities	Must be interpreted first; limited
Recognizing patterns and relationships	Fast, easy to explain	Machine learning still not as good as people in most cases, but in some cases better than people
Reasoning	Making use of wide context of experiences	Good only in narrow, focused, and stable domains

Intelligent systems show up in a number of places, some of them surprising, as the following examples illustrate:

- A good session player is hard to find, but UJAM (*www.ujam.com*) is always ready to rock. This web app doubles as a studio band and a recording studio. It analyzes a melody and then produces sophisticated harmonies, bass lines, drum tracks, horn parts, and more.

  Before UJAM can produce accompaniment, the app must figure out which notes the user is singing or playing. Once UJAM recognizes these, its algorithms use a mix of statistical techniques and programmed musical rules to search for chords to match the tune.
- To the human eye, an X-ray is a murky puzzle. But to a machine, an X-ray—or a CT or MRI scan—is a dense data field that can be assessed down to the pixel level. AI techniques currently are being applied aggressively in the field of medical imaging.

  New software gathers high-resolution image data from multiple sources—X-rays, MRI scans, ultrasounds, CT scans—and then groups together biological structures that share hard-to-detect similarities. For instance, the software can examine several images of the same breast to measure tissue density. The software then colour-codes tissues of similar densities so humans can see the pattern as well.

  The software finds and indexes pixels that share certain properties, even pixels that are far apart in one image or in a different image altogether. This process enables medical personnel to identify hidden features of diffuse structures as well as features within a region of tissue.
- The human brain receives visual information from two eyes. Google's AI system receives visual information from billions of smart phone camera lenses. The company collects these images from users of Google Goggles (*www.google.com/mobile/goggles*), a mobile service that lets users run web searches by taking pictures. Snap a barcode, and Goggles will shop for the item's best price. Take a picture of a book, and users will be linked to, for instance, a Wikipedia page about the book's author. Photograph the Eiffel Tower and Goggles will give you historical background on the landmark.

  The software behind Goggles coordinates the efforts of multiple object-specific recognition databases. There is a database for text, one for landmarks, one for corporate logos, and so on. When an image arrives, Goggles transmits it to each of these databases, which in turn use a variety of visual-recognition techniques to identify potential matches and compute confidence scores. Goggles then applies its own algorithm to decide which result(s), if any, go back to the user. Goggles' next category? Identifying plants.
- Professor Chris Eliasmith and his team have built a model of the human brain at the University of Waterloo, in Ontario. The model uses 2.5 million virtual neurons, and it takes a supercomputer at the university two hours to run the programs that create 1 second of simulation for the virtual brain, called Spaun. The virtual brain can do several functions, primarily working with numbers (such as searching for patterns in a string of numbers). It can also do visual recognition, such as copying and identifying numbers that are handwritten. One difference about this brain simulation is that it also simulates problems that humans have, such as difficulty in remembering the middle numbers in a long string of numbers. The researchers hope that by modelling a brain that is close to human functioning, it can be used for drug testing (for example, by simulating what happens when neurons die), for disease testing, and for creating a computer that humans will more readily be able to interact with.

before you go on...

1. What is artificial intelligence?
2. Differentiate between artificial and human intelligence.

TG 4.2 Expert Systems

When an organization has to make a complex decision or solve a problem, it often turns to experts for advice. These experts have specific knowledge and experience in the problem area. They can offer alternative solutions and predict whether the proposed solutions will succeed. At the same time, they can calculate the costs that the organization may incur if it doesn't resolve the problem. Companies engage experts for advice on such matters as mergers and acquisitions, advertising strategy, and purchasing equipment. The more unstructured the situation, the more specialized and expensive is the advice.

Expertise refers to the extensive, task-specific knowledge acquired from training, reading, and experience. This knowledge enables experts to make better and faster decisions than nonexperts in solving complex problems. Expertise takes a long time (often many years) to acquire, and it is distributed unevenly across organizations.

Expert systems (ESs) are computer systems that attempt to mimic human experts by applying expertise in a specific domain. Expert systems can either *support* decision makers or completely *replace* them. Expert systems are the most widely applied and commercially successful intelligent systems. A fascinating example of an expert system is IBM's Watson.

Example TG 4.1

As the amount of data increases, so do companies' needs to access data quickly and efficiently. Consider the need for speed when searching for information to answer customer questions, like a technical support worker, or to do legal research on behalf of clients that is billed by the hour. Like many business processes, the function of answering questions is becoming increasingly automated.

Since 2007, IBM scientists have been trying to automate one of the most human of abilities: answering questions asked in everyday language, or *natural language*. They even gave their technology a human name: Watson. But unlike Watson's cousins, search engines such as Google and Bing, Watson must supply a precise, factual, correct answer, not merely list hundreds or even thousands of documents that might contain the answer.

Another aspect that separates Watson from search engines is that it has its own knowledge base that needs to be populated with information; it doesn't search the information on the Internet. In fact, it's not even connected to the Internet. IBM employees have to input millions of documents into Watson—including books, reference manuals, dictionaries, encyclopedias, novels, plays, the Bible, and many other information sources. It "knows" only what has been input into its knowledge base.

In order to simulate human thinking, Watson uses more than 100 algorithms, whereas other question-answering systems use only a few, limiting the number of possible answers the technology can provide. Watson analyzes a question in different ways, providing hundreds of possible answers. If several of these answers are similar, other algorithms tell Watson how to rank them by plausibility, suggesting the answers that are the most probable.

One promising application of Watson is in the field of medical diagnosis, requiring knowledge of vast amounts of information on ailments and symptoms. In mid-2011, IBM was training Watson in medicine by inputting medical textbooks and journals. The team planned to link Watson to hospital electronic health records in the United States. In addition, medical students are sending sample questions to Watson to help train it.

When Watson appeared as a contestant on the television show *Jeopardy!*, it had to produce only one correct answer to each question. The medical Watson, in contrast, uses its multiple algorithms to the fullest, offering several possible diagnoses, ranked in order of plausibility. The IBM team designed the medical Watson this way because physicians want to see a list of options, especially since there is always a chance that someone might have a rare illness that doctors might not consider too seriously. The medical Watson will have a diagnosis application and a treatment application.

When Watson completes its virtual medical residency and graduates to the equivalent of an MD, IBM envisions several uses:

- Allowing doctors to interact with Watson virtually using speech-recognition technology and cloud computing
- Acting as a knowledge base for the most advanced research in cancer and other fields
- Serving as an always-available second opinion

Medical Watson does have competition. Isabel Healthcare (*www.isabelhealthcare.com*) offers Isabel, a private medical database already used by several multihospital health systems. Isabel purportedly performs roughly the same functions as the medical Watson system.

Expert systems are also used by human resources management to analyze applicants for available positions. These systems assign "scores" to candidates, lessening the workload for HR managers in the hiring process. Human HR managers still make the final decision, but the expert system provides useful information and recommendations.

The previous examples demonstrated the usefulness of expert systems in a relatively narrow domain. Overall, however, expert systems may not be as useful as users would like. Consider the Microsoft Windows troubleshooting software located in the help section in the taskbar menu. Microsoft has designed its expert system to provide solutions, advice, and suggestions to common errors that users encounter in the operating system. But we have all found that, in some cases, the help section does not provide particularly useful advice.

An ES typically is decision-making software that can perform at a level comparable to a human expert in certain specialized problem areas. Essentially, an ES transfers expertise from a domain expert (or other source) to the computer. This knowledge is then stored in the computer, which users can call on for specific advice as needed. The computer can make inferences and arrive at conclusions. Then, like a human expert, it offers advice or recommendations. In addition, it can explain the logic behind the advice. Because ESs can integrate and manipulate enormous amounts of data, they sometimes perform better than any single expert can.

An often overlooked benefit of expert systems is that they can be embedded in larger systems. For example, credit card issuers use expert systems to process credit card applications.

The transfer of expertise from an expert, to a computer, and then to the user involves four activities:

1. ***Knowledge acquisition.*** Knowledge is acquired from domain experts or from documented sources.
2. ***Knowledge representation.*** Acquired knowledge is organized as rules or frames (object-oriented) and stored electronically in a knowledge base.
3. ***Knowledge inferencing.*** The computer is programmed so that it can make inferences based on the stored knowledge.
4. ***Knowledge transfer.*** The inferenced expertise is transferred to the user in the form of a recommendation.

The Components of Expert Systems

An expert system contains the following components: knowledge base, inference engine, user interface, blackboard (workplace), and explanation subsystem (justifier). In the future, ESs will include a knowledge-refining component as well. You will learn about all these components below. In addition, Figure TG 4.1 diagrams the relationships among these components.

Sources: Compiled from J. Fitzgerald, "IBM Watson Supercomputer Graduates from 'Jeopardy!' to Medicine," *The Huffington Post*, May 21, 2011; C. Thompson, "What is I.B.M.'s Watson?" *The New York Times*, June 14, 2010; *www.ibm.com/innovation/us/watson/index.html*, accessed April 4, 2013.

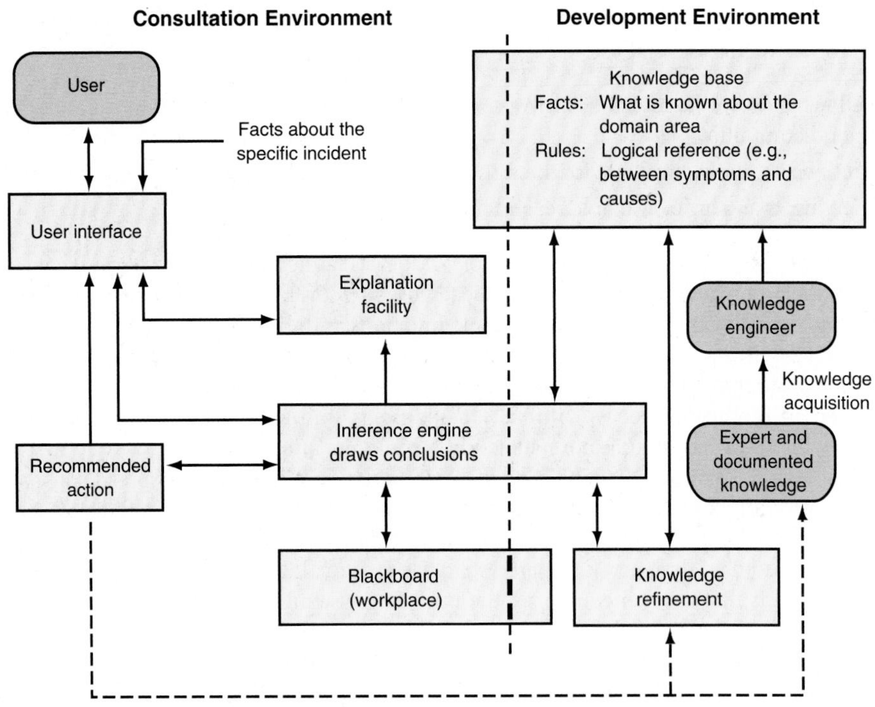

FIGURE TG 4.1 Structure and process of an expert system.

The *knowledge base* contains knowledge necessary for understanding, formulating, and solving problems. It comprises two basic elements: (1) *facts*, such as the problem situation, and (2) *rules* that direct the use of knowledge to solve specific problems in a particular domain.

The *inference engine* is essentially a computer program that provides a methodology for reasoning and formulating conclusions. It enables the system to make inferences based on the stored knowledge. The inference engine is considered the "brain" of the ES.

Here is an example of the reasoning that might be used by a medical expert system for lung cancer treatment:

IF lung capacity is high
AND X-ray results are positive
AND patient has fever
AND patient has coughing
THEN surgery is necessary.
IF tumour has spread
OR contraindications to surgery exist
THEN surgery cannot be performed.

The *user interface* enables users to communicate with the computer. The communication is carried out in a natural language, usually a question-and-answer format, and in some cases is supplemented by graphics. The dialogue between the user and the computer triggers the inference engine to match the problem symptoms with the knowledge contained in the knowledge base and then generate advice.

The *blackboard* is an area of working memory set aside for the description of a current problem, as specified by the input data. Thus, it is a kind of database.

Unique to an ES is its ability to *explain* its recommendations. This function is performed in a subsystem called the *explanation subsystem* or *justifier*. The explanation subsystem interactively answers questions such as the following: *Why* did the ES ask a certain question? *How* did the ES reach a particular conclusion? *What* is the plan to reach the solution?

Human experts have a *knowledge-refining* system; that is, they can analyze their own performance, learn from it, and improve it for future consultations. This type of evaluation is necessary in computerized learning as well so that the program can be improved by analyzing the reasons for its success or failure. Unfortunately, such a component is not available in commercial expert systems at the moment; however, it is being developed in experimental systems.

Applications, Benefits, and Limitations of Expert Systems

Today, expert systems are found in all types of organizations. They are especially useful in the 10 generic categories shown in Table TG 4.2.

During the past few years, thousands of organizations worldwide have successfully applied ES technology to problems ranging from researching AIDS to analyzing dust in mines. Why have ESs become so popular? The answer is, because they provide such a large number of capabilities and benefits. Table TG 4.3 lists the major benefits of ESs.

Despite all of these benefits, expert systems present some problems as well. The difficulties involved with using expert systems include:

- Transferring domain expertise from human experts to the expert system can be difficult because people cannot always explain how they know what they know. Often they are not aware of their complete reasoning process.
- Even if the domain experts can explain their entire reasoning process, automating that process may not be possible: It may be either too complex (requiring too many rules), or too vague.
- In some contexts, there is a potential liability from the use of expert systems. Humans make errors occasionally, but generally are "let off the hook" if they took reasonable care and applied generally accepted methods. An organization that uses an expert system, however, may lack this legal protection if problems arise later. The usual example of this issue is medical treatment, but it can also arise if a business decision driven by an expert system harms someone financially.

Table TG 4.2

Ten Generic Categories of Expert Systems

Category	Problem Addressed
Interpretation	Inferring situation descriptions from observations
Prediction	Inferring likely consequences of given situations
Diagnosis	Inferring system malfunctions from observations
Design	Configuring objects under constraints
Planning	Developing plans to achieve goal(s)
Monitoring	Comparing observations with plans, flagging exceptions
Debugging	Prescribing remedies for malfunctions
Repair	Executing a plan to administer a prescribed remedy
Instruction	Diagnosing, debugging, and correcting student performance
Control	Interpreting, predicting, repairing, and monitoring systems behaviour

Table
TG 4.3

Benefits of Expert Systems

Benefit	Description
Increased output and productivity	ESs can configure components for each custom order, increasing production capabilities.
Increased quality	ESs can provide consistent advice and reduce error rates.
Capture and dissemination of scarce expertise	Expertise from anywhere in the world can be obtained and used.
Operation in hazardous environments	Sensors can collect information that an ES interprets, enabling human workers to avoid hot, humid, or toxic environments.
Accessibility to knowledge and help desks	ESs can increase the productivity of help-desk employees, or even automate this function.
Reliability	ESs do not become tired or bored, call in sick, or go on strike. They consistently pay attention to details.
Ability to work with incomplete or uncertain information	Even with an answer of "don't know," an ES can produce an answer, although it may not be a definite one.
Provision of training	The explanation facility of an ES can serve as a teaching device and a knowledge base for novices.
Enhancement of decision-making and problem-solving capabilities	ESs allow the integration of expert judgement into analysis (for example, diagnosis of machine malfunction and even medical diagnosis).
Decreased decision-making time	ESs usually can make faster decisions than humans working alone.
Reduced downtime	ESs can quickly diagnose machine malfunctions and prescribe repairs.

before you go on...

1. What is an expert system?

2. Describe the benefits and limitations of using expert systems.

TG 4.3 Neural Networks

A **neural network** is a system of programs and data structures that simulates the underlying concepts of the biological brain. A neural network usually involves a large number of processors operating in parallel, each with its own small sphere of knowledge and access to data in its

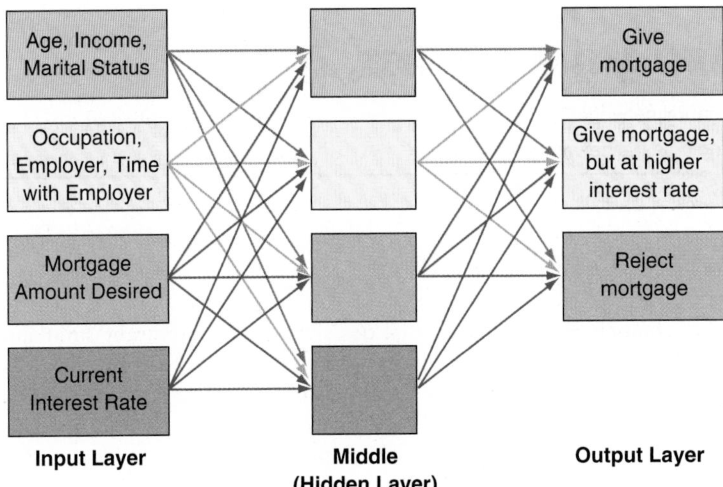

FIGURE TG 4.2 Neural network.

local memory (see Figure TG 4.2). Typically, a neural network is initially "trained" or fed large amounts of data and rules about data relationships.

Neural networks are particularly adept at recognizing subtle, hidden, and newly emerging patterns within complex data, as well as interpreting incomplete inputs. Neural networks can help users solve a wide range of problems, from airline security to infectious disease control. They are the standard for combating fraud in the credit card, health care, and telecom industries, and they are becoming increasingly important in today's stepped-up international efforts to prevent money laundering.

Neural networks are used in a variety of ways, as illustrated by the following examples.

- The Bruce nuclear facility in Ontario has eight nuclear reactors, making it the largest facility in North America and the second largest in the world. The plant uses a neural network in its checkpoint X-ray screening system to detect weapons concealed in personal belongings. The system also identifies biologically dangerous liquids.
- Neural networks are used in research into diseases like Alzheimer's, Parkinson's, and epilepsy. Researchers build robots with simulated rat brains that mimic the rats' neural activity. The researchers then can study the brain's function and its reaction to stimuli.
- Investors employ neural networks to forecast the performance of stock index futures, currencies, natural gas and oil stocks, treasury bond futures, gold stocks, and other major investments.
- In banking systems, neural networks help detect fraud in credit card transactions and insurance claims, fight crime, and gauge customer satisfaction.

Figure TG 4.2 illustrates how a neural network might process a typical mortgage application. Note that the network has three levels of interconnected nodes (similar to the human brain): an input layer; a middle, or hidden, layer; and an output layer. When the neural network is trained, the strengths, or *weights*, of its connections change. In our example, the input nodes are age, income, occupation, marital status, employer, length of time with that employer, amount of mortgage desired, and current interest rate. The neural network has already been trained with data input from many mortgage applications, successful and unsuccessful. That is, the neural network has established a pattern as to which input variables are necessary for a successful mortgage application. Interestingly, the neural network can adjust as both mortgage amounts and interest rates increase or decrease.

before you go on...

1. What are neural networks?
2. Describe how neural networks function.

TG 4.4 Fuzzy Logic

Fuzzy logic is a branch of mathematics that deals with uncertainties by simulating the processes of human reasoning. The rationale behind fuzzy logic is that decision making is not always a matter of black or white, or true or false: It often involves grey areas where the term *maybe* is more appropriate.

A computer programmed to use fuzzy logic precisely defines subjective concepts that humans do not define precisely. For example, for the concept "income," descriptive terms such as "high" and "moderate" are subjective and imprecise. Using fuzzy logic, however, a computer could define "high" incomes as those exceeding $200,000 per year, and "moderate" incomes as those ranging from $150,000 to $200,000 per year. A loan officer at a bank then might use these values when considering a loan application.

Fuzzy logic has also been used in financial analysis and Internet searches. In accounting and finance, fuzzy logic allows you to analyze assets expressed in imprecise values (for example, intangible ones like goodwill). Google uses fuzzy logic to find answers to your search terms, based on your perception of the topic as reflected in how you phrase your query, which determines the relevance of the web pages that Google delivers to you.

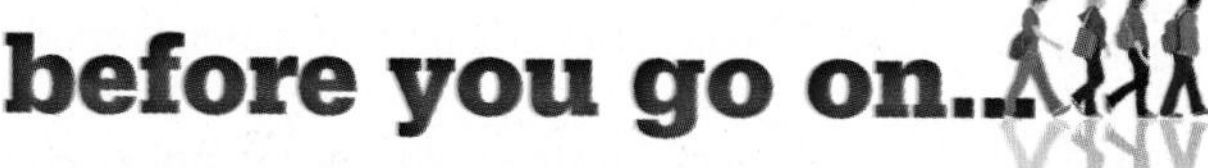

1. What is fuzzy logic?
2. Give some examples where fuzzy logic is used.

TG 4.5 Genetic Algorithms

An algorithm is a problem-solving method expressed as a finite sequence of steps. A **genetic algorithm** mimics the evolutionary, "survival-of-the-fittest" process to generate increasingly better solutions to a problem. That is, a genetic algorithm is an optimizing method that finds the combination of inputs that produces the best outputs. Genetic algorithms have three functional characteristics:

- Selection (survival of the fittest): Giving preference to better and better outcomes.
- Crossover: Combining portions of good outcomes in the hope of creating an even better outcome.
- Mutation: Randomly trying combinations and evaluating the success (or failure) of an outcome.

Genetic algorithms are best suited to decision-making environments in which thousands or millions of solutions are possible. Genetic algorithms can find and evaluate solutions intelligently, and they can process many more possibilities more thoroughly and faster than a human can. Users do have to tell the genetic algorithm what constitutes a "good" solution, which could be low cost or high return, or any number of other results. Let's look at some examples:

- Boeing uses genetic algorithms to design aircraft parts such as the fan blades on its 777 jet. Rolls Royce and Honda also use genetic algorithms in their design processes.

- Retailers such as Marks and Spencer, a British chain that has 320 stores, use genetic algorithms to manage their inventories more effectively and optimize their store displays.
- Air Liquide, a producer of industrial gases, uses genetic algorithms to find optimal production schedules and distribution points in its supply chain. The company, with 40 plants and 8,000 client sites, must consider factors such as power prices and customer demand projections, as well as the power costs and efficiency of each plant.

before you go on...

1. What is a genetic algorithm?
2. Give examples of the use of genetic algorithms.

TG 4.6 Intelligent Agents

An **intelligent agent** is a software program that assists you, or acts on your behalf, in performing repetitive computer-related tasks. Intelligent agents often use expert systems and fuzzy logic behind the scenes to create their seemingly intelligent behaviour.

You may be familiar with an early type of intelligent agent—the paper clip ("Clippy") that popped up in early versions of Microsoft Word. For example, if your document appeared as though it was going to be a business letter—that is, if you typed in a date, name, and address—the animated paper clip would offer helpful suggestions on how to proceed. Users objected so strenuously to this primitive intelligent agent that Microsoft eliminated it from subsequent versions.

There are many intelligent agents (also called *bots*), used for a wide variety of tasks. The following sections examine three types of agents: information agents, monitoring-and-surveillance agents, and user or personal agents.

Information Agents

Information agents search for information and display it to users. The best known information agents are buyer agents. A **buyer agent**, also called a **shopping bot**, helps customers find the products and services they need on a website. There are many examples of information agents. We present a few illustrative cases below.

- The information agents for Amazon.ca display lists of books and other products that customers might like, based on past purchases.

- Google and Ask.com use information agents to find information, and not just when you request it. Google, for example, sends Googlebots out to surf all the websites in Google's index. These bots copy individual pages to Google's repository, where Google's software indexes them. This process means that when you perform a Google search, the search engine builds a list of all the pages that have the keywords you specify and presents them to you in PageRank order. Google's PageRank algorithm sorts web pages based on the number of links on the web that point to each page. That is, the more web links that point to a particular page, the higher that page will be on the list.
- The U.S. Federal Electronic Research and Review Extraction Tool, or FERRET, was developed jointly by the U.S. Census Bureau and the U.S. Bureau of Labor Statistics. Americans can use FERRET to find information on employment, health care, education, race and ethnicity, health insurance, housing, income and poverty, aging, and marriage and the family. In Canada, you can accomplish similar functions at *www.servicecanada.gc.ca/eng/home.shtml*.

Monitoring-and-Surveillance Agents

Monitoring-and-surveillance agents, also called **predictive agents**, constantly observe and report on some item of interest. There are many examples of predictive agents. Consider the following:

- Allstate Insurance uses monitoring-and-surveillance agents to manage its large computer networks 24/7/365. Every 5 seconds, the agent measures 1,200 data points. It can predict a system crash 45 minutes before it happens. The agent also watches to detect electronic attacks early so that they can be prevented. Uptime Software (*www.uptimesoftware.com*) is a company headquartered in Toronto that sells software that includes these types of capabilities.
- Monitoring-and-surveillance agents can watch your competitors and notify you of price changes and special offers.

- Predictive agents can monitor Internet sites, discussion groups, and mailing lists for stock manipulations, insider trading, and rumours that might affect stock prices.
- These agents can search websites for updated information on topics of your choice, such as price changes on desired products (e.g., airline tickets).

User Agents

User agents, also called **personal agents**, take action on your behalf. Let's look at what these agents can do (or will be able to do shortly).

- Check your e-mail, sort it according to your priority rules, and alert you when high-value e-mails appear in your in-box.
- Automatically fill out forms on the web for you. They also will store your information for future use.

before you go on...

1. Define "intelligent agents," "information agents," "monitoring-and-surveillance agents," and "user agents."
2. Explain the uses of each type of intelligent agent.

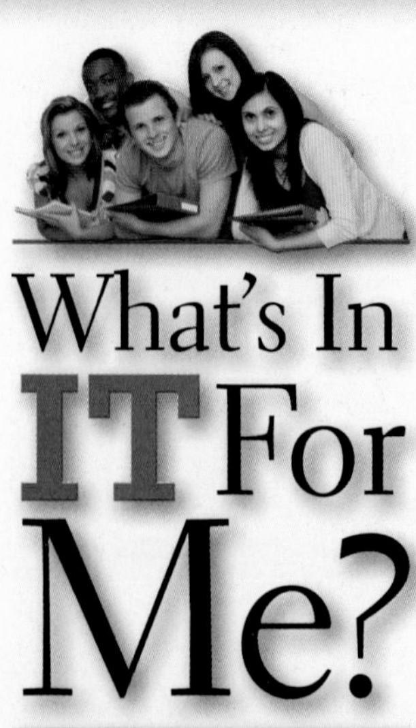

What's In IT For Me?

For the **Accounting Major**

Intelligent systems are used extensively in auditing to uncover irregularities. They are also used to uncover and prevent fraud. Today's accountants use intelligent systems for many of their duties, ranging from risk analysis to cost control. Accounting personnel also use intelligent agents for routine tasks such as managing accounts and monitoring employees' Internet use.

For the **Finance Major**

People have been using computers for decades to solve financial problems. Innovative intelligent applications have been developed for activities such as making stock market decisions, refinancing bonds, assessing debt risks, analyzing financial conditions, predicting business failures, forecasting financial trends, and investing in global markets. Often, intelligent systems can facilitate the use of spreadsheets and other computerized systems used in finance. Finally, intelligent systems can help reduce fraud in the use of credit cards, and other financial services.

For the Marketing Major

Marketing personnel use intelligent systems in many applications, from allocating advertising budgets to evaluating alternative routings of salespeople. New marketing approaches such as targeted marketing and marketing transaction databases are heavily dependent on IT in general and on intelligent systems in particular. Intelligent systems are especially useful for mining customer databases and predicting customer behaviour. Successful applications appear in almost every area of marketing and sales, from analyzing the success of one-to-one advertising to supporting customer help desks. With customer service becoming increasingly important, the use of intelligent agents is critical for providing fast response.

For the Production/Operations Management Major

Intelligent systems support complex operations and production decisions, from inventory to production planning. Many of the early expert systems in the production/operations management field were developed for tasks ranging from diagnosing machine failures and prescribing repairs to complex production scheduling and inventory control. Some companies, such as DuPont and Kodak, have deployed hundreds of ESs in the planning, organizing, and control of their operational systems.

For the Human Resources Management Major

Human resources personnel employ intelligent systems for many applications. For example, recruiters use these systems to find applicants' resumes on the web and sort them to match needed skills. Expert systems are also used in evaluating candidates (tests, interviews). HR personnel use intelligent systems to train and support employees in managing their fringe benefits. In addition, they use neural networks to predict employee job performance and future labour needs.

For the MIS Major

The MIS function develops (or acquires) and maintains the organization's various intelligent systems, as well as the data and models that these systems use. In addition, MIS staffers sometimes interact with subject-area experts to capture the expertise used in expert systems.

[Summary]

1. **Differentiate between artificial intelligence and human intelligence.**

   Table TG 4.1 differentiates between artificial and human intelligence on a number of characteristics.

2. **Define "expert systems," and provide examples of their use.**

   Expert systems are computer systems that attempt to mimic human experts by applying expertise in a specific domain. Tables TG 4.2 and TG 4.3 offer examples of expert systems.

3. **Define "neural networks," and provide examples of their use.**

   A neural network is a system of programs and data structures that simulate the underlying concepts of the human brain. Neural networks are used in many applications, such as to detect weapons concealed in personal belongings, to conduct research on various diseases, to carry out financial forecasting, to detect fraud in credit card transactions, and to fight crime.

4. **Define "fuzzy logic," and provide examples of its use.**

Fuzzy logic is a branch of mathematics that deals with uncertainties by simulating the processes of human reasoning. Fuzzy logic is used in financial analysis, to measure intangible assets like goodwill, and to find answers to search terms in search engines such as Google.

5. **Define "genetic algorithms," and provide examples of their use.**

A genetic algorithm is an intelligent system that mimics the evolutionary, "survival-of-the-fittest" process to generate increasingly better solutions to a problem. Genetic algorithms are used to design aircraft parts such as fan blades, to manage inventories more effectively, to optimize store displays, and to find optimal production schedules and distribution points.

6. **Define "intelligent agents," and provide examples of their use.**

An intelligent agent is a software program that assists you, or acts on your behalf, in performing repetitive, computer-related tasks. Intelligent agents are used to display lists of books or other products that customers might like, based on past purchases; to find information; to manage and monitor large computer networks 24/7/365; to detect electronic attacks early so that they can be prevented; to watch your competitors and notify you of price changes and special offers; to monitor Internet sites, discussion groups, and mailing lists for stock manipulations, insider trading, and rumours that might affect stock prices; to check your e-mail, sort it according to your priority rules, alert you when high-value e-mails appear in your in-box; and to automatically fill out forms on the web for you.

[Technology Guide Glossary]

artificial intelligence (AI) A subfield of computer science that is concerned with studying the thought processes of humans and recreating the effects of those processes via machines, such as computers.

buyer agent (or **shopping bot**) An intelligent agent on a website that helps customers find products and services that they need.

expert systems (ESs) Computer systems that attempt to mimic human experts by applying expertise in a specific domain.

fuzzy logic A branch of mathematics that deals with uncertainties by simulating the processes of human reasoning.

genetic algorithm An approach that mimics the evolutionary, "survival-of-the-fittest" process to generate increasingly better solutions to a problem.

information agent A type of intelligent agent that searches for information and displays it to users.

intelligent agent A software program that assists you, or acts on your behalf, in performing repetitive, computer-related tasks.

intelligent systems Commercial applications of artificial intelligence.

monitoring-and-surveillance agents (or **predictive agents**) Intelligent agents that constantly observe and report on some item of interest.

neural network A system of programs and data structures that simulates the underlying concepts of the human brain.

personal agents (see **user agents**)

predictive agents (see **monitoring-and-surveillance agents**)

shopping bot (see **buyer agent**)

Turing test A test in which a man and a computer both pretend to be women (or men), and the human interviewer has to decide which is the real human.

user agents (or **personal agents**) Intelligent agents that take action on your behalf.

[Discussion Questions]

1. Explain how your university could employ an expert system in its admission process. Could it use a neural network? What might happen if a student were denied admission to the university and his or her parents discovered that an expert system was involved in the admissions process?
2. One difference between a conventional business intelligence system and an expert system is that the former can explain *how* questions, whereas the latter can explain both *how* and *why* questions. Discuss the implications of this statement.

[Problem-Solving Activities]

1. You have decided to purchase a new video camcorder. To purchase it as inexpensively as possible and still get the features you want, you use a shopping bot. Visit several of the shopping bot websites that perform price comparisons for you. Begin with MySimon (*www.mysimon.com*), BizRate.com (*www.bizrate.com*), and Google Product Search. Compare these shopping bots in terms of ease of use, number of product offerings, speed in obtaining information, thoroughness of information offered about products and sellers, and price selection. Which site or sites would you use, and why? Which camcorder would you select and buy? How helpful were these sites in making your decision?
2. Access the MyMajors website (*www.mymajors.com*). This site contains a rule-based expert system to help students find majors. The expert system has more than 300 rules and 15,000 possible conclusions. The site ranks majors according to the likelihood that a student will succeed in them, and it provides six possible majors from among 60 alternative majors that a student might consider.

   Take the quiz, and see if you are in the "right major" as defined by the expert system. You must register to take the quiz.
3. Access Exsys (*www.exsys.com*), and click on the Corvid Demo(*www.exsyssoftware.com/CORVID52/corvidsr?KBNAME=../Download2/DownloadForm.cvR*). Provide your e-mail address, and click on the link for "Student—Needed for Class." Try the various demos, and report your results to the class.

Technology Guide 5

Protecting Your Information Assets

[LEARNING OBJECTIVES]

1. Explain why it is critical that you protect your information assets.
2. Identify the various behavioural actions you can take to protect your information assets.
3. Identify the various computer-based actions you can take to protect your information assets.

[CHAPTER OUTLINE]

TG 5.1 Introduction
TG 5.2 Behavioural Actions to Protect Your Information Assets
TG 5.3 Computer-Based Actions to Protect Your Information Assets

[WEB RESOURCES]

Student Companion Site

wiley.com/college/rainer

- Student PowerPoints for note taking
- Complete glossary

WileyPlus

All of the above and

- E-book
- Mini-lecture by author for each chapter section
- Practice quizzes
- Flash Cards for vocabulary review
- Additional "What's in IT for Me?" cases
- Video interviews with managers
- Lab Manual for Microsoft Office 2010
- How-to Animations for Microsoft Office 2010

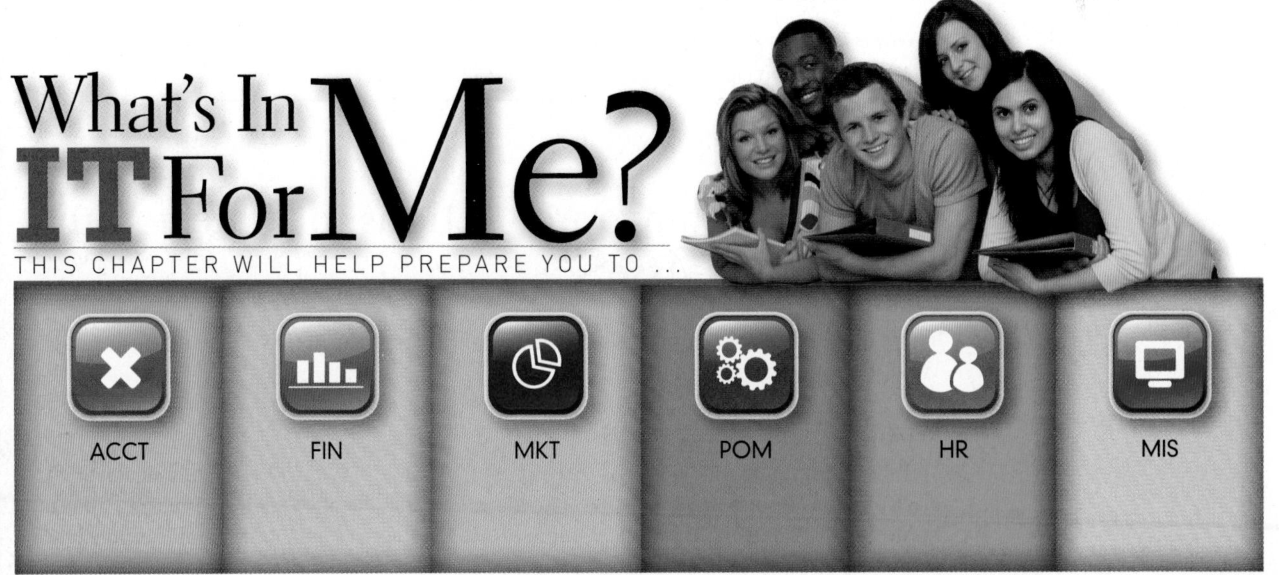

TG 5.1 Introduction

While travelling in our jobs or working from home, we access the Internet from home and from hot spots for various purposes—shopping, planning trips, gathering information, or staying in touch with friends and family. Unfortunately, every time you access the Internet, you risk exposing both professional and personal information to people looking to steal or exploit that information. This Technology Guide explains how you can protect your information assets whether you are computing at home or "on the road." The level of protection needs to be geared toward the type of information that is being stored or transported. Your term paper requires a different level of protection from your banking records and identification information. Information that you are a custodian of (such as your employer's customers' data) requires a high level of protection, while other information, such as pictures of your cat, requires less security.

When you connect at work or access your organization's network at home or on the road, you have the advantage (we hope!) of the "industrial-strength" information security implemented by your organization's IS department. In all other cases, however, you are on your own, so it is your responsibility to protect yourself. Protecting yourself is more critical than ever today because organized crime is increasingly turning its attention to home users. Because businesses are improving their information security, consumers are now the next logical target. According to Symantec (*www.symantec.com*), which manufactures the Norton Internet security products, in 2003 an unprotected personal computer connected to the Internet would be attacked within 15 minutes. Today, that same computer will be attacked within seconds.

The first step to any security actions you take is to make an inventory of the types of information you are using, storing, or accessing. Then, you need to consider what could go wrong if the information were to be copied or stolen. That will be your guide as to the level of protection you need to put in place.

You can take two types of actions to protect your information assets: behavioural actions and computer-based actions. Behavioural actions are those that do not specifically involve a computer. Computer-based actions relate to safe computing. If you take both types of actions, you will protect your information and greatly reduce your exposure to fraud and identity theft.

before you go on...

1. Why is it so important for you to protect yourself?
2. What are the two types of action that you can take to protect yourself?

TG 5.2 Behavioural Actions to Protect Your Information Assets

There are many behavioural actions that you should take to protect your information assets. We discuss these actions in this section.

General Behavioural Actions

You should never provide personal information to strangers in any format—physical, verbal, or electronic. As discussed in Chapter 13, you are vulnerable to social engineering attacks at home as well as at work. It is critical, therefore, to be on guard at all times. For example, always verify that you are talking to authorized personnel before providing personal information over the telephone. To do this, hang up and call the person or company back at a number that you obtain independently from another source. Whenever a call is fraudulent, the number that the caller gives you also will be fraudulent. Credit card companies usually make their numbers available on the back of the card and on every statement, as well as on the company's website.

A critically important behavioural action that you can take is to protect your social insurance number. Unfortunately, far too many organizations use your social insurance number to uniquely identify you. When asked to provide this number, ask why you could not just substitute some other combination of numbers and letters. If the person asking for your social insurance number—for example, your physician's receptionist—is not responsive, then ask to speak with a supervisor. There is a movement underway to avoid using social insurance numbers everywhere for identification. If this movement is successful, then you might have to remember many more identifiers. However, your information security would improve. Remember, you have to take the initiative.

Because fraudulent credit card use is so widespread, another critical consideration involves securing your credit cards. Some credit cards have the cardholder's picture on them. Although cashiers probably cannot read your signature on the back of your card, they certainly can compare your picture to your face. For example, in the United States, the Bank of America will place your picture on several of its credit cards for free. To view this service, visit *https://www.bankofamerica.com/privacy/accounts-cards/credit-debit-card-security.go*, and click on the Security Features link. Since credit cards with photo identification were not yet available in Canada, it might be an easier alternative to not sign your credit card, and place the words "ask for photo identification" in the signature space. This means that every time that you use your credit card, you will need to provide photo identification. While this may be cumbersome, it makes your credit card harder to use by an unauthorized person if it is lost.

You also may want to use virtual credit cards, which allow you to shop on-line with a disposable credit card number. For no extra charge, you sign up at your credit card provider's website and typically download software onto your computer. When you are ready to shop, you receive a randomly generated substitute 16-digit number that you can use at the on-line store. The number can be used only once or, in some cases, repeatedly, but only at the same store. The card number can also be used to buy goods and services over the phone and through the mail, although it cannot be used for in-store purchases that require a traditional plastic card. Two U.S. card issuers that offer virtual cards are Citibank and Discover. (Recall our discussion of virtual credit card numbers in Chapter 5.)

Also, pay close attention to your credit card billing cycles. You should know, to within a day or two, when your credit card bills are due to arrive. If a bill does not arrive when expected, call your credit card company immediately. If your credit card is stolen, the first thing the thief does is change the address on the account so that you no longer receive the bill. Fortunately, you can view your credit card bills on-line. Further, most credit card issuers offer the option of receiving credit card bills via e-mail. This process eliminates postal mail theft as a problem.

Finally, if you pay your bills by cheque, particularly your credit card accounts, do not write your complete account number on the "For" line of your cheque. Instead, write only the last four digits.

Another important action is to limit your use of debit cards. Debit cards are linked to your bank account, so a person who steals your debit card and personal identification number (PIN) can clean out your bank account. With proof of identity theft, your bank will return the funds, but it could take weeks or months. With credit cards, in contrast, your liability is usually zero (or a small amount). Credit card companies bear the liability for fraudulent charges, provided that they are notified within 60 days of the theft. However, it is good practice to notify them as soon as you are aware of anything unusual happening with your account. One way to limit your risk is to reduce the number of credit cards you have, and hold only a relatively small credit limit, such as $500 to $2,000, on each credit card.

It is important to be aware of what is happening with your financial accounts, as the source of identity theft could be someone hacking into the places where you bank or conduct your transactions. For example, in 2006, a breach was reported in the Bank of Canada accounts that handle automatic payroll deductions for Canada Savings Bonds.

Depending on the type of traffic in the area where you live, you might choose to avoid using a personal mailbox at your house or apartment for anything other than catalogues and magazines. You could use a private mailbox or a Post Office box. It is far too easy for thieves to steal

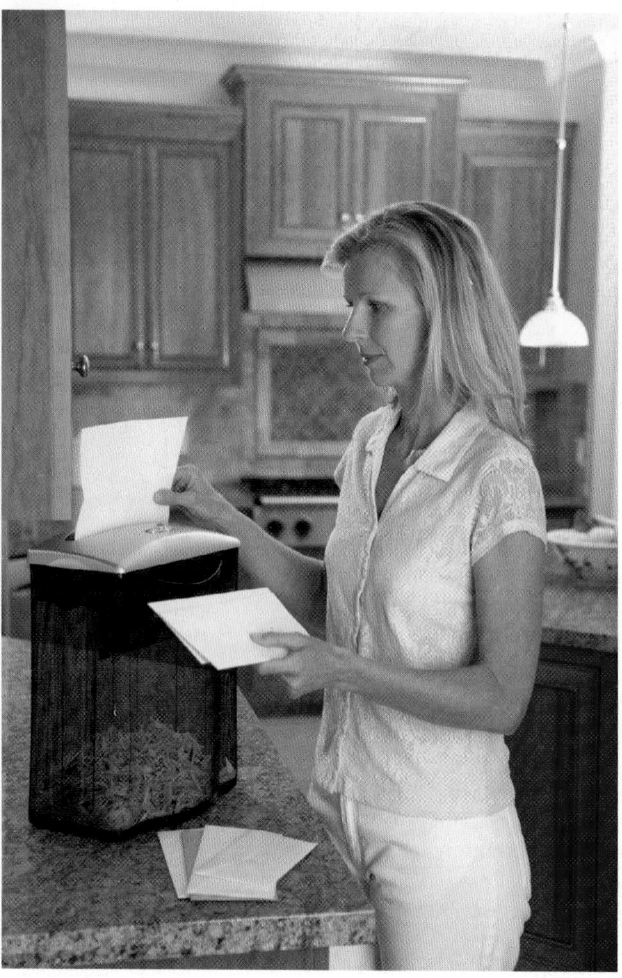

Care should be taken when discarding mail and old records.
(*Source:* Gene Chutka/iStockphoto)

mail from home mailboxes when no one is home for much of the day. Think about the wealth of information that could be stolen from your mailbox: credit card statements, bank statements, investment statements, and so on.

When you discard mail or old records, use a cross-cut or confetti shredder to cut them up. Recall our discussion of dumpster diving in Chapter 13. A single-cut shredder is not sufficient because, with enough time, a thief can reassemble the strips.

As you take these actions, consider your financial exposure. Do you live in a rental unit and regularly have more than $500 in the bank (rental units cannot have a false mortgage placed upon them in your name, and the lower your bank balance, the less can be stolen)? What if someone took out a student loan in your name? What is the value of your assets that could be mortgaged, or used as collateral? If you live in a home that is worth several hundred thousand dollars without a mortgage, someone could place a mortgage on your home. This could be protected by title insurance at a relatively low one-time cost. Do you have stocks and bonds? How much are they worth? As you decide the actions you are going to take to protect yourself, the context should be the amount of money you could lose, or the amount you would have to pay in legal fees and other costs to recover your assets if they were stolen by someone else assuming your identity.

Another security option is to sign up with a company that provides proactive protection of your personal information. Examples of such companies are LifeLock (*www.lifelock.com*), TrustedID (*www.trustedid.com*), and CardCops (*www.cardcops.com*).

LifeLock and TrustedID state that they enable customers to lock their credit files so that new lines of credit cannot be opened unless customers first unlock their existing files. Locking credit files means that merchants and banks must have verbal or written permission from customers before opening new credit lines in their names. Ordinarily, the locking process involves sending registered mail to each of the two major credit agencies every 90 days. These two agencies are Equifax Canada Inc. (*www.consumer.equifax.ca/home/en_ca*) and TransUnion (*www.transunion.ca*).

Security protection organizations claim to provide an early warning service that notifies its customers that the company has found their personal information circulating on the Internet. They may also collect compromised data on the Internet and make them available to customers and to merchants. Be sure to check the quality of the organization that you want to sign up with first.

What to Do in the Event of Identity Theft

In 2012, there were more than 12.6 million victims of identity theft reported in the United States, and over 22,000 in Canada. If you follow the behavioural and computer-based actions recommended in this Technology Guide, you will greatly reduce, but not eliminate, the chances that your identity will be stolen. If your identity is stolen despite these precautions, follow these steps to recover it:

- If your social insurance number has been compromised, contact Service Canada; in the event of passport theft, contact your local passport office.
- If you believe your mail is being diverted, contact your local Canada Post office.
- Cancel all affected credit cards and obtain new credit card numbers.

More than 22,000 Canadians were victims of identity theft in 2012.
(*Source:* MotoEd/iStockphoto)

- Consult a lawyer for the type of paperwork that may be required to deal with disputes with financial institutions or credit-granting organizations.
- Get organized. Keep a file with all your paperwork, including the names, addresses, and phone numbers of everyone you contact about this crime.
- File a detailed police report. Send copies of the report to creditors and other agencies or organizations that may require proof of the crime.
- Get the name and phone number of your police investigator and give it to your creditors.
- In all communications about the crime, use certified, return-receipt mail. Report that you are the victim of identity theft to the fraud divisions of both credit reporting agencies: Equifax and TransUnion. Due to the increased incidence of identity theft, federal law now gives you the right to have one free credit report per year. If you request your free annual credit report from both of the agencies, you will receive one free report every six months.
- Be sure to get your unique case number from each credit agency, and ask each agency to send your credit report.
- Tell each agency to issue a fraud alert. The fraud alert requires mortgage brokers, car dealers, credit companies, and other lenders to scrutinize anyone who opens an account in your name for 90 days.
- Get the document that you need to file a long-term fraud alert, which lasts for seven years and can be cancelled at any time.
- Ask the credit agencies for the names and phone numbers of lenders with whom recent accounts have been opened in the affected time frame, so you can identify fraudulent accounts that have been opened.
- Point out all entries generated due to fraud to each agency. Ask each agency to remove the specified fraudulent entries.
- Tell each agency to notify anyone who received your report in the last six months (or the affected time frame) that you are disputing the information.
- You may be able to order a "credit freeze" with the two major credit agencies. This freeze requires lenders, retailers, utilities, and other businesses to get special access to your credit

report through a PIN-based system. It also helps prevent anyone from getting any new loans or credit in your name.

- Be alert for change-of-address forms in your mail. The post office must send notifications to your old and new addresses. If someone tries to change your mailing address, it is a major indication that you have been victimized.
- If debt collectors demand payment of fraudulent accounts, write down the name of the company as well as the collector's name, address, and phone number. Tell the collector that you are the victim of identity theft. Send the collection agency a registered letter with a completed police report. If this does not work, refer the agency to your lawyer.

In addition to these behavioural actions, the computer-based actions we discuss in the next section will help you further protect yourself.

before you go on...

1. Why is it so important for you to protect your information assets?
2. Describe behavioural actions you can take to protect your information assets.

TG 5.3 Computer-Based Actions to Protect Your Information Assets

You can take many computer-based actions to increase the security of your information. We first discuss how to determine what sites users of your computer have visited on the Internet. Next, we briefly explain how to access social networking sites safely.

We will look at how to detect malicious software (malware) on your computer and what actions to take to prevent such infections. We then discuss protection of portable devices—for example, laptops and flash drives—and the information they contain. We follow with other valuable computer-based actions to protect your privacy when using the Internet and e-mail, how to recover from a disaster, and how to protect your system when computing wirelessly.

Determining Where People Have Visited on the Internet Using Your Computer

At home, you may have a single computer or several computers connected to a network. Although you may practise "safe computing," other users of your computer (for example, roommates or their friends) might not. You cannot be certain that these individuals take the same safety precautions that you do. You can, however, identify the Internet sites that anyone who uses your computer has visited. To do this, check the browser history. (Note that all modern browsers have a "private browsing" mode in which the viewing history is not recorded. You will not be able to check the browser history of someone who uses private browsing on your computer.)

The Dangers of Social Networking Sites

You should never post personal information about yourself or your family in chat rooms or on social networking sites. In fact, you should review any entries that you have made on these websites. The reason for these precautions is that potential employers may search these websites for information about you. Well-known social networking sites include Facebook, Twitter, LinkedIn, YouTube, MySpace, and Flickr.

Social networking websites do have features that give users more control over their information. Unfortunately, the privacy settings are not always easy to find and use. Your first decision is whether to make your profile publicly available or to keep it private. More than one third of adult users allow everyone to see their profiles. In contrast, nearly two thirds restrict access in some way.

One company, Reputation.com (*www.reputation.com*), claims to search out all information about you on the Internet and present it to you in a report. Then, at your command, it claims that it can "destroy all inaccurate, inappropriate, hurtful, and slanderous information about you." Remember, though, that website data are frequently archived, so companies like Reputation.com would be incapable of deleting archives or data controlled by others.

Determining Whether Your Computer Is Infected

There are several signs to look for if you think your computer system is infected with malicious software, or malware (discussed in Chapter 13). These signs include:

- Your computer shuts down unexpectedly by itself.
- Your computer refuses to start normally.
- Your computer exhibits erratic behaviour, displaying some or all of these characteristics:
  - Your system unexpectedly runs out of memory on your computer's hard drive.
  - Your system continually runs out of main memory (RAM).
  - Programs take longer to load than normal, or run very slowly.
  - Programs act erratically.
  - Your monitor displays strange graphics or messages.
  - Your system displays an unusually high number of error messages.
  - Your e-mail program sends messages to all the contacts in your address book without your knowledge or permission.

If you note any or all of these signs, your computer might be infected with malware. You can then take the computer-based actions discussed later in this Technology Guide to get rid of this software. Taking the actions discussed in the next section, however, will reduce your system's chances of being infected in the first place.

Computer Actions to Prevent Malware Infections

Many of the actions discussed in this section are common sense, but surprisingly large numbers of people do not pay attention to them. Taking these steps will help prevent a malware infection of your computer system.

We begin by considering things that you must *never* do on your computer. Never open unrequested e-mail attachments, even if the message is from someone you know and trust. The sender's computer may have been compromised without his or her knowledge, in which case the e-mail could be a phishing attack. Recall from Chapter 13 that a phishing attack involves tricking people into visiting a phony website and, once there, providing confidential information.

Never open attachments or web links in e-mails from people you do not know. These attachments can infect your system with a worm or virus. These web links also could be a phishing attack that may infect your system with a Trojan horse, turning your computer into a zombie or bot (short for "robot"). As we saw in Chapter 13, when this occurs your computer is no longer under your control.

Never accept files transferred to you during Internet chat or instant messaging sessions. These files usually are not from people you know, and they can infect your system with malware. You also should never download any files or software from websites that you do not know, or files or software that you have not requested.

Test Your System. It is a good idea to test your system. Several websites provide free security tests. These tests send different types of messages to your computer to evaluate how well it is protected from a variety of attacks. Free testing websites include HackerWhacker (*www.hackerwhacker.com*), ShieldsUP! (*www.grc.com*), Norton Security Scan (*http://security.symantec.com/NSS/GetNSS.aspx*), McAfee My SecurityStatus (*http://us.mcafee.com/MySecurityStatus/*), and AuditMyPC (*www.auditmypc.com*).

Microsoft provides a valuable scanning tool called the *Microsoft Baseline Security Analyzer*. This tool scans Windows-based computers for common security problems and generates individual security reports for each computer that it scans. The Microsoft Baseline Security Analyzer can be downloaded for free at this website: *http://technet.microsoft.com/en-us/security/cc184924.aspx*.

You can also run free malware scans on your computer. Several companies will scan your computer to identify viruses, worms, and other malware and will also offer suggestions about how to clean your system if it has become infected. These companies include:

- Trend Micro (*http://housecall.trendmicro.com*)
- McAfee (*http://home.mcafee.com/Default.aspx*)
- Panda Software (*www.pandasecurity.com/canada-eng/*)

Install a Security Suite on Your Computer. Security suites are software packages that contain various security products, such as anti-malware software, spam protection, e-mail fraud protection, spyware detection, intrusion detection, monitoring software, and others. These suites provide a great deal of functionality in one package. There is a question as to whether the individual functions in a security suite can match the combined functions of a group of individual products. Therefore, we discuss individual products in the next sections.

The following are well-known providers of security suites, but there are many others:

- ZoneAlarm (*www.zonealarm.com/*)
- McAfee (*www.mcafee.com/ca/*)
- Norton (*www.symantec.com*)

Install an Anti-Malware Product on Your Computer. You should install an anti-malware product on your computer and use it, ideally at least once per week. Remember to update your software's malware definitions every time before scanning your computer for malware. Typically, anti-malware product vendors automatically update malware definitions over the web.

Both free and commercial anti-malware products are available. In general, the free products are adequate, but the commercial products offer more functionality. Thefreecountry.com offers a great deal of information on free anti-malware products, as well as many other security products. For free anti-malware products, visit *www.thefreecountry.com/security/antivirus.shtml*.

Well-known commercial anti-malware products (among many others) include Norton Anti-malware (*www.symantec.com*) and McAfee Internet Security (*www.mcafee.com/ca*).

Install a Firewall on Your Computer. A personal firewall is software installed on your home computer that permits or denies communications to and from your computer based on your security settings. A personal firewall usually protects only the computer on which it is installed. Nevertheless, firewalls perform other essential functions.

Firewalls should make your computer invisible. This means that your firewall should not respond to Internet requests to ports (communications links to your computer) that are not intended for common Internet use. In effect, your computer operates in stealth mode on the Internet.

Firewalls also should alert you to suspicious behaviour. They should tell you when a program or connection is attempting to do something you have not instructed it to do, such as download software or run a program such as ActiveX. ActiveX (by Microsoft) executes programs downloaded from Internet Explorer, and it can be exploited by attackers trying to compromise your computer. Programs like ActiveX should be disabled on your computer.

Finally, firewalls block outbound connections that you do not initiate. That is, your firewall should not let your computer access the Internet on its own. If your computer tries to access the Internet by itself, it is almost certainly infected with malware.

As with anti-malware programs, firewall products can be free or commercially produced. Again, the free products are adequate, but the commercial products offer more functionality. For a list of free firewall software, visit: *http://netsecurity.about.com/od/personalfirewalls/a/aafreefirewall.htm*.

Many companies offer commercial firewall software. Some of the best-known commercial firewall products are provided by:

- ZoneAlarm (*www.zonealarm.com*)
- Norton (*www.symantec.com*)
- McAfee (*www.mcafee.com/ca/*)
- F-Secure (*www.f-secure.com*)
- Panda (*www.pandasecurity.com/canada-eng/*)

It is a good idea to test your firewall. It is best, however, to use only test websites that are run by actual firewall or security software companies. A good firewall test site is the McAfee HackerWatch site at *www.hackerwatch.org/probe/*. The HackerWatch site allows you to do a basic probe test on your computer to see if your firewall is blocking ports that may be vulnerable.

Install an Antispyware Product on Your Computer. As with anti-malware products and firewalls, free antispyware products are adequate, but commercial antispyware products offer more functionality. Free antispyware products include Ad-Aware Free Antivirus+ (*www.lavasoft.com*) and Spybot Search & Destroy (*www.safer-networking.org*).

Well-known commercial antispyware products include the following, although many others are available: VIPRE (*www.sunbeltsoftware.com*), Ad-Aware (*www.lavasoft.com*), and SpyCatcher (*www.tenebril.com*). Finally, several companies offer free spyware scans, including Norton (*www.symantec.com*).

Install Monitoring Software on Your Computer. Monitoring software logs keystrokes, e-mails, applications, windows, websites, Internet connections, passwords, chat conversations, webcams, and even screenshots. Companies that offer monitoring software include SpyAgent (*www.spytech-web.com*), SpyBuddy (*www.exploreanywhere.com*), WinSpy (*www.win-spy.com*), and SpectorSoft (*www.spectorsoft.com*).

Install Content-Filtering Software on Your Computer. Content-filtering software performs many functions. It can block access to undesirable websites, and it can record and view all of the websites that you or other users have visited. It also can record both sides of chat conversations from AOL Instant Messenger (AIM and AIM Triton), Yahoo! Messenger, and Windows Live Messenger.

Content-filtering software provides many filter categories, enabling you to selectively filter content. Companies that offer this software include CYBERsitter (*www.cybersitter.com*), Net Nanny (*www.netnanny.com*), and CyberSpy (*www.cyberspyware.com*).

For example, Internet Explorer's Content Advisor utility allows you to block access to websites that meet specified criteria and to set your own tolerance levels for various types of Internet content.

Install Anti-Spam Software on Your Computer. Anti-spam software helps you to control spam. The following are well-known commercial anti-spam products, among many others:

- Cloudmark (*www.cloudmark.com*)
- Total Protection (*www.mcafee.com/ca/*)
- Norton Antispam (*www.symantec.com*)
- SpamGourmet (*www.spamgourmet.com*)
- SpamAssassin (*http://spamassassin.apache.org*)

You might also want to set up multiple free e-mail accounts, such those on Hotmail and Gmail. Then, as you surf the Internet and are asked for your e-mail address, you use one of these accounts rather than your home or business e-mail account. When your free e-mail accounts are full of spam, you can close them and open new accounts.

Install Proactive Intrusion Detection and Prevention Software on Your Computer. Anti-malware software is reactive in nature, which leaves you vulnerable to zero-day attacks. Zero-day attacks take advantage of newly discovered, previously unknown vulnerabilities in software products. Perpetrators attack the vulnerability before the software vendor can prepare a patch for the vulnerability. For this reason, it is important to add proactive intrusion detection and prevention software to your defences. One such product is Prevx (*www.prevx.com*). You can download and install Prevx for free, and it will scan your computer for malicious software. If it finds any, it will activate a free 30-day cleanup account and remove the malware from your computer. Once this period runs out, Prevx will continue to scan incoming programs and protect your computer from them. If your system subsequently gets infected, however, and you want to continue using Prevx, you must pay for one year of protection.

Manage Patches. You should download and install all software patches (for example, patches for Windows) immediately. Companies typically release patches to repair security problems. If you do not download and install patches quickly (or enable automatic update), your computer will be vulnerable to attack.

Use a Browser Other Than Internet Explorer. You might consider using a browser other than Internet Explorer, such as Firefox (*www.mozilla.org*), Opera (*www.opera.com*), Safari from Apple (*www.apple.com/safari/*), or Google Chrome (*www.google.com/intl/en/chrome/browser/*). These browsers are not impregnable, but they are less prominent, and hackers, at least so far, have paid less attention to them. Even if you decide to use a browser other than Internet Explorer, however, you should still implement all of the security measures we have discussed. You should also keep your browser updated.

Use an Operating System Other Than Windows. The two main alternatives to Windows 8 and Vista are Apple's Mac OS X and Linux. These two operating systems are not invulnerable, but both are based on UNIX, which makes them inherently more secure than any version of Windows. (UNIX is an operating system developed by AT&T in the 1960s and 1970s that usually runs on servers rather than on desktops.) In addition, Linux and Mac OS X have smaller market shares than Windows and thus are less attractive targets for malware.

Protecting Your Portable Devices and Information

Theft or loss of laptops, notebook computers, tablets, smart phones, BlackBerry units, and thumb drives, as well as the data contained on these devices, is a significant problem. There are many proactive steps that you can take to protect portable devices and their data, including preventing their theft, using two-factor authentication, and encrypting your data. You can also take reactive steps after a theft or loss has occurred. We consider all of these actions in this section.

Before we discuss these steps, there are two common-sense precautions that many people forget. First, keep your laptop in an inconspicuous container. Laptop cases with a company logo simply draw the attention of thieves. Second, do not leave your laptop unattended in plain view; for example, in your car where it can be seen. Instead, lock it in the trunk.

One strategy to prevent the theft of a portable device is to use alarms. Laptop security systems operate by detecting motion, analyzing the motion to determine whether a threat exists, and, if it does, implementing responses. These alarms are battery-powered, are independent of the computer operating system, and operate whether the laptop is on or off. If a laptop armed with a security system is carried beyond a perimeter specified by the user, the system assumes the laptop is being stolen. It can then prevent access to the operating system, secure passwords, and encryption keys, and sound an audible alarm. One company that provides laptop security systems is Computer Security Products, Inc. (*www.computersecurity.com*). Two-factor authentication means that you must have two forms of identification to access your laptop or notebook. The first authentication factor is a token or a biometric. The second factor is your personal password.

A token generates a one-time password that you must enter within a specified time limit. This password typically consists of six digits, which appear on the token's LCD screen.

Companies offering tokens for two-factor authentication include Authenex (*www.authenex.com*), Kensington (*www.kensington.com*), and SecuriKey (*www.securikey.com*).

Fingerprints are the biometric most often used for two-factor authentication. The fingerprint reader is incorporated into the laptop itself. (Search the IBM (*www.ibm.com*) and Microsoft (*www.microsoft.com*) websites for more information.) You can also use fingerprint authentication on your thumb drive with the SanDisk Cruzer (*www.sandisk.com*), the Lexar JumpDrive Touch-Guard (*www.lexar.com*), the Sony MicroVault (*www.sony.net*), and the Kanguru Bio Slider (*www.kanguru.com*).

Take steps to protect portable devices like laptops and smart phones. (*Source:* greg801/iStockphoto)

Data encryption provides additional protection by turning data into symbols that can be deciphered only by an authorized person. You can encrypt some or all of the data on your computer by using your computer's built-in encryption, folder-based encryption, or full-disk encryption. Beachhead Solutions (*www.beachheadsolutions.com*) and Credant (*www.credant.com*; now part of Dell) also provide applications that allow you to encrypt files and folders.

Another step you can take to improve your security is to encrypt your entire hard drive, including your applications. See Check Point Software (*www.checkpoint.com/pointsec*), Mobile Armor from Trend Micro, (*www.trendmicro.com/us/enterprise/product-security/endpoint-encryption/mobile-armor/*), and the Kanguru Wizard (*www.kanguru.com*). If your laptop is lost or stolen, you can use laptop-tracing tools or device reset/remote kill tools. For example, the YoYo Laptop Tracking Software (*www.computersecurity.com*), PC Phone-Home (*www.pcphonehome.com*), and LaptopLocate (*www.laptoplocate.net*) provide transmitters that secretly send a signal to their respective company control centres via telephone or the Internet. This signal enables the company, with the help of local authorities, Internet service providers, and telephone companies, to track your computer's location.

You can also use device reset/remote kill tools to automatically prevent specified data on a lost or stolen laptop from being compromised or misused. This solution works even when other security software or encryption methods fail. Examples of companies providing these solutions are Trust Digital (now part of McAfee) (*www.mcafee.com/us/about/trustdigital/index.aspx*) and Beachhead Solutions (*www.beachheadsolutions.com*).

Preparing for Personal Disasters

Disasters are not limited to businesses. You can experience disasters such as fires and floods at home. Therefore, you should take certain steps to protect your information assets, whether they are stored on your computer (digital form) or in another form (hard copy). First and foremost, you should have a safety deposit box at your bank for your important papers. You also should have a fireproof safe at home where you can store other important papers. You should make regular backups of your key files and keep these backups off site. You also might want to encrypt your backup files if they contain sensitive information.

Wireless Security

Many home users have implemented a wireless local area network. The security considerations for wireless networks are greater than those for wired networks. The reason for this is simple. If you are computing and communicating wirelessly, you are broadcasting, and therefore, by definition, you are non-secure. The most common reason for intruders to connect to a non-secure wireless network is to gain access to the Internet. Intruders also might connect in order to use your network as a base for spamming or for other unethical or illegal activities. Finally, they may do so to gain access to your sensitive personal information.

Unfortunately, recent studies have indicated that three quarters of all home wireless users have not activated any security features to protect their information. Unless you take the steps discussed here, your information assets are extremely vulnerable.

Hide Your Service Set Identifier (SSID). Your wireless router, which connects your home network with your ISP, comes with a default SSID that is the same for thousands or millions of routers made by the manufacturer. Therefore, an attacker can search for wireless networks by looking for a relatively small number of default SSIDs. For this reason, you should (1) change your default SSID to a unique SSID, and (2) configure your wireless home network to stop broadcasting the SSID. A step-by-step guide to perform these security measures is available here: *http://netsecurity.about.com/od/stepbystep/ss/change_ssid.htm*.

Use Encryption. To avoid broadcasting in the clear, you must use encryption with your wireless home network. Wireless equivalent protocol (WEP) is an old protocol that is easy to crack and therefore should not be used. Instead, you should use Wi-Fi Protected Access (WPA2), which is the second generation of WPA. WPA2 is much stronger than WEP and will protect your encryption against attackers. (Note: Your wireless router must support WPA2. Otherwise, use WPA rather than WEP.) In addition, you should use a strong password of at least 20 random characters on your router. Chapter 13 provides specific instructions for creating strong passwords.

Filter Out Media Access Control (MAC) Addresses. Every piece of networking hardware has a unique identification number called a *media access control (MAC)* address that looks like this: 00-00-00-00-00-00. (Note that this MAC address is only an example.) You can compile the MAC addresses of all computers on your home wireless network, then instruct your router to connect only with these computers and deny access to all other computers attempting to connect with your network.

Limit Internet Protocol (IP) Addresses. You should instruct your router to allow only a certain number of IP addresses to connect to your network. Ideally, the number of IP addresses will be the same as the number of computers on your network.

Sniff Out Intruders. A variety of wireless intrusion detection systems will monitor your wireless network for intruders, alert you when they are on your network, display their IP addresses and their activity, and even inform them that you know that they are there. Commercial products include the Internet Security Systems (*www.iss.net*) wireless scanner and AirDefense Personal (*www.airdefense.net*). AirSnare is a free wireless intrusion detection system (see *http://home.comcast.net/~jay.deboer/airsnare*).

Take Precautions When Using a Public Hotspot. When you travel, remember that most public wireless providers and hotspots employ no security measures at all. As a result, everything you send and receive is in the clear and has no encryption. Many intruders go to public hotspots and listen in on the wireless computing and communications taking place there. If you must compute wirelessly at a public hotspot, there are several precautions you should take before you connect.

- Use virtual private networking (VPN) technology to connect to your organization's network (discussed in Chapter 13).
- Use Remote Desktop to connect to a computer that is running at your home.
- Configure your firewall to be "on with no exceptions."
- Visit only websites that use secure sockets layer (SSL) to conduct any financial or personal transactions.

Remember to surf in an encrypted mode when using your laptop wirelessly in a public "hotspot."
(*Source:* Bart Sadowski/iStockphoto)

Test Your Wireless Network. After performing all the necessary steps to protect your wireless home network, it is a good idea to test the network for vulnerabilities. eEye has created a free Wi-Fi vulnerability scanner that you can download here: *www.eeye.com/Downloads*. This tool scans your vicinity looking for wireless devices to test. When you run it, it generates a detailed report that outlines all of the security problems it finds.

Use Wireless Security Software. For extra security, you can purchase wireless security programs. McAfee (*www.mcafee.com/ca/*) includes Wi-Fi intrusion detection in its McAfee Mobile Security package, which also includes a personal firewall, antivirus software, antispyware software, the ability to check apps and lock your phone. The software warns you when an unknown user tries to access your wireless network. ZoneAlarm (*www.zonealarm.com*) has a line of products that automatically detect wireless networks and help secure them.

before you go on...

1. Why is it important to protect your mobile devices?
2. Describe three different tools that you could use to protect your devices, and the purpose of each tool.

[Summary]

1. **Explain why it is critical that you protect your information assets.**

   We live in a digital world. Unfortunately, every time we use our computers or access the Internet, we risk exposing both professional and personal information to people looking to steal or exploit that information. It is your responsibility to protect yourself in our hostile digital environment. Protecting yourself is even more critical today because organized crime is increasingly turning its attention to home users. Because businesses are improving their information security, consumers now have become the next logical target.

2. Identify the various behavioural actions you can take to protect your information assets.

- Do not provide personal information to strangers in any format (physical, verbal, or electronic).
- Protect your social insurance number.
- Where available, use credit cards with your picture on them.
- Do not sign your credit cards. Instead, write "photo ID required" on the back.
- Pay close attention to your credit card billing cycles.
- Limit your use of debit cards.
- Do not use a personal mailbox at your home for anything other than catalogues and magazines.
- Use a cross-cut, or confetti, shredder.
- Sign up with a company that provides proactive protection of your personal information.

3. Identify the various computer-based actions you can take to protect your information assets.

- Check to see the websites that anyone who may have used your computer has visited.
- Never post personal information about yourself or your family in chat rooms or on social networking sites. Use the privacy features provided by social networking sites to limit public access to your profile.
- Never open unrequested attachments to e-mail files, even those from people you know and trust.
- Never open attachments or web links in e-mails from people you do not know.
- Never accept files transferred to you during Internet chat or instant messaging sessions.
- Never download any files or software over the Internet from websites that you do not know.
- Never download files or software that you have not requested.
- Test your system.
- Run free malware scans on your computer.
- Have an anti-malware product on your computer and have it set for automatic updates.
- Have a firewall on your computer.
- Have an antispyware product on your computer.
- Have monitoring software on your computer.
- Have content filtering software on your computer.
- Have anti-spam software on your computer.
- Have proactive intrusion detection and prevention software on your computer.
- Manage patches.
- Use a browser other than Internet Explorer.
- Use a laptop security system.
- Use two-factor authentication.
- Use encryption.
- Use laptop-tracing tools or device reset/remote kill tools.
- Look for new and unusual files.
- Use strong passwords.
- Adjust the privacy settings on your computer.
- Erase your Google search history.
- Make backups, backups, backups!
- For wireless security:
  - Hide your service set identifier (SSID).
  - Use encryption.
  - Filter out media access control (MAC) addresses.

- Limit Internet protocol (IP) addresses.
- Sniff out intruders.
- Change the default administrator password on your wireless router to something not easily guessed.
- Use virtual private networking (VPN) technology to connect to your organization's network.
- Use Remote Desktop to connect to a computer that is running at your home.
- Configure your firewall to be "on with no exceptions."
- Visit only websites that use secure sockets layer (SSL) to conduct any financial or personal transactions.
- Use wireless security programs.

[Discussion Questions]

1. Why is it so important for you to protect your information assets? Can you assume that your organization's MIS department will do it for you?
2. Discuss the differences between behavioural actions that you should take and computer-based actions that you should take.

[Problem-Solving Activities]

1. Using one product suggested in this Technology Guide or a product you find, do the following:
   - Test or scan your computer for malware.
   - Test your firewall.
   - Scan your computer for spyware.
2. Prepare a personal backup plan (in the event that the hard drive on your computer fails).

Index